Academic Freedom in the Era of Trump

Academic Freedom in the Era of Trump

EDITED BY LEE C. BOLLINGER
and
GEOFFREY R. STONE

OXFORD
UNIVERSITY PRESS

OXFORD
UNIVERSITY PRESS

Oxford University Press is a department of the University of Oxford.
It furthers the University's objective of excellence in research, scholarship,
and education by publishing worldwide. Oxford is a registered trade mark of
Oxford University Press in the UK and in certain other countries.

Published in the United States of America by Oxford University Press
198 Madison Avenue, New York, NY 10016, United States of America.

Library of Congress Cataloging-in-Publication Data
Names: Bollinger, Lee C., 1946- editor | Stone, Geoffrey R. editor
contributor
Title: Academic freedom in the era of trump / edited by Lee C. Bollinger,
Geoffrey R. Stone.
Description: New York : Oxford University Press, 2026. | Includes
bibliographical references and index.
Identifiers: LCCN 2026010194 (print) | LCCN 2026010195 (ebook) | ISBN
9780197854846 paperback | ISBN 9780197854839 hardback | ISBN
9780197854853 epub | ISBN 9780197854877
Subjects: LCSH: Academic freedom–United States | Trump, Donald, 1946- |
Higher education and state–United States | United States. Constitution.
1st Amendment | Constitutional law–United States
Classification: LCC KF4242 .A93 2026 (print) | LCC KF4242 (ebook)
LC record available at https://lccn.loc.gov/2026010194
LC ebook record available at https://lccn.loc.gov/2026010195

DOI: 10.1093/9780197854877.001.0001

The manufacturer's authorized representative in the EU for product safety is
Oxford University Press España S.A. of Parque Empresarial San Fernando de Henares,
Avenida de Castilla, 2 – 28830 Madrid (www.oup.es/en or product.safety@oup.com).
OUP España S.A. also acts as importer into Spain of products made by the manufacturer.

To Jean and Jane

And to the next generation:
Colin, Katelyn, Cooper, Sawyer, and Emma
Julie, Mollie, Maddie, Jackson, Amaya, and Leni

CONTENTS

LIST OF CONTRIBUTORS

Lee C. Bollinger, president emeritus and Seth Low Professor of the University, Columbia University

Erwin Chemerinsky, dean and Jesse H. Choper Distinguished Professor of Law, University of California, Berkeley School of Law

Nicholas B. Dirks, president and chief executive officer, The New York Academy of Sciences

Niall Ferguson, Milbank Family Senior Fellow, Hoover Institution, Stanford University; senior faculty fellow, Belfer Center for Science and International Affairs, Harvard University

Mary Anne Franks, Eugene L. and Barbara A. Bernard Professor in Intellectual Property, Technology, and Civil Rights Law, George Washington University Law School

Tom Ginsburg, Leo Spitz Distinguished Service Professor of International Law, Ludwig and Hilde Wolf Research Scholar, professor of political science, The University of Chicago Law School

Amy Gutmann, Christopher H. Browne Distinguished Professor of Political Science, School of Arts and Sciences, and professor of communication, Annenberg School for Communication, president emerita, University of Pennsylvania, retired US Ambassador to Germany

Aziz Z. Huq, Frank and Bernice J. Greenberg Professor of Law, The University of Chicago Law School

Olatunde Johnson, Ruth Bader Ginsburg '59 Professor of Law, Columbia Law School

Randall L. Kennedy, Michael R. Klein Professor of Law, Harvard Law School

Larry Kramer, president and vice chancellor, London School of Economics and Political Science

Leah Litman, professor of law, University of Michigan Law School

M. Elizabeth Magill, professor of law, Penn Carey Law School, University of Pennsylvania

Mary-Rose Papandrea, Burchfield Professor of First Amendment and Free Speech Law, George Washington University Law School

Steve Poskanzer, professor of political science and president emeritus, Carleton College

Robert C. Post, Sterling Professor of Law, Yale Law School

Louis Michael Seidman, Carmack Waterhouse Professor of Constitutional Law, Georgetown Law

Suzanna Sherry, Herman O. Loewenstein Chair in Law Emerita, Vanderbilt Law School

Robert Shibley, special counsel for Campus Advocacy, Foundation for Individual Rights and Expression

Ilya Somin, professor of law, Antonin Scalia School of Law, George Mason University

Geoffrey R. Stone, Edward H. Levi Distinguished Service Professor of Law, The University of Chicago Law School

Nadine Strossen, John Marshall Harlan II Professor of Law, Emerita, New York Law School

Cass R. Sunstein, Robert Walmsley University Professor, founder and director of the Program on Behavioral Economics and Public Policy, Harvard Law School

ACKNOWLEDGMENTS

We are deeply grateful to the many individuals whose efforts made this volume possible.

Above all, we thank the distinguished scholars and practitioners who authored these essays. Their insight, rigor, and commitment to the values of academic freedom and universities form the core of this project. Their contributions elevate the conversation in ways that will inform and challenge both experts and general readers, and we are indebted to them all.

We are also fortunate to have the support and partnership of Oxford University Press, and especially our editor, Gabe Kachuck, whose guidance and enthusiasm have been invaluable. Our home institutions, Columbia University and the University of Chicago, have provided the intellectual environment and institutional support that sustain this work. At Columbia, we thank Britt Hefelfinger, Director of Strategic Projects, and Meghan McLoryd, Associate Director in the Office of the President Emeritus, for their oversight of this project. We are particularly grateful to our research assistants, Peter Camardo, Oliver Kleen and Saul Roselaar, whose care and diligence helped bring the manuscript to completion.

Finally, and most importantly, we thank our spouses, Jean Magnano Bollinger and Jane Dailey. Their constant support and understanding make all this possible and are profoundly appreciated.

Opening Dialogue

LEE C. BOLLINGER AND GEOFFREY R. STONE

Bollinger: We are in a treacherous period for American democracy, and one area of danger involves our universities. You and I entered the academy in the very same year, 1973, and between us we now have over a century of experience with these extraordinary institutions. Of all the projects we have undertaken together—now ten in number—I think it is fair to say we know more about this subject—academic freedom and the First Amendment—than about any of the others. We have spent our professional lives understanding the constitutional principles of freedom of speech and press, all the while being inhabitants of the university.

The current threat to universities seems to me greater than at any other time in our lifetimes. We did not really know the McCarthy Era, but we were alive then and we have studied the period closely. It seems like the closest parallel to today. Faculty and students were hounded, and worse, on suspicions of having sympathies or affiliations with communism or socialism (as also happened to others outside of colleges and universities), and many were driven from the academy.[1] But McCarthy was merely one senator, and today it is the president of the United States and his entire administration. Furthermore, the government's reach into the university is now going far beyond attacks on single professors—at its most aggressive, it is attempting to intrude into the selection of students, the standards for hiring faculty, the management of academic departments, and beyond into the basic policies of the university (such as those involving diversity). The principal lever that has been engaged to establish this control is the massive funding of science, which has been the backbone of American research since the time just after you and I were born.[2] The official message now is: Let us seize control of your institution or we will take away your grants.

The primary question we and our authors explore in this volume is whether these and other attacks on universities abridge basic values of the nation, the

Lee C. Bollinger and Geoffrey R. Stone, *Opening Dialogue*. In: *Academic Freedom in the Era of Trump*. Edited by: Lee C. Bollinger and Geoffrey R. Stone, Oxford University Press. © Oxford University Press (2026). DOI: 10.1093/9780197854877.003.0001

First Amendment of the Constitution, and the norms of our democracy. Does academic freedom—or, as I like to call it, the principle of freedom of the university—stand as a barrier against these intrusions? If so, how do we define that fundamental principle? And from what or where do we derive it?

Largely because these current assaults are so unprecedented in degree and scale, we do not have as well-developed an idea of academic freedom as we need for this moment. We find ourselves, therefore, in a context of building, of extrapolating, of testing, and of arguing for and against uncertain positions. At the very least, that gives an excitement and a richness to the essays that compose this book.

I have recently tried my hand at this. In *University: A Reckoning*, I see the modern American university, as a system, as the institutional fulfillment of the First Amendment's commitment to the search for knowledge and truth. Over the last century, the university and the First Amendment have evolved in parallel to create extraordinary worlds where we temper our inclinations to believe what we happen to believe in favor of developing an openness to new ideas and knowledge, an intellectual character that we hope and expect will continue to improve our lives individually and as a society. This alignment should bring special protections under the First Amendment for universities. The closest analogy is that of the press, where over the same decades there has been a recognition by the Supreme Court of the unique role played by the press in informing the public and a corresponding need for elevated protections against government interference. Insofar as the press, under this vision, can be seen as the Fourth Branch of Government, the university can be appropriately regarded as the Fifth.[3]

You know as well as I that this thesis is built on assumptions and premises that are contested, so I acknowledge that we are writing for the future and not just applying what has been decided, although it is also true that there are more than just intimations in the jurisprudence to support the idea.

All that said, where should we start our dialogue here? Perhaps we should begin not with extolling the virtues of universities but rather with confronting the objections of our critics. I personally believe that the modern university is one of the most successful institutions in America, as measured by any standard (e.g., economic development, global power, more fulfilling lives). I challenge anyone to spend a day or week on a campus—attending classes, visiting a lab, hearing lectures, listening to discussions across the campus—and not come away deeply impressed by the seriousness of the overall inquiry into knowledge and truth and by the integrity of those who implement the mission. Still, there are criticisms that we have to confront and that, at least to some degree, are in my view valid. Let's put aside those directed at things like tuition and the costs of education and focus instead on those that purport to justify the present attacks on universities. I'm thinking specifically of the charge that faculty have become too uniformly left-leaning (politically), intolerant toward conservative viewpoints, too critical of America (even anti-American), and basically engaged in indoctrinating our youth in these ideologies. Why don't you start, and then I'll come in.

Stone: This is great, Lee. I'd like to focus on the claim that higher education today is wildly biased in favor of liberal views and that this seriously undermines the core aspirations of higher education. Is it true that college and university professors tend to be much more liberal than the general public? All of the evidence suggests that the answer to this is yes, especially, but not only, in the humanities and social sciences. The survey data from a range of sources indicate that more than half of faculty nationally identify as "liberal" and less than 30 percent identify as "conservative."[4] Moreover, at some institutions the gap is much greater than that.

Assuming these data are reasonably accurate, which they may or may not be, the first question—addressed by several of our authors—is why this is so? National surveys suggest that, among Americans generally, somewhat more identify as conservative than liberal.[5] If this is so, why is there a significant difference between the ideological views of citizens generally, on the one hand, and college and university professors, on the other?

One possibility is that, at least at the moment, liberal views are better grounded in serious, rigorous, thoughtful, respectful, and informed thought and analysis than are conservative views. After all, there is no reason to think that the views of the general public are always serious, rigorous, thoughtful, respectful, and well-informed. It may be that, at least in the current world, rigorous inquiry, deep knowledge, and open-mindedness are more likely to lead one to embrace what we currently regard as a "liberal" than a "conservative" perspective. On that view, a person with a deep exposure to history, science, political theory, principles of justice, economics, law, and philosophy might quite sensibly be more inclined in today's world to embrace "liberal" than "conservative" views, as compared to a person with only a high-school degree. If that is true, it would suggest that the seeming "bias" in higher education is simply due to the fact that highly educated people today are quite sensibly more likely to be liberal than conservative. That is not the result of bias, but of merit. That is clearly a provocative suggestion, but it's certainly possible. After all, education, debate, disagreement, and scholarship enrich one's knowledge, understanding, and thinking, and there is no reason to assume that they won't do so in ways that might quite sensibly affect how one sees the world and how one defines a "free, fair, and just" society. Needless to say, there are many people who will reject this hypothesis and who will insist that conservative ideas are just as meritorious as liberal ideas.[6] If that is accurate, then what explains the disparity between the percentage of liberal and conservative professors?

A second possibility is that, among equally and highly talented individuals, conservatives are less likely than liberals to enter the academy because they are more interested in earning money. Thus, they might be less likely than liberals to sacrifice substantial earnings in order to have an academic career. If that is so, it could have an incidental but significant impact on the ideological makeup of the academy.

A third possibility is that the current "bias" in higher education toward more "liberal" views is based not on the relative merit of the competing ideas or on the self-interest of potential academics but on unintentional bias by faculty in making hiring and promotion decisions. In other words, because professors make hiring and promotion decisions based on their own evaluation of a candidate's work and intellectual and scholarly potential, they may (without being aware that they are "discriminating") prefer liberal over conservative candidates because they are inclined to give greater respect to the views of those who agree with them. That would be a disappointing, even if unintentional, bias that could contribute significantly to the current disparity.

Another possible explanation is that the faculty members who make the hiring and promotion decisions are very much aware of the ideological views of the candidates and, in order to ensure an institution that is more rather than less in line with their own views, they intentionally discriminate against those whose views differ from their own. This would be an example of overt ideological discrimination, and, if based on ideology rather than merit, it would clearly be inconsistent with the values and aspirations of academic freedom.

One more possibility is the impact of DEI. By focusing on diversity, equity, and inclusion in making hiring and promotion decisions, faculty may have been more inclined to hire or promote candidates whose views were substantially more likely to be liberal than conservative. This might have been due not to an ideological bias but instead to an incidental, though not insignificant, effect of DEI.

Having said all this, the question is, wholly apart from the pressures of the Trump administration, what should colleges and universities do? Is the current ideological makeup of faculty—with its clear tilt toward liberals—acceptable in light of the overarching goals and values of academic freedom?

Bollinger: These are very important observations and hypotheses for what both of us know from personal experience is a reality: namely, that, taken as a whole, universities are populated by people who are generally significantly more liberal than most of the society. As you point out, the potential causes of that reality range from being completely acceptable and reasonable in terms of fulfilling the mission of the university to being problematic and in need of remedial attention.

I would add just a few thoughts here. Whatever the causes, it is important to approach this discussion with a proper sense of proportion. The fact that a poll taken of all faculty at any given institution might establish that there is a much higher percentage of Democrats than Republicans does not mean that the research or education in that institution is necessarily compromised. In many, maybe even most, fields of knowledge within a university, political leanings play no role whatsoever. Mathematics is mathematics whether pursued by a liberal or a conservative, and that is true of many other fields (physics, biology, chemistry, engineering, etc.). Furthermore, the liberal tilt of faculty is not really pronounced or present in a variety of social sciences. I'm thinking here specifically of the discipline of economics. It's really only in a select number of the social sciences and the humanities that we see this tendency. So, the upshot is that the "liberal" bias is irrelevant as a risk for most of what the modern university is or does.

But there's more. Even where there is a close alignment between what the professor believes politically and what the professor teaches, it is entirely possible for the professor to perform his or her role without engaging in political bias. The professor may believe with deep conviction that *Roe* was properly decided and yet teach the class with complete openness to alternative and contrary viewpoints. And my experience tells me that this happens regularly. Let me just add here that I would not accept the counterargument that only a "conservative" on the issue of abortion, or on any other highly controversial political question, can articulate fully the anti-*Roe* viewpoint.

All that said, I think (as I know you do) that it would be good to have people from across the political spectrum pursuing research and teaching and engaging in the dialogues that make up the disciplines that undergird our academic system. Every hiring committee in every field where it's appropriate and relevant to the academic mission should be on high alert to find that diversity of intellectual interests.

Now, we start with this general critique of universities and the analysis of its validity because it lies at the center of so much of the current debate about academic freedom and the current government's actions that seem to many to threaten it. Many on the right and the left see this as the core of the matter: Universities have lost their way and the present crisis is the result, whether justified or not. Several of our authors take this matter up directly, while for others it is implicit in what they write.

I must say that I think this critique, while having some truth to it, has been blown vastly out of proportion and used as a pretext for seizing control of universities because they represent the kind of independent thinking that authoritarian-minded parties find threatening. The same critique can be and now is being made against the general press, the so-called traditional media, against judges appointed by Democratic presidents, against certain law firms and businesses, against foundations and nonprofits, and against broad swaths of the federal civil service. This is a crisis of democracy, falsely justified by distortions of reality.

Stone: I definitely agree that the extent of this problem has been wildly exaggerated by those who wish to control our colleges and universities and to silence views with which they disagree. At the same time, though, we have to acknowledge that there is an issue. Indeed, data collected by the Foundation for Individual Rights and Expression suggest that both faculty and students these days tend to be cautious about expressing their own points of view because they fear the consequences.[7] That is certainly incompatible with our commitment to academic freedom. I suspect this is considerably worse today than in the past because of social media. It used to be the case that, if students or professors said something that offended others, they would not pay a serious price for doing so. It might lead to some disagreement, or even anger, but it would pass quickly. Today, though, with social media there is a fear that what one says will not stay within the bounds of one's classmates or colleagues, but will be broadcast to the world, with much greater potential harm to the speaker. I suspect that has led to the current chilling effect. To the extent that all this is real, higher education has to figure out how to address these concerns in a way that reinforces and promotes the aspirations of academic freedom.

Beyond all of this, a central focus of this book is whether and to what extent government can constitutionally regulate, manipulate, or incentivize higher education in an effort to shape the nature and content of academic discourse and inquiry. On the one hand, government officials, including the president, are free to state their own views on all sorts of issues, including criticizing higher education. Moreover, government has no constitutional obligation to provide financial support for academic institutions. The key question posed by the Trump administration, though, is the extent to which government can constitutionally attempt to shape—or manipulate—academic freedom and free speech on campus, whether through laws, regulations, or funding, in a way that furthers the administration's own ideological preferences. Most specifically, to what extent can the Trump administration constitutionally deny federal resources to specific colleges and universities that do not agree to adopt policies that limit academic freedom, in an effort to pressure those institutions to adopt what the administration says is a more "fair and balanced" intellectual environment? If it's clear that the government cannot compel private universities to advocate certain points of view or prohibit them from teaching opposing points of view, to what extent can it leverage its power over federal grants to compel those goals? This is, in my view, the most fundamental threat to academic freedom today, and it is the question that is most central to the essays in this volume.

Bollinger: I agree completely that intolerance toward other viewpoints and opinions is a curse for any society—certainly for a democracy—and even more so for a university. However natural it is for all of us to have beliefs and reject those who would challenge them, such closed-mindedness leads nowhere in terms of expanding human knowledge or building a healthy democracy—and this is what both the First Amendment and the university are dedicated to acknowledging and overcoming. But because such bias is so natural and pervasive in human affairs, we have no choice but to be on high alert for its presence and determined to root it out.

Now, with respect to the current threats to academic freedom, or the freedom of the university, I think we are in something of a state of shock. What has been revealed by the Trump administration's efforts to wield the enormous power of the government for purposes of stifling independent voices, whether in universities, the press, the law, or the civil service, is that there is a very sizable gap between the protections we thought we had in place to secure democratic values (through the Constitution, the rule of law, built-in procedures in existing laws such as Title VI, and extensive norms and customs of appropriate behavior) and their actual vulnerability in the face of those willing to draw on raw government power to breach those lines of defense. Cases take time to reach and work their way through the courts; doctrines like standing make forming cases very difficult; litigation is costly in time and expense; threats of investigations and lawsuits instill fear, and fear chills, and what may look like a clear legal "right" can turn out to be an illusion of protection against a determined government.

So, what we fear for universities, and what we will consider throughout this book, is emblematic of what we fear and should attend to in every other sector of the society. Everything here is representative of a much larger question about the integrity of the system of constitutional democracy as a form of government.

PART I

THE HISTORY OF ACADEMIC FREEDOM IN THE UNITED STATES AND THE ARRIVAL OF THE TRUMP ADMINISTRATION

1

The Assault on Academic Freedom

ROBERT C. POST*

Academic freedom rests on a bargain between society and institutions of higher education. Universities are granted independence so that they can produce two necessities of modern life: knowledge and education. This bargain has enabled American universities to flourish.[1] It has made higher education in the United States the finest in the world, drawing to this country many of the best minds on the planet.

American higher education has been so dominant for so long that it is difficult to remember that academic freedom is only as strong as the underlying bargain that sustains it. The multiple assaults on university independence that characterize the past decade, which we can call the Time of Trump, suggest that this bargain is beginning to fray. If those in power in America no longer care about knowledge or education, academic freedom is imperiled. It becomes merely an obstacle to the achievement of partisan political ends.

The American concept of academic freedom was forged early in the 20th century. It emerged from struggles between the newly professionalizing American professoriate and the governmental, business, and parochial powers that controlled American universities. Reflecting our native pragmatism, academic freedom came to be defined in terms of the liberty necessary for American higher education to achieve its twin purposes of increasing knowledge and educating students to think for themselves. Promises of academic freedom are today everywhere inscribed in contractual relationships between faculty and the institutions that employ them.

* Sterling Professor of Law and former dean at Yale Law School. I am grateful for the wise comments of Clifford Ando, Evelyn Douek, Malcolm Feeley, Matthew Finkin, Owen Fiss, Tom Ginsburg, David Hollinger, Amy Kapczynski, Christine Landfried, Frank Michelman, David Rabban, Kim Scheppele, Joan Scott, Amanda Shanor, Reva Siegel, Brian Soucek, and Keith Whittington.

Robert C. Post, *The Assault on Academic Freedom*. In: *Academic Freedom in the Era of Trump*.
Edited by: Lee C. Bollinger and Geoffrey R. Stone, Oxford University Press.
 DOI: 10.1093/9780197854877.003.0002

The most striking feature of the Time of Trump is that government is now seeking to override these contracts. It is attempting to regulate institutions of higher education in ways patently inconsistent with the academic freedom required for colleges and universities to succeed. This would have been unthinkable only a generation ago, but American colleges and universities are now enmeshed in explicitly partisan controversies, where short-term incentives propose to override the underlying bargain between universities and society. Existential threats to the health of American higher education have become so pervasive and so severe that faculty and universities are turning to courts for protection.

The question is whether such litigation can safeguard the precious inheritance of American higher education. The answer in part depends on whether courts can recognize a constitutional principle of academic freedom sufficiently powerful to constrain official efforts to control university research and teaching. The longstanding focus of our constitutional law on individual rights of freedom of speech impedes this recognition. Academic freedom does not involve individual rights, but instead the autonomous self-government of a scholarly profession dedicated to disciplinary excellence. Courts can fully defend the academic freedom of colleges and universities only if they are able to relearn the important lessons of academic governance that emerged during the struggles of the early 20th century. They can defend academic freedom only if they constitutionalize the bargain upon which it rests.

Creating the Bargain: The Emergence of Academic Freedom

Academic Freedom of Research

Before the American Civil War, institutions of higher education in the United States were charged chiefly with the task of equipping young men with the intellectual, cultural, and moral resources necessary to succeed in elite society. Academic freedom was virtually unknown, dismissed as "one of those vague catchwords used without clear ideas, and appealing more to the feelings than to the understanding."[2] But after the war, as industrialization took hold, American scholars traveled to Europe and encountered the German research university, which was dedicated to the expansion of *Wissenschaft*.

American academics became entranced with this ideal and sought to bring it back home to the United States. Johns Hopkins was the first American institution explicitly to adopt it, announcing that its mission was "to advance knowledge."[3] As this mission gradually permeated American higher education, the knowledge sought by universities became less a matter of high cultural literacy and more a matter of disciplinary expertise.[4] The authority to determine what constituted knowledge was parceled into distinct specialties like physics or economics or biology or history.

The stage was thus set for a sharp rivalry between traditional American elites, like successful businessmen or professionals, and practitioners of the newly established American academic disciplines. Each side claimed the epistemological authority to determine truth. At first, the advantage lay with traditional elites, who controlled universities. Institutions of higher education were, as a formal legal matter, corporations owned and operated by private proprietors (private universities, whose trustees were generally successful businessmen or professionals), or by the public (state universities, which were ultimately controlled by politicians), or by a church (parochial universities). Faculty were mere employees of these corporations. Most faculty were hired "at will," which meant that they could be fired for any reason or for no reason.[5]

The early 20th century witnessed a sharp conflict over epistemological authority between those who legally owned universities and the faculty employed by those universities. Professors were summarily fired for offending conventional beliefs—for demonstrating the evolution of the species, for example, or for questioning the gold standard. It became plain that faculty could not be free to expand expert knowledge so long as their scholarship could be judged and circumscribed by laypersons who were the legal masters of university corporations.

The distinctive American ideals of academic freedom were forged to adjudicate this conflict.[6] American professors banded together in 1915 to create the American Association of University Professors (AAUP), with John Dewey as its first president. The AAUP acted immediately to issue the *1915 Declaration of Principles on Academic Freedom and Academic Tenure*,[7] which explicitly asserts that a central function of universities is "to promote inquiry and advance the sum of human knowledge."[8] Because "progress in scientific knowledge is essential to civilization,"[9] the *1915 Declaration* argues that every true university is "a public trust" dedicated to the public interest in expanding knowledge.[10] The university is not "an ordinary business venture."[11]

From this premise, the *1915 Declaration* argues that faculty should not be categorized as mere employees of a university. They should instead be characterized as university "appointees."[12] The *Declaration* analogizes the status of university professors to that of appointed judges:

> [O]nce appointed, the scholar has professional functions to perform in which the appointing authorities have neither competency nor moral right to intervene. The responsibility of the university teacher is primarily to the public itself, and to the judgment of his own profession; and while, with respect to certain external conditions of his vocation, he accepts a responsibility to the authorities of the institution in which he serves, in the essentials of his professional activity his duty is to the wider public to which the institution itself is morally amenable. So far as the university teacher's independence of thought and utterance is concerned—though

> not in other regards—the relationship of professor to trustees may be compared to that between judges of the federal courts and the executive who appoints them. University teachers should be understood to be, with respect to the conclusions reached and expressed by them, no more subject to the control of the trustees, than are judges subject to the control of the president, with respect to their decisions; while of course, for the same reason, trustees are no more to be held responsible for, or to be presumed to agree with, the opinions or utterances of professors, than the president can be assumed to approve of all the legal reasonings of the courts.[13]

Just as the President does not and should not control the decisions of judges he appoints, so the owners of a university, whether they are private trustees, the state, or a church, should not control the scholarship of the faculty they hire. The university can fulfill its public trust of expanding knowledge only if faculty are free to pursue their scholarship according to the standards of excellence defined by their disciplinary specialties. Academic freedom does not exempt faculty from peer review and judgment, but instead requires the liberty to pursue the "scholar's profession"[14] according to the standards of the profession.

Because the purpose of universities is to expand *disciplinary* knowledge, the *1915 Declaration* asserts that the "liberty of the scholar within the university to set forth his conclusions, be they what they may, is conditioned by their being conclusions gained by a scholar's method and held in a scholar's spirit; that is to say, they must be the fruits of competent and patient and sincere inquiry."[15] Academic freedom, the *1915 Declaration* precisely notes, upholds "not the absolute freedom of utterance of the individual scholar, but the absolute freedom of thought, of inquiry, of discussion and of teaching, of the academic profession."[16] Academic freedom thus functions according to a radically different logic than freedom of speech, which is an individual right that attaches to individual speakers.

Academic Freedom of Teaching

The *1915 Declaration* breaks down academic freedom into three components: "freedom of inquiry and research; freedom of teaching within the university or college; and freedom of extramural utterance and action."[17] The *Declaration* justifies academic freedom of teaching in the same functional manner as it does academic freedom of research. The purpose of a college education, the *Declaration* argues, is not merely to fill students' heads with information. Nor is it to "provide . . . students with ready-made conclusions."[18] Instead the goal of higher education is to train students "to think for themselves,"[19] which can occur only if students and faculty are free to express the widest range of viewpoints consistent with the standards of rational inquiry and professional ethics.

Independence of mind, unlike information, cannot be handed directly from teachers to students. It can be inculcated in students only by inspiring them to internalize the intellectual independence of their teachers. The *1915 Declaration* thus asserts:

> No man can be a successful teacher unless he enjoys the respect of his students, and their confidence in his intellectual integrity. It is clear, however, that this confidence will be impaired if there is suspicion on the part of the student that the teacher is not expressing himself fully or frankly, or that college and university teachers in general are a repressed and intimidated class who dare not speak with that candor and courage which youth always demands in those whom it is to esteem. The average student is a discerning observer, who soon takes the measure of his instructor. It is not only the character of the instruction but also the character of the instructor that counts; and if the student has reason to believe that the instructor is not true to himself, the virtue of the instruction as an educative force is incalculably diminished. There must be in the mind of the teacher no mental reservation. He must give the student the best of what he has and what he is.[20]

The *1915 Declaration* emphasizes that teaching students to think for themselves is especially important for American democracy, where students will eventually become citizens who must exercise the consequential responsibility of choosing national leaders. The particular task of higher education "is to help make public opinion more self-critical and more circumspect, to check the more hasty and unconsidered impulses of popular feeling, to train the democracy to the habit of looking before and after."[21]

Academic Freedom and Federal Funding

The *1915 Declaration* offers a purposive account of higher education. As that account gained traction, a consensus emerged in favor of academic freedom of research and teaching. The consensus was codified in the *1940 Statement of Principles on Academic Freedom and Tenure*.[22] What ultimately cemented national support for this consensus, however, was the trauma of World War II, which definitively demonstrated the dependence of national security on the acquisition of scientific and technological knowledge. The war also made plain the need for expanding disciplinary expertise to sustain advances in medicine and industry. Suddenly research universities became essential engines of national development.[23]

No one expressed this new attitude toward universities more clearly or more effectively than Vannevar Bush, an MIT professor who was the wartime director of the Office of Scientific Research and Development. In 1945, Bush delivered an immensely influential report to President Truman, *Science: The Endless Frontier*, which argued that "Scientific progress is one essential key to our security as a nation, to our better health, to more jobs, to a higher standard of living, and to our cultural progress."[24] The clear implication was that the federal government should "accept new responsibilities for promoting the flow of new scientific knowledge and the development of scientific talent in our youth."[25]

Bush recommended investing in universities to train future experts[26] and to support "basic research."[27] Accepting the premise of the *1915 Declaration* that quality research could be produced only under conditions of academic freedom, Bush stressed that federal funds should be distributed in ways that preserved "freedom of inquiry."[28]

Bush was clear that "scientific progress" required "the free play of free intellects, working on subjects of their own choice, in the manner dictated by their curiosity for exploration of the unknown."[29] Hence "[s]upport of basic research in the public and private colleges, universities, and research institutes must leave the internal control of policy, personnel, and the method and scope of the research to the institutions themselves. This is of the utmost importance."[30] Federal support, Bush insisted, should depend upon criteria of disciplinary excellence.[31] Because science is universal, Bush recommended that the federal government "should take an active role in promoting the international flow of scientific information."[32]

Bush proved prophetic. His report became a "blueprint" for federal support of scientific and technological development, support that "established American technological and economic preeminence."[33] In the postwar world, American science, technology, and medicine became the international gold standard. The price of this success, however, was a growing dependence of American research universities upon federal funding.[34] Universities accepted this price because federal support seemed secure. It was profoundly beneficial to all concerned. Who would be foolish enough to kill a golden goose that produced such undiluted benefits, such unquestioned American dominance in the essential fields of scientific and technological development, as well as education?

Undoing the Bargain: Academic Freedom in the Time of Trump

Universities, Elites, and Partisan Politics

What Bush never foresaw was that universities would themselves become entangled in partisan controversy. At the time of the Bush report, higher education was the mark of elite status. University attendance may have been small—in 1937, just 8.4 percent of the 18- to 24-year-old population attended an institution of higher education[35]—but it was broad enough to encompass large swaths of the American ruling class, which on a bipartisan basis prized the higher education that distinguished it from the masses. Elite solidarity, which spanned the major political parties, made it inconceivable that universities would themselves become the object of partisan controversy.

The enactment of the GI bill after World War II altered this configuration. By supporting higher education for returning World War II veterans, the bill initiated a sweeping process of democratization that fundamentally changed the relationship of higher education to American class structure.[36] American colleges and universities lost their association with a narrow upper crust and became something closer to a common entitlement.[37] They grew into important shapers of mass public opinion and therefore implicated themselves in the cultural conflicts that began to characterize partisan American politics.[38] As a result, they evolved into potential targets of partisan disagreement.

The point is nicely illustrated by the changing politics of race. The struggle to overcome Southern apartheid reached its culmination in the monumental Civil Rights Act of 1964, which was a bipartisan effort. Universities gradually threw their considerable institutional weight behind that effort, eventually in many cases embracing affirmative action on grounds that were later to be explicitly endorsed by the Supreme Court in *Grutter v. Bollinger*: "In order to cultivate a set of leaders with legitimacy in the eyes of the citizenry, it is necessary that the path to leadership be visibly open to talented and qualified individuals of every race and ethnicity."[39]

Yet even as universities pursued these ends, the bipartisan national commitment to civil rights began to unravel. The success of Nixon's "Southern strategy" increasingly transformed the racial question into a partisan struggle between the major political parties. Universities were forced to choose sides, which made them participants in an ongoing war between the parties. As partisan differences over race gradually intensified over the succeeding decades, the position of universities grew increasingly vulnerable to partisan attack.

The culmination of these developments can be seen in legislation enacted by Florida in the Time of Trump. Attempting to wrest leadership of the Republican Party away from Donald Trump after the 2020 election, Governor Ron DeSantis of Florida pushed the Individual Freedom Act (IFA) through the Florida legislature in 2022.[40] The IFA prohibits faculty in Florida's public universities from educating students in ways that espouse, promote, or advance eight specific concepts about race and sex, including that of affirmative action.[41]

In court, Florida has defended the act on the ground that "When public employees speak pursuant to their official duties," as do professors in the classrooms of public universities, "that speech is *government* speech and thus not subject to First Amendment protection."[42] The implication of Florida's argument is that government can require faculty at public universities to teach whatever government instructs them to teach.[43] Asserting that faculty are mere employees, not appointees, Florida is now prepared officially and explicitly to deny an essential premise of the academic freedom that was established at the outset of the 20th century.[44]

The IFA is crafted to prohibit some faculty from disseminating the results of their research to students, thus undermining the dissemination of new knowledge.[45] The IFA is also designed to prevent some Florida faculty from modeling intellectual independence in their classrooms, thus undermining the goal of higher education to produce students who can think for themselves.[46] In these ways the IFA subordinates the goods of academic freedom to the imposition of partisan ideology.[47] The Republican Party of Florida is more concerned to capture higher education as a mouthpiece for conservative views than it is to preserve universities for the creation of new knowledge or for the education of independently thinking citizens.[48]

The Partisan Assault on Universities

In 2015, when Gallup first measured confidence in higher education, 57 percent of those polled had a great deal or quite a lot of confidence in higher education. By 2024, that number had dropped to 36 percent. In 2015, only 10 percent of adults had little or no confidence in higher education, but by 2024 that number had tripled to 32 percent.[49] Public attitudes toward higher education are dramatically changing due to emerging and intense partisan differences like those driving the enactment of the IFA.[50]

Between 2015 and 2024, the percentage of Republicans with a great deal or quite a lot confidence in higher education sank from 56 percent to 20 percent; the percentage of Republicans with little or no confidence quintupled from 11 percent to 50 percent.[51] Forty one percent of Americans with little or no confidence in higher education report that their lack of confidence is due to what they perceive is the biased liberal agenda of colleges and universities.[52]

In the Time of Trump, higher education has moved into the crosshairs of sharp partisan struggle. Vice President J. D. Vance made this very clear in his November 2021 address to the National Conservatism Conference. Vance explained to his audience that, because universities teach "progressive orthodoxies" that consist of "deceit and lies," conservatives must "honestly and aggressively attack the universities in this country."[53] According to Vance, the lies promulgated by universities include that it is liberating for women to work outside the home; that environmental justice is important; and that Critical Race Theory offers useful insights into the state of our society. "We are giving our children over to our enemies," Vance declared, "and it is time we stopped doing it."

It is important to note that the contemporary partisan attack on higher education transcends specific controversial issues, like gender or race.[54] When Vance asked his audience what gave Anthony Fauci the right to order people about, the answer was the "diploma" hanging on Fauci's wall. Because universities are empowered to certify expertise, it is expertise itself that is the ultimate target of Vance's speech. It has become clear to conservative activists that the epistemological authority of academic disciplines stands in the way of achieving many of their political goals,[55] in contexts ranging from epidemiology to climate change to tariffs.[56]

Almost immediately after assuming office in January 2025, Trump chose to emphasize this point. He announced a series of provocative appointments, like that of Robert F. Kennedy, Jr., to become secretary of health and human services, Linda McMahon to become secretary of education, and Tulsi Gabbard to become the director of national intelligence. These appointments unmistakably signaled that, in Trump's second administration, traditional disciplinary expertise would have little value.[57] Trump instead wanted a cabinet that would loyally follow his political decisions. Professional expertise could serve as a positive obstruction to Trump's partisan agenda.[58]

Academic freedom depends upon the value that society places on expertise and disciplinary knowledge. The second Trump administration set out to diminish that value by taking direct aim at the production of scientific expertise. In 2023, $59.6 billion of the $109 billion spent on university research in the United States came from the federal government.[59] Seeking to exploit this vulnerability, Trump moved immediately to have the National Institutes of Health cap at 15 percent all previously negotiated indirect-costs rates on all existing and future grants for biomedical research.

This was not an attack on specific kinds of research, but on research itself. It was an attack that produced an "imminent risk of halting lifesaving clinical trials, disrupting the development of innovative medical research and treatment, and shuttering of research facilities, without regard for current patient care."[60] The proposed cut was promptly enjoined as illegal due to its inconsistency with applicable statutory and administrative requirements.[61] Not to be deterred, the Trump administration proposed to slash NIH spending in 2026 by roughly 40 percent, a proposal that would constitute a "disaster . . . for American science & technology and our nation's continuing competitiveness."[62]

Trump also moved swiftly to impose on higher education the ideological substance of his racial agenda.[63] On February 14, 2025, the Department of Education issued a "Dear Colleague" letter clarifying the DOE's policy enforcing Title VI of the 1964 Civil Rights Act.[64] Purporting to implement the Supreme Court's 2023 decision in *Students for Fair Admissions v. Harvard* [*SFFA*],[65] which had struck down affirmative-action programs as inconsistent with the Equal Protection Clause, the letter stated:

> Educational institutions have toxically indoctrinated students with the false premise that the United States is built upon "systemic and structural racism" and advanced discriminatory policies and practices. Proponents of these discriminatory practices have attempted to further justify them—particularly during the last four years—under the banner of "diversity, equity, and inclusion" ("DEI"), smuggling racial stereotypes and explicit race-consciousness into everyday training, programming, and discipline.[66]

The letter threatened non-complying institutions with cancellation of federal financial assistance.[67] Stressing that "academic freedom . . . is of transcendent value to all of us," a federal district court enjoined the enforcement of the letter on April 24, 2025.[68]

Perhaps the most troubling aspect of the second Trump administration's explosive assault on higher education is its unabashed use of punitive measures to break the resistance of particular high-profile universities. After a quick and seemingly decisive victory over Columbia University, which acceded to administration demands in the hope of restoring $400 million in frozen federal funds,[69] the Trump administration quickly came to focus its attention on Harvard University, in the apparent belief that Harvard's collapse would bring the rest of the American higher-education establishment to heel.[70]

On April 11, 2025, the administration demanded that Harvard adopt and implement "merit-based" hiring and admissions policies and "cease all preferences based on race, color, religion, sex, or national origin"; that Harvard "reform its recruitment, screening, and admissions of international students to prevent admitting students hostile to . . . American values and institutions"; that Harvard ensure that "each department, field, or teaching unit . . . be individually viewpoint diverse"; that Harvard review departments and programs for antisemitism and "ideological capture"; and that Harvard "immediately shutter all diversity, equity, and inclusion (DEI) programs, offices, committees, positions, and initiatives."[71]

In essence, the Trump administration demanded that Harvard reform its faculty and students so that they would reflect the partisan ideological views of the president's party. It seems apparent that these demands were designed to force Harvard to resist, which it did. Harvard wrote the administration that, despite its threat to cancel "billions of dollars in federal funding critical to vital research and innovation that has saved and improved lives and allowed Harvard to play a central role in making our country's scientific, medical, and other research communities the standard-bearers for the world," "the university will not surrender its independence or relinquish its constitutional rights. Neither Harvard not any other private university can allow itself to be taken over by the federal government."[72]

Apparently relishing the opportunity to pound Harvard into submission, the administration immediately unleashed a barrage of coercive responses.[73] It threatened to revoke Harvard's tax-exempt status.[74] It announced that Harvard would receive no new federal grants until it complied with the administration's demands.[75] It canceled more than $2 billion in grants and contracts already allocated to Harvard.[76] It revoked Harvard's ability to certify foreign students to receive visas.[77] It announced an investigation of the accuracy of Harvard's disclosures of foreign gifts and contracts.[78] It threatened to strip Harvard of its patents.[79] It accused Harvard of "deliberate indifference" toward antisemitism in violation of Title VI.[80]

Traditional First Amendment Rights and the Assault on Universities

The violence and brutality of the assault makes clear that the second Trump administration is prepared to shatter the bargain that has for generations sustained the preeminence of American higher education. The administration does not want students who will learn to think for themselves; it wants students who will toe the conservative line.[81] The administration does not want research that expands knowledge; it wants research that supports conservative policies.[82]

The question is thus starkly posed, as it has never before been posed in this nation's history, whether fundamental principles of academic freedom can shield universities from government-based assaults. These principles were articulated in the *1915 Declaration* and in the *1940 Statement* as guidelines for how colleges or universities should organize themselves to facilitate education and research. The triumph of academic freedom after World War II meant that these principles were widely incorporated into contractual agreements between faculty and the institutions that employed them. The principles enabled American higher education to flourish. It is an entirely different question, however, whether these same principles of academic freedom can also serve as standards of constitutional law capable of constraining a government determined to force colleges and universities to kneel before the whip of state power.[83]

American courts have long referred in tantalizing ways to a distinctively constitutional concept of academic freedom,[84] even going so far as to announce that "Our Nation is deeply committed to safeguarding academic freedom, which is of transcendent value to all of us and not merely to the teachers concerned. That freedom is therefore a special concern of the First Amendment."[85] But judicial references to a constitutional concept of academic freedom have been largely vague and rhetorical, with the result that "no clear doctrines have emerged."[86] We simply do not know what the constitutional status of academic freedom might be.[87] When confronted with constitutional questions of academic freedom, courts have typically turned instead to generic First Amendment principles of freedom of speech.[88]

Ordinary First Amendment free-speech doctrine is sufficient to render unconstitutional many actions of the Trump administration. So, for example, if the Trump administration terminated Harvard's ability to enroll foreign students in retaliation for Harvard's "exercising its First Amendment rights to reject the government's demands to control Harvard's governance, curriculum, and the 'ideology' of its faculty and students," as Harvard plausibly alleges in its complaint,[89] the administration's actions would be unconstitutional.[90] As the Court recently emphasized, executive officials cannot rely on "'legal sanctions and other means of coercion . . . to achieve the suppression' of disfavored speech."[91]

Colleges and universities are what is known in ordinary First Amendment doctrine as "expressive associations."[92] It is black-letter law that "the First Amendment protects acts of expressive association,"[93] so that government cannot force an expressive association "to 'propound a point of view contrary to its beliefs' by directing its membership choices."[94] Colleges and universities exist to facilitate expression in both teaching and research. The messages that they send to the public are very much affected by whom universities and colleges choose to admit as students and by whom they choose to hire as faculty.[95]

A university is much more obviously an expressive association than is the Boy Scouts of America [BSA], which the Court held in its *Dale*[96] decision was constitutionally immune from the application of a state antidiscrimination statute on the ground that the BSA was an expressive association.[97] The Trump administration's efforts to force private institutions of higher education to abandon all forms of DEI in hiring and admissions are for this reason likely unconstitutional,[98] as are the administration's efforts to impose ideological diversity in hiring and admissions.[99]

It is true that the Trump administration is not directly regulating the hiring and admissions of colleges and universities; it is instead attempting to coerce those decisions by placing conditions on federal funding. But because the Court long ago created the doctrine of unconstitutional conditions to abolish the rights/privileges distinction, this is a distinction without a difference. The doctrine "holds that government may not grant a benefit on the condition that the beneficiary surrender a constitutional right, even if the government may withhold that benefit altogether."[100] The doctrine applies with special force to many recent Trump-administration actions, which threaten to withdraw *all* funding from a university even though only particular programs allegedly violate Title VI. Although government can certainly designate specific funds for specific purposes,[101] it cannot use official funds as leverage to "'prohibit[] the recipient from engaging in the protected conduct outside the scope of the federal funded program.'"[102] This is precisely what the Trump administration has attempted to do.[103]

Academic Freedom and Traditional First Amendment Rights

It is certainly effective lawyering to invoke generic First Amendment doctrine to challenge the assaults of the Trump administration. But a cost of this approach is that it leaves unresolved the constitutional status of academic freedom, which follows a logic that is quite different from that which underlies what the Court has called "ordinary First Amendment standards."[104]

Ordinary First Amendment doctrine condemns viewpoint discrimination as anathema, as "poison to a free society."[105] The doctrine postulates that there is "an 'equality of status in the field of ideas.'"[106] That is why, if an aspiring young astronomer publishes an editorial in the *New York Times* arguing that the moon is made of blue cheese, he cannot be sanctioned by the state for his outlandish hypothesis. Yet academic freedom within universities, even within public universities, depends upon a quite different approach. If a young astronomer were to seek tenure on the basis of such a preposterous hypothesis, his bid for promotion would and should be denied. Using methods that define the discipline of astronomy, faculty in the field would find the argument meritless.

In both public and private universities, academic freedom does not merely tolerate viewpoint discrimination; it *requires* viewpoint discrimination. Public universities appropriately exercise viewpoint discrimination to decide whom to hire, whom to promote, and who should receive grants.[107] Academic freedom depends upon viewpoint discrimination of this kind because it insists that evaluations of merit are essential to academic life.[108] Academic institutions aspire to produce *knowledge*, which, as Allan Gibbard reminds us, are those ideas upon which we have warrant to rely.[109] That warrant depends upon continuous and rigorous testing and evaluation. Academic freedom requires, however, that such evaluations be made *only* by those who are competent to judge the quality of professional scholarship and *only* on the basis of criteria relevant to the determination of that quality.[110]

At root, therefore, academic freedom involves "the absolute freedom of thought, of inquiry, of discussion and of teaching, of the academic profession,"[111] not of individual professors. If First Amendment rights of free expression attach to individual speakers, rights of academic freedom attach instead to the community of inquiry constituted by scholars.[112] "Historically speaking, the heart and soul of academic freedom lie not in free speech but in professional autonomy and collegial self-governance."[113] Academic freedom protects the disciplinary standards that constitute "the academic profession" and that make possible the expansion of expert knowledge.[114]

A similar point can be made about the doctrine of compelled speech. Ordinary First Amendment standards protect "the decision of both what to say and what *not* to say."[115] It is a "fundamental rule of protection under the First Amendment, that a speaker has the autonomy to choose the content of his own message"[116] and that government therefore may not "compel speech."[117] Yet both private and public universities routinely compel speech. Students must take examinations and complete assignments; faculty must publish or perish. Academic freedom allows speech to be compelled because education and research can be advanced only if speech is mandated. Academic freedom requires, however, that speech be compelled only as necessary to advance the university's mission of education and research.

The deep theoretical discrepancy between ordinary First Amendment standards and academic freedom is well illustrated by the doctrine of public-employee speech. As a matter of positive law, faculty in public universities are public employees. There is well-worked-out First Amendment doctrine that specifies the constitutional protections accruing to the speech of public employees. In *Garcetti v. Ceballos*,[118] the Court held that "when public employees make statements pursuant to their official duties, the employees are not speaking as citizens for First Amendment purposes, and the Constitution does not insulate their communications from employer discipline."[119]

When faculty teach or disseminate their research, it is typically pursuant to their official duties. The literal holding of *Garcetti* would thus seem to deprive faculty at public universities of individual First Amendment rights of freedom of speech in teaching and in disseminating the results of their research. The whole point of academic freedom, however, is to protect the ability of faculty to freely engage in these official duties.

This discrepancy reflects the fact that academic freedom follows a different logic than do ordinary First Amendment free-speech rights. Acknowledging this difference, the Court in *Garcetti* explicitly withheld judgment on whether its holding should apply to public universities, remarking that "academic freedom" might require a different rule in cases "involving speech related to scholarship or teaching."[120] But the lack of any well-developed constitutional account of academic freedom has rendered lower courts quite uncertain about how to apply *Garcetti* to institutions of higher education.[121]

Apart from *Garcetti*, well-established First Amendment doctrine holds that the speech of a government employee is not protected by the First Amendment unless it is about a matter of "public concern."[122] The criterion of "public concern," however, is theoretically irrelevant to academic freedom.[123] The obscure scholarship of a professor of Hittite deserves the same academic freedom of research as do the publications of a prominent expert in American constitutional law. It is not surprising, therefore, that the criterion of "public concern" has caused great "inconsistency and confusion" in lower courts that seek to apply ordinary First Amendment standards to cases involving higher education.[124] The disarray illustrates the persistent inability of American courts to work out a coherent constitutional theory of academic freedom.

Toward a Constitutional Concept of Academic Freedom

The Structure of Academic Freedom as a Constitutional Right

Recent assaults on higher education have been so crude and malign, so obviously motivated by animus, that ordinary First Amendment standards might indeed be sufficient to repulse them.[125] But a better result would be the construction of a coherent constitutional theory of academic freedom. Any such theory must depend upon the claim that academic freedom is necessary to preserve a functioning American democracy, which is an essential purpose of the First Amendment.[126] The theory would require at least two dimensions. The first would address constitutional limitations on the actions of public universities. The second would address constitutional limitations on government regulation of all universities, both public and private.

It is not difficult to specify the contents of the first dimension. Public universities already act in accordance with basic principles of academic freedom, even if such actions are forbidden by ordinary First Amendment standards. Like all institutions of higher education, public universities exercise content and viewpoint discrimination; they compel speech; they respect the academic freedom of faculty regardless of whether scholarship involves matters of public concern.[127] This is because public universities, like all universities, seek "to discover knowledge" and to teach their students to exercise "a mature independence of mind."[128] The principles of academic freedom expressed in the *1915 Declaration* and the *1940 Statement* codify the protocols necessary to achieve these ends, even if these protocols do not square with ordinary First Amendment standards.

There are existing doctrinal resources capable of explaining this anomaly. Although courts have not self-consciously theorized the point, they have in fact interpreted the First Amendment to authorize government, when it creates discrete managerial domains to accomplish specific goals, to regulate speech as necessary to achieve those goals.[129] That is why speech within courts, prisons, legislatures, bureaucracies, or schools is regulated quite differently than ordinary public discourse.[130] When the state creates public universities to educate students and to expand knowledge, therefore, these universities can regulate speech as necessary to achieve their purposes. Explicitly authorizing public universities to enforce standards of academic freedom would be consistent with these broad jurisprudential principles. Conversely, when public universities regulate speech in ways that violate standards of academic freedom, they act in ways that are inconsistent with the achievement of their own purposes and hence that are unconstitutional.

The second dimension of a constitutional theory of academic freedom requires a somewhat more ambitious doctrinal reform. Courts cannot protect universities from government abuse unless they possess a convincing account of the distinct constitutional function of universities. But the contemporary Court has great difficulty conceptualizing the First Amendment as protecting anything other than the rights of individual speakers, all of whom are conceived as exercising identical speech rights. So, for example, the Court can barely comprehend, and indeed often seems outright hostile to, any explanation of the specific constitutional function of the "press," even though the press receives explicit textual recognition in the First Amendment.[131] It will not be easy to induce the Court to develop a distinct constitutional theory of higher education, even if such a theory is necessary for colleges and universities to serve essential functions in our modern democracy.

Higher education was a rare phenomenon during the 18th century, when the First Amendment was ratified. But at that time the expert, disciplinary knowledge produced by contemporary universities was also almost unknown. In the 21st century, by contrast, nations cannot survive, either commercially or militarily, without deploying expert knowledge. If citizens in our democracy cannot assess for themselves the application of this knowledge, they cannot control the actions of their own government. This is true in almost all essential policy sectors, ranging from health to climate, from nuclear energy to AI. The distinct constitutional value that underlies academic freedom of research is therefore what I have elsewhere called "democratic competence,"[132] which refers to the principle that in a democracy the state cannot control the knowledge available to its citizens.[133]

The basic idea underlying democratic competence is simple. Democracy would become a farce, and the value of self-government meaningless, if the state could manipulate the knowledge available to its citizens. Although many institutions in American life create knowledge, only universities possess authority to reproduce and revise the disciplinary standards that *define* what counts as expert knowledge.[134] Although this was not the case in the 18th century, it is plain that, in the 21st century, if government can assert ideological control over university research and teaching, it can freely manipulate the content and nature of expert knowledge.[135] The government can render it impossible for the people to maintain epistemological independence from the state. It is for this reason that universities should receive distinctive constitutional protections that limit government control over research.[136]

In the context of graduate education, academic freedom of research often bleeds indistinguishably into academic freedom of teaching, since a major function of research is to determine how future experts should be trained. But in the context of undergraduate education, academic freedom of teaching also serves an additional constitutional value. The essential thought, which was well articulated in the *1915 Statement*, is that a modern democracy cannot survive unless its citizens are adequately educated.[137] Citizens who cannot think for themselves threaten democracy because their credulity is inconsistent with the rational deliberation that self-governance requires.[138] A successful democracy requires that citizens possess both critical-thinking skills and basic cultural and scientific literacies.

Although higher education was rare in the 18th century, American democracy at that time largely depended upon deference to the judgment of educated elites.[139] In the 21st century, by contrast, American democracy is controlled by a popular will that is increasingly vulnerable to techniques of mass-media manipulation. Our democracy is threatened if its citizens lack the capacity to free themselves from the thrall of misinformation and gaslighting. Education is required for this capacity, especially the kind of education widely offered by colleges and universities.

Constitutional protections for academic freedom of undergraduate teaching must therefore depend upon reasons like those advanced by Justice Felix Frankfurter more than seventy years ago in his eloquent concurring opinion in *Wieman v. Updegraff*:[140]

> That our democracy ultimately rests on public opinion is a platitude of speech but not a commonplace in action. Public opinion is the ultimate reliance of our society only if it be disciplined and responsible. It can be disciplined and responsible only if habits of open-mindedness and of critical inquiry are acquired in the formative years of our citizens. The process of education has naturally enough been the basis of hope for the perdurance of our democracy on the part of all our great leaders, from Thomas Jefferson onwards.
>
> To regard teachers—in our entire educational system, from the primary grades to the university—as the priests of our democracy is therefore not to indulge in hyperbole. It is the special task of teachers to foster those habits of open-mindedness and critical inquiry which alone make for responsible citizens, who, in turn, make possible an enlightened and effective public opinion. Teachers must fulfill their function by precept

> and practice, by the very atmosphere which they generate; they must be exemplars of open-mindedness and free inquiry. They cannot carry out their noble task if the conditions for the practice of a responsible and critical mind are denied to them. . . . They must have the freedom of responsible inquiry, by thought and action, into the meaning of social and economic ideas, into the checkered history of social and economic dogma. . . .

The functions of educational institutions in our national life and the conditions under which alone they can adequately perform them are at the basis of these limitations upon State and national power. These functions and the essential conditions for their effective discharge have been well described by a leading educator:

> Now, a university is a place that is established and will function for the benefit of society, provided it is a center of independent thought. It is a center of independent thought and criticism that is created in the interest of the progress of society, and the one reason that we know that every totalitarian government must fail is that no totalitarian government is prepared to face the consequences of creating free universities.[141]

Applying a Constitutional Right of Academic Freedom to Public Universities

The country is now in the throes of a populist eruption that strives to sweep away all sources of resistance to the will of the governing party. Universities possess an epistemological authority that competes with this political will,[142] and they are therefore targeted by an administration determined to erase all opposition.[143] Many of the President's actions are so ill-advised that they can be prevented by applying ordinary First Amendment standards, like those which forbid state interference with expressive associations.[144] But these standards do not directly or clearly address what is most deeply at stake in the contemporary assault on universities, and this failure is especially pertinent to government efforts to regulate state universities.

Public Law 113, which was recently enacted in Indiana,[145] well illustrates the point. The statute authorizes the board of trustees of public universities in Indiana to review faculty teaching with a view to denying tenure or promotion "if the faculty member is unlikely to foster a culture of free inquiry, free expression and intellectual diversity within the institution; [or] unlikely to expose students to scholarly works from a variety of political or ideological frameworks that may exist within and are applicable to the faculty member's academic discipline." The purpose of Public Law 113 is to counter a perceived liberal bias in the professoriate.[146]

The statute's author has stated that the purpose of the legislation is to restore "trust" in higher education,[147] but in fact the statute imposes on university teaching vague and politically charged criteria that will be enforced by laypersons who are answerable to a partisan authority. It is no wonder that the statute cast an instant and deadly chill over university pedagogy in Indiana.[148] The statute manifests the same populist impulse to colonize universities as is more obviously and crudely embodied in Trump's many executive orders.

Ordinary First Amendment doctrines, like those involving individual rights of freedom of speech, do not easily apply to a statute like Public Law 113. Because there are many forms of control over faculty speech that are appropriate and necessary, professors in public universities do not possess individual rights of free expression that categorically remove them from the supervision of their state employers. A faculty member in a physics department in a state university, for example, can properly be required to staff a science course instead of a class in musical theory that she may instead desire to teach. The fundamental difficulty with a paradigm of individual free-speech rights is that it lacks theoretical resources to distinguish between acceptable and unacceptable regulations of faculty speech in the classroom.[149]

Such distinctions can be usefully drawn only if the independence of public-university professors is conceptualized through an entirely different constitutional paradigm. We must shift our focus from individual professors to the organizations in which they are embedded. From this perspective, it is clear that no government organization can function if its members are free to say whatever they wish whenever they wish. All government organizations are therefore authorized to sharply limit the individual free-speech rights of their members. They can prohibit speech that is inconsistent with the ability of the organization to fulfill its mission. So, for example, if the federal government wishes to propagandize American values to the world, it can by statute establish the Voice of America (VOA), and employees of VOA cannot invoke individual First Amendment rights to undermine VOA's mandate when speaking as employees of the organization.

This is the logic that underlies Public Law 113. Trustees are the legal masters of Indiana's public universities. Public Law 113 empowers trustees to regulate faculty teaching to advance what the trustees regard as the mission of the universities they control.[150] The premise of Public Law 113 is that the mission of public higher education in Indiana is to be determined by the politically appointed trustees who are charged with supervising Indiana's public universities.

No theory of individual speech rights can dislodge this premise, for the expression of all individuals employed by government organizations is constrained for analogous reasons.

Although we often speak of constitutional rights of academic freedom as though they were analogous in form and structure to individual free-speech rights, in point of fact they embody a quite different kind of constitutional reasoning. They do not focus on individual liberties, but instead on organizational structure. The point of a constitutional right of academic freedom is to establish that the mission of a public university is not to be determined by the whim of its trustees, or even by the political will of a state legislature, but instead by the Constitution itself.

Whenever we speak about constitutional rights of academic freedom, what we mean is that for constitutional purposes the mission of public universities should be conceived as advancing knowledge and teaching students to think for themselves.[151] Higher education is, in this sense, truly a "public trust" under the protective umbrella of the First Amendment.[152] Although trustees may legally control a public university, they lack authority to alter the terms of this trust. So also does a state legislature. Government regulation of faculty teaching in a public university is thus constitutional if it is compatible with the mission of educating students to think for themselves, but it is unconstitutional if it is inconsistent with that mission.

It may sound strange to fix the constitutional purpose of a state institution in ways that are independent of legislation that regulates it. But courts do this all the time. Whenever a court decides the First Amendment rights of students in K–12 schools[153] or the constitutionality of government restrictions on the speech of lawyers in courts,[154] it assesses the compatibility of government regulation with the underlying mission of a government institution, and it does so independently of whatever particular state regulation happens to be at issue.[155]

So long as attendance is voluntary, nothing in the Constitution would prevent Indiana from creating an institution for the Propagation of Indiana Values, analogous to the VOA. Nothing would prevent the Indiana legislature from specifying the curriculum and teaching protocols of such an institution. But a constitutional concept of academic freedom would prevent Indiana from creating a university and requiring it to propagate the politically dominant values of Indiana.[156] This is because a constitutional concept of academic freedom specifies that the fundamental pedagogical purpose of a university, including a public university, is to inspire students to think for themselves.[157] Longstanding principles of academic freedom of teaching, as set forth in the *1915 Declaration* and the *1940 Statement*, form a prima facie guide for determining whether government regulation is consistent or inconsistent with this mission.

The Court came close to recognizing an independent constitutional principle of academic freedom when it acknowledged the potential need for a university exception to the generic rules of public-employee speech articulated in *Garcetti*.[158] Whether the generic rules of *Garcetti* apply to public universities depends upon whether the mission of public universities is independently grounded in the Constitution. If government were free to define the purpose of public higher education as it wishes, it would also be free to regulate the speech of faculty in the same comprehensive way as it regulates the speech of all other government employees.[159] But if the purpose of higher education is instead grounded in the Constitution, government cannot regulate faculty speech in ways that are inconsistent with that purpose. It cannot regulate speech in ways that are incompatible with academic freedom of teaching or research, because these forms of freedom are necessary for universities to fulfill their constitutionally given mission of expanding knowledge and teaching students to think for themselves.

The most important constitutional issue raised by Public Law 113, therefore, is whether Indiana has sought to create a public system of actual colleges and universities. If a court were to conclude that Indiana was serious about higher education, it would ask whether Public Law 113 is consistent with the classroom independence required by academic freedom of teaching.[160] A constitutional concept of academic freedom would prevent Indiana University from sailing "under false colors," to use the metaphor of the *1915 Declaration*.[161] Interpreted in this way, constitutional rights of academic freedom could be asserted either by individual Indiana faculty or by Indiana universities and colleges. The decisive question is not who could bring such a suit, but rather whether the substance of the rights asserted in the suit is designed to protect the fundamental academic mission of the university.[162]

With Freedom Comes Responsibility

Apart from formal questions of constitutional law, Public Law 113 raises a deep and fundamental question about the authority of academic freedom in the present age. At its root, academic freedom concerns the need for professional self-governance.[163] Academic freedom of research cannot exist unless research is judged by those competent to evaluate the quality of research, which is to say by the academic profession itself. Academic freedom of teaching cannot exist unless teaching is judged by those competent to evaluate the quality of teaching, which is to say by the academic profession itself. These elemental propositions have defined American academic freedom for more than a century.

As lawyers and doctors have discovered to their chagrin, claims to professional self-regulation have not fared well in this country. Such claims are viewed with a suspicion that is too often justified. It is obvious that self-interested professionals will often protect their colleagues from the application of otherwise appropriate standards. The *1915 Declaration* explicitly cautioned faculty against a failure of this kind. "It is conceivable," it said, "that our profession may prove unworthy of its high calling, and unfit to exercise the responsibilities that belong to it."[164] But the *Declaration* pledged that the newly founded AAUP would not only "earnestly guard those liberties without which [the profession] cannot rightly render its distinctive and indispensable service to society, but also that it will with equal earnestness seek to maintain such standards of professional character, and of scientific integrity and competency, as shall make it a fit instrument for that service."[165]

Public Law 113 suggests that in the Time of Trump significant sectors of the public no longer believe that the academic profession has fulfilled this high duty of self-regulation. They believe that they must impose external controls on universities because the academic profession has become self-serving and insulated. This perception is encouraged by sharp political polarization, which fuels widespread charges of liberal bias.[166]

These charges pose a serious problem for American higher education. If they are true, if universities have in fact failed to exercise the self-regulation pledged by the *1915 Declaration*, that dereliction must be rectified. But these charges cannot be ignored even if they are false. Once the public comes to believe that higher education indoctrinates rather than educates, it will, in the absence of constitutional restraints, seek to impose external controls that will compromise the necessary self-regulation of colleges and universities. Once the public comes to believe that the research produced by higher education expresses the biases of liberal ideology instead of actual knowledge, it will, in the absence of constitutional restraints, seek to suppress and control that research.[167]

The clear implication is that the academic community ignores public opinion at its peril. American faculty thus face a delicate conundrum. On the one hand, if faculty allow the vagaries of public opinion to control their teaching and research, they betray the essential purpose of their profession. But if, on the other hand, faculty entirely disregard public opinion and imagine that support for academic freedom descends as an immaculate mandate from heaven, they risk a backlash that will sweep away academic professionalism and independence through statutes like the IFA or Public Law 113, or through the many Trump executive orders that seek to crush the autonomy of American higher education. Academic scholarship, like every profession, ultimately requires some measure of public acceptance and support.

There is no ideal solution to this tension, which requires tact and statesmanship for its negotiation. In this respect, faculty are in the same difficult position as judges who must decide highly controversial questions of constitutional law. The obligation of a judge is to decide cases according to law rather than public opinion, and yet law decreed by a judge must ultimately be vindicated by public opinion.[168] As Professor Paul Freund once observed, in such circumstances judges must be aware of "the climate of the age" even if they rightly refuse to be "influenced by the weather of the day."[169] University faculty must walk an analogous tightrope.

In the face of the present assault, institutions of higher education have remained shockingly silent and passive. They seem paralyzed, unable to mount an effective public defense of university research and education. Apparently the fundamental importance of these goods has been so widely assumed for so long that universities have forgotten how to make the case for the bargain that underwrites academic freedom. Yet it is now vital that universities speak up for that bargain. Unless the public is convinced that higher education is necessary for our democracy, courts are exceedingly unlikely to interpret our Constitution to protect it.[170]

In the last analysis, the boundaries of permissible government regulation of universities will be set by courts, which must balance the necessity of academic autonomy against the potential for academic abuse and overreach. Courts have many techniques for maintaining such a balance,[171] but these techniques are rudderless unless courts clearly apprehend the social and constitutional goods produced by universities. These goods are obscured if constitutional questions of university regulation are seen only through the lens of individual First Amendment rights. And these goods are rendered constitutionally impotent if they lack widespread public support. That is why constructing a lucid and convincing defense of the constitutional doctrine of academic freedom is so important.

If it is possible for a silver lining to emerge from the cruel chaos that characterizes the Time of Trump, it is that the courts and the public might at last come to a clearer and more trenchant grasp of what it means to defend academic freedom. If colleges and universities are indeed a public trust, it is time for the judiciary to remove them from the crossfire of partisan appropriation. But if, in the absence of public trust, colleges and universities cannot depend upon a measure of judicial protection, America risks losing its most powerful engine for its scientific, economic, and cultural development. American democracy risks taking a long step backwards.

2

"Our Money or Your Life!" Higher Education and the First Amendment

CASS R. SUNSTEIN*

Money doesn't talk, it swears.

—Bob Dylan

Introduction

Did it all start with William F. Buckley, Jr.? There is a good argument that it did. More particularly, it might well have started with Buckley's 1951 book *God and Man at Yale.*[1] Buckley wrote that book right out of college (Yale, more specifically). He offered two main claims. First, that Yale was hostile to Christianity. Its faculty consisted of atheists who cast contempt on religion.[2] Second, that Yale was hostile to capitalism and free markets. Its faculty consisted of socialists who looked down on the engine of national prosperity (and a fundamental location and source of freedom).[3]

The book offered an assortment of details. It asked: How could one of the nation's greatest universities reject Christianity and despise economic liberty? How could it be so anti-American? Buckley wanted Yale to change, and he did not think that Yale would change itself. It needed external pressure. Its values, he thought, were not our country's values. Nor were they the values of Yale's graduates. Buckley made a plea for the exercise of economic influence: Yale's graduates

* Robert Walmsley University Professor, Harvard University. My thanks to Benjamin Eidelson, Richard Fallon, Stephen Sachs, and Geoffrey Stone for terrific comments on an earlier draft. Thanks too to Regina De Nigris for superb research assistance.

Cass R. Sunstein, *"Our Money or Your Life!" Higher Education and the First Amendment*. In: *Academic Freedom in the Era of Trump*. Edited by: Lee C. Bollinger and Geoffrey R. Stone, Oxford University Press.
© Oxford University Press (2026). DOI: 10.1093/9780197854877.003.0003

should use their financial might to pressure Yale to reform itself.[4] Of course, Buckley's ultimate target was much broader. He was not focused only on Yale; his target was higher education as a whole.[5]

While Buckley addressed economic support for Yale in the form of alumni contributions, he did not focus on possible action by the federal government, which has since come to give an extraordinary amount of money to colleges and universities.[6] If it threatens to withhold some of that money, it might be able to achieve what Buckley sought. More broadly, it can create serious risks to educational institutions, perhaps even existential risks, and it can use its power to move institutions in its politically preferred directions.[7] May it use the power of the purse, and related authorities, to alter what those institutions do? To what extent? May it achieve some or all of Buckley's ends? What about the ends of those on the left, if the executive branch leans left in the future? May it deny funds to institutions that have violated the law? Which law? May it deny funds to institutions that do not protect speech? To institutions that act in accordance with values or moral commitments that federal authorities dislike or abhor? If an institution is unpatriotic, antisemitic, right-leaning, or left-leaning, may it be deprived of money for that reason? If an institution does not see civil-rights issues in the same way that the federal government does, may it be brought into line through the use of federal funds? Is there a right to academic freedom, and what does it entail?

These issues are not at all new, but they started to come into newly sharp relief in 2025. On March 7 of that year, the Department of Education, the Department of Health and Human Services, and the General Services Administration announced a pause or termination of federal funding to Columbia University.[8] On March 13, the same institutions sent another letter to the same university, suggesting that it "has fundamentally failed to protect American students and faculty from antisemitic violence and harassment in addition to other alleged violations of Title VI and Title VII of the Civil Rights Act of 1964."[9] They added that certain steps are "a precondition for formal negotiations regarding Columbia University's continued financial relationship with the United States government."[10]

The specified steps were these:

- ***Enforce existing disciplinary policies.*** *The University must complete disciplinary proceedings for Hamilton Hall and encampments. Meaningful discipline means expulsion or multi-year suspension.*
- ***Primacy of the president in disciplinary matters.*** *Abolish the University Judicial Board (UJB) and centralize all disciplinary processes under the Office of the President. And empower the Office of the President to suspend or expel students with an appeal process through the Office of the President.*
- ***Time, place, and manner rules.*** *Implement permanent, comprehensive time, place, and manner rules to prevent disruption of teaching, research, and campus life.*

- ***Mask ban.*** *Ban masks that are intended to conceal identity or intimidate others, with exceptions for religious and health reasons. Any masked individual must wear their Columbia ID on the outside of their clothing (this is already the policy at Columbia's Irving Medical Center).*
- ***Deliver plan to hold all student groups accountable.*** *Recognized student groups and individuals operating as constituent members of, or providing support for, unrecognized groups engaged in violations of University policy must be held accountable through formal investigations, disciplinary proceedings, and expulsion as appropriate.*
- ***Formalize, adopt, and promulgate a definition of antisemitism.*** *President Trump's Executive Order 13,899 uses the IHRA definition. Anti-"Zionist" discrimination against Jews in areas unrelated to Israel or Middle East must be addressed.*
- ***Empower internal law enforcement.*** *The University must ensure that Columbia security has full law enforcement authority, including arrest and removal of agitators who foster an unsafe or hostile work or study environment, or otherwise interfere with classroom instruction or the functioning of the university.*
- ***MESAAS Department—Academic Receivership.*** *Begin the process of placing the Middle East, South Asian, and African Studies department under academic receivership for a minimum of five years. The University must provide a full plan, with date certain deliverables, by the March 20, 2025, deadline.*
- ***Deliver a plan for comprehensive admissions reform.*** *The plan must include a strategy to reform undergraduate admissions, international recruiting, and graduate admissions practices to conform with federal law and policy.*

This letter was followed by others to other universities, most prominently including Harvard.[11] On April 11, 2025, a letter to Harvard offered its own conditions, meant as the foundation for a "binding settlement agreement."[12] These included the following:

- ***Discontinuation of DEI.*** *The University must immediately shutter all diversity, equity, and inclusion (DEI) programs, offices, committees, positions, and initiatives, under whatever name, and stop all DEI-based policies, including DEI-based disciplinary or speech control policies, under whatever name; demonstrate that it has done so to the satisfaction of the federal government; and demonstrate to the satisfaction of the federal government that these reforms are durable and effective through structural and personnel changes.*
- ***Viewpoint Diversity in Admissions and Hiring.*** *By August 2025, the University shall commission an external party, which shall satisfy the federal government as to its competence and good faith, to audit the student body, faculty, staff, and leadership for viewpoint diversity, such that each department, field, or teaching unit must be individually viewpoint diverse. This audit shall begin no later than the summer of 2025 and shall proceed on a department-by-department, field-by-field,*

or teaching-unit-by-teaching-unit basis as appropriate. The report of the external party shall be submitted to University leadership and the federal government no later than the end of 2025. Harvard must abolish all criteria, preferences, and practices, whether mandatory or optional, throughout its admissions and hiring practices, that function as ideological litmus tests. Every department or field found to lack viewpoint diversity must be reformed by hiring a critical mass of new faculty within that department or field who will provide viewpoint diversity; every teaching unit found to lack viewpoint diversity must be reformed by admitting a critical mass of students who will provide viewpoint diversity.

- ***International admissions reform.*** *By August 2025, the University must reform its recruitment, screening, and admissions of international students to prevent admitting students hostile to the American values and institutions inscribed in the U.S. Constitution and Declaration of Independence, including students supportive of terrorism or anti-Semitism. Harvard will immediately report to federal authorities, including the Department of Homeland Security and State Department, any foreign student, including those on visas and with green cards, who commits a conduct violation.*

Requirements of this kind raise evident legal questions.[13] The first of these are statutory: Do existing enactments permit the federal government to impose requirements of this sort? The second questions are constitutional: Do steps of this sort violate some constitutional provision?

My goal in this essay is to explore a subset of the relevant questions involving the First Amendment.[14] Much of the analysis will abstract from questions of the current moment. My hope is that the analysis will help to clarify relevant principles, which can be applied in any moment. As we shall see, some important things are relatively clear, and other important things are unsettled. Here are three propositions that are relatively clear: (1) the federal government can generally speak as it wishes, free from the constraints of the First Amendment; (2) the federal government is generally not permitted to engage in viewpoint discrimination in its funding decisions, as, for example, by funding faculty research projects except those that are right of center; (3) the federal government may not impose unconstitutional conditions, as, for example, by leveraging its power over federal funds to discourage speech that it dislikes or to encourage speech that it likes. I shall spend some time on (1), (2), and (3).

Here are three open questions: (1) When and how may the federal government use its money to require colleges and universities to respond to and to prevent alleged or actual violations of federal law? (2) Should the void-for-vagueness doctrine apply to funding decisions? (3) Is there a principle of academic freedom restricting government's authority to interfere with the administration of institutions of higher education, and if so, what restrictions does that principle impose?[15]

With respect to (1), I shall argue that the government has a great deal of authority, but that it ought to be bound by a proportionality principle, forbidding it from seizing on isolated or particular violations of the law as the basis for broad or global withdrawals and funding. With respect to (2), I shall argue that the void-for-vagueness doctrine should indeed apply to funding decisions, in order to protect fair notice and to prevent the arbitrary exercise of discretion. In recognition of the distinctive nature of the funding context, I shall also suggest that its restrictions are more lenient in the funding context than in the context of criminal punishment. With respect to (3), I shall argue that there is no *freestanding* principle of academic freedom, but that some interferences with academic institutions abridge the First Amendment, and that the forbidden interferences include not only certain restrictions on speech but also certain restrictions on the self-governance of academic institutions (though the scope of that principle is not entirely clear). I shall also contend that the Avoidance Doctrine and the Major Questions Doctrine are highly relevant in assessing what the executive branch is permitted to do. As we shall see, there are other open questions as well, some involving the idea of freedom of association as applied to higher education.

For the most part, I propose to analyze and answer these questions with the help of simple scenarios, designed to put the underlying puzzles and principles in sharp relief. A general lesson is that certain uses of federal funding, here and on the horizon, raise novel issues about the relationship between the First Amendment and academic freedom, an idea that the Supreme Court has endorsed but not specified.[16] It is clear that the First Amendment protects the freedom of speech of administrators, professors, and students. What is less clear is whether and to what extent the First Amendment at least presumptively protects academic institutions, as such, from government interference. Consistent with my arguments with respect to (2), I shall sketch some reasons to think that the First Amendment provides that presumptive protection against imaginable intrusions on their autonomy.

Three Kinds of Restrictions

For orientation, it will be useful to begin with a basic point, which is the importance of distinguishing among three kinds of restrictions on speech: viewpoint-based, content-based, and content-neutral.[17] A viewpoint-based restriction is one that punishes people because of the point of view that they embrace.[18] For example, such a restriction might say that while faculty members may praise the Civil Rights Act of 1964, they may not criticize the Civil Rights Act of 1964. Or it might say that while faculty members may speak favorably of the creation of the state of Israel, they may not speak unfavorably of the creation of the state of Israel. A content-based but viewpoint-neutral restriction is one that punishes people because of the content of their speech.[19]

All viewpoint-based restrictions are content-based, but some content-based restrictions are viewpoint-neutral. For example, a content-based restriction might say that law-school classes may not discuss the Civil Rights Act of 1964, without proscribing any point of view about the Civil Rights Act of 1964. A content-neutral restriction applies regardless of what is being said.[20] A time, place, and manner restriction would count as content-neutral. For example, such a restriction might say that between the hours of midnight and six a.m., no speeches of any kind on any topic will be allowed in dormitories. Or it might say that no one may take over campus buildings for any reason at any time.

In general, viewpoint-based restrictions face a strong presumption of invalidity.[21] They are almost always invalid. Congress or the executive cannot ban, punish, or disincentivize speech that favors critical race theory while allowing speech that criticizes critical race theory. To be sure, we might be able to imagine cases in which a viewpoint-based restriction is acceptable—say, in the context of a serious, imminent threat to public safety or national security, in which certain kinds of speech might be banned because of their viewpoint. Someone might be prevented from saying "Kill that man" when there is an imminent threat of violence, even if no one is prevented from saying "Do not kill that man." Someone might be forbidden from saying, "Let's fix prices," even if no one is forbidden to say, "Let's not fix prices."[22] But in general, viewpoint-based restrictions are impermissible.[23]

Content-based but viewpoint-neutral restrictions also face a heavy burden of justification, and they are usually struck down.[24] A state cannot forbid people from discussing civil rights or an ongoing war effort. But the burden of justification can sometimes be met in general,[25] and in the educational setting in particular, not least because education necessarily involves the establishment of content (and so content-based judgments). Universities can tell history professors that they have to teach history, not climate change, in their history courses. Universities judge faculty members in terms of the content of their work, and faculty members judge students on the basis of the content of their papers and their exams. It is generally to be hoped, and required, that assessments of this kind are viewpoint-neutral, but we can imagine testing cases.[26]

Content-neutral restrictions, such as time, place, and manner restrictions, are subject to a balancing test.[27] The balancing test depends largely on four factors: (1) the strength of the interest in preventing the speech (is the goal to prevent a genuinely serious problem or to eliminate a minor inconvenience?); (2) the extent of the adverse effect of the regulation on people's ability to communicate; (3) the presence of alternative ways, or channels, by which people can get their message across; and (4) the possibility that officials can achieve their legitimate goals through means that are less restrictive of speech.[28] A rule that prohibits faculty and students from taking over buildings, or from engaging in political activity in quiet areas, is likely to be upheld as permissible content-neutral regulation.

There are questions, of course, about the relationship between federal funding and standard doctrine with respect to the three kinds of restrictions. Let us now turn to that relationship. In the process, we will engage with the difficult questions flagged above, involving proportionality, the role of the void-for-vagueness doctrine in the context of federal funding, and the nature and existence of a general right to academic freedom.

Funding and Free Speech: Ten Scenarios

1

The federal government wants to spend its money in support of critical race theory. It publicly adopts an official project, sponsored by the White House and strongly supportive of critical race theory. Its officials write reports that are consistent with that project. The White House publicizes those reports.

Is there a First Amendment violation? The answer is clear: There is not. In general, government can speak as it likes.[29] It can endorse a particular viewpoint without offense to the Constitution. This proposition follows from *Rust v. Sullivan*.[30] Insofar as it is a speaker, the government can use taxpayer money to support its preferred causes. As the Court put it in *Rust*: "When Congress established a National Endowment for Democracy to encourage other countries to adopt democratic principles, it was not constitutionally required to fund a program to encourage competing lines of political philosophy such as communism and fascism."[31] There are few and perhaps no constitutional restrictions on government speech.[32]

2

The federal government creates an institution, the National Endowment for the Arts, through which it makes grants to universities to "promote public knowledge, education, understanding, and appreciation of the arts." A new regulation states that no grants shall be given for work that "is unpatriotic" or that "casts the United States of America in an unfavorable light."

This is viewpoint-based funding, and it is probably unconstitutional under *National Endowment for the Arts v. Finley*[33] and successor cases.[34] In *National*

Endowment for the Arts, the Court did uphold a statutory provision directing the NEA to "tak[e] into consideration general standards of decency and respect for the diverse beliefs and values of the American public."[35] The Court emphasized the breadth and generality of the provision ("decency and respect for the diverse beliefs and values") and the fact that it is a mere "take into consideration" requirement and no more.[36] At the same time, the Court made it clear that it would invalidate a provision that "directed viewpoint discrimination."[37] The Court went out of its way to suggest that "[i]f the NEA were to leverage its power to award subsidies on the basis of subjective criteria into a penalty on disfavored viewpoints, then we would confront a different case."[38] The strong implication of *National Endowment for the Arts* is that government subsidies, no less than penalties, may not discriminate on the basis of point of view.[39] Subsequent decisions, discussed immediately below, have so held, and indeed have made the basic principle relatively clear.[40] Still, it must be said that some Justices on the Court have rejected the view that viewpoint discrimination is impermissible in the funding context,[41] and we cannot rule out the possibility that the law will shift on this question in the future. We could imagine a reading or extension of *Rust v. Sullivan* that would justify that shift.

3

The federal government develops a general funding program for colleges and universities. But it states that it will not fund Muslim organizations. It asserts that "Muslim organizations do not deserve funding at this time."

The exclusion of Muslim organizations is a First Amendment violation. In *Rosenberger v. Rector and Visitors of University of Virginia*,[42] the Court invalidated a University of Virginia policy that allowed payment from the Student Activities Fund for the printing costs of student publications, but not for any publication that "primarily promotes or manifests a particular belief in or about a deity. . . ."[43] As the Court saw it, this was a form of impermissible viewpoint discrimination. Distinguishing and significantly narrowing *Rust*, the Court said that the government there "did not create a program to encourage private speech but instead used private speakers to transmit specific information pertaining to its own program."[44] The Court "recognized that when the government appropriates public funds to promote a particular policy of its own it is entitled to say what it wishes" but stated that "it does not follow . . . that viewpoint-based restrictions are proper when the University does not itself speak or subsidize transmittal of a message it favors. . . ."[45] On the contrary: "Having offered to pay the third-party contractors on behalf of private speakers who convey their own messages, the University may not silence the expression of selected viewpoints."[46]

The word "silence" is a bit tendentious. Selective funding does not silence anyone. But the principle is clear: Viewpoint-discriminatory funding is a First Amendment violation. To be sure, the government might be able to evade the principle by funding private speakers to "transmit specific information" that it favors. But the distinction drawn in *Rosenberger* is not simply semantic. The government can create a program celebrating (say) the Clean Air Act and hire private speakers to transmit information pertaining to that program. But as the law now stands, it cannot fund people who will celebrate the Clean Air Act while denying funding to people who are critical of the Clean Air Act.

The same lesson emerges from *Legal Services Corporation v. Velazquez*.[47] At issue there was a statute that prohibited LSC-funded lawyers from challenging the constitutionality of existing welfare laws. The Court struck down the prohibition, holding that it was a form of viewpoint discrimination and impermissible for that reason. The Court again read *Rust* narrowly, stating that while the Court there did not emphasize that the counseling activities were a form of government speech, it has come to ground the decision "on [that] understanding."[48] As the Court had it, the viewpoint-based funding decisions would be upheld if (and only if) (a) the government was speaking or (b) the government enlisted "private speakers to transmit information pertaining to its own program."[49]

While (b) could be a large category in principle (potentially covering anyone who receives federal funds), the Court plainly understood it to be small, and not to include cases in which the government disbursed funds only to those whose point of view it likes.[50] Thus, government might create a program extolling the virtues of democracy, and fund private speakers who agreed to spread information relating to that program. But government could not run a grant program open only to those who agreed to speak in favor of particular views on immigration.[51] Admittedly, the distinction might seem thin, but it should not be obscure. As the law now stands, a grant program limited to those with a certain point of view is illegitimate, even though the government can speak as it likes and enlist people to offer information related to its program.

4

The federal government adopts a funding program for colleges and universities. It will fund Democratic student organizations but not Republican student organizations.

This form of selectivity is impermissible. In principle, it is the same case as (3). Viewpoint discrimination is not permissible in government funding. But we do have to introduce a complication here. Suppose that the government creates a grant program focusing on air pollution. Suppose that it funds an assortment of applications that study the effects of lead on human health, but is unreceptive to, and will not provide grants to, applications that hypothesize that lead has no adverse effects on human health. The government might urge that it is not really discriminating on the basis of viewpoint here, any more than it would be if it said that it would fund studies on the effects of gravity while denying funding to those who hypothesize that gravity is an optical illusion. The question is whether the government can point to some kind of consensus about matters of fact and rule certain positions out of bounds. Surely it can, but there will be some hard line-drawing problems here.

5

The federal government refuses to fund certain departments of psychology. It believes that such departments are doing bad work and do not serve their students.

Whether the denial of funding is lawful depends on its justification. The government need not fund programs that are failing to serve their students. The government need not fund an Astrology Department or a Department for the Study of Space Aliens Among Us. (Recall, in this light, the complexity of the ban on viewpoint discrimination. It would be permissible not to fund those things while also funding studies of why people wrongly believe in astrology or space aliens.) Note the breadth of the underlying principle: The government can refuse to fund silly or failing programs in the first instance, and it can also stop funding such programs at any time. But the ideas of "silly" or "bad work" or "failing," and "not serving students," need to be unpacked, and cannot be a smokescreen for what we must call illegitimate viewpoint discrimination. If the government stops funding because it wants to punish a particular point of view, there would be a constitutional problem. Imagine, for example, a decision to stop funding a psychology department because a faculty member spoke out in favor of more immigration, or opposes the current president, or does not believe in God, or thinks that Freud is full of rubbish. That would offend the First Amendment, unless the speech were unprotected by the First Amendment (suppose, for example, that it were libelous, or that it consisted of a "true threat").[52]

We could imagine further cases that would press hard on the concept of viewpoint discrimination in this context. Suppose that the federal government believes that the relevant psychology departments are placing an undue emphasis on the work of Daniel Kahneman,[53] or on subjective well-being,[54] or on feminist issues. Some such judgments are plausibly characterized as viewpoint-based and could also run afoul of principles of academic freedom, taken up below.

6

The federal government suspends federal funding, in toto, to universities with faculty members who do not support critical race theory. To obtain federal funding, universities must require all faculty members to sign a pledge: "I support critical race theory and will speak out in its favor."

That is unconstitutional. Federal funding is, in that case, accompanied by an *unconstitutional condition.*[55] *Rust v. Sullivan* itself makes the category clear, emphasizing that "our 'unconstitutional conditions' cases involve situations in which the government has placed a condition on the *recipient* of the subsidy, rather than on a particular program or service, thus effectively prohibiting the recipient from engaging in the protected conduct outside the scope of the federally funded program."[56] In support of that conclusion, the Court pointed to *FCC v. League of Women Voters of California,*[57] where the Court struck down a federal law banning noncommercial television and radio stations receiving federal grants from "engag[ing] in editorializing."[58] In that case, the constitutional problem was that a recipient of federal funds was "barred absolutely from all editorializing," because it "is not able to segregate its activities according to the source of its funding," and thus "has no way of limiting the use of its federal funds to all noneditorializing activities."[59] As a result of the law, "a noncommercial educational station that receives only 1% of its overall income from [federal] grants is barred absolutely from all editorializing."[60]

Note that the law invalidated in *League of Women Voters of California* was content-based, not viewpoint-based. A viewpoint-based law saying that, in order to receive federal funds, noncommercial stations must agree to support a presidential initiative or must agree not to speak favorably of critical race theory, would be self-evidently unconstitutional.[61] The same principle protects institutions of higher education. The executive branch could not say that in order to receive federal funds, its faculty must agree to support the current president or to take a particular position on climate change or immigration.

The distinction between the relevant cases should be relatively straightforward.[62] The government is free to speak as it likes and also to hire agents to speak on behalf of X and Y but not Z. That is the lesson of *Rust v. Sullivan.* But it is generally not permissible for the government to say that in order to receive funds for X and Y, a university must agree that its faculty members will speak for or against Z.[63] The problem with an unconstitutional condition is that the government is *leveraging its power over federal funds to stop people from saying (or to get people to say) what they would otherwise say (or not say), independent of the exercise of that leverage.*

We do have to offer some qualifications. A great deal depends on what Z turns out to be. If Z is unprotected speech, there is no problem. It is not unconstitutional for the government to use its power over federal funds to discourage false commercial advertising, criminal conspiracy, sexual harassment, fraud, true threats, or bribery. But if Z is protected speech, we have an unconstitutional condition.

7

An executive agency says this: "If you do not have programs in place to deal with sexual harassment, as defined by law, we will remove federal funding, in toto." The basic idea is that unless universities have programs minimally necessary to prevent sexual harassment, as defined by law, they will lose federal funds.

Case (7) raises statutory questions: Does enacted law allow the executive to do that? Under what circumstances, and subject to what processes? It also raises a First Amendment question: May the federal government broadly deny federal funding to a university if it fails to have relevant programs in place to ensure compliance with federal law? The answer is less obvious than it might seem. Note first that the government's rationale is viewpoint-neutral: Its goal is to promote compliance with federal law, not to ensure conformity to a point of view. If a university fails or refuses to comply with federal law in some egregious or general way—if it treats federal law as a matter of indifference—the government would seem to have a strong justification, plausibly characterized as viewpoint-neutral, for denying federal funds.

Nonetheless, case (7) raises two questions:

First, is there a proportionality principle here? Would it be permissible to deny federal funds in toto because of infrequent, or de minimis, or occasional, or perhaps localized, violations of federal law in domain X or Y or Z? Under existing law, there is no clear answer to this question; we are in uncharted territory. But it would be plausible to say that there is indeed such a principle, so long as the government's action implicates speech. We might see the relevant issue as one of a content-neutral restriction on speech (acknowledging that uses of funding may or may not qualify as "restrictions"). The question would be whether the denial of funding to (say) a medical school and a business school is justified as a response to violations of federal law by (say) an economics department. A reasonable answer would be that it cannot be so justified. By hypothesis, institutions that have not discriminated are being punished for acts for which they have no responsibility and over which they have no control. To be sure, we might think that the university, as such, has control over all of its components. But suppose that the unlawful acts were not favored or promoted by the university, and that it sought to discourage and punish them. If anything like this is so, it is reasonable to suggest that the legitimate purpose of sanctioning noncompliant actors, or even a noncompliant department, is adequately served by sanctioning those actors and that department, not by sanctioning parts of the university that have not violated any law. For that reason, we might well be speaking of an impermissible form of content-neutral regulation in cases of disproportionate responses to what are, by hypothesis, admitted forms of unlawful behavior. Of course, the facts matter. If the central university favors that behavior, or does not do anything about it, the analysis might be different.

Second, might there be a problem of impermissible selectivity? Suppose that the federal government focuses on some subset of violations of federal law, and nothing else. Is that a problem? It might be. In *R.A.V. v. City of St. Paul,*[64] the Court said that "the government may proscribe libel; but it may not make the further content discrimination of proscribing *only* libel critical of the government."[65] The Court added that the proposition "that a city council could enact an ordinance prohibiting only those legally obscene works that contain criticism of the city government or, indeed, that do not include endorsement of the city government" was "a simplistic, all-or-nothing-at-all approach to First Amendment protection . . . at odds with common sense and with our jurisprudence. . . ."[66] The basic proposition is that even within the category of unprotected speech, the government may not draw impermissible lines.

It follows that, if the government denied federal funds only for violations of federal law that in some sense reflected a disfavored viewpoint, and not for any other violations of federal law, there would be a legitimate *R.A.V.* problem. We could imagine cases in which that problem would be severe. Suppose, for example, that the government targeted (unprotected) speech directed at Jews, but did not target (unprotected) speech directed at Muslims or Christians. Or suppose that the government imposed special penalties on libel of Republicans as compared with libel of Democrats. The government's best response to any objection of this sort would be to insist that, in the circumstances, there is no viewpoint discrimination or even content discrimination, because it is focusing on the most serious or egregious violations of federal law. If, for example, the government is responding to a great deal of anti-Semitic action in violation of federal law, it need not respond to anti-Christian action if there is very little of that. If this is a convincing response on the facts (a potentially big if), the First Amendment objection would not be at all easy to sustain.

8

An executive agency says this: "If you do not have sufficient safeguards in place to deal with anti-Semitism, we will remove federal funding, in toto." The basic idea is that, unless universities do not stop anti-Semitism, they will lose federal funds.

This problem[67] is similar to that in (7), but it has some distinctive features. First, it broadly targets anti-Semitism, which it does not define; for that reason, the restriction might be void for vagueness. The term "anti-Semitism" can mean any number of things and must be specified.[68] Second, some forms of speech that are or arguably are anti-Semitic are protected by the First Amendment. ("Jews are more concerned about money than are most people.") Third, the restriction in question, as written, discriminates on the basis of viewpoint; it forbids "anti-Semitism" but it does not forbid "pro-Semitism." Is that a problem? It might be, once we specify what the relevant terms mean.

Begin with vagueness. Does the void-for-vagueness doctrine apply to funding restrictions, as well as to civil or criminal sanctions? Surprisingly, that immensely important question appears to be unresolved. In *National Endowment for the Arts v. Finley*,[69] the Court's highly ambiguous discussion can be taken to have suggested either (1) that the doctrine does not apply or (2) that the doctrine does indeed apply but its strictures are less severe. The Court said this: "The terms of the provision are undeniably opaque, and if they appeared in a criminal statute or regulatory scheme, they could raise substantial vagueness concerns. It is unlikely, however, that speakers will be compelled to steer too far clear of any 'forbidden area' in the context of grants of this nature."[70] It follows that a degree of opacity is acceptable—more so than in a criminal statute or regulatory regime. The Court explained that "when the Government is acting as patron rather than as sovereign, the consequences of imprecision are not constitutionally severe."[71]

One reason for that is that when we are dealing with selective subsidies, "it is not always feasible for Congress to legislate with clarity. Indeed, if this statute is unconstitutionally vague, then so too are all Government programs awarding scholarships and grants on the basis of subjective criteria such as 'excellence.' . . . To accept respondents' vagueness argument would be to call into question the constitutionality of these valuable Government programs and countless others like them."[72] Perhaps more cautiously, the Court concluded that because the statute "merely adds some imprecise considerations to an already subjective selection process . . . [i]t does not, on its face, impermissibly infringe on First or Fifth Amendment rights."[73] Justice Scalia went further, or at least was more explicit, flatly stating that the "constitutional rule against vague legislation . . . has no application to funding."[74] Perhaps that what was the majority said; but perhaps not.

Lower courts have not read *Finley* to endorse Justice Scalia's position. On the contrary, they have accepted vagueness challenges to funding restrictions.[75] One court distinguished the vague (!) language in *Finley*, which involved "only another factor to be considered in an inherently subjective evaluation alongside 'artistic excellence and artistic merit,'" from the "Equity Termination Provision" that was challenged in the case, which "render[ed] categorically ineligible for funding any contract or grant based on the single determination of whether it is 'equity-related' without any guidelines as to what that term might mean."[76] In the court's view, the term "equity-related" was simply too open-ended. It is not clear that that distinction works; "artistic excellence" is not exactly a model of clarity. Still, we could imagine a ruling that *Finley* should not be understood to foreclose vagueness challenges to funding provisions. There is a good argument that it should not be so understood.

Imagine, for example, a statutory provision stating that the executive branch could cut off federal funds "whenever it believed it appropriate to do so, on whatever grounds it chooses." Such an open-ended grant would raise the two concerns that animate the void-for-vagueness doctrine.[77] First, it would fail to give people fair notice about what they are supposed to do. Those who were seeking to obtain funding, and those who were seeking to ensure that funding is not cut off, would not know what course of action to take. Second, such an open-ended phrase would allow the executive branch to pick and choose, and perhaps to favor its enemies and to punish its friends. We should agree that the strictures of the void-for-vagueness doctrine are loosened in the context of funding; but we should not agree that they are eliminated.[78]

Apart from vagueness, (8) seems to cover constitutionally protected speech and also to discriminate on the basis of viewpoint. At least it might do so if the definition of anti-Semitic speech is broad and if it forbids (for example) criticism of Israel while also permitting positive statements about Israel. But we could imagine a variation on (8), or an understanding of (8), that targets unlawful discrimination against Jews, specifically defined by statute or regulation, and not anti-Semitic speech in general. Let us stipulate, then, that we are dealing with some violation of new or existing civil-rights laws, and so *"If you do not have sufficient safeguards in place to deal with unlawful discrimination against Jews, we will remove federal funding, in toto."* That restriction would meet the same objections as in (7). With respect to proportionality: Suppose that there have been incidents of discrimination against Jews in the psychology department but not elsewhere. Is it acceptable to deny funds to the medical school, the business school, the law school, and the divinity school because of those incidents? That is an unresolved question, and there is a good argument that it should not be acceptable. With respect to selectivity: Why has the government singled out this form of discrimination and not others? This is the *R.A.V.* problem. Perhaps the government could show that discrimination against Jews is a more serious problem than other forms of discrimination. But it would be obliged to make that showing.

9

The federal government says this: "If you do not put your English department in some kind of receivership, you will lose all federal funds."

To know whether there is a First Amendment problem, we need to know why the government is saying that. Consider these possibilities:

(a) The government disapproves of the fact that the English department is right-of-center. That would be impermissible. Federal funding cannot be stopped as a way of punishing disfavored speech. See (6).

(b) The English department is found to have engaged in pervasive sexual harassment, and the federal government is attempting to stop that. That might well be acceptable under the First Amendment. See (7). The challenge is that the government is not merely directing the university to comply with federal law; it is specifying the means by which it must do so. Here again we are in uncharted waters. We might be drawn to this principle: The federal government is permitted to ensure that federal funds do not go to an institution that is violating federal law, subject to a possible proportionality principle, but it is not permitted to specify the means by which institutions come into compliance with federal law. In a phrase from regulatory policy: performance standards, not design standards.[79] I take up this principle below.

(c) The English department is terrible, by objective standards. The faculty is undistinguished, and the students are not learning anything. If so, there is a statutory question: Can the federal government respond to poor quality by withholding federal funds? On First Amendment grounds, the federal government might well be on safe ground here, so long as it is acting in a viewpoint-neutral way. See (5).

10

The federal government says this: "To receive federal funds, colleges and universities must promote viewpoint diversity. Institutions that do not promote viewpoint diversity will not receive federal funds."

At first glance, the issue might seem tricky, a kind of brainteaser. A goal of the First Amendment is to promote viewpoint diversity, so how can it possibly violate the First Amendment to require viewpoint diversity? But the issue actually is not tricky at all. It is unacceptable to deny funds to institutions that do not promote viewpoint diversity. On its face, that is an unacceptable form of regulation on the basis of content, and in application, it will inevitably turn into a form of viewpoint discrimination, which could well be taken, because of the word "inevitably," to be viewpoint-discriminatory, or the functional equivalent of viewpoint discrimination, on its face.

A relevant case is *Miami Herald Publishing Company v. Tornillo*,[80] decided in 1974. There the Court struck down a statute that created a "right to reply" to criticism, by the press, of a candidate for nomination or election. The Court ruled that the government could not require that kind of viewpoint diversity in the newspapers. "The choice of material to go into a newspaper, and the decisions made as to limitations on the size and content of the paper, and treatment of public issues and public official—whether fair or unfair—constitute the exercise of editorial control and judgment."[81] Those words are about newspapers, not universities. But they easily could be invoked by an institution of higher education objecting to a requirement of viewpoint diversity. From *Miami Herald*, it is clear that a legislature could not require "viewpoint diversity" in newspapers or on websites. We could readily imagine this conclusion: "The choice of material to go into an academic setting—whether fair or unfair—constitutes the exercise of academic control and judgment."

Still, a newspaper is one thing; a university may be another. In addition, a mandatory right of reply is one thing; a withdrawal of federal funds may be another. *Miami Herald* is suggestive, and perhaps more than that, but it does not resolve the issue. Nonetheless, there are two potential problems with a requirement of viewpoint diversity imposed on institutions of higher education. The first is that it might be unconstitutionally vague.[82] The second is that, even if it is not void for vagueness, it might constitute an impermissible kind of content discrimination, interfering with the freedom of (private) institutions of higher education to make their own judgments about what shall and shall not be taught.

Begin with vagueness: What is "viewpoint diversity"? How do we know if we have it? If a computer-science department is committed to viewpoint diversity, what should its faculty be expected to teach? A physics department? Should a biology department be expected to offer courses showing that Darwin was 100 percent right and also 100 percent wrong? Should a history department be required to hire Marxists, or people who think the Holocaust did not happen? What would an English department be expected to look like? Should a law school be required to hire Kantians, critical race theorists, originalists, Communists, Nazis, libertarians, economic analysts of law, devotees of behavioral economics, common good constitutionalists, or (and?) people who agree with Ronald Dworkin? Should an economics department be required to hire Hayekians and also people who believe in central planning, Keynesians, Marxists, rational-choice theorists who follow Gary Becker, people who believe in behavioral economics, and also people who think that behavioral economics is nonsense? Should a divinity school be required to hire atheists? Mormons? Jews? In short: The range of "viewpoints" is impossibly wide, and any requirement of "viewpoint diversity" is impossibly vague. It does not give people fair notice. It would inevitably allow government to pick and choose. These are the canonical problems with vague edicts.

At the moment, the idea of viewpoint diversity is being wielded by followers of Buckley who think, not at all unreasonably,[83] that certain conservative points of view are underrepresented on campus.[84] But the requirement of viewpoint diversity greatly outruns that reasonable thought. (If we are genuinely committed to viewpoint diversity, we should want all sorts of points of view, not simply conservative ones.) To require "more conservative voices" would be a self-evidently unacceptable form of viewpoint discrimination. (More on that below.) To require "viewpoint diversity" more broadly is to require—well, who knows?

Here is a fundamental problem: The range of "viewpoints" is very wide, and in deciding which ones are required by a commitment to "viewpoint diversity," any government overseer will have to discriminate on the basis of viewpoint. If that suggestion seems obscure, consider what counts as viewpoint diversity in a philosophy department. Must the department have Kantians? Utilitarians? Aristotelians? Followers of Ayn Rand? Followers of Foucault? Followers of John Rawls? Followers of Robert Nozick? Supporters of animal rights? Skeptics about animal rights? (And these are just questions about political philosophy.)

Now put vagueness to one side. Suppose that a university—Notre Dame, for example—defines its mission in certain terms which are associated, broadly speaking, with the point(s) of view of those who gave rise to or oversee the institution. Suppose that the government does not believe that Notre Dame has enough in the way of viewpoint diversity; perhaps it does not have enough (or any) faculty members who (sufficiently) emphasize racism, sexism, Marxism, or colonial exploitation. The objection is that, if the government requires it to show viewpoint diversity in specified ways, it is plausibly intruding on the university's First Amendment rights. Imagine, for example, that the federal government insists that Notre Dame's political-science department must have courses with a Marxist point of view, or unambiguously celebrating the United States.

Does a withdrawal of federal funds make a difference? The answer is no. The government could not say that it will give out federal funds only to universities that agree to require their faculty members to support a particular political party, or to establish their patriotism, or to pledge their enthusiasm for diversity, equity, and inclusion. As we have seen, viewpoint discrimination in the use of federal funds runs into serious obstacles. To be sure, we can imagine testing cases. A prohibition on discrimination on the basis of race might, for example, spill over into control of viewpoint, or it might not. But the basic conclusions should be clear: (1) An insistence on viewpoint diversity, implemented through a threatened withdrawal of federal funds, would be void for vagueness, so long as the void-for-vagueness doctrine applies in some form to federal funding (as it should). (2) An insistence on viewpoint diversity, implemented through a threatened withdrawal of federal funds, would be an impermissible form of content discrimination.

Mandatory Processes and Academic Freedom

In this light, we may turn to the letter from federal agencies to Columbia quoted above.[85] The fundamental goal is "to protect American students and faculty from antisemitic violence and harassment in addition to other alleged violations of Title VI and Title VII of the Civil Rights Act of 1964."[86] To say the least, that is an unobjectionable goal. Nonetheless, the word "alleged" is not ideal here; if federal funds are to be withheld, it should be because of actual violations, not alleged violations. The term "should be" in that sentence might even have constitutional foundations. A still fundamental problem is that the requested actions seem to go well beyond what is necessary to ensure compliance with federal law. For present purposes, the question is whether doing that is a constitutional problem. That question raises in turn an assortment of issues about the nature and the constitutional status of the idea, broadly endorsed but never specified by the Supreme Court, of academic freedom.

A

Consider this: "The University must complete disciplinary proceedings for Hamilton Hall and encampments. Meaningful discipline means expulsion or multi-year suspension." Or this: "Abolish the University Judicial Board (UJB) and centralize all disciplinary processes under the Office of the President. And empower the Office of the President to suspend or expel students with an appeal process through the Office of the President." Or this: "Implement permanent, comprehensive time, place, and manner rules to prevent disruption of teaching, research, and campus life." Do these directives violate the First Amendment? Do they implicate freedom of speech at all? All of them seem to affect speech, and the third quoted sentence does so most broadly. To be sure, time, place, and manner rules, designed to prevent disruption of academic life, need not violate the First Amendment.[87] *But are they necessary "to protect American students and faculty from antisemitic violence and harassment in addition to other alleged violations of Title VI and Title VII of the Civil Rights Act of 1964"? And may government agencies direct academic institutions to issue such rules as a condition for receiving federal funds?*

We have to make some distinctions here. As a private university, Columbia is not subject to the First Amendment; it can regulate speech however it likes. The problem, if there is one, is that federal agencies are directing a university to regulate speech. Whether such a direction violates the First Amendment depends on its content. If the federal government directed Columbia to punish "unpatriotic speech," or even "anti-Semitic speech," it would indeed be violating the First Amendment, because such a direction would be unconstitutionally vague[88] and overbroad.[89] The question is whether the directives can be understood in a way that does not conflict with the First Amendment. Perhaps they can be. And more generally, it might be argued that most of the directives in the letter are targeting processes to combat discriminatory action in violation of existing law, not protected speech as such, and that insofar as the directed processes might implicate speech, what is implicated is unprotected by the First Amendment. On that view, the letter is not forbidding anyone at Columbia from engaging in constitutionally protected expression, which might seem to mean that there is no First Amendment issue.

B

To approach this argument, we need to slow down. The first problem involves the relationship between process requirements and freedom of speech. Suppose that the federal government says that a university must commence and complete disciplinary proceedings against those who engage in "dangerous" or "unpatriotic" speech, or that it must establish a centralized disciplinary process to deal with such speech. If the underlying speech is protected by the First Amendment, any requirement, imposed by the federal government, of establishing or maintaining some process to punish that speech would itself be a violation of the First Amendment. We need not speak of academic freedom to reach this conclusion. But this point does not establish that the directives quoted above are unconstitutional. It establishes only that requiring processes to punish speech can be a First Amendment violation if the government's purpose is to punish protected speech.

To make it a bit harder, suppose that the federal government said that unless universities adopt specified processes to deal with allegations of (say) sexual harassment, they will lose federal funds. Might such requirements violate the First Amendment? That is not clear. To be sure, the federal government could say that unless universities adopt processes to deal with such allegations, they will lose federal funds. The problem lies with the word "specified." If the specified processes go beyond what is necessary to deal with such allegations, they might intrude on protected speech—by, for example, requiring complex and burdensome investigations in cases in which there is, in fact, no sexual harassment. The Supreme Court has not spoken to this question, but there is a strong argument that some mandatory processes designed to prevent or punish unprotected speech could amount to a First Amendment violation if they end up having a serious adverse effect on protected speech.

The second and broader problem involves a much larger issue: academic freedom, taken to constitute a presumptive right of institutions of higher education to be free from government intrusion.[90] The nature, grounding, and scope of that right are unsettled,[91] and in coming years, it might well be tested. We should be able to agree that insofar as professors and administrators are engaged in speech, relevant restrictions raise First Amendment issues. That point is obvious, and to make it, we need not speak of academic freedom as such. We are speaking of "the freedom of speech."[92] What is less clear is to what extent academic institutions, as such, have constitutional protection against government interference with their operations, over and above the ordinary protection that speakers have as speakers.[93]

The Supreme Court has spoken firmly and sometimes stirringly of such protection, especially in the 1950s and 1960s, in the aftermath of the McCarthy period.[94] It did so with a constitutional method that did not speak of the original public meaning, or with any kind of the history-and-tradition test,[95] which may make the relevant opinions look like relics of a foregone era. And some of the discussions seem alarmingly loose, perhaps especially by contemporary standards. In *Sweezy v. New Hampshire*,[96] decided in 1957, the Court said this: "It is particularly important that the exercise of the power of compulsory process be carefully circumscribed when the investigative process tends to impinge upon such highly sensitive areas as freedom of speech or press, freedom of political association, and freedom of communication of ideas, *particularly in the academic community*."[97] Why the italicized phrase? The Court referred to "liberties in the areas of academic freedom and political expression—areas in which government should be extremely reticent to tread."[98] It added:[99]

> The essentiality of freedom in the community of American universities is almost self-evident. No one should underestimate the vital role in a democracy that is played by those who guide and train our youth. To impose any strait jacket upon the intellectual leaders in our colleges and universities would imperil the future of our Nation. No field of education is so thoroughly comprehended by man that new discoveries cannot yet be made. Particularly is that true in the social sciences, where few, if any, principles are accepted as absolutes. Scholarship cannot flourish in an atmosphere of suspicion and distrust. Teachers and students must always remain free to inquire, to study and to evaluate, to gain new maturity and understanding; otherwise, our civilization will stagnate and die.

Justice Frankfurter elaborated the point, arguing for "the exclusion of governmental intervention in the intellectual life of a university."[100] He continued: "It matters little whether such intervention occurs avowedly or through action that inevitably tends to check the ardor and fearlessness of scholars, qualities at once so fragile and so indispensable for fruitful academic labor."[101] He referred with enthusiasm to a statement from South Africa, pointing to "'the four essential freedoms' of a university—to determine for itself on academic grounds who may teach, what may be taught, how it shall be taught, and who may be admitted to study."[102] Justice Frankfurter appeared to think that the "four essential freedoms" could be rooted in the First Amendment, but it is not exactly clear how to do that.

In 1967, the Court spoke in similar terms, insisting, "Our Nation is deeply committed to safeguarding academic freedom, which is of transcendent value to all of us and not merely to the teachers concerned. That freedom is therefore a special concern of the First Amendment, which does not tolerate laws that cast a pall of orthodoxy over the classroom."[103] The Court has pointed to a right to academic freedom on various occasions,[104] though its sources and content remain less than clear.[105]

C

To test intuitions, suppose in this light that government agencies said that in order to receive federal funds, *all* of the nation's colleges and universities must agree to accept some kind of federal receivership, in which those agencies specified mandatory processes, to be followed by all such institutions and to be overseen by federal authorities, for dealing with alleged violations of federal law. We could imagine that such a step would intrude directly or indirectly on protected speech; to know, we would need to know the details. But it is also possible that such a step would intrude into academic freedom, taken as an inference from the First Amendment.[106] The basic claim is that the First Amendment is best taken to give academic institutions something like presumptive immunity against government intrusion, so that they can engage in their various speech-related activities and exercise freedom of association.[107] If there is a general right to academic freedom,[108] mandatory processes would face a heavy burden of justification, simply because they intrude on academic institutions. Such processes would of course be more likely to be upheld if they leave academic institutions with room to identify their own ways to respond to, or to avoid, violations of federal law.[109]

Consider some other examples. Suppose that the federal government required, as a condition for the receipt of federal funds, a specific governance structure—say, a president and a provost, and no more than three specific offices, dedicated (for example) to admissions, alumni relations, and athletics. Or suppose, to make it still more extreme, that the federal government required, as a condition for the receipt of federal funds, an exceedingly spare governance structure—say, a president and a provost, and no one else. Suppose that colleges and universities could not receive funds unless they followed the prescribed model. Or suppose that colleges and universities could not receive funds unless they abolished the institution of tenure or gave everyone tenure.[110] Or suppose that colleges and universities could not receive funds unless they named all of their buildings after specified American politicians. Or suppose that colleges and universities could not receive funds unless they followed certain procedures for admitting students.

We could imagine variations on such cases that would make the First Amendment violation clear—for example, a mandatory office for patriotism, or for reckoning with racism, or for promoting diversity, equity, and inclusion. Mandatory offices of this kind would involve unconstitutional conditions, in the form of funding requirements accompanied by "strings" that embed viewpoint discrimination or impermissible content discrimination. In such cases, we would be dealing with intrusions on speech, where the idea of intrusions is specified by reference to established law. But suppose that viewpoint discrimination and impermissible content discrimination are not involved. All that is involved is specification of a certain governance structure. That would put the question of academic freedom in sharp relief.[111] Extreme cases are the most revealing: If government said that universities cannot receive federal funds unless they agree to a governance structure that essentially disables their operations, we should be able to insist that there is a First Amendment violation, if there is indeed a right to academic freedom as such.[112] One of the leading treatments urges that "academic freedom should be understood to include only rights unique or necessary to the functions of higher education."[113] Note that under this formulation, certain interferences with structure or governance could amount to a First Amendment violation *even if speech is not targeted or directly at risk.*

How might that conclusion be defended? That is a large question, and I restrict myself to some general remarks here.[114] On one view, it is a legitimate inference from the protection of freedom of speech itself. Structure or governance that is a precondition for the exercise of freedom of speech by academic institutions is itself protected by freedom of speech. Justice Frankfurter's four freedoms might be defended on this light: the freedom of an academic institution "to determine for itself on academic grounds who may teach, what may be taught, how it shall be taught, and who may be admitted to study."[115] Two of these do involve speech itself ("what may be taught" and "how it shall be taught"), and the other two seem to be preconditions for the relevant speech ("who may teach" and "who may be admitted to study").

On another view, we are speaking of freedom of association.[116] Suppose that a group of people created an Organization for Climate Science, or an Association for Shakespeare Studies, or an Institute for Academic Freedom, or an Alliance for Educating Young People. Suppose that the government would fund such institutions if and only if they agreed to have a president, a vice president, and an associate director as the leadership team. It might be plausible to say that conditions of this kind would be a violation of freedom of association, at least if we see the relevant institutions as associating for a political, educative, or similar purpose. So too, perhaps, with certain interferences with the structure or governance of colleges and universities. Admittedly, we are (again) in uncharted waters here.

Consider in this light this directive: "*The plan must include a strategy to reform undergraduate admissions, international recruiting, and graduate admissions practices to conform with federal law and policy.*" If it were shown that some institution violated federal law and policy—if, for example, an institution were shown to have discriminated on the basis of race in those specific domains—a requirement of this sort might plausibly be defended as a remedy for past legal wrongs. But if such a requirement is imposed without a showing of recurring or systematic violations of federal law, it would be more difficult to defend. (Recall Justice Frankfurter's reference to "who may be admitted for study.") If there is a presumptive right to academic freedom, not freestanding but rooted in the

First Amendment's protection of freedom of speech, there is a plausible argument that mandatory production of a strategy to conform with federal law cannot lawfully be compelled in the absence of a demonstration of either (1) the inadequacy of the current strategy or (2) past nonconformity. And again: performance standards, not design standards.

Canons

As a matter of law, two canons of construction might also matter. The first is the Avoidance Canon. The second is the Major Questions Doctrine.

The Avoidance Canon has a weak version and a strong version. The weak version states that if a court is presented with two interpretations of a statute, one of which would be constitutionally valid and one of which would be invalid, and if the statute is ambiguous, the court should adopt the interpretation that is valid. The strong version says that if a court is presented with two interpretations, one of which is unquestionably valid and one of which would raise a serious constitutional issue, and if the statute is ambiguous, the court should choose the interpretation that is unquestionably valid.[117] The strong version is evidently stronger than the weak version. It suggests that even if an interpretation would not necessarily violate the Constitution, it should be avoided if it would raise a serious constitutional issue. Here is the implication: If an agency decision to withhold federal funds would raise a serious constitutional question, relevant statutes should be construed so as not to allow that withholding, so long as those statutes are genuinely ambiguous.

Suppose, in this light, that statutes may or may not give the executive branch the authority to do what it is doing. Suppose, as seems plausible, that what the federal government is doing raises serious First Amendment issues. Under the Avoidance Canon, ambiguous statutes must be interpreted so as not to raise those issues.

The Major Questions Doctrine is much newer than the Avoidance Canon.[118] It remains in a process of development.[119] Under the Major Questions Doctrine, agencies are not allowed to act in ways that have extraordinary "economic and political significance" unless Congress has clearly authorized them to do so, above all if the contemplated actions are "unheralded" and "transformative."[120] This is ordinarily understood as a nondelegation principle: If agencies are doing something extraordinary, they had better point to clear authorization from Congress.

There is little doubt that what is now being done, or contemplated, by relevant agencies has extraordinary economic and political significance. It has extraordinary economic significance because we are speaking of a great deal of money (billions of dollars). It has extraordinary political significance; that is self-evident. What is being done is also (and this may be more fundamental) "unheralded" and "transformative." Administrations have done a great deal to police civil-rights violations on campus,[121] of course, but we have never seen anything of this scope. It follows that what is happening would count as a massive transformation of the role of the national government with respect to universities, and if anything, that understates matters. For example: (a) Federal regulators have never overseen plagiarism at universities they fund. (b) Federal regulators have never asked for a third-party assessment of viewpoint diversity. (c) Regulators have never asked to abolish diversity, equity, and inclusion programs as such.

The whole is at least as big as the sum of its parts. In some ways, it is bigger. The federal government can be seen to be coming close to asserting the authority to run the universities it funds. If it has the authority to do what current agencies are seeking to do, an administration with very different political convictions (say, left or far left) could almost certainly do all kinds of things to press the nation's universities in its preferred directions. However that may be, the Major Questions Doctrine naturally applies to the recent actions.

Conclusion

We are in a period in which the federal government is using its authority over funds to move institutions of higher education in its preferred directions. It is clear that government speech, as such, is unconstrained by the First Amendment. It is clear that so long as government and its agents are not speaking, federal officials are severely restricted in their ability to fund programs in a way that involves viewpoint discrimination. It is clear, finally, that the government may not impose unconstitutional conditions, as, for example, by saying that in return for receipt of federal funds, a university must agree to require its faculty members to endorse behavioral economics, or to write an annual paean to Franklin Delano Roosevelt, Ronald Reagan, or Olivia Rodrigo.

More challenging questions arise when federal agencies use federal funding to punish or prevent actual or alleged violations of federal law. At first glance, such efforts need not raise First Amendment questions at all, at least if they are not directed at protected or arguably protected speech. If a university repeatedly allows such violations, and does not do anything to stop them, federal authorities can surely withhold federal funds, subject to a possible requirement of proportionality. If a university "allegedly" commits or allows such violations, it is a fair question whether and how federal authorities may respond; there should be an obligation to ensure that the allegations are not groundless or are based on fact. I have also suggested that the First Amendment should be taken to embody a proportionality principle: Eliminating all federal funding because of isolated or occasional unlawful acts might well be an impermissible content-neutral restriction on academic institutions.

I have urged as well that the void-for-vagueness doctrine does indeed apply to federal funding decisions, though its strictures are relaxed. The reason is that the doctrine is needed to ensure fair notice and (more emphatically) to prevent arbitrariness and favoritism on the part of those who make funding decisions.

If federal authorities seek to require certain processes, they may be on firm ground insofar as they are not regulating protected speech. But even if so, they may run up against principles of academic freedom whose scope has yet to be specified and whose very existence remains to be unambiguously established. In some cases, those principles are firmly and directly rooted in the First Amendment, because speech and speakers are involved. In other cases, we might be speaking of freedom of association, or perhaps of an inference from protection of freedom of speech, because academic freedom, as such, is a precondition, for members of the relevant communities, for the exercise of that freedom.[122]

Two canons of construction are highly relevant. The Avoidance Canon counsels in favor of construing relevant statutes so as to avoid constitutional doubts. The Major Questions Doctrine argues against construing statutes so as to give agencies "unheralded" and "transformative" authority. Both doctrines offer a potential way to approach the relevant agency actions without confronting the hardest constitutional questions.

3

Academic Freedom, Ideological Capture, and the Autonomy of the University

NICHOLAS B. DIRKS*

In universities we speak often about academic freedom and how it is a core value of university life. It has become an article of faith, a critical confessional component in the university catechism for administrators and faculty alike. It has also become the "line in the sand" as university boards and presidents negotiate with the Trump administration over charges ranging from allowing "anti-Semitism" to flourish on college campuses to engaging in preferential practices around student admission and faculty hiring. But as universities attempt to honor this commitment, it is increasingly unclear what academic freedom really means and when we can say it has been abridged or abrogated.

Academic freedom is traditionally glossed as the right of the university to pursue truth without constraint or control by outside forces. For most observers, however, it is clear neither why it is linked primarily with issues of academic governance, nor what relationship it has with First Amendment guarantees about freedom of speech. Unfortunately, this lack of clarity threatens to render the concept inadequate to meet the current assault on the university.

The idea of academic freedom goes back not to the US constitution but to early modern Europe, most notably in the Netherlands, where the University of Leiden offered faculty relative freedom from religious and political restrictions, and Germany, where the University of Göttingen during the late eighteenth century proclaimed the need for academics to determine what

* Nicholas B. Dirks is President and CEO of the New York Academy of Sciences. He was the tenth chancellor of the University of California, Berkeley, and is author of the recent book *City of Intellect: The Uses and Abuses of the University* (Cambridge Univ. Press, 2024).

Nicholas B. Dirks, *Academic Freedom, Ideological Capture, and the Autonomy of the University*. In: *Academic Freedom in the Era of Trump*. Edited by: Lee C. Bollinger and Geoffrey R. Stone, Oxford University Press.
 DOI: 10.1093/9780197854877.003.0004

they would teach. Academic freedom was an important element in the 1811 founding of the University of Berlin, which declared the foundational importance of *Lehrfreiheit* (freedom to teach) and *Lernfreiheit* (freedom to learn). Thomas Jefferson advocated for the importance of academic freedom ("here we are not afraid to follow truth wherever it may lead") when he founded the University of Virginia in 1819, but the idea was strengthened even further in the United States because of the growing influence of the idea of the university in Germany, where many American academic leaders did their own graduate studies in the second half of the nineteenth century. Over time, academic freedom came to be cherished both as an ethical imperative and as a necessary intellectual condition for advanced and innovative research.

By the late nineteenth century, general commitments to academic freedom were widely shared in the US academic community, if not always understood in common ways. Meanwhile, control over university matters was still firmly in the hands of trustees, major donors (and founders), and presidents, who often hired and promoted faculty and set curricula with little in the way of formal faculty input. Nevertheless, when the University of Wisconsin Board of Regents in 1894 rejected an effort to expel Richard Ely, a professor of economics who had been accused of promulgating socialism, it used soaring rhetoric to justify its decision: "In all lines of academic investigation it is of the utmost importance that the investigator should be absolutely free to follow the indications of truth wherever they may lead. . . ."[1] Despite this broad invocation of academic freedom, however, Ely significantly toned down his criticisms of capitalism (and capitalists) after his trial in order to keep his job.

It was Ely's former student, Edward Ross, who features more prominently in the canonic history of academic freedom in the United States. Ross taught at the newly established Stanford University, and alienated its sole trustee, Jane Stanford, widow of Leland Stanford, the founder—and primary funder—of the university. Ross was a socialist and a political firebrand as well as a eugenicist, who made incendiary statements opposing the importation of "cheap" Asian labor to work on the railways at the expense of American workers. Mrs. Stanford was troubled by his political outspokenness and especially his condemnations around immigration, given the role of Chinese labor in building her husband's fortune through the transcontinental railroad. But Ross was a popular teacher and an influential academic, and Stanford's president, David Starr Jordan, defended him repeatedly. However, after Ross gave two fiery speeches in 1900, one about the railways and the other about Chinese immigration, Stanford insisted that he be fired, and Jordan complied. Some prominent faculty resigned in protest, including the philosopher Arthur Lovejoy, who moved to Johns Hopkins, where in 1915 he helped to form, with Columbia's John Dewey and other academic notables such as the Columbia economist Edwin Seligman, the American Association of University Professors (AAUP).

The founding principles of the AAUP were laid out in a "Declaration of Principles on Academic Freedom and Tenure." It defined academic freedom as consisting of three elements: "freedom of inquiry and research," "freedom of teaching," and "freedom of extramural utterance and action." At first, the declaration had only symbolic value, as illustrated by the fact that several college presidents, including Nicholas Murray Butler at Columbia, fired faculty for their opposition to US entry into World War I. But with the growing power of an increasingly professionalized faculty, the AAUP principles became far more widely accepted and set the terms for the establishment of rules and conventions around academic employment (and, in time, tenure). Most importantly, the AAUP vested its principles in the professional judgments of faculty "peers," not university presidents or trustees, making faculties the arbiters not just of "truth" but of matters having to do with teaching, the choosing of curriculum, and the evaluation of colleagues for appointment and promotion. In so doing, the AAUP declaration secured its principles as much in protocols of governance as in more general ideals, declaring that faculty bodies were the only appropriate arbiters of academic freedom.

The emphasis on governance reflected the extent to which the AAUP was in part a lobbying organization for faculty and in part an umbrella professional organization, committed to conferring authority over academic matters to the newly professionalized community of academics, denominated by and organized through their respective fields of specialization and expertise. This was the era when disciplinary organizations were first formed—organizations that continue to the present day to host the meetings and publish the journals that define these disciplines. Between 1880 and 1910, "American Associations" of history, economics, political science, sociology, anthropology, and language and literature, among others, were created to help strengthen the disciplines formally and to advocate for their recognition as vital for the research as well as teaching mission of the university. Although presidents and trustees maintained rights of final approval over most university concerns, they did begin to cede some significant control in response to faculty pressures. As academic freedom became increasingly a set of principles grounded in the professionalization of the faculty, it also compromised the extent to which presidents, and even trustees, would need to continue to take responsibility, along with faculty departments, disciplines, and governing bodies, for upholding the ideals of academic freedom.

Faculty mobilized in these collective bodies in part to press for their political right to free expression, and in part to express their concern that administrators were subject primarily to political and financial pressures. John Dewey, who wrote a statement about the critical nature of academic freedom as early as 1902, was especially concerned about the role of founders and big donors. As he observed, "The great event in the history of an institution is now likely to be a big gift, rather than a new investigation or the development of a strong and vigorous teacher. Institutions are ranked by their obvious material prosperity, until the atmosphere of money-getting and money-spending hides from view the interests for the sake of which money alone has a place."[2] But Dewey was also aware that while money was especially important for fields like the sciences, given the cost of laboratories and scientific equipment, the fields that required the most protection from the possible abuses against academic freedom were in the humanities and social sciences.

Dewey wrote that, "There is another group of sciences which, from the standpoint of definitive method and a clearly accepted body of verified fact, are more remote from a scientific status. I refer especially to the social and psychological disciplines, and to some phases of linguistic and historical study—those most intimately associated with religious history and literature." Dewey saw that since the public did not understand the scientific character of these disciplines, they met any pronouncement about public issues that came from them "with little but skepticism or hostility or, what is worse, sensational exploitation." As a consequence, he believed that "the only way in which the more backward subjects can possibly reach anything like the status of mathematics and mechanics is by encouraging to the utmost freedom of investigation." But even as he believed that the applied social sciences would gain—given the right conditions—scientific status over time, he was well aware not just that controversies over any policy-related questions would continue, but that even the older controversies in science had not disappeared. Indeed, the AAUP was officially formed in part as a response to the firing in 1913 of the philosopher John Mecklin from Lafayette College for teaching evolution, a controversy that would famously flare up as a national issue in the Scopes Trial of 1925.[3]

During the first decades of the twentieth century, the flash points for academic freedom concerned the kind of "extramural" speech that got Ely, Ross, and most of the faculty who lost their jobs in the years around World War I, in trouble. But the larger struggle, if not as newsworthy, was over faculty control of academic matters in the university, especially what faculty were teaching their students. Even when the Cold War "Red Scare" led to controversies over loyalty oaths (as at the University of California in 1949) and pressure to fire individual faculty (as happened especially during Joseph McCarthy's Senate hearings and the House Un-American Activities Committee's red-baiting investigations), there was a deep concern about what students were learning in college. The problem with hiring someone who had been a communist in the past was less what they were saying in public than the worry that at some future time they would smuggle in leftist or even socialist views to the teaching of impressionable young people in the university classrooms. That is where subversion would take hold.

The first major Supreme Court ruling about academic freedom in fact concerned a guest lecture given at the University of New Hampshire in 1954 by Paul Sweezy, a well-known Marxist economist who had taught at Harvard and was the author of important articles and books. After Sweezy was briefly imprisoned in New Hampshire for subversion, his conviction was reversed by the Supreme Court in 1957, the opinion of the plurality having been written by Chief Justice Earl Warren.[4] According to the ruling, government interference in the intellectual life of the university created "an atmosphere of suspicion and distrust" antithetical to free inquiry. The case responded specifically to the New Hampshire charge that Sweezy should be forced to testify about his views because of his Marxist ideology, and to produce his lecture notes in response to the investigation. In its invocation of academic freedom, the court referenced both the relevance of free-speech protections and the integrity of academic governance over matters of intellectual content.

If the court's elevation of the idea of academic freedom, with its affiliation with the First Amendment, was at least in part a response to the excesses of McCarthyism, it did not put an end to the controversies over university life. It was only a few years laterthat Ronald Reagan, castigating Warren's alma mater, the University of California (UC) at Berkeley, would make the political excesses of campus life a major focus of his campaign for California's governorship in 1966. The precipitating event for Reagan's attention was the Free Speech Movement of 1964, in which Berkeley students staged protests and occupied buildings to secure the right for free and open political speech on campus. This right had been disallowed under earlier provisions that prohibited most political speech on university campuses, along with political organizing, rallies, and recruiting. Following prevailing notions of "in loco parentis," university boards and administrators argued that no public university should take political positions or encourage formal political activity, in order to achieve political neutrality. While the prohibition on formal political advocacy is still a requirement for administrators—and for the use of campus resources—the idea that students should avoid any political activity changed after Mario Savio and other Berkeley students, told that they could not recruit students to join them in civil-rights work in the American South, set up their tables on campus and demanded their right to do so given the protections of the First Amendment.

In time, Clark Kerr, president of the University of California, supported student demands around free speech on campus, but the scenes of student protest were ripe for political appropriation by their opponents. Reagan used Berkeley's unrest skillfully, blending together a picture of anarchic protest, student licentiousness, and left-leaning faculty to justify his campaign pledge to clean up the mess at Berkeley. But although Reagan won, and quickly fired Kerr, Berkeley only became more political. As student protests erupted around the war in Southeast Asia in the late 1960s and early 70s, with scenes from Columbia, Berkeley, Kent State, and the University of Wisconsin broadcast regularly on the nightly news, campus politics became a focus of calls for government intervention and the need for law and order by Nixon and subsequent Republican leaders, including Reagan when he finally moved into the White House in the 1980s. The focus of their concern increasingly turned from issues around free speech to the college curriculum. Significantly, however, these conservative leaders never threatened to punish universities by cutting federal funding for science.

Although the "culture wars" were in many respects the inevitable outcome of efforts to reflect social and cultural changes in the faculty, the student body, and American society more broadly,[5] new courses, and changes in old ones, began to elicit significant attention and controversy in the 1980s. One pronounced example of this escalating debate took place at Stanford, when, in 1986, several Stanford student groups, led by the Black Student Union, complained that the Western Civilization course was dominated by texts by white men. Protests followed, with national political figures such as Jesse Jackson in attendance, accompanied by chants such as "Hey, hey, ho, ho, Western culture's got to go!" In 1988, after long deliberations, Stanford's faculty senate yielded to student demands and voted to change the course.[6] Reagan's secretary of education, the outspoken William Bennett, came to Stanford soon thereafter to argue that the diminution of focus on Western Civilization in the core curriculum was a tragic abandonment of moral values. Hosted by conservative Stanford students led by a young Peter Thiel, Bennett decried what he claimed was the evisceration of the course in response to the bullying of students who used charges of racism and sexism to get their way.[7] He complained that Stanford was committing "intellectual suicide" and was "closing [the] Stanford mind," alluding to the recent book *The Closing of the American Mind*, by the University of Chicago philosopher Allan Bloom, to suggest the gravity of Stanford's decision.[8]

Bloom's book, published in 1987, quickly became a bestseller, attracting enormous attention. It became a sensation because of its feverish attack on university professors who, so he claimed, had carried on the student revolution of the 1960s by introducing doctrines of relativism and nihilism to college campuses (even though much of the book was an abstruse account of early Greek literature and thought and its subsequent philosophical legacy). Bloom argued that the demise of reverence for Western civilization was the cardinal sin of the university, presided over by tenured radicals who promulgated the end of truth, beauty, and universal ideals. Over the next few years, Bloom's book was followed by a spate of similar opinion pieces, articles, and books filled with denunciations of the professoriate who were seen as having taken over elite universities in the United States, both private and public. The syndicated columnist George Will wrote that the curricular wars in universities were "related battles in a single war, a war of aggression against the Western political tradition and the ideas that animate it."[9]

If the hyperbolic moral panic about curricular changes in the 1980s and '90s routinely raised the rhetorical stakes of faculty and student matters on campus, it tapped into a larger cultural unease about changes in American society, using college politics as a proxy for larger political forces.[10] In fact, courses in Western Civilization had only really emerged in the wake of World War I, the cataclysm that both brought America into alliance with Europe and made abundantly clear that European civilization was in major crisis. Judging from the outrage about curricular changes, one would have thought that these courses had been in place for centuries, and yet, increasingly, wars about curriculum provided a steady diet for conservative outrage and political appropriation. Although the first student protests specifically for new programs and departments in ethnic and African American studies took place at San Francisco State University and UC Berkeley in the late '60s, there would be continual agitation for curricular change in subsequent years, picking up steam again after the Stanford controversy of the late 1980s. At Columbia, for example, students would go on a hunger strike in 1996 to demand the creation of an ethnic-studies department, followed by another hunger strike in 2007 demanding that the program that had been created be given full departmental status and resources to match. And in 2004 Columbia witnessed a full-scale media assault when a group of students—aided by an off-campus organization that called itself the "David Project"—complained about bias and political persecution on the part of professors in the department of Middle Eastern Studies.

Andrew Hartman, in his excellent 2015 book *A War for the Soul of America,* about the culture wars of the last decades of the 20th century, declared that the wars largely concluded after the 1990s. But if campus politics were relatively quiet in the first years of the 21st century, when political protest was largely directed against the war in Iraq and the "war" on "terror," they picked up steam again after the great recession of 2008–09, especially when student protesters joined forces with the Occupy movement. Concerns about race—and specifically police violence against African Americans—escalated with the Black Lives Matter movement, which launched after the death of Trayvon Martin in 2012 and became a national movement after the 2014 death of Michael Brown in Ferguson, Missouri. Concerns about sexual harassment and assault meanwhile also grew on college campuses, with a steady proliferation of scandals, publicized in films such as *The Hunting Ground* released in 2015, that took off during the Me Too movement especially around accusations concerning Harvey Weinstein in 2017. The second decade of the century also saw the rise of emphasis on "safe spaces," "micro-aggressions," and, increasingly, the use of social media to prosecute speech codes.[11]

Meanwhile, even as long-neglected tensions on campus came to the fore, the liberal consensus that had prevailed on college campuses during the convulsions of the '60s and '70s began to unravel. Some faculty and students rejected the premise of free speech, noting that when power inflected all social relations, there was nothing like a level playing field; universities, they argued, should side with those lacking power and limit the speech of the powerful. Concerns about the ways in which prejudice was expressed in everyday interactions, often through unintentional or "mild" slights and statements, surfaced as priorities for administrators and were often converted into speech codes and protocols. A new language of "harm" was used to prosecute new canon wars, target faculty who offended students in the normal course of teaching, and deploy a new range of techniques to censor, punish, or "cancel" other members of the university community.[12] The rise of social media helped to enable a variety of movements and causes that were seen as "calling out" unfair practices, but such activism could also be used to jockey for power on the playing field of identity politics. The police murder of George Floyd in May of 2020 brought concerns about racial justice to a boiling point. "Systemic racism" became a broadly shared term, and investments in programs and initiatives having to do with "diversity, equity, and inclusion" mushroomed in universities, corporations, governmental bodies, and nonprofits. The widespread recognition of racial injustice also contributed to the intensification of campus politics around identity, in this case concerning which voices should be given priority and which should not.

The first presidential campaign of Donald Trump had capitalized on the reaction against "political correctness" while using, and celebrating, precisely the kind of verbal abuse that had been the object of social concerns about civility, and of student monitoring, in the first place. Conservative political discourse used the slogan of "free speech" to justify attacks on universities, even as the First Amendment was weaponized both to allow limitless expenditures of money by candidates, citizens, and corporations in the context of political campaigns and to defend the speech of incendiary right-wing figures such as Milo Yiannopoulos and Richard Spencer. As Trump came to power, these and other speakers were provocatively recruited to visit college campuses by organizations such as the Young Americans for Freedom, Breitbart, and local-level college Republicans. Predictably, many college students reacted against these outside speakers and called for university administrators to disinvite or cancel their campus appearances. Conservatives were handed a gift by these controversies, as they proceeded to publicize what they claimed were hypocritical double standards about free speech.

Trump and his allies jumped on the contradictions and limits around commitments to free speech, however, precisely to build a narrative that the university, rather than the political right, was the chief threat to the First Amendment.[13] Fox News and conservative social-media channels publicized protests and denounced the new generation of student activists as simultaneously repressive and "snowflakes." State after state introduced legislation, drawing on a template devised by the conservative Goldwater Institute, purportedly to defend free speech but also to enact strict (and in some cases draconian) protocols for disciplining students who engaged in campus protests deemed to prevent others from speaking.[14] At least twenty-three states now have statutes conferring some level of authority on state legislatures to monitor free speech on campus, demanding yearly reports on the subject and imposing harsh new rules for student discipline.[15] Ironically, however, although the Goldwater template focused on student discipline—anticipating the current Trump administration's focus on student policing and punishment—it also introduced the idea that conservative students should have greater political rights to counter the left-wing ethos of college campuses. This idea, which appeared as the animating idea behind the critique of "safe spaces" and student protests, has only grown, along with concerns about the need for stronger student discipline. Over the last few years the term "politically correct" has been replaced by "woke," a term that once meant being aware about issues of race and justice, but that now has now been turned into a meme for everything from resentment about having to change the way in which one speaks or tells jokes to not being admitted to one's favorite college or getting a job. Increasingly, "woke" refers not just to issues around race but also to the accusation from the right that the focus on race and identity is part of a Marxist rejection of American values. The term became ubiquitous in the presidential campaign of 2024, as Elon Musk railed against the "woke mind virus," gaining traction both because of the contested politics of race and the declining support for and trust in universities.[16] That decline in trust had first been driven by the effects of the great recession of 2008–09, especially because of the accelerating cost of college and the perception that college did not prepare students for lucrative jobs. Increasingly, however, it has been driven by narratives around wokeness and the disruption caused by campus radicals. Republican politicians began to include denunciations of universities in their talking points following from the 2021 speech by J. D. Vance, when he declared, "we have to honestly and aggressively attack the universities in this country."[17]

Positioning himself for a presidential run, Florida Governor Ron DeSantis began to do precisely that in his home state of Florida. He signed the Stop WOKE Act (HB 7) in 2022, prohibiting the teaching of any concept that might occasion "guilt" or "distress" on the part of students based on their race or gender.[18] Florida began to review course syllabi, first in American history, then in Middle Eastern history, as well as in ethnic and other identity-based studies programs. And in early 2023, DeSantis appointed six new conservative trustees for the state's liberal-arts college, New College, including the activist Christopher Rufo. The new trustees fired the president for ideological reasons, reviewed course syllabi, and presided over what Rufo had called for: a process of ideological recapture of the college that, in his view, had been taken over since the 1960s by radical left Marxist socialist revolutionaries like so many other colleges. Notably, the idea that advocacy for free speech was what defined this movement dissolved in a new and aggressive effort to take back control of universities through government actions that suppressed rather than liberated free expression.

The architect for the new effort to "recapture" public universities in Florida, and increasingly for the ideological attack on elite universities across America, was the conservative activist Christopher Rufo. He successfully identified and caricatured "critical race theory" (CRT) as the intellectual justification for governmental intervention. Rufo used a term for a specific and influential legal theory developed during the 1970s and '80s by law professors Derrick Bell and Kimberlé Crenshaw (among others), holding that racial discrimination was not always explicit but nevertheless systematically encoded in both laws and practices in the United States, including zoning laws and "redlining," judicial sentencing, and bail policy. Critical of liberal legal ideas, Bell and others held that core beliefs concerning individual rights and meritocratic procedures often disguised structural ways in which race was used and abused, while Crenshaw argued that race was often used in conjunction with gender, sexuality, and other identities—a phenomenon labeled by her as "intersectionality"—to constitute an even greater obstacle to social justice and equal treatment under the law.[19]

Rufo in turn charged that any effort to use the idea of race to critique the legal system was itself prejudicial, working against whites, men, and other groups that had been victimized, in his account, by nefarious attacks on common-sense notions of equal rights. He helped to whip up a frenzy of political attacks not just on the legitimate provenance of critical race theory but on anything even vaguely connected to the use of race for what he invariably considered prejudicial purposes. Having introduced critical race theory to American political discourse, he then went after anything connected to "diversity, equity, and inclusion" (DEI). As part of his own personal "influence" campaign, Rufo wrote an entire book on the intellectual antecedents of CRT and DEI theories and initiatives, claiming that universities are now controlled by Marxist intellectuals with dark agendas and revolutionary philosophies.[20]

At first glance, the book seems to be a successor to a spate of conservative attacks on university intellectual life, beginning back in 1987 with Allan Bloom's bestseller. In fact, it is far more insidious, accusing a small set of revolutionary intellectuals and their radical compradors of undertaking a long, relentless effort to promulgate their ideological viewpoints through their "capture" of our top universities. He focuses on four intellectuals: Herbert Marcuse, Angela Davis, Paulo Freire, and Bell himself. Leaving aside Rufo's tendentious and inaccurate framing of the meaning and influence of the work of these figures, it is hard to understand how Marcuse, Davis, and Freire deserve to be classified along with

Bell. Bell was the only one of the four who spent the bulk of his career at major institutions of higher education wielding important academic influence on the development of a consequential field of study (if not nearly as radically or successfully as Rufo claims).[21] Marcuse was an important German philosopher who, after working for the Office of Strategic Services during the war, taught at Brandeis, later moving to UC San Diego, when his contract was discontinued. Angela Davis, a student of Marcuse's, was fired by the UC Board of Regents after teaching at UCLA for only a year, though years later she was hired by UC Santa Cruz to teach in a boutique graduate program. Paulo Freire only taught in the United States for a year.

The problem is not so much that Rufo provides a deeply flawed account of the rich intellectual history of the university, but rather that he has no qualms about using a spurious historical and theoretical argument to justify precisely what he has accused left academics of doing: engaging in a *political takeover* of the university. And his book charts a path forward to do precisely that, as recent actions from the Administration have amply demonstrated. His book makes a case for no less than an American cultural revolution. Rufo argues that his account of the radical "ideological capture" of the American university by figures like the ones he writes about fully justifies—in fact, necessitates—a revolutionary response.

Gradualism is apparently no longer a reasonable playbook for conservatives. Rufo's language has permeated both conservative critiques of elite universities and the language used by the Trump administration in its new "Dear Colleagues" letter and in its recent missives to Columbia and Harvard (containing threats to cancel billions of dollars of federal grants). He has unabashedly told the *New York Times* that he wants "to set them [elite universities] back a generation or two," laying out a plan for destruction given his diagnosis that the entire system is rotten and requires rebuilding from the ruins of the contemporary university rather than anything resembling gradualist reform.[22]

Ironically, although Rufo's playbook has been used not just around CRT and DEI but also around anti-Semitism, there is not a single mention of anti-Semitism as a concern in his 2023 book. Those who have charged that the Trump administration has used anti-Semitism as an opportunistic issue for prosecuting its case against universities can certainly make the case that it was only after October 7, 2023, that anti-Semitism became a stated concern for many on the right wing, certainly those in Trump's orbit.

Rufo's plan for action is a direct assault on "academic freedom," though in fact it is much more than that as well. Since, so the argument goes, radical professors have used academic freedom to insulate themselves and their revolutionary agendas from any outside influence—even from university presidents and trustees—academic freedom is a ruse, and in fact a fundamental part of the problem. Whether as a direct adviser to Ron DeSantis, as a trustee of the New

College of Florida, or as a critical influence on recent actions taken by Trump's Department of Education, Rufo has targeted faculty control over teaching and learning as well as over faculty hiring, evaluation, and promotion. And he has used the role of trustees and boards in public universities as the launch pad for what he intends to be a much more invasive effort on the part of the government to assert control over university curricula, hiring, and admission, all key elements of academic freedom.

Although Rufo wrote in broad terms about using the suspension of public funding to exert pressure on universities, he did not explicitly advocate for the government to be the agent of change. Rather, he exhorted the public to "lay siege to the institutions that have lost the public trust" with the goal of "reanimating the eternal principles and reorienting the institutions toward their highest expression." The public should direct the university to protect "the humble values and institutions of the common man: family, faith, work, community, country.... Excellence over diversity, equality over equity, dignity over inclusion, order over chaos."[23] And yet Rufo's "counter-revolution" has been anything but a grassroots movement. Prosecuted by the most heavy-handed government intervention in higher education in US history, the counterrevolution he calls for has been far more a coup from above than a groundswell from below.

Rufo has been extremely influential for another architect of the Administration's assault on the university, Max Eden, the author of many of the Project 2025 proposals about universities. A senior fellow of the American Enterprise Institute (he was formerly a fellow at the Manhattan Institute, where Rufo currently works), he not only targeted CRT and DEI, but expanded Rufo's proposals to suspend public (government) support for universities in order to pressure universities to comply, suggesting, among other things, that it would be inspiring to put Lee Bollinger, former president of Columbia University, in an "orange jump suit."[24] He has called for strict enforcement of the Supreme Court decision of 2023 on college admissions (at Harvard and the University of North Carolina). He has also suggested using anti-terrorism laws and protocols to demand information about every student who participated in campus protests, reforming accreditation bodies to put additional pressure on universities and their adherence to "woke ideology," and soliciting adjunct professors across the country to partner with states to sue universities for discrimination in hiring and promotion. He has directly advocated for lowering the "overhead" rate on federal research grants to 15 percent and increasing the federal tax on endowments to the level of either individual or corporate tax rates.

The Trump administration has largely followed this playbook, peremptorily canceling billions of dollars in research grants, choosing Columbia as its first target of attack and then training its sights on Harvard, while also demanding access to private student information and imprisoning noncitizen (including permanent resident) students who have been seen as critical either of Trump's policies or Israel's actions in Gaza. Again, the attack has been on much more than academic freedom, and yet the rhetoric no longer depends entirely on "extramural" speech, instead targeting decisions about who gets access to these universities (through admission as well as hiring) and what is taught within them (since DEI courses may be as worrisome as DEI bureaucracies). The principal objective is to dismantle the apparatuses of "woke" mind control that have taken over the universities, so as to facilitate a new open and free exchange of fresh ideas, or so we are told. The mantra is to "Make our universities great again"—that is, as great as they were before they diversified their students, faculty, and curricula. Of course, this nostalgic look to the past also seeks to reclaim universities before they became, thanks to massive federal support, world-class centers for research and innovation.

In the recent attacks on some of our nation's leading universities, research funding has not only been cut to exclude anything related either to diversity or climate but used as ransom for extortionate government demands. These demands, as made clear both by Rufo and Eden (not to mention Trump and Vance), are about much more than simply dismantling DEI and discontinuing the teaching of subjects related to critical race theory. The administration seeks both to stifle protest and to encourage the cultivation of patriotism, which is defined as recovering the founding myths of American democracy. As Rufo has put it, "History must once again serve as nourishment for society, and its highest symbols—the Founders, the Constitution, the Republic—must inspire a renewed and unashamed defense . . . allowing [the common citizen] to live as an equal, raise a family, participate in the Republic, and pursue the good, the true, and the beautiful."[25] Although the "true" gets a formulaic mention, the emphasis here is not on following the truth wherever it may lead. What the DOE letters to universities suggest instead is that what is needed for the counterrevolution is addressing the issue of lack of "viewpoint diversity."

On the face of it, viewpoint diversity, like any diversity, seems a fine idea. I am among those who have often criticized the insularity of professional protocols within the university and how they have occasioned less intellectual diversity than optimal in many faculty arenas. Academics have a propensity to hire colleagues who share their professional interests and perspectives. As an academic administrator, I could recount many instances of protectionism on the part of faculty who would rather make a decent hire decided by them than a spectacular hire suggested by someone from outside their immediate decision-making body. I have accordingly been a critic of departmental autonomy and have argued that faculty need to think far more broadly about how to identify, evaluate, and recruit other colleagues for the sake of advancing cutting-edge research and teaching. I would even agree that the problem of how to achieve an appropriate diversity of "views" (whether methodological and theoretical perspectives or attitudes reflecting different professional/disciplinary backgrounds, experiences, and interests) raises questions for the framing of academic freedom as it has been defined by the AAUP, given its deference to professional communities of judgment.

Academic disciplines have been largely unchanged since their emergence in the late 19th and early 20th centuries. We are now well aware that some of the most original scholarly and scientific work emerges from cross- and non-disciplinary work. In that context, it is an open question how best to define a professional community for the purposes of determining expertise, judgment, and course content. How might we choose appropriate "peers" for review? How could we encourage not just interdisciplinary work but work that genuinely transcends disciplinary boundaries and communities? And how might we strive to include new kinds of "professional" voices, including entrepreneurs, innovators, artists, writers, practitioners with limited or different formal educational credentials, and public intellectuals whose work has been acclaimed by other kinds of professional bodies (journalistic, literary, etc.)?. In fact, many universities have managed to reform evaluative procedures and ensure broader forms of faculty governance while also continuing to follow the basic principles of academic freedom. Nevertheless, these questions must continue to be debated within universities, for the sake of both expanding the professional relevance of the university and upholding a capacious understanding of the meaning of the relationship between faculty governance and academic freedom.

These are not, however, the kinds of questions that are raised by Trump's Department of Education when it calls for viewpoint diversity, as was immediately made clear by the letter from the administration to Harvard University. The letter of April 11, 2025, instructed Harvard to "commission an external party, which shall satisfy the federal government as to its competence and good faith, to audit the student body, faculty, staff, and leadership for viewpoint diversity, such that each department, field, or teaching unit must be individually viewpoint diverse."[26] At the same time, the letter demanded that Harvard "abolish all criteria, preferences, and practices, whether mandatory or optional, throughout its admissions and hiring practices, that function as ideological litmus tests." And yet, in what appeared to be in total contradiction to the abolishment of ideological testing, the letter went on to demand that "every department or field found to lack viewpoint diversity must be reformed by hiring a critical mass of new faculty within that department or field who will provide viewpoint diversity; every teaching unit found to lack viewpoint diversity must be reformed by admitting a critical mass of students who will provide viewpoint diversity."

The language here neither defines viewpoint diversity nor acknowledges that academic standards and criteria are critical in both hiring and admissions. For while many academics would agree with the idea of broadening the disciplinary contexts for evaluation and selection, they would also insist that it is critical to use formal academic criteria for hiring faculty. What the letter suggests instead is that "viewpoint" diversity be monitored by the government, which will judge the "competence and good faith" of university decisions. But what criteria would it use to do this, or to "audit" students, faculty, or staff? We have already seen examples that suggest that the administration takes viewpoint diversity to mean the exclusive hiring of conservative faculty members who will promote its own ideological views on a range of issues in history, culture, and science. Besides, one need not opine about the current administration in terms of decisions made about the overriding importance of loyalty over competence for key appointments to be cautious about giving this (or any) government supervisory control over university hiring and admissions. Academic freedom, whatever the precise definition, has always been understood as deferring to a core conviction: that academic standards, decisions, and modes of governance must be articulated, activated, and monitored by academic experts within the university, not by the government or any other political agency.

Rufo's and Eden's agenda for ideological "recapture" is thus obscured in the language of viewpoint diversity. To be sure, there is a blurring, even at the best of times, between scholarship and political convictions in many fields in the humanities and social sciences (and, occasionally at least, the sciences too). Sharp distinctions between power and knowledge are hard to make, given the limits of the ideal of objectivity and the associated conceit that ideas are inherently free of values. As Joan Scott has written, "Academic freedom was aimed at resolving conflicts about the relationship between power and knowledge, politics and truth, action and thought by positing a sharp distinction between them, a distinction that has been difficult to maintain."[27] The slippery nature of this distinction is an issue for the exercise of academic freedom when applied to teaching and research, and there have certainly been occasions when academics have lost touch with the boundaries between scholarship and advocacy, as conservative and liberal columnists alike have noted (e.g., Ross Douthat and Tyler Austin Harper).[28] However, that is precisely why universities have been so deeply committed to the use of bureaucratic protocols to evaluate scholarship—convening numerous academic committees, soliciting multiple expert evaluations, and following conservative conventions to make decisions about most academic procedures and personnel. And, relatedly, the protection of extramural speech deliberately includes advocacy of any kind, free of any political control or constraint, as long as it takes place outside of the specific academic contexts of teaching and research.

Unresolved tensions between professional organizational structures and broader intellectual goals and convictions, or for that matter between professions of objectivity in judging scholarship and the intrusion of political pressures, values, and perspectives from outside (donors and the public as well as government), are endemic to institutional life. And yet, academic freedom as a principle and a protocol has the unique responsibility to anchor the relationship between the idea of the university and its actual operation, whatever the specific modes of academic governance. Academic freedom, defined in this way, protects the core functions of the university: preserving the established knowledge of the past, transmitting the cutting-edge knowledge of the present, and producing new knowledge for the future through open exploration, experiment, and discovery.

Looking back at the televised debate in 1988 between Secretary of Education William Bennett and Stanford President Donald Kennedy about the Stanford core course, we now see who is getting the last laugh. Kennedy was measured—appropriately presidential—in the conversation. Amused by the idea that as a university president he had any real say in the outcome, he was clearly driven by a belief that the faculty had made a deliberative and reasoned decision to change the core course curriculum. Bennett looked unhappy, aggressive, and angry even when expounding his defense of classical wisdom. But he also looked weak, unable to think of forms of pressure to reverse Stanford's decision beyond his repeated insistence of the danger of abandoning Western Civilization

Now that Bennett has morphed into Linda McMahon under the dispensation of the Trump administration, times have changed. The government has decided that it has all the cards and that it should use them. As deals are struck, university by university, academic freedom is no longer either a rhetorical flourish or an imperative value. Instead, it is being cast as the erstwhile fetish of a finally disempowered faculty that finds itself on the wrong side of history.

Unfortunately, this moment of history portends the steady erosion and diminishment not just of academic freedom but of the comparative distinction and excellence of American universities. The culture wars have now been elevated to a subject of national politics, resulting in the administration's efforts to control free speech, punish universities for the expression of any political ideas it objects to or deems dangerous, and use federal funding of universities to force them to proclaim its own views of history and culture. The attack on universities is part of a larger assault on the fundamental institutions that have supported American democracy over its history and constitute the basic fabric of a free and open civil society. The second Trump administration has not only activated earlier threats against universities; it has targeted media and the press, law firms and other legal institutions, and selected corporations, making extortionate demands while using capricious forms of federal power to exact loyalty and subservience, whether from CBS or the Paul, Weiss law firm. And the same assault has been taking place within the government, as experts and career civil servants are replaced by loyalists, sycophants, and many clearly unqualified people.

Across our institutions, the university holds a special place. It is the critical site for the production and preservation of truth and—more to the point—those who seek the truth. We know from history that far more than the university would be grievously and irrevocably damaged by the assumption on the part of the government that it, instead of universities themselves, should start dictating what might stand in for the truth, wherever it might lead. That is not a path we wish to go down again.

4

Executive Authority and Academic Freedom

NIALL FERGUSON*

When a head of state picks a fight with a university, you generally expect the university to lose. Even the richest university—say, Harvard—does not have pockets as deep as the government. And as for armed force, to paraphrase Stalin, "How many divisions does the president of Harvard have?"

And yet the pen is sometimes mightier than the sword, the gown more powerful than the crown. King James II learned this the hard way in 1687, when he attempted to impose a new president on the fellows of Magdalen College, Oxford. Each year, at its Restoration dinner, the college celebrates its victory over the last Stuart monarch.

The president of Magdalen College, Henry Clerke, died on March 24, 1687. Early the following month, King James II nominated one Anthony Farmer to be the College's next president. Farmer was in multiple ways an unsuitable—indeed ineligible—candidate, as Macaulay tell us in his *History of England*:

> This man's life had been a series of shameful acts. He had been a member of the University of Cambridge, and had escaped expulsion only by a timely retreat. He had then joined the Dissenters. Then he had gone to Oxford, had entered himself at Magdalene, and had soon become notorious there for every kind of vice. He generally reeled into his college at night speechless with liquor. He was celebrated for having headed a disgraceful riot at Abingdon. He had been a constant frequenter of noted haunts of libertines. At length he had turned pandar [pimp], had

* Milbank Family Senior Fellow at the Hoover Institution at Stanford University and a Senior Faculty Fellow at the Belfer Center at Harvard University.

Niall Ferguson, *Executive Authority and Academic Freedom*. In: *Academic Freedom in the Era of Trump*.
Edited by: Lee C. Bollinger and Geoffrey R. Stone, Oxford University Press.
© Oxford University Press (2026). DOI: 10.1093/9780197854877.003.0005

exceeded even the ordinary vileness of his vile calling, and had received money from dissolute young gentlemen commoners for services such as it is not good that history should record. This wretch, however, had pretended to turn Papist. His apostasy atoned for all his vices; and, though still a youth, he was selected to rule a grave and religious society in which the scandal given by his depravity was still fresh.

> As a Roman Catholic he was disqualified for academical office by the general law of the land. Never having been a Fellow of Magdalene College or of New College, he was disqualified for the vacant presidency by a special ordinance of William of Waynflete [the founder of Magdalen]. William of Waynflete had also enjoined those who partook of his bounty to have a particular regard to moral character in choosing their head; and, even if he had left no such injunction, a body chiefly composed of divines could not with decency entrust such a man as Farmer with the government of a place of education.[1]

The fellows petitioned against Farmer, and, on the last statutory day, elected John Hough, a London-born fellow of the College, whom the Visitor at once admitted. But the fellows were cited before the Court of Ecclesiastical Commission. Hough's election was annulled on June 22. The vice president was suspended and, on August 14, the fellows were instructed to admit Samuel Parker, the Bishop of Oxford, who—although an Anglican and obviously a less disreputable figure than Farmer—was also unqualified by statute.

A few weeks later, the king came to Oxford and harangued the fellows in Christ Church. Here is Macaulay again:

> When they appeared before him he treated them with an insolence such as had never been shown to their predecessors by the Puritan visitors. "You have not dealt with me like gentlemen," he exclaimed. "You have been unmannerly as well as undutiful." They fell on their knees and tendered a petition. He would not look at it. "Is this your Church of England loyalty? I could not have believed that so many clergymen of the Church of England would have been concerned in such a business. Go home. Get you gone. I am King. I will be obeyed. Go to your chapel this instant; and admit the Bishop of Oxford. Let those who refuse look to it. They shall feel the whole weight of my hand. They shall know what it is to incur the displeasure of their Sovereign." The Fellows, still kneeling before him, again offered him their petition. He angrily flung it down. "Get you gone, I tell you. I will receive nothing from you till you have admitted the Bishop."
>
> They retired and instantly assembled in their chapel. The question was propounded whether they would comply with His Majesty's command.

> Smith was absent. Charnock alone answered in the affirmative. The other Fellows who were at the meeting declared that in all things lawful they were ready to obey the King, but that they would not violate their statutes and their oaths.
>
> "Will you submit," said the Bishop [of Chester], "to our visitation?" "I submit to it," said Hough with great dexterity, "so far as it is consistent with the laws, and no farther." "My Lords," said he, "you have this day deprived me of my freehold: I hereby protest against all your proceedings as illegal, unjust, and null; and I appeal from you to our sovereign Lord the King in his courts of justice."[2]

On October 20, three Royal Commissioners (with three troops of horse) arrived to visit the college. After declaring Hough no longer president, they struck his name out of the Buttery book. When the Court of Ecclesiastical Commission met again on the 25th, it installed Parker by proxy and broke into the Lodgings. On November 15, twenty-five fellows were expelled and declared incapable of receiving any preferment. A few submitted and remained. After the sudden death of Parker in March, the installation as president of Bonaventure Giffard—a Catholic priest whom James had already made vicar-apostolic of the midland district—meant that seven more fellows rebelled and were deprived of their fellowships. Now only two of the original fellows remained.

Here again is Macaulay: "The college was turned into a Popish seminary. . . . The Roman Catholic service was performed in the chapel. In one day twelve Roman Catholics were admitted Fellows."[3]

Three centuries later, these events find an echo on the other side of the Atlantic. On April 3, 2025, Harvard University received a letter from the federal government, signed by representatives from the Department of Health and Human Services, the Department of Education, and the General Services Administration.[4] The letter stated that Harvard had "fundamentally failed to protect American students and faculty from antisemitic violence and harassment in addition to other alleged violations of Title VI and Title VII of the Civil Rights Act of 1964."[5] In particular, Harvard had permitted a hostile environment for Jewish students, in violation of Title VI.

Eight days later, Harvard received another letter from the federal government.[6] This one demanded that the university take a long list of actions as a condition of receiving continued federal funding. Here are some highlights of the government's demands. Harvard must:

- Hire a third party to audit certain programs, identify faculty members who contributed to anti-Semitism on campus, and sanction them "within the bounds of academic freedom and the First Amendment";
- "Carry out meaningful discipline" for conduct violations since 2023;

- Implement merit-based hiring and admissions reforms, to be audited by a third party;
- Immediately report any conduct violation by an international student to the federal government (on top of providing ongoing information to the Department of Homeland Security);
- Shutter all DEI programs and offices;
- Ban masks;
- Reform governance to "reduc[e] the power held by faculty (whether tenured or untenured) and administrators more committed to activism than scholarship"; and
- Ensure through a series of audits, hires, and transfers that "each department, field, or teaching unit [is] individually viewpoint diverse."[7]

Not long after, the Department of Education suspended $2.2 billion in multiyear federal grants and $60 million in contracts, claiming that Harvard had rejected its policy demands relating to anti-Semitism and racial discrimination. The Department of Homeland Security also threatened to revoke Harvard's eligibility to host international students.

Nor was that all. On May 2, President Donald Trump published one of his regular "truths." "We are going to be taking away Harvard's Tax Exempt Status," he wrote on his own social-media platform. "It's what they deserve!"[8] Like nearly all universities, Harvard has 501(c)(3) tax-exempt status as an educational institution, which means it does not pay income taxes on net earnings and its donors get income-tax deductions. But that status could be revoked if an audit found that it had violated the relevant rules. On June 30, a Trump-administration investigation found that Harvard had indeed violated the federal civil rights of Jewish students, faculty, and staff.[9]

One possibility is that Harvard's admissions policies and/or its tolerance of anti-Semitism violate public policy. That is the standard the Supreme Court set in 1983, when it upheld an IRS decision to revoke the tax-exempt status of Bob Jones University, in Greenhill, South Carolina, over the school's racially discriminatory policies, which included rules against interracial dating and marriage.[10] (BJU regained its tax-exempt status in 2017, having abandoned the interracial dating rule in 2000.)

Now, Harvard's endowment is massive, in excess of $50 billion. But, as Jim Hankins has pointed out, most of it is tied up in donor-restricted funds, and, in any case, it covers only 37 percent of Harvard's annual operating costs of $6.5 billion.[11] For the rest, the university relies on tuition (20 percent), federal grants (11 percent), current gifts from alumni and other donors, and borrowing.[12] So the Trump administration's actions are not trivial threats to its financial stability.

Like the fellows of Magdalen in 1687, Harvard has resisted the government's encroachment on its traditional privileges. On April 21, the university filed a lawsuit against the Trump administration.[13] The suit argues that the government has "violate[d] Harvard's constitutional rights" and "threaten [its] academic independence."[14] The university's President, Alan Garber—the John Hough figure in my analogy—has said that the threat to revoke the school's tax-exempt status is "highly illegal" and "destructive to Harvard."[15]

"Tax-exempt status is granted to educational institutions to enable them to successfully carry out their mission of education and, for research universities, of research," he told the *Wall Street Journal* on May 2.[16] "Obviously that would be severely impaired if we were to lose our tax exempt status. . . . The message that it sends to the educational community would be a very dire one . . . that political disagreements could be used as a basis to pose what might be an existential threat to so many educational institutions."

In response, in May 2025, Education Secretary Linda McMahon informed Garber that the federal government would no longer provide grant funding until the university complied with its demands.[17] The following week, the Trump administration cut an additional $450 million in grants.[18] Department of Homeland Security Secretary Kristi Noem announced that Harvard's Student and Exchange Visitor Program certification had been revoked, barring Harvard from hosting international students.[19] On May 30, the State Department ordered all US embassies and consulates to conduct "comprehensive and thorough vetting" of anyone seeking to visit Harvard from abroad.[20] On June 4, Trump issued a proclamation restricting international students from studying at Harvard, and directing the State Department to consider revoking the visas of current international students.[21]

Harvard again took legal action, arguing that the government had no right to forbid it to enroll foreign students, and a judge granted a temporary restraining order. On June 20, Harvard was granted an injunction allowing it to continue hosting international students as litigation continues.[22] And, on September 3, District Judge Allison Burroughs ruled that the Trump administration's freezing of research funding "violated Harvard's free-speech rights as well as the U.S. Civil Rights Act."[23] The issue has of course become political, just as the case of the presidency of Magdalen did. On May 2, Senate Minority Leader Chuck Schumer asked the Internal Revenue Service inspector general to investigate whether Trump has violated the law and if the IRS has begun auditing nonprofits based on White House requests.[24]

At the time of writing, Harvard and the Trump administration appear to be negotiating the kind of "deal" that has characterized Trump's trade negotiations with sovereign states. At the end of September, Trump himself claimed that he had "reached a deal with Harvard today," which would involve Harvard paying $500 million, operating trade schools, teaching artificial intelligence, and other unspecified actions.[25]

There is even giddy talk of establishing an equivalent of the Hoover Institution at Harvard—presumably to play the part that entity plays at Stanford, as a semi-autonomous research center with foundational commitments to constitutional government and free-market economics that are regarded by the rest of the university as appallingly conservative. It is noteworthy that all previous attempts to establish an analogous institution at Harvard have been stymied on the spurious grounds that it would be "too political."[26]

Although the Trump administration's attack on Harvard is its most spectacular move against a university, it is clearly intended *pour encourager les autres,* and has been accompanied by similar though somewhat less drastic challenges to other institutions, including Columbia University. Indeed, Columbia, Brown University, the University of Pennsylvania, and the University of Virginia have already cut deals with the administration.[27] However, confronted with a broader ten-point compact, at least six of the nine universities to which it was sent have—in the spirit of Magdalen—refused to accept it.[28]

As Macaulay relates, James II made a mistake in taking on the fellows of Magdalen, unlikely heroes though they were:

> The nature of the academical system of England is such that no event which seriously affects the interests and honour of either [ancient] University can fail to excite a strong feeling throughout the country. Every successive blow, therefore, which fell on Magdalene College, was felt to the extremities of the kingdom. In the coffeehouses of London, in the Inns of Court, in the closes of all the Cathedral towns, in parsonages and manor houses scattered over the remotest shires, pity for the sufferers and indignation against the government went on growing.[29]

So, the question arises, should all professors—indeed everyone concerned about the health of higher education—defend Harvard against the American equivalent of James II, in the same way that the wider English public rallied to the side of the fellows of Magdalen? Greg Lukianoff of the Foundation for Individual Right and Expression says that we are obligated to, "on principle":

> When the federal government is exceeding its power, or claiming new powers that it never previously had, we have to step in. We have to defend against it. . . . Its demands of Harvard would catastrophically undermine academic freedom, free speech, and institutional independence on campus. . . . The federal government dictating the hiring, admissions, and

> academic freedom of a college is no solution to either the problem of Harvard in particular or anti-Semitism on campus in general.[30]

Greg has argued that:

- The government is ignoring established procedures for its proposed sanctions. . . . The government cannot freeze funding to impose punitive sanctions on an institution without determining, through the appropriate processes, that those punishments are warranted.
- Some of what the government seeks to do is beyond its lawful authority, even as part of proposed sanctions.
- The federal government attempting a hostile takeover of a private institution is a bad idea.
- [T]he list of research funding being suspended by the government . . . includes research into infectious diseases, neurology, toxins, microbiomes, military advancements, and cancer.[31]

Indeed, Atul Gawande points out that "More than 90% of the nine billion federal dollars for Harvard that are now in danger supports life sciences, primarily through the National Institutes of Health. . . . Three-quarters of it goes to five independent Boston hospitals affiliated with its medical school: Brigham and Women's Hospital, Massachusetts General Hospital, Boston Children's Hospital, the Dana-Farber Cancer Institute, and Beth Israel Deaconess Medical Center."[32] As one of my children was born—by emergency cesarean section—at Brigham and Women's, I would surely be a hypocrite if I shrugged my shoulders and said: "Too bad."

And yet, I believe we all must think twice before we uncritically embrace FIRE's narrative that Trump is the villain, like James II, and the professors of Harvard the heroes, like the fellows of Magdalen.

On April 29, the Harvard Presidential Task Force on Combating Antisemitism and Anti-Israeli Bias published its report. It made for sobering reading:

> A Harvard faculty member who works closely with students reported to us that some Jewish students choose to hide their identities on campus, which was something the faculty member could not have imagined would ever be the case at Harvard. . . . We have heard from many dozens of non-Jewish students, faculty, and staff who were profoundly troubled at what they described as an intolerance that has crept into higher education and that is also on display at Harvard. . . . [Many people] saw Harvard as a place where, over time, many students' politics become more radical and where students become less tolerant of people who disagree with them.[33]

According to the report, "student activists [attempt] to drive Israeli students (and Jewish students who feel connected to Israel) out of student life. This often takes the form of 'shunning.'"[34] And: "American Jewish students told us . . . they felt pressure to condemn Israel to prove they were 'one of the good ones' (meaning, an 'anti-Zionist Jew'), and faced social consequences when they refused."[35] Moreover, "Jewish students told us stories of Harvard-run 'privilege trainings' where they were told that they were deemed to be privileged not only by dint of being identified as White but also because of their Jewishness."[36]

Here is a gem, from page 150 of the report:

> A session in four sections (out of 28) of a required course for all [Harvard Graduate School of Education] students . . . included the following graphic about White supremacy. . . . The graphic labels opposition to the Boycott, Divestment, Sanctions (BDS) movement as considered "coded genocide," placing it alongside the Anti-Defamation League (ADL). Both are positioned merely one step removed from "overt genocide," which includes examples like lynching and the KKK. . . . The instructor displayed the graphic on screen for an extended period without addressing its problematic characterization of Jewish organizations and perspectives.[37]

I don't think there can therefore be any doubt that Harvard—once, not so long ago, notable for the high proportion of Jewish faculty and students—now has a serious anti-Semitism problem. "Nationally," according to FIRE research, "55% of students said it would be difficult to have an open and honest conversation about the Israeli/Palestinian conflict. At Harvard, it's 67%. Among faculty nationwide, according to our 2024 Faculty Survey, 70% have a hard time talking openly and honestly about the conflict. At Harvard, it's 84%."[38]

And that is not Harvard's only problem. It has an anti-conservatism problem, too. According to the Harvard Crimson's 2023 survey, only 2.5 percent of faculty respondents identified as conservatives, with more than three-quarters identifying as liberal.[39] More than 90 percent of political donations from Harvard employees go to the Democratic Party," Greg Lukianoff notes.[40] According to the *Harvard Crimson*, "More than half of the Class of 2027–65%—identified as progressive (45.2%) or very progressive (19.5%), while only 8.4% of the class identified as conservative or very conservative."[41] Predictably, 86.8% had a negative view of Donald Trump; 3.6% favorable.[42] Not surprisingly, "while 41% of liberal students reported feeling comfortable discussing controversial topics, only 25% of moderates and 17% of conservatives felt similarly."[43]

And let us not forget Harvard's systematic anti-Asianism in its admissions policy, first exposed by Ron Unz and culminating in the 2023 Students for Fair Administrations case, which led the Supreme Court to rule that college affirmative-action programs were unconstitutional.[44] Has that led to reform? Don't ask me; ask liberal commentator Matthew Yglesias. "It is, of course, difficult to know exactly what happens in the black box of college admissions," he wrote recently.[45] "But Harvard and most other elite schools do not appear, in practice, to have dramatically altered their admissions practices."[46] That should not surprise us. According to the *Harvard Crimson*, 85.6 percent of the Class of 2027 agree that "Harvard Should Strive to Create a Diverse Student Body."[47] And two thirds (66.5 percent) support affirmative action.[48]

Harvard is blighted by anti-free-speechism, as well. Here's the *Harvard Crimson* again, from February 10: "Only one-third of Harvard's last graduating class felt comfortable expressing their opinions about controversial topics during their time at the College, the University's 2024 senior survey found, reporting a 13 percent decrease from the Class of 2023. . . . more than a quarter of the class of 2024 respondents said they only like to engage socially with people who share their political beliefs. Only 29 percent disagreed or strongly disagreed with that statement."[49] Moreover, only 19.2 percent of the Class of 2028 are very concerned or concerned about free speech.[50]

Harvard students are pretty woke, it is clear. And yet they are not complete outliers. On the contrary, as surveys by Heterodox Academy and FIRE show, they are fairly representative. Take the issue of Israel and the Palestinians. According to Pew, a third of Americans under 30 say their sympathies lie either entirely or mostly with the Palestinian people, while 14 percent say their sympathies lie entirely or mostly with the Israeli people.[51] For adults as a whole, the shares are 16 percent (pro-Palestinian) and 31 percent (pro-Israeli). For over-64's, 9 percent and 47 percent.[52]

Americans aged 18–29 have the lowest approval of Trump of any generation—34 percent approval vs. 66 percent disapproval—compared with 47 percent to 55 percent for all ages. They're also least proud to be American (46 percent vs. 62 percent for all ages). And they're the most opposed to Trump's handling of DEI (66 percent disapprove vs. 56 percent all ages). These findings are all from an NBC Poll, published on April 27.[53]

As has long been obvious, there is a fairly seamless continuum that leads from illiberalism to outright authoritarianism. We should therefore not be surprised that Generation Z is also turning away from democracy. According to a new More in Common survey, 75 percent of Americans, including 80 percent of Democrats and 85 percent of Republicans, say the Constitution should be "widely respected because it has provided stability."[54] Sixty-three percent of Americans, including 79 percent of Democrats and 69 percent of Republicans, say democracy is "definitely the best" form of government for America. But nearly half of Gen Z Americans (47 percent) agree that "sometimes it's okay for leaders to set aside democratic principles (e.g., constitutional checks and balances) to fix the economy," compared to 29 percent of all Americans. A quarter of Gen Z (25 percent) say they "don't really care" about the Constitution. And only four in ten Gen Z-ers (42 percent) say democracy is "definitely the best" form of government for America.[55]

All this is what the higher-education establishment has wrought—no doubt with some help, as Jonathan Haidt argue, from social-media apps and smartphones. Harvard merely exemplifies the rot that permeates the entire system. In this context, I do not find much to object to in the Trump administration's ten-point "Compact For Academic Excellence In Higher Education." To be clear, I am unambiguously in favor of these principles:

1. "[N]o factor such as sex, ethnicity, race, nationality, political views, sexual orientation, gender identity, religious associations, or proxies for any of those factors shall be considered, explicitly or implicitly, in any decision related to undergraduate or graduate student admissions or financial support," and all applicants to undergraduate programs should take standardized tests.
2. Universities shall "adopt a policy protecting academic freedom in classrooms, teaching, research, and scholarship. Such policies also shall recognize that academic freedom is not absolute, and universities shall adopt policies that prevent discriminatory, threatening, harassing, or other behaviors." They shall not "knowingly: (1) permit actions by the university, university employees, university students, or individuals external to the university community to delay or disrupt class instruction or disrupt libraries or other traditional study locations; (2) allow demonstrators to heckle or accost individual students or groups of students; or (3) allow obstruction of access to parts of campus based on students' race, ethnicity, nationality, or religion." They shall "adopt policies prohibiting incitement to violence, including calls for murder or genocide or support for entities designated by the U.S. government as terrorist organizations."
3. "[N]o factor such as sex, ethnicity, race, national origin, disability, or religion shall be considered in any decision related to the appointment, advancement, or reappointment of academic, administrative, or support staff at any level."
4. "[A]ll university employees, in their capacity as university representatives, will abstain from actions or speech relating to societal and political events except in cases in which external events have a direct impact upon the university." University members should be "encouraged to comment on current events [only] in their individual capacities."
5. "[A] grade must not be inflated, or deflated, for any non-academic reason, but only rigorously reflect the demonstrated mastery of a subject that the grade purports to represent."

6. "Women's equality requires single-sex spaces, such as bathrooms and locker rooms, and fair competition, such as in sports. Institutions [shall] commit to defining and otherwise interpreting 'male,' 'female,' 'woman,' and 'man' according to reproductive function and biological processes. Otherwise, immutable characteristics, particularly race, do not permit unequal treatment, including in grading as well as access to buildings, spaces, scholarships, programming, and other university resources." Disciplinary standards shall "apply equally to all students, faculty, and staff. These standards should promote fairness, due process, and equal treatment."
7. "[U]niversities that receive federal funds have a duty to reduce administrative costs as far as reasonably possible and streamline or eliminate academic programs that fail to serve students.... [T]he effective tuition rates charged to American students [shall be frozen] for the next five years." And "any university with an endowment exceeding $2 million per undergraduate student will not charge tuition for admitted students pursuing hard science programs."
8. "[N]o more than 15 percent of a university's undergraduate student population shall be participants in the Student Visa Exchange Program, and no more than 5 percent shall be from any one country." And "all universities shall promptly and fully disclose all funding from any foreign institutions and individuals. No foreign funding may in any way encourage or restrict the hiring of any persons or the teaching of any particular perspective or the admission of any foreign student or group of students."
9. "[A] religious institution may maintain preferences for religious affiliation or belief in hiring and admissions, a single-sex institution may maintain sex-based preferences, and any institution may maintain preferences in admissions for American citizens."
10. "On an annual basis the university's President, Provost, and Head of Admissions shall be required to certify the University's adherence to the principles.... The university annually shall conduct... an independent, good faith, empirically rigorous, and anonymous poll of its faculty, students, and staff, providing them the opportunity to evaluate the university's performance against this compact."[56]

These seem to me quite reasonable demands to make of universities—not only Harvard—that for years have acted in diametrically opposite ways. They have engaged in all kinds of discrimination in their admissions policies. They have rendered academic freedom an oxymoron. They have engaged in race and sex discrimination in their hiring and promotion policies too. On numerous political issues, there was an almost complete absence of institutional neutrality at many universities. There was rampant grade inflation. The exaltation of "transgender rights" made a mockery of women's sports. The inflation of tuition costs was out of all proportion to inflation for the economy as whole. Far too many foreign students were admitted. And the lack of transparency about all these offenses against the most basic principles of the university as an institution for the advancement of knowledge and learning—for the pursuit of truth—has been shameless.

I wish only that it had not been necessary for the federal government to offer such a compact. Yet I have no illusions that the established universities would have spontaneously introduced such reforms.

The irony of the story I am telling is that Harvard today has become what Oxford once was. For Oxford in the late 17th century was anything but a stronghold of intellectual adventure—quite the contrary. As Salter and Lobel tell us in their 1954 history of the university:

> When the king had begun to realize the effects of his folly, he allowed the Visitor to restore Hough and the fellows. This restoration took place on October 25, 1688. The names of the intruders were struck out of the books and Charnock was expelled.
>
> The "Golden Election" of demies [scholars] in 1689, under the victorious Hough, augured well for the intellectual harvest of the coming century, which, however, even in its better years, bore sadly little fruit.

Hough lived to the ripe old age of 90 and went on to hold three bishoprics (Oxford, Lichfield and Worcester). But I doubt many people regularly read the thirty published sermons of his that you can find in the Bodleian Library. Magdalen remained a grand but stagnant institution—the same one where, in 1752–53, the historian Edward Gibbon spent fourteen months. They proved "the most idle and unprofitable of my whole life," he wrote in his memoirs:

> In my sixteenth year I was not devoid of capacity or application; even my childish reading had displayed an early though blind propensity for books; and the shallow flood might have been taught to flow in a deep channel and a clear stream. In the discipline of a well-constituted academy, under the guidance of skilful and vigilant professors, I should gradually have risen from translations to originals, from the Latin to the Greek classics, from dead languages to living science: my hours would have been occupied by useful and agreeable studies, the wanderings of fancy would have been restrained, and I should have escaped the temptations of idleness, which finally precipitated my departure from Oxford.[57]

I wonder how many of today's most gifted Harvard students feel the same way as Gibbon. I know a few who certainly do. Yet in the days of James II and

John Hough, Harvard was still a relatively young institution, founded in 1636 to cater to the needs of the nearly 10,000 Puritans who had migrated to New England in search of religious freedom. Like the University of Austin in our time, Harvard sprang from a rebellion against a suffocating orthodoxy, even if it swiftly embraced—to the extent of witch-hunting—an even more rigid one. (The original motto was *Veritas Christo et Ecclesiae.*) It started small, with a library of just 400 books.

My great fear is that, as happened in the case of James II and the fellows of Magdalen, too forceful an external challenge to Harvard's vices will have the unintended consequence of entrenching them. One may think here of Harvard as being a bit like Canada—a country whose chronically woke Liberal Party has been saved from political oblivion by none other than Donald Trump. My recurring nightmare is that the worst culprits in the downfall of Harvard will now reemerge from their conspicuous silence to pose, alongside President Garber, as the heroic upholders of academic freedom and integrity.

The conclusion I draw is that, on the whole, it would probably be better for universities to eschew the temptations of government money, alluring though it may be to take it. For there seems no other way to uphold academic freedom and standards than through an absolute independence. The fellows of Magdalen did not have it (and they have it even less today). Nor do the professors of Harvard. We may pretend that the intrusion of politics into the American academy began with President Trump, but it is a hollow pretense. The legally dubious threats of Barack Obama's administration to withdraw federal funds pressured universities to change their rules on sexual assault and harassment in ways that led to egregious injustices in the 2010s. Did any academics speak up then against the executive branch's intrusion into the sequestered groves of scholarship? Of course not. Long before, the universities had entered into a tacit compact with the Democratic Party. They are paying the price for that compact today.

But the lesson of history is not that defiance will be rewarded. It is that, if reforms are not forced upon them, the American universities will quickly lapse back into the corrupt ways of the recent past—just as the fellows of Magdalen did after their seeming triumph over James II.

PART II

THE AUTHORITARIAN PLAYBOOK ON ACADEMIC FREEDOM

Federal Funding

5

The Trump Administration's Assault on Academic Freedom

Controlling Funds as a Way to Impermissibly Control Universities

ERWIN CHEMERINSKY*

The United States has the greatest system of higher education in the world, and in its first months the Trump administration has inflicted enormous damage to it. The Trump administration realizes that American universities have three financial vulnerabilities: they are very dependent on federal money for research; they are very dependent on foreign students; and they are very dependent on philanthropy. It has targeted all of these sources of revenue.

For example, in its first months, the Trump administration has cut off billions of dollars of federal assistance for research, including for vital medical research.[1] In addition, the administration has imposed massive cuts in funding to many elite universities: Harvard, Columbia, University of Pennsylvania, Northwestern, Cornell, UCLA, and others. Federal district courts in Massachusetts and California found that the termination of funds to Harvard University and to University of California faculty violated the Constitution and federal law.[2]

The context for this is the tremendous dependence of American universities on federal funds for research. It is estimated, for example, that 48 percent of MIT's budget comes from federal money; the figure is 42 percent for Johns Hopkins, 31 percent for Duke, 29 percent for University of Michigan, 29 percent for Northwestern, and a significant part of every major university's revenues.[3]

* Dean and Jesse H. Choper Distinguished Professor of Law, University of California, Berkeley, School of Law.

Erwin Chemerinsky, *The Trump Administration's Assault on Academic Freedom*. In: *Academic Freedom in the Era of Trump*. Edited by: Lee C. Bollinger and Geoffrey R. Stone, Oxford University Press.
 DOI: 10.1093/9780197854877.003.0006

President Trump and those around him have been explicit as to their goal in cutting off funds: they see colleges and universities as too liberal and seek to impose a conservative ideology upon them. In a post on his Truth Social platform, President Trump said he will reform universities that are "now corrupting our Youth and Society with WOKE, SOCIALIST, and ANTI-AMERICAN Ideology."[4] As Christopher Rufo, who has helped shape Trump's policies on higher education, has stated, the goal is to make universities experience "existential terror" and put them in "significant recession."[5] Secretary of Education Linda McMahon has added that "universities should continue to be able to do research, as long as they're abiding by the law and are in sync . . . with the Administration and what the Administration is trying to accomplish."[6]

The United States has a highly decentralized system of higher education, and schools always have been largely able to make their own choices about a myriad of matters including student admissions, faculty hiring, governance structures, curriculum, and programs. To be sure, there are some limits on universities; the Constitution and federal law prohibit discrimination. But overall, schools have enjoyed enormous autonomy.

This autonomy is reflected, even embodied, in the concept of academic freedom. The central tenet of academic freedom is that, consistent with professional competence and ethics, professors are entitled to full freedom in research and in the publication of results, freedom in the classroom to teach and discuss the topics in which they have professional expertise, and freedom to convey their knowledge and expertise to the public at large. These principles, codified early in the 20th century, are central to the creation of modern American universities. Colleges and universities could not do the important work of creating and transmitting advanced knowledge unless there were robust protections for scholarly inquiry and expression, bounded by professional expectations of competent and ethical behavior.

As the then-new American Association of University Professors (AAUP) put it in its original "Declaration of Principles on Academic Freedom and Academic Tenure" in 1915: "It is highly needful, in the interest of society at large, that what purport to be the conclusions of [those] trained for, and dedicated to, the quest for truth, shall in fact be the conclusions of such [experts], and not echoes of the opinions of the lay public, or of the individuals who endow or manage universities."[7]

The Supreme Court has been explicit about academic freedom as "a special concern of the First Amendment."[8] Indeed, more than seventy years ago it powerfully declared:

> The essentiality of freedom in the community of American universities is almost self-evident. No one should underestimate the vital role in a democracy that is played by those who guide and train our youth. To

> impose any strait jacket upon the intellectual leaders in our colleges and universities would imperil the future of our Nation. . . . Scholarship cannot flourish in an atmosphere of suspicion and distrust. Teachers and students must always remain free to inquire, to study and to evaluate, to gain new maturity and understanding; otherwise, our civilization will stagnate and die.[9]

But what the Trump administration has done in trying to control universities is at odds with schools being able to decide for themselves a myriad of matters. In this essay, I want to focus on how the administration is using leverage over federal funds in a manner inimical to academic freedom. I want to focus on two examples of this: the termination of funds to researchers and to universities, and the Trump administration's proposed "compact" with higher education. Both are grave threats to universities and academic freedom. Both are unconstitutional, though it is unclear what the outcome in the courts ultimately will be.

As this is written less than a year into the second Trump presidency, it is unclear how far the administration will go and how successful it will be in controlling universities. It cannot be known at this point how much damage it will do. But there is every reason to be very scared.

The Termination of Funds

Beginning January 20, 2025, President Trump issued executive orders (EOs) directing agencies to terminate grants, including those related to disfavored topics, such as diversity, equity, and inclusion (DEI). Many federal agencies implemented the president's orders by abruptly and unlawfully terminating grants *en masse*. They selected grants for termination using keyword searches for what they deemed forbidden terms and concepts and terminated them via form letters without any reasoned explanation. Additionally, grants with no apparent connection to DEI concepts were also terminated via form letters without any reasoned explanation.

For example, the Trump Administration directed federal agencies to "terminate" previously awarded grant funds through a series of EOs to that effect. For example, his first DEI EO, titled "Ending Radical and Wasteful Government DEI Programs and Preferencing," instructed the attorney general and others to "coordinate the termination of all discriminatory programs, including illegal DEI and 'diversity, equity, inclusion, and accessibility' (DEIA) mandates, policies, programs, preferences, and activities in the Federal Government, under whatever name they appear." Additionally, the DEI EO directs each federal agency head to "terminate, to the maximum extent allowed by law, all . . . 'equity-related' grants or contracts" within sixty days.[10]

His second DEI EO, titled "Ending Illegal Discrimination and Restoring Merit-Based Opportunity," addresses purported "immoral race- and sex-based preferences under the guise of so-called [DEI] or [DEIA]." The order requires the Director of the Office of Management and Budget to "[e]xcise references to DEI and DEIA principles, under whatever name they may appear, from Federal acquisition, contracting, grants, and financial assistance procedures" and to "[t]erminate all 'diversity,' 'equity,' 'equitable decision-making,' 'equitable deployment of financial and technical assistance,' 'advancing equity,' and like mandates, requirements, programs, or activities, as appropriate."[11]

An EO titled "*Defending Women from Gender Ideology Extremism and Restoring Biological Truth to the Federal Government*" [Gender EO] directed that "[f]ederal funds shall not be used to promote gender ideology," instructing federal agencies to revise grant conditions accordingly, and defining "gender ideology" as a "false claim" that "replaces the biological category of sex with an ever-shifting concept of self-assessed gender identity," and that "includes the idea that there is a vast spectrum of genders that are disconnected from one's sex."[12]

The executive orders are explicit that their goal is to exercise control over universities and change their policies in a conservative direction. But control was ordered over federal funds in another way as well. An EO titled "Establishing and Implementing the President's 'Department of Governmental Efficiency'" [First DOGE EO] required the head of each federal agency to establish a team of at least four DOGE employees within their agency. As per the EO, DOGE would be "dedicated to advancing the President's 18-month DOGE agenda."[13]

An EO titled "Implementing the President's 'Department of Governmental Efficiency' Cost Efficiency Initiative" [Second DOGE EO] purports to begin the Executive's "transformation in Federal spending on contracts, grants, and loans." This EO required federal agencies to review all existing grants with an eye toward termination.[14] According to DOGE's self-described "Wall of Receipts," as of May 31, 2025, federal agencies had terminated over 15,000 grants, totaling roughly $40 billion in "savings."[15]

For example, from January 20 to early June 2025, the federal government terminated over $324 million in grants to the University of California system.[16] This is a significant underestimate, as it is limited to what was listed on the Department of Government Efficiency website, which was incomplete and also did not include instances where University of California researchers received sub-grants that were terminated.

All of these EOs seek to cut off funding for research with a perceived viewpoint at odds with the Trump administration's conservative ideology. But terminating grants because of the perceived viewpoint of the research violates the First Amendment. As the US Court of Appeals for the Ninth Circuit explained:

> We are bound by the bedrock principle that the government cannot "leverage its power to award subsidies on the basis of subjective criteria into a penalty on disfavored viewpoints" or "aim at the suppression of dangerous ideas" in the provision of subsidies. The government does not dispute that it terminated the subject grants because they promoted DEI, DEIA, or environmental justice. . . . Because the current record suggests that the government aimed at the suppression of speech that views DEI, DEIA, and environmental justice favorably, the government has not shown that it is likely to succeed on the merits of its claim that the district court abused its discretion when it concluded the agencies likely terminated the grants based on viewpoint.[17]

Although the government has great latitude in what to fund, the Supreme Court has said that Congress cannot constitutionally "discriminate invidiously in its subsidies in such a way as to 'aim[] at the suppression of dangerous ideas.'"[18] One of the most difficult issues in First Amendment law arises when the government inevitably must make content-based choices. The government cannot fund all research, of course, and it must make choices based on the content of the research. Where is the line to be drawn between permissible and impermissible choices? For example, I think all would agree that the government cannot choose to fund only researchers who endorse Donald Trump or whose research supports the MAGA agenda. But at the same time, the government can decide not to fund research on climate change, instead putting its money elsewhere.

From a separation-of-powers perspective, these should be choices for Congress to make in deciding what to fund, and not for the President to refuse to spend money appropriated by Congress. That, of course, does not address the First Amendment issue. From that perspective, the government can choose to fund some activities but not others—say, coal research but not solar research. The Court made this point in *Rust v. Sullivan*.[19] *Rust* involved a challenge to a federal regulation that prohibited recipients of federal funds for family-planning services from providing "counseling concerning the use of abortion as a method of family planning or provide referral for abortion as a method of family planning."[20] The regulations prohibited recipients of federal money from referring a pregnant woman to an abortion provider, even upon specific request. Also, the rules "broadly prohibit a [recipient of funds] . . . from engaging in activities that 'encourage, promote, or advocate abortion as a method of family planning.'"[21]

Chief Justice Rehnquist, writing for the Court, upheld the regulation on the ground that the government could decide what activity to subsidize. He wrote: "[The] Government can, without violating the Constitution, selectively fund a program to encourage certain activities it believes to be in the public interest, without at the same time funding an alternate program which seeks to deal with the problem in another way. *In so doing, the Government has not discriminated on the basis of viewpoint*; it has merely chosen to fund one activity to the exclusion of another. 'A legislature's decision not to subsidize the exercise of a fundamental right does not infringe the right.'"[22]

But that is quite different from the government cutting off grants because of the perceived viewpoint of the research. In *National Endowment for the Arts v. Finley*, the Court explained that if an agency "were to leverage its power to award subsidies on the basis of subjective criteria into a penalty on disfavored viewpoints, then we would confront a different case."[23] In *Finley*, the Court upheld federal restrictions on the funding of artists. The federal statute creating the National Endowment of the Arts gives it substantial discretion in awarding funds; it is empowered to give money based on "artistic and cultural significance, giving emphasis to American creativity and cultural diversity," "professional excellence," and encouragement of "public knowledge, education, understanding, and appreciation of the arts."[24] In 1990, the statute was amended to provide that the NEA also should "tak[e] into consideration general standards of decency and respect for the diverse beliefs and values of the American public."[25]

Justice O'Connor's opinion for the Court rejected the claim that the law was impermissible viewpoint discrimination. The Court stressed that the government must make choices among applicants, and it said that the statute's language does "not engender the kind of directed viewpoint discrimination that would prompt this Court to invalidate a statute on its face."[26] The Court said that there was no allegation of viewpoint discrimination in the application of the law and that facially the law was constitutional. The *Finley* Court stressed that the government was not wielding its purse to "penal[ize] disfavored viewpoints," "manipulat[ing]" the subsidies "to have a coercive effect," or canceling those subsidies to "drive certain ideas or views from the marketplace."[27]

But that is precisely what the Trump administration has done. As the federal district court found in the case on behalf of University of California researchers, the government "terminated pre-existing grants *en masse* across the federal government for touching on prohibited topics."[28] The agencies did so in compliance with the president's executive orders, requiring agencies to terminate "to the maximum extent allowed by law" "*all* . . . 'equity-related' grants or contracts" for the purpose of "end[ing] today" "diversity, equity, and inclusion" programs, which the Order described as "immoral" and "shameful," as well as requiring agencies to terminate "*all* 'diversity,' 'equity,' . . . and like . . . programs[] or activities[,]" in order to "combat" and "end" "diversity, equity and inclusion programs," which are described as "dangerous, demeaning, and immoral."[29]

This attempt to use federal funds to control the ideological content of research is unprecedented and a serious threat to university autonomy and academic freedom. In addition, there has been the termination of funds to selected universities: $400 million cut off to Columbia, $2 billion to Harvard, $594 million to UCLA. Again, the Trump administration is seeking to use these terminations of funding to change the policies of the universities.[30]

Nor can the termination of grants based on furthering diversity be justified based on the Supreme Court's decision in *Students for Fair Admission v. President and Fellows of Harvard College*.[31] The Court held that colleges and universities cannot use race as a factor in admissions decisions to benefit racial minorities and to advance diversity. But quite crucially, the Court did not hold that colleges and universities cannot pursue diversity in other constitutionally permissible ways. Nothing in that decision, explicitly or implicitly, prevents schools from seeking to have diverse faculty and students, from promoting equity within their campuses, and from seeking to be inclusive for all. And, of course, nothing in the decision limits the ability of universities and their administrators and faculty from expressing their support for DEI.

A federal district court found that the termination of funds to Harvard violated the First Amendment. The court concluded that the Trump administration "urged and threatened Harvard . . . to hire faculty and make curricula and research choices that better aligned with the government's preferred viewpoints, to the detriment of professors and researchers with competing views."[32] The district court further held that the Trump administration violated the First Amendment by retaliating against Harvard for its statements refusing to accede to the Trump administration's demands.

I have no doubt that the Trump administration singled out Harvard, in part, because of its prestige and wealth, believing that if Harvard could be forced to capitulate, every university would fall in line. Interestingly, of the several universities that had funds cut off, only Harvard filed suit in federal court. The University of California, for example, did not file suit when $594 million for UCLA was cut off. My sense is that universities are intimidated and afraid that, if they sue, there will be retaliation and even larger cutoffs of funds.

The purported justification for the cutoff of funds to Harvard and other universities is their deliberate indifference to anti-Semitism. But it is clear that this is a pretext to exercise control over universities. Agreements reached with universities have little to do with combating anti-Semitism. Brown University, for example, agreed to pay $50 million to Rhode Island workforce-development organizations, to adopt the Trump administration's definition of male and female, and to end gender-affirming care for minors at its hospital.[33] Brown also agreed to provide detailed admissions data to the federal government about students who apply to and are admitted to the university, with information about their race, grades, and standardized-test scores. The data will be subject to a "comprehensive audit" by the government.[34] Secretary of Education Linda McMahon said, "The Trump Administration is successfully reversing the decades-long woke-capture of our nation's higher education institutions."[35]

This, of course, is not about fighting anti-Semitism at all. All of it is about furthering a Trump agenda totally unrelated to how Jews are treated on campus.

Similarly, the agreement with Columbia University, which was based on claims of fighting anti-Semitism, goes far beyond remedying anti-Semitism. It includes Columbia's agreeing to restrict the number of international students, to give the federal government oversight over admissions, to hire faculty in particular departments, and to pay the federal government $221 million.[36]

The demand letter to Harvard, also based on an assertion of fighting anti-Semitism, sought great federal control of the university. The letter required changes in faculty hiring and student admissions, including mandating "viewpoint diversity in admissions and hiring." This included that Harvard "shall satisfy the federal government as to its competence and good faith, to audit the student body, faculty, staff, and leadership for viewpoint diversity, such that each department, field, or teaching unit must be individually viewpoint diverse." The letter further stated, "Every department or field found to lack viewpoint diversity must be reformed by hiring a critical mass of new faculty within that department or field who will provide viewpoint diversity."[37]

This is not about anti-Semitism; it is about federal control over Harvard. The Trump administration has been explicit that it wants from Harvard what Columbia has agreed to and desires that Harvard be a "template" for what it wants to do to other universities. It clearly believes that if it can force these wealthy, elite schools to capitulate, other universities will quickly follow.

If the Trump administration was serious about this being about anti-Semitism, it would follow the law in this area. The law is explicit that if the government believes that a recipient of federal funds has been deliberately indifferent to a hostile environment on the basis of race or ethnicity, in violation of Title VI of the 1964 Civil Rights Act, there are procedures that must be followed.[38] The institution must be given notice and a hearing before any cutoff of funds. There must be findings of violations of law. The House and the Senate must be given thirty days advance notice before cutoff of funds. The funds can be cut only for that part of the program deemed in violation of the law.

The Trump administration has done none of this. Nor would it likely have succeeded. It is difficult to prove that campuses were deliberately indifferent in dealing with anti-Semitism, and even if they were, the law would not allow the massive cutoff of funds that the Trump administration has imposed on schools without any semblance of due process.

This is not to deny that there have been anti-Semitic incidents on campuses. I have personally been targeted for being Jewish. But my campus was not "deliberately indifferent" to this and has worked hard to protect Jewish students and faculty. That is true of other universities as well. To be sure, more can and should be done. But that is not what the Trump efforts are about.

The federal district court in the Harvard case powerfully expressed this:

> Defendants and the President are right to combat antisemitism and to use all lawful means to do so. Harvard was wrong to tolerate hateful behavior for as long as it did. The record here, however, does not reflect that fighting antisemitism was Defendants' true aim in acting against Harvard and, even if it were, combatting antisemitism cannot be accomplished on the back of the First Amendment. We must fight against antisemitism, but we equally need to protect our rights, including our right to free speech, and neither goal should nor needs to be sacrificed on the altar of the other. Harvard is currently, even if belatedly, taking steps it needs to take to combat antisemitism and seems willing to do even more if need be. Now it is the job of the courts to similarly step up, to act to safeguard academic freedom and freedom of speech as required by the Constitution, and to ensure that important research is not improperly subjected to arbitrary and procedurally infirm grant terminations, even if doing so risks the wrath of a government committed to its agenda no matter the cost.[39]

The termination of grants was about exercising control over universities in a manner that is blatantly inconsistent with their autonomy and academic freedom. The decisions by the federal district courts in Boston and San Francisco should be precedents followed by other judges when there are challenges to the termination of federal money.

The Compact for Academic Excellence in Higher Education

Another Trump-administration assault on higher education and academic freedom is the proposed "Compact for Academic Excellence in Higher Education" that was sent to nine universities on Wednesday, October 1, 2025. Secretary of Education Linda McMahon said that ultimately it would be extended to all schools, and indeed it was offered to all schools within two weeks after the initial letters were sent.[40]

The proposed compact is a stunning and unprecedented effort by the federal government to assert control over colleges and universities. It is inconsistent with the most basic notions of academic freedom and institutional integrity.

Any institution that violates the Compact would lose all federal funding for a year. The Compact provides that universities agreeing to the Compact will receive federal funds, and implies that those rejecting it will not have access to this money. The letters sent to these schools say that institutions that agree to the Compact would receive "multiple positive benefits," including priority access to federal funds and looser restraints on overhead costs. But the threat to universities that don't agree is explicit in the letters: "Institutions of higher education are free to develop models and values other than those below, if the institution elects to forego federal benefits."[41] No major university can afford to forgo federal funds.

What is so objectionable about the Compact?

It violates the First Amendment. The Compact requires that universities revise their governing structures and abolish institutional units that "belittle . . . conservative ideas." Treating conservative ideas differently from liberal ones clearly violates the First Amendment. And there is a First Amendment right to belittle or criticize any idea. The very core of the First Amendment is that the government cannot regulate speech based on the viewpoint expressed. As the Supreme Court has forcefully declared: "If there is a bedrock principle underlying the First Amendment, it is that the government may not prohibit the expression of an idea simply because society finds the idea itself offensive or disagreeable."[42]

The Compact requires that there be a "broad spectrum of views not just in the university as a whole, but within every field, department, school, and teaching unit." Although this is a laudable goal, it would violate the First Amendment to require schools to admit students or hire faculty—or refuse to do so—based on their views. This provision of the Compact would give the federal government the ability to monitor and regulate the ideological composition of the student body and the faculty in "every field, department, school, and teaching unit." University control over admissions and faculty hiring, core aspects of institutional autonomy, would be lost.

The Compact says that "all university employees, in their capacity as university representatives, will abstain from actions or speech relating to societal and political events except in cases in which external events have a direct impact on the university." Does this mean that faculty in their classes cannot discuss social or political events because, by definition, they are acting in their official capacity? Does an op-ed, or even this essay, violate the Compact because it lists my official title and institutional affiliation?

The Compact also requires universities to establish "conditions of civility" and regulate "threatening" speech. If speech constitutes "true threats," as defined by Supreme Court,[43] then it is not protected by the First Amendment. But there is no indication that the Compact is limited to expression that meets this constitutional standard. Also, the government cannot mandate that speech conform to "civility." A public university that did this would violate the First Amendment; a requirement that people speak only with civility certainly would violate the First Amendment. For the federal government to impose this on all universities is unconstitutional. In the early 1990s, over 350 colleges and universities adopted hate-speech codes, and every one that was challenged in court was declared unconstitutional.[44]

Harming students' education. The Compact would impose great financial harm on universities, prohibiting them from raising tuition for five years and limiting the number of international students. It would require that schools with large endowments provide free education for students in the STEM fields.

This would mean a substantial loss of revenue for schools. Campuses raise tuition because costs are increasing. International students bring invaluable perspectives and also are a crucial source of revenue for schools. At Harvard, for example, 27 percent of the student body is from foreign countries. When schools' revenue decreases while costs rise, there is no choice but to cut the quality of educational programs. The Compact takes away the institutional autonomy of schools to set their tuition and to recruit international students.

Discrimination against transgender students. The Compact also includes a requirement that universities adhere to the Trump administration's strict definitions of gender, which deny the existence of transgender students and prohibit the provision of gender-affirming care. I would hope that no university would throw its transgender students under the bus in this way. It also likely would be illegal to do so, as the Supreme Court has held that the prohibition of sex discrimination in federal laws, such as employment-discrimination statutes, forbids discrimination based on gender identity.[45]

Denying institutional autonomy. All of the Compact involves the federal government's trying to control choices that should be made by educational institutions. A provision requires that undergraduate institutions require students to take a standardized test, such as the ACT or SAT. There are arguments on all sides of requiring tests, being test-optional, or not having standard tests considered at all. But that is a choice that each institution should make for itself, not the federal government.

This is an effort by the Trump administration to use federal funds to force schools to adhere to its ideological agenda. Nothing like this ever has been seen in the United States. If schools capitulate to this, the Trump administration can come back next year, or even next month, with another series of demands.

My hope is that all colleges and universities will reject the Compact. If any agree to it, there remains a strong argument that, even though it is a "voluntary" agreement, it is still unconstitutional. First, it exceeds the power of the federal government, and especially the President, to impose such conditions. Congress has the power of the purse, and Congress can put conditions on federal money so long as it meets requirements specified by the Supreme Court. The President has no authority to create additional conditions on federal funds.

But even when it is Congress itself putting strings on federal grants, the Supreme Court has said that the conditions must be clearly stated, they must relate to the purpose of the program, and they cannot be unduly coercive. In *South Dakota v. Dole,* a federal law sought to create a 21-year-old drinking age by withholding a portion of federal highway funds from any state government that failed to impose such a drinking age.[46] Specifically, 5 percent of federal highway funds would be denied to any state that did not create a 21-year-old drinking age. The Court, in an opinion by Chief Justice William Rehnquist, approved this condition on federal money. The Court emphasized that the condition imposed by Congress was directly related to one of the main purposes behind federal highway money: creating safe interstate travel. The Court recognized that, at some point, "the financial inducement offered by Congress might be so coercive as to pass the point at which pressure turns into compulsion."[47]

Following this, the Supreme Court enforced an important limit on Congress's ability to put conditions on grants to state and local governments: Such conditions cannot be unduly coercive. In *National Federation of Independent Business v. Sebelius,* the Court declared unconstitutional provisions of the Patient Protection and Affordable Care Act that required that states receiving federal Medicaid funds cover within their Medicaid programs those within 133 percent of the federal poverty level.[48] The federal government pays 100 percent of these costs until 2019 and 90 percent thereafter. Any state that failed to comply would lose all of its Medicaid funds.

Chief Justice John Roberts, writing for the Court in a 7–2 decision, said that "[i]n this case, the financial 'inducement' Congress has chosen is much more than 'relatively mild encouragement'—it is a gun to the head."[49] The Court explained that "Medicaid spending accounts for over 20 percent of the average State's total budget, with federal funds covering 50 to 83 percent of those costs. . . . The threatened loss of over 10 percent of a State's overall budget, in contrast, is economic dragooning that leaves the States with no real option but to acquiesce in the Medicaid expansion."[50]

The Compact, which would deny all federal funding to a university that breached its terms and apparently would deny funding to schools that do not agree to it, is truly a "gun to the head" of universities. Given their dependence on federal funds, it is every bit as coercive as the conditions in the Affordable Care Act. As mentioned earlier, for some schools, more than 30 percent of all their revenues come from the federal government.[51]

The Compact would be unconstitutional for a separate reason: it would be an unconstitutional condition on federal funds. The unconstitutional-conditions doctrine is the principle that the government cannot condition a benefit on the requirement that a person forgo a constitutional right. The corollary is that the "government may not deny a benefit to a person because he exercises a constitutional right."[52]

Speiser v. Randall is a classic example of the application of the unconstitutional-conditions doctrine.[53] A California law provided that, in order for an individual to receive a veterans' property-tax exemption, he or she had to sign a declaration disavowing a belief in overthrowing the US government by force or violence. The Court said that "[t]o deny an exemption to claimants who engage in certain forms of speech is in effect to penalize them for this speech."[54]

Conditioning a benefit on a requirement that individuals give up their First Amendment rights obviously pressures individuals to forgo constitutionally protected speech. The *Speiser* Court explained that the condition "will have the effect of coercing the claimants to refrain from the proscribed speech."[55] Put another way, the unconstitutional-conditions doctrine prevents the government from penalizing those who exercise their constitutional rights by withholding a benefit that otherwise would be available. In *Perry v. Sindermann*, the Court, in explaining that the government could not deny employment to a person for exercising First Amendment rights, declared: "For if the government could deny a benefit to a person because of his constitutionally protected speech or associations, his exercise of those freedoms would in effect be penalized and inhibited. This would allow the government to 'produce a result which it could not command directly.'"[56]

For example, the Court applied this in *Federal Communications Commission v. League of Women Voters of California*.[57] The Supreme Court declared unconstitutional a federal statute that prohibited any noncommercial educational broadcasting station that received a grant from the Corporation for Public Broadcasting from engaging in editorializing. The Court said that the government could not condition funds on a requirement that the stations relinquish their right to editorialize.

But that is exactly what Trump's proposed Compact does: condition federal money, upon which universities are dependent, on their giving up their academic freedom, which is protected by the First Amendment. It is impossible to imagine a more blatantly unconstitutional condition. If any university capitulates to the Compact, a court challenge should be brought by faculty and students, and the condition should be declared unconstitutional.

Conclusion

The first year of the Trump presidency has been unprecedented in American history in the extent of its blatantly illegal and unconstitutional acts, its efforts to expand the power of the presidency, and its use of government power for retribution. It also has been unprecedented in the assault on academic freedom. As this is written, it is uncertain how this confrontation will turn out. But it is safe to say that the future of American universities as we have known them—and thus the future of academic freedom—will turn on the outcome of this battle.

6

Money, Money, Money

Universities, Government Funding, and Academic Freedom

MARY-ROSE PAPANDREA*

Since the federal government began its large-scale funding of research at the start of World War II, the United States and American universities have been in a mutually beneficial relationship. The federal government has reaped the benefits of countless scientific, social-science, and technological discoveries that have promoted national security and served the general welfare. In return, American universities have developed extraordinary research enterprises that are regarded as among the best in the world.

From the outset of this relationship, however, scientists and university administrators have expressed concern that federal funding would interfere with institutional autonomy and academic freedom. President Trump's current attacks on higher education reveal that these concerns were well justified, albeit to a degree these early critics could have scarcely imagined. Assuming federal research funding will continue—and there is every reason to believe it will continue, even if diminished—it is likely that this funding will come with even more limitations and conditions that require universities to bend their missions and research priorities to secure this funding. Elite private universities are now facing, and will continue to face, some of the same kind of pressure that public universities in red and purple states have faced for several years. As state universities well know, however, there is no easy resolution to the conflicts that arise when the government holds the purse strings.

* Burchfield Professor of First Amendment and Free Speech Law, The George Washington University Law School. The author thanks Matthew O'Connor for his outstanding research assistance.

Mary-Rose Papandrea, *Money, Money, Money*. In: *Academic Freedom in the Era of Trump*.
Edited by: Lee C. Bollinger and Geoffrey R. Stone, Oxford University Press.
 DOI: 10.1093/9780197854877.003.0007

Government Funding and Institutional Autonomy

Federally funded research is a central endeavor of the leading universities in the United States, but this was not always the case. The history of federal funding for universities illustrates the tensions between the government and universities that rely on federal funding to achieve their research mission.

The first four US presidents proposed the establishment of a national university, but this never occurred, for a variety of reasons. Not only did the early federal government lack funds to establish a university, but the Constitution also made no mention of education. Pursuant to the colonial tradition, states were left in charge of chartering schools.[1] States chartered many private colleges of various types and sizes; while there were a handful of public universities in the early years of this country, the vast majority of universities prior to the mid-1800s were private, and most had religious affiliations.[2]

The federal government began supporting higher education during the Civil War, and this led to the growth of public state universities. The Morrill Act of 1862—the Land-Grant College Act—provided both land and money for states to establish colleges specializing in agricultural and mechanical engineering.[3] This support had no strings attached; the federal government did not even require an accounting for the expenditure of these funds.[4] A second Morrill Act of 1890 required states with segregated universities to provide equal opportunities to Black students in agriculture and mechanical engineering, which led to the creation of Historically Black Land-Grant Colleges and Universities (HBCUs).[5] The Hatch Act of 1887 provided support for the establishment of agricultural experiment stations in the states to conduct agricultural research and disseminate their findings; recipients were required to submit annual financial reports.[6]

Through the mid-18th century, the early elite colleges like Harvard and Columbia primarily taught undergraduates and some law, medicine, and theological students. Johns Hopkins, founded in 1876, was the first American university to focus on research rather than undergraduates.[7] This early research was largely funded not by the government but by private capitalists like Andrew Carnegie and John D. Rockefeller.[8] As late as the 1930s, the research enterprise at universities remained modest and relied primarily on small grants from corporations and foundations,[9] unlike in most other democracies, including France and Germany, where the government funding of universities included their research enterprises.[10]

Until World War II, the US government was not significantly engaged in research and development, aside from some military scientific labs and agricultural research.[11] In June 1940, as Hitler marched across Europe, several leading US scientists, led by Vannevar Bush (the president of the Carnegie Institute in Washington and former dean and engineering professor at MIT), convinced President Roosevelt to create the National Defense Resource Committee (NDRC).[12] Rather than constructing federal laboratories and staffing them with "scientist-soldiers," as the United States had done during World War I, the government entered into research contracts with nongovernment entities, including universities.[13] The group of prominent scientists working with Bush to organize the scientific community had long been concerned about political interference with science and disagreed about whether the government could be trusted.[14] But the urgency of the wartime need that neither the government nor universities could meet on their own led them to overcome this hesitation.[15]

In 1941, it became clear that the wartime research effort would require Congressional appropriations. The NDRC was dissolved into a new entity called the Office of Scientific Research and Development (OSRD).[16] This wartime research most famously produced atomic energy and the hydrogen bomb, but it also led to the mass production of penicillin, ballistic missiles, radar, and remote-controlled fuses, among many other discoveries.[17] American universities "were poised to become the greatest in the world,"[18] and the public and politicians were coming to regard science discovery as the key to American health, prosperity, and security.[19]

When the war concluded, Vannevar Bush drafted his landmark book *Science: The Endless Frontier*, arguing for ongoing federal support of scientific research.[20] This suggestion was not without controversy, particularly with respect to the details of how peacetime research would proceed. Scientists who had worked with the military during the war were eager to get back to setting their own research agendas without political interference; however, President Truman refused to sign any legislation creating the National Science Foundation (NSF) that did not give the executive branch ultimate oversight authority.[21] Even more fundamentally, those who were involved in the process of developing the federal funding apparatus disagreed as to whether the funding should be mission-driven, with priorities set by Congress, or should instead fund "basic research" driven by "curiosity," which would lead, over time, to new technological advances and practical applications.[22] The latter view would promote academic freedom and minimize government interference.[23] Tensions between these different approaches to federal funding delayed the passage of legislation for several years.[24] Though a compromise between these views was ultimately reached, tensions between advocates of academic freedom and political control remained.[25] As Jonathan Cole has pointed out, "[t]he potential for political interference was built into the postwar system for funding science."[26]

By the time the NSF was founded in 1950, several other government agencies had already ramped up their postwar research efforts. The National Institutes of Health (NIH), located within the US Department of Health and Human Services, is the leading federal agency for biomedical and health research, and in recent years it has provided half of all federal research funding.[27] Like the NSF, the research priorities of the NIH are established with some direction from Congress, as well as consultation with external stakeholders from the scientific and health-care community, other federal agencies, and the general public. At various times Congress has provided specific appropriations for particular health issues, such as cancer, HIV/AIDS, and Alzheimer's,[28] but decisions about research priorities are largely left to the internal NIH processes and peer-review process.[29]

How Congress and NIH should set their research priorities is an issue that members of Congress, NIH leaders, and scientists have debated since NIH's founding.[30] Early on, members of Congress objected to the peer-review process, which favored more elite institutions in a handful of states.[31] In addition, various members of Congress have objected to particular grants and projects.[32] Since the passage of the Dickey-Wicker Amendment of 1996,[33] the federal government has not funded any research that involves the creation or destruction of any human embryos. Since that time, Republican presidents have placed significant additional restrictions on stem-cell research.[34]

Universities have obviously benefited enormously from federal funding. Federal research funding has supported the massive growth of American universities. NIH funding has led to the expansion of university medical schools and hospitals.[35] Other parts of the university, such as schools of public health, science departments, engineering schools, area studies programs, economics, and education schools, have all benefited substantially from federal funding. The funding universities have received in the form of "indirect costs" to cover overhead and other administrative burdens of doing research has been used to support other parts of the university enterprise. The passage of the Bayh-Dole Act in 1980, which permits universities to own and license the patents for federally funded research discoveries, promoted the commercialization and public availability of new inventions.[36] Although the primary purpose of this law was to promote the useful applications of new discoveries rather than to enrich universities, some universities make millions of dollars each year from patent licenses.[37]

Of course, not all parts of the university mission have benefited substantially from federal funding, at least not directly. Federal research funding for the humanities is meager.[38] Critics also argue that universities are disproportionately interested in research to the detriment of their teaching mission.[39] As Derek Bok has noted, research has brought "unprecedented riches to many universities, but it has also given rise to problems of overall balance and equitable treatment."[40]

Over time, the conditions placed on research contracts in the name of promoting accountability and protecting research subjects have grown substantially. These requirements, although clearly well-intended, are onerous and undermine the ability of researchers to do their work. In one survey, grant recipients reported they spend 40 percent of their time writing grants, getting approval for their work, hiring personnel, and doing grant administration.[41]

Efforts to provide federal support for students began with the 1958 National Defense Education Act. This legislation created low-interest student loans and graduate fellowships for students studying national-defense-related disciplines.[42] The law required beneficiaries to pledge loyalty to the US government and sign an affidavit that they had not been a member of any subversive organizations.[43] Conservatives argued that loyalty requirements made perfect sense because the funding had a limited purpose of supporting defense; in addition, they pointed out, the law did not require students to actually put their degrees to use to serve defense interests.[44] But thirty-two institutions—including Brown, Princeton, Harvard, Yale, and the University of Chicago—refused to participate in the program, expressing concern that these requirements undermined principles of free inquiry and institutional autonomy, and governing boards at 162 other colleges and universities expressed objections to the loyalty requirements.[45] The loyalty requirements were ultimately repealed in 1962, but the debates about them revealed tensions between academic freedom and demands that federal funding to universities serve government priorities.[46]

As the federal government expanded support for students, antidiscrimination laws followed. Title VI of the Civil Rights Act of 1964 prohibits any program that receives federal funding from engaging in discrimination on the basis of race, color, or national origin.[47] Title IX of the Education Amendments of 1972[48] prohibits discrimination on the basis of sex, and Section 504 of the Rehabilitation Act of 1973 prohibits discrimination on the basis of disability.[49] The Supreme Court has read Title VI expansively to cover discrimination not just by the university itself but by anyone on campus, subject to certain conditions (including a showing that the university was "deliberately indifferent" to this discrimination).

The Trump administration, in demanding concessions from universities, has relied extensively on alleged violations of Title VI and Title IX. However, no one seriously argues that the administration has followed the detailed procedures set forth in these acts, and it is not even clear that the universities have actually violated Title VI to the extent the administration claims. Nevertheless, interpreting these laws expansively through executive orders and "Dear Colleague" letters is a well-trodden path. For example, under President Obama, universities were required to create extensive bureaucracies to resolve sex-discrimination and hostile-environment claims.[50] Universities did not push back, even though they could have made good legal arguments that the executive did not have the authority to make these changes.[51]

It seems simple enough to argue that Trump's demands on universities are unconstitutional conditions, but that doctrine is notoriously fuzzy. The case law specifically addressing funding conditions placed on universities is slim. The first obstacle is convincing a court that a condition even violates a university's First Amendment rights. In *Rumsfeld v. FAIR*,[52] the Court upheld the constitutionality of the Solomon Amendment[53] over the First Amendment claims of universities that allowing military recruiters on campus interfered with their expressive and associational rights.[54] In that case, the Court apparently thought the university's institutional academic-freedom arguments were so meritless that it did not even bother to address them in its unanimous opinion.[55] In *Moody v. NetChoice, LLC*,[56] the Court suggested in a footnote that the *FAIR* case might have come out differently if the Solomon Amendment interfered with what happened in classrooms.[57] Though this footnote perhaps provided some comfort to universities, it also could be interpreted as embracing a rather narrow view of institutional autonomy that does not include (for example) the student disciplinary code and procedures, the structure (or even existence) of faculty governance bodies, or the structure of university administrative offices.

Furthermore, even if a court concludes that federal funding conditions do implicate a university's First Amendment rights, the court would have to determine whether the conditions are within the contours of the funded program and not "conditions that seek to leverage funding to regulate speech outside the contours of the program itself."[58] The Supreme Court itself has recognized that "[t]he line is hardly clear, in part because the definition of a particular program can always be manipulated to subsume the challenged condition."[59] While some of the conditions the Trump administration has demanded in its resolution agreements with universities, such as banning masks or transgender medical procedures, have no apparent relevance to the funding program, other requirements demanding a robust campus discourse culture are not so easily discounted. Discrimination and a stifled atmosphere can undermine the very creative thinking universities are providing on their side of the bargain.

Of course, the reality for universities is that these legal arguments are virtually beside the point. The Trump administration has used universities' enormous reliance on federal support to put pressure on them to cave to longstanding conservative demands, which many have appropriately called extortion.[60] A significant problem for universities is that even if they are successful in their legal fight to have federal funding restored, there is no guarantee that their legal challenges will be successful in the future. This is especially true as the federal government develops justifications for canceling and refusing funding that are less susceptible to legal attack.[61] In addition, Congress could significantly scale back appropriations for research, as President Trump has proposed.[62]

Furthermore, in addition to cutting off direct research funding, the Trump administration has threatened other mechanisms by which the federal government has traditionally supported universities. Several agencies have announced they will reduce to 15 percent (from as high as 69.5 percent[63]) the "indirect costs" percentage paid as part of a research grant to support things like building overhead, laboratory maintenance, and administrative staff support.[64] Universities also rely on federal funding for their students, many of whom would not be able to attend without federal grant and loan assistance. The Trump administration now requires that all universities receiving federal funding turn over their admissions data to ensure compliance with the Supreme Court's decision in *SFFA v. Harvard*.[65] The federal government also controls the entry of foreign students to study within the United States. These students bring to campus diverse backgrounds and experiences that enrich the campus culture and academic endeavors, but they also provide significant additional tuition revenue.[66] At some universities, international students make up over one-third of the student population.[67] Although the recent headlines have focused on the reliance of private universities on foreign students, public research universities have also dramatically increased their reliance on full-tuition-paying international students in the last twenty-five years to cushion the effects of declining state appropriations.[68] In 2017, Congress levied a 1.4 percent endowment tax on universities with endowments of at least $500,000 per student.[69] In 2025, in the "One Big Beautiful Bill Act," Congress increased the tax by as much as 8 percent for the wealthiest universities.[70] President Trump has also threatened to review universities' tax-exempt status as 501(c)(3) entities, which allows donors to make tax-deductible charitable donations.[71]

Given the leverage the federal government has, it is no surprise that the presidents of the top US universities violently disagree about how to respond to these extraordinary threats.[72] Elite universities face the difficult choice of complying with these new federal conditions, rejecting federal support, or bringing legal challenges. For example, the Trump administration demanded as a "precondition" for continued federal funding that Columbia University overhaul its disciplinary procedures, restrict protests on campus, place a department under academic receivership, adopt a broad view of anti-Semitism, and reform its admissions policies.[73] Columbia agreed to most of these conditions (and made additional changes the Trump administration did not request),[74] while Harvard University, when faced with a similar choice, decided to sue instead. The Trump Administration has also extended an offer to several universities for federal funding preference in exchange for intrusive institutional changes that would align the universities with conservative priorities.[75]

In one particularly disturbing example, the Trump administration demanded that the president of the University of Virginia resign in order to resolve Title VI claims against the school.[76] The Department of Justice claimed that President Jim Ryan needed to resign because he had supported widespread diversity initiatives on the campus even after the Court's decision in *SFFA v. Harvard* held that affirmative action in student admissions is unconstitutional.[77] Rather than challenge this extraordinarily aggressive and unprecedented use of federal power, Ryan resigned for the good of his university, expressing concerns that unless he resigned, Trump would strip the university of federal funding.[78]

Concerns About Academic Freedom and Shared Governance

Questions about whether and how outside funding interferes with institutional autonomy and academic freedom are not new concepts to higher-education scholars. These concerns were voiced as soon as discussions began about the possibility of the federal government funding university research. University presidents expressed concern that federal funding would come with political interference.[79] University of Chicago President Robert Maynard Hutchins warned, "It is sad but true that when an institution determines to do something in order to get money it must lose its soul, and frequently it does not get the money."[80]

Some of these concerns reflected the tension—apparent in Vannevar Bush's postwar *Endless Fronter*—between the government's research priorities and the priorities of universities (and "curiosity" of their professors). Russell Kirk argued that universities in the United States "exhibit less independence and strength of opinion" than they did before they received over half of their funding from the federal government.[81] Perceptively, Kirk noted that safeguards have been put in place to protect against interference from state and local authorities and corporate interests, "[b]ut there are no present sure guarantees against the novel influence of foundations and of the federal government."[82] Kirk argued that because there are other millionaire donors but only one government, it was incumbent upon the universities to take grants "only after reflection—and only when certain that the largess is consonant with freedom of teaching and enquiry, calculated to raise the level of humane and scientific disciplines, and to respect the dignity of the scholar."[83]

Clark Kerr echoed these concerns in his essay *The Realities of the Federal Grant University*.[84] Kerr noted that when federal agencies offer to fund a project, a university does not have to accept, but as a practical matter it is unlikely to turn down the funding. As Kerr noted, universities are not likely to tell their faculty they cannot work on a project for which they have received funding. As a result, a university may find itself letting government funding influence its choice of research priorities, professors' teaching loads and contact hours, and the allocation of research and office space.[85] As Kerr perceptively comments, the fact "[t]hat [these impacts] are subtle, slowly cumulative and gentlemanly makes them all the more potent."[86] Universities are free to refuse federal funds, but accepting funds can undermine institutional autonomy.

Federal funding can also influence the academic freedom of individual professors. On the one hand, federal funding can support academic freedom by enabling professors to undertake research they simply would not be able to do without that support. But on the other hand, the very importance of federal funding means that professors are more likely to engage in research for which they can get the money they need to do it. Scientific research requires money to pay for labs, equipment, personnel (such as research assistants and post-docs), and other essential resources. Professors can also use funding to "buy out" their teaching time. The sciences and social sciences expect professors will bring in outside money to support their work, and the reputations of professors and their departments and universities are based on their federal funding success. As a result, it is natural that professors might decide to take on research projects because outside funding is potentially available.

In addition, the terms of the federal research grant may require professors to alter their research agendas in some ways to make them more likely to receive the grants, or even to be eligible for the grants. For example, the National Institutes of Health (NIH) used to promote biomedical research that sought to address structural racism and systematic barriers for underrepresented groups and aimed to increase the participation of diverse populations in clinical trials. Faculty who wanted to compete for these federal dollars crafted research proposals that satisfied those terms. Under the Trump administration, in contrast, research that serves "DEI" (not defined) is not funded. Now that the Trump administration has targeted all "diversity" research, professors are scrubbing their research in hopes of maintaining their funding (or qualifying for new funding). The American Association of University Professors [AAUP] has recognized that "[t]he intense competition for private or governmental funding can affect the choice of research subjects, and in some instances scientists in academic medicine are finding it difficult to secure funding for unorthodox research or research on matters that are politically sensitive."[87]

Furthermore, university reliance on grants can pervert the scholarly process, as administrators hire and promote professors on the basis of the number and amount of federal grants they have rather than on the quality and quantity of their work and publications.[88] Federal grants are preferred because they come with indirect resources that can help fund the operation of the university.[89] Administrators pressure faculty to make research choices based on whether they are likely to receive grant money, which is inconsistent with the very basic understanding of academic freedom.[90]

At the same time, federal funding can obviously promote academic freedom by providing resources for research (and relief from teaching duties) that the university might not be able to provide on its own. Federal funding helps promote important discoveries and research more quickly and perhaps more directly connected to public need than if universities tried to figure out on their own what would best serve the public good. Professors may find that if they are able to obtain funding for research, they can force a university to support their research agenda, even if the university otherwise might not regard that research as a priority. Federal research dollars can also make it easier for a scholar to obtain a tenure-track position and ultimately tenure itself.

The pressure that federal funding places on academic freedom is not necessarily all that different from the many other kinds of pressure that professors face when making decisions about what subjects to study and in what manner. Some of these financial pressures may impact the quality of scientific research. For example, private industry may tempt professors to spend more time performing research for lucrative financial gain, and universities have profited from patents on their professors' discoveries since the passage of the Bayh-Dole Act in 1980. Universities have developed policies to blunt the distracting impact of private industry on their academic mission, such as rules prohibiting professors from working more than one day a week on outside activities, and studies have shown that scientists have continued to perform standard scientific research.[91] Concerns remain regarding conflicts of interest—including the toleration of contract provisions giving industry control over the publication of the research—and excessive secrecy of research findings.[92]

Depending on how their universities respond, faculty members may (or may not) feel that their academic freedom is supported. For example, some professors have expressed concern that their universities do not support their research that relates to diversity, equity, and inclusion.[93] But as Williams College discovered when it refused to accept any additional NSF or NIH grants until the federal government clarifies its ban on "DEI," an institution that stands up to the federal government can be hailed as "taking a moral stand and living up to its values," or it can be condemned as "signaling it doesn't care about research."[94] Colleges and universities are finding themselves in a no-win situation.

To the extent that some universities have conditioned faculty compensation on outside funding, professors may find that their economic security—an essential part of academic freedom—is undermined. Tenure itself provides some aspect of economic security, in that it protects ongoing employment, but tenure without salary protections provides an empty form of economic security. The AAUP's *1940 Statement* provides that "tenure is a means to an ends," including "sufficient degree of economic security to make the profession attractive to men and women of ability."[95] The *1940 Statement* specifically mentions that "[t]ermination of a continuous appointment because of financial exigency should be demonstrably bona fide," but nothing in the *Statement* refers to what level of salary is required for economic security or when a university can reduce a professor's salary.[96]

In addition, the *1940 Statement* is entirely silent on whether professors have any sort of right to university facilities or support. In 2024, the Supreme Judicial Court of Massachusetts sent back to the trial court claims by Tufts professors that their university had violated their rights to economic security by slashing their salaries, reducing their lab space, and reducing them to half-time status when they failed to obtain external grant funding to support their salaries.[97] The salary cut was based on a "salary modification plan" that Tufts adopted in 2009, which provided that full-time basic-science professors had to generate external funding to cover their salaries; professors who did not meet this requirement would have their salaries cut and be reduced to part-time.[98] The court concluded that the meaning of the term "economic security" in the tenure documents was "ambiguous" and sent the case back to the trial court for additional discovery and fact-finding "regarding the customs and practices and reasonable expectations related to salary and full-time status for tenured professors at [Tufts University School of Medicine], and even other universities and medical schools."[99]

The court rejected, however, the professors' challenge to the closure or relocation of their lab space, holding that "a reassignment or reduction in lab space does not directly threaten the economic security of a tenured professor."[100] In addition, the court noted that lab space is expensive; as a result, "[p]roviding such lab space to those who have grants to support the use of the space, rather than those who require Tufts to incur such costs, appears to be well within the authority of Tufts to control its affairs."[101] This conclusion is based on an unwillingness to interfere with the institutional autonomy of a university. Importantly, the court noted that Tufts still gave the professors access to some lab space and continued to promise additional lab space as part of any future grant applications.[102] Nothing in the court's opinions indicated that the professors' ability to conduct research was meaningfully impaired in any way.[103]

Contributing to tensions between institutional autonomy and the faculty's academic freedom is that some universities are doing more than they have been asked or need to do to avoid the federal government's attention. If the government explicitly or implicitly threatens a university with the loss of federal funds unless the university gives up some protected expressive activity, including the expression of its professors and students or even the university itself, the university might have a jawboning claim under *National Rifle Association of America v. Vullo*.[104] It is very possible that many universities around the country have received such threats, especially behind closed doors.

But it is highly probable that at least some universities have not received any threats or had any direct contact with the Trump administration. Instead, university administrators are aware of what is happening to sister universities around the country and want to avoid the federal government's attention by proactively taking steps. The AAUP and scholars of authoritarianism have called this "anticipatory obedience."[105] In this circumstance, the university is not likely to have a First Amendment claim against the federal government. Professors and students at private universities will not have First Amendment claims against their institutions because they are not state actors; their only claims will be under contract or perhaps collective-bargaining agreements (if applicable). Public-university professors and students might have claims against their institutions if the university's decisions independently violate their First Amendment rights. But determining the scope of these rights is itself a difficult task, especially in light of some claims that universities should have some flexibility as special institutional actors to have different First Amendment rules.

For example, the University of North Carolina System Office issued a memo shortly after Trump took office in January 2025 that all constituent universities had to eliminate mandatory curricular and program requirements "related to diversity, equity and inclusion."[106] This change to curricular requirements was made without consulting the faculty at any constituent university,[107] even though curricular changes are typically regarded as squarely within the domain of faculty governance. The UNC System felt it was essential to make this curricular change, explaining that "[e]ven though some form of additional federal guidance is expected, and the law in this area remains unsettled, the risk of jeopardizing over $1.4B in critical federal research funding is simply too great to defer action."[108] It is certainly possible that the Trump administration would argue that curricular requirements violate anti-discrimination laws, but the executive order did not make this claim.[109]

The idea of institutional autonomy is intended to protect universities from outside third parties, but sometimes it is difficult to tell whether a university is acting as a result of pressure from the outside or for its own independent reasons. Trump's executive orders and more specific demands to Harvard and Columbia came at the same time universities were already evaluating existing policies. This complicates efforts to blame the federal government for changes the faculty does not like. In *AAUP v. DOJ*,[110] for example, a federal district court judge rejected the claims by the AAUP and American Federation of Teachers against various federal actors, repeatedly noting that the real beef Columbia professors have is with Columbia.[111] The court held that the preliminary record indicated that Columbia had already been considering and planning some of the changes it agreed to implement before it received the federal government's demand. In addition, the court held, most of the things Columbia agreed to do differed in material ways from the requests the government made.[112] When universities do more than the government asked them to do, or implement changes they were already considering prior to any formal or informal request from the federal government, it is challenging to make a successful jawboning argument.

The pressures the Trump administration has placed on university funding reveals how fragile the faculty's role in "shared governance" is as a matter of practical reality. In 1915, when the American Association for University Professors was born, the primary concern was interference from governing boards;

in 1940, the primary concern was state actors. Both documents predate the era of massive federal support for both public and private universities. The 1966 *Statement on the Governance of Colleges and Universities*—jointly issued by the AAUP, the American Council on Education, and the Association of Governing Boards of Colleges and Universities—attempted to delineate who had primary responsibility for what on university campuses. This document called for "shared governance" of higher education. In part, this conclusion rested on the recognition that both public and private universities were losing autonomy due to the funding mechanisms for higher education:

> [B]uildings, research, and student tuition are supported by funds over which the college or university exercises a diminishing control. Legislative and executive governmental authorities, at all levels, play a part in the making of important decisions in academic policy. If these voices and forces are to be successfully heard and integrated, the academic institution must be in a position to meet them with its own generally unified view.[113]

Aside from arguing for "shared governance" within the university, however, this statement explicitly did not attempt to provide any guidance for "relations with those outside agencies that increasingly are controlling the resources and influencing the patterns of education in our institutions of higher learning: for example, the United States government, state legislatures, state commissions, interstate associations or compacts, and other interinstitutional arrangements."[114] Instead, the statement simply hoped its guidance would be "helpful" to outside forces as they "consider educational matters."[115]

What constitute "educational matters" is very unclear. The AAUP's 1966 *Statement on the Government of Colleges and Universities* and the American Association of Higher Education's (AAHE) 1967 *Faculty Participation in Academic Governance* articulate broad visions of the faculty's role in institutional governance. The AAUP's statement recommends that faculty have "primary responsibility" over "those aspects of student life that relate to the educational process," without defining or limiting what might *not* fall within this category.[116] At the same time, fiscal matters are left to university administrators, governing boards, and, in the case of state institutions, state legislatures. The AAHE statement concludes that campuses should embrace the concept of "shared authority" between the faculty and administrators.[117]

The current crisis highlights existing weaknesses of faculty governance. Some universities, including Harvard, do not even have a centralized faculty senate that could advise the administration about how to handle the Trump attacks.[118] Instead, the Harvard administration and Corporation Board engage in ad hoc communications with faculty. Faculty play a very limited role in determining how to respond to the Trump administration's direct threats. Even if a university decides to fight the Trump administration, it has to figure out precisely what to fight, what arguments to make, and what terms to accept (if any) to settle these disputes. These are essential institutional leadership questions that the faculty is not well suited to make.[119] Furthermore, the faculty are deeply divided about how to handle these new threats. The Trump attacks pit scientists against humanities professors.[120] The scientists want to protect their grants and preserve their research; most professors in the humanities do not rely on federal funding and are not as desperate for its restoration and preservation.

As Trump came into office, the AAUP suggested that faculty "[r]eview handbooks and contracts to strengthen and reinforce faculty rights in the areas of curricular reform and course approval; academic program discontinuance; and faculty appointments, reappointments, promotions, and dismissals."[121] These efforts are important and could help overcome some of the changes to the curriculum that universities are undertaking in "anticipatory obedience." Strengthening faculty (and staff) governance can also be important as universities figure out who, what, and how much to cut in the face of dramatically reduced federal support.[122] But in determining whether to settle with the government, and what the terms will be, these mechanisms are likely to be of little value.

What State Universities Have Known for a Long Time

Although issues regarding federal control over public and private universities are relatively new, "[s]tate control over universities has been a real problem" for decades.[123] Private universities are now facing the sorts of political pressures many state universities have been dealing with for a very long time.

State universities are often at the mercy of their state legislatures. State universities are creatures of the state, which means they are also subject to the control of the state. The practical reality is that public universities, even those with constitutional autonomy, remain dependent on state appropriations, which creates a significant incentive to remain responsive to elected officials and state policy priorities. Any claim that a university might have to institutional autonomy—which can be weaker or stronger depending on the state—is balanced against the need for accountability and the public interest, often leading to ongoing negotiation between universities and state governments.

Funding decisions by state legislatures often implicate "core" academic matters, such as decisions to fund—or to stop funding—new schools, initiatives, programs, and majors. Even in states like Michigan and California, which have strong constitutional provisions protecting the autonomy of their public universities, political funding decisions necessarily impact the operations of the schools.[124] Private donors, corporations, and foundations often dictate the content and direction of the programs, schools, research, and professorships they fund, and as a result, universities may change their curriculum and hiring priorities in ways they might not have otherwise prioritized absent the funds.[125] The constitutional limits on what a state legislature can do to form a distinct identity for its universities is not clear. States clearly can allocate resources for different types of institutions and programs, from community colleges to research centers.

As a practical matter, it is impossible to wall off government funders from some level of interference with faculty and institutional governance. It is also not obvious that completely separating the academic enterprise from politics is desirable.[126] Federal funding of university research began because there was a dire political need for it.

Given its massive financial investment, the public has a right to make sure universities are serving the public interest. If the state has a large tech start-up community, it makes sense for the state to support new higher-education programs in technology. If it has several military bases, it makes sense to support a veterans' legal clinic. The list of perfectly understandable public goals goes on and on.

Drawing lines between what political actors can and cannot do to their state universities is extremely difficult, and potentially subject to a "we know it when we see it" kind of test. For example, Keith Whittington has offered that "viewpoint-based discrimination" is "especially suspect." He argues that it is permissible for state officials "to determine that a given university will concentrate its offerings on the sciences and not the humanities or will be home to a law school but not a medical school."[127] Professor Whittington allows that it might be permissible for a state university to "authorize particular programming or even particular classes and course materials in which professors might choose to participate."[128] Under this view, the university is permitted to "supplement[] the regular academic offerings of the university" as long as it "does not restrain or crowd out the freedom of members of the faculty to express countervailing ideas in the course of their teaching and scholarship."[129] He analogizes this to the "adequate alternative channels" requirement of the time, place, and manner doctrine.[130] But, Whittington contends, once a university has a law school, it cannot make rules about the viewpoints of the professors who are hired or promoted or the content of the courses.[131]

Whittington's approach is helpful, but only to a point. It is helpful when a state like Florida passes clearly viewpoint-based "anti-woke" legislation that is directly aimed at what is taught in the classroom. It is not helpful, however, when the legislature refuses to fund a much-needed new law-school building because it is unhappy with a faculty member who criticizes the legislature in a weekly newspaper column, and expands its business and medical schools instead. It certainly does not help if a state legislature dramatically cuts the state university's budget. These funding decisions are viewpoint-neutral, but the reality is that they are very much based on whether the legislatures are happy—or not—with what is being taught at the school and what the professors are saying in public.

The governing bodies of state universities—as well as state legislatures—have increasingly claimed a role in making even core academic decisions relating to the curriculum and promotion and tenure of faculty. Governor DeSantis's destruction and recreation of the New College of Florida reveals how far a state could go to remake a public institution. This assault has brazenly ignored and even mocked the norms of academic freedom and faculty governance.[132] This assault on academic freedom and institutional autonomy is spreading throughout the country, especially in "red" states where disdain for "elite" universities and their faculty runs rampant. Dividing institutional governance into "academic" and "fiscal" affairs ignores the reality that each of these spheres is entangled in the other. Because universities—and states—do not have unlimited funds, they must make allocation decisions. Whether to offer certain majors or programs, how many students to admit, and who to hire, promote, or tenure are all decisions that have profound fiscal impacts.

State universities are constantly trying to convince their state legislatures—and the public—that their financial investment is worthwhile. This is a difficult undertaking because universities are massive, and their very nature—a commitment to free inquiry—means that there is almost always some research, class, extramural speech, or student protest that politicians find troubling.[133] At the University of North Carolina, where I taught for a decade, the political fight is a daily undertaking. UNC would surely prefer that the legislature just make giant appropriations for the university to use as it sees fit, but that is not realistic. As mentioned earlier, UNC administrators act proactively—and sometimes controversially—to blunt political intrusion into university affairs. They have expanded programs supporting first-generation students, members of the military, and students from all areas of the state. The university has developed programs like Carolina Across 100—a name that refers to the 100 counties in North Carolina—to use its resources to assist the entire state. Its communications office tries to convince lawmakers and the public alike that its research is worth the investment costs. UNC also battles perceptions that the university engages in ideological "indoctrination" and is politically unbalanced. This is not an easy task, and it is more difficult in these polarizing times. But it is essential if the university is to keep the lights on.

Conclusion

Universities are facing a much different calculus today as the federal government asserts the authority not merely to influence but to control their operations and thereby undermine their institutional autonomy as well as the academic freedom of their faculties. The federal government's current attempts to exercise control over and force accountability from universities is ham-fisted, deeply threatening to the norms of academic freedom and institutional autonomy. These efforts also appear to violate Title VI both procedurally and substantively.[134]

The history of federal funding of research reveals, however, that since World War II, universities (and professors) have had to make some compromises to maintain a favorable relationship with the government. Though the conditions the federal government has placed on universities have grown over time, this tension between the need for public accountability and institutional autonomy has always been present. Universities have some difficult days ahead, but in deciding what path to take, they should be clear-eyed that federal funding has always required compromises. The question is how many compromises they are willing to make.

7

The End of the Cold War University

AZIZ Z. HUQ*

Introduction

In 1854, the trustees of Columbia University denied a faculty appointment to the distinguished chemist Oliver Wolcott Gibbs on the ground that his Unitarianism was at odds with their Episcopalian aspirations for the institution. By this time, Gibbs was widely viewed as among the first rank of American physical chemists for his work on chemical compounds called cobalt bases. Upon hearing of Gibbs's rejection, a special committee of the US Senate sent a letter to the board of trustees, which then included six clergymen, asking whether it had ever rejected a candidate "on account of his peculiar tenets in matters of religion."[1]

Flash-forward to 2025, and the threat to free speech and inquiry at Columbia has a different complexion. On March 7, 2025, the second Trump Administration peremptorily cancelled $400 million in federal grants and contracts that the university had already obtained. Five days later, three of the federal agencies involved in those grants sent the university's president a list of nine demands to be met by March 20, "as a precondition for formal negotiations regarding Columbia University's continued financial relationship with the United States government." The demands "closely tracked lists that had been disseminated in prior weeks by Columbia's own faculty members and alumni groups concerned that the university was not doing enough to protect Jewish and Israeli students." In the following weeks, four noncitizens who had participated in Gaza-related protests at Columbia and Barnard were targeted by immigration authorities for arrest and deportation, plainly in retaliation for constitutionally protected

* Frank and Bernice J. Greenberg Professor of Law, University of Chicago. Research for this essay was supported by the Frank J. Cicero Fund. Thanks to Sue Stokes for comments, and to Jacqueline Hillman for editing support.

Aziz Z. Huq, *The End of the Cold War University*. In: *Academic Freedom in the Era of Trump*.
Edited by: Lee C. Bollinger and Geoffrey R. Stone, Oxford University Press.
 DOI: 10.1093/9780197854877.003.0008

speech. In relation to those arrests, a deputy attorney general suggested that the university might face prosecution for "harboring" undocumented persons. The legality of the funding cutoff, the conditions on negotiations, the arrests, and the threatened prosecution were all sharply contested. Powerful, even conclusive, arguments are available to the effect that all of them flouted either the First Amendment or statutory bounds to presidential authority. Yet at the end of March, Columbia's president, facing right-wing press reports that she had expressed views at odds with her public stance in internal meetings, resigned under some apparent pressure from the board of trustees. To many internal observers, it appeared that "the Trump administration [had] effectively forced out Columbia's president." At the end of July, the new president entered a "settlement" with the administration, which included a $200 million payout and no admission of fault.[2]

The federal government's multipronged attack on Columbia's autonomy, leadership, policies, and curriculum was echoed at a number of other prominent universities, including Harvard, the University of Pennsylvania, and Northwestern. These attacks unfolded, moreover, against the backdrop of a broader rescission of federal funding for biomedical, scientific, and public-health research. In the first half of 2025, for example, Johns Hopkins lost some two-thirds of its federal funding—without, it should be noted, any predicate accusation of wrongdoing of the sort that had been vaguely and unpersuasively leveled at Columbia—forcing a radical scaling back of research and hiring.[3] Subsequent legislated cuts to science funding and to Medicaid—an important element of many teaching hospitals' fiscal bases—are likely to make Johns Hopkins's dilemma exemplary rather than unique, at least for the duration of Trump's second term in office. The effect of such changes is unlikely to remain confined to the science-related units, as provosts and presidents use the opportunity of forced austerity to push through unrelated agendas of institutional transformation.

There is no dearth of disparities between the nature of threats to free inquiry in 1854 and 2025. A striking irony, for example, is the way in which the airing of allegations of discrimination within the university have transformed from a shield for protecting academic freedom of faculty like Gibbs into a blade to be shoved into the side of the university's institutional autonomy. The effect now is to stifle, as a predictable side effect, the discursive freedom of faculty with officially disfavored views that antidiscrimination norms once sheltered. But perhaps the most striking variance between then and now is the starkly different posture of the federal government toward the autonomy of academic bodies.

In 1854, the government had limited authority to negate trustee decisions, and would have had to scramble to find a legal hook in the university's charter. In 2025, by contrast, the federal government is a substantial underwriter of university research via federal grants and contracts. Its historical forbearance from taxing university endowments (cut short, at least for some institutions, by the 2025 budget legislation) and its generous credit facilities for students also count as measures of needful support for universities. Federal monies, though, turn out to be a double-edged sword. What had enabled the university to thrive could—in the medium term—be used to choke it into submission. The federal government's pivot, moreover, reveals the underlying vacuity of complaints about "cancel culture," "snowflake" students, and informal speech codes: These supposedly censorious intramural dynamics—often, in truth, more properly described as vigorous critiques of previously hegemonic positions and figures—turned out to work not as threats to academic freedom (which they never really were) but as invitations for the actor with the true leverage (i.e., the federal government) to exercise by flexing its suppressive fist.

Given these gulfs between then and now, it might seem that we (advocates for the academy) have little to learn from history. Worse, it may be dangerous and misleading to look to history, because the patterns of the past are liable to mislead when the present assaults launched against academic freedom have changed so much. Indeed, one of the distracting ironies of the present moment is a historical reversal of sorts. It is the way in which a history of endogenous challenges to free speech on campus from the left—which presented tricky questions, but never a large threat—has been flipped and intensified and transformed into an existential challenge from the right against the universities. History can be dissonant as well as accordant. And yesterday's advocacy for free speech has been seized upon and redeployed by enemies of free speech today in a devastating, foundational assault.

Yet I think it would be a mistake to reject history's relevance in thinking about the present predicament of universities, even if we cannot transpose the templates of past threats to academic freedom mechanically to the present day in order to identify appropriate responses. My aim in this chapter is to offer a reading of that history that may be useful for wrestling with some of the ethical and moral dilemmas faced by university administrators in the second Trump administration. At a minimum, this history, even in the form of the cursory sketch offered below, can illuminate the way in which certain dilemmas arise in the first instance, and cast light on the pathways that remain open to universities today. With a measure of simplification, I offer a capsule history of the American research university as ground for two currently salient lessons. To begin with, the origins of universities' present dilemma in the Cold War undermines the argument offered by proponents of the federal assault that universities have obtained an unfair and unwarranted free ride and that the time for payback for their "abuse" is nigh. History teaches instead that universities have not been mere parasites, but have more than reimbursed the public for its support through their contributions to the security and economic strength of the nation.

But even if universities are not at moral fault for exploiting the federal government or the taxpayer, their present dependency upon the national state's purse is very much a matter of their own choice. And even if they have not unfairly gained from that decision, it remains the case that the relationship was freely forged. Yet history suggests that, in deciding whether to walk away from the advantages of a close relation to the federal government, certain universities might do well to recognize a genuine choice between a return to a pre-Cold War status quo ante and a pivot to a novel form of dependency upon the federal state in which such institutional affordances as academic freedom no longer obtain. Rather than pointing to one of these pathways as obviously preferable, I suggest that the choice is a genuinely difficult one, implicating certain core moral and professional judgments about what it means to be a home for scholars and scholarship.

Excellence, and Then Preeminence, as Distinct Virtues of the American University

Excellence and global preeminence are separate virtues of the American university. They can be distinguished in the sense that they arose at different times and for distinct reasons. American universities developed the institutional conditions for excellence in the late 19th and early 20th centuries. While the federal government played a role, it was a relatively peripheral one. Many of those same universities attained a global preeminence only in the context of the Cold War—this time abetted substantially by the federal government. Nevertheless, excellence of a kind was not just a function of government funding.

Neither excellence nor global preeminence existed at the beginning. If you had visited a college classroom throughout much of the nineteenth century, you would have found it a dreary place. Students rarely had any choice about subjects or professors. Most instruction proceeded through tedious daily rituals, punctuated by riotous objections from students. With the exception of a handful of schools such as Harvard, Yale, and Dartmouth, most colleges were obscure, inefficient institutions employing between six and eight faculty members, with student bodies ranging between fifty and 100. Most were sectarian, and like Columbia, enforced their doctrinaire beliefs as firm guardrails on academic inquiry. Not surprisingly, such dismal offerings attracted few young minds. In 1826, one in 1,513 men of college age attended a college. By 1855 this figure had actually fallen to one in 1,689, and by 1869—when one might have anticipated a postwar boom—to one in 1,927.[4]

American colleges started to make marked progress in the 1880s thanks to a group of ambitious university presidents pursuing a larger vision. Andrew White (Cornell), Charles William Eliot (Harvard), G. Stanley Hall (Clark), William Rainey Harper (Chicago), and David Starr Jordan (Stanford) set out to leave their mark on their institutions. Eliot, for example, started with about a thousand students and sixty teachers in an institution with a $2.5 million endowment. By the time he left Harvard, it had some 4,000 students, 600 teachers, and an endowment of more than $200 million. A few years before his presidency began, Congress had enacted the Morrill Act, which made millions of acres of federal land available to agricultural and mechanical colleges, with the announced purpose of advancing "the liberal and practical education of the industrial classes in the several pursuits and professions in life."[5] Alongside this public recognition of secular purpose, the sectarian character of universities also ebbed. The number of clergy sitting on university boards, for example, slowly fell; the number on Harvard's board dropped from seven in 1874 to one in 1894.[6]

All this set the ground for the emergence of excellence in higher education. Starting with Johns Hopkins's founding in 1876, administrators at the best schools in the country drew upon and combined the German model of the advanced research institution with the British model of tertiary education organized around the undergraduate college. Taking the best of the two systems, American universities improved on both: by most accounts, less rigid and hierarchical than the German system, thanks to the centrality of departments rather than chairs, but more open to opportunity on the student side than the British system.[7] In a relatively short time, American universities transformed themselves into a model emulated around the world. This transformation, it is worth noting, largely unfolded—exceedingly quickly in some instances, such as the University of Chicago—without any meaningful government intervention. However, even at the end of this period the basic scientific research upon which US industry relied tended to be carried out in Europe.

American higher education underwent a second transformation starting in the 1940s with World War II, which gathered pace in the 1950s. As a consequence of a massive inflow of government funds in the form of both direct funding for research and indirect support via loans for student tuition, universities in this period went from being merely excellent to being globally preeminent. The dramatic quality of this change was in part a function of the absence of federal action before the early 1900s. Law played a role here. Until the beginning of the 20th century, the federal government was not in any position to intervene broadly in higher education in this fashion. While it owned land (which it could distribute through measures like the Morrill Act), it lacked financial clout and administrative capacity. In consequence, until the early 20th century, private universities relied on their endowments and philanthropy for research support, while state universities could look to their state's legislatures. This pattern changed with the Sixteenth Amendment of 1913, which overturned the *Pollack v. Farmers Loan and Trust* decision of the Supreme Court and vested Congress with the power to tax income. The New Deal and the Second World War then saw the emergence of bureaucratic capacity at the national level capable of intervening in—and shaping—the national economy. Constitutional fetters previously cast by the US Supreme Court's understandings of federalism and liberty of contract also fell away, allowing a more aggressive national role in higher education.

In the historical literature, it is standard to speak of the emergence of a "Cold War university." Yet such a conception ignores the fact that federal spending on scientific research had already shot up from $23 million in 1938 to more than $1.6 billion in 1945.[8] At the same time, this new federal role was inflected by America's geopolitical environment, and in particular by its involvement in hot and cold wars. The Soviet launch of Sputnik in 1957 is often described as a clarifying moment for American policymakers for the light it cast upon the strengths of scientific research behind the Iron Curtain. By the end of the Cold War, thanks to the funding flows that followed, American universities dominated the league tables of global higher education. This was especially true for its research universities—institutions that served only a minority of undergraduate students but that produced the bulk of national research output. Whereas many nations had only one or two research universities, America, by one count, was home to some 150 among its 4,800 higher educational institutions.[9] At the same time, perceptive observers such as Jonathan Cole and Rodney Nichols noted that, just as the Berlin Wall was falling, generous federal funding had led to an "increasing dependence" and raised questions about how universities could be characterized as autonomous.[10] Their worries would in time prove prescient.

The latter part of the 20th century is thus a litany of federal generosities aimed at academia. An example of significant early federal fiscal involvement was the June 1944 G.I. Bill, which would enable some 15 million World War II veterans to obtain university degrees. By 1947, more veterans were enrolled in higher education than the total number of college students a decade before. As part of the Manhattan Project, the University of California managed the Los Alamos facility in New Mexico under a government contract. Federal involvement changed in scale after Sputnik. Between 1957 and 1972, Congress created a "cacophony of federal programs" channeling money to American higher education, resulting in an explosion of federal funding.[11] Between 1940 and the end of the century, the nation's research and development (R&D) expenditures increased ninetyfold in inflation-adjusted terms. Universities played a large role in this explosive growth. In 1953, universities accounted for $273 million, or 5.3 percent, of the nation's total R&D expenditures. By 1965, this had risen to 7.3 percent, by 1975 it was at 10 percent, and by 2004 it was at 13.6 percent of total R&D spending. Key to this funding was the 1958 National Defense Education Act, passed in the shadow of *Sputnik*. In the two years after *Sputnik*'s launch, indeed, the budget of the National Science Foundation alone was increased by some 250 percent. The result was a tidal wave of support for the hard sciences in particular. Whereas in

1953 the federal share of research was 54.6 percent, with industry responsible for 7.7 percent, by 1970 the national government was responsible for 69.7 percent, industry's share having fallen to 2.7 percent.[12]

While the humanities did not benefit from the same levels of state support, other strands of social-scientific research did benefit from the Cold War. Area studies, which were focused on specific geographic zones, expanded dramatically at the same time and for similar reasons. The first Russian Institute was established at Columbia University in 1946, staffed by former members of the Office of Strategic Services [OSS]. A year later, the Russian Research Center was established at Harvard with a grant from the Carnegie Corporation. From 1953 to 1966, the Ford Foundation gave $270 million for area and language studies at thirty-four universities, offering "immediate" support for national-security policymaking through the training of specialized personnel. In 1958, as mentioned above, further federal funding spigots opened thanks to the National Defense Education Act.[13] In yet other ways, the Cold War engendered whole new fields of academic study. Behavioral science, systems theories, and modernization theory were all interdisciplinary fields that emerged out of a wartime matrix of concerns.[14] A series of leftist critics, such as Noam Chomsky, Frances Stonor Saunders, and Christopher Simpson, polemicized against US higher education for its statist and militaristic orientation—in effect, paying sidelong tribute to the large role played by the national state in the new educational landscape. In more measured terms, the historian Mark Solovey observed that "Cold War politics helped to determine what science was, what it did, and what it meant."[15]

Federal funding for higher education, of course, was not supplied out of some naive benevolence. It was, from its inception, linked closely to the federal government's national policy ambitions. In 1945, President Roosevelt asked MIT engineer Vannevar Bush to report on what would happen to American science after the war. Bush's report, *Science: The Endless Frontier*, advocated for a National Research Foundation to support basic research as a public good that would be predictably undersupplied by the market. It further argued that public monies should be deployed to support research universities, rather than building up that capacity within the state, as a way to link research and teaching closely. Bush argued that the mechanisms of research support ought to be consistent with the norms of academic practice.[16] As a result of Bush's visionary efforts, universities have indeed "become the engines of innovation and discovery in our society."[17] All twenty-six Nobel Prizes awarded in Physics between 1950 and 1975, for example, were won outright or shared by Americans; six of the eight Nobels in Economics awarded from the award's inception in 1969 through to 1975 also went to Americans.[18]

The federal government had economic as well as security-related reasons for investing in higher education. Multiple studies "repeatedly reported finding a significant positive relationship between higher educational attainment and per capita income and employment growth in the United States." In the United States, a rigorous study identified "positive growth effects of exogenous shocks to investments in four-year college education, for all states." Studies of the firm-level effects of tertiary education on productivity also found "significant" positive effects.[19]

In sum, the American research university would not exist in its current form in the absence of the plentiful support for research and for tuition that has flowed from the government's purse since the 1950s. But that is not to say that the tertiary education sector would have been a failure absent federal funds. There is no transhistorical and universally shared benchmark for what counts as a "successful" university. But it is striking to observe that, even in the absence of significant state support, American universities at the end of the 19th century had already carved out a niche through institutional innovation.

Cold War Universities and the End of the Cold War

The Cold War ended, and yet the Cold War university soldiered on. Why, and how, can federal support for higher education be explained or justified in the absence of the threat that initially motivated lawmakers to step in? Before turning to the normative questions raised by the second Trump administration's assault on the American research university, it is worth considering why the latter persisted for so long without the sort of potential transformative challenge witnessed in 2025. In brief, we should not imagine the university to be akin to a Looney Tunes character careering off a cliff with his legs still spinning before pausing to look down and cogitate the absence of terra firma. The persistence of the superlative American research university can be explained by familiar political economies, and it rests upon reasonably robust normative justifications. Wile E. Coyote it is not.

The persistence of federal funding for universities after the Cold War should not surprise, solely as a matter of political economy. Political scientists such as Paul Pierson have demonstrated that legislated programs entailing predictable spending tend to survive, because they create constituencies that then lobby Congress for their renewal.[20] Universities create large pools of wage earners who have strong sentimental ties to their alma maters. Where once their governing boards had clergy, now they have CEOs and former cabinet secretaries or senators as their members. Many universities are anchor tenants for their local economies, especially given the growing economic importance of health care. Thus, the persistence of universities as favored wards of the national state needs no subtle explanation.

Yet this is not to say that universities became parasitic once their Cold War function ended. Basic research remains as important to productivity today as it did in the 1950s and 1960s. Even absent a national-security justification for federal funding for academic work, there would be a powerful economic case for subsidies of "basic" scientific research in particular. A 1980 industry-specific study of basic R&D's effect on productivity found a "significant and direct" connection. The absence of adequate levels of basic research, by contrast, generates large distortions in investment and meaningful welfare losses.[21] The geographic proximity of universities, moreover, tends to stimulate both the supply and debate for human capital.[22]

Nor have the geostrategic implications of the university disappeared. Universities are a kind of national standard-bearer. Geostrategic competition today has not ebbed, but has been redirected along different axes. Most importantly, the United States and China now perceive themselves (rightly or wrongly) in competition for hegemonic status in the South China Sea and beyond. A central front of this new "cold war" concerns the rate of technological development, and in particular, national capacity in cutting-edge digital technologies such as semiconductors, data centers, and artificial intelligence.[23] To be sure, much of the development of these tools occurs in a corporate context (a shift that is particularly pronounced in cutting-edge artificial intelligence, which often requires access to processing power that corporations but not universities possess). Yet it is hard to see how national innovators in the digital sphere could flourish without a steady supply of well-trained computer scientists and engineers emerging from doctoral programs. OpenAI and Anthropic, that is, need employees. The programs that generate qualified personnel have emerged historically at research universities sustained in large part by federal dollars.

An additional justification turns on the global reputation and prestige of leading research universities. Particularly among international students, this creates the potential for skill-based export of a commodity (education) that by helping a nation's current-account balance can act as a substitute for declining manufacturing. It is also arguably a form of "soft power," which can be instrumentalized by states to advance foreign-policy goals through persuasion and influence. One measure of the importance of higher education as a form of "soft power" is the large investment by the Chinese state in "Confucius Institutes" in the United States and around the world.[24] It is hard to see why China would make these investments if it did not think "soft power" mattered too.

No country of which I am aware has developed a world-class university sector without significant government funding. The United Kingdom, since 2010, may be distinctive insofar as its austerity program, with its sweeping effect on higher education, has done much to weaken what had been among the world's best universities. Its example, however, goes to show that foolish governments locked into myopic and rigidly ideological ruts can do profound, perhaps irreparable damage to the very institutions upon which national prosperity depends (so nothing new there). It is hardly an advertisement for denying state support to the tertiary educational sector.

The persisting centrality of universities to the geostrategic competition over digital technologies, to national exports, and to soft power creates a puzzle: Why has a political movement that styles itself as putting "America first" engaged in a root-and-branch assault on institutions that are, by any measure, central to its own economic and geopolitical goals? It seems counterproductive for a regime that wishes to reduce the national trade deficit to go after a sector of the economy that is quite successful in exporting goods. A government worried about Chinese dominance of new digital technologies would surely beef up its endogenous capacity to nurture technological talent, or to lure it from overseas.

One way of thinking about the Trump administration's assault on higher education would be to regard it as a result of the triumph of domestic over geopolitical priorities. The case for maintaining strong research universities, which rests largely on concerns about America's place in the world, may run headlong into a vision within the Trump coalition for a dramatic social transformation within the United States driven by resentment and anger at those perceived as carpetbagging "elites." The aim of this transformation can be described in various ways, but it centrally entails abrogation of the decades-long dismantling of racial and gender hierarchies, and institutions that have pursued that just and noble mission. To the extent that universities are perceived as anchor tenants of an older political order, aligned with liberal, inclusive values in respect to historical forms of domination, they are natural targets of opportunity. That this is at odds with the putative economic and geostrategic goals of the movement is simply a reflection of the fact that many political formations comprise fractious and fissiparous alliances, and that the emotive claims of some factions can triumph over the coolly rational claims of others.

The Cold War University in the Trump Era

History offers no conclusive answers to the dilemmas posed by the renewed assault on higher education that followed the 2024 election. But history, and in particular a distinction between the roots of American universities' excellence and their global preeminence, offers a clearer sense of the criticisms that in fact have merit, as well as the options that remain legitimately open to academic leadership.

The Myth of University Abuse

One of the architects of the 2025 assault on universities, Christopher Rufo, has justified the measures taken by the Trump Administration in terms of the academy's "responsibility to follow the law and to uphold basic academic standards," given the "reality . . . that American taxpayers subsidize the universities to the tune of more than $150 billion per year." Until now, Rufo argues, the universities have been "abus[ing]" ordinary taxpayers by drawing these funds without any payoff. In effect, Rufo's argument is that universities have been parasitic on the public purse to the detriment of the American people.[25] There are, to be sure, many elements of this framing that are worth disputing as profoundly dishonest (including charges of toleration of discrimination[26]), but I want to focus here on the notion of "abuse" and the lessons of the history I have just told.

Reflection on history suggests that Rufo's polemical terms, such as "abuse," are misleading or fallacious. Higher education did not require federal funds to become excellent. Instead, the state looked to universities first in World War II and then during the Cold War as the essential suppliers of national public goods related to national security and economic growth. Rufo's presentation omits that history, making it seem that universities have not (and have never) contributed to the United States. This is simply false. Rather, they were and are central to national security, and they remain pivotal to any plausible strategy to increase labor productivity in the United States. The sort of arguments that Rufo makes trade, I think, on a perceptual sleight of hand. Look at the "woke" elites who staff universities, he argues, and believe that they are the only ones who benefit from federal funding. This argument implicitly relies on the fact that the *most visible* beneficiaries of universities are not the *only* beneficiaries of higher education. Rather, the gains from scientific research, and from a more clear-eyed understanding of our history, society, and world, are diffused among people at large.

There is another, subtler deception embedded in Rufo's argument. He omits the terms on which the original bargain between the government and academia was struck, as reflected in Vannevar Bush's *Science: The Endless Frontier*. In that influential framing document, Bush envisaged universities as "engines of innovation and discovery in our society"—but on terms that accorded with the existing norms of academic independence. In fashioning federal support for higher education, Congress acquiesced to that understanding. In effect, Rufo and the officials following his cues want the benefits of that deal while repudiating the government's side of the bargain. Rather, they urge that the federal government, having established a mutually beneficial relationship, take advantage of the trust and dependency fostered in universities.

In this context, the fact that Rufo refers to the tactics he proposes as inflicting "existential terror" on universities is telling.[27] It is telling because the cuts in funding to Columbia, Harvard, and other institutions do not merely harm the institutions as such. They disrupt, and at times derail, the lives and expectations of students, faculty, and administrators who have little or no say over, and had no role in shaping, the policies to which he objects. Demands such as the ones leveled at Columbia (often in violation of federal law) must therefore be understood as a species of blackmail: in effect, "Comply with our ideological dictates or we will harm innocent members of your core communities." In this light, I think it is tolerably clear where the "abuse" is happening.

I should stress that there are real arguments to be made against the (false) claim that universities were violating statutory law through diversity initiatives. And there are other, equally important points to be made about how the attack on "DEI" by Rufo and others is, in practical effect, an effort to assert white, male dominance over institutions, and to marginalize or exclude racial minorities' and women's voices. And there is a need to challenge the corrosively false and misleading way that Rufo and his allies use the term "institutional neutrality" to mean "conformity with our racist and misogynistic belief system." Those, however, are arguments that will need to be made someplace else; the narrower point here is how history gives the lie to claims of "abuse."

History and the Burden of Present Choice

Assume that those who assail and aim to capture academic institutions are unlikely to heed either logic or history (as, I think, seems tolerably clear). Even then, the historical trajectory of universities over the 20th century clarifies certain important points about the choice structure now facing administrators at Columbia, Harvard, and elsewhere. It is easy to imagine that the responsible thing to do is to find some path of compromise by acceding to some federal demands. But history generates some countervailing considerations. These may or may not be conclusive, but I think they cannot be dismissed out of hand.

To begin with, university administrators might bear in mind that what is at stake in the threats to Columbia and their ilk is not the loss of academic excellence as such. Long before the advent of significant federal funding, American universities had created a model successfully integrating elements of the German research university and the British college system—the University of Chicago was a notable example—and by iterating and improving upon this synthesis managed to match, in a matter of decades, what some European institutions had taken centuries to build. The elimination of federal funding would, at least in the absence of any (likely unlawful) efforts at vindictive harm, mean a return to an early-twentieth-century model, a succès d'estime even if it was not yet globally preeminent.

Moreover, those administrators might bear in mind that the assault on Columbia represents a repudiation of the historic bargain struck in the 1950s and reflected in the Bush report. Quite apart from the (questionable) legality of this adjuring, such a rupture is a signal that the federal government is no longer a trustworthy partner. Once a government in the wrong hands has shown that it can walk away from its commitments and take advantage of vulnerabilities that it has fostered, how can it reestablish its credibility? Even if other universities follow Columbia's example in striking a deal, how can they be assured that the agreement will represent the end of federal demands? A very plausible response to the breach of trust by the federal government would be to view the latter as a henceforth unreliable partner, one that presents an irremediable future risk of abuse or betrayal. On this construal of the 2025 assault upon universities, there is cause for deep skepticism about the relationship even if lost federal funding is eventually restored, and ample reason to view future funding streams with distrust. Even if the second Trump administration is taken as an outlier (and its successful radicalization of the Republican Party at large suggests that it is not), what guarantee is there that federal funding will not again be used to subvert academic institutions, albeit on different grounds? Something done for the first time simply can't be undone. At minimum, there will be good grounds to diversify fiscal structures, and ultimately perhaps even to eschew federal funding (however vital it currently seems).

Finally, assume that federal funds were offered originally in exchange for the production of intellectual public goods and human capital that redounded to the benefit of all. Their withdrawal today raises the question of who the university should henceforth benefit. That is, if universities are no longer being supported in such a way that they can achieve these goals, aimed as they are at the general welfare, then should they reconsider their aspiration to be universally beneficial? There is nothing, after all, intrinsic in the definition of the university that implies that institutions must be of uniform or universal service. Prior to the reforms of the 1880s and 1890s, indeed, universities had narrow sectarian ends (as, indeed, do many religious institutions of higher learning today). And even once they broke from that sectarian past, universities might go on to serve narrow intellectual elites rather than society at large.

I do not mean to suggest that universities should go back to their pinched and parochial sectarian pasts. Nor do I think it desirable that universities, stripped of federal funding, should pivot to the education of the already wealthy (as some have suggested would likely happen).[28] But consider this: We are, plainly, in a world in which many people no longer believe in free and unfettered inquiry, and are willing to use the awesome powers of the modern state to act upon this aversion. Rejection of rigorous epistemic procedures—and distrust in the institutions that employ such procedures—has percolated from the margins of society not only into the center of public discourse but into cabinet offices (with Trump's secretary of health and human services being a notorious and clear example). Under these conditions, a university might plausibly say that it is no longer compatible with its educational model to welcome those who a priori reject the principled and disciplined scientific and social-scientific approaches to inquiry that have characterized the academy since the beginning of the 20th century. If higher education is to be rationed, that is, why should it not be assigned to those who accept and will work with (rather than against) its epistemic predicates and foundational practices? In a world in which the academy has enemies, and where it cannot serve all, that is, why should it aid and advance those who are ex ante antipathetic to its basic mission?

I also do not mean to suggest that there is one pathway suited to all universities. Seeking a return to institutional forms of excellence that predated the rise of federal funding will fit some institutions better than others. In some universities such a project could take years, but for others it could take decades. Universities with large medical wings, especially those that serve large indigent communities, may have no option but to accede to federal demands. Their best option might entail a split between their medical wings and their undergraduate and even graduate components. Other universities are deeply invested in the hard sciences, for which there may be no short-term alternative to federal funding. Severing bonds with the federal government may make little sense for them; in effect, it might instead represent a functional death sentence. Rather than making a categorical claim, I am simply suggesting that—at least for some universities, at some time in the future—the pathway of institutional and fiscal independence should be taken very seriously. We should have the courage to imagine the world as starkly different from what it is—and history can help us in that endeavor.

Severance is not an option to be taken lightly, especially given its potential spillover costs for forms of academic work functionally dependent on federal funds. But it should also not be taken off the table.

Conclusion

The global preeminence of American universities was a contingent by-product of World War II and the Cold War. There was never a reason to think it would last forever, and there is now some reason to think that it began to break down in 2025. Yet the end of the Cold War university need not be a cause for comprehensive dismay. Rather, the history of the American university across the 20th century suggests that there are multiple paths that can be followed. Different institutions will need to pick which one fits them—but their choices should not be artificially foreclosed by an ignorance of what the university has been, and might be again.

What is impossible, however, is a return to the prelapsarian world in which the federal government, looking to universities as natural supports for its foreign and economic policy ends, can be trusted to keep its end of the bargain struck at the beginning of the 1950s. We are no longer in the era of the Cold War university; in other words, Wile E. Coyote has, in an important sense, already run off the cliff's edge. Rather than spinning our legs in midair, we who believe in the epistemic model of the university need to imagine a new future. And in that endeavor, paradoxically, we cannot proceed far without a sure grasp of the past.

PART III

THE AUTHORITARIAN PLAYBOOK ON ACADEMIC FREEDOM

Civil Rights and Antidiscrimination

8

Title VI Rights and Wrongs: Campuses Must Bar Discrimination Against Both Identities and Ideas

ROBERT SHIBLEY AND NADINE STROSSEN*

Overview

The Trump administration has deployed multiple tools in its unprecedented, multi-pronged[1] crackdown on the institutional autonomy of universities and the free-speech rights of individual members of university communities. One headline-grabbing example was its March 2025 arrest and detention of several foreign students based on their pro-Palestinian speech after the October 7, 2023, Hamas attack on Israel and ensuing war in Gaza,[2] citing potential damage to "foreign policy" from their continued presence in the United States. In the same vein, the administration revoked student visas from more than 1,800 foreign students on hundreds of campuses (at least temporarily[3]) and even stripped Harvard University *entirely* of its ability to host foreign students (though a judge quickly restored it while litigation progressed[4]). These measures, accompanied by the freezing and cancellation of billions in federal grants to Harvard, Columbia, and other major universities, represent extraordinary assaults on not only the free-speech rights of individual students and faculty members but also

* Nadine Strossen is the John Marshall Harlan II Professor at New York Law School and a Senior Fellow with FIRE, the Foundation for Individual Rights and Expression. Robert Shibley is FIRE's special counsel for campus advocacy and author of Twisting Title IX (Encounter Books, 2016). For research assistance, the authors thank Molly Nocheck, FIRE's Vice President of Student Development, and FIRE's 2025 summer interns; and for answers to specific queries, they thank Kenneth S. Stern, Director, Bard Center for the Study of Hate.

Robert Shibley and Nadine Strossen, *Title VI Rights and Wrongs: Campuses Must Bar Discrimination Against Both Identities and Ideas*. In: *Academic Freedom in the Era of Trump*. Edited by: Lee C. Bollinger and Geoffrey R. Stone, Oxford University Press. © Oxford University Press (2026).
DOI: 10.1093/9780197854877.003.0009

the academic freedom of educational institutions, which includes the right to select their students. And the resulting chilling impact has undermined the free-speech rights not only of foreign students but also of American members of the campus community who benefit from the opportunity to listen to and engage with students from abroad.

The purported primary justification for nearly all of these speech-suppressing efforts has been to fight discrimination on campus, particularly against Jewish and Israeli students, in the name of enforcing Title VI of the 1964 Civil Rights Act. Title VI requires campuses that receive federal funding to counter "discrimination because of race, color, or national origin," and it has been interpreted to extend to discrimination "based on shared ancestry," including anti-Semitic and Islamophobic discrimination. Campuses found to have violated Title VI may be stripped of all federal funds unless they settle with the government. Beyond appropriately pressuring campuses to counter illegal discriminatory conduct or expression—such as assaults, vandalism, and threats—the Trump administration also has inappropriately pressured campuses to suppress expression conveying (allegedly)[5] discriminatory views, on the rationale that such expression constitutes constitutionally unprotected "hostile environment harassment."[6] Yet the First Amendment famously protects "freedom for the thought that we hate,"[7] including hateful, discriminatory thoughts.

To be sure, the Supreme Court has held that expression—particularly if it accompanies other conduct—may constitute impermissible hostile-environment harassment in context-specific factual circumstances. In contrast, any restriction that targets expression due to its discriminatory viewpoint, absent any one or more of the required contextual factors, violates the First Amendment's cardinal "viewpoint neutrality" principle, which bars government from restricting speech solely due to its disfavored viewpoint or message.[8]

The Trump administration's suppression of certain constitutionally protected campus expression through an exaggerated concept of hostile-environment harassment has garnered significant attention and criticism, though certainly less than the more "exciting" fights over deportation, detention, and defunding. Yet it may end up proving the most damaging from the longer-term legal perspective. Indeed, the very same tactic was used by both the Biden and Obama administrations in the context of fighting sex discrimination under Title IX of the Education Amendments of 1972, provoking similar criticism—albeit not necessarily from the same segments of the campus community that are now objecting to Trump's use of it.

In fact, campuses began to enforce unconstitutional concepts of harassing expression on their own initiative even earlier, in the late 1980s. Anti-harassment policies became a vehicle for implementing the "hate speech codes" that were then being advocated by many members of campus communities with the goal of countering discrimination against racial, ethnic, and other traditionally excluded or marginalized groups.

Along with other advocates of both free speech and nondiscrimination on campus, both of us have long maintained that any form of unconstitutional "speech code" which restricts expression solely because the views expressed are deemed discriminatory—including through an overly broad concept of harassment—is the worst of both worlds. Not only do such restrictions violate freedom of speech; they are also at best ineffective, and at worst counterproductive, for promoting equality and pluralism in our democratic society.[9] While courts have consistently struck down campus speech codes whenever they are challenged, most go unchallenged.

For the last several decades, overly broad concepts of unprotected harassing expression have constituted a major vehicle—according to some experts, *the* major vehicle—for unduly restricting campus free speech. As one of us wrote in 2019, if campuses were to "properly" answer the critical question, "When does conduct among students cross the line from being annoying . . . or offensive into being actual harassment?," that "would likely represent the greatest advance for free speech on America's campuses in a generation."[10] That statement has gained added salience since October 7, 2023, as the ensuing campus protests have unleashed further efforts to suppress constitutionally protected campus expression on the hostile-environment harassment rationale.

Given the attention and criticism that the Trump administration's speech-stifling misuse of Title VI has engendered, being forced to contend with this strategy should prompt campuses to finally correct the longstanding, broader problem that it illustrates.

Part I of this essay analyzes the Supreme Court's sole precedent defining expression that constitutes constitutionally unprotected hostile-environment harassment in the education context. Part II outlines the history of measures suppressing disfavored campus speech through overly broad concepts of impermissible harassing speech, which violate that decision. Part III highlights how campuses' essential goal of eliminating identity-based discrimination is undermined by idea-based discrimination, including through exaggerated concepts of harassing expression. Finally, Part IV recommends actions that universities should take to promote the important identity-based antidiscrimination goals reflected in federal civil-rights statutes, consistent with the First Amendment's ban on viewpoint-based discrimination.

The Supreme Court's Definition of Hostile-Environment Harassment in the Education Context: Davis v. Monroe County Board of Education

The Supreme Court has issued only one decision squarely discussing what expression constitutes impermissible hostile-environment harassment in the context of federally funded education programs: 1999's *Davis v. Monroe County*

Board of Education.[11] The *Davis* complaint alleged a mix of "verbal" (speech) and other conduct, including physical touching, so the Court's analysis applies to the overall course of conduct that included both.

Recognizing the differences between educational and employment settings, including the greater importance of free speech in the former, the Court crafted a more exacting standard for hostile-environment harassment in the educational context: it must be *"so severe, pervasive, and objectively offensive, and . . . so undermine[] and detract[] from the victims' educational experience, that the victim-students are effectively denied equal access to an institution's resources and opportunities"* (emphasis added). In contrast, the Court had previously specified that, for workplace harassment to violate the ban on employment discrimination under Title VII of the 1964 Civil Rights Act, it only had to be "sufficiently severe or pervasive to alter the conditions of [the victim's] employment and create an abusive working environment."[12]

The *Davis* decision repeated its more demanding, education-specific standard for hostile-environment harassment no fewer than five times, with only slight variations in the phrasing, and with all five iterations incorporating the exact phrase "severe, pervasive, *and* objectively offensive" (emphasis added), clearly requiring *all three* criteria to be satisfied. Likewise, all four of the Court's references to the requisite harm element used synonymous terms to describe the impact that the complained-of conduct (including expression) must have on the complainant's educational opportunities—"bars," "deprives," and "denies"—in contrast with a less demanding potential alternative such as "limits," "reduces," or Title VII's "alters."[13]

Notwithstanding the majority's narrow definition of hostile-environment harassment in the education context, its holding that this definition potentially applies to expression prompted the dissent's concern that the definition could function as a viewpoint-discriminatory "speech code."[14] The majority opinion responded several times to this concern, underscoring the limited scope of its definition, and noting that there could be no categorical ban even on "insults, banter, teasing, . . . gender-specific conduct that is upsetting, . . . name-calling," or other "offensive" expression, while recognizing that, in certain factual circumstances, the First Amendment might permit some such expression to be restricted.[15]

Davis's speech-protective approach is underscored by the plaintiff's factual allegations. The complained-of conduct was a far cry from the constitutionally protected expression about pressing public-policy issues that has too often been suppressed as hostile-environment harassment on campus. In *Davis,* a fifth-grade boy repeatedly subjected his classmate, LaShonda Davis, to a five-month-long pattern of "vulgar" sexual propositions and unwelcome physical contact, for which he ultimately pled guilty to a criminal charge of sexual battery. In holding that these facts satisfied its newly articulated definition of hostile-environment harassment in an educational setting, the Court was hardly approving speech codes even for the elementary school at issue, much less in the much more speech-protective campus environment.

Flagging key distinctions between universities and elementary schools, *Davis* indicated that universities would have reduced obligations to control the behavior and expression of "free adults,"[16] such as those on campus. *Davis*'s definition of unprotected expression should therefore be viewed as the First Amendment's bare-minimum campus standard. When government or campus officials invoke federal civil-rights laws as ostensibly justifying—indeed, *requiring*—measures that violate the First Amendment, they squarely violate this governing precedent.[17]

Campuses' Unconstitutional Viewpoint-Based Discrimination in the Name of Reducing Identity-Based Discrimination

Campuses' Adoption of Overly Broad Harassment Rationales to Justify Unconstitutional Hate-Speech Codes

Starting in the 1980s, campuses began to adopt policies intended to restrict hateful, offensive, or discriminatory expression on the basis of such identity factors as race, ethnicity, and sex. Many advocates of civil liberties and civil rights opposed these codes, concluding that they not only violate fundamental free-speech principles but also are ineffective in countering discrimination, and likely even counterproductive.[18] The ACLU promptly challenged one of the earliest such codes to be enacted, leading to the first court ruling[19] of many, all consistently recognizing the codes' fatal First Amendment flaws.[20]

After the Supreme Court's 1986 recognition of sexual harassment as a form of sex discrimination under federal civil-rights statutes, campus speech codes often assumed the form of overly broad policies targeting not just sexual but also other forms of discriminatory harassment. To be sure, the courts that have reviewed anti-harassment policies that impose viewpoint-based speech restrictions have consistently struck down these policies.[21] After all, as the Third Circuit noted in an opinion authored by then-Judge Samuel Alito, "[t]here is no categorical 'harassment exception' to the First Amendment's free speech clause."[22]

Yet, to this day, campuses have continued to maintain unconstitutional, speech-suppressive anti-harassment policies. Such policies helped propel the 1999 founding of FIRE, the Foundation for Individual Rights in Education (in 2022, the name was changed to the Foundation for Individual Rights and Expression, signaling the expansion of FIRE's free-speech work beyond campus). Although FIRE has brought successful First Amendment lawsuits against many campus harassment policies that suppress constitutionally protected speech, students and faculty members willing to sue the institutions that educate or employ them are difficult to find. Self-funded suits are rarer still, as damages awards in speech cases are rarely substantial, and issues of standing, mootness, and qualified immunity further complicate the process of becoming a "prevailing plaintiff" for purposes of recovering attorney fees under pertinent civil-rights statutes.

Annually since 2006, FIRE has evaluated speech policies on hundreds of America's largest and most prestigious campuses. As of 2025, 14.7 percent of the 490 campuses evaluated continue to receive "an overall 'red light' rating for maintaining policies that clearly and substantially restrict free speech," with another 68.8 percent "earn[ing] an overall 'yellow light' rating for maintaining policies that impose vague regulations on expression." Only 16.5 percent of schools earned a "green light" rating for having no written policies that "seriously imperil speech."[23] While the 2025 percentage of red-light schools had greatly declined from its 2009 peak of 74.2 percent, FIRE's 2024 report observed that the most prevalent policies "that put protected speech at risk" that year, as well as every year since the ratings' inception, continued to be "overbroad policies on harassment,"[24] a trend that persisted in 2025.

The Obama and Biden Administrations' Unconstitutional Definitions of Punishable Sexually Harassing Expression Under Title IX

In 2011, the Obama administration launched a campaign to change what it perceived as "a culture on college campuses that often breeds student-on-student sexual violence."[25] The starting gun of this campaign was an April 4, 2011, "Dear Colleague" letter [DCL] sent to all US campuses by the Department of Education's Office for Civil Rights [OCR],[26] implicitly threatening campuses with being found in violation of Title IX, and ultimately stripped of all federal funding, if they didn't abide by its terms.[27]

The 2011 DCL turbocharged campuses' misuse of harassment policies to suppress constitutionally protected speech. It conspicuously omitted any reference to campuses' obligations to implement their anti-harassment policies only in ways that strictly comply with the First Amendment, as the George W. Bush OCR had strongly reaffirmed in a 2003 Dear Colleague Letter.[28] The 2011 DCL also undermined fundamental due-process protections for those accused of sexual harassment and other misconduct, which had provided some guardrails against punishing constitutionally protected expression (as well as against other types of unjustified punishments).[29]

That the DCL's speech-suppressive impact was no accident became unmistakable in 2013, when OCR, along with the Department of Justice's Civil Rights Division, released a joint-findings letter and resolution agreement regarding their Title IX investigation of the University of Montana. Declaring itself "a blueprint for colleges and universities throughout the country to protect students from sexual harassment and assault,"[30] the "blueprint" removed any doubt that the federal government intended to use Title IX to regulate campus speech.

Rather than invoking the Supreme Court's *Davis* standard, the blueprint instead defined sexual harassment in sweeping terms: "any unwelcome conduct of a sexual nature,"[31] including "verbal conduct"[32] (speech), was deemed harassment, even when not part of a larger course of harassing conduct. Moreover, the government demanded that campus "policies and procedures ensure the elimination of sexual harassment."[33] Considered collectively, these provisions required campuses to adopt "policies and procedures that ensured the elimination" of "any unwelcome" speech "of a sexual nature." As First Amendment scholar Eugene Volokh put it, the government was "telling universities to institute speech codes,"[34] just as the *Davis* dissenters had feared. Along with other speech codes that reviewing courts had invalidated, these government-prescribed harassment-style speech codes embodied multiple First Amendment flaws: undue vagueness, substantial overbreadth, and viewpoint discrimination.

During the first Trump administration, the Department of Education (ED) rescinded the Obama-era documents[35] and replaced them with formal Title IX regulations that repaired much of the damage.[36] These 2020 regulations incorporated *Davis*'s speech-protective definition of hostile-environment harassment and added significant due-process protections. Although the Biden OCR in turn adopted new regulations in 2024 that would have largely restored the Obama-era speech-eroding standards, federal judges blocked them from going into effect in a majority of states on various legal grounds (including the First Amendment). A federal judge ultimately struck down the Biden regulations nationwide in January 2025, and the ED returned to enforcing the 2020 Title IX regulations.[37] But by then, a new threat to campus speech in the name of preventing harassment had arrived.

The Biden and Trump Administrations' Unconstitutional Definitions of Punishable Anti-Semitic Expression Under Title VI

After October 7, 2023, both the Biden and Trump administrations invoked Title VI's restrictions on race, color, and national-origin discrimination to counter what they saw as anti-Semitic and anti-Israeli discrimination stemming from the widespread pro-Palestinian protests that erupted on campuses across the country.[38] Many colleges faced accusations that they were not punishing offenses such as assault and vandalism, and that they were giving a pass to constitutionally unprotected anti-Semitic and anti-Israel expression, including threats and disruptive protests that violated reasonable, viewpoint-neutral time, place, and manner regulations. These accusations came to a head in a December 5, 2023, congressional hearing that ultimately led to the resignation of two of the three Ivy League presidents who testified.

Under Title VI, federal grant-making agencies have the same duty as under Title IX—to investigate and make findings about violations of the laws. Invoking this duty, both the Biden and Trump administrations reran the same playbook previously used by the Obama administration: misusing civil-rights laws to target protected expression solely because it conveyed allegedly discriminatory or violent views.

Both the Biden and Trump administrations have pursued two major strategies to facilitate their unjustified targeting of constitutionally protected speech under Title VI. The first is a yearslong effort to pressure campuses to adopt an unduly vague and broad definition of anti-Semitic expression that the International Holocaust Remembrance Alliance (IHRA) had promulgated for an entirely different purpose. The second is a newly invented concept of "cumulative harassment" that forces campuses to consider imposing campus-wide speech restrictions after each and every allegation of discrimination—even when the particular allegation regards clearly protected speech.

The IHRA Definition of Anti-Semitism

In 2019, President Trump issued an executive order that required executive-branch agencies administering Title VI to consider the IHRA's "non-legally binding working definition of antisemitism" and illustrative examples.[39] The Biden administration left this order in effect (as has the second Trump administration).

Kenneth Stern, the definition's principal author during his twenty-five-year tenure as Director of the American Jewish Committee's Division on Antisemitism and Extremism, has explained that the definition's purpose was to facilitate expert tracking of anti-Semitic incidents in European countries, not to guide law enforcement.[40] The definition is especially unsuitable in the context of speech regulations because its vague, broad language dramatically departs from the "narrow tailoring" that the First Amendment requires for any speech restriction, in order to avoid an undue chilling impact. IHRA's all-encompassing language states:

> Antisemitism is a certain perception of Jews, which may be expressed as hatred toward Jews. Rhetorical and physical manifestations of antisemitism are directed toward Jewish or non-Jewish individuals and/or their property, toward Jewish community institutions and religious facilities.[41]

Under this definition, literally any expression may be classified as anti-Semitic—or not. If anti-Semitism is "a certain perception" of Jews that "may be expressed as hatred towards Jews," it also may *not* be so expressed. Likewise, anti-Semitism may be "directed at Jewish or non-Jewish individuals and/or their property," explicitly including *all* persons and property.

The definition's speech-stifling impact, when misapplied in the Title VI enforcement context, is compounded by the definition's Appendix, which lists examples that "may serve as illustrations" of anti-Semitism (meaning that they also may *not* so serve). These examples include expression about public-policy issues—the very "political" speech that the Supreme Court consistently has held entitled to the highest level of First Amendment protection—such as "[d]rawing comparisons of contemporary Israeli policy to that of the Nazis," and "[d]enying the Jewish people their right to self-determination, e.g., by claiming that the existence of a State of Israel is a racist endeavor."

President Trump's executive order attempted to avoid the First Amendment pitfalls of using IHRA's definition for enforcement purposes, saying agencies were bound only to "consider" the definition, and to use its examples only "to the extent that any examples might be useful as evidence of discriminatory intent," claiming that such use "shall not diminish or infringe upon any right protected under . . . the First Amendment."[42] Predictably, however, these boundaries have been disregarded by both government and campus officials, who have been working to enshrine its use in campus speech codes.[43]

The "Cumulative Theory" of Harassment

The Biden Administration Adopts the Cumulative Theory

After the wave of post-October 7, 2023, pro-Palestinian protests provoked a flurry of complaints about anti-Semitism on campuses across the nation, the Biden administration introduced a new standard for determining whether a hostile environment existed: it required educational institutions to "assess whether incidents individually *or cumulatively* created a hostile environment" (emphasis added),[44] explicitly obligating the institutions to conflate constitutionally protected speech with impermissible conduct and expression. In a December 2023 article, Berkeley Law School Dean Erwin Chemerinsky and UC Irvine Chancellor Howard Gillman explained and critiqued this novel approach:

> [U]niversities have been advised . . . by the Department of Education that protected speech, including speech that would not meet the definition of harassment, can create a hostile environment that universities are obligated to address. . . . Universities have been advised that statements . . . such as "From the river to the sea, Palestine will be free"—which are clearly constitutionally protected—likely create a hostile environment for Jewish students . . ., thus requiring investigations

> and mitigation efforts. . . . [W]e know that some Muslim, Arab and Palestinian students similarly feel threatened by protesters who chant "We stand with Israel." Do they also require investigations and mitigation efforts? . . . The Department of Education should make it clear that, on college campuses, a discriminatory educational environment cannot be created merely through exposure to objectionable ideas and speech that is protected by the First Amendment.[45]

To be sure, the Biden ED said that campuses should not impose any disciplinary sanction on students for constitutionally protected speech, instead directing universities to "address" such speech through alternative measures, such as speaking out against certain viewpoints or reaching out to both speakers and offended individuals to discuss the speech's negative impact.[46] Although these interventions do not impose punitive sanctions such as suspension or expulsion, they nonetheless have a similar stigmatizing and deterrent impact on speakers. For this reason, several federal courts have struck down analogous campus measures, such as "bias response teams," under the First Amendment.[47]

But when the ED's OCR first issued findings in its post-October 7 Title VI investigations, it was not content to rely on this chilling impact alone. Most concerningly, OCR's resolution letter to Lafayette College conveyed its view that perhaps nothing short of outright censorship would suffice.[48] OCR's own findings concluded that Lafayette made at least *some* attempt to intervene after every reported anti-Semitic incident, even those involving social-media posts that the college correctly recognized could not be punished because doing so would pose "a free speech issue."[49] OCR nevertheless faulted Lafayette for not making a determination, after every incident, as to whether that incident "individually or collectively created or contributed to a hostile environment."[50]

This asserted duty to investigate even protected speech has the very same repressive, chilling impact as the other purportedly nonpunitive measures already discussed: it pressures universities to err in favor of deeming even constitutionally protected speech to constitute punishable harassment; and it thereby also deters members of the campus community from exercising their free-speech rights to avoid being subject to investigation. The very process of being investigated is itself punitive—exacting both tangible and intangible costs—even if the investigation affirms that the speech was indeed constitutionally protected; such an investigation therefore "abridges" free speech.[51]

The Trump Administration Continues Its Use

Just two weeks into President Trump's second term, administration officials announced their "priority to root out antisemitic harassment in schools and on college campuses,"[52] echoing the Obama OCR's demand that campuses "ensure the elimination of sexual harassment."[53] Although the Trump administration has paid lip service to the *Davis* standard, it has continued to enforce the speech-suppressing cumulative theory of harassment that the Biden administration had introduced.

On May 22, 2025, the respective Offices for Civil Rights of the Department of Health and Human Services (HHS) and the Department of Education issued a "joint findings letter"[54] asserting that Columbia University had violated Title VI by failing to properly respond to allegations of anti-Semitic harassment and discrimination from October 2023 through January 2025. The agencies' extensive list of "background, allegations, and facts relevant to [their] investigation"[55] included some clear violations of law or Columbia rules, and even some incidents of violence. Yet the list also included multiple instances of protected expression from different places and times, including the presence of a sign saying, "Ivy League Funds Genocide" at a November 2023 demonstration;[56] students' distribution of literature that said "Globalize the intifada" in March 2024;[57] and chants such as "Al-Qassam, you make us proud, kill another soldier now," and "Yes Hamas, we love you, we support your rockets, too"[58] at other, unspecified protests. The government made no effort to connect the incidents other than by the ideology expressed. Nevertheless, the agencies wrote, "taken together, these actions by students and others on Columbia University's campus from October 7, 2023, through the present denied Jewish students equal access to certain educational opportunities or benefits," violating Title VI.[59]

HHS's OCR issued a similar findings letter to Harvard on June 30, 2025, again concluding that multiple unrelated incidents combined to create a hostile environment under Title VI, although some such incidents apparently involved only constitutionally protected expression. Among allegations of "antisemitic acts of vandalism,"[60] for example, HHS included not only the criminal acts of "smash[ing] the ground-floor windows to University Hall and cover[ing] the John Harvard statue in red paint," but also an instance of clearly protected expression in which "student and faculty groups at Harvard posted to Instagram an antisemitic cartoon 'show[ing] a white hand, marked with a dollar sign inside a Star of David, tightening nooses around the necks of a Black man and an Arab man.'"[61]

Court Rulings That the IHRA Definition and Cumulative Harassment Theory Violate the First Amendment

Our preceding discussion explains our conclusions that the First Amendment bars enforcing Title VI in accordance with either the IHRA definition or the cumulative-harassment theory. These conclusions have been reaffirmed by the only courts that have addressed these issues to date: the single court that has addressed the IHRA issue, and the two courts that have explicitly engaged in a legal analysis of Title VI claims based on the cumulative-harassment theory.

Notwithstanding these consistent court rulings, they afford no guarantee that either government or campus officials will abide by their First Amendment holdings. After all, as we have discussed, government and campus officials have failed to abide by the Supreme Court's sole precedent governing hostile-environment harassment in the educational context. Therefore, supporters of free speech—and of meaningful equality and inclusivity—must take proactive steps, such as the ones we recommend in Part IV.

Courts and the IHRA Definition

In October 2024, a federal district court in Texas issued preliminary rulings in a First Amendment challenge to the speech policies of several Texas universities that had incorporated the IHRA definition into their speech policies,[62] in compliance with Texas Governor Greg Abbott's March 2024 executive order directing campuses to use that definition "to guide university personnel and students on what constitutes antisemitic speech."[63] The challenged policies provided that "any . . . violations of state or federal law or university policy that was committed because of antisemitism or the offender's bias or prejudice against [any identity group] will be subject to discipline . . . including possible termination/expulsion."[64]

The plaintiffs argued that the challenged speech policies violated the cardinal First Amendment bar on viewpoint discrimination, and the court's order concluded that the plaintiffs had a "likelihood of success on the merits" of their claim. In fact, the university defendants didn't even dispute the viewpoint-discriminatory nature of the new policies using the IHRA definition, arguing instead that viewpoint discrimination is legally permissible if university officials "rightfully forecast [that] the proscribed speech will be a substantial disruption." Although the court did not accept this misstatement of the governing legal standard,[65] the court assumed for the sake of argument that the defendants' standard was the correct one, and nonetheless concluded that the speech policies likely violated the First Amendment. As the court explained, the asserted "forecast" of "substantial disruption" was based solely on the controversial nature of the targeted, allegedly anti-Semitic, viewpoints—in other words, it amounted to nothing more than blatant viewpoint discrimination.[66]

Given the Trump administration's pressuring of campuses nationwide to adopt the IHRA definition, paralleling the Texas governor's pressure on his state's campuses, we can expect that many other universities will incorporate that definition into their speech policies, as Columbia, Harvard, and NYU (among others) have already done. Therefore, it is worth considering an extended excerpt from this sole pertinent judicial ruling so far:

> [T]he Court finds the incorporation of this specific definition of antisemitism is viewpoint discrimination. In general, including the word "antisemitism" in speech policies, . . . in the context of protecting students from discrimination and harassment, is not inherently a First Amendment violation. . . . But here, the speech policies do not leave "antisemitism" open to constitutional definitions and interpretations, because [the executive order] mandated a specific definition. . . . That definition, by incorporation of the IHRA's examples, labels "calling the State of Israel a racist endeavor" and "drawing comparisons of contemporary Israeli policy to that of the Nazis" as antisemitic. . . . Through the connection to these examples, the policies make that speech punishable, thereby chilling it. . . .
>
> The revised university policies chill a kind of expression that is a hallmark of university activity. . . . Defendants emphasize the spring [pro-Palestinian] protests, arguing that . . . this speech is a substantial disruption. . . . But the Court disagrees, finding the prohibition of this expression more akin to "a mere desire to avoid the discomfort and unpleasantness that always accompany an unpopular viewpoint." . . . For example, a student could calmly express she finds Israel's policies similar to that of the Nazis while seated in a classroom. . . . Yet under [the] revised polic[ies], . . . her expression is defined as antisemitism and could be punished as "harassment . . . committed because of antisemitism."[67]

The unduly vague, broad IHRA anti-Semitism definition will predictably have the speech-suppressive impact that the Supreme Court's narrow-tailoring requirement is designed to avoid. Especially given the enormous adverse consequences of a finding that a campus has violated Title VI—or even a charge that it has done so—campuses will err in favor of over-restricting speech about Israel and Zionism. Likewise, members of campus communities will err in favor of excessive self-censorship on these topics.

As Columbia professor and Holocaust scholar Marianne Hirsch told the Associated Press shortly after Columbia announced it would adopt the IHRA definition, she was not sure she could competently teach her subject in an environment that "treats criticism of Israel as antisemitic."[68] "We learn by making analogies," she noted, adding, "Now the university is saying that's off-limits. How can you have a university course where ideas are not up for discussion or interpretation?" Faculty in particular may feel greater pressure not just to avoid accusations that they personally have engaged in anti-Semitic or anti-Israeli harassment, but also to avoid contributing to a finding that their institutions have violated Title VI under the newly minted "cumulative harassment" theory, discussed in the next section.

Courts and Cumulative-Harassment Theory

No educational institution has yet (as of this writing) challenged the government's application of the cumulative-harassment theory to find a campus in violation of Title VI. Yet this theory's constitutional flaws are demonstrated by the reasoning of two courts that recently ruled on private lawsuits alleging Title VI violations. In both *Gartenberg v. Cooper Union*[69] and *Landau v. Haverford College*,[70] plaintiffs based their Title VI hostile-environment harassment claims on an aggregation of allegedly anti-Semitic incidents not necessarily aimed at the plaintiffs themselves, some involving constitutionally protected expression. In both cases, the federal courts held that constitutionally protected political expression could not be considered as either constituting or contributing to Title VI violations.

The *Cooper Union* court noted that "many of the alleged instances of harassment detailed in Gartenberg's Complaint are examples of pure speech on matters of public concern."[71] These included students' holding a vigil to "grieve and honor all those killed by decades of Israeli occupation and imperial violence," and distributing fliers celebrating "the 36th anniversary of the First Intifada."[72] The court stressed that this speech "cannot itself support a claim for an objectively hostile educational environment under this Court's interpretation of [Title VI],"[73] including at a private institution like Cooper Union.[74] Contrastingly, the court did permit the plaintiffs to pursue their Title VI complaint to the extent that it alleged illegal conduct, including an alarming incident in which Jewish students were forced to hide from a hostile mob in the library while the school's president escaped from the same building through a back exit.[75]

In the *Haverford* case, the court observed that plaintiffs attempted to establish a Title VI hostile environment claim "by citing some 25-plus incidents purportedly impacting the collective consciousness of 50-plus mostly unnamed individuals."[76] As in *Cooper Union*, the court noted that "several of Plaintiffs' allegations involve protected political expression, and cannot be regulated under the guise of nondiscrimination."[77] The court also pointed out that "[o]nly one allegation here involved speech targeted at a particular Plaintiff."[78] It captured the fundamental flaw in the cumulative theory of hostile-environment harassment in memorable terms, observing that combining multiple unrelated incidents into a "*gestalt* pleading cannot be employed as a strategy to avoid scrutiny."[79] Yet the essence of the cumulative theory of harassment is precisely that a campus's *gestalt*—its general quality or character—is being investigated and held against it.

As already indicated, the excessively vague, broad cumulative-harassment theory has the very same chilling effect on campus expression about the Israel-Gaza conflict as the excessively vague, broad IHRA definition. University officials are pressured at least to investigate—and perhaps also to punish—*any* expression about this topic, and students and faculty members are pressured to self-censor any such expression, for fear of increasing the likelihood of adverse consequences under Title VI not only for themselves individually, but also for their universities.

Far from Promoting Antidiscrimination Goals, Overly Broad Concepts of Harassing Speech May Well Undermine These Goals

Counterproductive Impacts of All Hate-Speech Codes

Like other campus speech codes, concepts of harassment that extend to expression beyond *Davis*'s definition inevitably suffer from undue vagueness and overbreadth, as reviewing courts have consistently ruled. They vest too much discretion in enforcing authorities, who predictably (in democratic societies) wield them disproportionately against minority voices and views—ironically, the intended beneficiaries of the restrictions. For this reason, many human-rights advocates worldwide have opposed "hate speech" restrictions, even when such restrictions are permitted by their countries' free-speech standards.[80]

The fact that hate-speech laws inevitably endanger views and speakers across the political spectrum is confirmed by recent experience under such laws in European countries. Journalist Glenn Greenwald cited many in a 2017 essay titled, "In Europe, Hate Speech Laws Are Often Used to Suppress and Punish Left-Wing Viewpoints." As he observed:

> Many Americans who long for Europe's hate speech restrictions assume that those laws are used to outlaw and punish expression of the bigoted ideas they most hate: racism, homophobia, Islamophobia, misogyny. Often, such laws are used that way. . . . But hate speech restrictions [in Europe] have frequently been used to constrain and sanction a wide range of political views that many left-wing censorship advocates would never dream could be deemed "hateful," and even against opinions which many of them likely share.[81]

Human-rights advocates have also opposed hate-speech restrictions because, far from advancing their desired goal of reducing hate speech's potential impact, they too often have the opposite effect: increasing the attention that the speech receives, and increasing sympathy for the speakers, who are celebrated by some who hear their messages as free-speech martyrs or heroes.

Unduly speech-restrictive concepts of hostile-environment harassment can also exacerbate rather than reduce discriminatory attitudes for another reason. By suppressing robust discussion about pertinent issues—including anti-Semitism, Islamophobia, and the Israel-Gaza war—these speech restrictions foreclose a constructive outlet for expressing, and possibly reducing, hostile emotions and ideas.

Counterproductive Impacts of an Overly Broad Concept of Harassing Expression Under Title IX

As explained above, universities (as well as the Obama and Biden administrations) have misinterpreted Title IX's ban on gender discrimination as authorizing or even requiring the suppression of all speech about sex and gender that any member of the campus community finds subjectively offensive—even when it has an important academic purpose, and even when it has a feminist perspective. A 2017 report by the American Association of University Professors documented and critiqued universities' "tendency to treat academic discussion of sex and sexuality as contributing to a hostile environment."[82]

One of the best-known and most egregious examples of Title IX's warped enforcement to suppress pro-feminist expression is the monthslong Star Chamber-style harassment investigation to which Northwestern University subjected film professor Laura Kipnis in 2015 because of an article she published in the *Chronicle of Higher Education*.[83] Not only was that article self-evidently academically important, given the respected forum in which it was published, but Kipnis was then charged with violating Title IX based on the very same distorted concept of sexual harassment that her article had criticized.[84]

Even beyond universities' widespread incorporation of an unduly broad concept of sexual harassment into their policies, such a concept has become widely accepted in campus culture. Too many students and faculty members avoid discussing topics related to sex and gender for fear of being accused of making someone "uncomfortable" or causing them "harm" (even if unintentionally).

Surveys consistently confirm the rampant campus self-censorship about these topics, even when they entail key public-policy issues. For example, in a 2023 comprehensive survey of university students, conducted for FIRE by College Pulse, almost half—49 percent—named abortion as a topic about which it is "difficult to have an open and honest conversation" on their campus. Likewise, 42 percent of respondents said that it is difficult to candidly discuss transgender issues on their campus. Even more concerning, considering Title IX's goal of promoting women's equal participation on campus, female students were substantially more likely than male students to say that they could not candidly discuss abortion (53 percent of female students vs. 45 percent of male students) or sexual assault (40 percent of female students vs. 29 percent of male students).[85]

Surely an essential component of equality for women and gender minorities on campus is the meaningful exercise of free-speech rights to discuss topics related to sex, sexuality, and gender. Accordingly, it is sadly ironic that Title IX, which aims to increase campus gender equality, has been twisted into a tool for suppressing such discussion.

Counterproductive Impacts of an Overly Broad Concept of Harassing Expression Under Title VI

Just as the overly broad concept of harassing expression about gender under Title IX (and campus policies) has caused substantial campus self-censorship, the same is true of the overly broad concept of harassing expression about race and ethnicity under Title VI. In the same 2023 College Pulse survey discussed above, 43 percent of students said that they couldn't candidly discuss "racial inequality." After the October 7, 2023, Hamas attacks, more than 26 percent of students said that they couldn't candidly discuss "the Israel/Palestinian conflict." Notably, liberal students were significantly more likely than moderate or conservative students to say this (30 percent, 22 percent, and 21 percent, respectively).[86]

Even beyond self-censorship, and even before Donald Trump took office, FIRE documented an "alarming" number of attempts to sanction constitutionally protected campus expression about the Israeli-Palestinian issue, many of which were successful. In October 2024, FIRE issued a report on the instances of such speech suppression that it had been able to document through June 15, 2024. Sean Stevens, FIRE's Senior Research Fellow in Polling and Analytics, summarized the eight-month-long record:

> Since Oct. 7, FIRE has recorded 138 deplatforming attempts targeting expression about the Israeli-Palestinian conflict. That's about three a week, or one every other day. . . . We've also recorded 77 attempts to sanction scholars for expression about the Israeli-Palestinian conflict, and 11 terminations. . . . [Moreover, there have been 167] recorded attempts to sanction students and student groups for expression regarding the Israeli-Palestinian conflict. That is four attempts to sanction students a week,

> and . . . half of these . . . succeed. This is likely just the tip of the iceberg, because our student data only reflect the publicly reported incidents that we've been able to review up to June 15, 2024. We are aware of many more since then, but their sheer number, in combination with sometimes limited information and/or lengthy adjudication processes, means that we are often one step behind when it comes to keeping up with the outcomes of these student sanction attempts. This means that it is likely that some kind of expression regarding the Israeli-Palestinian conflict was sanctioned on a college campus almost every single day in the past year.[87]

Again, there is a striking parallel between the misuse of Title IX to suppress expression about sex/gender and the misuse of Title VI to suppress expression about the Israel-Gaza war, as well as issues of anti-Semitism, Islamophobia, and other forms of discrimination. Compelling antidiscrimination goals are hindered, not helped, by distorting the laws into unconstitutional speech codes, suppressing the constructive dialogue that is essential for reducing hatred, hostility, and discrimination.

Recommended University Actions to Comply with Antidiscrimination Laws' Important Goals, Consistent with the First Amendment

Universities must adopt, enforce, and educate all community members about the specific concept of hostile-environment harassing conduct, including expression, that the Supreme Court set out in *Davis* as affording the baseline level of free-speech protection on campus: any such conduct must be "so severe, pervasive, and objectively offensive that it effectively bars the victim's access to an educational opportunity or benefit." Students must develop the understanding that merely being annoyed or offended does not give rise to a harassment claim, and that because their own expression will inevitably annoy or offend *someone,* they all benefit from this vital speech protection.

Universities must not include the IHRA "non-legally binding working definition" of anti-Semitism, or the examples included in its Appendix, in any policy.

Universities must resist government pressure to use the cumulative theory of hostile-environment harassment, above all refusing to use it to limit constitutionally protected speech. At the same time, universities must consistently enforce rules against violence and lawbreaking, as well as reasonable time, place, and manner rules, without regard for the viewpoints being expressed. If the rules are not needed, they should be repealed, not held in abeyance at officials' discretion.

Universities must pursue strategies for discouraging self-censorship and promoting vibrant discourse about even—indeed, especially—the most controversial and sensitive issues; they must support all members of the campus community in airing and considering the full range of perspectives on these issues. The most effective means for pursuing these goals are the very tools of liberal education that are (or should be) in every campus's wheelhouse. Examples include Harvard's 2025 decisions to explicitly prohibit grading based on political or ethical beliefs, and to enforce a non-attribution policy for classroom speech.

Crucially, these efforts must include intensive teaching about the principles and importance of academic freedom, free speech, and civil discourse. Throughout all of their interactions with actual and potential members of the campus community, universities must stress these themes, beginning with their recruitment and application materials, continuing with orientation programs for new students and faculty, and carrying through curricular and cocurricular programming. One example is Harvard's recently required short-answer question on its application form: "Describe a time when you strongly disagreed with someone about an idea or issue. How did you communicate or engage with this person? What did you learn from this experience?" Not only should students be able to answer these kinds of questions when applying to college, but even more importantly, their college education should continually increase the breadth and depth of their answers.

Conclusion

For decades, colleges have tried to curb identity-based harassment and discrimination through speech codes that single out disfavored viewpoints, despite repeated court rulings forbidding such censorship and a lack of evidence that the suppression had the desired effect. The most persistent strategy for perpetuating this censorship has been the mislabeling of First Amendment-protected speech as hostile-environment harassment, first under Title IX and now under Title VI. This approach, fueled by the Obama, Biden, and Trump administrations alike, continues to suppress expression and to subvert full-fledged inclusion.

Current resistance to the Trump administration's Title VI excesses offers a chance for all parties to course-correct. While the Obama administration prioritized reforming campus culture to curb sex discrimination, and the Trump administration has prioritized reforming campus culture to curb anti-Semitism, the priority henceforward—for all administrations and all educational institutions—must be to reform campus culture to curb discrimination against any members of the campus community while also curbing censorship and self-censorship. Campuses must not tolerate discrimination based on either identities or ideas.

9

Equal Protection and Academic Freedom

OLATUNDE JOHNSON*

Introduction

Equal-protection principles have unexpectedly emerged as a constraint on academic freedom in the United States. As the current US presidential administration takes steps to assert control over the governance, hiring, and curriculum at public and private schools and universities, it has invoked Title VI of the 1964 Civil Rights Act and enforcing the equal-protection clause as motivations. Federal agencies have claimed authority to terminate or threaten federal funding to institutions, contending that schools are engaged in "illegal DEI" and that they are failing to take adequate steps to counter anti-Semitism on their campuses. Enforcement of antidiscrimination law has become the new rationale for constraints on speech on college campuses.

The administration's unprecedented invocation of agencies' substantive and procedural authority under Title VI presents a new chapter in a long-running negotiation between equality values and free expression on campuses. Some of the Supreme Court's pronouncements on the meaning of academic freedom have come in equal-protection cases. In his concurrence in *Regents of University of California v. Bakke* (1978), Justice Powell asserted that universities could pursue race-conscious affirmative action to advance diversity. He argued that advancing diversity was consistent with the "academic freedom" that was essential to the flourishing of universities and a "transcendent value to all of us."[1] This concurrence famously contended that "[t]he atmosphere of 'speculation, experiment and creation'—so essential to the quality of higher education—is widely believed to be promoted by a diverse student body."[2] Academic freedom, affirmed

* Olatunde Johnson is the Jerome B. Sherman Professor of Law at Columbia Law School.

Olatunde Johnson, *Equal Protection and Academic Freedom*. In: *Academic Freedom in the Era of Trump*. Edited by: Lee C. Bollinger and Geoffrey R. Stone, Oxford University Press. © Oxford University Press (2026). DOI: 10.1093/9780197854877.003.0010 and expanded in *Grutter v. Bollinger* (2003),[3] provided the legal and normative grounding for higher-education affirmative action at least until the 2023 decision in *SFFA v. Harvard,* which acknowledges the worthiness of diversity as a goal for academic institutions but says that pursuit of this goal cannot meet the high standard necessary for justifying explicitly race-conscious admissions.[4]

In *Bakke,* equal-protection principles existed in harmony with academic freedom and First Amendment principles. The tension between the two concepts, however, was evident in other domains. Anti-harassment policies and "speech codes" were enacted to address racism on college campuses and manage the tensions on racially and ethnically diverse campuses. In the late 1980s and the 1990s, hate speech and anti-harassment codes faced First Amendment challenges, and several lower courts struck down university speech codes for violating the First Amendment.[5] These cases highlighted the potential tension between the First Amendment and antidiscrimination goals. They also showed the indeterminacy of the mere invocation of "academic freedom," which could be called on both in support of and against speech codes and anti-harassment policies. And then, more recently, the Supreme Court's decision in *SFFA v. Harvard* upended *Bakke*'s compromise of values by barely mentioning "academic freedom" (it comes up only twice in the majority opinion when summarizing *Bakke*) and proclaiming "diversity" "not sufficiently coherent for purposes of strict scrutiny."[6]

The current actions by the administration take a new turn in this contestation between equality and academic freedom. Arguably, the administration invokes equal-protection principles to constrain academic freedom. The centerpiece has been to address anti-Semitism, arguing that, even beyond slurs, threats, or insults to Jewish and Israeli students, universities' failure to adequately respond to the Israel-Gaza antiwar protests and to harassment of Jewish students in 2023–24 provide a rationale for increased federal review of university governance, hiring, and curriculum. The administration also deploys the *SFFA* ruling on race-conscious admissions as an opening not just to direct admissions processes but also to alter on-campus programming and teaching ("illegal DEI") that it sees as "toxically indoctrinat[ing] students" and "stigmatiz[ing]."[7] Title VI's equal-protection goals are thus enlisted to control schools and universities.

This chapter examines the legal implications of the administration's enlisting of Title VI and equality law to assert control over schools and universities. It puts these actions in a larger context, examining their relationship to the expansion of executive power in the United States and polarized racial politics. The current actions against universities are connected to subnational movements over the past decade that give parents and school administrators more authority to ban particular books from K–12 schools and libraries and legislative efforts to forbid the teaching of "critical race theory" and of "divisive concepts" around race, gender, and sexuality.[8] The actions of the federal administration against universities since January 2025 represent an escalation of these tactics invoking Title VI's conditioned spending regime and the *SFFA* case. They take place alongside efforts to control the "knowledge institutions" of democratic society, which—as commentators have noted—are those institutions that produce research, promote inquiry, and allow dissent and protest that are often threatening to anti-liberal political regimes.[9] And they are made possible by an expansion of the power of the executive branch. This chapter contends that these efforts to control universities reflect more than the policy preferences of the current administration. They also stem from longer-running contestations in a diverse society over who controls knowledge production at elite institutions, speech and protest on campuses, and how admissions and access to these institutions should be structured. The chapter analyzes these challenges and offers provisional paths forward for advancing the goals of equality and the "atmosphere of speculation, experiment and creation" at schools and universities.

The Threat to Academic Freedom

The executive branch and federal agencies are currently invoking equal-protection and antidiscrimination law, regulation, and norms to exert greater control over universities and colleges. An opening salvo was the February 14, 2025, letter from the federal Department of Education to all educational institutions that receive federal funds, using its authority pursuant to Title VI of the Civil Rights Act of 1964, which prohibits discrimination on the basis of race and national origin in federally funded institutions. According to the letter, the *SFFA* decision applied "broadly," forbidding not just race-conscious admissions programs but all use of "race in decisions" relevant to financial aid, administrative support, housing, graduation ceremonies, and "all other aspects of student, academic, and campus life."[10] The letter states that the administration would now scrutinize admissions and outreach programs to rid them of "illegal diversity equity and inclusion," forbid "racial stereotypes" in training and discipline, and examine curriculum and training programs that "toxically indoctrinate students with the false premise that the United States is built upon 'systemic and structural racism' and advanced discriminatory policies and practices."[11] The letter purports to forbid universities from adopting programs that "teach students that certain racial groups bear unique moral burdens that others do not." The letter directs federal-funding recipients to comply with civil-rights law as interpreted by the letter, announces the possibility of agency investigation, and encourages reporting of violators through a Department of Education website. (As discussed below, the letter has, as of this writing, been enjoined by a district court.)

The next key move took place in March 2025, when the Trump administration sent a letter to Columbia University stating that, because the University had failed to protect "American students and faculty from anti-Semitic violence and harassment," $400 million of federal funds to the university would be paused or terminated.[12] According to the letter, regaining the funding would require the university to comply with a number of demands, including changes to student disciplinary policies and procedures stemming from campus protests; placement of the Middle Eastern, South Asian, and African Studies department "under academic receivership"; and reform of admissions to various schools within the university. The university did not legally challenge the letter but entered into negotiations with the administration, which were settled on July 23, 2025.[13] The administration took even more dramatic action against Harvard, freezing $2.2 billion in federal grants against Harvard, a matter that is being litigated as of this writing.[14] Then, in June 2025, the administration pressed for the resignation of the president of the University of Virginia based on what it alleged were violations of Title VI in its admissions programs and efforts to address racial and ethnic inequality on campus.[15] And in August 2025, the administration demanded that the president of George Mason University personally apologize for diversity, equity, and inclusion (DEI) efforts that the Administration deemed to violate Title VI.[16] As of this writing, the Administration is investigating the University of California system for violations of the Fourteenth Amendment and Title VI of the Civil Rights Act of 1964, 42 U.S.C. § 2000d (Title VI), and threatening the system with the loss of $1 billion in federal funding.[17] Title VI is the thread running through these directives. And thus the scope and reach of Title VI, and its relationship to academic freedom, free expression, and the First Amendment, will be determined through the resolution of these purported violations in the coming years.

Title VI conditions federal funding, and the claim is that universities have discriminated against Jewish and Israeli students after the campus protests of 2023 and 2024, or that universities are engaged in "illegal DEI" in violation of the *Students for Fair Admissions* ruling.[18] It is not unusual or out of bounds to use Title VI to investigate and redress anti-Semitism or racial discrimination. What makes the invocation of Title VI remarkable in this context is the violation of the procedural requirements of the statute, the breadth of the charges, and the remedy sought, which intrudes broadly into admissions, curriculum, on-campus programming, hiring, and governance. Simply put, no administration has in the history of Title VI effectuated or even attempted the termination of federal funds on this scale.

An example of the scope and threat to academic freedom is evident in the agreement that the administration struck with Columbia. To settle claims under Title VI, the administration placed conditions on faculty hiring, curriculum, faculty governance, admissions (including the admission of international students), and student discipline and protest policy. Though any of these changes may be worthy for a university to pursue on its own, this deal now requires the university to make these changes or give up a sizable amount of federal funding. Because of universities' reliance on federal funding for grants and student-loan programs, the effect is to create strong pressures to comply with the government's demands regardless of the legality of the process or remedies sought.[19]

While definitions of "academic freedom" vary, government control of teaching, hiring, and admissions is central to almost any conception of the term. A "foundational principle of academic freedom" is that faculty, not government, "should determine professional standards for the academy" and determine curriculum.[20] Scholars have described academic freedom as a notion distinct from "freedom of speech": "Academic freedom has a more specific purpose. It protects the pursuit and dissemination of knowledge through free inquiry and ensures that university research and teaching is authoritative and unbiased."[21] In *Sweezy v. New Hampshire*, the authoritative case on academic freedom under the First Amendment, the Supreme Court emphasizes that: "[t]eachers and students must always remain free to inquire to study and to evaluate," and "scholarship cannot flourish in an atmosphere of suspicion and distrust." The Supreme Court and lower courts have also interpreted "academic freedom" to extend to university governance, including "autonomous decision-making"[22] and the right to "manage an academic community and evaluate teaching and scholarship free from [government] interference."[23] As discussed in more detail below, in addition to the freedom of institutions to control teaching, curriculum, and research, some of the federal-agency actions also risk harm to free speech and expression by individual faculty and students.

These efforts at government control take place within a larger context of democratic erosion in the United States.[24] Doctrinally, academic freedom is frequently recognized as a core component of democracy. *Sweezy* notes that American universities play a "vital role in a democracy" and goes further in contending (perhaps dramatically) that, without thriving and free universities, "civilization will stagnate and die."[25] More recently, academics have characterized the Trump administration's efforts to control universities as part of a larger pattern of restrictions against "knowledge institutions."[26] Scholar Vicki Jackson has connected the attack on universities to attacks on the media and courts—institutions that all produce knowledge, contest the State's control of information, and seek to hold arbitrary state power accountable.[27] Executive-branch efforts to control universities are a trans-national phenomenon, as political leaders in other countries experiencing executive aggrandizement and democratic erosion have attacked academic and universities considered to be places of intellectual dissent and student protest."[28]

Relatedly, the focus on race that is exhibited in the demand letters and executive orders reflect this administration's particular investment in (re)shaping who has access to elite institutions and to the dissemination of ideas around questions of race. In particular, it can be connected to a broader effort by Trump and conservative social-movement leaders to shape the teaching of history in ways that de-emphasize slavery and racial inequality,[29] and to mobilize white identity politics either for the sake of political gains or to advance an ethno-nationalist conception.[30]

Even as these frameworks of academic freedom and democratic erosion are useful for understanding the attacks on higher-educational institutions, they are made possible by disagreement about the role and operation of higher education in the United States, particularly at elite institutions. The administration's actions exploit divisions within and external to universities on matters such as race, anti-Semitism, and viewpoint diversity. And these attacks take place at a moment of broader distrust of elite expertise and concerns about the cost and value of higher education.[31] Contradictorily, higher education is criticized as deepening inequality—the divide between those who attend college and those who do not—and as not providing a sufficient return on investment.

Keeping this broader political economy in mind, this chapter next takes up the legal implications of the administration's use of Title VI. First, it examines the use of Title VI's conditional-spending structure in a way that unsettles the long-standing relationship between the federal government and universities and the separation of powers. Second, it looks at the leveraging of *SSFA* to reshape admissions, outreach, curriculum, and "DEI" programs. And lastly, it considers how the use of Title VI reopens unresolved questions about how to balance free expression and antidiscrimination law and values.

Title VI and Executive Power

The demands placed on universities are justified as enforcing Title VI of the 1964 Civil Rights Act. The choice of Title VI is connected to executive aggrandizement in the United States. Scholars have noted that democratic erosion occurs through the exploitation of constitutional tools such as executive power,[32] even as these aggrandizements announce a fealty to law, or at least the performance of legality—a type of "autocratic legalism."[33] Two features of Title VI are useful along those lines: (1) the statute gives power to the executive branch, specifically through the leveraging of federal spending by agencies; and (2) Title VI is an antidiscrimination statute which appeals to moral as well as legal authority.

Title VI, enacted as part of the Civil Rights Act of 1964, forbids discrimination on the basis of race, color, and national origin in programs and activities that receive federal financial assistance (42 U.S.C. 2000d et seq.). It applies to a broad range of programs and activities (such as education, environment, housing, agriculture, and health) and to state and local government as well as to private actors that receive federal funds. The goal of the statute, as expressed by the drafters, was to leverage federal funding to advance equal-protection principles. As President John F. Kennedy stated when he introduced the Civil Rights Act: "Simple justice requires that public funds, to which all taxpayers of all races contribute, not be spent in any fashion which encourages, entrenches, subsidizes, or results in racial discrimination."[34] As Congress was expanding federal aid to elementary and secondary schools through the Title I program for poor schools, Title VI allowed agencies to put pressure on K-12 school districts that refused to desegregate. Professor Gerald Rosenberg's famous study of Title VI shows that *Brown v. Board of Education* had little effect on desegregation in much of the South until the passage of Title VI gave the federal Department of Health, Education and Welfare (HEW) the ability to threaten the loss of federal funding to school systems.[35] Title VI also applies to higher-education institutions, and it would play a role in the desegregation of Southern universities, though only after civil-rights groups brought litigation against the federal government for its failure to implement the statute.[36] Commentators credit Title VI enforcement, though initially slow, with the development of desegregation plans in higher-education institutions throughout the South.[37]

The federal government's power to terminate funding makes Title VI one of the most powerful civil-rights statutes.[38] Providing that amount of power to the executive branch was controversial from the statute's inception. Southern congressional members opposed Title VI for a range of reasons, including the expansion of executive power and concerns about intrusion in subnational government authority.[39] The resulting statutory compromise to address these concerns makes the Trump administration's present use of Title VI against universities startling. To begin, the termination of federal funding contravenes the language of the statute, which lists specific procedural steps that agencies have to follow before terminating federal funds. The statute requires agencies to first negotiate a compliance agreement for settling the discrimination complaints. The agency can then terminate federal funds only if the university does not reach a compliance agreement or fails to adhere to one. At that point, the statute requires a hearing and an express finding of noncompliance, which must be determined "on the record" by an administrative law judge.[40] There is still more process. Any administratively adjudicated finding of noncompliance can only become final thirty days after the agency has filed a "full written report" with the relevant congressional committees specifying the basis for termination.[41] That process was not followed in the Harvard and Columbia cases.

Congress put in place these procedural protections for the precise purpose of limiting executive power. When Congress was drafting Title VI, the termination authority was a key point of contention.[42] Civil-rights advocates argued that the threat of termination was important in order to get K-12 Southern school districts to desegregate after years of not adhering to *Brown*.[43] But some members of Congress feared that the capacity to terminate funding was too much power to leave in the hands of the executive branch.[44] The compromise was to allow funding termination but only after the steps described above—requiring negotiation, a hearing, a finding on the record, and congressional review.[45] Congress also inserted a requirement that limited the power of termination to the specific program that engaged in discrimination.[46] Congress retained this "pinpoint" requirement for funding termination even after it amended the statute in 1988. This amendment is significant in that it came after the *Grove City College v. Bell* (1984) case, in which a religious institution contested the federal government's application of Title IX (modeled on Title VI) against the university. In *Grove City*, the Supreme Court limited the substantive reach of Title IX to the program or activity receiving federal funds.[47] In other words, if the federal funds involved a student-loan or -grant program, then only the financial-aid office would be covered. Overriding the veto of President Reagan, Congress in 1988 amended the statute to override the *Grove City* decision and to provide that when *any* part of a school received federal funds, the entire school was covered by Title IX or Title VI.[48] This was the position urged by civil-rights groups, because it expanded the reach of Title VI. Significantly, however, Congress did *not* allow termination to extend beyond the specific program or entity in which the civil-rights violation occurred: it specifically retained the pinpoint provision for funding termination.[49]

The other check on executive power in the statute is its emphasis on voluntary resolution—the development of negotiated compliance agreements between schools and the agency. As Judge David Tatel, a former chair of the agency who led the Office of Civil Rights at HEW from 1977 to 1979, recently expressed in a declaration appended to an amicus brief opposing the funding cuts to Harvard, the point of the termination tool was that it would rarely be needed, since the funds were necessary for schools and students.[50] Negotiated compliance leveraged federal funds to promote student inclusion, but the agency took care not to threaten the very existence of public or private institutions and to take into account their institutional context when seeking compliance. Judge Tatel described this balance as necessary "because college and university leaders knew their systems better than the federal government and to respect the independence and autonomy of the state higher educational systems."[51]

Administrative history is also relevant here: it was only in a few instances in the entire history of Title VI that federal funds were terminated to institutions (including to institutions that refused to desegregate over decades).[52] And there is no evidence that funds were ever terminated to an institution because of a hostile educational environment (which is the claim advanced by the Trump administration, discussed below), much less one that required balancing the rights and norms of academic freedom and free expression. The scope of the remedies sought for the alleged Title VI violations by universities, remedies that extend to curriculum, hiring, and governance structures, also go far beyond the remedies it has negotiated to resolve Title VI complaints in the past. Thus, there appears to be no administrative precedent for interpreting the statute in this way, violating core requirements of regularity in the exercise of administrative power.[53]

In addition to the violations of Title VI itself, the Administration's actions raise other problems of separation of powers. The executive branch lacks constitutional power to create new conditions on federal funds that Congress has not written into the statute. Specifically, the Constitution gives Congress, not the executive branch, power to spend money and condition its use.[54] Any legislation enacted through the spending clause of the US Constitution (part of the authority for Title VI) would need to give recipients "clear notice" of the funding terms and conditions in order to limit agency power, protect federalism principles, and avoid the infringement of grant recipients' due-process rights.[55] The executive branch's effective additions of new conditions violate these limitations on spending.

The Supreme Court has also made clear that no branch of the federal government can place conditions on federal funds that violate other provisions of the US Constitution. This "unconstitutional conditions" doctrine thus prohibits the federal government from leveraging federal funds to engage in viewpoint discrimination against universities or coercing them into engaging in viewpoint discrimination.[56] Professors Evelyn Douek and Genevieve Lakier argue in addition that the Trump administration's enforcement of Title VI creates a related constitutional risk in its use of executive power to coerce regulated entities into violating the First Amendment rights of third parties. They argue that the Trump administration is using Title VI to force academic institutions into violating the First Amendment rights of students and faculty—a practice known as "jawboning."[57] Both unconstitutional conditions and jawboning are implicated here only to the extent that the First Amendment has indeed been violated, a matter taken up in the next section.

What this analysis shows so far is that executive-branch interpretations of Title VI violate the statute itself, and that they risk violations of separation of powers. It is not the first time, certainly, that the executive branch has been accused of overreach in its enforcement of an antidiscrimination spending statute. Title IX, Title VI's sister statute, which prohibits sex discrimination in programs and activities that receive federal funds, has faced recurring criticism. The *Grove*

City case, discussed above, arose when a religious school objected to having to certify compliance with Title IX. The college's arguments were supported by religious organizations and by President Reagan, who objected to agencies' coercive enforcement of Title IX as an example of government overreach and unwarranted intrusion into private schools.[58] Both President Biden and President Obama faced criticisms for their Title IX guidance. Commentators and some university leaders criticized the Obama Department of Education for its aggressive use of Title IX to address sexual assault on campus.[59] Several state attorneys general filed suit against the Biden Administration for its interpretation of Title IX to reach discrimination based on gender identity.[60] Disputes over the limits of executive power over schools and universities are not new.

The Trump administration's use of executive power to enforce Title VI, however, differs from these examples in the scale and breadth of the funding termination and termination threats and in its sidestepping of the statute's procedural requirements. The next step may be that courts step in to curb the administration's actions. This has already happened in one instance, when a district court held in September 2025 that the Harvard funding termination violates Title VI and due process.[61]

If courts do not step in, there is a risk that the administration will continue to use the statute to pressure universities. In theory, Congress could play a role to address executive-branch overreach. It could hold hearings that focus not just on actual incidents of anti-Semitism on college campuses but also on the threats to academic freedom. This might provide some political check on the executive branch's assertion of authority. But it seems unlikely that Congress will assert its own institutional power in this way in the absence of partisan change.

Title VI and Free Expression

The executive branch's enforcement of Title VI revives long-standing questions about how to balance antidiscrimination law values with free expression. The administration's enforcement of Title VI is largely centered on the claim that universities are creating a "hostile educational environment" for Jewish and Israeli students. After the Hamas attacks of October 7, 2023, and the widespread protests against the ensuing military efforts by Israel, the Department of Education received an increase in the number of civil-rights complaints by Jewish and Israeli students alleging harassment by peers.[62] Though the Department of Education also received a large number of complaints from Palestinian, Arab, Middle Eastern, and Muslim students after October 2023, these are not the focus of the current Administration's enforcement efforts.[63] Note that while Title VI does not prohibit discrimination based on religion, its prohibition of discrimination based on race and national origin has been held to extend to claims based on "shared ancestry."[64] The Department of Education for the past decade has interpreted Title VI to apply to Muslims and Jewish students under this shared-ancestry argument.

The aspect of Title VI that is at issue is the requirement that universities take steps to address a "hostile educational environment"—highly offensive behavior and speech by students against their peers. This standard took shape in the wake of harassment of students of color, primarily black students, on newly integrated college and university campuses in the 1980s.[65] The standard for peer harassment in schools and universities derives from the harassment standard developed by the Supreme Court in a fair-employment sexual-harassment case, *Meritor Savings Bank, FSB v. Vinson.*[66] Drawing on *Meritor,* the Supreme Court held in *Davis v. Monroe County,* a Title IX case, that to be actionable, student-on-student harassment must be "so severe, pervasive, and objectively offensive, and [] so undermine[] and detract[] from the victims' educational experience, that the victim-students are effectively denied equal access to an institution's resources and opportunity."[67] The Department of Education adopted this standard for federal grantees under Title VI, stating that the speech or conduct must be "severe or pervasive" (using the disjunctive)[68] enough to deny or limit a student's ability to participate in or benefit from the educational program.[69]

The danger of harassment law is that it can infringe on First Amendment-protected speech. Drawing the line between harassment and free speech became an issue on college campuses in the 1980s. Responding to student harassment, some schools adopted campus speech codes that prohibited speech that created an "intimidating, hostile or demeaning" environment or that "stigmatizes or victimizes an individual" on the basis of their identity. And in prominent cases involving public institutions, those speech codes were struck down by lower courts as violating the First Amendment.[70] At the time, the codes did not limit themselves to what is now defined as harassment under federal civil-rights law. Instead, they reached into speech that "victimizes" or "stigmatizes" without the severity, frequency, and objective-offensiveness requirements articulated in cases such as *Meritor* and *Davis.* These codes were struck down as violating the First Amendment. As one scholar summarized the doctrine at the time: "Every campus . . . hate speech code that has been challenged on First Amendment grounds in court has been ruled unconstitutional."[71]

Universities responded to these decisions by limiting their speech codes to the type of severe or pervasive behavior that would violate civil-rights law. And to some legal analysts this was an appropriate response, because speech that meets that high threshold for harassment is not protected speech.[72] But even assuming that this general approach may suffice for the facial legality of campus speech codes, it does not answer whether the application of Title VI's hostile-environment standard in any particular context violates the First Amendment. For one, the hostile-environment standard is broad and its application is fact-dependent. Assuming that slurs, threats, and epithets directed at an individual could be prohibited consistent with the First Amendment, can Title VI prohibit speech more broadly if it gives serious offense?[73] What if the offensive speech is not an epithet or slur and is not targeted at an individual, but stems from political protests opposing Israel's actions in Gaza? This was the case for a portion of the civil-rights complaints received by universities and the Department of Education in 2023 and 2024. The hostile-educational-environment standard doesn't by its own terms create a limiting principle that avoids First Amendment problems, by, for instance, excluding political or academic speech. And the Department of Education's guidance even prior to the current administration did not provide a clear test for when application of harassment law should be avoided so as to protect political or academic speech. The Department's administrative guidance indicated that it would interpret Title VI to align with the First Amendment, stating, for instance, that views on a country's policies or political protests will not "typically implicate Title VI" and that it would open an investigation for classroom comments or protest signs [only] if they involved "offensive stereotypes" or "targeted specific Jewish students using ethnic stereotypes."[74] But given the thicket of First Amendment issues implicated by the 2023–24 protests, the guidance could have done much more to clarify what types of speech would be immune from Title VI investigation, regardless of their subjective or objective offensiveness to students. The prior language in the guidance seems to be drawing a line between targeted and non-targeted speech, but it does not fully elaborate. And in its discussion of "offensive stereotypes," the guidance risks the kind of vagueness that was at issue in the cases involving campus speech codes.

Balancing harassment and free speech is difficult from a normative and doctrinal perspective and had been the subject of much debate even before the current administration's enforcement action. But attending to the First Amendment concerns becomes even more urgent given the threat of federal funding loss. The termination threat creates incentives for institutions to adopt rules that discipline or limit speech that may otherwise be protected in order to avoid retribution from the current administration. And as noted above, the agreements that the administration seeks against universities are not tailored to remedying alleged harassment against students (such as by expediting disciplinary proceedings, increasing staffing for affected communities, or improving anti-harassment training), but go further into the operation and governance of universities.

Given the administration's aggressive invocation of Title VI, it will likely be the courts that determine the First Amendment limits on the application of Title VI's hostile-environment standard. A trial court in New York has already weighed in.

In a suit brought in federal district court in 2024 against Cooper Union in New York City, a judge ruled that Title VI should be read consistently with the First Amendment, and that it had no application to political speech.[75]

The First Amendment is also implicated not just in the definition of prohibited harassment but in federal agencies' use of Title VI to coerce universities into adopting academic or political priorities that mirror the executive branch. Also, because the remedies sought by the administration against universities extend beyond discipline or training related to anti-Semitism and reach hiring, curriculum, and governance, they implicate the First Amendment. The district court in the Harvard case found this when it held that, in addition to violating the statutory procedural requirements of Title VI, the administration was directly violating the First Amendment rights of Harvard by seeking to control hiring and curriculum and by coercing Harvard into violating the First Amendment rights of campus stakeholders.[76]

Extending SFFA

The other move that permits extensive intrusion into universities is the executive branch's broad interpretation of the *SFFA* case to alter admissions practices and to influence hiring, curriculum, and program under the banner of "illegal DEI." In *SFFA*, the Supreme Court held that it violated Title VI and the Equal Protection Clause to consider an applicant's race and ethnicity as factors in admission for the purposes of advancing diversity. Moving away from its 2003 decision in *Grutter v. Bollinger*, the Supreme Court stated that diversity was not a coherent or sufficiently compelling government interest for purposes of the strict-scrutiny test demanded by the Equal Protection doctrine. Title VI's prohibition on discrimination is read coextensively with the Equal Protection Clause; thus, the ruling opens the door for enforcement of *SFFA*'s prohibition of race-conscious affirmative action to all federally funded programs. Because of Title VI, the *SFFA* ruling affects not just public schools but any independent and private institutions that receives federal funding.

In contention, however, is the question of whether *SFFA* goes as far as the administration urges. The *SFFA* decision explicitly addresses only admissions decisions, which the Court argues are necessarily "zero sum."[77] But the administration's guidance purports to reach "financial aid, administrative support, housing, graduation ceremonies" and "all other aspects of student, academic, and campus life."[78] The administration's February 14th guidance letter also invoked *SFFA* as a way to curb "illegal diversity equity and inclusion" programs, and forbid unspecified programs and curriculum that advance "racial stereotypes" or that "toxically indoctrinate students with the false premise that the United

States is built upon 'systemic and structural racism' and advanced discriminatory policies and practices."[79]

One of the administration's goals seems to be creating an admissions system solely reliant on GPA and standardized test scores. The administration's agreement with Columbia University required it to adopt "merit-based admissions," to surrender racial and ethnic data on admissions. Then, in August 2025, the Administration essentially applied this requirement to the entire country when it issued an executive order that requires all schools that receive federal funds to report detailed racial data to the federal government. The executive order articulated the concern that universities are using "overt and hidden proxies" in a way that thwarts the goal of "ridding society of shameful, dangerous racial hierarchies."[80] Under Title VI, the administration would have authority to investigate credible claims that universities are continuing to consider race as a factor in admissions. The move into what the administration calls "proxies," however, is much murkier. The *SFFA* decision explicitly allows universities to continue to evaluate whether a particular applicant has overcome hardship. Specifically, the opinion states that "nothing in this opinion should be construed as prohibiting universities from considering an applicant's discussion of how race affected his or her life, be it through discrimination, inspiration, or otherwise."[81] The administration's interpretation threatens the notion that universities have freedom in shaping their student body as long as it does not violate the Constitution or Title VI.

The forbidding of teaching about forms of inequality particularly, while not well-explained, is suggested to violate Title VI and *SFFA* because it creates stigmatic harm to students. This is sufficiently vague and far afield from *SFFA* that it seems unlikely to withstand judicial scrutiny. Indeed, as of this writing, a court has already enjoined this aspect of the February 14th guidance letter for being "arbitrary and capricious" under the Administrative Procedure Act and for violating the First Amendment rights of faculty and staff. More generally, the administration's efforts to purge what it calls "illegal DEI" from campuses threatens free expression and academic freedom. DEI is not a legally precise term; it could be used to refer to anything from compliance programs in response to discrimination to anti-bias training to programs that seek to promote cross-cultural or ethnic/racial solidarity. And programs such as the aforementioned do not generally violate civil statutes or equal-protection law, and could do so only if they deny a person access to particular services on the basis of a characteristic that is explicitly protected by civil-rights law.

The broader goal of the executive branch seems to be advancing a very expansive notion of colorblindness that forbids efforts to address or understand racial inequality.[82] Universities are now the terrain in which those ideas of colorblindness are being advanced.

Higher Education and Inclusive Democracy Going Forward

The executive-branch actions described so far may be stopped by courts. Rulings may protect academic freedom and free expression and limit executive-branch power over universities. But the administration's actions raise more enduring questions about the law and policy governing higher education, and the values served by higher education in a democracy.

The first important question that will demand attention regards the power that statutes such as Title VI give the executive branch over higher-education institutions. If the current administration is indeed overreaching its power, as this chapter suggests, then this raises questions about how to create more resilient constraints on the use of spending to exert control over universities. Title VI is already quite clear about the procedural steps that must be followed before terminating funds. However, it may be that even stronger statutory protections—for instance, an explicit statutory limitation on the ability of the executive branch to require institutions to change research, hiring, curriculum, or governance—will be needed to explicitly protect free expression and academic freedom. This would allow statutes like Title VI to continue to exist, but with sharper constraints. As a practical matter, it may be unrealistic to expect the current Congress to adopt such rules, but it seems a worthy focus for higher-education reformers concerned about academic freedom.

A second issue goes beyond legal constraints to the relationship between the federal government and universities. Executive-branch efforts to control universities raise the question of whether universities should rely less on federal funding. While most institutions would be wise to rethink the extent of their reliance on federal funds, it is unlikely that any research institution could wholly reject federal funds and remain capable of producing scientific research. Since the middle of the 20th century, the funding pact between federal government and universities (both public and private) has driven scientific research, and it is not clear that there is another equally viable source of funding.[83] And in any event, universities and colleges do not simply want to disavow federal funding entirely, as the federal government also provides aid to students in the form of Pell Grants for very low-income students. If, in the near term, universities continue to need federal funds, it will need to be evident (and made clear to public) how these funds are not just an exercise in elite opportunity hoarding but redound to the public good.

A third subject is that of admissions, which the current administration is trying to remake. It puts on the table questions that go far beyond the balance between standardized tests and qualitative factors. At issue is how admissions should be structured at top research institutions. Race-conscious affirmative action has always provided a limited answer to the question of universities' role in advancing social mobility. Other questions should be on the table, including efforts to reduce the cost of higher education, models to increase the size of the student body at the more selective institutions, and models that are fair and legitimate for assessing merit and ability to excel at college-level work. The approaches of selective and research universities to inclusion and to addressing structural barriers would need to explore efforts that go beyond admissions. For instance, the conception of universities as "anchor institutions" fuels the creation of university partnerships in their surrounding communities, especially with high schools and community colleges, and the development of joint teaching and research that provides opportunity to students and faculty beyond the formal walls of an elite campus.[84] This may seem far afield from the questions of academic freedom, but the attack on selective, elite, and research institutions that receive federal funds invites a reassessment of the extent to which elite and selective universities are entrenching or exacerbating forms of inequality that run counter to the inclusive goals that birthed Title VI.[85]

Lastly, there are the fraught issues of expression on campuses, given the range of identities and social backgrounds on any campus, and the perspectives and ideas they bring to academic and political discourse. As the doctrinal questions involving free expression and Title VI remain unsettled in courts, universities could take on the work within their own campuses of balancing inclusion and free-expression values. The battles over campus free speech and protests are reoccurring, and the more recent disputes reflect conflicts within university communities. The administration's ability to pressure universities is built on decades-long battles over speech, identity, and inclusion on campuses, as well as more recent concerns from students, faculty, and alumni that universities in 2023–24 were too tolerant of protesters and of anti-Semitic incidents on campus.[86] In this context, it is worthwhile for universities to develop their own ideas, strategies, and programs that promote the flourishing and participation of all students on campus while also allowing the expression of ideas, research, and speech that advances knowledge. This might involve shoring up viewpoint-neutral rules for disruptive activities and protests, and then dealing with the harm or hurt caused by debates over political or academic speech through a less punitive framework. Universities have an interest in developing students who can fully participate in learning and in campus activities, and who can interact with each other and their faculty critically, ethically, and as "confident pluralists."[87] Building these qualities in students and in campus discourse will involve every aspect of how university life is structured, from teaching to orienting students (and faculty and staff) and building a sense of cohesion among stakeholders in a university. Given the state of political polarization in the United States, one cannot be naive or romantic about what this work will entail.[88] Yet if campuses are to thrive in the way imagined by cases such as *Sweeney* and *Bakke*, it seems necessary.

10

Little Fascists Everywhere

The National Socialist Playbook of Trump's War on Universities

MARY ANNE FRANKS*

Introduction

A word frequently used to describe the second Trump administration's comprehensive and devastating assault on free speech generally and academic freedom in particular is "unprecedented." While it is true that there is no real predecessor in US history for the breadth and depth of the MAGA movement to destroy higher education—even the McCarthy period pales in comparison in fervor and scope—the Nazification of German universities in the 1920s–30s provides eerie and instructive parallels. The Nazification movement, like the MAGA movement, was organized around unquestioning obedience to a single leader and, correspondingly, hostility toward democratic ideals. The frontline soldiers of Hitler's war on universities were students resentful of progressive changes to higher education, and the tactics they used to convert German universities into right-wing propaganda factories closely resemble the ones used today to lay siege to American universities: disrupting classrooms, surveilling professors, and monitoring curricula for "undesirable" ideas; countering the "liberal indoctrination" of students with external speakers promoting far-right talking points; purging "degenerate" books from schools and libraries; and organizing watchlists, harassment campaigns, and public exposures of allegedly biased or

* Eugene L. and Barbara A. Bernard Professor in Intellectual Property, Technology, and Civil Rights Law, George Washington Law School; President and Legislative & Tech Policy Director, Cyber Civil Rights Initiative. My thanks to Jishan Ahmed for excellent research assistance.

Mary Anne Franks, *Little Fascists Everywhere*. In: *Academic Freedom in the Era of Trump*.
Edited by: Lee C. Bollinger and Geoffrey R. Stone, Oxford University Press. DOI: 10.1093/9780197854877.003.0011

immoral professors, with the goal of having them removed from their positions. And, in a crucial moment in their push for totalitarian control, the Nazis used the murder of a young, charismatic Party member known for his provocative debate style as a pretext to escalate their ruthless repression of dissent and violence against critics of the regime.

"Alone among the inhabitants of the academic world of the 1930s," writes Michael Steinberg,

> the Nazis seemed to have a clear idea of where they and the universities were going. The universities were not equipped to deal with violence, disorder, or serious attacks on the professors' right to teach freely. They were confronted by a student generation that had little use for past tradition, and they found themselves unable to deal with them. There were few voices courageous enough to warn . . . that if the enemies of liberty were permitted to operate without challenge their appetites would only grow until the inevitable disaster.[1]

German institutions of higher education did not fall to the Nazis because of the force of their numbers. The majority of administrators, professors, and students were not Nazi Party members. But the non-Nazi majority largely stood by as the rhetoric and the conduct of the Nazi student minority became increasingly violent, racist, and extreme. Their passivity was partly explained by the widespread belief that most Nazi students, and Hitler himself, were actually moderates who would temper and eventually prevail over the more radical factions of the Party. Conservative students who embraced nationalism but rejected many aspects of the National Socialist agenda "viewed the Nazis as a section of the nationalist movement which they could not afford to alienate" and "preferred to seek out their enemies on the Left."[2]

Many professors similarly preferred to criticize the aggressive political activities of left-leaning groups while accepting the increasingly implausible claims that Nazi student leaders were engaged in a noble and apolitical defense of Germany's educational and cultural traditions. Beneath their endorsement of "nonpartisan nationalism" lay "an undercurrent of hostility to democratic institutions and a nostalgic sympathy for prewar hierarchical government."[3] A final factor was the professors' confidence in their own pedagogical powers to tame the misguided fervor of the Nazi students: "The notion that the Nazis' apparent freedom to commit violence with impunity might positively encourage them later to yet greater trials of strength, attacking the very heart of the university, was one that was too painful to contemplate, for it would signify a complete renunciation of the professors' self-respect and their belief that they could still influence the students for the good. It would be tantamount to an admission of failure as a teacher."[4]

Among the urgent and important lessons to be learned from this historical precedent is that totalitarian impulses cannot, in fact, be tamed, and that when universities succumb to them, the rest of society will follow. The preservation of democracy requires the uncompromising rejection of all efforts to interfere with academic freedom and to zealously defend the autonomy of institutions of higher education.

Academic Freedom and the Texas A&M University Firing Squad

In September 2025, a nationwide controversy erupted over a classroom confrontation between a student and an instructor that culminated in the firing, demotion, and resignation of several members of the Texas A&M University (TAMU) faculty and staff. During the 2025 TAMU summer term, Melissa McCoul was teaching the class "Literature for Children," which she had previously taught at least a dozen times at TAMU since 2018. According to the course catalog, the class is about "representative writers, genres, texts and movements," a topic that McCoul, who holds a Ph.D. in English from the University of Notre Dame with a specialty in children's literature and a graduate minor in gender studies, has focused on throughout her career. The syllabus for the class advises that "[s]ome of the material in this class might be controversial, and it is likely differing opinions will emerge. You are certainly not required to agree with me (or your peers), or to adhere to any particular viewpoints," and emphasized that respectful dialogue was required.[5]

Early on in the semester, while discussing a paper about academics who are accused of having a "gay agenda" for presenting "diverse identities in literature," McCoul identified herself as a lesbian.[6] A few days later, on July 9, an anonymous user of the social-media site X (formerly Twitter) with the handle @Son_of_Aragorn made a post about McCoul, referring to her as "a Lesbian and self admitted crusader for LGBTQ" and accusing her of "getting kids to read the worst filth."[7] He followed that post with posts that included a photo of McCoul and a link to her faculty profile.[8] On July 10, he posted that he was gathering more information to distribute about McCoul.[9] That day, the user posted four "TEXAS A&M WOKE UPDATE[s]" focused on McCoul, accompanied by images purporting to be of her class slides.[10] In each post, @Son_of_Aragorn tagged Texas state representative and Texas A&M grad Brian Harrison (R–Midlothian), who had served in the first Trump administration and whose X account has over 80,000 followers, along with Texas A&M alumni accounts, the senior editor at the far-right publication *The Blaze*, and a conservative advocacy-organization publication called the *Texas Scorecard*. The user claimed that McCoul's course was "pushing LGBTQ & Sexually Inappropriate books on students. Its [sic] a full onslaught of woke propaganda from Professor Dr. Melissa McCoul."[11] In the fourth "update," @Son_of_Aragorn urged his followers to make "respectful but determined contact with TAMU English Department Head Dr. Emily Johansen," followed by Johansen's email address, phone number, and photo.[12]

Three weeks into the semester, the students were reading *Jude Saves the World*, a novel featuring a nonbinary protagonist. On July 29, as McCoul was discussing ways to present the concepts of gender identity, expression, and sexuality to young children, a student raised her hand and made the following statement:

> I just have a question, because I'm not entirely sure this is legal to be teaching, um. Because according to our president, um, there's only two genders, and he said that he would be freezing, um, uh, agencies' funding programs that promote, promote gender ideology. Um, and this also very much goes against I, not only myself but a lot of people's religious beliefs.[13]

The student then announced, "Um, and so I am not going to participate in this because, um, it's, it's not legal and I don't want to promote something that is, um, against our president's laws as well as against my religious beliefs."[14]

McCoul replied that the student was mistaken about the subject matter of the class discussion being illegal. The student offered to read her "President Trump's executive order"; McCoul declined, but informed the student that she had the right to leave if she was uncomfortable in the class and that she could take her issue up with the administration. The student told her she had already been in contact with the president of the university and that she was meeting with him in person "to show all of my documentation." After McCoul noted that she, McCoul, had professional expertise in the course topic, she told the student that "it's time for you to leave."

The next day, July 30, the student met with Texas A&M University's president, Mark A. Welsh III. President Welsh "pushed back on the student's arguments that the course material was illegal and inappropriate," noting that there is a "professional reason" to teach LGBTQ+ content to people who want to become psychologists or clinical counselors, because "they want to understand the issues affecting the people that they're going to treat." The student accused McCoul of being "discriminatory" and voiced her confusion about why McCoul would be allowed to continue to teach, prompting Welsh to ask, "What do you expect us to do? Fire her?" When the student replied, "Yes," Welsh told her, "Well, that's not happening."[15]

On August 1, 2025, McCoul's class was canceled. Johansen, the department head, informed students in an email that the class was ending "[i]n light of the circumstances that have impacted your class this semester and the emotions that they have generated." According to the *Texas Tribune*, Welsh told a small number of faculty members that he had been contacted by state officials about the course, which he characterized as "'almost entirely LGBTQ-themed and expanded into 'social and psychological aspects of transgender identity' without being listed as such." Welsh and the provost of the university instructed College of Arts and Sciences Dean Mark Zoran and the head of the English department to change McCoul's class from a core curriculum class to an elective. McCoul was scheduled to teach in the fall semester, which began on August 21.[16]

On September 8, Brian Harrison, the Texas state representative tagged in @Son_of_Aragorn's posts, posted a twenty-three-part thread on X that began "CAUGHT ON TAPE: TEXAS A&M STUDENT KICKED OUT OF CLASS AFTER OBJECTING TO TRANSGENDER INDOCTRINATION . . . and A&M President defends 'LGBTQ Studies.'" The thread included "hidden camera video and audio" of the student's exchanges with both McCoul and Welsh. Harrison stated that he was referring Texas A&M University "to the Trump administration for investigation" and called upon Governor Abbott to "instruct his Regents at all public universities to immediately end all DEI and LGBTQ indoctrination."[17] Harrison's letter to Governor Abbott, which he also shared on social media, specified that Abbott should "direct your politically appointed regents at Texas A&M to immediately fire this professor and President Welsh."[18]

The post received millions of views and retweets, including from US Assistant Attorney General for Civil Rights Harmeet Dhillon, who wrote "This is deeply concerning" and promised that the Department of Justice Civil Rights Division "will look into this."[19] @Son_of_Aragorn also reposted the tweet, claiming that "[o]ur daughter, & the girl speaking, recorded this and other videos. We fought TAMU & their former Obama appointed CSAF [Chief of Staff of the United States Air Force, a reference to the position Welsh held in the Obama administration]. This was a Children's Literature class for crying out loud. Nothing happened to prof. or head of English Dept. Stay tuned... TAMU is about to have a very bad week."[20] In a video posted to the social media site TikTok, a TAMU student who had also been enrolled in the Children's Literature summer class and may be the "daughter" @Son_of_Aragorn referenced in his post, expressed her support for the student who had confronted McCoul. "If you haven't seen the video, I encourage you to go watch it, because the girl in the video is just respectfully asking, like, how does this apply to children's literature?" the student, Savannah Landers, says in her video.[21] "Melissa McCoul was wrong for teaching this kind of thing in a children's literature classroom. Children deserve to maintain their innocence as long as they can, and whenever we're shoving this kind of stuff in their face that's ripping away their innocence."[22]

That evening, the Texas A&M X account posted a statement from President Welsh announcing that he had removed the dean and the department head from their administrative positions because he had learned that afternoon that they had "approved plans to continue teaching course content that was not consistent with the course's published description," stating that students rely on these descriptions "to make important decisions about the courses they take in pursuit of their degrees. If we allow different course content to be taught from what is advertised, we let our students down. When it comes to our academic offerings, we must keep our word to our students and to the state of Texas."[23] Governor Abbott reposted the statement the next day, commenting: "Good. Now, fire the professor who acted contrary to Texas law."[24] Representative Harrison replied, "Not 'good' enough. The President must also be fired,"[25] following up with a post that included what he described as "MORE BOMBSHELL AUDIO: Texas A&M President admitted WEEKS AGO to knowing about transgender indoctrination . . . and told the conservative student 'THERE'S NOT A PROBLEM WITH TEACHING IT!'"[26]

On the morning of September 9, @Son_of_Aragorn posted about McCoul again on X: "UPDATE: Professor Melissa McCoul is shown to be teaching ENGL 104 freshman class and also ENGL 361 Young Adults Literature this semester."[27] One user responded, "Record her classes [sic] students. Release on X if she goes woke."[28] Another commented, "Of course they're targeting 18 year olds just barely establishing a new footing away from parents and HS. These are predators SPECIFICALLY placed there to ensnare Americas youth."[29] A user with the handle @Aggie_Vet wrote, "Son of Aragorn is on a mission, and I love it. Eradicate this cancer."[30] @Son_of_Aragorn replied to this post with the words "For America" accompanying a GIF of the *Lord of the Rings* character Aragorn going into battle. Later that afternoon, @Son_of_Aragorn posted again, tagging Rep. Harrison and Governor Abbott: "UPDATE: Teacher in question is NOT a professor, but rather a 'Senior Lecturer'. It looks like that is a NON-TENURED position. Meaning, it would be easy to deal with her administratively."[31]

In the evening, Welsh announced that he had fired McCoul.[32] Welsh characterized McCoul's summer class as "contain[ing] content that did not align with any reasonable expectation of standard curriculum for the course" and that college leadership had "made changes to ensure this course content does not continue in future semesters."[33] Welsh stated that he "learned late yesterday" that "the college continued to teach content that was inconsistent with the published course description for another course this fall," which led to his termination of McCoul. He once again emphasized student reliance on course descriptions: "If we allow different course content to be taught from what is advertised, we break trust with our students. When it comes to our academic offerings, we must keep faith with our students and with the state of Texas." According to Welsh, "This isn't about academic freedom; it's about academic responsibility."[34]

It was a strange and troubling claim for a university president to make. Teachers' autonomy in their classrooms lies at the very core of academic freedom. As expressed in the *1940 Statement of Principles on Academic Freedom and Tenure*, endorsed by nearly 300 national scholarly and educational associations, academic freedom "in its teaching aspect is fundamental for the protection of the rights of the teacher in teaching and of the student to freedom in learning. . . . Teachers are entitled to freedom in the classroom in discussing their subject."[35] This freedom is essential to "the free search for truth and its free exposition" on which the "common good" of higher education depends.[36]

In a letter to President Welsh, the AAUP Chapter at Texas A&M University—College Station urged him to reverse the decision to terminate McCoul. The group asserted that the firing of McCoul not only violated AAUP's principles of academic freedom but also "contradict[s] the university's written policies and stated commitment to academic freedom." The organization emphasized that instructors "should have control over the content and structure of the academic course, free from outside influence. . . . [I]nstructors need the freedom to teach, so that students have the freedom to learn" in the classroom."[37] The chapter pointed to Texas A&M University Rule 12.01.99.M1, section 2.1, which explicitly states that "[e]ach faculty member is entitled to full freedom in the classroom in discussing the subject being taught." Because McCoul's dismissal seemed "to have been implemented in direct response to pressure from Texas political leaders and the governor," the group added, it appeared to have "bypassed essential faculty input and procedures that protect the integrity of personnel decisions." The AAUP chapter concluded that the firing demonstrated "a clear disregard of the rights of faculty and sends a chilling message to the entire academic community in Texas."[38]

The US Supreme Court has repeatedly affirmed that teachers' freedom to teach is vital to democracy. In his concurring opinion in *Wieman v. Updegraff* (1952), Justice Felix Frankfurter wrote that "[i]t is the special task of teachers to foster those habits of open-mindedness and critical inquiry which alone make for responsible citizens, who, in turn, make possible an enlightened and effective public opinion. Teachers must fulfill their function by precept and practice, by the very atmosphere which they generate; they must be exemplars of open-mindedness and free inquiry."[39] In *Sweezy v. New Hampshire* (1957), the Court reiterated that "[t]he essentiality of freedom in the community of American universities is almost self-evident. No one should underestimate the vital role in a democracy that is played by those who guide and train our youth. To impose any strait jacket upon the intellectual leaders in our colleges and universities would imperil the future of our Nation. . . . Teachers and students must always remain free to inquire, to study and to evaluate, to gain new maturity and understanding; otherwise our civilization will stagnate and die.'"[40] In *Keyishian v. Bd. of Regents of Univ. of State of N.Y.* (1967), the Court emphasized the intimate connection between academic freedom and the First Amendment, decrying antidemocratic efforts to "cast a pall of orthodoxy over the classroom."[41]

But the story did not end with President Welsh's egregious violation of McCoul's academic freedom. Republican state officials, including Harrison and Lt. Governor Dan Patrick, continued to criticize Welsh's handling of the situation. Patrick posted on X that Welsh's "ambivalence on the issue and his dismissal of the student's concerns by immediately taking the side of the professor is unacceptable."[42] On September 18, little more than a week after Harrison posted his initial thread, Texas A&M University announced Welsh's resignation. Harrison immediately took credit for the decision, claiming that "You've seen everything I've caused in one week by doing it the way that I firmly believe Texans want."[43]

The chair of the Texas A&M University System Board of Regents, which holds the authority to remove university presidents and whose members are appointed by the governor, vehemently denied that political pressure had influenced how the board addressed the controversy over McCoul's class. According to Robert Albritton, "the real issue" was that "a student should know what they're getting into. . . . You can't bring a student into a class on one pretense and have another pretense talk, OK. That's the rub in all of this."[44] McCoul's class, he claimed, "broke the law."[45]

Albritton did not specify which law he believed the class had broken, which is unsurprising given that no laws forbid college instructors from teaching about gender issues. Contrary to the student's claim that McCoul was violating "our president's laws," the president has no power to make laws. The executive order to which the student was presumably referring during her confrontation with McCoul instructs federal agencies not to fund the promotion of "gender ideology"; it is not addressed to institutions of higher education and makes no reference to course curricula or instruction.[46] There are no current federal or state laws that prohibit classroom discussion of gender or sexuality at colleges and universities, despite the best efforts of Republican lawmakers such as Rep. Harrison, who has unsuccessfully attempted to ban public universities from offering classes with topics relating to LGBTQ+ subjects, diversity, or inclusion.[47]

The Trolling of the University and the Coddling of the Conservative Mind

Two months after the publication of the classroom and office videos, the identity of the complaining TAMU student had not been revealed to the public. According to the *Texas Tribune*, which published a comprehensive article about the controversy on September 19, the student refused to be interviewed or to answer a list of questions it provided. The newspaper chose not to name the student in its piece, noting that she was "concerned for her safety."[48] Despite being nameless, the TAMU student was effusively praised by conservative lawmakers, influencers, and pundits in the wake of the videos. Christin Bentley, a Texas state Republican executive committeewoman, posted on X that the "A&M student in this video is brave for speaking up and exposing" why "teachers graduating from Texas universities are pushing highly sexualized content on children."[49] David J. Harris, host of a show on the pro-Trump channel Newsmax with more than 800,000 followers on X, posted the student's video of her confrontation of McCoul with the comment, "This is what courage looks like! We need more of this."[50] Internet personality Josiah Alipate posted the video on Facebook to his 1.4 million followers with the caption "Texas A&M student chose bravery over conformity."[51]

The praise heaped upon a student who interrupted a class lecture to announce that she was personally offended by the instructor's views on gender and who then proceeded to push to have that instructor fired is in illuminating contrast to the widespread vilification and punishment of college and graduate students who have protested external speakers on the basis of their views on gender. For example, students who protested a speech by a lawyer from the extreme anti-LGBTQ+ organization Alliance Defending Freedom at Yale Law School were accused of imposing a "heckler's veto"; they were mocked, denounced, and "canceled" from consideration as clerks by several prominent conservative federal judges. Stanford Law School students who disrupted a speech by a far-right conservative federal judge, Kyle Duncan, were similarly lambasted for their "intolerance" and similarly excluded for consideration for federal clerkships by conservative judges. These incidents have been frequently cited as examples of "snowflake students" trying to shut down discussion of topics they find personally offensive or unpleasant. In 2016, the founder of the Heritage Foundation described liberal students who protested conservative speakers as both "little snowflakes demand[ing] 'safe spaces' where they can be protected from words" and the "little dictators" of the campus.[52]

No one, however, has accused the anonymous Texas A&M student of being a "little dictator," despite her hysterical and erroneous assertion that a viewpoint she found offensive—presented in a classroom setting by an expert on the subject being taught—was "illegal" and her announcement that she would be reporting the professor to the administration for that reason. None of the conservative cancel-culture warriors have described the student as disrupting the class or heckling the professor, even though these descriptions fit her actions far more than they fit the actions of student protests of external speakers. None of them have characterized her successful campaign to have an instructor fired for speech they didn't like as "cancel culture." In contrast to students who participated in pro-Palestine campus protests, no one has called for the A&M student to be disciplined, expelled, or reported to law enforcement for breaking university rules, which she appears to have done by making surreptitious recordings of a class lecture and her conversation with administration officials. TAMU's Guidelines for Recording Lectures indicate that students must get permission from instructors to record lectures. They clearly state that recordings cannot "be used for any purpose other than as a supplement for notes taken in class"; that recordings are to be deleted "at the conclusion of the course"; and that unauthorized recording is considered misconduct under TAMU Student Rule Section 6.06.[53] That rule prohibits recording people "without their prior knowledge or without their effective consent" when they have a "reasonable expectation of privacy and/or such recording is likely to cause injury or distress," including, explicitly, "administrative meetings with *University officials*."[54]

What conservatives hailed as a heroic act was a narcissistic young woman's hijacking of a college classroom to act out a calculated performance of bratty, ignorant grievance. In the words of a fellow student in McCoul's class, the student's outburst was "an ambush" that "felt performative," pointing out that the student "could've done that on her own time or like emailed the professor" rather than interrupting class.[55] By recording the exchange, the student breached the privacy and the trust not only of the professor she arrogantly attacked but also of her peers in the classroom. While the student directed her comments at the professor and later at the university president, her real audience clearly lay outside the university: the MAGA community, unified in its contempt for any institution or idea that does not flatter its leader, Donald Trump.

The TAMU student's tantrum is only one of the most high-profile and destructive acts of the malicious surveillance that are becoming increasingly commonplace on college campuses. University of North Carolina—Wilmington Professor Kevin McClure has highlighted "a growing trend of students recording professors and posting clips online to try to get them fired."[56] As the anonymous individual behind the @Son_of_Aragorn account proclaimed as the online outrage he helped manufacture began to seriously disrupt the university, "This shows the power of X (thank you @elonmusk) and a focused effort. . . . We're not done here, but it is a good time to point out what is possible."[57] Conservative students in particular have at their disposal a robust far-right outrage information ecosystem of politicians, pundits, and parents who amplify each other online and off on "anti-woke" social-media platforms and media outlets such as X, College Fix, Fox News, and the Daily Caller, recasting breathless anecdotes into seemingly significant stories that are then covered by the mainstream media. Students are offered notoriety and validation in exchange for monitoring and reporting on their professors' and peers' ideological impurities, incentivizing them to perform for outside audiences rather than sincerely engaging with their academic communities.

Surreptitious recording and the activation of online mobs have been tactics of the far right's attacks on education and other institutions perceived as "liberal" for more than a decade, ramping up under Donald Trump's first administration. "This atmosphere, which intensified as social media culture evolved, changed how students and professors interact," according to Peter Lake, director of the Center for Excellence in Higher Education Law and Policy at Stetson University College of Law. "When you step in the classroom, you might as well be in the studio. . . . People are going to record what you're saying, they may publish it, they may take it out of context, they may share it with your enemies—anything can happen now and it frequently does."[58]

In 2016, Turning Point USA, an organization founded by podcaster Charlie Kirk in 2012 to spread conservative ideology on college campuses, began explicitly encouraging students to "expose and document college professors who discriminate against conservative students and advance leftist propaganda in the classroom" by reporting them to its newly created "Professor Watchlist."[59] According to the Professor Watchlist website, "students, parents, and alumni deserve to know the specific incidents and names of professors that advance a radical agenda in our lecture halls."[60] The tip form provides several options for users to select in describing the professor, including "anti-law enforcement," "anti-Second Amendment," "climate alarmist," "foreign influence," "socialism," and "identity politics."[61] When colleges and universities moved classes online in March 2020 because of the Covid pandemic, Kirk encouraged students to take advantage of the situation by recording their professors: "To all college students who have their professors switching to online classes," Kirk posted on the social-media platform then known as Twitter, "Please share any and ALL videos of blatant indoctrination with @TPUSA. . . . Now is the time to document & expose the radicalism that has been infecting our schools. Transparency!"[62] Around 300 professors and instructors are currently included on the list for various perceived transgressions against conservative ideology; many of those named have reported being harassed, doxed, and threatened after being placed on the list.

According to Lake, the watchlist "was part of a shift that made 'what had been a semi-private space—the classroom—into a place where statements or discussions could get national attention.'"[63] As a professor who was placed on the Watchlist shared in 2016, "These types of attempts to influence campus culture and teaching . . . create[] an environment where the very idea and understanding of academic freedom and first amendment rights are called into question—not only by students, but also by well-funded outsiders with agendas."[64] By encouraging students "to report on, rather than engage with, other perspectives,"[65] organizations like Turning Point coddle conservative youth, training them "to not engage their education critically, but to combat anything or anyone that does not promote or teach with a conservative viewpoint."[66]

Like so many other "provocateurs" who helped create and capitalized on the moral panic over campus free speech that took off in 2015, Kirk had no expertise in higher education. Kirk had applied and been denied admission to West Point, a rejection that seemed to have served as the true "turning point" in his life. Kirk insisted, without evidence, that the academy chose "a far less-qualified candidate of a different gender and a different persuasion" over him.[67] Kirk dropped out of community college after one term and never gained any experience as a scholar, a teacher, a researcher, or an administrator. Kirk's method of engagement with academic communities was to show up on "liberal" college campuses and challenge students to debate him about controversial topics. He would then selectively edit video recordings of these events and use them to mock and attack "liberal" students on various platforms.

Kirk, in other words, was not a sincere interlocutor seeking the truth through reasoned debate; he was a troll, both online and offline. He inserted himself into communities and conversations where he was neither welcome nor qualified to contribute, with the sole purpose of disrupting, distracting, and draining the attention and energy of those interacting in good faith. He attacked academic communities while desperately wanting to be taken seriously by them, never seeming to realize that the only thing that would have made that possible was the one thing he seemed incapable of doing: demonstrating a genuine openness to learning from people unlike him. University trolls, from Kirk to the TAMU complainant to the seemingly vast stable of professional campus "provocateurs" who attained notoriety during the manufactured "college free speech crisis," make ideal foot soldiers in Trump's war on higher education: entitled, incurious, intolerant mediocrities who view the opportunity to serve the whims of an authoritarian leader as the honor of a lifetime.

The Original Totalitarian Playbook: The Nazi Student Movement

But Trump's troll army were not the originators of the totalitarian playbook to destroy higher education. Obvious forerunners include the 1971 Powell Memo and Senator Joe McCarthy's "Red Scare" witch hunts, but the true masters of the strategy are found further back in history: the National Socialist student associations of the 1920s and '30s. These groups laid the groundwork for the Nazi Party's seizure of power by destroying German universities from within and without.

Nationalist students and their supporters vilified the intellectual traditions of the university; disrupted lectures and surveilled classrooms for "undesirable" ideas; countered "liberal" class instruction with external speaker series and other campus events that promoted nationalist propaganda; demanded changes to rid the university curriculum of "socialist" and non-Aryan influences; removed "degenerate" books from libraries and bookstores and destroyed them in public; and targeted left-leaning professors with blacklists, boycotts, and campaigns to have them terminated from their positions. By the time the Nazi Party was in power and had passed the infamous Law for the Restoration of the Professional Civil Service in 1933, the students' efforts had ensured that no university would offer serious resistance to the purging of "undesirable" faculty and students. Within two years, over a thousand faculty members were dismissed from their positions and government quotas had dramatically reduced the number of non-Aryan and female students at German universities. The most powerful bulwark against totalitarianism in any society—the academic freedom and independence of higher-education institutions—had been dismantled.

University students in the Weimar Republic were "caught up in a society which offered them conflicting expectations. On the one hand, the university appeared to promise traditional social status; on the other, it in fact promised very little, since employment prospects were limited and the elite status of professionals had been undermined economically by inflation and psychologically by democracy."[68] The response of many students was to blame democratic institutions for depriving them of the stability and identity to which they believed they were entitled, and to gravitate toward "antidemocratic theories and political views which promised to restore security and status.[69]

In 1919, the student committees of all the German universities merged to form the *Deutsche Studentenschaft* (DSt), or German Student Union. The DSt began as a democratic student-governance organization, but began moving farther and farther to the right in the late 1920s while keeping up the pretense of nonpartisanship. The DSt was increasingly dominated by members of the National Socialist German Students' League (*Nationalsozialistischer Deutscher Studentenbund*), which had been founded in 1926. Prior to 1930, Nazi student activists disguised their nationalistic and antidemocratic sentiments as neutral intellectual pursuits, making the strategic choice to "emphasize national and academic issues rather than exclusively racial appeals, and to give lip-service to the ideals of academic freedom and university autonomy."[70] The DSt compiled and circulated lists of Nazi Party speakers to invite to campuses "to provide 'expert' knowledge about those subjects which interested students."[71]

By 1930, when the Nazi Party had gained increasing support within German society, Nazi student activists began using much more aggressive and openly partisan tactics against professors of Jewish descent, professors who had expressed "anti-German" views, and professors known to be "tough examiners." They disrupted their lectures, called for them to be investigated, and pressured the universities to fire them.[72] The case of Hans Nawiasky, professor of Law and Political Science at the University of Munich, was one notorious example. During a lecture on June 23, 1931, Nawiasky made comments that appeared to frame the Treaty of Versailles in a positive light. The remarks angered Nazi students who were in attendance, and an inflammatory article about Nawiasky featuring out-of-context quotations from his lecture appeared in the National Socialist newspaper on June 25. On June 26, because of rumors that Nazi students were planning to disrupt his lectures, Nawiasky's class was moved to a smaller hall. Crowds of protesting students appeared at both locations, and Nawiasky had to be escorted out of his classroom by the rector. The Munich student council asked the university Senate to investigate Nawiasky for his "anti-German" views. Even after he met with the complaining students to explain his remarks, demonstrations against his classes and attacks in the National Socialist newspaper continued. In two lectures delivered in front of hostile student audiences on June 30, Nawiasky "defended academic freedom and warned that classroom demonstrations and publication of lecture quotations without permission and out of context threatened the necessary trust between students and faculty." Protesting students interrupted Nawiasky's second lecture multiple times, prompting the rector to send police to clear the hall and to close the university until order could be restored.[73]

Other examples included the targeting of theologian Günther Dehn because of his antiwar views. After demonstrating against him for two years, University of Halle students finally succeeded in driving Dehn out of the university in 1932.[74] Later that year, Nazi students began protesting a newly appointed professor, Ernst Cohn, to the University of Breslau law faculty because of his Jewish background. While Cohn's colleagues defended his right to teach, the university suspended his classes in response to student pressure.[75]

After Hitler was appointed Chancellor on January 30, 1933, Nazi government officials and Nazi student organizations began collaborating on "a more organized campaign against undesirable professors," employing detailed lists created by individual university student unions for the purpose.[76] The Law for the Restoration of the Professional Civil Service was passed in April, mandating that all individuals of non-Aryan descent and all who held views contrary to the Party be removed from university faculties as well as from a host of other professions, with exceptions made for veterans of the First World War. Student government officers "were directed to carefully compile a list of all professors to whom the law might apply," including Jews, socialists, "professors who had criticized 'the national Führer, the movement of national upheaval, or the front soldiers,'" as well as "all liberal or pacifist professors . . ., so that students might organize boycotts of instructors not covered by the law."[77] Nazi students closely monitored the lectures and social interactions of their professors for signs of disloyalty or ideological nonconformity.[78]

The Nazi government also collaborated with the DSt to address the issue of undesirable students as well as faculty. The DSt recommended prohibiting "Jews and Communists" from accessing student buildings and participating in student activities in March; the government enacted a law "against the overenrollment of German schools and universities" in April, limiting the number of Jewish students at each educational institution to 1.5 percent.[79] The Nazi government was also hostile to Weimar Republic efforts to increase female students' access to higher education, which had led to women making up 18.5 percent of the student body prior to the Nazi takeover. Accordingly, the Nazis imposed a 10-percent cap on female students in 1933, a development celebrated in right-wing circles: "The female intelligentsia type, the creature armed with horn-rimmed spectacles demanding equal rights, the terror of every male student, will disappear."[80]

The DSt's newly created Main Office for Press and Propaganda announced a nationwide "Action against the Un-German Spirit" in April 1933 that would conclude with public book burnings throughout Germany on May 10. The DSt instructed students to "cleanse" their personal libraries, university libraries, and public libraries of "leftist" books, including those that contained "the trash and filth of the Jewish spirit of decomposition."[81] As part of this campaign, Nazi members of the Berlin DSt looted the library and archives of the Institut für Sexualwissenschaft (Institute for Sexual Research), a groundbreaking nonprofit research institute headed by Magnus Hirschfeld. In addition to pioneering research on gay, transgender, and intersex topics, the Institute provided a wide range of public education and health services, including marital counseling, contraceptives, and treatment for venereal diseases. The Institute's library contained thousands of books, photographs, research documents, and other objects pertaining to sexual practices and identities. On May 10, the plundered materials were dragged into the Opernplatz in Berlin. More than 40,000 Germans watched while the students sang the Horst Wessel song, chanted "fire oaths," and threw the books into a large bonfire. Goebbels himself attended the event, shouting, "No to decadence and moral corruption!" and "Yes to decency and morality in family and state!" as more than 20,000 volumes went up in flames.

In his inaugural lecture as rector of the University of Freiburg in May 1933, the philosopher Martin Heidegger announced that the "much celebrated 'academic freedom' is being banished from the German university; for this freedom was not genuine, since it was only negative. It meant primarily freedom from concern, arbitrariness of intentions and inclinations, lack of restraint in what was done and left undone. The concept of freedom of the German is now brought back to its truth."[82] In a speech to students a few months later, Heidegger made clear what this "truth" entailed: "The Führer alone *is* the present and future German reality and its law."[83] This was an affirmation of the *Führerprinzip,* or "Leader principle," according to which all of society is structured as a hierarchy with one supreme leader at the top. Subordinate leaders, also called "Führers," pledged unquestioning obedience to the Leader. Heidegger himself had by the time of this speech officially become the "Führer of the university": a little dictator serving the will of the Great Dictator.

Conclusion

One of the rising stars of the National Socialist student movement in the late 1920s was Horst Wessel. Wessel had joined a variety of far-right youth groups as a teenager and founded his own at age 15. He developed a reputation for engaging in physical conflicts with Social Democratic and Communist youth groups. While enrolled as a law student, Wessel joined the paramilitary *Sturmabteilung* (SA, or Storm Detachment, also known as the Brownshirts). He became known as a charismatic debater who was skilled at converting working-class people to join the Nazi cause, "a good bridge builder between traditional conservative leaders and theoretical Nazis."[84] Wessel wrote a song called "Die Fahne hoch" (Raise the Flag), later known as the "Horst Wessel Song," which soon became the Nazi anthem. In 1929, Wessel dropped out of university to focus exclusively on promoting the Nazi cause, speaking at dozens of National Socialist events in 1929. His efforts earned him the attention and admiration of Joseph Goebbels, who appointed him to a leadership position in the SA that year.

On January 14, 1930, at age 22, Wessel was shot in the head. He was taken to a hospital but died soon after. As soon as Goebbels learned of the shooting, he immediately blamed the attack on "degenerate communist subhumans" and quickly embarked on a campaign to turn Wessel into a martyr for the Nazi cause. The circumstances of the shooting were never entirely clear, but it is generally believed that he was shot by a group of Communists in a dispute over unpaid rent. The Nazi Party announced a two-month period of mourning for Wessel, while high-ranking members of the Party eulogized him in soaring, religious language: "A divine element works in him, making him the man he is and causing him to act in this way and no other," wrote Goebbels. "One man must set an example and offer himself up as a sacrifice! Well, then, I am ready!" Adolf Hitler praised Wessel as "a 'blood witness' whose song had become 'a battle hymn for millions,'" whose sacrifice for the Nazi cause was "'a monument more lasting than stone and bronze.'"[85] The Nazis used Wessel's murder to inflame hatred against leftist activists, portray Nazi Party members as victims, and to justify the atrocities that followed their seizure of power.

While speaking at an outdoor Turning Point event on September 10, 2025, Charlie Kirk was shot and killed. Within hours of his death, prior to the identification of the shooter and any possible motive, President Trump blamed the rhetoric of "those on the radical left" for Kirk's death, asserting that comparisons between "wonderful Americans like Charlie" and Nazis are "directly responsible for the terrorism that we're seeing in our country today." Trump vowed that his administration "will find each and every one of those who contributed to this atrocity, and to other political violence, including the organizations that fund it and support it."[86] In an interview on Fox two days later, Trump openly called for violence against Americans on the basis of their political views: "We have radical left lunatics out there, and we just have to beat the hell out of them."[87] Trump followed these statements with an increasingly unhinged set of executive orders and statements threatening violence, investigation, arrest, and imprisonment of "left-wing" individuals and organizations.

Threats of censorship, retaliation, and punishment for criticizing Kirk were repeated by several MAGA officials. Trump's deputy secretary of state, Christopher Landau, threatened to strip visas from individuals if they celebrated Kirk's death.[88] Republican Congressman Clay Higgins vowed to use his congressional authority to permanently ban people who "belittled the assassination of Charlie Kirk" from social media and to "go[] after their business licenses and permitting, their businesses will be blacklisted aggressively, they should be kicked from every school, and their drivers licenses should be revoked."[89] Trump's attorney general, Pam Bondi, threatened to use the Department of Justice to prosecute people for not praising Kirk as a martyr. As soon as the shooter was identified as a young, white man from a conservative family, far-right influencers began to push the narrative that universities and professors were responsible for "indoctrinating" him, despite the shooter's having spent barely more than a semester in college.[90]

Effusive tributes to Kirk poured in from Donald Trump and other MAGA politicians, pundits, and celebrities, but also from individuals across the political spectrum, including numerous think pieces and commemorations by self-identified liberals who praised Kirk as a champion of civil dialogue and free speech. Kirk and Turning Point were lauded for modeling good-faith debate on college campuses, prompting pushback from those actually familiar with the surveillance and silencing tactics Kirk popularized. In a development for which the term "ironic" does not seem nearly strong enough, individuals who criticized Kirk, or did not endorse his posthumous beatification enthusiastically enough, or who merely quoted some of his more notorious statements vilifying and advocating violence against those he disagreed with, were harassed, doxed, threatened, and fired from their jobs, including dozens of professors and teachers.[91]

A century before the Nazis came to power, the Jewish German author Heinrich Heine presciently asserted, "Where they burn books, they will ultimately burn people too." Government threats to academic freedom and attempts to seize control of educational institutions are a hallmark of totalitarianism. Put more positively, universities are the best defense against totalitarianism: "the one reason that we know that every totalitarian government must fail is that no totalitarian government is prepared to face the consequences of creating free universities."[92] But universities can only exist as bulwarks against totalitarian impulses when their communities—professors, students, staff—are vigilant in identifying and denouncing those impulses before it is too late.

PART IV

THE AUTHORITARIAN PLAYBOOK ON ACADEMIC FREEDOM

Courts and Immigration

11

Courting Higher Ed

How Right-Wing Attacks on Higher Education Mimic Their Attacks on the Courts

LEAH M. LITMAN*

The second Trump administration has higher education in its sights, using the federal government's considerable leverage to go after various schools for a variety of reasons. The administration attempted to suddenly and drastically reduce the costs that universities would be reimbursed for under research programs. The president illegally froze hundreds of millions of dollars in funds to universities such as Columbia, Northwestern, University of Pennsylvania, and Harvard.[1] As a misguided attempt to stave off further funding freezes, Columbia entered into a deal that did not completely stave off further threats and coercion.[2] When Harvard University refused to enter into a similar deal, the federal government launched an all-out, all-government war against the school, attempting to prohibit Harvard from admitting international students and threatening its endowment and tax-exempt status, among other things.[3]

Although these measures are extreme and high-profile, the war on higher education did not begin with Donald Trump or the Trump administration. Trump is merely the latest manifestation in a long-running effort to diminish the power of higher education, which has been an important engine of social and economic mobility in the United States and a vehicle for producing the kind of independent, free-thinking citizens who can challenge executive overreach and catastrophic government policies. Undermining higher education also undercuts civic institutions that can function as independent sources of authority and knowledge and, in so doing, constrain government power.

* Professor of Law, University of Michigan. Co-host of Strict Scrutiny, a Supreme Court podcast.

Leah M. Litman, *Courting Higher Ed*. In: *Academic Freedom in the Era of Trump*.
Edited by: Lee C. Bollinger and Geoffrey R. Stone, Oxford University Press.
 DOI: 10.1093/9780197854877.003.0012

The Trump administration is running a playbook that is not unique to higher education. People familiar with the Republican Party's decades-long effort to take over the Supreme Court will recognize some elements of that campaign in the Party's efforts to do the same with higher education. Like the targeted campaign against higher education, Trump's ability to select Justices who delivered on many of the goals of the right-wing legal movement and the priorities of the Republican Party did not emerge from nowhere; it was the product of a carefully orchestrated, decades-long effort that was pursued in particular ways.

This short piece identifies some of the parallels between the right-wing attacks on higher education and the Republican Party's successful takeover of the courts. Recognizing the parallels suggests that progressives and moderates should be wary of certain lines of attack and certain seemingly innocuous overtures; it also underscores the importance of recognizing the measures for what they are before it is too late. Part I outlines the shared origins of the attacks on higher education and the courts; Part II shows how the attacks on both kinds of institutions rely on similar tactics.

Origins

The right-wing interest in higher education and the courts have the same origin story. The ties are evident in the 1971 "Powell memorandum," written by future Supreme Court Justice Lewis Powell, who was, at the time, a director and member of the executive committee of Philip Morris, the tobacco company. As a corporate lawyer, Powell defended the company through lobbying.[4] The US Chamber of Commerce asked him to prepare a memo as part of those efforts. The memo laid out a blueprint for how corporate America could fight back against the burgeoning environmentalist movement and rising public support for consumer protection.[5] Most relevant for these purposes is how the memo focused on two areas that purportedly required corporate America's attention—the education system and the courts.

The premise of the Powell memo was "that the American economic system" was "under broad attack."[6] Powell outlandishly claimed that "[b]usiness has been the favorite whipping-boy of many politicians for many years."[7] Perhaps even more ridiculously, he wrote that "[o]ne does not exaggerate to say that, in terms of political influence with respect to the course of legislation, the American business executive is truly the 'forgotten man.'"[8]

These supposed travesties, Powell argued, could be traced to higher education. Powell labeled "[t]he most disquieting voices" in the attacks on corporate America as those coming "from the college campus," which "often are the most articulate, the most vocal, the most prolific."[9] The memo ventured that "there is reason to believe that the campus is the single most dynamic source" of "[t]he assault on the enterprise system."[10] It faulted American business for supporting higher education, and for displaying what Powell called "appeasement, ineptitude and ignoring the problem."[11]

Powell considered and rejected some possible solutions to the purported problem with higher education. The memo conceded that "[i]t would be fatal to attack . . . academic freedom" as a principle.[12] It viewed "independent and uncoordinated activity by individual corporations" as "[in]sufficient." It urged that "strength lies in organization, in careful long-range planning and implementation, in consistency of action . . . [and] in the scale of financing available."[13]

The memo offered a few recommendations to this end. Powell zeroed in on the purported lack of "balance" on campuses, "with relatively few members being of conservative or moderate persuasion and even the relatively few often being less articulate and aggressive than their crusading colleagues."[14] The memo maintained that addressing the imbalance could be persuasively folded into a strategy that coded as pro-academic freedom rather than anti-.[15] Powell suggested that organizations such as the Chamber of Commerce establish a staff of "highly qualified scholars" and "speakers of the highest competency." He concluded with the recommendation that the Chamber demand "equal time on the college speaking circuit" and "urg[e] . . . for faculty balance."[16]

Powell's memo also recommended a focus on another institution—the courts. His writings maintained that "the judiciary may be the most important instrument for social, economic and political change."[17] As a possible model for what corporate interests could do with the courts, the memo pointed to the fact that the American Civil Liberties Union "initiates or intervenes in scores of cases each year," including by filing amicus briefs at the Supreme Court.[18] The courts, Powell concluded, were "a vast area of opportunity for the Chamber, if . . . business is willing to provide the funds."[19]

And so they did.

Tactics

The parallels between the right-wing measures directed at the courts and those directed at higher education are not limited to an origin story. They persist to this day with shared tactics. Some of the tactics were outlined, in part, through the Powell memo, including the heavy reliance on corporate money, now often dark money. The efforts also include Trojan-horse-like crusades that amount to efforts to smuggle in an ideological project under the guise of something superficially banal.

Corporate Money, Dark Money

Higher Education

Jane Mayer's astonishing book *Dark Money* details much of the story concerning right-wing dark money and academia.[20] Mayer traces the focus on higher education to an event that occurred shortly before the Powell memo—a protest at Cornell University during parents' weekend when several Black students seized the student union (some with guns).[21] A Cornell alum and former Cornell trustee, John Olin, became heavily involved in the right-wing efforts that followed "to wrest control of higher education in America" and "fund an ambitious offensive to reorient the political slant of American higher education to the right."[22] As Mayer documented, by 2005 the John M. Olin Foundation had "spent half of its total assets of $370 million bankrolling the promotion of free-market ideology and other conservative ideas on the country's campuses."[23]

Olin, like Powell, "regarded the campus as overrun by scholars 'with definite left-wing attitudes and convictions.'" He sought advice from people at the Koch and Scaife Foundations, among other places, about how to respond. (The Koch Foundation is associated with the petrochemical billionaire Koch family, and the Scaife Foundation with the billionaire heir to the Mellon banking and oil fortunes.)[24] To lead the Olin Foundation, Olin selected William Simon, who, again like Powell, warned that "our freedom is in dire peril" because of the "secret system" of academics who, he maintained, were running the country. Simon, again echoing Powell, emphasized the "need" for "a counter-intelligentsia" and urged private and corporation foundations "to funnel desperately needed funds to scholars, social scientists and writers who understand the relationship between political and economic liberty,"[25] insisting that "They must be given grants, grants, and more grants."[26]

Other individuals involved in the Olin Foundation were Michael Joyce and James Pierson. Together, Mayer writes, the two generated the "beachhead theory" that sought to place conservative groups at "the most influential schools in order to gain the greatest leverage" without "rais[ing] questions about academic integrity."[27] To carry this out, the Olin Foundation began offering funding for programs with particular fields of study, or fellowships for people pursuing certain arguments, or conference programs centered on particular ideas. And, Mayer assessed, "[t]he Olin foundation's most significant beachheads . . . were established in America's law schools."[28]

At George Mason University, the Charles Koch Foundation helped set up the Mercatus Center and the Institute for Humane Studies, two anti-regulatory, libertarian-focused programs.[29] Leonard Leo, the longtime vice president of the Federalist Society, later helped broker a deal that awarded a lot of money, some of which came from the Koch foundation, to George Mason's law school, which resulted in the school's being renamed the Antonin Scalia Law School.[30] The school has since launched the C. Boyden Gray Center for Study of the Administrative State, which files frequent anti-regulation amicus briefs.[31] *The Intercept* reported that Leo bestowed more than $20 million on Texas A&M's law school as part of an agreement that required the school to establish a center, though the precise terms are less clear.[32]

The money for much of the beachhead programming that Mayer unearthed came from "the Charles Koch Foundation, the Searle Freedom Trust, ExxonMobil, [and] Shell Oil."[33] One of the latest funding mechanisms is Donors Trust, which *ProPublica* reporter Andy Kroll described as the "dark-money ATM of the conservative legal movement." Donors Trust has structured itself to avoid disclosure requirements, and its directors are also the directors for major conservative organizations such as the Koch-supported Heritage Foundation and Institute for Justice. Donors Trust has funded the Federalist Society, among other organizations. In 2022 alone, it spent more than $200 million on such groups.[34]

The Trump administration's repeated threats to federal funds for higher education work in tandem with these efforts. When schools cannot depend on the federal government for grants, they will have to look elsewhere—perhaps to the wealthy corporate interests with money to throw around (such money will come with some conditions, of course). That is particularly true when the federal government yanks or freezes funding in the midst of projects with little to no notice, as the Trump administration has done.[35] As a result, schools may become more receptive to overtures from private, corporate donors with ideological agendas.

Courts

The Olin Foundation also helped with right-wing efforts targeted at the courts. Some of that happened via funding at law schools. But it happened in other ways as well: The foundation provided early money—$5.5 million, according to Mayer—to the fledgling Federalist Society, the group to which the Trump administration would largely outsource its judicial selections. Even before Trump, the Federalist Society had provided support for the Bush administration's judicial nominations, and, even earlier, a pathway to opportunities in the Reagan administration.[36] Mayer quoted the Federalist Society president as saying the organization "possibly wouldn't exist at all" without the support of the Olin Foundation.[37]

Koch money has funded other organizations that have their eyes on the courts, including the Judicial Education Project, which files amicus briefs and hosts gatherings for lawyers and judges.[38] Democratic Senator Sheldon Whitehouse has unearthed the striking number of briefs filed at the Supreme

Court that are funded with dark money.[39] And an investigation by *Politico* found that a notable percentage of amicus briefs filed in support of right-wing causes were filed by groups associated with Leonard Leo.[40]

As Powell envisioned, libertarian funders have also poured large amounts of money into legal nonprofits with libertarian angles that have brought cases, filed briefs, and funded public intellectuals.[41] They have done the same via 501(c)(4) social-welfare organizations, which generally need not disclose their donors. Charles Koch donated more than $4 billion to a single 501(c)(4) in one year.[42] Leonard Leo recently established a new 501(c)(4) social-welfare organization, the Marble Freedom Trust, which entered into a transaction with American businessman Barre Seid in which Seid donated 100 percent of the shares in an electrical-device manufacturing company to the nonprofit. As a result, when the company sold for $1.65 billion, all of that money went to the Marble Freedom Trust, which, in turn, gave some of the money to Donors Trust.[43]

Corporate money and dark money have also been directed at the courts in other ways. In 2025, political action committees affiliated with Elon Musk spent more than $20 million in a Wisconsin Supreme Court race.[44] In the same year, Musk also maxed out contributions to Republican politicians who supported efforts to impeach judges who ruled against the Trump administration.[45]

The Olin Foundation model has been successfully replicated by other groups, including the Bradley Foundation, which in a single year (2012) awarded more than $32 million in grants.[46] As the Olin Foundation did with the Federalist Society, the Scaife Family Charitable Trust provided some of the early money to the Heritage Foundation, at the time a new conservative think tank. "Scaife [eventually] became its largest backer, donating $10 million more" over the years 1975–1985.[47] Charles Koch similarly gave somewhere between $10 to $20 million to the Cato Institute in its early years.[48]

Bad-Faith Campaigns and Trojan Horses

The campaigns themselves, not just their funding, have proceeded in similar fashion. In particular, the efforts directed at the courts and at higher education raise seemingly neutral, unobjectionable criticisms that, in fact, conceal an ideological agenda. The right-wing projects on both fronts have proposed superficially neutral and even superficially plausible agendas and sets of reforms that, on closer inspection, also mask political aims. As outlined below, there is both a negative, critical aspect to the attacks on courts and higher education and a positive, affirmative one.

Negative, Critical

As to the courts, the long-running, right-wing, Republican complaint has been (loosely) that judges and courts were engaged in judicial activism. The basic critique was that judges, when they ruled in ways the Republican Party did not like, were making the law reflect the judges' policy preferences rather than the law itself. Along these lines, as both a presidential candidate and as president, Republican Ronald Reagan campaigned against judicial activism and promised to appoint federal judges who engaged in judicial restraint.[49] Reagan spoke about "judicial activism" as a "liberal phenomenon" whereby judges "thought it was their right to make the law, not just interpret it."[50] He depicted judicial restraint as the alternative to courts' and judges' using the law as "vehicles for political action and social experimentation."[51]

But the notions of judicial activism and judicial restraint were woefully underspecified, such that it was hardly clear what such terms meant, just as they remain unclear today. In operation, it seems that the Supreme Court justices who were selected by Republican presidents who railed against judicial activism and who professed support for judicial restraint did not avoid judicial activism, or at least any coherent, plausible account of it. To the extent that courts were said to be making law, not interpreting it, there are very pointed examples of Republican appointees ignoring that principle. Take *Shelby County v. Holder*, the 2013 decision invalidating a portion of the Voting Rights Act [VRA].[52] The Republican appointees in the majority relied on a constitutional principle, the notion of equal sovereignty, which purportedly generally requires Congress to impose requirements on all states. Yet that principle appears nowhere in the text, is belied by history, and has little to recommend it in other constitutional sources.[53] Indeed, in order to establish the existence of the principle of equal sovereignty, the opinion had to insert a misleading ellipsis into a quotation from a prior case to change its meaning.[54]

To the extent that the judicial-activism/judicial-restraint critique reflected a sense that courts were invalidating federal laws too freely, the Roberts Court doesn't exactly shy away from that, either. *Shelby County* is one example; the various decisions striking down campaign-finance laws are others.[55] The Republican appointees affirmatively invited the parties to argue that a campaign-finance law was unconstitutional when the parties initially framed the case in terms of statutory interpretation; the justices did something similar in a pending challenge to another provision of the VRA, inviting a constitutional challenge.[56] As for the objection that courts were invalidating too many state legislative enactments on the basis of ambiguous constitutional provisions, the Roberts Court doesn't seem immune to that criticism, either. The Court's Second Amendment decisions are examples; so too are the First Amendment decisions chipping away at civil-rights protections for the LGBT community.[57] There are also the First Amendment decisions invalidating state efforts to ensure the separation of church and state.[58]

If the critique was that courts were being undemocratic (another somewhat underspecified accusation), the decisions striking down myriad legislative enactments, let alone the myriad decisions invalidating or narrowing voting-rights protections, or cases prohibiting federal courts from remedying partisan gerrymanders, suggest that the Roberts Court hasn't avoided that criticism.[59] In part because Republican appointees seem to have defied all of these possible definitions of judicial restraint and avoiding judicial activism, those phrases really seem to have functioned like stalking horses for Republicans' preferred results in the courts, permitting Republican elected officials to avoid having to say that that's what they look for in nominees.

In the context of higher education, the objection proffered by right-wing Republicans has, at times, been allegations of anti-Semitism. The Trump administration initially threatened funding of both Columbia University and Harvard University by suggesting that the schools had not done enough to counteract anti-Semitism on campus and were accordingly in violation of federal civil-rights laws.[60] The focus on anti-Semitism as a method of criticizing schools and as a way of stripping their funding has its origins in Project Esther, an initiative spearheaded by the Heritage Foundation.[61] The Heritage Foundation is one of the dark-money-funded groups that has played a role in facilitating right-wing attacks on courts and Republicans' takeover of the courts, as well as the efforts directed at higher education.[62]

The *New York Times*'s extensive investigation into Project Esther uncovered an origin story of a campaign with designs to censor curriculum, remove faculty, deport foreign students, and more—all to ensure that campuses featured less criticism of Israel and fewer expressions of support for Palestine.[63] A group of conservative supporters of Israel helped the Heritage Foundation launch a national task force that included, in their statement of purpose, a definition of anti-Semitism that appears to encompass broad, general criticisms of Israel.[64]

Here too, the selectivity of Republicans' and conservatives' concerns about anti-Semitism should have revealed that the motivating force behind these efforts was not rooting out anti-Semitism. Recall that during the first Trump administration, then-President Trump refused to condemn the Unite the Right rally in Charlottesville, Virginia, at which protesters chanted "Jews Will Not Replace Us."[65] Trump insisted there were good people on both sides at the rally.[66] That is the person and the administration that the Project Esther movement coalesced around. NPR has "identified three Trump officials with close ties to anti-Semitic extremists, including a man described by federal prosecutors as a 'Nazi sympathizer,' and a prominent Holocaust denier."[67] Trump nominated Paul Ingrassia to lead the Office of Special Counsel; Ingrassia attended a rally for Nick Fuentes, a Holocaust denier, after Fuentes was removed from a

Turning Point USA gathering. At the rally, NPR reported, "supporters chanted 'down with Israel.'"[68] (Trump hosted Fuentes at Mar-a-Lago, together with Kanye West.[69] West had made a series of anti-Semitic comments the same year (and before), and would go on to make even more later.[70]) Trump has also said that Jewish Democratic Senator Chuck Schumer is "not Jewish anymore" but instead "a Palestinian."[71] He has thrown out anti-Semitic slurs such as "shylock."[72]

One of the many examples of the Heritage Foundation-organized Project Esther's selective concern about anti-Semitism came from the Heritage Foundation itself. In the course of insisting that speech and organizations critical of Israel and supportive of Palestine were part of an anti-Semitic movement, the group seemed to imply that the anti-Semitic movement was a conspiracy orchestrated by Jews themselves. The *New York Times* described how Heritage "finalized a national strategy that aimed to convince the public to perceive the pro-Palestinian movement in the United States as part of a global 'Hamas Support Network' that 'poses a threat not simply to American Jewry, but to America itself.'"[73] As orchestrators of the movement, Heritage "singled out" several groups, among them "Jewish Voice for Peace." Heritage also "presented an illustration of a pyramid topped by 'progressive "lites" leading the way,' which included Jewish billionaires such as the philanthropist George Soros and Governor JB Pritzker of Illinois."[74]

Even the officials who are ostensibly pressing on schools because of anti-Semitism on campus sometimes give away the game. Trump's secretary of education, Linda McMahon, made some media rounds after Columbia agreed to enter into a settlement with the administration. As part of that victory tour, she didn't focus only or even primarily on vindicating the civil rights of Jewish students and addressing anti-Semitism. Instead, her subject was ideological diversity; anti-Semitism got a passing reference: "This is a monumental victory for conservatives who wanted to do things on these elite campuses for a long time because we had such far left-leaning professors. . . . Our campuses are now what they should be. They're places for debate, for education. They're not places for left-leaning riots and anti-Semitism."[75]

Positive, Affirmative

Right-wing efforts to control the Supreme Court and to take over education also supply positive, affirmative visions for proposed reforms. Each effort advances a superficially neutral agenda—originalism in the case of the Court and ideological diversity in the case of education—that on closer inspection masks a deeper ideological project.

For the courts, the Republican Party's positive vision was originalism. Especially in recent decades, originalism has been pitched as a way of constraining judicial discretion and ensuring that judges will follow the law rather than their own politics and personal preferences. In part because originalism promises to bind decision-makers to a supposedly determinate source of law, the implication was that the methodology did not favor one political view or ideology over another. Indeed, common defenses of originalism point to originalist decisions that do not seem to favor traditionally Republican, right-wing interests.[76] Typical examples include Justice Antonin Scalia's decisions on the confrontation clause and the right to a jury trial favoring criminal defendants over government prosecutors.[77]

The origin story of originalism, as well as its application in the modern Court, however, complicates this picture. The notion that judges went awry when they did not follow the original understanding of the Constitution was initially trotted out as segregationists criticized the Supreme Court for invalidating segregated public schools in *Brown v. Board of Education*.[78] It picked up steam during the administration of Ronald Reagan, as officials in the administration fused the administration's views on social policy with the jurisprudence of originalism. Reagan administration officials, including the attorney general, championed originalism as a way of combating the civil libertarianism and egalitarianism of the Warren Court.[79] They also outlined how originalism provided a way to implement the administration's views on social issues, including support for private education, particularly religious education and sometimes segregated education.[80] Originalism was also championed as a way of overruling *Roe v. Wade* at a time when the Republican Party was actively seeking to cultivate voters who were anxious about the feminist and civil-rights revolutions of the 1960s and 1970s.[81]

In operation, originalism in the hands of the Roberts Court has managed to produce results that just so happen to track the Republican Party's preferences on a range of high-profile issues that are of particular value to, and particular priorities of, the Republican Party. That includes the end of *Roe v. Wade*, ending affirmative action, and reviving the Second Amendment. Even applied neutrally, originalism seems to lend itself to the views of a party that has promised to Make America Great Again—and return the country to some past time period that must be restored.[82]

For higher education, the right wing's proffered positive vision has been ideological diversity and balance.[83] Recall that Powell's original memo had recommended that the Chamber of Commerce demand "equal time on the college speaking circuit" and "urg[e] . . . faculty balance."[84] Mayer similarly described how members of the Olin Foundation sought to push a "beachhead theory" that would place conservative individuals, groups, and thinkers on campus without "rais[ing] questions about academic integrity."[85] But their goal was not academic freedom as such; framing the campaign in that way was merely done to avoid allegations and perceptions that the carefully organized campaign was an attack on academic freedom. The ultimate goal was to prop up support for corporations and their power and interests.[86] Recall McMahon's triumphant claim that the Columbia settlement was "a monumental victory for conservatives who wanted to do things on these elite campuses for a long time."[87]

Assailing schools as insufficiently balanced while demanding that they amplify more right-wing voices has become a deafening chorus from this administration. Journalists have written about the "nonstop right-wing attacks on what they call 'indoctrination.'"[88] The foreword to *Project 2025*, the ambitious blueprint for the hoped-for second Trump administration, is illustrative. It reads, "With or without an Education Department," the next Republican administration "should promote educational opportunities *outside the woke-dominated system of public schools and universities*."[89] In their push for ideological diversity, however, the people instigating these fights recognized that it was important to ensure that their preferred academics would not be labeled as ideological: "[I]t was 'essential for the integrity and reputation of the programs that they be defined not by ideological points of view.'"[90]

One of the more successful efforts to counterbalance the progressive tilt of higher education, one which has likely had spillover effects onto courts and the law, occurred in law schools: the law and economics movement. As Jane Mayer described, one of the Olin Foundation's leaders "admitted that the beauty of the program was that it was a stealth political attack and . . . the country's best law schools didn't grasp this."[91] "I saw it [law and economics] as a way into the law schools—I probably shouldn't confess that," he admitted to the *New York Times* in the early 2000s.[92] "Economic analysis tends to have conservatizing effects."[93] "If you said to a dean that you wanted to fund conservative constitutional law, he would reject the idea out of hand. But if you said you wanted to support Law and Economics, he would be much more open to the idea," he said.[94] "Law and Economics . . . like many disciplines, it seems neutral, but it isn't in fact," because, in his view, it tended to reach what are regarded as conservative conclusions.[95] And at least in some hands, it could be deployed intentionally to do so.

A right-wing takeover of education is not the goal of everyone involved in the beachhead programming or similar efforts. Nor is everyone in those circles part of a coordinated campaign. But the same could be said of the right-wing efforts directed at the courts, at least with respect to certain organizations such as the Federalist Society, and that didn't keep the overall effort from being brutally effective.

***

Both the attacks on higher education and the attacks on the courts have troll-ish tones to them. In the case of higher education, the administration and its ideological allies have often pretextually and unlawfully invoked Title VI, the federal law prohibiting discrimination in education, as a basis for cutting off federal funds to schools. But the efforts are a front in a larger campaign that is targeting minority groups on campus (and elsewhere). By demanding admissions data from schools and treating the presence of racial minorities in higher education as evidence of illegal affirmative action and racial discrimination, the Trump administration and its ideological allies are threatening access to equal education. It is a vindictive and insulting use of federal antidiscrimination protections to deploy them as a weapon for facilitating discrimination.

So too with the courts. After decades of railing against lawless judicial activism, Republicans and the right-wing legal movement seem to have learned to love it—at least when it benefits them. And the Republican-dominated Supreme Court, which is engaged in its own lawless antics, continues to act as if the real threat to the rule of law today is not an executive branch that is engaged in brazen, systematic legal violations and antidemocratic behavior, but the lower federal courts that are attempting to uphold the law and enforce the law as that happens.[96]

Part of what makes the affirmative visions offered by right-wing politicians so appealing and effective is that, in the abstract, they are onto something: It *would* be a concern if the federal courts were too activist, whether that means departing from the law to impose their own preferences, invalidating democratic enactments, or something else, just as it would be a concern if academia lacked the kind of diversity that would facilitate effective research and teaching. That is, there may be something to both critiques: We may want the elected branches to be exercising more power relative to the federal courts, and we may want more diversity in certain aspects of academia.

The problem is in the application of the principles—that is, what the principles appear to mean in practice. In practice, calls against judicial activism seem to be code for criticizing the courts for doing things the Republican Party and right-wing movement don't like. Reforming and remaking the federal courts to address that concern and implement a right-wing agenda isn't something to embrace. So too with the calls for ideological diversity in academia. In practice, ideological diversity seems to mean something like hiring faculty whose worldviews and policy preferences track those of the Republican Party. But when the Republican Party is embracing false claims about voter fraud or climate change, how does that enhance the mission of research universities that are committed to enhancing knowledge? Again, it might be the case that academia would benefit from certain kinds of diversity of viewpoints, such as methodological diversity. It would also be good if academia did not discriminate against people for their ideological or political beliefs. But the picture is vastly more complex when some of the ideological beliefs or political beliefs run counter to the academic enterprise, including the search for truth, a commitment to facts and evidence, and a willingness to engage with people of different identities. When those are the relevant ideologies or politics, then we couldn't and shouldn't expect institutions of higher education to be actively cultivating them.

Mutual Reinforcements

The campaigns to take over the courts and education are related in other ways as well—the two reinforce one another. Consider the calculus facing some schools that find themselves in the crosshairs of the Trump administration. Sure, a school may reason, the administration's actions are illegal, and on multiple grounds.[97] But if and when that case came to the Supreme Court, they wonder, what would the Court do, given its willingness to be flexible on the law in more than a few cases?[98] Universities may not be sure, especially given how often the Court has given the Trump administration what it has asked for on the shadow docket.[99] A similar calculus probably informs universities' assessments about whether the Court would even force the administration to comply with decisions ordering it to release frozen funds to schools, given the Court's willingness to overlook the administration's defiance of lower-court orders.[100]

The takeover of the courts has advanced the right-wing movement's goals for higher education in other ways as well. There have been several high-profile instances of federal judges announcing "boycotts" of hiring law clerks who attend law schools that are perceived to be insufficiently friendly to Republican appointees and Republican views.[101] Here, too, Republicans are able to leverage their power over the courts into a kind of power over higher education.

***

Surveying some of the wreckage a few months into the second Trump administration, journalist Will Bunch observed that "[t]he American Dream of higher education" had "soared" at a time of "major government support" for higher education, whereas now the country has "devolved into a nation where public trust in our universities is at an all-time low." There are myriad contributing causes, including rising economic inequality coupled with the cost of higher education, as well as right-wing efforts to amplify excesses and mistakes of left-leaning students, faculty, and administrators. But as Bunch astutely observed, "the real threat" "has always been from a too powerful government and a hostile right-wing that has come to oppose the very idea of higher education."[102]

Too many people saw the right-wing efforts to take over the Supreme Court too late—when the takeover had already succeeded. Ideally, that mistake would not be repeated for higher education. To fight back and to resist, academics and universities will have to engage in public(-facing) education—to combat misinformation about higher education, to make information and education accessible, and to make the case for the value of education. All of that is necessary to combat the campaign against academia. To carry it out, schools will have to combine the expertise of different kinds of faculty, specializing in different fields. And they will need to embrace principles of academic freedom that will protect academics and universities as they make the case for their continued existence.

12

How Speech-Based Immigration Restrictions Threaten Academic Freedom

ILYA SOMIN*

Since he returned to office in January 2025, President Donald Trump's administration has engaged in a systematic effort to deport noncitizen university students and academics who express views contrary to those of the US government on a number of issues. This is far from the first time the US government has engaged in speech-based deportations. But this effort is the most significant in many years, and is notable for specifically targeting university students and employees. Litigation over these attempted deportations has focused on First Amendment free-speech issues.[1] But speech-based deportations of students and university employees also threaten academic freedom. This chapter explains how and why.

As of 2024, there were some 1.1 million foreign students studying at US colleges and universities.[2] US universities also employ large numbers of recent immigrants and other noncitizens as academics and researchers, though the exact percentages are not easy to determine because available data doesn't separate out foreign-born noncitizens from immigrants who have become naturalized.[3] Thus, these academic-freedom issues directly affect large numbers of people. They also have large indirect effects on the academic freedom of US-citizen students, academics, and researchers.

Part I briefly summarizes the Trump administration's campaign of speech-based deportation of noncitizen students and academics. That campaign focuses

* Professor of Law, George Mason University. For helpful discussions and suggestions, I would like to thank Lee Bollinger, Geoffrey Stone, Eugene Volokh, and Keith Whittington. A few passages here were adapted from posts published on the Volokh Conspiracy, a law and politics blog hosted by *Reason*.

Ilya Somin, *How Speech-Based Immigration Restrictions Threaten Academic Freedom*. In: *Academic Freedom in the Era of Trump*. Edited by: Lee C. Bollinger and Geoffrey R. Stone, Oxford University Press. © Oxford University Press (2026). DOI: 10.1093/9780197854877.003.0013 primarily on students with anti-Israel and pro-Palestinian views regarding the ongoing war in Gaza. But its logic could just as easily justify targeting a wide range of other viewpoints. Many kinds of speech could easily be depicted as justifying violence, terrorism, or anti-Semitism, or as being inimical to US foreign-policy goals.

Part II presents an overview of the idea of academic freedom. That principle is related to, but distinct from, freedom of speech. In some respects, it is narrower than the latter; for example, faculty and researchers must be evaluated based on the quality of their work, which may entail action against those who publish works advocating positions that fail to meet disciplinary methodological standards. Faculty and student in-class speech is also subject to restrictions that would be seen as violating freedom of speech if imposed by the government on the general public. But academic freedom does nonetheless require faculty and researchers to be able to consider and express a wide range of viewpoints on the issues they work on, and to be free of sanctions for viewpoints they express outside of the context of their academic work.

Part III explains how speech-based deportations undermine the academic freedom of both noncitizens subject to deportation and US citizen scholars and students. The former effect is obvious. The latter is more indirect, but nonetheless large. Speech-based deportations of foreign students and academics chill the speech of their US-citizen colleagues, and also deprive the latter of the opportunity for valuable interactions that could enhance their research, teaching, and learning. What is true of speech-based deportations is also true of speech-based exclusions of potential migrants even before they are allowed to set foot in the United States. While First Amendment legal precedent distinguishes between the two situations, their implications for academic freedom—and free speech—are similar.

Finally, Part IV considers multiple possible rationales for speech-based deportations. Ironically, some of these rationales—currently advanced by a right-wing administration—turn out to be similar to traditional left-wing rationales for restrictions on "hate speech." Whether deployed by the right or the left, the rationales are badly flawed. If correct, they cannot logically be limited to suppressing speech by noncitizens. Bigoted or otherwise reprehensible speech by US citizens gives rise to comparable or greater dangers.

The Trump Administration's Campaign of Speech-Based Deportations

Since returning to office, the Trump administration has repeatedly made clear its intentions to target anti-Israel and pro-Palestinian noncitizen students and university employees for deportation. Both the President and other officials have said as much. Moreover, the rationales for deporting these individuals go beyond the specifics of the Gaza War and the Israeli-Palestinian conflict and could easily justify deporting people for espousing a wide range of views.

In an executive order issued on his first day in office, Trump announced his intention to bar noncitizens who "commit terrorist attacks, threaten our national security, *espouse hateful ideology*, or otherwise exploit the immigration laws for malevolent purposes" (emphasis added).[4] Later, Trump, Secretary of State Marco Rubio, and other high officials repeatedly indicated that they sought to target those expressing anti-Israel and pro-Palestinian views.[5]

The statute the administration most relies on allows deportation of any "alien whose presence or activities in the United States the Secretary of State has reasonable ground to believe would have potentially serious adverse foreign policy consequences."[6] If mere speech attacking Israel, opposing the government's position on the Gaza War, or expressing "anti-Semitic" views qualifies as an "activity" with "potentially serious adverse foreign policy consequences" justifying deportation, the same would be true of a wide range of other speech on a vast range of issues. For example, virtually any criticism of US policy or that of a US ally can be seen as having "potentially serious adverse foreign policy consequences." Espousing pacifism could be described as having such consequences for defense policy and for deterring attacks against the United States. And so on.

In 1996, Federal District Judge Maryanne Trump Barry—ironically, the late sister of President Donald Trump—issued a decision striking down the statute because its standards are so unclear as to be unconstitutionally "void for vagueness."[7] Her ruling was overturned on appeal, based on procedural grounds.[8] But her point about vagueness—and the resulting potential for abuse—was well-taken.

The Trump administration also cites a statute which bars "any alien who . . . endorses or espouses terrorist activity or persuades others to endorse or espouse terrorist activity or support a terrorist organization."[9] This, too, is a vague standard. What counts as "terrorist activity," and especially what counts as "endorsing" or "espousing" it, is a matter of long-standing dispute. Among other things, there is an ongoing debate over when violent resistance to government authority is justified.[10]

In the context of the Israel-Hamas War, it is not clear whether this means (1) only speech directly defending Hamas's terrorist attacks, or also includes (2) speech supporting the establishment of a Palestinian state (which is one of Hamas's objectives in the current conflict), and (3) speech attacking Israel's conduct of the war, including claims that Israeli forces are committing war crimes such as genocide. Speech in categories 2 and 3 can be seen as "supporting" Hamas by helping it achieve its objectives, even if it doesn't directly endorse the group's terrorist actions.

Speech restrictions like this are also readily susceptible to discriminatory enforcement. For example, the Trump administration claims to be targeting "Hamas sympathizers,"[11] but is not similarly seeking to deport supporters of Russia's invasion of Ukraine, which has resulted in atrocities comparable to those of Hamas but on a larger scale.[12] Those who support or justify Russian atrocities are far more aligned with the Trump administration's own positions (the Trump administration notoriously refuses to even admit that Russia is the aggressor in the conflict[13]) than those who support Hamas. The administration acts accordingly. Similarly, Trump's executive order no. 14188, which seeks to deport "aliens" involved in promoting anti-Semitism,[14] promises to "punish anti-Jewish racism in leftist, anti-American colleges and universities," but makes no similar commitments regarding right-wing anti-Semitism.[15]

As of this writing (October 2025), there have been multiple court cases involving attempted deportations of students and academics, applying these vague standards.[16] And these cases do not even necessarily involve clear endorsements of any kind of "terrorism" or defenses of Hamas or the horrific atrocities that terrorist group perpetrated in its October 7, 2023, attack on Israel.

For example, the attempted deportation of Tufts University graduate student Rümeysa Öztürk was, as a federal court ruled,[17] motivated by her publication of an op-ed in a student newspaper that made no mention of Hamas and did not endorse its attacks, but merely demanded that the university "acknowledge the Palestinian genocide, apologize for University President Sunil Kumar's statements, disclose its investments and divest from companies with direct or indirect ties to Israel."[18] I do not agree that Israel's actions in the Gaza War amount to genocide, nor do I support the call for universities to divest from companies with ties to Israel. But nothing in the op-ed qualifies as an endorsement of Hamas or terrorism; indeed, Hamas is not even mentioned. Öztürk was detained for weeks under terrible conditions before a court ordered her released.[19]

The Trump administration has indicated that it intends to engage in other speech-based deportations and exclusions. For example, its proposed "Compact for Excellence in Higher Education" would require universities to "screen out students who demonstrate hostility to the United States, its allies, or its values."[20] This pretty obviously covers a vast range of speech. Protesting American "values" is a subjective standard, subject to all kinds of dispute. "Hostility to the United States, its allies, or its values" could potentially include even such things as criticism of repression in authoritarian US allies, such as Egypt and Saudi Arabia. So far, every school to address the matter has refused to participate in the compact, including the Massachusetts Institute of Technology, Brown University, the University of Pennsylvania, the University of Virginia, the University of Arizona, and the University of Southern California.[21] But the compact is clearly part of an effort to pressure universities into enforcing speech-based restrictions on foreign students, by restricting federal funding to universities that refuse to comply.[22]

The Administration has also rescinded visas issued to at least six foreign nationals based on what it claims are inappropriate online comments about the September 2025 assassination of conservative activist Charlie Kirk.[23] If such policies continue, they too could sweep up a vast range of speech. And, as with anti-Semitism and terrorism, there is a clear ideological bias here. The Administration has not attempted to impose similar restrictions on visa holders who support or make light of right-wing political violence.

The Concept of Academic Freedom

Academic freedom is closely related to freedom of speech, but also distinct from it. The famous *1915 Statement of Principles of Academic Freedom* by the American Association of University Professors (AAUP), as amended in 1940, states that "Teachers are entitled to full freedom in research and in the publication of the results."[24] Similarly, the statement also states that, "When they speak or write as citizens, [professors] should be free from institutional censorship or discipline," though it also cautions that "they should at all times be accurate, should exercise appropriate restraint, should show respect for the opinions of others, and should make every effort to indicate that they are not speaking for the institution."[25]

These principles are essential to ensure that academics can engage in free inquiry on their subjects, and also discuss issues within their expertise in broader discourse that can reach the general public. In addition, if professors can be dismissed or otherwise punished for expressing political views outside the academic context, that necessarily chills public debate on important issues and reduces the range of views that can be considered in public and academic debate. If, for example, people who express right-wing political views can be fired for doing so, then those views are not likely to be effectively represented in academic debates over key issues. Modern scholarship on academic freedom largely agrees on these points.[26]

Academics' rights to academic freedom do not include free-speech rights against university officials as broad as those that they—and the general public—enjoy against government censorship. As the AAUP recognizes, faculty members' academic-freedom rights are "subject to the adequate performance of their other academic duties," which usually include meeting professional standards in their research, teaching, and publications.[27] Some views may be so erroneous or ridiculous as to fall short of disciplinary standards, if expressed in academic publications or teaching. For example, as legal scholars Erwin Chemerinsky and

Howard Gillman point out, a university can choose not to hire a Holocaust denier to teach World War II history.[28] Similarly, a geography department can refuse to hire a supporter of "flat earth" theory, and a biology department can refuse to hire a person who rejects genetics or the theory of evolution.

Such restrictions are essential to the academic enterprise. But it is also worth noting that they can be abused. Ideological and other biases can affect academics' and administrators' perceptions of what views are so incompetent as to fall outside disciplinary boundaries. That is especially likely in fields that address ideologically disputed issues, such as law, political theory, and history.

When it comes to classroom speech, universities can also require both faculty and students to focus on the subject at hand rather than extraneous issues. The AAUP statement, for example, notes that instructors "should be careful not to introduce into their teaching controversial matter which has no relation to their subject."[29] Even the introduction of relatively noncontroversial matters may be appropriately barred if it distracts from focusing on the subject the class is supposed to be about. For example, when I teach a constitutional-law class, the university can appropriately discipline me if I instead spend class time discussing professional football—even if the students and I might find that subject more interesting than the issues we are supposed to be covering.

What is true of faculty speech also applies to students, and to nonfaculty researchers affiliated with universities. They, too, must be free to pursue professional research topics unfettered by censorship, though subject to disciplinary standards. And they, too, must be free to express opinions outside of class and outside their research responsibilities. The AAUP and other academic organizations have endorsed these ideas in their "Joint Statement on Rights and Freedoms of Students," originally drafted in 1967 and revised since then.[30]

Students and nonfaculty researchers—in their capacities as research assistants, as coauthors of articles and books, and in other ways—play crucial roles in promoting academic inquiry. When acting in these capacities, they must be free of censorship for much the same reasons as professors. Similarly, if students and nonfaculty employees engaged in research can be punished for expressing political views outside of class, such punishment—like that of professors—chills expression and limits the range of views that can be considered in academic and public debate.

It is also obvious that, in many situations, students play a key role in classroom debates and discussions. If, say, right- or left-wing students can be expelled from the university for publicly expressing those views, then that will narrow the range of opinions likely to be effectively represented in classroom debate and discussion. While faculty members generally play a key role in leading classroom discussions, student participation is usually essential to their effectiveness. That effectiveness is greatly reduced if students holding certain views are systematically excluded from the university.

As with professors, students' academic freedom in the classroom and while doing assignments is not as extensive as their free-speech rights against the government. Like faculty, students and nonfaculty researchers can be disciplined or (in extreme cases) even dismissed for advancing views in publications that fall short of disciplinary standards. Similarly, students taking exams or writing class assignments may get lower grades if they advocate positions that are clearly erroneous and fall below disciplinary standards. For example, a student who defends Holocaust denial or flat-Earth theory in a paper written for a class may appropriately receive a lower grade, even a failing grade. As with faculty, evaluations of student work may sometimes be influenced by ideological or other biases. But that does not mean universities can or should abjure such evaluations altogether.

How Speech-Based Deportations and Exclusions Undermine Academic Freedom

The above elaboration of the principles of academic freedom suggests multiple ways in which speech-based deportations of academics and students undermine those principles. The same is true of speech-based exclusions of potential students and university employees who are never allowed to enter the United States in the first place.

Allowing deportation based on the types of vague standards used by the Trump administration could easily chill speech on a wide range of issues involving armed conflict, international relations, US foreign policy, and much more. And the effect is not limited to the speech of immigrants and foreign students. Other students and faculty may decline to discuss these subjects on campus for fear of exposing international students or noncitizen immigrants to danger if the latter participate in the relevant discussions.

For example, in my constitutional-law classes I teach segments on the use of racial profiling for national-security purposes (e.g., in the War on Terror), executive war powers, immigration, and other issues related to foreign and security policy. If a noncitizen student participates in class discussion or writes a paper on one of these topics, there is a chance that they might say something the administration defines as supporting terrorism, endorsing a "hateful ideology," or having "adverse foreign policy consequences for the United States," and thereby be targeted for deportation. To forestall that danger, instructors must either avoid such topics altogether or forgo discussing them in the presence of noncitizen students.

That concern applies to both in-class discussions and less formal interactions elsewhere on campus. If there is a chance that federal officials might learn of the discussion and the viewpoints expressed, there will be incentives to avoid issues and viewpoints that might attract the ire of the administration in power.

Similar points apply to scholars researching and writing on such issues in collaboration with noncitizen students or faculty. Speech-based deportations prevent US-citizen students and academics from pursuing some types of research projects with noncitizen colleagues. Any topic that might lead to expressions of viewpoints contrary to those of the administration in power could lead to deportation of the noncitizen coauthor. Thus, there would be a strong incentive to avoid such collaboration.

These kinds of chilling effects are an obvious threat to free speech on campus, to the academic enterprise of teaching and research, and to academic freedom more generally. At any university with noncitizen students, faculty, or research employees, such issues are likely to arise so long as speech-based deportations continue.

Much the same issues arise with speech-based restrictions on initial entry to the United States. Current judicial First Amendment precedent is more deferential to government on initial exclusion than on deportation.[31] Elsewhere, I have argued that this distinction is wrong.[32] The First Amendment is a generalized limitation on federal-government power, whose application is not limited by the citizenship of the people the government is targeting or by their location.

But whatever may be true of First Amendment doctrine, speech-based exclusions clearly undermine academic freedom in much the same way as do speech-based deportations. Such exclusions obviously curtail the academic freedom of the noncitizen academics and students who are barred as a result. In order to forestall exclusion, the latter are either deprived of opportunities to pursue research and education that may not be available elsewhere or incentivized to avoid expressing certain views or researching certain topics.

Speech-based exclusions of foreign students and academics also curtail the academic freedom of their potential US-citizen classmates and colleagues, who are deprived of opportunities to pursue research projects with the foreigners in question, at least insofar as some research collaborations require the latter to be present in the United States.

They are also deprived of the classroom discussions and informal interactions that often stimulate learning and the development of new research projects. Even in an age of remote digital communication, such informal in-person discussions are often crucial, and sometimes not easily replicable online. Among other things, an in-person presence facilitates more informal, spontaneous discussions, stimulates increased neural activity (which may lead to better reasoning), and makes it easier to take account of tone and nonverbal communication.[33]

These academic-freedom issues apply not only to scholars working at universities but also to those at other types of research institutions, such as think tanks, research institutes, and non-university laboratories. Such institutions likewise need venues for unfettered discussion and analysis of ideas, and they very often rely on the contributions of recent immigrants and other noncitizen scholars and researchers.

When I was a visiting professor at a Chinese university in 2014, I noticed how students and faculty faced constant difficult trade-offs in deciding which topics were safe to discuss and which might bring down the wrath of the authorities in that repressive authoritarian state.[34] The rules on this score were far from clear, much like the standards the Trump administration currently seeks to apply to foreign students and academics in the United States. As a foreign professor, I faced fewer constraints than Chinese academics, because running afoul of the authorities was less dangerous for me than for them. But I still had to worry about whether covering certain topics or expressing certain views might lead to sanctions against my Chinese students and colleagues or to my own expulsion. For example, I carefully considered whether, in my course on property rights, I should do a lecture on the harm caused by Mao Zedong's collectivization of agriculture, which led to a famine that killed millions of people.[35] Experts on China gave conflicting advice on whether this was safe to do.[36]

Routine use of speech-based deportations and exclusions would create similar dilemmas in American academic institutions. Just as vague government-imposed speech restrictions had an obvious chilling effect there, the same is likely to be true in the United States if the Trump administration's policies take root.

Addressing Possible Objections

There are a number of potential objections to the argument developed so far, and I will go over each in turn. All have serious flaws, and if applied consistently, many would also justify extensive restrictions on the speech and academic freedom of US citizens.

Perhaps the most obvious justification for speech-based exclusions and deportations is the idea that only American citizens have any right to influence American political and intellectual discourse, and thus noncitizens have no entitlement to academic freedom or freedom of speech in the United States. This, however, ignores the fact that speech-based migration restrictions threaten the academic freedom and speech rights of US citizens as well as those of migrants and non-citizens.[37]

Even more fundamentally, this argument founders on the reality that the quality of an idea is not dependent on its origin. There is no good reason to think that ideas generated by Americans are necessarily better (or worse) than those generated by citizens of other countries. As the great Nobel Prize-winning economist F. A. Hayek put it, "[t]he growth of ideas is an international process. . . . It is no real argument to say that an idea is un-American, un-British, or un-German, nor is a mistaken or vicious ideal better for having been conceived by one of our compatriots."[38] Universities and other research institutions should strive to seek out the best ideas, regardless of origin. That means extending principles of academic freedom not just to Americans but to noncitizen scholars and students. The United States was founded, in large part, on Enlightenment liberal ideals, developed primarily by European thinkers.[39] It would be foolish to arbitrarily cut off our universities and other intellectual institutions from developing ideas with the participation of noncitizens.

In some cases, the ideas and viewpoints in question might be well-represented by native-born students and academics. But that often will not be the case. The United States has only about 4.2 percent of the world's population.[40] Although it develops a disproportionate percentage of world innovation, a large proportion of the best new ideas will inevitably be developed by non-US citizens, and our universities and other research institutions can inevitably benefit greatly from the contributions of noncitizen scholars and students.

Another prominent justification for speech-based deportations and exclusions is the concern that foreign academics and students might spread particularly pernicious ideas, such as the support for "terrorism" and anti-Semitism cited by the Trump administration.[41] Such fears have a long history, going back to the fears of the 1790s that Western European immigrants might spread dangerous French Revolutionary ideas,[42] and the early-20th-century fears that Jewish and other immigrants might spread socialism and anarchism.[43]

This argument has been repeatedly disproven by history, insofar as previous waves of immigration have not in fact led to the deterioration of liberal democratic institutions in the United States[44] or to any particularly pernicious spread of harmful ideas. It also overlooks standard objections to government control of political speech, including that government cannot be trusted to separate out harmful ideas from beneficial ones, and is instead likely to use its censorship authority to target ideas inimical to those in power at the moment.

Moreover, any rationale for suppressing the spread of harmful ideas cannot be limited to those generated by immigrants and other noncitizens. If the government is justified in suppressing the spread of a dangerous idea, then it can do so with respect to citizens as well. Indeed, the spread of harmful ideas by citizens is, as a general rule, actually more dangerous than similar activity by immigrants or foreign students, because citizens have much more political influence than noncitizens do, and longtime residents have greater influence than recent immigrants (even those who are citizens).[45] If the goal is to stop the spread of harmful ideas, we must target those advocates most likely to be effective in spreading them widely throughout society, which in most cases will not be noncitizen immigrants or foreign students.

Closely related to the argument that foreign students or academics may spread harmful ideas is the concern that they might cause harm by engaging in bigoted "hate speech," such as by spreading racial, ethnic, or gender prejudice. The Trump administration's claim that it is targeting anti-Semitic speech appeals to such considerations.

Ironically, right-wing immigration restrictionists who cite bigoted expression as justification for speech-based deportations are making claims similar to those advanced by longtime left-wing advocates of government suppression of "hate speech," who have long argued that such speech must be censored so as to prevent the spread of bigotry and alleviate the pain it causes minority groups.[46] Suppression of supposedly bigoted speech by migrants and other noncitizens is subject to all the same objections as other attempts to censor "hate speech," including that such repression violates human rights, that governments cannot be trusted to separate out hate speech from more legitimate speech, and that censorship is not actually an effective way to combat bigotry.[47]

If we conclude that the supposed benefits of restricting hate speech outweigh the harms, there is no reason to target speech by noncitizens specifically. To the contrary, like other supposedly harmful speech, hate speech is likely to be more dangerous if engaged in by native-born citizens than by noncitizens or recent immigrants. The former have greater political influence and more ability to promote their views with both the general public and government policymakers. Thus, consistent advocates of anti-hate-speech laws must advocate either a general censorship regime to suppress it, or one that prioritizes targeting those advocates that have the greatest influence on public and elite opinion. Ultimately, arguments that we should engage in speech-based deportation and exclusion of noncitizens because the ideas they spread are harmful collapse into arguments for a much broader censorship regime.

A standard response to the view that speech-based deportations and exclusions violate the Free Speech Clause of the First Amendment is that, even if noncitizens have a right to free speech, they do not have a constitutional right to be in the United States. Thus, deporting them for their speech doesn't violate the Constitution. In defending the Trump administration's policy, Secretary of State Marco Rubio stated that "This is not about free speech. This is about people that don't have a right to be in the United States to begin with. No one has a right to a student visa."[48]

One can deploy the same argument against academic-freedom objections to speech-based deportation and exclusion. A person who does not have a general legal right to be in the United States cannot raise academic-freedom objections to exclusion.

But, in virtually every other context, it is clear that depriving people of a right as punishment for their speech violates freedom of speech, even if the right they lose does not itself have constitutional status and can be withheld for a range of other reasons. For example, there is no constitutional right to get Social Security benefits, and Congress can lower them anytime it wants.[49] But a law that barred critics of the president from getting those benefits would obviously violate the First Amendment. In *Perry v. Sindermann* (1972), the Supreme Court held that "even though a person has no 'right' to a valuable governmental benefit, and even though the government may deny him the benefit for any number of reasons, ... [i]t may not deny a benefit to a person on a basis that infringes his constitutionally protected interest, especially his interest in freedom of speech."[50] The Court therefore concluded that a state university may not refuse to renew the contract of an instructor based on his constitutionally protected outside-of-class speech, despite the fact that he had no contractual or constitutional right to continued employment, and could potentially be fired for any number of other reasons.[51]

This logic applies to academic freedom no less than to freedom of speech. Even if academics or students can be deprived of a given right or opportunity for other reasons, taking it from them for expressing opinions unsympathetic to the government is still a violation of academic freedom. People do not have a general constitutional right or other legal right to be academics or university students. Universities can refuse to employ applicants for academic jobs (or fire those already employed, unless they have tenure) for any number of reasons. Similarly, they can reject applicants for student slots for a wide range of reasons, such as a lack of academic credentials or extracurricular skills. Students already at the university can be expelled for various reasons, such as falling short of academic requirements or violating university rules. But it would still violate the First Amendment—and academic freedom—if rejection was based on the academics' or students' political views or expression thereof.

The same logic applies in the immigration context. Even if an academic or student does not have an inherent constitutional or other legal right to be in the United States, deportation or exclusion based on their views on political or social issues would still violate both freedom of speech and academic freedom.

Critics of US universities, particularly right-of-center critics, might argue that the higher-education sector's appeal to academic freedom is fundamentally hypocritical, because many schools do not genuinely respect that freedom themselves. For example, in recent years, many institutions have required applicants for faculty positions to submit "diversity statements" committing themselves to controversial political stances on racial and gender issues.[52] A 2020 study of recent faculty job postings found that 19 percent required applicants to submit diversity statements, including one third of postings at "elite" institutions.[53] Some universities have also sought to impose speech codes restricting "hate speech" and some other forms of expression offending left-progressive sensibilities. The Foundation for Individual Rights and Expression (FIRE), a leading higher-education free-speech research and advocacy group, gives 166 of 257 surveyed institutions failing grades for their campus free-speech policies.[54] Such speech restrictions often impact not only freedom of speech but academic freedom as well.

If many colleges often don't respect academic freedom themselves, one could argue that they cannot appeal to that value in opposing speech-based deportations and exclusions of foreign academics and students. But the fact that many schools fail to fully respect academic freedom cannot justify the government's undermining that freedom further. Government-imposed restrictions make the situation worse, not better.

Moreover, government policies imposed nationwide are a bigger menace to free speech and academic freedom than policies imposed by individual schools. If some universities have badly flawed policies on academic freedom, others are much better. FIRE, for example, praises the speech policies of a number of schools, such as Claremont McKenna, Vanderbilt, and Dartmouth.[55] Faculty and students have the option of "voting with their feet" for schools with good policies, or at least relatively better ones.[56] Over time, schools with stronger academic-freedom protections are likely to outperform those with weak ones, and to have greater success in attracting top scholars and students, research grants, and the like.

There are also potential benefits to having schools with a diverse range of policies on speech and academic-freedom issues. It increases the range of options available to students and potential employees and fosters competition. We would not necessarily want every school to feature the same, internally diverse, range of opinions. Having some more homogeneous schools can increase the diversity of options in the system as a whole, promoting what legal scholar Heather Gerken calls "second-order diversity."[57]

For example, many religious schools may foster a climate of support for the views of their particular religious denomination. Thus, some Catholic schools seek to maintain a distinctively Catholic atmosphere, while Brigham Young University promotes a Mormon ambience. It would be bad if all or most schools promoted a particular religious or ideological ethos. But having a few that do so usefully expands the range of options available in the higher-education system as a whole and make useful contributions to debates over various issues.

By contrast, a censorship policy imposed by the federal government constrains all universities throughout the nation. There is no exit option short of leaving the country entirely. And, far from fostering potentially useful competition and second-order diversity, it stifles them. For reasons already discussed,[58] even if the censorship only directly targets noncitizen academics and students, it necessarily undermines the academic freedom of US citizens as well.

Finally, there are a variety of arguments for immigration restrictions that do not focus on migrants' speech or political opinions. These include fears that immigrants will take jobs from natives, overburden the welfare state, increase crime and terrorism, undermine political and economic institutions, spread disease, "swamp" the native population, and cause environmental destruction. Elsewhere, I have argued that these concerns are almost always unjustified and greatly overstated, that they do not outweigh the many benefits of immigration (including those for native-born citizens of receiving countries), and that in any event they can be addressed by "keyhole" solutions that do not require exclusion.[59] For example, if immigrants indeed threaten to overburden the welfare state, that could be addressed by restricting the range of welfare benefits they are eligible for.[60]

If such considerations do justify some immigration restrictions, they do not justify deportation or exclusion based on migrants' speech or political views. Rather, they can only justify barring those migrants likely to create or exacerbate the problem at issue, such as crime, terrorism, or burdens on the welfare state.

Conclusion

Speech-based deportations and exclusions of noncitizen students and academics constitute a grave threat to academic freedom, including that of US citizens. Possible justifications for these policies are badly flawed. If applied consistently, many of them would actually justify much broader censorship policies that would target native-born US citizens as much as or more than immigrants and foreign students.

PART V

UNIVERSITY CULTURE AND ITS CONTRIBUTION TO THE DEMISE OF ACADEMIC FREEDOM

13

The American Attack on Academic Freedom in Comparative Perspective

TOM GINSBURG*

Everyone has seen the numbers. Democracy is in trouble everywhere, with two straight decades of declines in the number of democratic countries and the percentage of humanity living in free societies. The United States is obviously not immune from this trend, and the second Trump administration is acting as an accelerant for democratic decline at home and abroad. The use of illegal authoritarian tactics at home is combined with active alliance with dictators, populist strongmen, and demagogues abroad, posing a grave threat to liberty in many spheres.

This chapter considers the impact of democratic decline on academic freedom. Global indices of academic freedom show a decline similar to that seen in democracy measures, particularly exacerbated by anti-pluralist political parties.[1] The first few months of Trump 2.0 have followed this trend, as we have seen a series of high-profile attacks on academic institutions. These were foreshadowed in 2021 by J. D. Vance, who declared that "universities are the enemy" and promised to "honestly and aggressively attack the universities in this country."[2] Some of the strategies used by Trump 2.0 mirror those of other populists, especially the use of material resources to coerce substantive changes. But others may represent innovations, which in turn may diffuse to other countries around the world.

One reason the Trump attacks have come so fast and furious is that, relative to other countries, academic freedom is relatively weakly institutionalized in the United States. In the US Constitution, in contrast with others more recently

* Tom Ginsburg is the Leo Spitz Distinguished Service Professor of International Law and Professor of Political Science and the University of Chicago Law School.

Tom Ginsburg, *The American Attack on Academic Freedom in Comparative Perspective*. In: *Academic Freedom in the Era of Trump*. Edited by: Lee C. Bollinger and Geoffrey R. Stone, Oxford University Press. © Oxford University Press (2026). DOI: 10.1093/9780197854877.003.0014 drafted, there is no discrete provision protecting the rights of scholars or scientists to pursue inquiry, or the right of citizens to enjoy the fruits of scientific research. Nor is there a national-level statutory scheme. There is nevertheless a rich body of institutional norms and practices, as well as law that has arisen at the sub-constitutional level.[3] As the United States turns in a more authoritarian direction, however, these norms are coming under severe and sudden threat. Authoritarians in any country do not want an engaged citizenry, nor an autonomous public sphere that might breed political opposition.[4] We in the US academy can learn from the experience of our colleagues around the world about trajectories and vectors of attack and defense.

The chapter is organized as follows: First, we briefly describe the American framework for academic freedom from a comparative perspective. We next consider the pathways of attack by authoritarians, with a taxonomy of techniques. Importantly, the threats to academic freedom have long been conceived of as top-down, with the material dimension being critical. But in fact the threats to academic freedom also come from below, using the tools of civil society itself. Here the United States has been something of a leader in recent years, through a series of energized activists on both left and right who seek to advance political agendas. The trend, though it is accelerating through social media, is structurally similar to that of the fascist period in Europe, when a symbiosis between fascist politicians and a mob of followers squeezed the air out of German academia. The final section concludes with some preliminary thoughts on counterstrategies.

Protecting Academic Freedom

Academic freedom is a complex idea, rooted in the 19th-century German notion of freedom of teaching and freedom of research. It includes both individual and collective components, in that it can be invoked not only by an individual professor pursuing knowledge but also by collective entities such as universities that seek to insulate themselves from state interference. Jacob Levy nicely describes it as a complex associational right that depends on freedoms to associate with others in formulating norms and standards particular to disciplinary communities.[5] After all, academic freedom cannot be exercised alone: it depends on complex institutional structures for its realization.

If one includes various textual formulations, academic freedom is protected in more than half of constitutions in force today.[6] This number has risen, particularly in the last few decades, and some countries have strong institutional structures to protect academic freedom. In Germany, for example, violations of academic freedom can be challenged before administrative courts.[7] In some countries, the collective right of university self-governance is the primary focus;

in others, it is conceived of as a right of individual scholars to pursue knowledge.[8] Some countries are part of supranational systems that also guarantee academic freedom: the European Union Charter of Fundamental Rights states that "The arts and scientific research shall be free of constraint. Academic freedom shall be respected."[9]

Unlike many other constitutions, however, the US Constitution contains no right to scientific knowledge, to academic freedom, or even to education. Other than allowing Congress to establish intellectual-property rights "to promote the progress of science and useful arts," the text leaves these matters to the private sphere or to the several states.[10]

As David Rabban has recently recounted, the idea of academic freedom in the United States started as a set of professional norms, developed within universities and crystallized by the American Association of University Professors (AAUP).[11] It gradually developed into a set of legal rights, stitched together under the First Amendment protection for freedom of speech along with contract law. Two AAUP documents are touchstones for almost every discussion: the *1915 Declaration of Principles on Academic Freedom and Tenure*, and the *1940 Statement of Principles on Academic Freedom and Tenure*. These have been widely endorsed and often voluntarily incorporated into faculty handbooks.

Yet legal protections remain weak and are being sorely tested under the Trump administration. The key constitutional question is whether state-university leaders run afoul of the First Amendment when they restrict or coerce academic speech. In *Garcetti v. Ceballos*, the Supreme Court held that public-employee speech does not receive full First Amendment protection when made pursuant to official duties.[12] Since state-university teachers in the classroom are pursuing their official duties, this would imply that government actors could dictate the content of their speech; however, the Court declined to rule on this point, since it was not the issue before it.[13] While the Supreme Court has never returned to the issue, lower courts have applied the more general Pickering-Connick test, which provides First Amendment protections to employees who speak on matters of public concern.[14] Several circuit courts of appeals have announced exceptions to the *Garcetti* standard, providing more protection for academic freedom.[15]

There are also state-constitutional protections, which can be grounded in state-level free-speech guarantees.[16] These in turn can exist at the constitutional or statutory level. California's Leonard Law, for example, extends free-speech guarantees even to private universities that operate within the state. California's constitution also establishes state universities as autonomous entities, providing a degree of collective academic freedom. In other states, state courts have interpreted constitutional language to provide protection for academic freedom. But this creates a patchwork set of protections for academic freedom that depends on whether one is in a private or public institution, and whether in a tolerant or intolerant jurisdiction.

Pathways of Attack

Knowledge is power, and authoritarians understand that independent institutions that produce knowledge can form a major threat to official narratives. "Knowledge institutions" of whatever kind are not to be allowed to be autonomous. In country after country, we see populist and demagogic leaders attacking the media, manipulating government information, and attacking academic freedom. One can classify the techniques used to squeeze academia as either individual or collective threats.

Start with individual threats. Most obviously, an unjust firing infringes on the academic freedom of the fired teacher as a direct matter. But disciplinary processes can be effective even if the final result is not termination. Students and faculty have been disciplined around the world for speech critical of the government. The effects of such action are not limited to the targets, as other faculty and students may be intimidated or silenced, and in this sense infringements on the individual right to academic freedom can, and are often designed to, have general effects.

The techniques used range from crude violence, such as wrongful arrest and detention or physical attack, to revocation of rights to reside (for foreign scholars), travel restrictions preventing scholars from leaving the country, and loss of position.[17] General restrictions on free speech can be abused when academics are targeted. For example, in 2019 the Polish-Australian professor Wojciech Sadurski was charged with criminal libel by Poland's ruling Law and Justice Party in connection with comments he made about its members' similarity to Nazis.[18] In Thailand, American academic Paul Chambers was arrested for violating the country's strict *lèse majesté* laws for comments he made about the Thai military. Though he was released, his visa was revoked and his academic position was terminated.[19] Others have been silenced into submission.

Collective threats may address a particular university or the system of higher education as a whole. Sometimes this involves restrictions on subjects that can be researched; more often it involves increases in government scrutiny of scientific funding. In Albania, Japan, and Poland, for example, research funding has been put under closer government oversight. In 2018 Poland's Law and Justice Party adopted a major legislative reform, which it followed with an "Academic Freedom Package" in 2021. This sought to undermine academic control of debates by introducing a new disciplinary procedure and mandating tolerance of religious and ideological beliefs and convictions. While this seemed to support academic freedom, it actually represents a politically motivated broadening of debates and an attempt to take them out of the control of academics.

Anatole France once said that the rich man and the poor man enjoy equal rights to sleep under bridges at night. This comment highlights the fact that rights of every type always depend upon certain material conditions for their effectuation. A long debate over the relative priority of civil and political rights versus economic and social rights illustrates the tension: Can one truly be free to speak on an empty belly? But how can one address material inequities without a right to speak freely?[20] One needs a material base for the exercise of rights, and the existence of that base itself depends on rights.

The exercise of academic freedom is particularly sensitive to material factors. The right to be free to research depends on some fundamental economic conditions that are, to say the least, unevenly distributed around the world. One cannot research effectively in a library with no books. The situation of many public universities in Africa reflects the effective starvation of institutions by politicians who have little interest in independent institutions that might foment student activism.[21]

This means that the effective scope of academic freedom is highly variable. One may enjoy a right to be free from interference at the retail level for one's scholarship, but even under conventional understandings, one does not have a right to any particular level of research support, teaching load, or particular course assignment. Nor is there any right, outside of contract, to be employed in a particular department. When universities close departments for budgetary reasons, they often will fire all the academic employees. Administrative reorganization is a powerful tool that looks to be increasingly viable in an era of profound financial crises at universities.

Both individual and collective threats occur in a political context. In this regard, it is important to note that threats of both types are not only top-down, but can also come from social forces outside the university, and sometimes from students themselves. In India, affiliates of Hindu nationalist groups such as the Rashtriya Swayamsevak Sangh (RSS) have waged a campaign against many organizations and individuals deemed to be insufficiently nationalist. For example, in 2024 members of several groups attacked Professor Ch. Chengaiah, head of the electrical-engineering department at Sri Venkateswara University, an advocate of Dalit rights who was accused of promoting Christianity by a group called the Legal Rights Protection Forum.[22] In another incident, RSS activists disrupted a film festival, and critics of the government routinely receive threats. In October 2024, Argentine President Javier Milei vetoed the University Financing Law, which led to large student protests around the country; in response, unknown groups threatened protesting students, using pepper spray in some cases, and some faculty received threatening calls.[23]

Student groups themselves can threaten academic freedom. Fights between student activists on left and right are becoming more common. Early in 2025, a French antifascist group called Raised Fist fought with right-wing student activists at the Mirail campus of University of Toulouse-Jean Jaurès around the time of student-council elections. Similar fights have occurred elsewhere in Europe as well.

The rise of militant student groups can put pressure on faculty. The most prominent historical example was that of the Nazi Party, which in 1926 created the National Socialist German Students' League. These students became frontline enforcers of the "Law for the Restoration of the Professional Civil Service," passed soon after the Nazi electoral takeover in 1933. The Law required the dismissal of all non-Aryan civil servants as well as political opponents of the government. The Students League bullied and intimidated Jewish students and faculty members, disrupting lectures and organizing book burnings, and more than 1,000 faculty members were terminated.

In short, threats to academic freedom can come at the individual or collective level. The former involve disciplinary tools and selective legal challenges; the latter typically involve funding. In addition to these top-down threats, which rely on government or university administrators to effectuate, there is in some contexts a kind of bottom-up pressure that emerges from society itself.

The United States

How do such pressures manifest in the case of the United States? Trump has wielded the material tools at his disposal with astounding swiftness. American universities had relied on a benevolent bargain with the federal government dating from World War II, when the Office of Scientific Research and Development was created to conduct military research. Its director, Vannevar Bush, conceived of a broad partnership between government and research universities, whereby government would outline broad priorities for research, which would then be conducted by university faculty on a competitive basis.

The model contributed to victory in World War II and produced the greatest university system in the world, as well as countless scientific discoveries. But it always carried the risk of government pressures. Some prescient analysts and scholars warned about the risks of this bargain, emphasizing the different incentives of the two parties. University of Chicago President Robert Maynard Hutchins criticized the G.I. bill after World War II on the grounds that government funds would diminish the autonomy of universities. In an essay entitled "Massive Subsidies and Academic Freedom" in 1963, conservative scholar Russell Kirk emphasized the different incentives of the two parties to the government-university bargain.[24] Beginning with the observation that "to kill with kindness is quite possible," he noted a serious risk that funders, like the proverbial payer of the piper, would call the tune. Both the federal government and the large foundations that played such an important role in the second half of the 20th century were highly bureaucratized and "monolithic" endeavors, which would "resent unusual talents or insubordinate opinions among scholars."[25]

Whatever the merits of these arguments, they were decisively rejected by managers of universities. Federal spending on research expanded; Hutchins eventually acceded to competitive pressures and decided to accept government research funds. Government priorities in turn shaped education opportunities. Many of our individual intellectual trajectories are ultimately traceable to government funding. In my own case, as a scholar of East Asia, I benefited from the rise of area studies, which was originally funded by the Office of Strategic Services and later by a series of private foundations, most notably the Ford Foundation. The 1957 National Defense Education Act (later modified in the Higher Education Act of 1965) provided funding for area studies at US universities and for scholarships in Foreign Language and Area Studies (FLAS), intended to encourage students to study languages and cultures of foreign societies. This system was still in place when I was an undergraduate; as a graduate student, I won a National Science Foundation scholarship, without which I could never have completed my PhD.

Somehow, this grand bargain has unraveled, largely as a result of conservative politicians who view universities as hotbeds of liberal ideology. The attack has proceeded using three sets of tools: the formidable powers of the federal government, state legislative power, and, perhaps most disturbingly, the mobilization of society itself to undermine the classroom.

Start with the federal government. The Trump administration has slashed budgets for scientific research and for government-funded medical care provided by many university hospitals. Funding and staff cuts have crippled the National Institutes of Health, the National Science Foundation, and the National Endowment for the Humanities, as well as other sources of federal research monies. The One Big Beautiful Bill has significantly reduced investment in research, and it is not clear that these funds will ever return.

Another set of tools is the abuse of investigative powers granted under federal antidiscrimination law. Before Trump, prior administrations had deployed veiled threats to cajole universities into adopting favored policies. The Obama administration, for example, used a technically nonbinding "Dear Colleague" letter to push universities into setting up large and sometimes overzealous bureaucracies to combat sex discrimination and sexual harassment. The Trump administration used this technique but has gone further and faster, most notably in the headline-making attacks on Ivy League universities. Weaponizing antidiscrimination law under Title VI of the Civil Rights Act, the administration has withheld money from universities that was due under existing grants and contracts. While Title VI does allow withholding of funds after an investigation and an extensive set of procedures, the Trump government has followed none of these. Threatened with existential funding cuts, several universities nevertheless agreed to settlements on such issues as DEI policies, admissions, eliminating trans women's participation in sports, and fighting anti-Semitism. (The Trump administration also issued a "Dear Colleague" letter of its own, prohibiting the use of federal work-study funds to support voter registration and other activities.)

In the fall of 2025, the Trump administration reframed its approach as being one of carrots rather than sticks. It offered a select set of nine universities a special opportunity for preferential access to federal research dollars in exchange for signing a "Compact for Academic Excellence in Higher Education." This included a mix of unobjectionable requirements, including nondiscrimination on the basis of race or sex, but also a freeze on tuition and a limit on the number of foreign students. It also demanded that schools close departments hostile to conservative ideas and adopt institutional neutrality, the policy adopted in the 1967 Kalven Report at the University of Chicago. In exchange for these promises, universities would get more funding but also be subject to unilateral suspension of benefits. The Compact failed, in that no schools agreed to its terms and several rejected it.[26] But it indicates the administration's continued desire to use research funds to cajole universities into broad structural changes that are beyond the scope of government power to order in a free society.

Additional challenges to higher education are occurring in red states. Republican legislatures are competing with each other to cripple state universities with new requirements coupled with severe funding cuts. A major target is the teaching of so-called "divisive concepts," such as race and Middle Eastern politics. Politicization of oversight by governing boards has put academic freedom at risk. In Indiana, all state universities now have post-tenure review processes that include evaluation of faculty on their ability to foster free speech and viewpoint diversity in the classroom. The process includes a complaint mechanism whereby students can report on their professors, and at least one professor has already been sanctioned[27] for political speech.

This leveraging of students to monitor their professors is a particularly insidious technique in the campaign, because it undermines the trust necessary for pedagogy. A chilling incident happened in early September 2025 at Texas A&M university, hardly a hotbed of progressive thought. A student interrupted a lecture,[28] claiming that the discussion was illegal because the president had declared in an executive order that there are only two genders. Governor Greg Abbott weighed in, and the lecturer was fired, while two deans lost their administrative positions. This was not enough for the local GOP, and soon the university's president was forced to resign on account of his slow response. The broader story is that GOP politicians are incentivizing students to monitor their own professors and engage in "gotcha" games that go viral, deeply undermining the trust needed for effective pedagogy.

On September 10, 2025, Charlie Kirk was assassinated on the campus of Utah Valley University. Conservatives who had recently decried left-wing "cancel culture" began calling for the firings of anyone who was insufficiently reverential toward Kirk or had reacted positively to the murder. Many lecturers and administrators have been fired, along with some tenured professors, often for very bland expressions of disagreement with Kirk's controversial views. While these efforts to squelch speech might seem like the opposite of what Kirk would have wanted, one of the hallmarks of Turning Point USA was the mobilization of students to identify professors for supposed pedagogical or ideological violations. Its Professor Watchlist program regularly highlights so-called "woke" professors and encourages students to shame them, often on the basis of a single tweet. Today's students can feel that they are empowered in the Republican ecosystem, even as they undermine the institutions they are paying tuition to. In this sense, Kirk embodied another trend of our times, namely the exploitation of university environments by outside actors who are not directly engaged in academic debate. The social-media era has crumbled the already-low walls of the ivory tower, and Turning Point USA has been an active agent in this process.

The charge of hypocrisy against the currently ascendant right wing, however, reveals that bottom-up attacks on academic freedom are not the exclusive province of just one side of the aisle. Observers of "cancel culture" for the past decade have noted how students, like others in society, are quick to pounce on any perceived deviation from orthodoxy. Demands for cancellation and even firing of professors began to appear with frequency around 2014, and the Foundation for Individual Rights and Expression reports that more faculty have been fired in the past few years than in the entire McCarthy period of the 1950s. Much of this activity preceded the Trump administration.[29]

The trend toward bottom-up social pressure on academic freedom makes the United States a bit more like India than Hungary. Whereas attacks on academic freedom in the latter have been top-down, the United States and India have seen a pincer attack by a highly mobilized social movement allied with an energetic state. This is a far more dangerous situation, in that it suggests a more sustained, structural attack whose consequences will be harder to reverse.

This is not to say that professors should be unaccountable. Exercising First Amendment rights outside the classroom in the form of extramural speech properly opens one up to criticism, and professors should not get a free pass in the public sphere. But once "monitoring" enters the classroom, there is a massive risk that faculty (and other students) will be intimidated and chilled by fear of recorded or leaked conversations. Every student becomes a potential enemy. It is this undermining of society, an attack on university life from below, that has terrified faculties in many American states.

Conclusion

As institutions devoted to truth and knowledge, universities play an essential role in democracy.[30] They conduct the fundamental research that can serve as the basis of policy debates; they educate students in citizenship; and they serve as inherently plural open spaces of exchange that reflect the open society.[31] As embodiments of a liberal public sphere, they represent prime targets for illiberal actors who seek to control public narratives and shrink the space for opposition.

It is conventionally understood that attacks on academic freedom come primarily from the state. For 19th-century advocates of academic freedom, the state and the church were the primary concerns. While the church has receded from view, the threat from the state has expanded, as public research funds have become a lifeblood of many university systems. The state can restrict research and manipulate public funding to steer knowledge in particular directions. It can insist on the firing of particular professors with disfavored views. And it can in some cases deploy libel law to intimidate critics on campus. These and other threats have materialized in many countries in recent decades.

What the United States is experiencing, however, is something that has emerged only in a few authoritarian contexts. It reflects a set of social forces that comes from both above and below and features students as foot soldiers. Buoyed by a social-media ecosystem that feeds on performative outrage, and acting under the reasonable banner of accountability, students have sought to constrain faculty and to treat the classroom as an arena for political combat. In this, they act in close partnership with outside civil-society groups, which take advantage of the inherent openness of university campuses. Such a two-pronged attack, from above and below, reflects a substantial set of structural concerns and will not be reversed with a single election victory.

What tools are available to those who wish to defend the university? One important idea is to return to professionalism as a norm. Claims of professional expertise were present at the founding of the American Association of University Professors in the early 20th century. The central idea of academic freedom is that academic merit is to be judged not by politicians or state bureaucrats but by other academics acting within their disciplinary competence. These norms of professional knowledge are deeply entrenched in the United States, though, like the university itself, they are also under threat in an era of social media and disinformation. Without a recommitment to professionalism, academic freedom will continue to wither in the face of populist and authoritarian forces.

14

Academic Freedom and the Progressive Crackup

LOUIS MICHAEL SEIDMAN*

Before we can understand the status of the constitutional right to academic freedom in the Age of Trump, we must first understand the Trump revolution itself and its overall impact on progressive constitutionalism.

The ultimate fate of Trumpism remains to be determined. Trump himself may be undone by hubris, by incompetence, by external events, or by sustained political opposition. But for what it is worth, I'm convinced that even if Trump fails, there will be no restoration of the old order. Trumpism marks a decisive victory for populist forces and the collapse of the progressive coalition that has dominated American politics for almost a century. If Trumpism is defeated, it will be replaced by something new—perhaps a left populism.

Of course, my prediction may be off base. But if it is correct, then the populist victory over progressivism will have a major impact on our conception of academic freedom. As I will argue below, the constitutional protection for academic freedom is a progressive project, and populism has been its longtime enemy.[1] If academic freedom is to survive in this new environment, it must shed its constitutional underpinnings. Parts I, II, and III of this chapter explain why. In the Age of Trump, supposed constitutional commands cannot and should not do the work of providing actual reasons why the government should respect academic independence. To survive in this new atmosphere, academic freedom must be radically reconceptualized and then defended in new ways. In Part IV I suggest some reforms that might make the academy more attractive to ordinary Americans.

* Carmack Waterhouse Professor of Constitutional Law, Georgetown University Law Center.
Thanks to Peter Byrne, Martin Lederman, Lara Schwartz, Jessica Seidman, Geoffrey Stone, and Mark Tushnet for comments on an earlier draft of this chapter.

Louis Michael Seidman, *Academic Freedom and the Progressive Crackup*. In: *Academic Freedom in the Era of Trump*. Edited by: Lee C. Bollinger and Geoffrey R. Stone, Oxford University Press. © Oxford University Press (2026). DOI: 10.1093/9780197854877.003.0015

Populism, Progressivism, and Academic Freedom

Historically, American populism has been identified with both the left and the right. Its roots lie in the early-19th-century Jacksonian revolution, but it did not take its modern form until the end of that century. By then, it had become the voice of the anxieties and anger of rural and lower-class Americans who felt left out by the forces of urbanization and industrialization.[2] For them, the primary problem was the corruption of political institutions by the moneyed interests. The solution was decentralization and direct democracy—power exercised by the people themselves, who would take down the old system and return the country to a (largely mythic) state when the people ruled.[3]

In contrast, progressivism attracted middle- and upper-class voters who were predominately urban rather than rural. Whereas populists thought that the problem was government and that the solution was decentralization, progressives tended to look to centralized government for answers.[4] Effective government, run by experts, was necessary to control the forces of private capital, and, to do their job, the experts had to be shielded, at least to some extent, from popular democracy.[5] Whereas populists yearned for a lost past, progressives thought that science and expertise could guide us to a brighter future.

At least since the New Deal, progressives have dominated American politics. In the domestic arena, they created a greatly enlarged "administrative state" populated by thousands of professionals who provided government services and regulated large swaths of the economy. In the international arena, they established a series of alliances united in opposition to communist expansion and promoting ever-increasing integration and trade. As a cultural matter, they consolidated the power of urban, coastal elites who arbitrated standards of truth and taste. And, importantly, they dominated American universities.

When conservatives were in power, they trimmed the margins of the progressive regime but left its central features intact. The regime held together a fragile coalition by promising ever-improving standards of living to working-class voters and protection from discrimination to a variety of vulnerable minority groups. It was bolstered by mildly redistributive government regulation authored and administered by knowledgeable specialists who could get things done without stymieing growth and innovation or triggering the exodus of capital. The regime satisfied socially liberal but economically conservative suburbanites by supporting reproductive choice and gender equality while holding off revolt from socially conservative but economically vulnerable lower-class voters by protecting safety-net programs like Social Security, Medicare, and Medicaid.

The progressive coalition has been under strain for years, but with the election of Donald Trump it has collapsed. It was undone by the hollowing out of rural America, by declining real wages, and by growing inequality.

These forces were amplified by an epistemic crisis especially relevant to the problem of academic freedom.[6] The crisis resulted in part from deceit and in part from technological change. The deceit: Political leaders told Americans that victory was just around the corner in Vietnam,[7] that Watergate was a "third rate burglary,"[8] that Bill Clinton "did not have sexual relations with that woman,"[9] that there were weapons of mass destruction in Iraq,[10] that it was necessary to bail out big banks to save us from economic disaster.[11] Leading academics were forced to retract scientific papers or even admit to fraud.[12] Newspapers were caught peddling phony stories.[13] Religious institutions covered up grave abuses by clergy.[14]

Things got still worse during the Covid epidemic.[15] Americans were told that "within a couple of days [Covid] is going to be down to close to zero,"[16] that masks were or were not necessary to control the spread of Covid,[17] and that keeping children out of school was or was not a necessary preventive measure.[18] As a result of these and other breaches of faith, arbiters of truth and common sense lost credibility.

The technological change: The Internet decentralized and democratized sources of knowledge and standards of truth. Memes, rumors, and outright lies now circulate on the web with lightning speed and without filter. "Deep fakes," newly assisted by artificial intelligence, have become much more difficult to detect.[19]

All these trends threaten traditional notions of academic freedom. But because academic freedom is often defended in constitutional terms, the Trump revolution's impact on law is especially relevant. The legal expression of progressivism was liberal constitutionalism. Liberal constitutionalists attempted to depoliticize important and explosive questions that divide Americans by treating them as issues of constitutional law, to be finally resolved by reference to the Constitution, usually as interpreted by the Supreme Court.

Liberal constitutionalists shared the more general progressive preference for top-down solutions, formulated by experts shielded from popular control. They distrusted the ability of popular majorities to reach wise and humane conclusions on subjects like racial justice, crime control, the influence of fundamentalist religion on educational institutions, gender equality, family relationships, and reproductive freedom.

Liberal constitutionalism's most vigorous expression is associated with the Warren Court, which thought that it had the solution for these and other problems. Although the Warren Court triggered a backlash that trimmed some of its supposed excesses, its approach remained remarkably resilient for years, and to this day some progressives nostalgically imagine that, if only the right justices were appointed, we might return to its glory days.

But despite these delusive hopes, liberal constitutionalism, too, is gone for the foreseeable future. It cannot survive without the progressive political coalition that supported it. It is hard to imagine the circumstances under which Warren Court liberal constitutionalism, undone for the short term by Trump's three appointments to the Supreme Court and for the long term by growing rejection of undemocratic "solutions" formulated by legal elites, might again capture the American imagination.

How does this revolution relate to the status of academic freedom? Obviously, defending universities and what they do is much more difficult in an environment dominated by skepticism about expert opinion and hatred toward elites. That does not mean that the defense is impossible, but defenders must be ready to reform universities in answer to justified criticism, and to demonstrate, more effectively than they have so far, why we all benefit from academic work.

What is impossible, though, is a revival of the old strategy that rested on constitutional protection for academic freedom. An effective defense requires persuasion, not the arrogant insistence that persuasion is unnecessary because the Constitution mandates academic independence whether people are persuaded or not. The authoritarian insistence that people shut up and obey constitutional commands is what helped produce Trumpism in the first place. It is uniquely ill-suited to defeating Trumpist attacks.

That said, a nonconstitutional version of academic freedom linked to free-speech traditions emphasizing a "free marketplace of ideas" might be attractive precisely because it is compatible with populism. Justice William Brennan once gave voice to this version (albeit in a constitutional setting) when he wrote that "[t]he Nation's future depends upon leaders trained through wide exposure to that robust exchange of ideas which discovers truth 'out of a multitude of tongues, [rather] than through any kind of authoritative selection.'"[20]

A populist version of academic freedom that emphasized a "multitude of tongues"—the equal status of different ideas and access to equal means of persuasion—might meet the current moment. Modern populists angrily reject the ability of economic and cultural elites to make an "authoritative selection" of which ideas should be taken seriously. One can imagine a version of academic freedom that promoted broad, popular access to academic institutions, which would in turn produce an anarchic assortment of theories, ideologies, and worldviews as varied as the American people themselves. Reforms that moved universities closer to that vision might persuade more people that universities are doing something valuable. In Part IV, I suggest some specific measures that universities might take to meet this goal.

But as our two leading commentators on academic freedom, Peter Byrne[21] and Robert Post,[22] have pointed out, the populist version bears little resemblance to how universities currently function or to what defenders of university autonomy mean when they champion academic freedom. If populist reforms were taken seriously, they would threaten the very values that academic freedom, as currently understood, is designed to preserve. Universities are all about the "authoritative selection" of ideas. Their hiring, tenure, and publication decisions regularly enforce standards that lead to the endorsement of some ideas and the rejection of others. The maintenance of these standards is at the core of the academic mission as currently understood, and academic freedom is meant to insulate these standards from outside attack.[23]

The current version of academic freedom therefore stands for the opposite of the unfettered exchange of ideas that populists might endorse. For that reason, Post has argued that protection for universities must rest instead on the privileging of the kinds of ideas that meet academic standards. Post emphasizes the crucial role these standards play in the production of knowledge.[24] On this theory, universities must be accorded a measure of autonomy from political forces that might interfere with the academic enterprise and so with the production of knowledge.

This sort of autonomy fits easily within the more general progressive worldview, and it is therefore no surprise that the most eloquent judicial defenses of constitutional protection for academic freedom came during the Warren Court period.[25] Academic freedom makes sense if one believes that experts—whether on the bench, housed in administrative agencies, or on university campuses—should be left undisturbed in their pursuit of wise public policy.

But it makes much less sense in the Age of Trump. Trumpism asks why the claims made for academic freedom should not be subject to democratic contestation. The current version of academic freedom might yet win such a contest, but it would have to do so on its merits—or, more precisely, on how its merits were judged by the people and their representatives.

To prevail in such a struggle, defenders of academic freedom must respond to two criticisms. First, Trumpists argue, we should not take at face value the self-presentation of academic experts as disinterested seekers of truth. Their views, like everyone else's, are situated and influenced by politics, class, and culture. Second, academics engage in the pursuit of, at best, only a certain kind of truth. There is scientific truth, but there are also rival cultural, traditional, moral, and religious truths. Trumpism insists that self-government entails the right of a people to choose for itself the kind of truth it wishes to prioritize.

The first challenge grows out of the collapse of epistemic consensus discussed above. Consider, for example, Justice Thomas's observations in his opinion concurring in the Court's conclusion that a ban on gender-affirming care for children is constitutionally permissible:

> This case carries a simple lesson: In politically contentious debates over matters shrouded in scientific uncertainty, courts should not assume that self-described experts are correct.

> Deference to legislatures, not experts, is particularly critical here. Many prominent medical professionals have declared a consensus around the efficacy of treating children's gender dysphoria with puberty blockers, cross-sex hormones, and surgical interventions, despite mounting evidence to the contrary. They have dismissed grave problems undercutting the assumption that young children can consent to irreversible treatments that may deprive them of their ability to eventually produce children of their own. They have built their medical determinations on concededly weak evidence. And, they have surreptitiously compromised their medical recommendations to achieve political ends.
>
> The Court today reserves "to the people, their elected representatives, and the democratic process the power to decide how best to address an area of medical uncertainty and extraordinary importance. That sovereign prerogative does not bow to major medical organizations. Experts and elites have been wrong before—and they may prove to be wrong again."[26]

Justice Thomas may or may not be right about the (now threatened[27]) expert consensus on gender-affirming surgery, and he is certainly wrong when he feeds broader intolerance of trans people. But he is just as certainly right that academic experts "have been wrong before . . . and . . . may prove to be wrong again." For years, the academy championed "scientific racism" and "eugenics."[28] World-renowned academic experts fell victim to the crude "Piltdown Man" hoax that, they claimed, indisputably established the truth of Darwin's theories.[29] Leading figures in the academy supported the Vietnam War[30] and claimed that the effort to empower newly freed African Americans in the Reconstruction South led to nothing but corruption and misgovernment.[31] In recent years, there has been an explosion of retracted academic papers that were based on shoddy evidence or, occasionally, outright fraud.[32] Of course, universities have also produced important advances in human understanding, but there are enough examples of missteps and blunders to raise questions about whether constitutional law should insulate academic methods from popular control.

The second challenge raises questions about the nature of truth. Put crudely, some people find truth by looking through a microscope, while others find it by getting on their knees and praying. Whereas disputes about, say, "scientific racism" might be settled by careful examination of the evidence, disputes about the nature of truth itself are not susceptible to empirical resolution. Truths that are rooted in tradition, in culture, in ways of living, and in faith cannot be proved or disproved by academic methods. They stand as an external challenge to the system of belief that the academy promotes and, therefore, cannot be judged by criteria derived from the premises they reject.

On occasion, academics have gotten into trouble by prioritizing science over these other sources of truth. For example, no one today defends the Tuskegee experiment, which left almost 400 African American males untreated for syphilis as part of a scientific study.[33] In response to criticism, universities have reformed many practices relating, for example, to informed consent and humane treatment of animals, but the very fact that some of the reforms resulted from outside pressure throws doubt on the ideal of academic independence. Moreover, it remains the fact that a certain type of truth rooted in empiricism, standard logic, and scientific falsifiability lies at the heart of the academic enterprise, and that other sources of truth, rooted, for example, in intuition, revelation, faith, or folk wisdom, are systematically excluded.

Taken together, these two criticisms demonstrate the way that the label "academic freedom" obscures and depoliticizes the conflict that lies at the concept's core. "*Academic* freedom" assumes that we already know what an "academy" looks like and that a particular conception of the academy is permanent and outside the realm of legitimate contestation. "Academic *freedom*" assumes the answer to another contested question: Whose "freedom" should we protect? Affording freedom to some people and institutions limits the freedom of other people and institutions. The word "freedom" assumes that we already know whose freedom deserves protection, and that protection of the freedom of other people is off the table.

The next two sections discuss how this conflict plays out on a more granular level.

Which Academy?

Academic institutions come in a bewildering variety of shapes and sizes.[34] Some are state-sponsored and -controlled; others are private. Some are huge, with thousands of students; others are tiny. Some are run by large bureaucracies, while others are controlled by small groups, and still others are administered by elected or appointed government officials. The mission of some academic institutions is to advance a particular set of religious doctrines, while others are secular in orientation. Some academies have been established to shield whites from integration. The mission of others is to provide educational opportunities principally to people of color or women, while still others are coeducational and purport to be race-neutral. Some academies offer liberal-arts education, while others train their students to be soldiers, farmers, or engineers. Some are nonprofit and supported by private philanthropy. Others are government-run and supported by taxpayer dollars. Still others are profit-making. Some view their primary mission as research and graduate education, while others prioritize teaching undergraduates.

This bewildering diversity of American education is consistent with a populist vision. Its strength lies in its decentralization and its openness to people with different needs and values. Unfortunately, though, the constitutionalization of academic freedom often blinds us to this strength. When its defenders speak of the constitutional right to "academic freedom," they have in mind a particular kind of academy—schools that are engaged in the academic exercise as they define it. As a practical matter, that means liberal-arts colleges or universities whose faculty engage in scholarship, research, and teaching. But institutions that fit this description educate only a minority of students. Most students attend trade schools, religiously affiliated institutions that do little or no research, community colleges, or liberal-arts colleges where faculty are not expected to engage in scholarship.[35]

Defenders of academic freedom are unwilling to defend, and sometimes actually attack, these other kinds of academies. For example, defenders of "academic freedom" often oppose government subvention of religious or racially discriminatory institutions, and they are uninterested in protecting trade schools. They favor heavy regulation of profit-making schools. Importantly, they envision a particular conception of how knowledge is gained and transmitted. Historically, the kind of institutions that supporters of academic freedom favored were dominated by upper-class, Protestant elites and were closed to people of color, to Jews, and to people of modest means. Even today, these institutions have an important role in reproducing a cultural, political, and economic hierarchy.

Because constitutional protection for this version of academic freedom is no longer plausible, its defenders must explain why the particular types of academic institutions they favor are entitled to special protection. No doubt, the study of the mysterious behavior of subatomic particles, the causes of the French Revolution, Kantian philosophy, and the relationship between the Pre-Raphaelites and modern art are all important, but it will require some effort to explain to ordinary Americans why these pursuits are relevant to their lives. They are more interested in skills and knowledge that will help them pursue ordinary careers in fields like business, service, manufacturing, computer programming, marketing, and administration. It is and should be a political question whether "academic" study should be privileged over these other endeavors.

Whose Freedom?

Suppose we limit our inquiry to the kinds of academies that defenders of academic freedom favor—liberal-arts colleges and research universities. Defense of academic freedom is also complicated by the failure to specify just whose freedom is being protected. Freedom for some people in the academy means coercion for others. To understand how academic freedom cashes out, we need to examine these groups individually. We can start at the bottom of the hierarchy and work up.

Staff

Years ago, critical scholar Duncan Kennedy suggested that law professors and janitors temporarily switch jobs.[36] One doesn't have to endorse this proposal to worry about the stark contrast between the way universities treat faculty and students and the way they treat the staff that keeps universities running. Virtually no one thinks that staff deserves constitutional protection. Universities treat cleaning staff, cafeteria workers, secretaries, and security personnel in the same way that large corporations treat comparable employees. These workers are often not unionized and enjoy little bargaining power regarding their jobs and working conditions. They have no input into how universities are run. The constitutional tradition of academic freedom has nothing to say to or about them. Yet they are the frontline workers who make academic research possible.

This behavior is rooted in class bias. Universities are hierarchical institutions, and everyday interaction between, say, students and faculty on the one hand and cafeteria workers on the other reinforces notions of who is on top and who is at the bottom—who is worthy of respect and who is not.

The hierarchy is rooted in the constitutional conception of academic freedom that universities defend. For those steeped in this traditional conception, it would be unthinkable for staff to receive protection, because, after all, they are not engaged in—and are not capable of engaging in—the academic enterprise. A secretary who answers phones does not understand and cannot possibly be made to understand nuclear physics or what Heidegger meant when he wrote about *Dasein*.

Unfortunately, this bias blinds us to possibilities for including staff within the academic enterprise. No, janitors and law professors should not trade places. But it is not utopian to imagine that, in addition to serving students, staff might also become students. They too might be given the opportunity to learn about physics and Heidegger. Some universities offer tuition reduction and time off for education to staff, but much more could be done to integrate them into the academic community. Staff might be invited to participate in scholarly events or be offered automatic admission to the institutions where they work. As detailed below, universities might broaden what they teach or how they teach it, so as to make being a student more attractive to staff. And even if none of that is possible, universities can do much more to accord equal respect to people within their community who pursue lives not dominated by academic thought.

Undergraduates

As universities have become more consumer-oriented, they have catered more to the desires of their students. That has meant devoting more money to nonacademic matters. Universities competing for students build more luxurious dormitories, fancier student centers, and better athletic facilities. Football coaches receive huge salaries and star athletes, large scholarships.

Some of these expenditures might be compatible with a populist conception of academic freedom. Still, one cannot help but notice the hypocrisy. Universities truly devoted to the disinterested search for truth as filtered through rigorous academic standards would not devote substantial shares of their budgets to fancy dorm rooms. This allocation of resources suggests a much uglier reality: That universities compete to provide a select group of young people with a pleasurable introduction to the exercise of power and networking opportunities that they can use to cement that power in later life.

What happens when students do engage in the academic exercise? Undergraduates are emphatically there to learn what others teach them, not to think for themselves. Universities pride themselves on training students to have open minds and allowing them to experiment with new ideas. But students who take that offer seriously end up being punished for doing so. A student who writes on a final exam that Darwin was wrong and creationists are right, that the Constitution's reference to "We the people" should be interpreted to include only white people, that human-induced climate change is a hoax, or that the best way to understand history is through the lens of rigid Marxism is unlikely to receive good grades.

Graduate Students

In theory, graduate students are supposed to engage in research that, when freely undertaken, can lead to surprising and heterodox conclusions. In fact, though, they are among the most vulnerable members of university communities. They are often required to assume large teaching responsibilities with little compensation, and universities have strongly resisted their efforts to unionize. More importantly, they are at the mercy of their dissertation committees, which can facilitate or block their access to tenure-track jobs. There is no appeal from the judgment of these committees, and, not surprisingly, their untrammeled power produces abuse.[37] There are disturbing reports of sexual abuse[38] and of faculty plagiarism of student research.[39] It is doubtful that these practices are common, but what *is* common is the enforcement of academic orthodoxy. No sensible graduate student would write a dissertation ridiculing the work of the gatekeepers to her career. Independent student thought is confined to a narrow bandwidth established by the faculty members who control the fate of their mentees.

Faculty

When its defenders speak of academic freedom, this is the group they are thinking about. But how much freedom do faculty members have?

Universities are increasingly reliant on adjunct faculty and faculty with temporary appointments, who are typically short-term and at-will employees. They are often poorly paid, are not expected to do research, and have little or no prospect of joining the tenure track. Universities unashamedly use them along with graduate students to cheaply process large numbers of students. Their job has nothing to do with the kind of free, heterodox, and creative thought that defenders of academic freedom prize.

Tenure-track faculty are usually expected to do independent and creative research. That does not mean, though, that they can reach just any conclusion that free thought leads them to. Faculty working in the hard sciences are dependent on grants, usually from the government, that support some kinds of research and leave other inquiries unfunded. A faculty member who fails to attract grants will often find her job or salary at risk.[40]

More generally, and as emphasized above, academic freedom insulates craft norms, not individual thought. As the name implies, academic disciplines *discipline* people who depart from those norms. These standards are historically and culturally contingent. On occasion, they are challenged, and when the challenge is successful, the standards change. But a faculty member who departs from the standards is taking a huge risk. The chances of a successful revolt are small, and the consequences of failure large. And even when revolts are successful, they do no more than substitute a new orthodoxy for the old.

Tenured faculty are generally freed from the threat of discharge, but we have seen that even they can be disciplined when their teaching and writing get too far out of line with prevailing orthodoxy.[41] Moreover, the very protection that tenure affords tends to limit creativity in a different way. As they age, many faculty members become "deadwood" who have not made meaningful contributions to their field in many years.

Administrators

Most universities are not governed by their faculties. The most important decisions are made by often self-perpetuating boards of directors, deans, and administrators. These are the people with ultimate authority about how money is allocated among departments, who gets tenure, which students are admitted, what gets taught, and who does the teaching. And even they are not free actors. They must be responsive to large donors, to *U.S. News* rankings, and to market forces. Because the board of directors, deans, and administrators are the people who actually run colleges and universities, they are the actual beneficiaries of the insulation that academic freedom affords. But in state-run institutions, at least some of these people are government officials. It is nonsensical to say that government officials should be free from government control.[42] Moreover, even in private institutions, many of the people who run colleges and universities are not academics at all, or long ago left their academic positions. They view their jobs as managing large, complicated businesses, and often share the values and concerns of business executives more generally.

What Is to Be Done

Nothing I have said above should be interpreted to mean that we should not mobilize to defend universities. Attacks on DEI, on the teaching of critical race theory and post-colonial studies, and on students and faculty opposing Zionism are demagogic and often racist. More broadly, Professors Post and Byrne are right to claim that the academic method has produced important advances in human understanding. Much would be lost if traditional colleges and universities were destroyed. More broadly still, the Trump administration's assault on academia should be understood as part of a larger attack on civil society. It conforms to standard authoritarian tactics designed to eliminate centers for dissent and consolidate regime power. It must be stopped.

The issue, then, is not *whether* we should defend universities, but *how* we should go about mounting the defense. The first rule should be, "Do no harm." That means abandoning the reliance on judicial enforcement of a supposed constitutional right to academic freedom that plays into the hands of Trumpists. For reasons I have already discussed, constitutional defenses reinforce the toxic perception that elites run the country through an exercise of power that they cannot defend.

If academic freedom is to survive, it must be defended on the merits. Part of that defense entails regaining the trust of the American people, which, in turn, requires reforms of academic institutions that make them more worth defending. The reforms look in two directions that, concededly, are in tension with each other. On the one hand, colleges and universities need to take more seriously the values that they claim to stand for. On the other, they need to open themselves up to other values and make themselves more attractive to people not devoted to the academic exercise as currently defined.

Taking Academic Values Seriously

How might colleges and universities accomplish the first objective? They cannot successfully defend themselves against outside pressure when they themselves seem to be abandoning the very ideals that they are defending. Embracing those ideals means reinstituting distributional, liberal-arts, and general-education requirements for all students, relying more on full-time faculty engaged in research and writing to teach students, providing meaningful protection for graduate students, resisting pressure from donors, instituting faculty governance, and funding research not supported by grants from government and private sources.

Universities should also be more open to people with a variety of ideas. At their best, universities are sites of tumult and argument, both inside and outside the classroom. There is a long tradition of student protest, teach-ins, rallies, and marches. This tradition is part of academic freedom, and it should be respected. No one has the right to bully or intimidate others or to disrupt ongoing operations, but everyone on a university campus has the right to express unpopular views that make others uncomfortable. It is a mistake to treat this right as rooted in constitutional command, but it is no mistake to defend it. Universities must do a better job at resisting outside pressure to curb student and faculty expression about controversial issues.

What about academic freedom as expressed in the classroom and in academic writing? The problem here is more complex. There is no way to resolve the dilemma posed by disciplinary limits on thought and debate. Academic institutions pride themselves on maintaining high standards, but the commitment to these standards entails the power to define what the standards are. A university where anything goes—where anything at all counts as "good" scholarship—is not worth defending.

It does not follow, though, that nothing can be done to free the academy from groupthink and orthodoxy. Critics of colleges and universities have a point when they complain about deadening and depressing academic uniformity. Educated undergraduates need to read Ta-Nehisi Coates, but they should also read Thomas Sowell. They need to take courses with both "Postcolonial" and "Western Civilization" in their titles. And while academic institutions should not abandon academic standards, there should be more openness to faculty and students who challenge those standards. Imagine, for example, a university where every academic department had a designated chair to be filled by someone appointed to challenge standard disciplinary norms. Perhaps this proposal is utopian or unwise, but even if it is, universities need to find other ways to include within their communities more iconoclasts and disrupters of all ideological stripes and fewer defenders of normal science.

Democratizing the University

Too often, the right to free inquiry that colleges and universities claim to value is enjoyed only by elites thought capable of doing the inquiry. Admissions officers at academic institutions control access to future economic, political, and cultural power. They grant the power to a few who are more or less insured successful lives, while denying it to many who lack the resources, connections, aptitudes, or backgrounds to gain admission. Unsurprisingly, the rejected majority resent their rejection, and their anger helps to fuel the Trumpian revolt.

Elite academic institutions need to be more democratic. Unfortunately, universities no longer have the legal power to do much about racial and ethnic diversity,[43] but that does not mean that there is nothing else they can do. At a minimum, elite universities should end legacy admissions, admit fewer students who attend posh private schools, and recruit more rural and low-income students.

Even if these reforms were implemented, they would not by themselves deal with the unaffordability of much higher education. Unfortunately, publicly funded student aid has produced unintended consequences. Too often, colleges and universities have captured public subvention intended for students by raising tuition. The extra money, in turn, has produced a bloated administrative apparatus that contributes little to the academic enterprise. The best way to deal with this problem is to couple publicly funded aid to students with government-imposed price controls on tuition.

Here is a more radical proposal. Elite colleges and universities should offer new majors in subjects like plumbing, electrical work, construction, and administration. Students majoring in these subjects would take the same liberal-arts distributional courses required of students with more traditional majors, but their advanced courses would be very different.

An obvious response to this proposal: This function is already served by community colleges and less prestigious institutions. Moreover, even fancy universities offer specialized majors in "less academic" areas like communications, business, and computer sciences. One might think, therefore, that the proposal is a solution in search of a problem.

In fact, though, there is a problem, and it is serious. Elite universities do more than educate their students. As noted above, they provide a credential and a set of connections that facilitate entry into the ruling class. This is just the sort of privilege that fuels the anger behind the Trump revolt. Offering aspiring plumbers and electricians a Harvard degree might dispel some of this anger, promote class mobility, and produce a more democratic culture.

Admitting these students into the academic community offers another advantage. Defenders of the academy beginning with Thomas Jefferson have insisted that an educated citizenry is a necessary precondition for democratic engagement.[44] From Jefferson's time to our own, many have believed that only a select few can benefit from that education. But if it is true that education is necessary for citizenship, and if it is also true that only a few will benefit from education, it logically follows that only a few are capable of engaging in democratic self-governance.

That is a view that some progressives were comfortable with and that might have prevailed in a different political environment. But it will not prevail in the Age of Trump. At its core, the new populism is devoted to ending elite control of our politics and culture. Even those frightened by what the new populism might produce must come to grips with the fact that dictation by the privileged is no longer possible. There is no choice, then, but to bet on the possibility that liberal education might better equip ordinary Americans to make wise political decisions. That means offering large numbers of people the kind of academic training that they need to be engaged citizens. And that means funneling them to the institutions that are the best at providing this training.[45]

Conclusion

Academic institutions are in peril. Faced with this danger, their defenders understandably reach for rhetoric and doctrine associated with an earlier period of stress that accompanied the McCarthyism of the 1950s. But despite McCarthy's efforts, the progressive coalition, and with it, liberal constitutionalism, managed to prevail during that period. Colleges and universities were therefore able to substitute constitutional commands for the kind of reasoned argument that might persuade ordinary Americans that they were right. The Trump revolution has ended that possibility. Trumpism is fueled, rather than contained by, the claim that legal and academic experts have a constitutional right to control the country. That means that defenders of the academy can no longer rely on lazy and ultimately authoritarian constitutional rhetoric. If the academy is to survive, it must defend academic work on its merits and convince the country of its value. It can do so only by giving up the crutch of constitutionalism and embracing reforms that make the academy attractive to the people it is supposed to serve.

15

Academic Freedom and Academic Orthodoxy

SUZANNA SHERRY*

> *"Freedom of inquiry, freedom of discussion, and freedom of teaching—without those a university cannot exist."*
>
> —Robert M. Hutchins[1]

Academic freedom is crucial to the mission of a university. At its core, the mission of a university is to discover truth and to expand and disseminate knowledge. Universities select faculty and students, and structure departments and curricula, with this goal in mind. (Although other goals exist, they are—or should be—secondary to this primary mission.) The system of tenure both reflects and protects this mission at the individual level: research and teaching are the traditional bases for awarding tenure, and tenured faculty are free to explore the most controversial topics without fear of losing their jobs. The idea of academic freedom thus encompasses both the freedom of individual faculty members to shape their own research and teaching, and the university's ability to determine the best way to fulfill its own mission.

Academic freedom, then, can be described as the absence of any imposed orthodoxy. Justice Robert Jackson's observation about American constitutional democracy is equally apt in the context of a university:

> If there is any fixed star in our constitutional constellation, it is that no official, high or petty, can prescribe what shall be orthodox in politics,

* Herman O. Loewenstein Professor of Law Emerita, Vanderbilt University.

Suzanna Sherry, *Academic Freedom and Academic Orthodoxy*. In: *Academic Freedom in the Era of Trump*. Edited by: Lee C. Bollinger and Geoffrey R. Stone, Oxford University Press. © Oxford University Press (2026). DOI: 10.1093/9780197854877.003.0016

> nationalism, religion, or other matters of opinion or force citizens to confess by word or act their faith therein.[2]

President Donald Trump's attempts to blackmail universities into aligning their decisions about faculty, students, research, and curricula with his own political agenda thus pose an existential threat to universities and their mission. Like the McCarthyism of the 1950s, Trump's threats are a blatant attempt to impose orthodoxy on universities. And because universities and their tenure-protected faculties—along with the media and lawyers, also under attack by Trump—are some of the institutions most able to expose and oppose governmental abuse or corruption, Trump's campaign of intimidation also represents an existential threat to democracy itself.

But although Trump's actions undermine both universities and democracy, violate the First Amendment, and substitute an axe for a scalpel when addressing actual university problems, I want to make a different point in this essay. Many universities, especially the so-called "elite" universities, have betrayed their mission by adopting an orthodoxy of their own. Instead of protecting academic freedom, these universities promote particular worldviews and punish those who espouse others. And because the new university orthodoxy is also inherently anti Semitic, it serves as a wedge for Trump's attacks. The current catastrophe, then, is partly of the universities' own making.

After describing the source and effects of universities' abandonment of academic freedom—and thus the betrayal of their own mission—as well as the anti-Semitism that accompanies the new orthodoxy, this essay will explain how we got here and then suggest how universities should respond, even while legitimately decrying Trump's attacks.

The New Orthodoxy and Its Anti-Semitism

The source of universities' betrayal of their mission goes by many names, including anti-racism, social justice, and "woke" culture. These movements have both a unified ideology and an operational arm that puts the ideology into practice. The diversity, equity, and inclusion (DEI) movement, which has taken over universities during the last decade or two, is the operational arm. For convenience, this essay will use "DEI" as a shorthand for both the underlying ideological principles and the implementing practices. Both are directly opposed to the truth-seeking mission of a university. DEI is fundamentally authoritarian, seeking to impose an orthodoxy that is antidemocratic and, not coincidentally, anti-Semitic. It is no surprise that Trump is using the pervasive, and increasing, anti-Semitism of elite universities as his excuse for bludgeoning them into submission. (Trump's repeated praising, welcoming, and pardoning of multiple outspoken anti-Semites proves that anti-Semitism is merely an excuse and not Trump's real motivation.)

The conflict between DEI, on the one hand, and democracy and universities, on the other, stems from the essential principles underlying each. Both American democracy and the modern American university rest on the universalist values of the Enlightenment: objectivity, rationality, individualism, and freedom of thought. Or, as one scholar described it forty years ago, higher education is "a process of individual development, through the acquisition of objective knowledge in a process of rational and open-ended discussion."[3] The diversity, equity, and inclusion movement explicitly rejects those Enlightenment values. In both principle and practice, DEI adherents at American universities reject objectivity and rationality as "white" ways of thinking, trade individualism for tribalism and identity politics, and reject freedom of thought in favor of enforced orthodoxy.

A side note: DEI is *not* the same as affirmative action, although many people (including Trump) mistakenly conflate them. Affirmative action is a practice that predates DEI—and its predecessors—by decades. It was blessed by the Supreme Court in 1978 and again in 2016, then sharply limited by that court in 2023. While controversial, it is meant as an ameliorative practice and can be defended without recourse to DEI's core rejection of Enlightenment principles. What differentiates DEI is that it is not merely a single remedy but instead a complete worldview with a specified orthodoxy and a condemnation of any contrary beliefs as heresy. For that reason, John McWhorter has argued that DEI and its cognates are, in all but name, a religion.[4] It is the embrace of this all-encompassing aspect of DEI that represents a betrayal of universities' mission.

Begin with DEI's rejection of objectivity and rationality. DEI adherents have argued that "objective, rational linear thinking" is an aspect of whiteness,[5] and that objectivity is part of "White Supremacy Culture."[6] What this means in practice is that teaching and scholarship are viewed as advocacy, or as just another form of partisan politics.[7] In all fields—from history to law to chemistry—traditional scholarship represents white (and male) ways of thinking. Even libraries are simply "sites of whiteness."[8] The role of the progressive scholar is to expose and undermine that scholarship by showing how it exemplifies white racist cultural norms.[9] In other words, DEI weaponizes academic ideas for partisan political purposes.

To the extent that universities embrace or reward that view, they abandon the proven Enlightenment tools for discovering knowledge, reverting instead to a worldview in which the validity of knowledge depends on the identity (especially the racial, ethnic, or gender identity) of those who propound it. History should teach us the dangers of that worldview. As Thomas Keneally recounts, the commander of a Nazi camp ordered a Jewish architectural engineer shot when the engineer argued that the foundation of a new barracks needed to be replaced, because, according to the commander, it was a "first principle that you never listened to a Jewish specialist."[10] A similar disaster arising from the politicization of knowledge (although not based on identity politics) occurred with the Soviet endorsement of Lysenkoism, which, by denying biological reality about genes and inheritance in order to conform to Stalinist principles, set Soviet scientific progress back by decades.[11]

The rejection of objectivity also leads to the DEI conclusion that there is no such thing as objective merit. The DEI Glossary (used by many universities) defines "merit" as "embedded in the ideology of Whiteness and uphold[ing] race-based structural inequality."[12] In other words, no one earns success, which is instead granted or withheld by the white male power structure. Note that the DEI critique of merit—based on the rejection of objectivity—is qualitatively different from a more conventional argument that our current *measures* of merit are flawed. It is instead a denial that there is any such thing as objective merit, and a claim that *any* purported attempt to measure it is merely a way for the powerful to advance their own interests at the expense of others, especially minorities.

The DEI view of merit not only interferes with universities' ability to fulfill their mission—by depriving them of any rational way to evaluate students or faculty—but also turns out to be anti-Semitic (and anti-Asian) when followed to its logical conclusion. If merit is always unearned, and instead bestowed by those in power, it is impossible to explain why Jews (and many groups of Asian Americans) in the United States outperform non-Jewish whites on almost every measure of success. Those measures include both academic accomplishments and economic stability, some of the very things that DEI claims are denied to people of color by a racist America. In other words, DEI does not quarrel with the definition of "success" but merely claims that it is distributed on the basis of power, not merit.

The DEI explanation for Jewish success cannot be that Jews have earned it or that Jewish culture prizes traits that are in fact useful in modern society. Both of those explanations depend on some version of objective merit. Nor can it be that Jews happen to value the same traits and behaviors that powerful whites value; that might explain success, but cannot explain why Jews surpass members of the supposed white power establishment who have rigged the system in their favor. The only explanations available under the principles of DEI invoke longstanding anti-Semitic tropes: that American society and culture are actually controlled by powerful Jews, that Jews are collaborators who benefit from white racism, or that Jews allow themselves to be used as pawns so that the white power structure can point to them as evidence that "minorities" can succeed in a purportedly nondiscriminatory America. Similarly, under the DEI account of merit, Asian American success cannot be explained except through anti-Asian stereotypes.[13]

The orthodoxy on objectivity and merit fits well with another DEI precept: that the world is divided into oppressors and oppressed, further confirming that racial, ethnic, or gender identity is the key defining feature of every person. This simplistic bifurcation of the world into oppressors and oppressed is bad enough as a general philosophy because it promotes tribalism. It is especially problematic when it comes to Jews. For centuries, Jews have been scapegoated, persecuted, and murdered solely because of their religion. But they have nevertheless persevered and succeeded. (There is a Jewish joke that every Jewish holiday can be described with the words "They tried to kill us, we survived, let's eat.") So, are Jews oppressed or oppressors? For DEI, the answer is clear: Jews are successful and therefore they must be white (or "white-adjacent") . . . and whites are by definition oppressors.[14] There are, of course, Black Jews, Asian Jews, and Hispanic Jews, to say nothing of the common Semitic heritage of Jews and Arabs—but the DEI worldview does not allow such subtleties to get in the way of its conclusions. It is ironic that, in the many centuries when being white was considered a good thing in the Western world, Jews were often categorized as non-white; now that DEI has made being white a bad thing, Jews are white.

Here it is necessary to include a few words about "anti-Semitism." Anti-Semitism, as I use it here, is hostility, prejudice, or discrimination against Jews based their religious, ethnic, or cultural identity. I need not enter into the debates about whether anti-Zionism is equivalent to anti-Semitism—although many people, Jewish or not, have argued that it is, including Martin Luther King.[15] The anti-Semitism of DEI stems not from any association with anti-Zionism, but instead from its own principles, which both label Jews as oppressors and necessarily deny that Jews have earned their success. And it is reflected in the campus protests, which go well beyond condemning Israel's policies: protesters chanting "From the river to the sea" and "Globalize the intifada" are contending, respectively, that Israel has no right to exist (and thus that the Jews living there have no right to do so) and that Jews all over the world should be at best subjugated and at worst murdered. Moreover, labeling Jews as oppressors is, as a Harvard law professor has noted, "far too close for comfort to the antisemitic tradition of singling out Jews as uniquely deserving of condemnation and punishment, whether in its old religious form or its Nazi iteration."[16] These protests—and the university's failure to enforce its own rules against the protesters—have in turn enabled the Trump administration to claim that its actions against universities are necessary to protect Jewish students from unlawful discrimination.

It is not surprising that DEI's reversion to tribalism has redounded to the detriment of Jews. Historically, attacks on the Enlightenment have been coupled with anti-Semitism,[17] and Jews in turn have been instrumental in bringing Enlightenment values to American intellectual traditions, providing a secular and cosmopolitan perspective.[18]

The final Enlightenment value rejected by the DEI movement is freedom of speech and thought. From "cancel culture" to "microaggressions," those who dare to challenge the DEI orthodoxy do so at their peril. Universities have canceled lectures, revoked offers of admission, suspended students, driven out (by firing or constructive firing) tenured faculty members, and otherwise disciplined those who do not toe the DEI party line.[19] But when Jews became the victims of both verbal and physical attacks, universities looked the other way.[20] As one anonymous Berkeley faculty member wrote: "For years, our DEI police and their faculty deputies have taught us to denounce dog-whistle politics, recognize and decry microaggressions, acknowledge stolen land that we have no intention of returning, and always be sure to specify our preferred pronouns, all the while ignoring or dismissing the frequent fog horns and macroaggressions of antisemitism."[21]

Anti-Semitism—and anti-Enlightenment, antidemocratic thought—is thus inherent in the university culture wrought by the DEI movement. And so we have seen Jewish students harassed, threatened, excluded from campus organizations, and physically barred from portions of campus; DEI administrators exchanging anti-Semitic text messages during a panel on Jewish life; and university presidents unable or unwilling to condemn anti-Semitic speech despite their frequent and public condemnation of protected speech that conflicts with the DEI orthodoxy. As one observer described the situation at Columbia: "Jewish students faced ostracism and bullying that, if experienced by any other group of students on campus, would be universally regarded as unacceptable."[22] A federal judge pulled no punches in issuing a preliminary injunction against UCLA:

> In the year 2024, in the United States of America, in the State of California, in the City of Los Angeles, Jewish students were excluded from portions of the UCLA campus because they refused to denounce their faith. This fact is so unimaginable and so abhorrent to our constitutional guarantee of religious freedom that it bears repeating, *Jewish students were excluded from portions of the UCLA campus because they refused to denounce their faith.*[23]

His words could have applied to many other universities; several university task forces have found "pervasive" anti-Semitism at their institutions.

No one should be surprised by any of this, nor by the fact that after Hamas terrorists tortured, raped, and murdered more than 1,200 Israeli civilians, including the very old and the very young, and took some 200 innocent hostages, including children, the response on college campuses was blatantly anti-Semitic—even before Israel fought back.[24] Anti-Semitism had been simmering for years, stoked by the principles underlying DEI. And it will continue until universities reclaim their stance against orthodoxy.

What's the Big Deal?

Some readers might be tempted to minimize the effect that DEI has had on university culture. They might also suggest that what this essay has described is a few rare instances of the most extreme forms of DEI, not reflected in DEI as it is practiced at most universities.

The problem with that response is twofold. First, the underlying principles—what might be called the logic of the DEI enterprise—push in the direction of extremism, especially in the current polarized climate. Many of the students and faculty who act on DEI principles are not only convinced that they are on the side of the angels but are dismissive of the Enlightenment focus on rational debate, so they cannot help but demonize those who disagree with them. (DEI adherents, of course, are not alone in demonizing their opponents, but they are the ones who explicitly deny the usefulness of rational debate and are also the ones in control of our universities at the moment.) Second, it does not take many extreme incidents to change a university's culture by chilling further discussion or dissent. With that chilling effect in mind, consider some of the broader effects of DEI on campus.

First is the widespread adoption (now perhaps waning, partly in response to Trump) of "diversity statements" for faculty hiring and promotion. Faculty candidates were—and in many universities still are—required to submit a statement regarding their knowledge of, and support for, DEI principles. Those statements are graded pursuant to a rubric that awards low marks for such benign sentiments as treating everyone equally or welcoming all students, as well as for vague and nonspecific endorsements of diversity in principle.[25] For some universities, candidates are required to provide very specific statements about their own plans, such as identifying "two or more strategies for contributing to advancing racial equity and eliminating systemic racism" or naming "at least three inequities" and describing how the candidate would address those inequities.[26] The diversity statements thus serve as an ideological litmus test for faculty hiring. Worse still, at some universities, candidates have been eliminated solely because of the weakness of their diversity statements, without any consideration of their scholarship or teaching.[27]

The diversity litmus test—combined with the tendency of many faculties to replicate themselves—has had the desired effect: a dearth of conservative faculty, and even a diminished number of moderates.[28] The enforced orthodoxy has also substantially dampened the willingness of both students and faculty to give voice to controversial ideas.[29] One study found that 88 percent of undergraduates at two elite universities admitted to having pretended to hold more progressive views than they actually held, in order to succeed socially or academically.[30] The same orthodoxy infects what is actually taught. Another study examined thousands of college syllabi to determine what works were assigned on three controversial topics. Each topic had in fact generated competing arguments and viewpoints among respected scholars, but the syllabi almost uniformly assigned *only* a work taking the most progressive stance.[31]

Finally, faculty concerns about the potential consequences of saying the "wrong" thing, even inadvertently, are warranted, as my own experience illustrates. In 2019, after a single student complained, I was under investigation by my university's DEI office for two months. The investigation concluded without any punitive action, but only, I was told, because it was my first offense. What egregious conduct triggered the complaint and the investigation? I allowed a student to quote from—and then quoted from myself—a 1968 case that used the word "Negro." Never mind that in 1968 it was considered a term of respect and preferred by most African Americans. (No, the complaining student had not misheard it as a different word beginning with "N"; she reported it accurately.) In more than thirty-five years of teaching at three different universities and lecturing to faculty and students at many more, including previously using that word and teaching controversial subject matter, this was the first time I was ever subjected to investigation.

I realize that "data" is not the plural of "anecdote," but my experience is far from unique, and even a few such incidents can be enough to make people change what they say or do not say. For example, in 2022 the incoming director of Georgetown Law School's Center for the Constitution was placed on leave after a tweet criticizing President Biden's promise to appoint a Black woman to the Supreme Court.[32] In 2020, a professor at the USC business school was removed from teaching his class, investigated, and excoriated by the dean in a school-wide email, all for using (in an appropriate context) a Chinese word that students thought sounded like what is euphemistically called "the n-word."[33] Another USC professor characterized the incident as part of a trend: "Fundamental values—freedom of speech, intellectual freedom, equality—have largely fallen out of fashion in most elite universities, including USC. This has created a climate of terror among faculty."[34] In addition to the cases that make headlines, there are numerous similar stories that go unreported but are widely circulated among faculty, creating an atmosphere of fear. For example, one law-school professor (not at my university) was criticized for quoting Justice Harlan's famous dissent in the 1896 case of *Plessy v. Ferguson* that "[o]ur Constitution is color-blind."[35] Students were upset that she failed to condemn Harlan, because advocating color blindness ignores the lived experience of racial minorities and thus exhibits unconscious racism.

It does not take many such incidents to create a culture in which faculty and students feel compelled to stay silent and change their teaching and scholarship to avoid running afoul of the prevailing orthodoxy. Today's universities reflect such a culture: Hiring decisions turn on DEI loyalty oaths. Conservatives have all but disappeared from campuses. When surveyed anonymously, students and faculty say that are afraid to speak their minds. And students can and often do trigger investigations and retaliation by university administrators against faculty for speech the students dislike. We can thus be confident that the culture of universities has changed—and not for the better.

How Did We Get Here?

None of this developed overnight. Although DEI suddenly gained momentum after the murder of George Floyd in 2020, and campus anti-Semitism seemed to come out of nowhere in October 2023, there were warning signs much earlier. The DEI movement has its roots in critical race theory of the late 1980s and 1990s. DEI adopted the critical-race-theory views that there is no such thing as objective merit, that knowledge is subjective (and dependent primarily on race, gender, or ethnicity), and that Enlightenment values have served merely to advance straight white males and hold back everyone else.

The impetus for the development of critical race theory was the failure of traditional legal remedies to produce enough progress in narrowing the gap between white and Black success in the United States. Critical race theorists therefore pivoted from the conventional view that unequal outcomes were the result of prejudice and discrimination, arguing instead that the cause was structural (or systemic) racism. The DEI Glossary echoes this, defining structural racism as:

> The normalization and legitimization of an array of dynamics—historical, cultural, institutional and interpersonal—that routinely advantage Whites while producing cumulative and chronic adverse outcomes for people of color. Structural racism encompasses the entire system of White domination. . . .[36]

Over the next two decades, critical race theory gradually seeped beyond legal academia and into progressive politics. It formed a cohesive, convenient intellectual framework that allowed adherents to avoid hard questions about the causes of inequality by blaming every bad outcome on structural racism. Indeed, even asking those hard questions, or raising any objections against critical race theory, was itself seen as racist. Anyone not aligned with the critical race theorists was racist, just as anyone not aligned with the oppressed was a privileged oppressor. One critical race theorist, for example, denounced the "white male" backlash against critical race theory and dropped a footnote citing *only* scholarship by one white man, one white woman, and one Taiwanese man who had moved to the United States at the age of 6.[37] The latter two were lumped in with white males presumably because they had a taken a stand against critical race theory.

Critical race theory was just that, however: a theory. But soon those dissatisfied with racial progress began to turn the theory into practice, eventually calling for diversity, equity, and inclusion. Each term both resonated with critical race theory and offered a concrete path forward.

The embrace of diversity had two quite different sources. The first was Justice Lewis Powell's solo opinion in *Regents of University of California v. Bakke.*[38] Powell provided the pivotal fifth vote to invalidate the University of California Medical School's quota system, but to allow race to be taken into account in admissions decisions, thus placing the Court's imprimatur on what came to be known as affirmative action. Crucially, Powell denied that affirmative action could be justified as a remedy for past societal discrimination. Instead, he wrote, "the attainment of a diverse student body"[39] was a sufficiently compelling governmental interest to warrant the use of some forms of affirmative action. This was apparently the Supreme Court's first linkage of race and diversity. But universities quickly began to justify their existing (and growing) affirmative-action programs in terms of diversity, and by the early 2000s most people were probably unaware of its origins.

The second source for diversity as a goal was critical race theory itself. Powell's opinion in *Bakke* lauded racial diversity but did not explain why racial—as opposed to ideological—diversity was necessary in a university. By positing that knowledge was subjective and that it varied depending on the knower's racial or ethnic identity, critical race theorists provided that explanation and laid the groundwork for DEI. A university cannot seek or transmit identity-based knowledge unless it has a sufficient number of students and faculty with access to that knowledge—and the only people with that access are those with the correct racial, ethnic, or gender identity. The irony here is that as elite universities became more racially and ethnically diverse, they became less ideologically diverse. At Harvard, for example, one study in 2023 found that more than 75 percent of the faculty identify as "liberal" or "very liberal,"[40] and another found that less than 15 percent of students in the class of 2024 identified as "conservative" or "very conservative."[41]

The idea of equity also flowed directly from critical race theory and its discontents. Antidiscrimination theorists originally focused on *equality*, specifically equality of opportunity. Through residential and educational segregation, redlining, confinement to menial jobs, formal and informal obstacles to voting, and other explicitly discriminatory practices, Black Americans had been denied the opportunity to succeed. The promise of *Brown v. Board of Education*[42] and transformative federal statutes including the Voting Rights Act of 1957 and the Civil Rights Act of 1964 was that removing those barriers would solve the problem.

It didn't work out that way. Even as the initial protections against explicitly discriminatory practices were expanded—by barring neutral practices with a disparate impact on Blacks and by engaging in affirmative action that sought to increase Black representation in most American institutions—Blacks made progress, but they still lagged behind whites.

Critical race theorists blamed the failure on systemic or structural racism. For their DEI successors, then, the solution also had to be systemic and structural. Enter "equity." Equality means equal opportunity, but equity means equal results. For example, Ibram X. Kendi proposed an anti-racist constitutional amendment to enshrine the idea that "racial inequity is evidence of racist policy,"[43] with "inequity" defined as unequal outcomes[44] and "racist policy" described as his more precise substitute for what others call systemic or structural racism.[45] Translation: All unequal outcomes result from structural racism. Thus, as equity replaced equality as the goal for DEI adherents, every racial disparity in achievement became evidence of racism and demonstrated the need for remedies that produced more racially balanced results. The remedies ranged from eliminating standardized tests or making them optional, to providing segregated "safe spaces" (including separate dormitories, orientation programs, and graduations) for students of color, to policing microaggressions.

Finally there is inclusion. It sounds harmless—who could be against inclusion?—but in practice it has meant that students of color must be protected from any and all discomfort, because that discomfort always stems from white America viewing them as "other" and systematically excluding them from truly belonging. For example, a student in a course on global art history complained about the showing of a 14th-century Islamic painting of Muhammad, despite the fact that students had been warned multiple times that this would occur and were given the option of not viewing the painting. The student nevertheless felt excluded: "As a Muslim, and a Black person, I don't feel like I belong." The DEI machinery was invoked, the lecturer's contract was not renewed, and the president of the university sent a university-wide email proclaiming that "respect for the observant Muslim students in that classroom should have superseded academic freedom."[46]

Although the president's admission that the university chose inclusion over academic freedom is rare, the conflict between the two is not. Especially in an age of microaggressions, when students are taught to take offense at the slightest provocation, discussion of all but the blandest topics is bound to cause discomfort. But discomfort is an inherent part of education. As Hanna Holborn Gray, former president of the University of Chicago, put it, "education should not be intended to make people comfortable, it is meant to make them think."[47] Nevertheless, DEI has trained students to translate discomfort into exclusion, and to tearfully demand that university administrators make it stop. Even worse, that discomfort, as one commentator notes, "has come to be defined in the medicalized vocabulary of safety,"[48] so protecting students' physical safety now includes forbidding any speech that makes them uncomfortable.

There is thus a direct path from critical race theory to today's DEI juggernaut. But where critical race theory was impotent in practice, the diversity, equity, and inclusion movement has had real consequences. Universities are now reaping that whirlwind.

What Is to Be Done?

One possibility is that nothing *can* be done, at least not by universities themselves. DEI critic David Reiff argues that the university has always been a reflection of the larger culture: "The liberal university has collapsed because liberalism as the governing consensus of US . . . society has collapsed."[49] He continues: "Vile though it is, and destructive as it is within . . . academe, DEI is a manifestation of the collapse, not its cause."[50] Alternatively, the golden age of universities as bastions of free thought and seekers of knowledge may have been a fluke, bound to end eventually, given America's essential anti-intellectualism.[51] Finally, asking university administrators to curb faculty impulses toward DEI authoritarianism might be a hopeless cause: no one becomes a university president by opposing the zeitgeist.

But I am not yet willing to concede that universities cannot heal themselves. Because so many faculty and students at elite universities (and other universities as well) have swallowed the DEI dogma, it is up to university administrators—especially presidents and provosts, whose jobs do not depend directly on the existence of the DEI bureaucracy—to protect the university, its mission, and its academic freedom, from *all* who seek to impose orthodoxy. Although there are specific steps that should be taken, they all boil down to two directives: Don't bend the knee to Trump, but be the grown-up in the room against childishly simplistic (but dangerous) progressive orthodoxy.

The implementation of the first directive is obvious. Do not follow the example of Columbia or Brown. Refuse to take the devil's bargain, and if necessary turn to the courts for assistance. There may be pain in the short run, but in the long run it is better than giving up independence and with it the university's *raison d'être*.

The second directive is harder. Before I turn to several concrete steps that universities might take to accomplish it, I want to suggest a few things that they should *not* do. They should be careful not to punish mere speech, no matter how obnoxious, offensive, or anti-Semitic. Only those who violate content-neutral regulations (by blocking access, disrupting classes, and the like) should be subject to discipline. And universities should err on the side of allowing speech—even purely verbal harassment of Jewish students should be prohibited only where it is pervasive enough to interfere with the university's educational mission. To do otherwise would be to tread too close to a censorship as bad as, although opposite to, what has been occurring because of DEI. Similarly, faculty should be free to teach from any perspective unless they do so in a way that is totally divorced from the topic of the class (for example, praising Hamas in calculus class). Finally, universities should avoid doing what Trump and some state legislatures are trying to make them do: either impose anti-DEI (or pro-Enlightenment) loyalty oaths, or broaden their ideological diversity by implementing a sort of affirmative action for conservatives.

The first thing that universities *should* do is easy: follow the example of the University of Chicago and adopt both the principles of free speech endorsed by the Report of the Committee on Free Expression[52] and the principle of institutional neutrality proclaimed by the Kalven Report.[53] As the former notes:

> [T]he University's fundamental commitment is to the principle that debate or deliberation may not be suppressed because the ideas put forth are thought by some or even by most members of the University community to be offensive, unwise, immoral, or wrongheaded. . . . As a corollary to the University's commitment to protect and promote free expression, members of the university community must also act in conformity with the principles of free expression. Although members of the University community are free to criticize and contest the views expressed on campus, and to criticize and contest speakers who are invited to express their views on campus, they may not obstruct or otherwise interfere with the freedom of others to express views they reject or even loathe.[54]

Or, as Oliver Wendell Holmes put it when defending freedom of speech from government censorship, universities should allow even the "expression of opinions that we loathe and believe to be fraught with death."[55] Freedom of speech and thought for members of the community also requires neutrality on the part of the university itself, as the Kalven Report concludes: "The neutrality of the university as an institution . . . arises out of respect for free inquiry and the obligation to cherish a diversity of viewpoints."[56]

Though it will be somewhat more difficult than adopting these two University of Chicago statements of principle, universities should faithfully apply their own rules and therefore discipline faculty and students who break those rules. Although both students and faculty have the right to speak and to protest, they do not have the right to ignore reasonable content-neutral university rules, to disrupt university functions, or to exclude others from public spaces. The line between protected speech and rule-breaking may sometimes be hard to discern, but elite universities seem to have ignored the line entirely, letting students and faculty disrupt university events or occupy university spaces and exclude others from those spaces for weeks or even months with impunity. Even worse, universities have enforced their own rules selectively, punishing some rule breakers but not others, apparently based on the views the rule breakers express.[57] As two commentators suggest, in the easy cases there is an easy test: If white supremacists engaged in the conduct, would they be punished? If so, then anti-Semitic protesters should suffer the same fate.[58]

The hardest, but still necessary, step is to dismantle the DEI bureaucracy that has been established over the past few decades. But the dismantling must be done thoughtfully and carefully, unlike Trump's blunderbuss attempts to accomplish the same thing. Because every university—and therefore every DEI bureaucracy—is different, I can only offer general guidance on how universities should proceed.

Essentially, universities must seek out and eliminate the myriad offices, practices, and rules that were put in place to accomplish DEI objectives. Just as several universities have recently carried out internal examinations of their own anti-Semitism, universities should ask a task force to identify all of the DEI tentacles and to recommend how they should be neutralized. Importantly, universities must still leave in place a process—and an apparatus, such as an antidiscrimination office—for resolving complaints by students, faculty, and staff that they have been discriminated against. But there must be safeguards to prevent ideological capture or replication of the DEI regime. The details of those safeguards must be worked out on a university-by-university basis.

Even with the safeguards, there is still no guarantee that complaints of discrimination will always be handled appropriately. Nor can an internal audit identify or erase all traces of DEI. No institutional arrangement is better than the people who staff it, and the DEI mentality is so deeply entrenched in elite universities that it may not be possible to eradicate it completely. In particular, because so many faculty members have bought into the DEI agenda, it perhaps cannot be rooted out without causing irreparable harm to the fundamental concept of faculty governance—one of the aspects of academic freedom that is already too often being undermined by bloated university administrations. Nevertheless, universities should at least dilute the DEI orthodoxy, if only to avoid being forced by federal or state authorities to adopt an opposite one.

Finally, despite the need to adopt the University of Chicago principles, to retake control over the university campus, and to dismantle DEI in order to reclaim academic freedom from its stifling orthodoxy, universities should remain at the forefront of solving the very real problems that DEI—and critical race theory before it—were misguidedly invented for.

Instead of repeating the DEI canon, universities should do what they do best: ask hard and controversial questions about race (and gender and everything else). The DEI party line, that white racism is the one and only reason Blacks as a group lag behind whites on almost every measurable outcome and that anyone who says otherwise must be a racist protecting his or her own privilege, prevents universities from investigating other possibilities. Maybe Black American culture is somehow dysfunctional, or maybe psychological or sociological factors trigger maladaptive behaviors.[59] Maybe the answer is both of the above and more, including the legacy of slavery and discrimination. Investigating other related questions relevant to DEI, currently taboo in academia, might also be of practical use: Why are American Jews (and some groups of Asian Americans) so successful despite a long history of discrimination against them? Why are there so few women in STEM fields? Why have gays, so long subject to both legal and social discrimination, melted so seamlessly into the ranks of the successful? But as long as the DEI orthodoxy reigns, professors will be afraid to engage in research on these issues, and universities will be unwilling to support it.

We cannot fix a problem unless we know what is causing it. A university free of orthodoxy would be free to search anywhere for causes—and maybe eventually find a solution. The final irony, then, is that in addition to its anti-Semitism and its threat to academic freedom, the DEI orthodoxy creates obstacles to accomplishing its own laudable goals.

16

Committing to Intellectual Fallibility

The Improper Use of Academic Freedom to Limit Speech

LARRY KRAMER AND LEE C. BOLLINGER

Bollinger: Larry, thank you for being part of this project. You've had a distinguished career–now as president of the London School of Economics, and before that president of the Hewlett Foundation, dean of the Stanford Law School, and law professor at NYU, Chicago, and Michigan (where we were colleagues). Your scholarly expertise in American constitutional law and history, together with the important roles you have assumed, give you a singular perspective on the primary subject of this volume: What are the rights and responsibilities of universities in the United States, and how are they being threatened by actions of the new Trump administration? The essays collected here address various aspects of this crisis. Some explore the idea that universities deserve to have a special standing in society, an autonomy derived from political theory or constitutional law. The now century-long assertion of rights of academic freedom provides the roots of this idea. But everyone agrees that all these claims and arguments are underdeveloped and need deeper explanations.

Other essays focus on how the strategies of the Trump administration—largely built around new interpretations of Title VI of the 1964 Civil Rights Act and the withholding of federal funding and grants, primarily in fields of science and engineering, until universities accede to various changes in faculty hiring, student admissions, student discipline, practices and policies around diversity, and other areas traditionally regarded as within the realm of university self-governance—are inconsistent with law and various norms of government/higher education relations; and are part of a general authoritarian-style strategy of suppressing independent thought and voices in the society. Still other authors examine topics such as the origins and development of the federal

Larry Kramer and Lee C. Bollinger, *Committing to Intellectual Fallibility*. In: *Academic Freedom in the Era of Trump*. Edited by: Lee C. Bollinger and Geoffrey R. Stone, Oxford University Press. © Oxford University Press (2026). DOI: 10.1093/9780197854877.003.0017 government's deciding in the aftermath of World War II to create a national scientific-research enterprise through federal funding to universities; and the roles that universities have played in achieving racial justice in the decades following the Supreme Court's momentous decision ending racial segregation in public schools in *Brown v. Board of Education* (1954) and the partial successes of the Civil Rights Movement of the 1960s. Finally, some essays here argue that, while universities are entitled to special protections according to the principle of academic freedom, too many universities have jeopardized their rights under that principle by becoming more ideological and politically partisan than scholarly and neutral on politically charged issues.

Given all this, where would you like to focus your attention and begin?

Kramer: Wow. There are a lot of issues there worth deep consideration, though I keep thinking about how many of the challenges we're facing today are unintended consequences of earlier choices that made sense at the time but played out in ways that have made universities vulnerable. Because we need to be honest: Trump is able to get away with this, for now at least, because universities have lost the kind of public support and respect they used to have.[1]

That's so for a lot of reasons. Partly, it's that so much of the research and scholarship we do seems abstruse and incomprehensible to laypeople, light-years removed from anything they think matters. Not so much in STEM fields, perhaps, but there is still a lot of jargon-heavy work coming from arts, humanities, and social-science departments (including law) that's ripe for mockery. Not because it's bad scholarship—some is, some isn't, as with scholarship generally. But both content and presentation are so inward-facing and ultra-refined that it's easily caricatured, setting universities up for attack.

The irony is that it's an unintended product of one of the best, most generous, most enlightened pieces of legislation in American history: the G.I. Bill. Enabling the generation of WWII veterans to attend college greatly increased the numbers attending, as well as helping generate a culture that carried forward to the next generation a belief that success comes from getting a college degree. The resulting surge in enrollment led to a surge in both the number and the size of universities.[2] All good, except now there were vastly larger numbers of scholars working in any given field—making it harder for a young scholar to make a name without finding some ever more minute, esoteric niche in which to say something novel. The work became narrower and more technical, increasingly accessible only to others within the priesthood. Put that together with the undeniable shift to the left that took place among university faculty, and the equally undeniable shift to focus on domination and oppression, and the stage was set for an attack like that of the Trump Administration to succeed.

That universities did so little either to respond to the critique or explain their value proposition didn't help. We neither showed people how much of what we do in fact does provide the kind of education they want or should want for their children nor explained how ideas that seemed bewilderingly irrelevant to them are not. It's one thing to assert a value like academic freedom as a reason for government and people outside the university to leave us free to do the research we want and develop ideas free from external constraint. It's another to insist they just take on faith that it's worth it.

Most of the discussion is about issues like these. Those of us in universities have a very deep hole to dig ourselves out of in reexplaining to the public why we matter—and the explanation, I should add, needs to be about more than just our contribution to economic growth. We need to reengage the public in seeing universities as centers for debate and discussion and the development of ideas that matter to social and political as well as scientific problems.

But recently I've come across a different use of academic freedom: not as a tool to preserve the freedom of academics to think, research, and write about whatever they choose (so long as it's lawful), but as a tool being used by academics to *shut down* disfavored ideas being promulgated by other academics.

Bollinger: These are very important and provocative thoughts. The phenomena you highlight of the vast expansion of universities over the past century (especially after World War II) and the subdivision of fields of research and teaching (along with the invention of new fields) are real and notable. Those of us who have lived as professors and academic leaders know these forces well. To those you note, I would add several others. First and foremost, there is the sheer fact that an institution devoted to expanding knowledge is inevitably going to grow (if the resources are available). Every advance opens up new possibilities to explore. When you couple that with the advances in technology relevant to investigating new knowledge, which we've seen in abundance over this same period, you have the potential for exponential increases in the pursuit of knowing more. Then there are the pressures to expand that are somewhat independent of the research agenda. Clearly, the felt need to educate more and more young people—to fulfill a social commitment to overcoming discrimination against women and minorities, for example—has been an irresistible force. Finally, I would point to the public desire, often manifest through policy choices and legislation, to explore and discover new knowledge, especially treatments and cures for certain diseases. With time, I'm sure we could point to many more causes of the expansionary course of American higher education over these now many decades.

Now, you also make two very compelling points that we need to address. One is the way in which academic work has tended to become more and more impenetrable to nonexperts—and not, I think you would say, always as an unavoidable consequence of the search for truth. Probably you would add that, in the social sciences, the humanities, and certain professional fields (e.g., law), there has been too often a casual disregard for choosing language and explanations that would make it easier for nonexperts to connect to the discussions in those important areas of knowledge. With that I would agree. But I would probably go further and say that, insofar as this has occurred, what is lacking is a sense of responsibility, which should inhere in the academic community, to ensure that there is as much translation of expertise as possible. My own view is that the very claim of a special standing in the society for universities, whether it is derived from the constitution or from notions of a public trust, depends on universities caring that the knowledge they possess is shared as widely as possible.

We do need to acknowledge, however, that it is to some significant degree impossible for any of us to know more than a fraction of what is known by experts, in any field. Perhaps a better way to say this, then, is to add to the injunction that we feel an obligation to share in the search for truth however much we can, that we also do all we can to help create trust in the expertise we will never be able to understand. That, too, should be a felt responsibility. There is so much more to say here, as well, but let's leave this for now.

But then we need to attend to your other point: namely, that we have not just failed to engage the broader public in our mission to the extent we should, but also that we have become so insular that we have betrayed the very core values that are the foundation for the special autonomy we are now so vociferously defending. Take us into what you are thinking.

Kramer: I agree with pretty much everything you say here. And you are right: I do think the use of abstruse jargon is less about conveying substance than it is a kind of intellectual virtue signaling—meant almost intentionally, I sometimes think, to limit accessibility to members of the academic clergy. I also agree that scholars should, rather, be doing as much as they can to make their expertise accessible to the wider public. But this isn't something we can compel or require, and academic freedom certainly includes the freedom to choose your audience and write and speak and communicate however you want.

This isn't a new problem. The notion that "real" scholars don't care about nonacademic audiences or real-world impact has been around for quite a long time. I'm sure you remember Harry Edwards complaining about this in the context of legal scholarship back in the early 1990s.[3] And when I was at Stanford, one of the school's most successful scholars—someone already tenured and very well established—told me he was reluctant to pursue a project focused on a practical problem because he feared his colleagues would view the work (and by extension him) with contempt. I encouraged him to do the project, because his academic bona fides were so strong, but I couldn't honestly tell him he was wrong.

That's starting to change, especially among younger scholars, who increasingly see "impact" as something they care about and want to achieve. But this has come with a worrisome side effect—namely, a shift among many academics to seeing scholarship as advocacy and the university as an institution that should actively promote social change. In some ways, that's a short and not illogical step from wanting scholarship to have impact, yet there is a difference between doing research to help point the way toward solutions to social problems and seeing the scholar's role—and the role of the institution—as calling for active participation. It's a difference that shows up in the voice used in writing and in how social media are employed, a difference that produces calls for the university to take public stances and issue statements on political matters having nothing to do with the university's mission—which, we are now urged, should include "social justice" as a direct purpose and goal. It's a difference that also shows up in teaching by faculty who view the classroom not as a space to expose students to different ways of thinking about a problem, but as a forum in which students should be pushed to think about the problem "correctly." The university becomes a place from which to pursue social activism, with teaching and scholarship as means to that end.

All this is, and should be, encompassed by academic freedom, while many—I daresay most—faculty do *not* see their role this way. But a shift has been taking place, and a debate about the role and purpose of the university is definitely underway. A senior former colleague of ours told me about a conversation he recently had with some junior faculty about just this difference. He and they were amicably going back and forth when he suddenly realized they were just humoring him, thinking to themselves something like, "Yeah, yeah, old man, soon enough you'll be gone, and we'll make this university into what it should be." I laughed, but then pointed out how we had been exactly the same when we were junior faculty, though our fight was over whether and how interdisciplinary to make the educational program. But make no mistake, we're in the midst of a contest for the heart, or maybe I should say the soul, of our universities.

This divide in thinking about the role of a scholar and the role of the university is behind much of the turmoil that has troubled our institutions in recent years: the growing polarization among faculty, particularly in the arts, humanities, and social sciences; the increasing stridency of debate and disagreement; the narrowing of ideological and methodological diversity in certain disciplines and departments; the appearance of cancel culture and the resulting silencing among both faculty and students. The silencing is serious and pervasive but also not all that surprising. Most faculty and students aren't interested in having every encounter turn into an ideological battle with life-or-death stakes, and they find it easier to just withdraw or say nothing when faced with the self-righteous fury of a culture warrior or a risk of being called out on social media.

This is not, it must be said, a problem of the left alone. In recent years, the loudest voices may have come from progressives, but the problem arguably began with the insistence by conservatives in the 1980s and '90s that schools needed to hire more conservatives—which I believe did a huge disservice by fostering a self-fulfilling sense that faculty would and should be pushing their ideology. And, as we are seeing now, conservative proclamations about the importance of free speech and the evils of cancel culture vanished the instant conservatives found themselves with the political power to shut down progressives.

This increasing politicization of scholarship and teaching has, in turn, had significant effects on academic freedom, and not just by testing its boundaries as a shield from efforts to squelch unpopular views. On the contrary, academic freedom is now being used in some quarters as a sword to do exactly that squelching.

The argument goes something like this: Free speech is about opinions, and everyone has the same free-speech rights. But academic freedom is something distinct and narrower, attached to speech based on scholarly expertise and therefore extending only so far as the speech is plausibly based on and drawn from that expertise. The boundaries of expertise, in turn, are defined by the accepted norms of the discipline in which the faculty member purports to be an expert. Statements outside of or inconsistent with those norms are, consequently, not protected by academic freedom. It follows not just that a faculty member who makes such statements can be denied tenure or a promotion or some other honor or award. Faculty can, in fact, be sanctioned or punished. On this view, it was appropriate for Stanford to censure Scott Atlas for his publicly expressed views on Covid. And a professor at LSE argued to me that faculty members holding gender-critical views could and should be condemned by the School on the ground that such views are not "scientifically valid." At a meeting I attended of university presidents from several countries, everyone in the room (but me) agreed that faculty could be removed for speaking in their roles as scholars while taking positions outside the boundaries generally accepted by others in the discipline. As one person put it to me, "Surely you'd remove someone from the geography department if they argued that the world is flat!"

In these and other examples I've come across, we see academic freedom being used as a principle to *limit* the expression of ideas, which is the opposite of what I had always understood to be its purpose.

Bollinger: Let's step back for a moment and make sure we know what you are saying here. I have three questions. The first is whether you are talking here about a minority of faculty believing this way about scholarship and teaching as representing a different form of the university than has existed up to now, or, let's say, in modern times? Or is it a majority, in which case the transformation has already occurred? I do wonder about keeping a sense of proportionality here. And, while I suspect that in this discussion we are focusing on faculty in a few departments in the social sciences and the humanities, by definition these are only a mere subset of the faculty in our universities.

Second, for those faculty who profess to believe that scholarship and teaching should be about achieving some version of social justice, or social impact, is this idea of the university inherently inconsistent with the traditional notions of the university you and I say we believe in? In other words, you and I have known, and admired, many highly distinguished faculty who have done brilliant scholarship, accompanied by equally brilliant teaching, in the sense of making creative contributions to their fields, and who have carried that knowledge into the public realm and there also had important, even profound, effects. Presumably, we are not saying they and others like them were abandoning the traditional university. If not, then what is the new line that some faculty today are crossing that might lead us into new, and troublesome, territory for the future university?

Finally, I read you as saying that it is okay for the university to take into account a faculty member's "wrong" ideas, as defined by the prevailing disciplinary or scholarly standards, for decisions about tenure and promotion, but not for imposing sanctions or other official condemnations (e.g., censure) outside of those classic moments of professional evaluation. If that is so, why should we draw such a line at that point?

Kramer: Let me take these in order. With respect to your first question, I do think this is a minority of faculty, but a significant one. And while these views are, as you say, concentrated in particular disciplines in the humanities and social sciences, they are not isolated or limited to them. There are people who share the same views across the university, including in the professional schools and hard sciences.

Nor is it the case that everyone who does not share this view of the university is opposed to it. As with most issues, there are proponents on both sides, but also a large number who are not sure what they think: academics who have not really focused on the question systematically and who, as a result, sometimes support one side, sometimes the other, in any particular controversy. If there is a majority for any position, it is probably this group, the undecided, which is why I say we are in the middle of a contest to determine the mission of our universities. And where we will land is not yet clear.

This middle group is important for another reason. We live in a highly polarized age, in which proponents for or against many issues turn arguments about them into virtual life-or-death struggles. This isn't true just in universities. It's a development in the larger society that has also seeped into university culture. After all, annoying metaphors about "ivory towers" notwithstanding, universities are made up of people who live in and come from the same society as everyone else, and what happens outside the university inevitably shapes what happens inside it. The result has been a lot of silencing, as the cost for many faculty and students of engaging in fights with people who can become angry, self-righteous, and highly moralistic—and in which engaging includes risks like getting called out on social media—is just not worth it. So they say nothing.

Your second question, about taking scholarship out into the world, is important. I firmly believe it is not just useful but important for scholars to take their ideas outside the academy. Obviously, that's not a requirement, and an academic may care only about communicating to fellow academics, or may be indifferent to having any audience at all. This, too, is an essential part of academic freedom. But I do deeply believe we have so much to contribute to the world in so many fields and in so many ways that I wholeheartedly support efforts by faculty to have their work seen and used. This is, in fact, core to the identity of LSE, which has from the beginning defined its mission as "understanding the causes of things for the betterment of society"—with that last clause taken seriously. Our founders were Fabian socialists who thought the path to a better world did not require revolution and could be achieved by education and reform within existing structures, which was a big part of the reason they founded a university.

That said, let me reiterate that, while I personally think it valuable and appealing for academics to want their work to matter in society, I recognize that intellectual influence can be indirect as well as direct—meaning something one hopes to see happen without needing actively to push it—and I fully respect academics who are entirely indifferent to the matter. All these views are legitimate, all are part of a university, and all have their proper place within it.

Matters get trickier when this straightforward effort by academics to take their own work into the world—something that is and should be protected by academic freedom—is extended to an argument that the university, as an institution, should promote a particular vision of social justice. That's "the new line that some faculty today are crossing that might lead us into new, and troublesome, territory for the future university."

The reasons this is problematic are familiar. While society has many organizations whose missions are focused on advocacy, the central task and animating reason for a university is to develop and support a community of critical thinkers who can and will, collectively, analyze and understand complex issues from multiple viewpoints. This makes us institutionally unique, because we are the *only* institution in society with that central mission. And if history and experience teach us anything, it's that serving such a mission works only if we maintain an institutional commitment to intellectual fallibility—to the possibility of discovering that today's conventional wisdom may turn out to be wrong.

Securing that mission entails recognizing that different institutions are needed to play different roles in society and preserving the unique role that universities play. If we let ourselves become just one more political institution, we will over time (and probably not too much time) lose our credibility, our ability to garner support from across society, our ability to attract student and faculty populations diverse enough to ensure a vibrant intellectual environment, and, eventually, our independence. I think what's happened in the past few years—and particularly what's happening in the United States right now—pretty much bears that out, don't you?

By the way, this isn't saying that the university can never take a position that is "political." There are some political issues a university cannot avoid because they go to internal matters of how the institution itself operates. So maybe "political" isn't the right word, but the line I see is between controversial issues involving matters outside the university and those that bear directly on how it operates. When it comes to the latter—whether to adopt affirmative action in hiring or admissions, for instance, or how to address the needs of transgender students and staff—the university cannot escape taking a position: not doing anything is, in fact, doing something. We must decide whether to embrace affirmative action, or how to configure our facilities for people who are trans or gender-fluid. And whatever position we take has the inevitable and unavoidable consequence of expressing a view about the debate happening outside the university. But we should keep these "political" exceptions as narrow as possible, limiting them to questions we cannot avoid because they directly affect our operations.

The most challenging arena in recent years has been around managing an endowment. The decision about whether to add a screen on certain kinds of investments unavoidably expresses a position on an external matter, but we are taking affirmative action by investing and so cannot escape making choices and acknowledging that these choices express a viewpoint. But, again, to preserve our credibility for the larger mission, we can and should keep such instances as rare and as narrow as possible. The fact that we cannot close a door completely does not mean that we must therefore throw it wide open.

There is another, still tricker issue that arises once we recognize that faculty are free to go beyond developing ideas and may engage in active advocacy: namely, how does that freedom apply to teaching? Is it okay for a teacher to make their classroom one in which there are "right" views about an issue—meaning students are encouraged and expected to adopt the professor's viewpoint? You and I likely agree that doing so is not good teaching, that good teaching is about exposing students to different arguments and viewpoints and helping them think critically about them, while leaving the students free to make up their own minds. There are, however, faculty today who believe otherwise and who—whether openly or not, self-consciously or not—make their classrooms a place to inculcate "correct" thinking on issues.

While I may not think this is good teaching, I believe academic freedom entitles a teacher to make his or her class "political," even in this strong sense. What it does not permit a teacher to do, however, is to present those ideas in ways that exclude or ostracize students who feel otherwise. Instructors are obligated to find ways to invite such students into the conversation and cannot punish them for holding different views (for example, in grading). Put another way, the contractual obligation faculty have to students who have paid money to learn affects the *manner* of teaching but not the substance.

In addition, and I don't think this is a controversial point, an instructor cannot claim academic freedom as a shield to make the course about topics and ideas outside the advertised subject matter. Students who register for a class are entitled to have that class be about what they were told it would be about (especially if it's required). And the university must be able to offer students the classes it deems necessary for its degree programs. Faculty must have their courses approved for this reason. The privilege of teaching may include the freedom to teach the material as the faculty member deems best (subject to the limitation on manner described above); it does not include the freedom to make the class a platform for other purposes.

All that said, and coming back to the idea that there is an ongoing contest over the nature of the university's mission, these are the sorts of issues and arguments we must thrash out. There is and should be room inside the university for people who believe differently than we do. Put another way, I would not do to faculty who want to politicize the university what they seem to want to do to people like us, which is to exclude us, shut us out. It's the application to academic freedom of the paradoxical First Amendment principle that freedom of speech includes protecting the speech of people who advocate eliminating freedom of speech.

Which brings me to your third question and gets to the heart of the matter we have been discussing. I said above that it's improper to impose sanctions or other official condemnations (e.g., censure) for a faculty member's "wrong" ideas, as defined by prevailing disciplinary or scholarly standards. Why, then, is it permissible—as I believe it is—to use these standards when it comes to decisions about hiring, promotion, and similar moments of professional evaluation?

A first principle here is recognizing that, while academic freedom attaches to the university as an institution and is meant to protect it from certain kinds of external interference (such as that coming from the Trump administration right now), it also attaches to the individual scholar and is meant to protect them from certain kinds of internal interference. The basic premise underlying academic freedom, which is essential if the university is to be what it should be, is that academics must be free to explore and argue and present their ideas and positions without fear of being punished. Most important, it means they should not be formally sanctioned for exploring unconventional ideas or taking unorthodox positions.

You are right, however, that I don't think this principle works when it comes to decisions like hiring, promotion, or the giving of awards. Not so much because the principle no longer applies, but because I don't know what it would mean to make such decisions without taking prevailing standards into account. The nature of the decision requires assessing the quality of work. It's one thing to ask for agnosticism about the content of work you think is fundamentally wrong, but agnosticism isn't an option when the decision involves whether to hire or promote someone. Those decisions are necessarily based on the quality of the work, and that's inescapably refracted through the lens of prevailing norms and criteria.

We should, of course, try our best to create a culture of openness to new and challenging ideas—that's healthy, and a way to keep thinking alive and changing. Ideally, hiring and promotion committees will do their best to be as open as possible to such ideas. But I don't know what it would mean to say you cannot judge work as inadequate based on existing disciplinary norms when assessing scholarship for hiring or promotion.

Plainly, this puts a thumb on the scale in favor of perpetuating existing orthodoxies. Which is precisely why it is all the more important to say it is *in*appropriate to censure or condemn a scholar for the content of their ideas outside these contexts. I cannot think of anything more damaging to the development of new ways of thinking than making it permissible to fire or censure a tenured scholar for staking out positions that are unconventional and unorthodox.

Which brings us back to my main point: calling out and criticizing what I believe is a new use of academic freedom as a sword that can be wielded to punish (and so discourage) unorthodox thinking. Inside the university, there should not be positions, whether moral or intellectual, as to which the institution determines there shall be no more debate. (It's worth noting in this regard that if earlier generations of scholars had applied such a standard, many of the scholars who advocate for doing so today would not be on the faculty.)

This position doesn't go down easily. Others to whom I have made the argument have suggested that I cannot really mean it. What if a faculty member argued the Earth is flat? one asked incredulously. Or published an article in favor of slavery? I acknowledge how hard it would be to exercise restraint in such circumstances, but I think we must do so. The truth is, cases this outrageous are unlikely to occur, particularly given our hiring and promotion standards, while the situations we have actually had to address—like Scott Atlas on Covid, gender-critical views, affirmative action, and the like—are nowhere near so extreme. But opening the door to the extreme cases unavoidably and inevitably opens the door to these, which then opens the door to still less extreme cases. It's a very slippery slope, and the negative consequences of sliding down it seem more likely and more dangerous to me than chancing these (theoretical) absurdities while leaving refutation to the usual processes of academic discourse.

That's not an argument based on deductive logic. It's a pragmatic judgment, balancing different risks and considerations with an eye toward preserving universities in the form that will best enable them to serve their larger role in society as a place where ideas are always open to reexamination. In this, academic freedom is like the broader principle of free speech: the existence of extreme cases tests the principle, and our willingness to tolerate them is ultimately what ensures the security and effectiveness of that principle in less extreme cases.

Bollinger: Thank you, Larry. I think that perfectly clarifies your idea of what academic freedom means within the university. Before we conclude, though, I want to explore a bit more what you are thinking about the idea of the university as it relates to social or political impact, or reform, or social justice. You see this idea emerging especially among younger faculty, and you say that it is a conception of the university at odds with the traditional notions of the role of scholarship and teaching. Indeed, you even go so far as to say that the "soul" of the university is in question with this debate.

Just to be clear, you draw a distinction between a world in which "academics (want) to take their own work into the world," something you approve of, and one where "the university, as an institution, should promote a particular vision of social justice." Let me use a real case to test what you are thinking.

Columbia, like Stanford, has established a new school devoted to studying the issues related to climate change. Clearly, all sane people agree that climate change is real, man-made, and more or less a permanent part of the human condition for years and years to come.[4] Because of it, there are a host of issues to be explored: How will the world evolve? What can and should be done about it? What works and doesn't work? And so on. A century ago, universities saw the need for more academic work directly focused on public health. In these and other instances, universities that established "schools" decided that the existing disciplinary structures were insufficient to address the public needs.

In this case, we would expect those who compose the faculty to "believe" in the "science" about the causes of global warming and climate change and the need of societies in the world to address the issues raised. Indeed, the university's purpose might well include a purpose of trying to push for more attention and action than currently exists. This might well be characterized by some as an "activist" orientation and, therefore, unacceptable for a university. I, myself, would reject that conclusion. Would you?

Now, within the faculty, there would be a host of scholarly "experts" who would take up different dimensions of a vast number of issues connected to climate change—the role of certain energy sources, matters of climate justice, the impact on glaciers and sea-level rise, and on and on. Each of these areas would inevitably lead to debates, sometimes passionate debates, about the choices presented and the choices to be made. There undoubtedly also would be differences of opinion within the faculty on every one of these issues. That would be regarded as a healthy intellectual environment. But collectively this would probably be, in effect, pushing the world to confront these issues and to come to terms with them.

For me, the question under the principle of academic freedom would be whether the research and teaching and public involvement all happened with what I refer to as the scholarly temperament—a mind that is reflective, is committed to full and honest engagement with the work of others, ready to give full and fair attribution to ideas that you are relying on, dedicated to advancing the knowledge we have, and genuinely open to listening to and being persuaded by arguments opposed to one's own, as reason calls for.

And what I would not say is consistent with the principle of academic freedom would be a faculty, or a school, that was closed-minded, confident in their own beliefs such that further discussion seemed unnecessary, and determined to change the world according to their particular viewpoints. To my mind, this is now not a university—it is a nonprofit advocacy organization.

Do you agree with that? Does it seem right?

Kramer: What a great example on which to end. Climate change is one of the most profound challenges of our time, and universities everywhere are trying to figure out how to address it—including LSE, which recently launched a Global School of Sustainability to support scholarship, teaching, and other activities looking at climate change, biodiversity, and sustainable development through a social science lens.[5]

I thought at first you were going to challenge the very idea of a school or formal university unit that presupposes climate as a problem to be addressed. After all, there are still some—including the President of the United States—who say climate change isn't real.[6] A stickler for consistency might argue that schools like Columbia's, Stanford's, or LSE's are inconsistent with the principle of institutional restraint, because they reflect an official university position on an external political issue.

You don't press that argument, because (you say) "Clearly, all sane people agree that climate change is real." I concur, notwithstanding what this implies about the current White House resident. But the other position is out there, so we are taking sides in a political controversy, aren't we? We might, I suppose, say climate deniers are, at most, a tiny fringe; and given the significance and importance of the problem, we cannot and should not let a negligible group of marginal actors have such an outsized effect. If ever there were a fitting instance of Emerson's cutting remark about "a foolish consistency" being "the hobgoblin of little minds," this would be it. It's an exception, to be sure, but one that is not just sensible but compelling. Rigid principles must be seasoned with a pinch of pragmatism from time to time, particularly when important and weighty conflicting concerns are at play.

That's where I started, and I was comfortable with that position. But as I thought about it more, I realized there isn't necessarily a conflict here at all. The university has traditionally been organized around disciplines, because that's how we provide the kind of deep training we try to deliver. But it's not unreasonable to think also about organizing around problems, both as a way to better prepare students for the kinds of work they will do when they leave and to facilitate multidisciplinary and interdisciplinary scholarship. Whatever one's view on climate change—including the view that it isn't real or has been exaggerated—there is no question that it is a major social concern worthy of study and research, as well as an appropriate area in which to prepare students for the work they will do and lives they will lead after they graduate.

Hence, schools like the School of Climate Change at Columbia or the Stanford Doerr School of Sustainability or our own Global School of Sustainability have been created to focus on the climate problem, but are presumably open to any and all arguments in that respect—including even the argument that this isn't really a problem after all. To that extent, such schools are entirely consistent with the views I've expressed about academic freedom.

To be sure, and as you and I both agree, when it comes to hiring or promoting staff or making decisions about how to allocate limited grant funding, choices must be made based on quality assessment, and it is unlikely that climate deniers will find much support. But if someone were already tenured in the School and concluded that warming was not a problem, or that humans were not a primary agent in causing it, they could not and should not be removed, censured, or otherwise punished. Our commitment to intellectual fallibility and the idea that no issue should be declared off-limits for debate applies here no less than on any other issue.

Which brings me to your last question about ensuring we preserve "the scholarly temperament." You define this as "a mind that is reflective, is committed to full and honest engagement with the work of others, ready to give full and fair attribution to ideas that you are relying on, dedicated to advancing the knowledge we have, and genuinely open to listening to and being persuaded by arguments opposed to one's own as reason calls for." You then say:

> ". . . what I would not say is consistent with the principle of academic freedom would be a faculty, or a school, that was closed-minded, confident in their own beliefs such that further discussion seemed unnecessary, and determined to change the world according to their particular viewpoints. To my mind, this is now not a university—it is a nonprofit advocacy organization."

I agree wholeheartedly with your elegant description of a scholarly temperament. The best scholars have precisely that temperament in my experience, and all scholars should strive to approach the craft this way. But I'm not sure what you mean when you say that a faculty or a school that lacks this temperament is "not consistent with the principle of academic freedom."

Let me start with the individual scholar. Obviously, the purpose of academic freedom isn't to foster closed-minded scholars who are uninterested in discourse with people who think differently and care only about pushing their viewpoints on others. But it doesn't follow that the principle of academic freedom would therefore not apply to or protect them. In this, the scope for academic freedom must be like the scope for free speech: we protect what many people see as "bad" speech so as to give "good speech" breathing room—because we know how difficult it can be to determine which is which, and know also how easy it can therefore be to slip into policing more and more of the good stuff. I would say the same about academic freedom and scholars who may lack a scholarly temperament.

Bear in mind there is no inconsistency or even necessary tension between being an activist and holding the academic temperament you describe. Academics can fully embrace your vision of a scholarly attitude while wanting to see the conclusions they reach in their scholarship embraced by their students and turned into action outside the academy. In my experience, this describes the vast majority of academics who see themselves as activists. And while that isn't my approach to teaching and writing, my disagreement is only with those who insist that the institution as such must also embrace their views.

I'm not sure what to make of your hypothetical of a whole school or faculty that might be closed-minded this way. If, as many seem to believe, this describes our current universities, or parts of them—if, that is, our universities are falling short in manifesting intellectual diversity and freedom of thought—the solution is to hold them to principles and work harder to make them places where all ideas can be freely expressed and debated. But I would not say they have ceased to be universities.

Freedom of thought and expression can, I suppose, be formally or explicitly restricted in a university's stated mission, or by requiring adherence to a particular ideology or belief system as a condition for employment or attendance. Religious institutions come to mind, though good religious universities don't limit freedom of thought and fully protect academic freedom. There have, recently, been efforts to launch universities with a specific commitment to promoting a conservative political ideology. Like you, I think this is a terrible idea and very bad approach. The solution to the perceived lack of intellectual diversity or room for free expression in our universities can't and shouldn't be to create still less diverse universities with a different set of blinders. Certainly, I'd never send my child to such a school, and I expect the research will lack credibility and influence beyond true believers. But apart from that, I'm not sure what it means to say "This is now not a university." For me, it's enough to say that a university that, either formally or culturally, fails significantly to manifest and protect academic freedom is failing to live up to its core mission.

Bollinger: Like any good conversation, it's best to leave off when there is still much to clarify and to explore in even greater depth. What is especially important here is that you have made the case for universities fostering an extraordinary openness of mind as a central or core intellectual characteristic, while recognizing there will be within the academic realm those who will challenge—sometimes uncomfortably, sometimes even crazily—the accepted norms of thought at the moment, and those, too, should be tolerated (outside of the necessary and inevitable judgments around tenure and promotion). I think you have also given strong voice to the idea of a university—as an institution—as being separate and distinct from other organizations in the society insofar as it limits its role as a political actor as much as possible (e.g., only to those matters directly affecting its own operations). It may be a home for such actions by individual faculty, but it must resist calls for it to take on the mantle of an advocate or actor for achieving political causes. We so appreciate having this perspective.

PART VI

THE FUTURE OF ACADEMIC FREEDOM

Understanding What's at Stake and Forming a Response

17

Private Universities, Freedom, and Federal Power in the Trump Era

The Case of Harvard

RANDALL L. KENNEDY*

The administration of President Donald J. Trump is pursuing a campaign against universities that it perceives to be ideological enemies. It is utilizing an array of formidable weapons, including threats to withhold federal funds, revoke tax-exempt status, and disable institutions from hosting foreign students, in order to mute disfavored beliefs while promoting and amplifying favored voices. This encroachment on the liberty, autonomy, and independence of the American university is more repressive, far-reaching, and thus alarming than anything seen since the wave of anti-communist repressions in the 1950s, though a good argument can be made that what is happening now is even worse than what transpired then.

Effective responses have been hampered by several tendencies. Because of a mostly amicable collaboration between the federal government and higher education since World War II, insufficient attention has been paid to the alarming prospect of the federal government making unwelcome, intrusive demands on its putative beneficiaries. Occasionally the specter of federal intervention has arisen. In the 1990s, for example, some institutions barred military recruiters from campus pursuant to objections to military discrimination based on sexual orientation. When the Supreme Court upheld the constitutionality of legislation requiring institutions to permit recruiters or else forfeit federal funding, schools typically acceded to the imposition without strong, durable resistance.

* Michael R. Klein Professor of Law, Harvard Law School.

Randall L. Kennedy, *Private Universities, Freedom, and Federal Power in the Trump Era*. In: *Academic Freedom in the Era of Trump*. Edited by: Lee C. Bollinger and Geoffrey R. Stone, Oxford University Press.
 DOI: 10.1093/9780197854877.003.0018

The same recurred during the Obama and Biden administrations when many universities acquiesced without much dissent to directives regarding responses to allegations of sexual misconduct on campus. Failures to vigorously resist prior encroachments helped to inculcate complacency within academia toward threats posed by governmental power.

There is another, related reason for the halting, confused responses to attacks on academia from Congress and the White House. Liberals have become used to supporting or accepting extensions of federal standards—meaning federal power—pursuant to constitutional provisions such as the Equal Protection Clause and legislation such as the Civil Rights Act of 1964. Memories of fierce struggles over matters of racial justice have made many liberals habitually suspicious of "private" prerogatives and habitually welcoming of governmental regulation. After all, not so long ago liberals successfully argued that, at least for purposes of elections, political parties should be seen as functionally equivalent to governmental instrumentalities and therefore subject to federal constitutional standards. Absent federal intervention, the "private" Democratic Party in Southern jurisdictions excluded African Americans from party primaries, thereby depriving blacks of an opportunity to influence the only elections that really mattered.[1] Similarly, liberals argued successfully that legislation ought to empower the federal government to withhold federal funds from any entity that engages in racial discrimination. Absent federal intervention, some educational institutions would have persisted in excluding or otherwise discriminating against African American students. The extension of federal standards thus seemed to be a tried-and-true highway to a fairer and freer society.

Many of the fiercest opponents of expansive federal regulation were white supremacists. Their ranks included prominent politicians such as Senators Richard Russell, Strom Thurmond, and Sam Ervin. When their prejudices were shamed by the civil-rights movement, they resorted to other more reputable ideas in service of their defense of racial hierarchy. They invoked localism, federalism, pluralism, and the specter of federal overreach. Expedient embraces of these values tainted them in the eyes of many, particularly those who reside on the leftward end of the political spectrum. It is now imperative, however, to recover an appreciation for certain values that have often been coded as "conservative." Trumpian encroachments underline the dangers of coerced federal standardization, diminution of private prerogatives, and improper policing of individuals and organizations perceived by governmental authorities to be obnoxious or subversive. Against the backdrop of these dangers, I urge private institutions to insist militantly upon their independence. I focus on private institutions because their distinct legal status is underappreciated.

***

Some critics of higher education maintain that universities are insufficiently open to diverse perspectives and propose using governmental power to force private universities to be more hospitable to heterodoxy. In 1991, Representative Henry Hyde, seconded by the American Civil Liberties Union, proposed the Collegiate Speech Protection Act, which would have granted "students at private colleges and universities those rights of free speech already possessed by their peers at public institutions."[2] The Act would have affected many private schools because it would have applied to any institution receiving any federal financial assistance. Although proposals for federal legislation have been floated from time to time, none thus far have been enacted. California, however, did enact a law that imposes upon private universities certain First Amendment requirements that govern public universities. The Leonard Law prohibits schools in California, public and private, from disciplining students for speech that, "when engaged in outside the campus," would be protected by the First Amendment.[3] Proponents of such legislation defend it as liberty-enhancing. They are insufficiently attentive, however, to the danger entailed by permitting government to regulate the private collegiate educational environment. They seem to assume that such intrusions will end with relatively innocent incursions aimed at making campuses more hospitable to free speech, and seem oblivious to the possibility of intrusions with more disturbing aims. Yet such obliviousness now seems grossly negligent in light of the Trump administration's regulation of the ideological environment on private campuses through the power of contract—"deals" elicited through threats to withdraw funding if institutions decline the administration's terms.[4]

All of these governmental measures to impose various versions of scholarly, ideological, and political virtue on campus are objectionable, because private universities ought to be able to determine for themselves the character of their communities. Neither federal nor state authorities should mandate, or be permitted to mandate, any particular regime governing discourse on a private campus. Any governmental effort to compel private institutions of higher learning to be "free" or "diverse" or "civil" constitutes a regrettable diminution of academic autonomy. Opposition to such measures should be based upon two key aims. One is to confine governmental power in order to secure a suitably wide space for the exercise of power by private educational authorities. The second is to reinforce proper respect for the independence of private institutions. A manifestation of that respect is permitting private schools leeway to diverge from norms constitutionally required of public institutions. It is one thing to demand that *public* colleges and universities conduct themselves pursuant to First Amendment rules that have been designed with the imperatives of democratic governance foremost in mind. It is another thing to demand that *all* colleges and universities conduct themselves according to those rules. Doing so would entail erasing the pedagogical diversity that can arise from permitting private institutions to express themselves by limiting the expression that they permit on their campuses. No one is forced to enroll in such an institution or to teach at one. Perhaps the marketplace for students and scholars will marginalize such schools. But the academic marketplace will be richer by allowing a place for private institutional nonconformity. Trump wants to use the power of the federal government to bulldoze nonconformity so as to achieve his conception of the good university. To counter that aim, opponents need to embrace anew the values of localism, federalism, idiosyncrasy, and private prerogative.

Some private universities impose upon themselves First Amendment obligations. Harvard is one such institution. A former president, Derek Bok, writes that he has difficulty understanding why "Harvard should have less free speech than the surrounding society—or than a public university."[5] A striking feature of this position is its willingness to distance Harvard from its status as a private institution. Private universities, however, ought to avoid relinquishing their difference from public institutions. Indeed, they should insist upon and take advantage of their distinctive status. The distinction between public and private universities should be accentuated and championed for the sake of facilitating and reaping the advantages of a healthy institutional pluralism within academia.

It is true that schools like Harvard that place themselves under First Amendment regulation are acting on their own, opting to be governed by the same standard that applies to public schools. In doing so, however, they are delegating authority over their scholarly-intellectual-cultural domain to the federal judiciary, the arbiters of what constitutes the First Amendment. Judges do have the advantage of professional immersion in an extensive case law that represents the distillation of deliberation about matters of free expression. But judges are bound to consider factors beyond what is best for a given institution. They consider, for example, the administrability by other tribunals of rules they design, or the relationship of the judiciary to other branches of government. By contrast, the administrators of a university are, or should be, free to focus narrowly on their own institution.

Administrators ought not allow themselves to be bullied into believing that a campus regime governed by federal First Amendment standards is necessarily better than an alternative governed by rules fashioned by the institution itself to foster the particular type of community that it prefers. For good reason, the chant "No Means Yes, and Yes Means Anal" is protected by the First Amendment and thus beyond censorship at a public institution.[6] But that ought not preclude administrators of a *private* institution from deciding to exclude from their campus the voicing of such a slogan. They ought to be able to decide that it is simply too demoralizing, too insulting, or too gross to accept, given their pedagogical ambitions.

Or consider an example with a different political valence. Offered by Cass Sunstein, it features a private university that believes that the members of its community should follow norms of patriotism. Insistent upon inculcating an ethic of national gratitude, "it might consider some speech to be beyond the pale even if that speech is protected by the First Amendment. If students or faculty say disloyal or harshly negative things about the United States of America, its traditions, and its values, such a university might be inclined to say: Some places, maybe, but not here." Sunstein, a strong free-speech liberal, is inclined to prefer a university that would "follow the First Amendment—period." But he rightly recognizes the defensibility of more than one path.[7]

It is essential to protect the First Amendment and apply its demands unflinchingly. Where it governs, it should be stringently applied. But the First Amendment ought not be seen as governing everywhere. Recognizing its limits is an important service on behalf of the academic pluralism and institutional autonomy that the Trump administration is placing under intense, unprecedented pressure.

***

A second action that institutions of higher education should undertake with renewed vigor is simple to state but difficult to achieve: making the government follow the law. One might have thought such an ambition too banal to mention. But that is because two realities have been overlooked. One is the possibility that there might arise an administration that is dismissive of legal formalities and willing to deploy law expediently with transparent deceptiveness.[8] The other is the cost—often the prohibitive cost—of vindicating rights through litigation aimed at forcing the government to follow the law.

The Trump administration has used Title VI of the Civil Rights Act of 1964 as its principal vehicle of attack. Title VI prohibits entities receiving funding from the federal government (which includes virtually all private and public research universities) from engaging in racial discrimination.[9] Title VI empowers the federal government, working through executive-branch agencies, to withhold federal funding from entities found to be engaging in racial discrimination. Segregationists and their allies worked hard to cabin Title VI with a panoply of procedural requirements that officials would have to satisfy before withholding funds. Officials were tasked with, among other things, providing recipients with notice and "an opportunity for a hearing," limiting any funding cutoff "to the particular program, or part thereof, in which . . . noncompliance has been . . . found," and submitting a report explaining the proposed funding cutoff to the relevant committees in Congress at least thirty days before any funds can be stopped.[10] The legislators mainly responsible for these requirements were segregationists and their allies, politicians who wanted to defend racial hierarchy and limit the efficacy of antidiscrimination measures. Although in terms of the racial politics of the 1960s they were villains, they subsequently turned out to be heroes in that they recognized the susceptibility of Title VI to misuse and took steps to forestall that possibility.

***

The Trump administration—the segregationists' ideological descendant in terms of its hostility toward African Americans—has shown, ironically, the segregationists' prescience, in that the White House's deployment of Title VI is a conspicuous example of overreach, indeed the most extreme in the legislation's history. The administration has paid scant attention to any of Title VI's procedural requirements. In its opening salvos against universities, it offered neither formal hearings nor detailed explanations prior to making threats and ordering cutoffs. Furthermore, the purported purpose behind the administration's invocation of Title VI—protecting Jewish students from discrimination—is a pretext. The Trump administration claims to be committed to rooting out anti-Semitic discrimination on campus and negligent or even complicitous toleration of such discrimination by university bureaucracies. Trump portrays his actions as the realization of a campaign pledge. "My promise to Jewish Americans is this," he declared. "With your vote, I will be your defender, your protector, and I will be the best friend Jewish Americans have ever had in the White House."[11] But many observers, including many Jews, have noted the bad faith that infects Trump's claim.[12] Michael S. Roth, the Jewish president of Wesleyan University, maintains that while "Jew hatred is real," Trumpian "anti-antisemitism isn't a legitimate effort to fight it." The White House targeting of anti-Semitism "is a cover for a wide range of agendas that have nothing to do with the welfare of Jewish people. All of these agendas—from dismantling basic government functions to crushing the independence of cultural and educational organizations to criminalizing political speech to legitimating petty presidential vendettas—endanger the principles and institutions that have actually made [America] great."[13] Trumpian duplicity when it comes to anti-Semitism is evident. There has been little change in the President's solicitude for notorious anti-Jewish bigots since his suggestion of a moral equivalence between neo-Nazi and anti-Nazi activists at the deadly Unite the Right rally in Charlottesville, Virginia, in 2017.[14]

It is insufficient, however, to point merely to Trump's bad faith. He could be making insincere allegations that are nonetheless accurate. There is a need, therefore, to assess charges of anti-Semitism on campus independent of motivations. The allegation that universities have facilitated or ignored anti-Jewish discrimination is the most damning of the criticisms that have been leveled against institutions of higher learning. Condemnations have been voiced by congressional committees, litigants, and commentators. That there is anti-Semitism on campuses is hardly debatable or surprising; tragically, prejudice against Jews is an ancient bigotry that arises in all manner of settings, high and low. The issue, though, is whether the extent and severity of anti-Semitism on a campus justifies governmental intervention.

The Trump administration argues that, on various campuses, intervention is warranted under Title VI. Title VI is violated when, as a matter of policy, a university subjects students to anti-Jewish discrimination or facilitates or permits a "racially hostile environment," meaning a setting in which Jews experience harassment that is so severe, pervasive, and objectively offensive that it effectively bars access to an educational opportunity or benefit.[15] An anti-Semitic incident, or indeed several, does not suffice alone to constitute the institutional misbehavior prohibited by Title VI. Essential is that severe anti-Jewish mistreatment be fairly attributable to university officials' actions or inactions.

It may be that some institutions have violated Title VI by facilitating or ignoring the plight of Jews on campus. Some credible accounts setting forth substantiating facts, not mere assertions, portray anti-Jewish misconduct and university inaction that is deeply disturbing.[16] If an institution is encouraging or tolerating anti-Semitic harassment, remedial intervention that might include enforcement of Title VI is surely warranted. Unwarranted, however, is careless vilification like that which has been aimed at the Trump administration's most prominent target: Harvard University.

President Trump and his allies have loudly and repeatedly accused Harvard of flagrant and illegal anti-Semitic misconduct.[17] The Administration's Joint Task Force to Combat Anti-Semitism announced, for example, that "After a thorough investigation, HHS [Health and Human Services] OCR [Office for Civil Rights] finds that Harvard University is in violent violation of Title VI. . . ." According to the Task Force, "Harvard has been in some cases deliberately indifferent, and in others has been a willful participant in antisemitic harassment of Jewish students, faculty, and staff."[18] Yet the evidentiary basis for this allegation is remarkably thin. It consists of hyperbolic accusations that became the predicate for additional allegations. It consists of the reported subjective feelings of Jewish students who express unease, including fear for their physical safety, without any rigorous effort to determine the breadth of such sentiments or to determine their authenticity. It also consists of instances of misconduct whose significance the Task Force massively exaggerates, presenting as menacingly common episodes that are highly atypical.

Charges of institutional anti-Semitism at Harvard are also based upon concessions made by university leaders. The starting point was some decisions made in the aftermath of Hamas's attack on Israel on October 7, 2023. Harvard was roundly criticized on account of an open letter written by students and endorsed by dozens of university-affiliated student organizations that blamed Israel exclusively for the horrific events surrounding the Hamas attack. Critics not only bitterly denounced the letter and its endorsers; they also bitterly denounced Harvard's president, Claudine Gay, for failing to respond with what they viewed as sufficient alacrity and force. She did in fact chastise the students two days after the publication of their infamous letter. But to her detractors, her response was tardy and weak.[19] They perceived it to be notably less impassioned than the response of university leadership to the killing of George Floyd or the invasion of Ukraine.

Stung by a rising chorus of condemnation from prominent members of the Jewish community at Harvard and beyond, President Gay began to make deprecating concessions. Observing that "antisemitism has a very long and shameful history at Harvard," Gay claimed that the university "has done too little to confront [anti-Semitism's] continuing presence."[20] That complacency, she declared, would last "No longer"—a remarkable dig at a university leadership that contained a significant number of Jewish officials. Gay's predecessor, Lawrence Bacow, is Jewish, as is Penny Pritzker, the head of the governing body of the university, the Harvard Corporation, as is the current president of Harvard, Alan Garber, as is the current provost of Harvard, John Manning, who was previously the dean of the Harvard Law School, who was preceded as dean by Martha Minow, who is Jewish, and succeeded as dean by John Goldberg, who also is Jewish. The presence, influence, and flourishing of Jews throughout the student body, administration, and professorial ranks at Harvard should have prompted skepticism toward the damning anti-Semitism narrative. But Gay nervously deferred to it, and indeed reinforced it by convening an advisory body to suggest ways to address the university's purported problem.[21] After Gay resigned, her successor, Alan Garber, likewise accepted the claim that anti-Semitism at Harvard was a major impediment. He, too, convened a group to explore the matter and offer remedies.[22] While neither Gay nor Garber agreed with the most extreme of the negative portrayals of Harvard, both proceeded as if anti-Semitism was a powerful presence at the university.

***

That response is attractive in certain ways. It shows abhorrence of prejudice and a self-critical reflex. It also exhibits a humility in offering apology even in the absence of a reason for guilt; the mere fact that members of the community are moved to express hurt often generates within school officials a desire to respond with a sympathy that includes an assumption of partial responsibility. Confronted by aggrieved students (and others) who accused the university of misdoings, officials habitually apologized because of a commendable impulse toward seeking to respect the pain of others. This response was also pragmatic. Accepting partial blame and expressing a commitment to make amends signaled a willingness to be self-critical and engage in self-reform. That gesture paid off handsomely when federal district court Judge Allison Burroughs ruled in Harvard's favor in subsequent litigation, adverting approvingly to the steps that had been initiated by Harvard's presidents.[23]

However, acquiescence to the misleading narrative of widespread anti-Semitism also reflected and furthered tendencies that should be disturbing. One is a willingness by academics purportedly committed to finding and telling the truth to accept, and even encourage, obfuscation. Rather than examine allegations of anti-Semitism rigorously, university officials preferred to palliate the accusers. Presidents Gay and Garber tried to get ahead of anti-Semitism allegations by offering gestures of apology and expiation, hoping that their actions would satisfy detractors. But to many onlookers, that strategy reinforced a misleadingly negative appraisal of the university. While some observers accepted the university presidents' deprecations as positive signals of enhanced attentiveness to anti-Jewish misconduct, determined detractors seized upon the concessions as evidence of guilt, signs of weakness, and opportunities for leveraging additional pressure.

From its outset, the Trump administration signaled an intent to besiege Harvard and make the university submit to its terms. On March 31, 2025, Harvard received a letter from the Justice Department's Task Force to Combat Anti-Semitism, which had been formed to effectuate Executive Order 14188, "Additional Measures to Combat Anti-Semitism." On October 20, 2024, shortly before Trump's election, Leo Terrell, who would become the head of the task force, announced that Harvard would lose "much" come January 2025.[24] On March 31, 2025, Harvard received a letter from the task force stating that more than $8 billion in federal funding was being reviewed in light of investigations "for potential infractions and dereliction of duties to curb or combat anti-Semitic harassment."[25] On April 3, 2025, Harvard received a letter setting forth "several broad, non-exhaustive areas of reform that the government viewed as necessary for Harvard to implement to remain a responsible recipient of federal taxpayer dollars." Maintaining that Harvard has "fundamentally failed to protect American students and faculty from antisemitic violence and harassment," officials acting on behalf of the General Services Administration, the Department of Health and Human Services, and the Department of Education stated, among other things, that "Programs and departments that fuel antisemitic harassment must be reviewed and necessary changes made to address bias, improve viewpoint diversity, and end ideological capture."[26]

On April 11, 2025, Trump-administration officials sent to Harvard officials an ultimatum that reiterated previous allegations but also dramatically broadened demands. The government insisted, for example, that the university "commission an external party . . . to audit the student body, faculty, staff, and leadership for viewpoint diversity, such that each department, field, or teaching unit must be individually viewpoint diverse," that the university "abolish all criteria, preferences, and practices . . . that function as ideological litmus tests," that the university reduce "the power held by faculty . . . more committed to activism than scholarship," and that the university "shutter" all DEI programs."[27]

Harvard University responded to the Trump administration's April 11 ultimatum by resisting in a fashion that could hopefully be emulated, at least to some extent, by other institutions. It rejected the Trump administration's extortionate "deal." It insisted that the government follow the law that it pretended to enforce. Harvard, through counsel, declared that it is "not prepared to agree to demands that go beyond the lawful authority of this or any administration." They averred that neither Harvard nor any other private university "can allow itself to be taken over by the federal government."[28]

Harvard backed up its declaration by suing the Trump administration. It complained that the government had failed to meet Title VI's procedural requirements, had failed to show that the university was out of compliance with Title VI, had encroached unconstitutionally upon protected First Amendment rights, and was behaving in an arbitrary and capricious fashion. Harvard insisted that it rejected—in principle and practice—illicit, invidious discrimination in all its forms.

On September 3, 2025, Judge Burroughs held overwhelmingly in favor of the university. Along with declaring that the government had utterly failed to comply with procedural requirements, she also concluded that "the government-initiated onslaught against Harvard was much more about promoting governmental orthodoxy in violation of the First Amendment than about anything else, including fighting antisemitism," that the Trump Administration had "impermissibly retaliated against Harvard for refusing to capitulate to the government's demands," that the government had "impermissibly imposed unconstitutional conditions on Harvard's receipt of federal funds," and that it had unconstitutionally sought to force Harvard to amplify the government's favored worldview.[29] The court also granted summary judgment to the university on its claim that the government acted arbitrarily and capriciously in issuing freeze orders that cut off funding to activities that had nothing to do with the administration's allegations of anti-Semitism. This part of Judge Burroughs' opinion is particularly significant because it discussed an aspect of the case that was otherwise obscured—the substance of the charge that Harvard had facilitated or tolerated the existence of an unlawful condition of anti-Semitic violence and harassment on campus. Because of the administration's utter procedural delinquency, there was no occasion for a full airing of the matter. The judge hints rather strongly, however, that, in her view, allegations of anti-Semitic harassment and university inaction were highly exaggerated. The judge observed that the record "contains no evidence that Defendants considered any of the steps

Harvard had taken to research or address anti-Semitism on campus before declaring that funding would be frozen because Harvard had failed to address the issue. The record reflected that Harvard was, in fact, working to respond to and ameliorate anti-Semitism, that it continued to do so each time the government raised concerns, and that it remained (and seemingly remains) open to dialogue as to what more it could do in the government's eyes to combat the problem."[30] In sum, the court concluded, "it is difficult to conclude anything other than that Defendants used antisemitism as a smokescreen for a targeted, ideologically motivated assault on this country's premier universities . . . and did so in a way that runs afoul of . . . the First Amendment and Title VI."[31]

Conclusion

Despite Judge Burroughs' ruling, there is good reason to remain deeply alarmed by the Trumpian attack on higher education. The Trump campaigns continue and Judge Burroughs' judgment will likely be appealed. Government repression, moreover, is destructive even when courts eventually offer relief. By the time that the district court enjoined the Trump administration in the Harvard case, scores of researchers had already been adversely affected by the government's threats or funding freezes. It is all too possible that discoveries that might have enhanced health care were lost or delayed. Furthermore, repression often exerts a chilling effect even upon parties' intent upon protecting and exercising their rights. Although Harvard resisted, it nonetheless changed its behavior to avoid further antagonizing the Trump administration. Soon after filing suit against the government, it suddenly and without serious explanation dropped the term "DEI" from its bureaucratic infrastructure, obviously in response to Trump-administration pressure. It also took steps in line with other Trumpist demands—dropping university support for affinity-group commencement celebrations, removing academic administrators with ideological views deemed to be obnoxious, and suspending programs deemed to be too "woke." Some of these actions probably reflected university officials' independent judgment; a faction within Harvard that believes the university has strayed from its mission had been pushing for desired changes independently. However, it is also undoubtedly true that some of the reforms that Harvard has quietly embraced were adopted mainly to propitiate the government.

Another reason to remain alarmed is the high cost—in many instances, the prohibitive cost—of resistance. Relatively few institutions are able to mount the well-resourced resistance that Harvard has modeled. Attorney fees alone would be out of reach for many schools that have to make a go of things without

Harvard's deep pockets. In the commentary about Trump's attacks on civil liberties, there has often arisen excessive moralizing in which resisters are portrayed as brave, while those who capitulate are portrayed as cowardly. But those categories flatten a situation filled with ethical complexities. The leaders of a university run organizations on which many people rely for education, livelihoods, and the products generated by skilled academics. Deciding what to do in the face of Trumpian extortion is no simple matter. The situation poses an excruciating dilemma. One response would be to resist to the utmost, a "brave" decision that could virtually destroy an institution on account of the expense of litigation, its typical tardiness, and the punitive withholding of funds prior to judicial relief, if such relief were even forthcoming. Conversely, one could strike a deal, a "cowardly" decision that might allow education to proceed, albeit under morale-depressing and freedom-infringing terms. There is no pain-free way of dealing with Trumpian authoritarianism. All of higher education, all of the country, is sadly subjected to it no matter the response.

In this trying and tragic moment, Harvard University has acquitted itself relatively well, though in some ways it has erred. School officials at private institutions should be directly engaged in curating campus discourse; that all-important task ought not be delegated to judicial arbiters of the First Amendment, and Harvard is mistaken in making that delegation. The university's error is demonstrated by the contradiction that undermines central assertions made by its recent presidents. Both Claudine Gay and Alan Garber have declared that the university does not tolerate anti-Semitism.[32] Yet the First Amendment (as interpreted by the Supreme Court) requires precisely such toleration.[33] Expression of anti-Semitism, like other forms of "hate speech," have been accorded constitutional protection. Thus, such expression, without more, cannot lawfully be censored by a public university and must thus be tolerated as well by Harvard.

President Gay was pilloried for saying in testimony before Congress that urging genocide might not be punishable under Harvard's code of conduct.[34] But inasmuch as that code is governed by First Amendment standards, what she said was accurate. A private university, however, should have the leeway to craft for itself a different regime than that to which a public university must accommodate itself. Private institutions unduly cabin their discretion by imposing First Amendment limitations that prevent them from excluding from their campuses conduct, including expression, deemed by their academic leaders to be detrimental to their pedagogical aims. A private institution should not be obliged to censor "hate speech"; there is good reason to refrain from doing so.[35] But if educational authorities at a private institution want to offer less latitude than their public peers, respect for pluralism and institutional autonomy should make room for that choice.

On the most important issue of the day, the matter of resisting governmental encroachment on university independence, Harvard has been outstanding. It rejected the administration's extortionate "deal" and sued to vindicate its statutory and constitutional rights. By taking that stand, Harvard will likely influence other universities to be more resistant than they might have been otherwise.

18

Persuading the Unpersuaded

M. ELIZABETH MAGILL*

The scenarios are familiar. A faculty member teaching a class on religion and public policy invites guest speakers to her class. One visitor represents a faith-based organization opposing access to abortion. Another faculty member, an historian of the family, writes an opinion piece in a national magazine arguing against the recognition of same-sex marriage. A third, a pediatrician in the medical school, gives a high-profile lecture at the university arguing that puberty blockers, hormone therapy, and psychological support for young people questioning their gender identity reduce their risk of depression, anxiety, and suicide.

The unhappy calls come. Some demand that the chair of the department of public policy forbid the class speaker on abortion or require another speaker be added. Others want a department chair to require the historian to address counterarguments in her next article. Some want the dean of medicine to call in the medical-school professor and caution her that she did not sufficiently discuss alternative arguments in her lecture. All callers want the university to distance itself from these views.

At many universities in the United States, these choices lie squarely within the faculty member's academic freedom. Academic leaders will not dictate content or require point-counter-point arguments in classes, professional writings, or public lectures. This defense, however, rarely persuades skeptical outsiders, even those friendly to the university. This chapter takes on that challenge: persuading the unpersuaded.

* Professor of Law, Penn Carey Law School. I appreciate the wise comments of Lee Bollinger, Martien Halvorson-Taylor, Don Herzog, Eric Feldman, Robert C. Post, Sophia Rosenfeld, Jim Ryan, and Geof Stone. Errors remain my own.

M. Elizabeth Magill, *Persuading the Unpersuaded*. In: *Academic Freedom in the Era of Trump*.
Edited by: Lee C. Bollinger and Geoffrey R. Stone, Oxford University Press. DOI: 10.1093/9780197854877.003.0019

Universities are singular institutions. They are not like private firms, public companies, nonprofits, or government agencies. Given the variety of stakeholders with decision-making roles, a city is a closer analogy—although universities, unlike cities, do not elect their leaders. In truth, there may be no helpful analogy at all. And when controversies arise, it can be difficult to explain and harder still to justify university-specific norms and practices to audiences outside the academy.

Many university norms and practices are perplexing. Consider elaborate and time-consuming systems for hiring and promotion of faculty, shared governance, involving every constituency in significant policy decisions, and the fact that university leaders do not direct faculty teaching or research to align with the university's strategic plan. To outsiders, these practices are, at best, odd and inefficient and, at worst, irresponsible, naive, or incompetent.

No norm is more difficult to explain and defend, however, than academic freedom and the systems, like tenure and peer review, designed to protect it. Many wise and learned minds have written about the history, scope, and threats to academic freedom. This chapter explores only a small corner of the subject. The goal is to articulate the strongest arguments to explain and defend academic freedom to skeptics outside the university.

*

To start, it's crucial to understand some fundamentals about academic freedom. According to the definition drawn from the American Association of University Professors (AAUP), some version of which many US universities have adopted as their own, academic freedom protects faculty in three ways.[1] First, faculty are free to pursue and publish their research, subject to other professional duties and applicable institutional agreements. Second, faculty may teach their subject as they see fit, so long as they remain within the subject matter of the course and reflect the state of knowledge in their field. The most contested of these freedoms is the third one, the right of faculty to speak as citizens.[2] This is speech that faculty engage in outside of their teaching or research responsibilities. The AAUP approach outlines this as a freedom that is accompanied by a responsibility. Faculty are free to speak as citizens and officers of the university without institutional censorship or discipline; that is, they are free to weigh in on university matters or the issues of the day outside of their teaching and research duties. But responsibility is linked to this freedom: as professors who teach at a university, they are expected to be accurate, exercise restraint, respect others, and clarify that they do not speak for the institution.

These freedoms are not absolute. The definitions themselves contain limits. The professor is free to teach her class, but that does not include her right to say whatever she likes in class about matters that have nothing to do with the subject matter. The professor can teach about her subject, the Hebrew Bible/Old

Testament, as she wishes; she is free to take an informed if controversial position in her work about who authored various portions of that Bible. But she is not free to teach her students that Russia should prevail in its war with Ukraine—or vice versa. She is also not free to say that the Bible was written yesterday, as that is not accepted knowledge or scholarly consensus.

Academic freedom is often shorthanded as a professor's right to say or write whatever she wants without consequence. That is far off the mark. Faculty are constantly subjected to career-defining judgments by others. Academic freedom and peer assessment go hand in hand. A faculty member's exercise of freedom is evaluated—sometimes blindly, sometimes publicly—by experts in the field. Tenure is the most visible example: after years of work, a faculty member undergoes rigorous review, often including a dozen detailed letters by outside experts assessing the quality and significance of their scholarship, as well as the assessment of their colleagues. Those who fall short are denied tenure every year. But peer scrutiny extends far beyond tenure. Publications, hiring, promotions, moves between institutions, induction into learned societies, endowed chairs, even annual raises—all are shaped by expert assessment. The hallmarks of an academic life are inseparable from constant peer evaluation.[3]

Finally, laws and university policies constrain a professor's conduct. If a faculty member embezzles funds or commits fraud, if a faculty member assaults, harasses, discriminates, or (at some universities) bullies others, they are not protected by academic freedom. There is no doubt that some lines are difficult to draw, such as those between a tough academic adviser and a bully, or between disturbing content and unlawful harassment. But when those lines are crossed, academic freedom does not protect a faculty member from the consequences.

The limitations noted above are formal limits on the exercise of academic freedom, but there are powerful informal limits that I do not explore here. Faculty members who pursue ideas that are against the grain in their chosen field face difficulties; they may have trouble getting hired in the first place or obtaining support for their work if they are hired.

*

The powerful arguments in favor of academic freedom grow out of the purposes of the university. Universities do many things, but their core missions are simple to state: producing knowledge and educating students. These missions are of great importance to society at large. And this is the faculty's task in a university.

The arguments for academic freedom are many: it advances the search for truth, it underpins functioning democracies, it promotes an educated population and critical thinking in multiple areas of modern life. The arguments vary, but each requires autonomy. Those who produce knowledge and educate students must have autonomy in their work so that it is not compromised by powerful interests.[4]

The grandest defense of academic freedom is that it promotes the pursuit of truth. This encompasses not just what counts as a genuine advance in knowledge, but also the methods that reliably advance our understanding. Both are the subject of intense debate in many fields, but the argument for autonomy is straightforward. Those who devote themselves to producing knowledge may encounter accepted ideas that strike them as incomplete or wrong. If they are not free to challenge those ideas, according to reliable methods as established by the field, we may never find out that those ideas are wrong or incomplete or be able to move beyond them. In other words, if we want knowledge to be accumulated in an ongoing pursuit of what is true, those engaged in that enterprise must be free to pursue their ideas.

There is an avalanche of historical support for the idea that those who produce knowledge must enjoy autonomy if we are to get closer to what is true. That idea rests on two facts about the world: our understanding of what is—and what ought to be—has changed over time, sometimes radically so; and it is no easy feat to challenge the orthodoxy of the day.

Understandings that were nearly universal in one time have proved to be wrong—dead wrong—in the next. Take some familiar examples: Many believed that the sun revolved around the earth and that disease was caused by foul air. Those who disagreed were dismissed or persecuted. But they turned out to be right—the earth revolves around the sun and germs, not miasma, cause many diseases. Consider, too, subjects like slavery, child labor, and suffrage. Our conception of what *ought* to be has also changed drastically over time, owing to those who were willing to question the prevailing view and argue for a different one. Some who are driven to advance new ideas can bear the scorn and retribution of their peers and those in power, but many cannot. In the modern university, academic freedom protects them all.

Both the argument that academic freedom is necessary to the development of critical thinking in students and the argument that academic freedom is crucial to democratic systems rest on the need for autonomy for those who generate knowledge and educate students. Whether it be the church, the crown, the oligarch, the authoritarian, or the democratically elected leader, those in power are generally not keen on independent sources of knowledge or opinion. The critic who provokes the leader to retaliate has ancient roots in the Western world, as the trial of Socrates for impiety and corruption of youth reveals. The Congregation of the Inquisition of the Catholic church prosecuted and convicted Galileo for his position that the earth revolved around the sun. Educating students who are taught independently of those in power—taught to understand and to think critically, even skeptically, about all sorts of ideas—is necessary to a functioning democratic system. And so are faculty who have the freedom, relying on their professional expertise, to question the orthodoxies of their peers or their rulers for the sake of the public good.

*

And yet, academic freedom is difficult to defend to those not already persuaded of its importance. The arguments for academic freedom rest on happy examples, heroic thinkers who persevered and have been vindicated by historical judgment. These are the unalloyed goods of the freedom to ask questions, develop ideas, and teach students to do the same. Socrates was unjustly persecuted; child labor is wrong; germ theory is correct; Galileo was right. We now agree.

But these are not the examples that drive the doubters. Leaders have a hard time defending academic freedom to those who are skeptical, because the full picture of what it does is not observable. Its upside is largely invisible while its perceived downsides are glaring.

The many upsides of academic freedom are with us today, but we mostly don't notice them. Academic freedom underwrites the everyday work of faculty. It makes possible the groundbreaking translation of an epic poem, an ironclad paper that overturns what we thought we knew, or the inventive class that captures a new idea and the imagination of the students. The rare autonomy that academic freedom provides enables faculty members' most celebrated accomplishments as well as their everyday successes.

Take Professor Emily Wilson's acclaimed translations of Homer's *The Iliad*, published in 2023, and *The Odyssey*, published in 2017. No doubt, her job description required that she do work that would be published and evaluated by experts in the field in which she worked. But as a tenured scholar, Dr. Wilson made every single choice about this project. Most importantly, she chose to take it on, not an easy or obvious decision. It kept her from taking up other projects and it took years of her professional life. She put the poems in verse, iambic pentameter, a daring choice that no other English translator had made. Like the hundreds of other choices she made, she did not need to seek permission to undertake this years-long effort, nor did she need to seek approval for the choices she made. In the end, those in her field would assess the success and quality of the finished work, and she perhaps sought advice from others on the weighty choices that she made. But permission or approval for this major undertaking and all its details? Not required.

Yet in these happy moments, academic freedom fades into the background. It is invisible. It is rarely credited for enabling either the faculty's everyday work or their crowning achievements. When Dr. Wilson received awards, the fact that she had this freedom to choose this project and make all the decisions, even the boldest ones, is unremarkable to those in the academy. It's just part of the air that academics breathe in places that respect the academic freedom of faculty, so pervasive it goes unnoticed. And it is not either obvious or interesting to others. Sometimes, when a faculty member is finally recognized for a now-vindicated breakthrough finding, those who celebrate it focus on the years when the idea was not accepted, highlighting the perseverance of the faculty member in remaining committed to their idea. But the fact that those faculty were free to pursue that unusual idea in the first place is just the familiar furniture of academic life. Everyone sees the outcomes but not what made them possible.

If the best of what academic freedom makes possible today is invisible, what is perceived to be the worst of it is glaring. University leaders never take an angry call, and students never agitate, about a faculty member's pathbreaking book or innovative, successful class. Those calls come when a faculty member has said or written something viewed to be offensive, absurd, or dangerous.

In our viral age, the offensive examples are familiar. A professor calls the victims of 9/11 "little Eichmanns"; another denies the Holocaust; another wishes for "white genocide" for Christmas; another speaks at the "Save America" rally on January 6, 2021.[5] Those outside the university (and some inside) are irate about such statements and shocked that they were uttered and tolerated. Many want the faculty member to be disciplined in some way.

But it's not just shocking statements that give rise to concerns by the skeptics. Some work is viewed as wrong—unsubstantiated, absurd, or dangerous. Here, too, there are many examples. In the late 1960s, Berkeley psychology professor Arthur Jensen published an article arguing that IQ differences across racial groups might have a genetic component. In the mid-1970s, Harvard biology professor Edward O. Wilson published a book arguing that certain negative human behavior had evolutionary and genetic roots. In the 1980s and 1990s, Berkeley molecular and cell biology professor Peter Duesberg argued that HIV was not the cause of AIDS; drug use was. In 2018, Brown assistant professor of the practice Lisa Littman argued that some rapid-onset adolescent gender dysphoria could be socially influenced. Portland State political-science professor Bruce Gilley argued in 2017 that colonialism had some beneficial effects. In 2022, Harvard law professor J. Mark Ramseyer argued that many Korean "comfort women" voluntarily entered sex contracts. Loads of critics expressed outrage at these positions.[6]

The invisibility of academic freedom's pivotal role in faculty accomplishments, and its visibility when faculty write or say something deemed offensive or wrong, are challenging for academic leaders. Skeptics see only outliers, imagining they are representative of the exercise of autonomy granted by academic freedom, and perhaps even the tip of an iceberg of similar examples. It makes the principle of academic freedom look primarily like a shield for those who are perceived as offensive or wrong. And, if judged only by these examples, academic freedom is indeed devilishly difficult to defend.

*

When the skeptic calls, the most compelling case for academic freedom must rest on an essential link between its perceived downsides and its celebrated upsides—the requirement of protecting what inspires praise and what provokes condemnation. Thankfully, there are strong arguments for this link. There are four distinct but connected arguments. Epistemic humility, or the Galileo problem, reminds us that we cannot reliably distinguish true from false ideas in real time. The chilling effect warns that punishing wrong ideas will deter others from pursuing unconventional but potentially fruitful ones. The attraction argument shows that the creative and risk-taking minds will only enter the profession if autonomy and professional disciplinary standards are assured. And the reliability argument demonstrates that knowledge becomes trustworthy not by excluding error but by exposing, testing, and correcting it. Taken together, these arguments explain why the bitter and the sweet of academic freedom are inseparable.

Epistemic Humility; or, the Galileo Problem

The most straightforward argument for this connection is that, in the moment, it is difficult to sort the false idea from the true one, or what's right from what's wrong. In fact, the "false" idea today may be conventional wisdom tomorrow. Such changes, in fact, rest on the autonomy of subsequent generations to argue for the acceptance of the previously dismissed idea. The key point, though, is that in the moment experts and nonexperts alike are often just plain wrong about what is right and what is not.

We are comfortable with this argument as a matter of history. To his contemporaries, it was not clear whether Galileo's position was ridiculous, dangerous, or ahead of its time. Our moral consensus has changed over time as well. Those who spoke out against practices like child labor and for the expansion of suffrage to all adults were ridiculed and repressed, until, that is, their views became a moral consensus. Charles Darwin's idea about natural selection challenged deeply held religious views about creation. Fully aware of that anticipated reaction, he spent more than two decades carefully gathering evidence before he published anything, and adopted a careful, humble tone in his presentation of his ideas. A Newtonian-physics-dominated discipline resisted Einstein's theory of relativity for years. Ultimately accepted, the theory transformed 20th-century physics.

But ideas traveling from the reject pile to conventional wisdom are not confined to the past. Take the case of the cause of peptic ulcers. In 1983, physicians Barry Marshall and Robin Warren claimed that stomach ulcers were caused by bacteria (*Helicobacter pylori*), and not by acidity in the stomach caused by lifestyle choices. Dr. Marshall went so far as to consume the bacteria to prove his case, causing an ulcer and curing it with antibiotics and acid-neutralizing medicine. First considered foolish, nearly fifteen years later the idea became the consensus. Marshall and Warren won the Nobel Prize in Physiology or Medicine in 2005, and treating ulcers with antibiotics is now standard therapy.[7]

There are many other stunning examples in the sciences. Dr. Alfred Wegener, in 1912, proposed that continents had once been a single landmass but drifted apart. For decades, the idea that continents drift was dismissed as speculation. Then, in the 1960s, evidence from the ocean floor forced a revolution: plate tectonics. The realization that Earth's crust is broken into moving plates overturned entrenched theories and, almost overnight, transformed geology into a science of a restless planet. Scientists now understood earthquakes, volcanoes, and mountain building in entirely new ways, and plate tectonics continues to provide the scientific basis for seismic standards that dictate everything from buildings to city planning.[8] Dr. Dan Shechtman, in 1982, discovered crystals with "five-fold" symmetry, the existence of which violated the accepted view in the field. He was dismissed by leading lights in the field. As other research confirmed the existence of such crystals, he was vindicated decades later, winning the Nobel Prize in Chemistry in 2011.[9] Dr. Stanley Prusiner in the 1980s claimed that certain neurodegenerative diseases were caused by what he called a prion, a misfolded and infectious protein. He was mocked, dismissed, and called delusional for a decade because infection caused by a protein was not thought possible. One scientist called prions "the cold fusion of infectious disease." Various studies started to show this as a possibility—the outbreak of mad cow disease in the 1990s was a key turning point—and he and his previously heretical view were awarded the Nobel Prize in Physiology or Medicine in 1997.[10] Dr. Katalin Karikó's position, dating from the 1990s, that messenger RNA could instruct cells to make therapeutic proteins, including vaccines, was rejected. She was denied grants, experts arguing that mRNA was too unstable and inflammatory to perform this task. After a series of significant discoveries with her research partner Dr. Drew Weissman and the rapid development of the Covid-19 vaccine, they together won the Nobel Prize in 2023 for the discovery.[11]

Nor is this phenomenon limited to the sciences. New findings in the humanities and social sciences have dramatically changed those fields; and evolving approaches to understanding a large range of fields have changed significantly over time.

New documents and new artifacts have reshaped many fields. The Dead Sea Scrolls, discovered in the mid-20th century, altered our understanding of the Bible in countless ways, revealing that multiple versions of it existed 1,000 years earlier than previously understood and that Judaism of the era was both diverse and contested. The 1971 publication of Ezra Pound's heavy edits of T. S. Eliot's *The Waste Land* demonstrated that it had been a collaborative project, not a solo act of genius. The Venona Papers, which were declassified in 1995, documented that Soviet espionage in the United States during World War II was more extensive than previously understood, forcing historians to reassess debates about that period. Göbekli Tepe, dating back to 9600 BCE, was excavated in Turkey in the 1990s. Before it was found, the accepted wisdom about human history was that agriculture, the development of villages, and social structure *predated* development of religion and collective rituals. But Göbekli Tepe's massive structures, and their dating, suggested something quite different: in human history, symbolic structures and ritual practices may have come before agriculture.[12]

Generations of scholars have ushered in new ways of understanding many fields. In literature, the focus moved from close reading in New Criticism to emphasizing author and reader response to literature to the computational analyses of digital humanities. In history, the turn to social history—the study of ordinary people—was resisted but is now mainstream. Clifford Geertz's interpretive "thick description," once dismissed as unscientific, has become a standard ethnographic method.[13]

Economists, likewise, have evolved in the way they understand their subject and its implications. John Maynard Keynes's pre-WWII argument, put forward fully in 1936, that government should intervene in the market during downturns to stimulate demand was dismissed, treated as heretical. But in the post-WWII era it approached consensus as the way to manage downturns. Herbert Simon, Daniel Kahneman, and Amos Tversky all challenged the assumption of rational actors as modeled in economics; initially dismissed as psychology and (therefore) irrelevant, their concept of cognitive bias is now a fundamental premise of economics. (Kahneman won the 2002 Nobel Prize in Economic Sciences.)[14]

The cognitive revolution in psychology is similarly striking. In the early to mid-20th century, the behaviorist approaches of John B. Watson and B. F. Skinner dominated. The dominant view was that scientists should study only observable behavior; studying the mind was unscientific and speculative. In the 1950s and 1960s, pioneers of the study of mind published their work in computer science, linguistics, and the study of memory. They all argued that the mind could be studied rigorously. The initial reception was skepticism and hostility, but over time the method attracted supporters and spread across many disciplines. By the 1970s, cognitive psychology dominated most departments, and it is mainstream today.[15]

Finally, consider important changes in political-science thinking. When some scholars started applying economic concepts, like the "rational actor," to voting behavior, legislation, and institutions, many in the field dismissed it as too simple to explain these complex phenomena. While academics still debate the matter, reliance on rational-actor models is a dominant approach in many fields. So too with "democratic peace" theory. The theory is that democracies rarely, if ever, go to war with one another. Some realist scholars treated this as naive, believing that the form of government did not explain the outbreaks of wars. While still debated, it is among the most widely accepted empirical findings in the study of international relations.[16]

These turnabouts across many disciplines provide a compelling argument for protecting the perceived good and bad, the sweet with the bitter, of academic freedom. When new ideas are offered, even the experts who apply professional standards and assess those ideas cannot reliably sort the false from the true and the right from the wrong. Nor can many others. Across many fields, new ideas once considered marginal have become the accepted position in subsequent generations. The history of the sciences is littered with accepted truths later understood to be provably false. In other disciplines, there is a similar pattern of newly discovered facts and deepened or different understandings of how to understand the field. And what we think we believe and know today, through the same process, is very likely to change in the future. It is, in short, hard to distinguish, reliably, the person who is wrong from the person who is the visionary. Academic freedom thus requires protection for both.

Chilling Effects

Not every unconventional idea matures into a discovery. Many claims that were implausible in 1900 remain implausible today. But the defense of academic freedom does not rest only on the hope that today's outlandish idea might prove true tomorrow. It rests on a more systemic concern. Even if we could identify the "wrong" arguments, sanctioning those who advance them deters others from pursuing work that might be right. This is the chilling effect.

The record is instructive. During the McCarthy era, the University of California required faculty to sign loyalty oaths disavowing membership in the Communist Party. Thirty-one tenured professors refused and were dismissed. Their individual cases mattered, greatly, but so too did the larger effect on those who remained. Research in areas associated with left politics—labor history, critiques of US foreign policy—was abandoned, not because the work lacked merit but because the risks of pursuing it were too high. In the Vietnam era, a series of prominent tenure denials for faculty outspoken against the war sent a similar message. Junior scholars quickly learned that criticism of US policy was professionally perilous. The punishment of a few reshaped the research agenda of the many.[17]

Examples drawn from other regimes are sobering. With Stalin's backing, Dr. Trofim Lysenko denounced as pseudoscience the then-accepted genetics framework (Mendelian genetics). In 1948, Soviet institutions banned teaching and research under that framework, closed laboratories, and silenced or imprisoned geneticists. For decades, whole branches of biology—especially in agriculture—were cut off from global science, leaving Soviet biology stagnant while the rest of the world advanced. Similarly, after the 2016 coup attempt in Turkey, thousands of academics were dismissed or arrested. Even those untouched by the purges narrowed their research agendas and avoided politically sensitive questions. In Hungary, the forced relocation of Central European University chilled scholarship on democracy and human rights across the country. The lesson is consistent: When scholars anticipate sanction, the range of inquiry contracts, and the society's capacity for self-understanding diminishes.[18]

The difficulty is compounded by the question of who decides what is beyond the bounds of academic freedom. Within a given discipline, scholars disagree, often vigorously, but they share standards of evidence and criteria of reliability. Nonscholars, such as political leaders or trustees, face important pressures, but ones that have little to do with truth-seeking. If the line is drawn by such figures, faculty will flee from topics that may prove unpopular or inconvenient, regardless of scholarly merit. Some good ideas are consequently never pursued.

It is in partly out of concern for this chilling effect that many universities have vested the authority for judgment of their peers in faculty themselves, through the pervasive practice of peer review and disciplinary oversight. These mechanisms are imperfect, in part because peers can be hostile to new ideas. But the mechanisms are designed to insulate scholarly evaluation from transient pressures. When faculty are accused of exceeding their bounds, it is their peers—those who know both the value of freedom and the obligations of rigor—who are best situated to assess their cases.

The chilling-effect argument thus adds a distinct strand to the defense of academic freedom. Even if we could confidently identify error, punishing it would have collateral costs: It would silence those who might have been right or who might simply have asked an important question that others had not. Protecting the eccentric and the mistaken is not indulgence. It is the necessary price of ensuring that the conditions for genuine discovery remain intact.

Attracting the Independent Minds We Need

A separate argument for taking the bitter with the sweet is that it creates conditions of employment that attract the people best suited to the university's mission. That mission is to open up new areas of inquiry, to generate reliable knowledge, and to teach the next generation. Like baseball pitchers or priests, those who thrive in this vocation are not interchangeable generalists but people with distinctive traits. They are obsessed with their subject, committed to its standards, unwilling to take convention on faith, sometimes able to see what others overlook. These are the independent minds whose peculiarities fuel new ideas. Without the promise of independence—anchored in shared methods for judging reliability—many would not enter the academy at all. Academic freedom is not merely a condition for their best work; it is a magnet that draws them in.

Other fields that depend on unusual talents make a similar bargain. Federal judges are granted life tenure not because we expect infallibility but because independence attracts candidates willing to make decisions informed by law even when they are unpopular. Central bankers are shielded from political pressure so that people with the temperament to resist short-term demands will take the job. Journalists similarly devote themselves to exposing powerful interests because they are promised independence from state control. Artists, entrepreneurs, auditors, and military commanders in the field, and physicians in their clinical practice with patients operate within domains where autonomy is a strong norm, sometimes protected by law. In each case, that autonomy is tolerated despite the risk of mistakes or abuse because it is a condition that draws in the very people capable of doing the work well.

The logic is perhaps clearest in the arts, where creativity is the driving force. A novelist must be free to explore disturbing characters, a painter free to ruin a canvas, a composer free to follow a jarring theme. Excess and failure are tolerated because they are inseparable from genius. Van Gogh painted canvases dismissed as incoherent; Joyce wrote a novel banned as obscene. And yet their work redrew the boundaries of beauty and meaning. Where autonomy is denied, the most daring simply turn elsewhere. Stalin silenced Shostakovich, forcing him to compose only in sanctioned veins, and Nazi Germany drove out "degenerate" artists—losing visionaries whose work might have reshaped their culture.

Scholarship shows the same rhythm. Of course there are differences, and they matter. Artists answer primarily to themselves and to audiences, whether contemporary or future. Academics are embedded in institutions whose credibility depends on their work. That is why academic freedom, unlike artistic freedom, is bounded by professional standards: peer review, methodological rigor, ethical rules. Scholars are expected to produce knowledge that others can contest, test, or replicate (or all three). Autonomy is granted, but it is autonomy within a discipline. Still, it is that autonomy that is a necessary precondition to the creativity needed to fuel breakthroughs.

The autonomy enjoyed by entrepreneurs is also instructive. Most new ventures fail—by some estimates, three-quarters of venture-backed firms do not return their capital. Yet investors tolerate this because only those comfortable with risk will invest in the first place, and the rare success more than compensates for the many disappointments. Amazon was mocked as a money-losing bookstore; Google and Airbnb were once dismissed as implausible. But autonomy to chase hunches and overturn orthodoxy draws entrepreneurs in. The independence entrepreneurs enjoy—to chase ideas that defy conventional wisdom, even to waste capital—is not an indulgence but a necessity. Joseph Schumpeter called them the agents of "creative destruction," advancing progress by overturning what is settled. Israel Kirzner emphasized their "alertness" to overlooked opportunities, possible only when individuals are free to act on hunches. The bargain is clear: Without the freedom to fail, or try out a risky idea, even the bold would not try.[19]

The analogy is again not exact. Entrepreneurs are disciplined by markets, which quickly eliminate what cannot survive. Universities do not have that mechanism, and for good reason. Instead, they rely on peer review and professional standards as their form of discipline. They do so because many of a university's functions would be distorted or even disappear if subjected to the market. Though too much autonomy can allow waste or abuse, both systems depend on tolerating error and disappointment as the price of discovery. The venture capital model works because investors expect failure, not despite it. Academic freedom works the same way. Without tolerance for error, universities would be filled with the cautious and conventional, losing out on the opportunity to attract the kinds of minds most capable of reshaping knowledge.

Those who flourish in academic life are not only creative and willing to take a risk on an idea but also deeply committed to disciplinary standards. They want freedom to follow unconventional ideas, but they also want those ideas tested, challenged, and made stronger by contest. That combination—independence joined to rigor—is what makes the academy attractive to them in the first place. Academic freedom is the bargain that draws them in.

Society's—and the university's—most valuable contributors are those who combine skepticism and restlessness with disciplinary rigor. They come because they are promised autonomy, and they stay because their ideas will be tested. That is why protecting the freedom to take intellectual risks is inseparable from the university's mission of producing knowledge and educating students. And it is also why the next argument follows: Reliable knowledge itself depends on allowing even mistaken ideas to circulate and be corrected.

Reliable Knowledge Requires Error

The pursuit of reliable knowledge over time also requires taking academic freedom's upside and its perceived downside together. Reliable knowledge does not come from shielding only the correct ideas. It comes from exposing wrong ones and forcing them through the gauntlet of criticism. A false theory, when tested and refuted, sharpens the methods and strengthens the standards by which better theories are judged. To purge the wrong at the outset would be to dismantle the very mechanism that makes knowledge reliable.

The history of phlogiston makes the point vividly. For more than a century, chemists believed that all flammable substances contained a fiery element called phlogiston, released during burning. Ash or "calx" was thought to be the substance left behind once its phlogiston was spent. The theory was wrong, but it was fruitful. It framed experiments, generated debate, and organized inquiry. Only when Antoine Lavoisier measured combustion precisely did the flaws become undeniable: Metals gained weight when they burned because they combined with oxygen, not because they lost phlogiston. Refuting the theory inaugurated modern chemistry. The very wrongness of phlogiston seeded the precision that made chemistry a modern science.[20]

Two examples discussed earlier also make this case. Marshall and Warren persisted in their view that ulcers were caused by bacteria; their claim was ridiculed before it was vindicated. The case of prions is similar: Prusiner's idea was derided as "science fiction," until it wasn't. The attacks and questioning of these ideas were essential to their eventual acceptance.

The same dynamic is visible outside the sciences. Mid-20th century psychology was dominated by behaviorism, which insisted that only observable behavior could be studied scientifically. Dismissing the study of the mind as speculative turned out to be wrong—but that error sharpened the critiques that launched the cognitive revolution. Economics likewise long relied on rational-actor models that critics claimed were too simplistic to capture real human decision-making. Their limits spurred the rise of behavioral economics. History's elite-focused narratives were "partial" in ways that opened the door to social history, women's history, and cultural history—fields that expanded what counted as knowledge.

The danger of suppressing error is equally clear. Soviet biology under Trofim Lysenko, as noted already, denounced Mendelian genetics as "bourgeois pseudoscience," banned its teaching and research, and purged its practitioners. As a consequence, wrong ideas could not be challenged because right ideas could not be spoken. Agricultural science stalled for a generation, with catastrophic human costs. Here, the effort to insulate knowledge from error destroyed the system's capacity to produce truth. What looked like quality control became institutionalized falsehood.

The reliability argument holds that even when ideas appear wrong, even when most are certain they are wrong, they must be allowed to circulate. For reliability depends on the full cycle of contestation, refutation, and correction. Knowledge is trustworthy not because it excludes error but because it has overcome it. The bitter is the precondition of the sweet.

*

Let's return to the opening vignettes: A policy professor invites a pro-life advocate to class. An historian publishes an op-ed against same-sex marriage. A pediatrician defends gender-affirming care in a campus lecture. The calls arrive, urging cancellation, compelled "balance," or administrative reprimand, and demanding that the university disown the views.

There is, of course, a lot the university leader can say. The university does not endorse the opinions of individual scholars or their guests; it protects their autonomy within standards that let faculty teach, write, and debate inside their fields. That autonomy is paired with discipline—formal and informal peer review, methodological rigor, and professional ethics.

But to the skeptical caller, the case is more powerful than that. The "wrongheaded" idea has to be protected because we cannot achieve the university mission without protecting it. In real time we often misjudge what is true; punishing the mistaken deters the promising; creative, rigorous minds will not join a profession that enforces conformity; and reliable knowledge emerges on the part of both faculty and students by testing and correcting error, not by trying to ban it.

*

Many readers do not need to be persuaded that broad protection for academic freedom is crucial. But to the skeptics, the challenge is this: Its benefits are often hidden, while its perceived costs are visible. Yet the two cannot be separated. If we care about the advancement of knowledge—about discovery, understanding, and truth—we must protect the freedom that makes both error and insight possible. The bitter and the sweet are bound together; to lose one is to lose them both.

19

Stances in Defense of Institutional Academic Freedom

STEVEN G. POSKANZER*

> "[T]he question of whether in the long run the vital autonomy of a university might be sacrificed in the search for funds must be examined with all candor. . . . If the majority of [the leading universities] should some day come to depend heavily on Congressional appropriations for their support, the present picture of higher education in the United States would be completely altered. The problem of maintaining the independence of our universities would then have to be worked out with a totally different framework."
>
> —James B. Conant, President's Report, Harvard University (1948)

> "The prospect of domination of the nation's scholars by Federal employment, project allocations, and the power of money is ever present and is gravely to be regarded."
>
> —Dwight D. Eisenhower, Farewell Address (1961)

Introduction

It's notlike we didn't see the risk. Even during the heady post-WWII creation of a system of federal support for university science, even in the midst of the Cold War, the dangers of university[1] overdependence upon government funding were recognized, including by supporters (like Conant) of the federal partnership forged with academe.

Universities were wise to work hand in hand with the federal government to support research, graduate training, undergraduate student access, and more.

* Professor of Political Science and President Emeritus, Carleton College.

Steven G. Poskanzer, *Stances in Defense of Institutional Academic Freedom*. In: *Academic Freedom in the Era of Trump*. Edited by: Lee C. Bollinger and Geoffrey R. Stone, Oxford University Press. © Oxford University Press (2026). DOI: 10.1093/9780197854877.003.0020

Over the succeeding decades, the partnership, on the whole, worked brilliantly to promote American preeminence. But maybe we should have listened a bit more carefully to those first cautionary notes sounded, because today universities seek respite from an anvil chorus of federal attacks on their operations and goals.

The major dilemma facing American universities is how to respond to this unprecedented governmental assault. What kinds of stances and actions can and should they take in return?

Even well-intentioned universities and their leaders often fail to think as carefully as they ought before plunging their institutions into political, economic, moral, and social controversies. I have argued elsewhere that a combination of (1) fidelity to the university's highest values and a sustained focus on its fundamental purpose, and (2) the wisdom and need of adhering to the university's "side" of a mutually beneficial social compact between the academy and larger society should ordinarily lead academic institutions to decline to take stances on disputes unrelated to their core mission.[2] But while universities should typically choose reticence, they must bravely stand up for themselves when it truly matters. They can and should take stances:

- when the university as an institution has especially relevant knowledge to share on public (particularly educational) issues;
- when a stance is required to ensure that the university can provide the necessary intellectual environment and resources for faculty and student work;
- when the mission of the institution is at issue; and
- when the very existence of the institution is at risk.

At present, an agglomeration of Trump-administration actions violates institutional academic freedom in ways that shred that admirable social compact. Accordingly, universities must take institutional stances—conceived of broadly, and extending far beyond issuing formal statements—to preserve their autonomy and the fundamental mission and strength of much of American higher education.

The Extent, Context, and Importance of Institutional Academic Freedom

Individual academic freedom may be more regularly invoked and valorized, but *institutional* academic freedom is equally essential. Justice Frankfurter, in *Sweezy v. New Hampshire,* spoke approvingly of "the four essential freedoms" of the academy, declaring that a university must be allowed to "determine for itself on academic grounds who may teach, what may be taught, how it shall be taught, and who may be admitted to study."[3] While this offers a useful starting point, I conceive of institutional academic freedom even more capaciously.

As a foundational matter, universities as institutions—using their own best judgment—must be allowed to define their scope and strategic thrust. Driven always by its core values, each institution must have the ability to set its overall profile (e.g., its location, size, and mix of programs) and its academic goals. Those goals should include what kind of student it aims to enroll; choices about the curriculum (and co-curriculum) that will best achieve desired educational outcomes; and the relative emphasis placed on research versus teaching.

With such goals and priorities firmly established, an institution next requires the freedom to *pursue* those mission-driven intellectual and pedagogical aims. This entails upholding chosen standards in student admissions and academic performance, and in faculty hiring, tenure, and promotion. The institution assumes an obligation—and thus must have the concomitant freedom—to enable faculty scholarship and teaching. It likewise must have the autonomy to meet legitimate student needs and expectations, ranging from providing a safe and supportive learning environment to delivering a promised baseline quality of instruction.

Moving beyond the central activities of research and teaching, institutional academic freedom must permit a university to decide for itself what public services to deliver (e.g., student volunteerism, extension offices, cultural and athletic events). And finally, institutional academic freedom surely extends to crafting and overseeing the school's long-range plans and safeguarding its effective operation, fiscal health, and public reputation. These tasks are the particular fiduciary province of senior administrators and trustees.

One complication universities face in asserting the central value of academic freedom is that the Supreme Court has never expressly decreed that such freedom (either individual *or* institutional) must receive discrete constitutional protection. While it has held that academic freedom is a "special concern" of the First Amendment,[4] that is not as unshakable a legal foundation as higher education might like.[5] Further, the case law fleshing out the contours of academic freedom is often murky and inconsistent. Still, there has long been wide acceptance of the notion that universities require meaningful legal and operational "space" to achieve their goals. Apart from its legal status, then, academic freedom also constitutes wise intellectual and educational policy.

Institutional academic freedom therefore recognizes and honors that the university is its own separate entity, with a life, responsibilities, and relationships that extend temporally and conceptually far beyond those of any individual faculty member or student. Such institutional autonomy is an essential part of the distinctively American—and heretofore distinctively successful—social compact between higher education and broader society.

The obligations, responsibilities, and benefits of that compact flow in both directions. The university generates and disseminates new ideas and discoveries, pushing back the boundaries of knowledge and understanding. It serves as a custodian of the world's intellectual heritage (e.g., through libraries and teaching and research on ancient civilizations). It produces thoughtfully educated graduates who become upwardly mobile and engaged workers, citizens, and leaders. Indeed, by awarding degrees and certificates, the university authenticates the skills these individuals have acquired. As part of its educational role, the university also endeavors to provide students with the knowledge they need to live *fulfilling* lives. Beyond the classroom and laboratory, the university provides a wide range of public service to its local community, state, and nation, and perhaps to global humanity. Prominent examples include sharing university expertise with industry and government, commercializing discoveries, and providing health care. Universities also offer cultural enrichment through the arts, speakers, and sport.

On *its* side of the compact, society provides funding through direct appropriations (especially to public universities), and—of singular prominence at the current moment—research grants and contracts. Since the creation of the National Science Foundation in 1950, the federal government has been the principal source of such faculty support. Significant targeted public payments also support academic health centers.[6] Broader society supports universities through favorable tax treatment (e.g., exemptions from real estate and income taxes; tax-deductibility of charitable donations) and a generally advantageous regulatory environment. A last and overarching feature of the traditional compact is a meaningful degree of operational and legal autonomy, embracing the fundamental notion that universities must be allowed to manage core academic domains in accordance with their own best judgment and long-term interests. Another way of describing this, of course, is institutional academic freedom.

This compact ultimately depends on mutual respect, tolerance, and care. The public needs to respect that universities will often be "out of step" with elements of society as they discover and teach potentially disruptive ideas. But universities need to respect the public's forward-looking generosity in embracing their work. Cities with universities must tolerate their impact on public services and local politics. But universities must tolerate in turn how their culture, operations, and stature—and especially any perceived privileges extended to them—can create resentment. Finally, society must carefully preserve the university's needed independence. But universities and their faculties must also be careful along several critical dimensions, always aiming for intellectual and institutional humility. All parties must recognize the compact's fragility—and purposefully tend to it.

I will address later some of the ways universities have failed to live up to this compact. But far more distressing is how the Trump administration is intentionally ripping it apart.

The Current Assault

The administration is consciously "flooding the zone" with a variety of punitive actions intended to bring higher education into a more conservative ideological line. Federal authorities may recognize that some of these measures will not pass legal muster. Nevertheless, they presumably calculate that the short-term political mileage from excoriating universities outweighs any longer-term costs to science, medicine, other research, student learning, and national competitiveness. The tactics being used include:

- *Issuing executive orders,* such as the decree banning "illegal" diversity, equity, and inclusion [DEI] discrimination, and increasing regulation of accreditors.[7]
- *Aggressive interpretation of the* Students for Fair Admissions v. Harvard *decision* [*SFFA* opinion] barring consideration of race, not just in admissions but also in financial aid, programming aimed at minority students, and faculty/staff hiring.[8]
- *Mass firings at the Department of Education* [ED].[9]
- *Agency regulations* eliminating disfavored rules (e.g., protecting transgender students).[10]
- *Investigations* of universities, with the *New York Times* reporting at least eight different investigations spanning at least six executive agencies at Harvard alone, including a Joint Task Force to Combat Anti-Semitism [Anti-Semitism Task Force].[11]
- *Canceling existing grants and contracts.*[12]
- *Cutting off future grants/contracts and eligibility therefor.*[13] This is universities' greatest current legal and operational vulnerability, with huge sums at stake. The crux of the problem is that universities have no right to prospective funding. The government can set its own priorities for what it wants to fund and impose conditions on such funding. Potential grantees/contractors can choose to either abide by those conditions or not take the money.
- *Threatening removal of tax-exempt status.*[14]
- *Blocking the enrollment of international students* by revoking a school's participation in the Student and Exchange Visitor Program [SEVP].[15]
- *Directing Immigration and Customs Enforcement (ICE) to raid campuses.*[16]
- *Encouraging individual plaintiffs to file* qui tam *suits against universities under the False Claims Act.*[17]

- *Using its "bully pulpit" to pillory targeted schools.*[18] Every avenging step taken by the government has been accompanied by press releases and/or social media ridiculing universities.

Significantly, recent Congressional actions hostile to higher education compound the animus of the executive branch. For example, the One Big Beautiful Bill Act substantially raised the endowment tax, eliminated or capped various loan programs, and conditioned schools' continued eligibility for loans upon their graduates' meeting earnings thresholds.[19] One can easily imagine a compliant Congress passing further legislation that holds universities' feet to the fire. Of course, belligerent Congressional hearings and investigations of universities also continue.

Let me add two more sobering and cautionary thoughts. Once the Rubicon of politicizing the social compact with universities has been crossed, all partisan actors may do the same. Government swords can cut in both conservative and liberal directions.

Second, what we are witnessing is not only a federal government dynamic. State attacks on higher education were its precursors and will be its likely successors. Consider how Florida's "Stop WOKE Act" prohibits any training or instruction in a list of concepts related to the intractability of systemic racism and sexism. Its "Anti-DEI Act" prohibits state universities from spending public monies on DEI activities and details which general-education courses can count for credit. Similar statutes limiting what faculty can teach are being enacted in other states.[20]

Perhaps the most aggressive examples of the Trump administration's approach to higher education are the omnibus demand letters to Columbia and Harvard.[21] They directly violate the institutional academic freedom of those universities by intruding deeply into faculty personnel and curricular decisions, admissions, intra-institutional governance, the co-curriculum, student conduct and discipline, and other aspects of campus culture, while further curtailing university autonomy with intrusive reporting and compliance requirements.

Lines of Resistance and Counterattack

Universities are completely justified in adamantly opposing these attacks. Taking strong institutional stances in opposition to these current challenges is entirely legitimate—and even necessary.

The first circumstance warranting an institutional stance is when the university as an institution has especially relevant knowledge or experience to share on pressing educational issues. If the university makes its opinions known on such matters, it could enlighten debate and lead to smarter policy choices. Taking stances on education-focused issues lets a university fulfill its core duties to society without treading into realms where it can subvert its mission or tear at the social compact. Because the institution is staying in its proper lane, formal positions that draw on and articulate its insights have both credibility and utility to external audiences.

Several Trump administration policies involve prominent educational matters. The "Dear Colleague" letter interpreting the *SFFA* opinion as requiring "colorblindness" in domains far afield from admissions raises topics on which universities can offer valuable commentary.[22] University views on how to create genuinely inclusive learning environments where all students can succeed should be aired and heard.

University analyses of the impact of staff cuts and restructuring at the Department of Education are also highly relevant. Higher education institutions understand what smooth and effective operation of federal loan programs and other oversight of K-20 education should entail. Likewise with new, ideologically driven, regulations being issued by various executive agencies. University experience with these matters should be taken seriously in crafting such rules.

Resisting Trump administration efforts to block enrollment of international students (e.g., barring those "hostile to the American values and institutions") is another prime example of an appropriate stance. The untrammeled flow of students and scholars is central to the work of academic institutions. Universities know that a global student body leads to better educational outcomes, and therefore they can forthrightly defend their recruitment of such students. They can also take issue with demands to single out foreign students by reporting any conduct violations they commit to federal authorities (presumably opening them up to easier deportation).

The second set of circumstances when an institutional stance is required is to ensure that the university can provide the necessary intellectual environment and resources for academic work. Universities create what I think of as the "nurturing soil" from which the faculty (and student) labor at the heart of the academy can flourish. The elements of such "soil" are many, starting with physical facilities such as laboratories, libraries, and classrooms. Such academic "soil" consists in part of talented colleagues on campus, along with access to leading scholars located elsewhere. It requires, as well, diverse and engaged students whose questions and comments help refine faculty ideas and educate their peers. And last, but by no means least, this "soil" depends upon a supportive culture that values and advances the institution's mission.

When internal or external challengers question the importance of any such elements, or compromise the ability of the institution to provide them, the university should take a stance in support of their value and their protection.

Thus, for example, universities should defend the academic freedom of faculty, the importance of the scientific method, and adherence to high evidentiary standards.

To date, the Trump administration has not directly attacked any of the foregoing. But a substantial number of its actions threaten the university's ability to provide the requisite environment and resources for academic success. Deep intrusions into the rules governing student behavior and discipline processes can seriously alter the campus climate. Federal insistence upon specific penalties for incidents extending back to 2023 is ludicrously meddlesome, but even government mandates to enact and enforce precise rules governing future protests should be resisted (e.g., required definitions of anti-Semitism, bans on wearing masks). Almost all institutions already have time, place, and manner rules to prevent disruptive protests, so federal calls for the adoption of such regulations are largely performative. However, centralizing student discipline under the purview of the university president is a patent attempt to cut potentially sympathetic faculty, staff, and fellow students out of the process in favor of a single target of federal accountability. In all of these ways, the Trump administration is interfering with what should be fundamentally academic decisions on how to educate students through internal discipline.

Federal mandates about goals, structure, and functioning of schools' cocurricular offerings will also damage the desired environment for learning. It should be the responsibility of the university, acting through both faculty and student-life professionals, to decide under what terms student groups should be officially recognized, allowed to select their officers, awarded funding (and for what purposes), and disciplined for violating institutional rules. All of these matters have a didactic purpose, which should be deferred to by the government. Yet the Harvard Letter totally undercuts this approach by demanding the University end recognition and support of specific groups and imposing many new constraints on prospective student activities and organizations.

Going further, federal commands, as in the Columbia and Harvard Letters, to create a more authoritarian and compliant campus climate by buttressing the presence and power of campus police and local law enforcement should be rejected unless they are truly welcome on educational grounds. Local academic leadership should set and nurture the desired campus culture.

While it is impossible to generalize without knowing their precise content, new federal regulations can dramatically affect the campus environment and distort educational outcomes. Think here of Title IX rules that marginalize transgender students, or that protect those accused of sexual misconduct. As an extreme example of potential interference with an open climate for learning, consider the fear and disruption generated by ICE raids. Apart from such intentionally created anxiety, federal investigations of universities can suck up vast amounts of time and money. Even lower-level federal harassment—such as encouraging individuals to file False Claims Act suits, intrusive reporting requirements (e.g., data requests, quarterly reports, audits)—can sap a university's spirit and purse. And, of course, public criticism of universities also erodes a healthy intellectual environment. When the academic soil is being contaminated, the university must respond.

The third critical instance when an institutional stance is required is when the mission of the university is at issue. Schools should always seek to advance their mission. As a corollary, universities must take a defensive position when their mission is being questioned. At such moments, those charged with a fiduciary duty to protect the long-term welfare of the university (especially the president and trustees) should forthrightly plead on its behalf. It would, in fact, be a breach of duty *not* to do so.[23] Attacks on institutional missions typically arise from external loci. And many of the recent actions taken by the Trump administration purposefully aim to alter the missions of universities and how they pursue their principal goals.

These assaults on institutional autonomy begin with restraints on the first of Frankfurter's "four essential freedoms" of the academy: Who may teach. Disturbingly, the aggressive push for Columbia to place its Middle East, South Asian, and African Studies Department into academic receivership (thereby blocking ordinary faculty hiring) is modest compared to the outrageous demands of the Harvard Letter. To begin, Harvard must stop any employment practices that award preferences on the basis of race, color, religion, sex, or national origin, or that "function as ideological litmus tests" (a concept never defined). Instead, it is to implement "merit-based hiring" (Harvard would surely claim it is already doing this). While these requirements go well beyond the *SFFA* opinion, that ruling does raise serious questions about the legality of affirmative action in faculty hiring.

But the Harvard Letter reaches new levels of brazenness when it demands that the University ensure, through a federally approved external review, that every academic department and teaching unit be "viewpoint diverse"—and that if one is not found to be so, a critical mass of new faculty be hired to bring such diversity. Putting aside the vagueness of the definitions and the practical ludicrousness of actually trying to implement such a scheme,[24] such an approach curtails autonomous institutional choices about faculty qualifications and the institution's needs. Yet another restriction would be placed on "Who may teach" by required external reviews of at least ten Harvard academic units—including the entire schools of Divinity, Graduate Education, Medicine, and Public Health—with reports about and federally approved sanctions for individual professors who discriminated against Jewish or Israeli students or incited student violations of university rules, as well as larger corrective reforms, all to follow. The intentional chilling effect on faculty and institutional academic freedom is clear. And as the cherry on top of its attack on faculty composition, the Harvard Letter calls for all current and prospective faculty to be reviewed for plagiarism.[25]

While posturing and litigation proceed over the Harvard Letter, simultaneous EEOC investigations of Harvard's hiring and recent executive orders "restoring merit-based opportunity" also arguably constrain faculty recruitment. However, since all universities were *already* prohibited from discrimination in employment, the now-banned "illegal DEI" was always unlawful.

Justice Frankfurter's second and third essential freedoms—What may be taught, and How it shall be taught—have heretofore been the target of *state* governments rather than federal authorities. Previously discussed legislation prohibiting instruction on designated "divisive concepts" or mandating coverage in certain classes impinge upon individual and institutional academic freedom in troubling ways. Pedagogical autonomy, of course, is closely related to scholars' freedom to pursue whatever topics they wish and to draw whatever conclusions seem warranted from their research. And that scholarly freedom is also being constrained. Unilaterally suspending or canceling research grants and government contracts constitutes direct interference with scholarship. Cutting off *future* grants and contracts in retribution for legally protected speech or actions, or imposing political litmus tests on individual or institutional eligibility therefor, also betrays long-accepted notions and practices of academic freedom. Even if the federal government can theoretically choose only to fund research on topics and from perspectives it favors, this would be a far cry from how world-class science has previously been carried out and supported in America.

The fourth of the academy's essential freedoms is to determine "Who may be admitted to study." This, too, is being dangerously limited. I have already explored the propriety of university stances supporting the enrollment of international students. Schools should oppose unwarranted and/or procedurally deficient attempts to cancel their participation in the SEVP program, as this impedes mission attainment. The same can be said about the administration's intrusions into other university admissions decisions, as seen in the Harvard Letter, with its demands for ending any admissions practices that are based on race, color, national origin, or proxies thereof, or that function as "ideological litmus tests." Instead, all Harvard schools and programs are instructed to implement "merit-based" admissions policies (again, something the University would say it has long done).

In a troubling parallel to its proposed intrusions on faculty hiring, the administration is demanding federally reviewed "viewpoint diversity" in the Harvard student body across all teaching units, with critical masses of students holding the requisite diversity of views to be admitted either by the unit itself or by a cognate unit capable of and willing to select applicants on such grounds. To facilitate future scrutiny of Harvard's admissions, the University must share, with the government and general public, detailed statistical analyses of admitted and rejected applicants, broken down by race, color, national origin, grade point average, and performance on standardized tests. A harbinger of how such data might be used is the current Justice Department investigation of whether Harvard's admissions policies defrauded the government in violation of the False Claims Act.

The Harvard Letter threatens further violations of institutional academic freedom by improperly inserting federal authorities into intra-university governance and the setting of institutional priorities. Demands for a redistribution of power away from students, untenured faculty, and faculty and administrators who are "more committed to activism than scholarship" and toward those tenured professors and senior administrators who are determined to be the "most devoted to the scholarly mission of the University and committed to the changes indicated in [the Harvard Letter]" fly directly in the face of established norms of shared academic decision-making and other features of a healthy institutional culture. Requiring analogous changes in student disciplinary structures also interferes with internal governance and arguably blocks accomplishment of the University's mission.

In contrast, there is nothing inherently wrong with the Anti-Semitism Task Force calling for reduction of administrative bloat, duplication, or harmful decentralization that might block needed reform. But when, as in the Harvard Letter, the government mandates that schools can no longer operate DEI programs even if such activities have been carefully determined to advance core academic goals and are conducted in ways that fully comply with the law, federal authorities are clearly and impermissibly trying to recast institutional values, cultures, and missions. It is then necessary for affected universities to take a stance in their defense.

I note in closing that other, more routine, administrative actions taken by the federal or state government may, singly or jointly, create sufficiently serious operational and/or financial pressures as to disrupt a university's mission. Depending upon the specifics, achievement of an institution's goals can be endangered by new agency regulations or investigations; by required testimony at hearings; by onerous data collection, reporting, compliance, and auditing requirements; and by new legislation. Schools were therefore correct in trying to limit the fiscal exactions and legal risks of the One Big Beautiful Bill Act. Further federal laws striking at institutional academic freedom should also be hotly resisted. And while I think stripping away a university's tax-exempt status is very unlikely, such removal would constitute a mortal blow.

Which brings me, finally, to the last and scariest scenario when institutional stances are required: When the very existence of the institution is at risk. The University of Chicago's Kalven Report warned of instances when the society, or segments of it, genuinely threaten the university and its values.[26] Here, the university must take a position in the hope of ensuring its survival.

The kinds of acute challenges I envision will almost always arise from external sources—most likely, political actors with broad power over the institution. Again, we do well to recall the Conant and Eisenhower admonitions. The critical point is that, when the university's ability to pursue its core functions is truly at risk, it must publicly assail and counter such danger. Leadership must take official positions defending not just that mission but the institution itself. Silence in the face of such peril would constitute a breach of one's fiduciary duty of loyalty.

I contend that when a university:

- is forbidden to hire the individuals it wants to serve on its faculty;
- is barred from enrolling the students it wants to teach;
- has its daily operations thwarted through intrusive oversight; and
- more generally, cannot make and implement the decisions that its leadership believes are in the institution's long-term best interests;

then the stewards of the institution must take public stances and even direct actions that preserve the resources and fundamental character of the institution. Although such predicaments may be extraordinary, brave and resolute positions by universities are imperative under such circumstances.

Of course, the central and inescapable difficulty in deciding whether to take a stance to preserve the university is determining whether you are indeed *in* an existential crisis. Hindsight is always 20/20, but it can be singularly hard to gauge the severity of a situation while you are dealing with it. If the university jumps in headlong to fend off potential disasters, it is likely to become entangled in a host of political, economic, moral, and social controversies that turn out not to be that critical, thereby tearing at the social compact and seriously harming the institution. But if it passively waits too long until the full crisis emerges in all its horror, there may no longer be a university to defend. While I ordinarily advise caution and am reluctant to classify a situation in this final category, *I regretfully conclude that we have reached such a rare tipping point.*

I have described how fundamental university decisions—all constitutive of institutional academic freedom—are being intentionally blocked, if not perverted, by the Trump administration. Every one of the listed existential tripwires is being triggered: control over faculty and student-body composition, the setting of intellectual and pedagogical foci, and the execution of operational and strategic priorities. From a financial perspective, it is impossible to successfully run a major research university today without robust and steady flows of federal research dollars. Such funding is a central pillar of the institutional economy. Canceling current grants and contracts and subjecting future ones to ideological litmus tests and political agendas cut to the very heart of university solvency and mission attainment. A second terrifying bludgeon would be cutting off or conditioning institutional eligibility for federal Title VI financial aid, especially Pell Grants for low-income students. These dollars are part of the economic lifeblood of research universities as well as public and private comprehensive and liberal arts colleges. While that weapon is still sheathed, it could easily be deployed by a committed executive branch to considerable destructive effect.

The savage public criticism of higher education for being disconnected from the real world, too expensive, hopelessly "woke," anti-Semitic, and fundamentally un-American is taking a heavy toll. Repeated mockery and denunciation of universities damage their reputations, cost them goodwill, alienate potential allies and patrons, and leave schools vulnerable to further media attacks.

The cumulative impact of all these negative actions is profound and potentially irreversible. As the mission of the university is under assault, its core animating values are questioned and shaken as well. When one fairly considers the unprecedented Trump administration onslaught, the ineluctable conclusion must be that many individual universities—and, perhaps soon, large swaths of American higher education—face an existential threat. Such a threat requires direct, full-throated, and bold stances in response.

Potential Institutional Responses

Fortunately, there are many ways for universities to fight back on legal, political, fiscal, educational, and other grounds. The menu of possible responses begins with statements from individually targeted institutions justifying their work and explaining their actions and legal positions. Public letters from Harvard's President Alan Garber have been a model in this regard.[27] A university might also launch an organized campaign to energize its alumni and other supporters and generate sympathetic media coverage (e.g., "Stand Up for Princeton").[28] There is likewise value in *collective* statements of support and advocacy, typically orchestrated by national higher-education organizations. Several hundred university and college presidents have signed a letter crafted by the American Association of Colleges and Universities and the American Academy of Arts and Sciences opposing administration policies.[29] Filing *amicus* briefs in lawsuits challenging federal actions is another version of joint stance. Of course, universities can also directly lobby government officials. The recent record here offers glimmers of hope, as the Senate has dialed back proposed hikes in the endowment tax and many state anti-DEI bills have been defeated.[30]

But even when institutional stances are warranted, they present practical difficulties. The need for a swift and unified response is at odds with the deliberative pace and decentralized, consultative character of much academic decision-making. Taking stances may exacerbate tensions between faculty and administration and between different academic units (e.g., scientists may be more anxious to preserve grant funding). Of course, multi-institutional coordination is especially complicated.

Lawsuits are another powerful avenue of resistance to Trump administration actions. To begin with, affected universities should have compelling breach-of-contract claims for grants and other agreements unilaterally cancelled without requisite notice and other procedural safeguards. On that same basis, schools can also assert *statutory* violations—e.g., of the Administrative Procedure Act.[31]

Of more relevance to institutional academic freedom, universities can legitimately allege infringements of their *constitutional* rights. Several plausible lines of counterattack are open under the First Amendment. Universities can claim that the government is impermissibly restricting speech on the basis of its viewpoint. Examples of viewpoint discrimination might include withholding funds in order to force universities to conform with Trump administration positions; prohibitions on teaching certain "divisive concepts"; mandated sanctions for particular campus protests or student groups; and, of course, federally enforced "viewpoint" diversity in faculty hiring or student admissions. Universities can also argue that they are being punished in retaliation for prior protected speech. Canceling research grants on now-disfavored topics could fit under this rubric, as might bans on future funding because a university continues to run DEI programs or because it publicly rejected Trump administration demands. Next, schools can assert that the government is unlawfully compelling speech by conditioning funding upon relinquishment of their (and their faculties') constitutional rights and upon adherence to the government's preferred policies (e.g., definitions of anti-Semitism, or "merit-based" selection procedures). Cutting to the chase, universities might also directly allege a violation of constitutionally protected academic freedom, hoping courts might more securely enshrine that norm irrespective of the current climate. As for other constitutional hooks, universities might aver violations of the Due Process Clause for reasons noted above, and—only for religiously affiliated institutions—the Free Exercise Clause.

While such litigation proceeds, universities should steal a page from President Trump's personal legal playbook by stalling for time and erecting procedural hurdles. They can file repeated motions that will delay any adverse judgments and provide further opportunities to appeal. However, as the government well knows, even if the institution eventually prevails, great harm will be incurred in the meantime. Vital research is being disrupted; the pipeline of scholarly talent dries up as junior scholars leave the academy and senior faculty seek greener academic pastures; and, of course, plaintiff universities spend enormous time and money both on litigation and in trying to hold their institutions together.

Although the Trump attacks on higher education can be cast in legal garb, and some may even rise to the level of constitutional violations, they are best understood as a politically motivated effort to undermine established academic policies, values, and culture. Therefore, universities must pursue other, nonlegal paths to expose the government's motivations, rebut unfounded allegations, and explain the looming adverse consequences—while more effectively pursuing their missions.

One set of aggressive countermeasures could include various refusals to cooperate with the government (e.g., declining to do any research for or to consult with federal agencies; cancellation of campus ROTC programs), but these steps might harm internal constituencies and would likely heighten external tensions.

The great temptation for many universities will be to cut the best deal they can—essentially paying tribute. This is what law firms, media corporations, and foreign nations fearful of punitive tariffs are doing . . . and what Columbia has now done as well.[32] It is an entirely predictable outcome when the Trump administration views relationships as entirely transactional, always up for renegotiation to eke out further concessions.

The Columbia resolution came at a hefty price of $221 million in fines. However, this sum pales in comparison to the $1.3 billion or more of federal funding that was at risk. The University can argue that it preserved its core values, including institutional and individual academic freedom. It made no admission of wrongdoing. It received written confirmation that the government does not have "authority to dictate faculty hiring, University hiring, admissions decisions, or the content of academic speech." Clearly this was *the* critical clause from Columbia's perspective. The school also obtained federal endorsement of previous actions taken (e.g., appointment of an administrator to review and strengthen all regional-studies programs; expanded support for Jewish student life; tighter restrictions on protests). The University will be eligible for future grants and contracts without disfavor.

Beyond the money, what else did Columbia give up? It agreed to comply with a variety of federal laws and regulations, including antidiscrimination mandates in admissions, hiring, and promotion decisions—but it was already required to do this. More worrisome, it committed to extensive and costly independent monitoring across the three-year term of the Resolution Agreement, including providing detailed annual admissions data. It is now also obliged to report any known arrests of its international students for criminal activity. Importantly, the government remains free to reopen the fiscal and legal floodgates should there be future violations (cynics would say that fresh allegations are almost certain).

As the government surely intends, the Columbia agreement sets a baseline for settlements with other schools. Indeed, it will likely create a "rush to the exit" problem, as universities that cut early deals increase pressure on peer institutions to do the same. Most troubling of all, though, the outcome with Columbia reinforces the notion that universities are just one more party to be squeezed.

To better protect themselves, universities must focus now on other, longer-term responses, beginning with *fiscal* remedies. Schools will inevitably seek new or expanded funding to fill the federal gaps. Private philanthropy will assume even greater importance, if that is even possible. For even if taxes take a bigger bite out of endowment earnings, the larger one's endowment, the higher the firewall against government incursions and the more institutional autonomy. Schools will also aggressively pursue enhanced corporate support, especially for scientific and medical discoveries. Yet experience cautions that such funding will favor applied rather than basic research. And where feasible, universities—especially public ones—will seek state dollars and legal protection, even as these come with parallel risks.

As tempting as securing additional financial support may be, universities will also try to insulate their operations from federal depredations and reduce their financial dependence on an unreliable national government. Academic medical centers and physician practice plans may provide some useful models. However, I envision creating independent research enterprises with arms-length contracts with universities and their faculty. Successful free-standing prototypes already exist—think of the non-profit Broad Institute and the for-profit Bell Labs.

Considering painful cuts in university research expenditures leads us to a second set of longer-range *academic* responses to the current dilemma. Here are some thought-provoking examples. Seizing inherent opportunity within this crisis, universities might refocus and prioritize their research profiles. It might be possible to coordinate or redistribute scientific emphases and intellectual coverage in conjunction with other schools. Widely distributed faculty could conduct research at a central hub, with shared graduate programs and allocated undergraduate research slots. Even bolder academic solutions to federal cuts could entail dramatic reallocations of intellectual foci and funding within a given university, such as eliminating majors, reducing faculty and staff, or slashing financial aid in order to help underwrite research. Schools might shutter money-losing intercollegiate sports programs and redeploy the savings.

Alas, however, even brave fiscal and academic responses are unlikely to fill universities' yawning budgetary gaps or end their political exposure. American higher education's fundamental problem is that, over time, it has become enormously vulnerable to an unprecedented, unilateral, and acrimonious termination of its partnership with the federal government.

Universities should seek to remedy this situation, ideally through a reconstituted, mutually cherished partnership. Fortunately, there is yet another singularly potent—albeit especially long-horizon—set of measures to be taken that lie largely within the control of universities themselves. In the end, nothing will help universities more than simply doing their core job of research and teaching exceptionally and consistently well—and demonstrating the same.

Higher education has lost much goodwill. Gallup polls report that the percentage of US adults with a great deal of confidence in higher education dropped from 57 percent in 2015 to 36 percent in 2024.[33] Therefore, in addition to showing the positive impact of university research, a vital counter to declining public faith would be longitudinal data demonstrating that an institution's graduates have more successful life outcomes (e.g., higher earnings, greater professional responsibility, healthier and more engaged and fulfilling lives) compared to those who did not attend. By virtue of delivering superior academic results, universities can garner new and more persuasive allies from industry, the military, the media, and elsewhere to help make their best case for government support and respect. They must also fully tap the loyalty of alumni and friends serving in the government or with political influence. Research universities in conservative states that are key economic drivers and sources of local pride might play an especially influential role.

However, even as universities show their enduring value, higher education must also acknowledge valid criticisms and forthrightly correct its shortcomings. As the socioeconomic distribution of students at too many institutions attests, we have not sufficiently prioritized college access and affordability for both low- *and* middle-income students. Most schools have not paid appropriate attention to helping new graduates get good jobs in their desired fields, much less assisting their alumni in navigating a fluid workplace across their careers. Surely, providing a superb education means students feel valued and can take full advantage of their schooling. Accordingly, institutions should adhere to the lawful goals that underlie their DEI programs. But promoting genuine inclusion should also mean that universities treat anti-Semitism or suppression of politically conservative views with the same gravity as they regard racism, sexism, homophobia, and other barriers to full participation in the academic community, always encouraging freewheeling intellectual exchanges where seriously offered ideas are responded to in kind. Carefully "righting our own ship" in these ways will be critical to securing a brighter future both for the nation's universities and for the nation itself.

20

What's the Danger of the Trump Administration's Demands on Universities?

AMY GUTMANN AND LEE BOLLINGER*

> "If a nation expects to be ignorant and free," Thomas Jefferson wrote to a Virginia legislator in 1816, ". . . it expects what never was and never will be."[1]

Gutmann: Lee, you asked me to assess the danger of the second Trump administration's demands on universities. I begin with Jefferson's warning because the evidence (a small fraction of which I will summarize below) keeps mounting that this administration's demands on American universities pose a profound danger both to universities and also to the freedom of Americans and to democracy in America. The administration is demanding substantial control over who universities hire and what they teach, while simultaneously attacking other knowledge-generating institutions for publicizing information that it deems disagreeable. If the administration's demands threatened only the freedom of American universities, that would be bad, but Jefferson's warning would seem overblown at this moment. Quite to the contrary, this administration's demands on universities—coupled with its attack on other knowledge-generating institutions—profoundly threaten to hollow out the freedom of all Americans to make informed personal and political choices on which our health, learning,

* For their helpful comments, we thank Sigal Ben-Porath, Christopher Eisgruber, Alan Garber, Stephen Macedo, Robert Post, and Penny Pritzker.

Amy Gutmann and Lee Bollinger, *What's the Danger of the Trump Administration's Demands on Universities?*. In: *Academic Freedom in the Era of Trump*. Edited by: Lee C. Bollinger and Geoffrey R. Stone, Oxford University Press. © Oxford University Press (2026). DOI: 10.1093/9780197854877.003.0021 prosperity, security, and American democracy ultimately depend. How effective this threat turns out to be will depend on how many university leaders (including presidents and trustees) along with other Americans speak out and peacefully challenge the administration's demands. I'll begin with a prime case in point.

On April 11, 2025, the administration sent Harvard University a letter with an extensive list of demands as a condition of the University's keeping its federal funding.[2] The letter made clear that over $2.2 billion that agencies of the federal government had designated for faculty research at Harvard—research concentrated in the sciences—would be canceled unless the University agreed to accede to the government's demands.[3]

The administration's demands of Harvard resembled some that it had directed to other prominent American universities, including the two universities we led, Columbia and Penn,[4] but extended much further, attacking all four of the essential freedoms of universities: who teaches, what they may teach, how they may teach, and who may be admitted to study.[5] Without due process, the Administration told Harvard that it must change its governance, hiring, and admissions.[6] It must use "viewpoint diversity" as a criterion in hiring faculty and admitting students.[7] It must "shutter all diversity, equity, and inclusion [DEI] programs."[8] It must report on all these changes quarterly to the administration.[9] It must also undertake an audit—by an administration-approved external auditor—of Harvard departments, programs, and individual faculty members "who discriminated against Jewish or Israeli students or incited students to violate Harvard's rules following October 7 [2023]."[10]

The most immediate danger of the demands is that of replacing a university's defining mission of pursuing scholarship and teaching according to scholarly standards of hiring and teaching with partisan political standards of what counts as "viewpoint diversity."[11] Demanding viewpoint diversity in faculty hiring and teaching may sound like nondiscrimination, but it is quite the contrary. It dictates who gets hired and what faculty teach according to their political viewpoints rather than their scholarly merits.

Harvard and other institutions targeted with Trump's demands are among the most eminent universities in the United States and the world. These universities carry out their defining purpose of scholarship and teaching far from perfectly but well enough to be the source of the most sought-after and productive human discoveries and the greatest number of Nobel laureates, by far, of any country in the world.[12] American universities are correspondingly the most well-respected universities worldwide.[13]

Research funding and other financial support from the government and private donors have contributed to making American universities greater powerhouses of scholarship and teaching than they otherwise could be.[14] The most powerful external sources of funding put American universities under the greatest potential pressure of compromising their academic standards.

The most prominent universities in China and other enterprising authoritarian countries are also well funded by their governments, and they have attracted some excellent scholars.[15] But these universities lack two essential, interrelated conditions of the eminence and institutional integrity of universities in the United States and other well-functioning democracies.[16] Authoritarian governments recognize neither the academic freedom of faculty nor the academic freedom of universities from political control over their scholarly and teaching standards and missions. When these freedoms are institutionalized, universities need not be afraid of contesting or otherwise calling into question what governments and their officeholders say and do, an essential condition of modern universities' being among the most reliable sources of human knowledge and learning the world has known.[17]

Academic freedom is not a household term, and as constitutional rights go in the United States it is undeveloped.[18] The relative obscurity of academic freedom makes it both important and urgent for universities to clarify what is at stake in protecting the academic freedom of universities from overreaching governmental demands.

The academic freedom of faculty members is to conduct their scholarship according to canons of truth of their scholarly disciplines without fear of sanction if they arrive at unpopular conclusions.[19] The academic freedom of the university is to determine the institutional environment that protects knowledge creation and dissemination from partisan political control and distortion.[20]

Because a nation can never expect to be "ignorant and free," the stakes of protecting academic freedom extend far beyond academia. Universities are a major source of knowledge in our democratic society—knowledge we rely upon for everything from everyday life choices to lifesaving medical discoveries—and the reliability of that knowledge depends on universities' being free from partisan political control over their research and teaching. This is why the stakes of universities' resisting Trump's demands—and the dangers of their not doing so—are far larger than the freedom of Harvard and thousands of other American universities. Absent ample resistance, the threats have multiplied and will continue to do so.

Although threats to the academic freedoms of American universities are not new, those in the Trump era are more extensive and showing no signs of abating.[21] The threat to Harvard alone ranged across standards of hiring faculty, admitting students, and conducting research and teaching.[22] The demands on Harvard are nothing less than existential threats, because the *defining purpose of universities is the pursuit of knowledge and teaching by scholarly, not political, standards.*

To better grasp these existential stakes for universities, we need imagine no further than an American university—call it Teaching and Research U (TRU for short)—facing this "either-or" ultimatum from the federal government: *Either* we will discontinue our massive federal funding of your faculties' scientific and biomedical research *or* you will grant us the authority to apply what we consider adequate viewpoint diversity in all your faculty hiring. Variations on this ultimatum carry similar existential stakes, as in the following "offer": You will be eligible for our massive federal government funding if you grant us the authority to apply what we deem adequate viewpoint diversity in your faculty hiring.[23]

In the pursuit of knowledge and understanding, TRU has established principles and policies of free expression on campus, which it prominently communicates. Its policies importantly include time, place, and manner rules to prevent disruption of its basic operations. In multiple ways, TRU teaches members of its campus community that they should welcome robust discussion of diverse perspectives, and they must not shout down people with whom they disagree or otherwise prevent them from speaking, no matter how offensive they may find their viewpoints.[24] With thousands of speakers on campus every year, TRU has dealt with a few incidents where a small minority of community members violated its open-expression policy. TRU treats even the rare occurrence as one too many. It enforces established disciplinary procedures for violations and reinforces communicating the importance of its principles. With input from its campus community, the University periodically updates and improves its content-neutral time, place, and manner rules. Regardless of the message speakers wish to convey, encampments or noise levels that were historically unanticipated (or overlooked because so rare and short-lived) are now impermissible.

Consistent with its commitment to nondiscrimination, TRU recognizes that diversity of scholarly approaches and perspectives serves the pursuit of knowledge and understanding. This is because scholarly subfields become insular—less creative and less self-correcting over time—without sufficient challenge, also on scholarly grounds. Fallible beings all, scholars share the human propensity to confirmation bias. TRU is committed to regularly conducting external peer reviews of departments, asking knowledgeable outside scholars for recommendations to improve their research and teaching excellence. External peer reviews ask whether *scholarly* approaches and perspectives that would improve its research and teaching excellence are missing in a department. True to its truth-seeking mission (and tax-exempt status as a not-for-profit association), the University stands strongly against imposing ideological litmus tests on faculty hiring, student admissions, or any other core activity. Nondiscrimination requires TRU to reject ideological litmus tests on its core activities, just as it must reject racial, religious, and gender-based litmus tests.

What then is the danger of a university's pursuing viewpoint diversity—more or less proportionally representing the range of public opinion—as such diversity is typically understood in the political domain? Unlike democratic governments, universities are not representative institutions. For the sake of achieving more viewpoint diversity, hiring biologists who deny climate change, immunologists who claim that vaccines cause autism and deny vaccine effectiveness, or historians who deny that the Holocaust happened or that slavery caused the Civil War is the scholarly equivalent of medical malpractice. In the name of viewpoint diversity, popular politicians—with public support—may pressure universities to hire faculty who represent these perspectives. Yet neither the public nor the scholarly community has any reason to trust a university as such if it itself imposes—or allows the government or any donor to impose—an ideological litmus test on faculty hiring or teaching. These are times when popularity and trustworthiness stand at odds.

At the same time, universities can and should work harder against the confirmation biases that make us all less critical of perspectives more like our own and more critical of opposing perspectives. When the American Association of University Professors [AAUP] declared its principles of academic freedom in 1915, it warned that, to the extent that faculty members display "uncritical and intemperate partisanship" in their work, they will "breed suspicions and recurrent controversies deeply injurious to the internal order and the public standing of universities."[25]

Fast-forward to 2025, and critics within the academy update the AAUP's warning while consistently rejecting Trump's demands. "Taboos, blind spots, groupthink and the politicization of scientific standards" make "academic research narrower" and also reduce "public confidence in higher education, not just on the right but across the ideological spectrum."[26] By recognizing that viewpoint diversity is not an ultimate aim of faculty hiring or teaching, universities can work against confirmation bias by including intellectual perspectives that expand and improve scholarly research and teaching.[27] To include more perspectives that are intellectually defensible, a university must be free to hire and assess faculty *by scholarly standards, not partisan political ones.*

Now imagine that, under enormous financial pressure from the federal government, TRU agrees to the government's determination of what counts as viewpoint diversity in its faculty hiring. TRU has just sacrificed an essential part of its identity as a university. It has surrendered its public trust, core to the AAUP's understanding of a university's mission in service to democracy. The freedom of universities to hire faculty by scholarly standards is an essential part of their public trust.[28] How so? The *trust* of universities is *to pursue their core mission* of scholarship and teaching in pursuit of knowledge and learning *free from partisan political demands*. The *public* nature of a university's trust is that by freely pursuing this core mission, universities *contribute mightily to the freedom, security, and prosperity of the democratic public.*

We need to be clear about the high stakes here, understanding the profound risk faced by TRU under the pressure that flows from the government's demands coupled with the university's dependency on federal funds. In his 1961 Farewell

Address, President Eisenhower noted that the federal government was funding an ever-increasing share of research propelling the technological revolution forward. Presciently, Eisenhower warned that "the prospect of domination of the nation's scholars by Federal employment, project allocations, and the power of money is ever present and is gravely to be regarded."[29]

The stakes could hardly be higher today: When a university accedes to alienating its core power and prerogative of faculty hiring, or firing, to an outside entity—whether a government or a lay board—it surrenders its academic freedom, which is essential to carrying out its public trust. This alienation of its core freedom differs from the university's need to follow discrete policy directives—whether deemed right or wrong—that honor due process and academic freedom. The federal government has placed strict export restrictions and reporting requirements on "dual-use" laboratory materials, which many universities think excessive while rightfully respecting and honoring the goal of national security. The federal government also requires and enforces antidiscrimination laws, which universities think necessary even if they sometimes disagree with the government's interpretation. In these cases, universities comply with governmental demands consistently with their public trust.

By contrast, a university's public trust critically depends on its being free from partisan political pressure in order to apply scholarly standards in hiring faculty (while observing duly promulgated nondiscrimination laws). A university's duty not to subject its scholarly standards to partisan pressure is why just one of the administration's many demands on Harvard posed no less than an existential threat to its identity and reputation as a university. Had Harvard made this concession—succumbing to partisan political standards of hiring or firing faculty—it would have entailed the loss of immeasurably more (core to its identity and reputation) than the threatened $2.2 billion retraction in federal research funding, massive as that monetary threat is.[30] Conversely, this is the reason why it would entail far less of a loss (although still an extremely regrettable one) to its core mission and to American democracy if Harvard instead agreed to pay a great deal of money, were it possible to do so with clear legal assurance that it could continue to carry out its core mission free from partisan political control.

President Trump was democratically elected, yet his mandate for Harvard and other universities, in bypassing due process and imposing the leader's favored ideological perspective of "viewpoint diversity" on an institution whose primary purpose is pursuing knowledge and learning according to scholarly standards, could have been taken out of an authoritarian playbook.

Like other universities subject to the administration's demands, Harvard reaffirmed its commitment "to fighting antisemitism and other forms of bigotry in its community . . . while fostering open inquiry in a pluralistic community free from intimidation and open to challenging orthodoxies."[31] Unlike other universities that were subject to a subset of similar demands, Harvard's responded with a resounding public rejection of the administration's rotten offer.[32] The offer was rotten, analogous to the reason some compromises are rotten, because it boiled down to "Cede us your core freedom or we will take back our federal funding of your scientific research."[33]

Harvard's exemplary response made clear what was at stake for the University: "The university will not surrender its independence or relinquish its constitutional rights. Neither Harvard nor any other private university can allow itself to be taken over by the federal government. . . . Harvard is not prepared to agree to demands that go beyond the lawful authority of this or any administration."[34] Harvard clearly signaled that it would go to court, if necessary, to defend its constitutional rights and independence.[35] Notably, its reply did not use the term "academic freedom." Preparing to argue its case in court, while also making its case to the public, Harvard pointedly referred to protecting both its constitutional rights and its independence from being "taken over" by the federal government. Referring to the protection of constitutional rights and freedom from government takeover signals that more is at stake in Harvard's successful defense than academic freedom, as important as that freedom alone is.

The evidence is overwhelming in this moment that, if we want to safeguard the freedom, security, and prosperity of the American people, we must protect the basic freedom of American universities. We are led to conclude this, first, by heeding Jefferson's warning that our nation cannot be both ignorant and free, and, second, by "connecting the dots" of the many threats both to American universities and to so many other institutions that produce and convey knowledge. At stake in defending the freedom of universities is nothing less than the ability of Americans to have a decent level of confidence in the knowledge we need for making decisions in our private and public lives. Our public decisions importantly include holding our government accountable.

Evidence that the threat to the freedom of universities extends to all Americans is that, not coincidentally, we are also seeing simultaneous attacks by the administration against many other knowledge-generating institutions, including the press and media outlets, the Centers for Disease Control and Prevention, the Bureau of Labor Statistics, the Federal Reserve, law firms, philanthropic foundations and other NGOs, and branches of the military and its academies.[36] Their missions range very widely, yet significantly converge in a core dedication to discovering and disseminating reliable information, regardless of how controversial it may be. These attacks unmistakably target institutions and people who are reporting information that displeases the president and that he apparently deems relevant to his success.

Consider a small but representative sampling of lead stories during one (normally slow) news week, the first week of August 2025—three examples of the administration's firing, defunding, or threats thereof in just a single week that relate in their rationale to its attack on the academic freedom of universities. What these stories (and many others) share is key to understanding the broader political stakes of the administration's attack on the academic freedom of universities.

August 1, 2025: "President Trump ordered the firing of Commissioner of the Bureau of Labor Statistics Erika McEntarfer, asserting without evidence that the government's jobs numbers have been manipulated for political purposes. . . . 'In my opinion, today's Jobs Numbers were RIGGED in order to make the Republicans, and ME, look bad,' Trump wrote in a subsequent [social media] post."[37] As the *Wall Street Journal* reported: "The president's move throws the quality of America's statistical apparatus into question."[38]

Also on August 1, 2025: "President Donald Trump on Friday upped his attacks on Federal Reserve Chair Jerome Powell [whom he appointed in 2017], calling for the central bank's policymakers to 'assume control' of the Fed's policy decisions. Trump . . . took to his Truth Social platform . . . to urge the Federal Reserve's Board of Governors to take control from Powell if he resists immediate interest rate cuts, writing: 'Jerome 'Too Late' Powell, a stubborn MORON, must substantially lower interest rates, NOW. IF HE CONTINUES TO REFUSE, THE BOARD SHOULD ASSUME CONTROL, AND DO WHAT EVERYONE KNOWS HAS TO BE DONE!'"[39]

August 6, 2025: "Health and Human Services (HHS) Secretary Robert F. Kennedy Jr.'s decision this week to cancel hundreds of millions of dollars in mRNA vaccine funding will leave the United States unprepared for the next pandemic and other public-health emergencies, public-health experts warned. 'I've tried to be objective & non-alarmist in response to current HHS actions—but quite frankly this move is going to cost lives,' President Trump's former surgeon general, Jerome Adams, said in a post on the social platform X."[40]

There is a common pattern, a playbook, to firing Commissioner McEntarfer based on the fabricated allegation of her rigging the data, to insulting and calling on the Board to topple Chairman Powell, and to canceling mRNA funding based on false claims about its dangers. The playbook is authoritarian. It uses political power to deny or suppress sources of information and evidence that support the freedom of citizens to hold their representatives accountable and to make decisions about their own lives. Undermining the knowledge basis of the freedom of American citizens is what these attacks have in common with the administration's threat to defund American universities if they don't compromise their academic freedom.

Every week before and since these attacks has typically brought new official threats or actions to defund, restrict, punish, and disparage informed sources of evidence, information, and expert judgment related to Americans' holding our political leaders accountable and making decisions affecting our lives, those of our children and community members, and other vulnerable individuals. Not all the threats and actions are carried through or successful, but many have been, and together they send a clear signal, worthy only of an authoritarian regime: Beware of publicly disseminating knowledge, information, or simply an opinion that displeases the President.

Sometimes, as in the case of denying the effectiveness of proven vaccines and defunding mRNA research, the knowledge is key to making life-and-death decisions, and the defunding will likely result in millions of lost lives.[41] In many other cases—such as disparaging and firing those who refuse to doctor expert economic evidence or stifle their own judgment to suit the President's political ambitions—the threat to freedom is more indirect but similarly profound.[42] It impedes the public's ability to understand the state of the American economy and further undermines trust in what appointed public officials tell them.

Circling back to the opening question: What's the danger of the Trump administration's demands on universities? A "fast thinking" response based on accumulated experience and expertise can answer a significant part of this question. We can observe some of the immediate and short-term harm done within the targeted universities. With research funding cut and endowment taxes about to be raised by billions, universities are laying off staff, reducing scholarship funding, becoming less desirable employers and less affordable to low-income and middle-income students.[43] International students are targeted for exclusion, and diversity, equity, and inclusion programs have been abandoned, altered, or renamed—often in anticipatory reaction to the administration's expected punitive actions.[44] The most vulnerable students, faculty, and staff are far more fearful and naturally feel excluded, no matter how much assurance university leaders give them about their ongoing commitments. Fear has become rampant.

Yet these dangers only begin to capture the damage in process of being done. To take a prime example: When the administration causes massive amounts of promising research to be halted for lack of funding or because it does not meet its ideological standards, untold discoveries will not be made that will slow down the American economy, and untold millions of lives will likely be lost that otherwise would have been saved.[45] We need only recognize that federal research funding enabled the discovery of the mRNA platform that in turn made it possible to quickly develop lifesaving vaccines during the Covid-19 pandemic, thanks also to the first Trump Administration's Operation Warp Speed.[46] What a sad irony that the very same president who launched Operation Warp Speed is now threatening the peer-review-based system of federal research funding that was essential to saving millions of lives during the pandemic.[47]

"Slow thinking"—careful consideration of long-term repercussions beyond universities—will more completely answer the question as posed: What's the damage (not only to universities) of the administration's demands on universities?[48] We also must consider the damage to freedom and democracy in America by the ongoing erosion of the foundations of public knowledge in our society. It will take a more extensive analysis, which I've only begun here, to assess how profoundly threats to the academic freedom of universities, coupled with concurrent attacks on other sources of knowledge, endanger freedom and democracy in America and beyond.

The endangerment of our freedom and of our democracy is likely to be profound, because both freedom and democracy become hollow shells without public access to reliable information and knowledge, which depend on politically independent sources. This is also why the commitment of universities to protect the scholarly freedom of their faculty is publicly important. When a major cause of the danger to freedom and to democracy becomes *insidious* knowledge deprivation and deception by government rather than outright censorship, the jeopardy is less likely to be obvious to most people.[49]

Consistently with believing that the world's best universities can do better in promoting the scholarly pursuit of truth[50]—and for many of the very same reasons—we must fervently oppose ceding to government the power to manage the basic scholarly functions of our universities, which centrally include hiring faculty, admitting students, and designing courses of study and research.[51] The more our government succeeds in controlling these defining features of universities, the more power they have in depriving the American people of knowledge, and the more "we the people" lose *the powers we need to make informed decisions by our own best lights.*

Among those essential powers in American democracy is the ability to criticize what our government is doing. Disinformation coupled with firing and defunding critics and the institutions that support them discourages, and in many cases demoralizes, people who might otherwise speak out. Justice Louis Brandeis famously said that American constitutional democracy depends on the power of a "courageous, self-reliant" people, people who neither "fear political change" nor "exalt order at the cost of liberty."[52] I call this power and virtue of democratic citizens "civic courage." In a stable constitutional democracy, civic courage requires gumption and resilience: it's risky but not life-threatening. By upping short-term risks, targeting critics and bearers of unwelcome information, the second Trump Administration is also upping the ante on civic courage.

Whatever we the people want to know in order to assess our leaders, those leaders and their enablers are undermining our freedom and disempowering us as citizens when they deprive, deceive, and threaten us about these matters. Just as our personal freedom depends on knowledge necessary to make informed decisions in our own lives, so our political freedom depends on knowledge necessary to hold our politicians accountable. That is why "if a nation expects to be ignorant and free, . . . it expects what never was and never will be."[53]

Governments, including American presidential administrations, generally seek to increase their power. This is one reason why both separation of powers and checks and balances in government are so important, when they work.[54] One omnipresent temptation of powerful public officials is to deceive people who might oppose them, including by depriving them of the knowledge needed to hold officials accountable for their decisions.[55]

Nothing I have said here about the second Trump administration should be taken to deny that other American presidential administrations have engaged in some degree of dangerous deception. University faculty, by virtue of their scholarly commitment and freedom from partisan political control, can discover deceptions and call them to the public's attention, including when their findings offend the widely shared convictions of their own colleagues.[56] Faculty also freely challenge their own colleagues. All their claims are subject to rebuttal in the public domain.

Degrees of deception matter. Pervasive political deception from the top challenges the general well-being of a democracy. To witness anything approaching the second Trump administration's combination of deception, its demands to directly oversee the core missions of universities, and its attempts at controlling other sources of reliable knowledge and information preservation, production, and dissemination, we need to return in American history to the days of McCarthyism and the Red Scare.[57] Princeton University President Christopher Eisgruber, not prone to exaggeration, characterized the Trump administration's demands of Columbia University as "presenting the greatest threat to American universities since the Red Scare of the 1950s. Every American should be concerned."[58] Eisgruber assessed the gravity of this threat before the administration delivered its more extensive threats to Harvard and other universities.[59]

The greatest threat to the freedom of universities since McCarthyism is contemporaneous with an extensive attack on the press and many other sources of knowledge that help American citizens hold our public officials accountable.[60] Accountability of the government to the people is a defining principle of constitutional democracy. Academic freedom and freedom of the press are irreplaceable means to democratic accountability.[61] Yet this democratically elected president and his administration generally speak and act as if the only people who should hold them accountable are those who agree, and are willing to publicly profess agreement, with the president. *This is the accountability principle of an authoritarian leader.*

Having identified some profound dangers to universities and more broadly to freedom and democracy in America, we need to ask how individuals and institutions can effectively resist and counter them.

While it's important to begin by publicly identifying the dangers of "competitive authoritarians,"[62] this is not enough. We must also find ways of countering and resisting the danger, by having the courage to speak out publicly against the threats. Because no less than the president and many in his administration are targeting critics with threats, demands, and penalties, exercising our freedom to speak out critically as democratic citizens takes a greater level of civic courage than usual. Still, such civic courage, unlike military courage, typically does not risk our lives or basic livelihoods. It impels us to speak up against threats to freedom and democracy, to call out the threats for what they are, and to do what we can to defend the endangered individuals and institutions. When we do so, as the findings of both political science and neuroscience demonstrate, we incentivize others to join in, exercising their freedom of dissent in the knowledge that they have allies.[63] Only when facing resistance are bullies likely to back down.

University leaders can resist demands to compromise the academic freedom of their university and join with other leaders to speak up in defense of their peers under threat, even when their institutions risk the loss of significant federal funding. Overcoming a far-ranging assault from the highest levels of government will take much more resistance and unity than we have yet seen. Publicly supporting resistance is an important way of incentivizing it. Seven out of nine university presidents clearly rejected the Trump Administration's offer of favorable treatment in the awarding of research funding on conditions such as abolishing units that "belittle" conservative ideas and "defining and otherwise interpreting 'male,' 'female,' 'woman,' and 'man' according to reproductive function and biological processes" (regardless of what anyone's academic expertise suggests). These provisions, among others, "would restrict academic freedom. . . . Additionally, a fundamental part of academic excellence is awarding research funding on the merits of the research being proposed."[64] Student along with faculties of these and many other universities have become exemplary defenders of academic freedom. But a unified chorus of university leaders across academia defending these universities' resistance—and communicating their contributions to the freedom, security, and prosperity of our country—would be more effective.

Judges and courts can uphold rights of due process and recognize the ever-increasing role that academic freedom plays in upholding the democratic public's First Amendment right to free speech.[65] Journalists and social-media influencers and mavens can spotlight inspiring exemplars of civic courage in these times. They can powerfully convey in stories what history amply demonstrates. Democracies under the threat of democratically elected authoritarians fare best when citizens and their civic leaders speak up and resist threats early and often, and when a significant percentage of a country's population publicly and peacefully demonstrates its opposition.[66]

Lee, what do you think universities and courts should do in these circumstances to contribute to this resistance, and why? Considering the threat that the Trump administration poses to academic freedom *and* to American freedom and democracy, how do you think universities and courts can best address these threats to the very foundations of knowledge, freedom, and democracy in America?

Bollinger: We are in agreement on every step of your argument. Universities seek to advance knowledge according to well-honed professional scholarly standards that emphasize independent thinking and reliance on objective information and reason. They are inherently nonpartisan, although the outcome of that scholarship will often bring important information and ideas into the public realm. They are a public trust. And citizens in a democracy depend on the yield of the scholarly endeavor to make important decisions about their future and to hold those in power to account. The efforts by the government to use the leverage of federal funding, especially of science, to gain control of the academic process is a direct assault on the enormously successful system of higher education.

As you rightly go on to say, this assault on universities is part of a broader pattern of attacks on officials and institutions in order to disrupt and seize control of the sources of information and knowledge we need and trust in to deliberate and make good collective decisions. The destruction of independently derived knowledge will eventually drain the vitality from our democracy.

The disturbing campaign is, by far, the worst we have witnessed in our lifetimes, and it is only the first eight months of the new administration. Where this will end, what resistance will arise and be necessary to halt and reverse the progress of this alarming authoritarian trend, it is difficult to say at this point.

One thing needed for sure is a much more robust conception of the role and rights of universities in the American system of constitutional government. As you note, in *University: A Reckoning* I have tried to draw together a deep understanding of universities—their unique and irreplaceable structure, their extraordinary vitality, their amazing contributions, and yet their fragility and vulnerability—with an equally strong grasp of the development of the First Amendment and its profound commitment to the search for knowledge and truth, and to see in the relationship an emerging principle of the freedom of the university (or academic freedom). The system, or network, of our colleges and universities is a constitutional good we should all recognize as so important to the nation that it should be embedded in a First Amendment principle, disallowing any government intrusion into academic decision-making unless the government can meet the highest burdens of constitutional law (namely, demonstrating a "compelling state interest"). To achieve this constitutional standing must be a long-term goal of our universities, but there are threads of support in the jurisprudence we can draw on.

We know that there are a variety of Supreme Court cases over the past century where the Court and individual justices have spoken powerfully about the importance of maintaining academic control over the various aspects of university life and shielding that process from government interventions.[67] But we do not have, as of yet, a well-developed and articulated constitutional vision for this notion of a principle of the freedom of the university. There is a close analogy to be drawn with the more developed idea of the "press" having a special standing under the First Amendment, of having rights distinctive to the institutions of the press. That too, however, is not firmly ensconced in our constitutional doctrines. The upshot is that there is work to be done in building the case for strong constitutional protections of universities (and the press). To my mind, this must be a key focus of universities now and for many years and decades ahead. To be honest, I wish universities right now would join together in trying to make that case.

Given our overlapping yet different scholarly backgrounds (mine in constitutional law and yours in political science and theory), it is not at all surprising that I would turn to the First Amendment for help and you to the foundational and functional ideas of American democracy. I am intrigued by your idea of conceiving of the principle of academic freedom in terms of a "public trust." That concept also has a rich, and even profound, history in our law and jurisprudence. But I sense that you are drawing on thinking in political science. Could you say more about that?

And could we spend some time thinking about your recommendation of standing up to call out and resist the troublesome trends we see unfolding, beginning with universities. I have to say that, given the many years both you and I spent leading universities, I believe we would have wanted to make urgent efforts to organize universities in mounting a more forceful resistance to what we are seeing. I also believe that effort would have tried to join with other sectors of the society also under threat (e.g., major law firms, corporations, press and media). What do you think?

Gutmann: We agree on the need for strong constitutional protections to safeguard the freedom of American universities, and freedom of thought. We both also urge university leaders—along with leaders in law, business, press and the media—to demonstrate the strength of their commitment to these freedoms by speaking out and uniting in opposition to partisan political attacks. That unity needs to take different forms, depending on what's likely to be most timely and effective—from filing lawsuits, signing amicus briefs, to speaking out as coordinated groups and also individually with clear and consistent messages. Communications need to access not only traditional but also new media outlets to reach diverse audiences.

You ask that I reflect a bit more here as a political scientist and democratic theorist—and I would add also as the daughter of a refugee from Nazi Germany—on the public trust of universities, which encompasses their rights and responsibilities under political threat. These reflections suggest why universities and their allies can and must do more in our present moment.

The academic freedom of universities conceived as a public trust in a democracy was core to the American Association of University Professors' founding *1915 Declaration*: "If the institutions of learning in a democracy are to serve the state and the public, they must be conceived as a public trust."[68] This conception finds grounding not only in American law but also, and most foundationally, in democratic politics.[69] I would trace the rights and responsibilities of university freedom to a core principle of democracy, the informed consent by the governed. "We the people" have a basic right to hold our governments accountable, and that right depends on the sources of our knowledge and understanding being independent of partisan political power.[70]

With their essential academic freedoms protected, universities generate the scientific and humanistic knowledge essential to many of our personal choices, as varied and important as health care, reading, and reproduction.[71] Academic breakthroughs become the basis for the productive economy upon which Americans rely for growing employment, prosperity, and opportunity for us, our children, and future generations.[72] Millions of talented young people graduate each year from American universities, likely the single greatest contribution these institutions make to our country's strength.

For American universities to serve all of these public purposes, they must be free from partisan political control over hiring faculty, teaching and research, and admitting students. Universities accept a corresponding responsibility to carry out their mission for the good of the American public. This idea of universities serving the public interest, not by external command but as a public trust, is deeply rooted in the modern political history of American universities.[73]

Starting with its earliest *Declaration of Principles* in 1915, the Association of American University Professors recognized not only rights to academic freedom of faculty members but also their responsibilities as "primarily to the public itself, and to the judgment of [their] own profession."[74] Tracing the roots of this understanding in American political history sheds light on its importance in both protecting American universities and advancing the public interest.

In 1915, amid surging threats to the freedom of universities and their faculty members during World War I, John Dewey, the most eminent American philosopher of democracy and education, became the first president of the newly formed American Association of University Professors.[75] An early impetus to creating the AAUP was the forced resignation in 1900 of a popular Stanford University sociology professor, Edward Ross. Ross had populist views on railroads and was vehemently anti-immigrant, calling (on racial and eugenic grounds, among others) for a complete prohibition on Japanese and Chinese immigration to the United States.[76] Strongly objecting to Ross's political views, university board member Jane Stanford, the widow of railroad magnate and university founder Leland Stanford, pressured Stanford's president, who in turn pressured Ross to resign. Seven Stanford faculty members resigned in protest with Ross, including the philosopher and historian of ideas Arthur O. Lovejoy, who would later partner with Dewey in cofounding the AAUP.

With the strong support and input of eminent faculty members nationwide, the AAUP issued its signature *Declaration of Principles of Academic Freedom and Academic Tenure* in 1915. That document recognized the university as essential to America's "public interest" and to the progress of "civilization."[77]

To serve the public interest and the progress of civilization, the AAUP recognized that a university needs to conceive of itself and be treated as a public trust. So conceived, a university has both the *right* not to be controlled in ways that interfere with its academic freedom and the correlative *responsibility* to exercise academic judgment in its academic operations. Those academic operations centrally include who a university hires and what, how, and whom it teaches. In short, *a university must serve society but not be subservient* either to political authorities or to the dominant public opinion in its defining missions of research and teaching.[78]

It follows from the university being a public trust that university leaders are responsible for resisting partisan and authoritarian threats to academic freedom. These ever-present threats surged in modern American democracy during World Wars I and II, and in the McCarthy era with a government-sponsored witch hunt against "un-American" Communist sympathizers.[79] Long before American universities faced today's surge of threats from the Trump administration, academic leaders had ample cause, informed by this history, to be perpetually on high alert.

This abbreviated political history helps explain why, at the first Global Colloquium of University Presidents in 2005—hosted by you at Columbia University—we helped organize other university presidents in the United States and worldwide to support the cause of defending the freedom of universities. Our first action was to draft and issue a joint public statement on the importance of academic freedom to all our societies, a statement that was signed by university presidents in societies as diverse as the United States, India, South Africa, Turkey, Australia, Germany, France, Israel, and the Palestinian West Bank.[80]

As university presidents, we both would have urgently wanted to fearlessly support universities and other civic allies in a unified resistance to today's authoritarian incursions in the United States, before the attacks escalated. What we would have done as university presidents today of course can only be speculative.

But it's not speculation that, as former presidents, immediately after learning of the Trump administration's assault on Harvard, we issued a strong public critique of that assault and defense of Harvard's academic freedom. Eighty colleagues joined us on a few hours' notice.[81] Many sitting university presidents reached out to us, expressing appreciation for incentivizing them to speak together in Harvard's defense, which they did a week later. Christopher Eisgruber of Princeton, Michael Roth of Wesleyan, Alan Garber of Harvard, and Gregory Washington of George Mason are prominent among those who continue to speak out in resistance, but too few sitting presidents appear to be doing so.[82]

To serve their public trust, university presidents along with their trustees need to be doing their darndest to join the cause of their universities with others and also with major law firms, small and large businesses, press and media, and any other civic associations under related attacks. The stakes become higher and successful resistance harder when the attacks escalate.

Here too I learned some essential lessons from the more extreme cases of authoritarian attacks on freedom, including the horrors that law-abiding citizens like my father witnessed in the early days of Nazism. Most German universities—once famous worldwide for their dedication to knowledge production (*Wissenschaft*) and its component freedoms of learning and teaching (*Lehrfreiheit* and *Lernfreiheit*)—became complicit, first by remaining silent and then by anticipating authoritarian directives and obeying out of fear if not agreement.[83] The attacks on freedom of speech and thought—and then on life itself—only escalated over time.

The threats to freedom in America today are not the same as even the earliest fascist threats in 20th-century Europe or the more recent authoritarian attacks by Hungarian President Orbán on the Central European University (CEU).[84] Yet we can learn essential lessons from how deference to political threats to and by universities contributes to the easier erosion, and later to the total destruction, of personal and political freedoms. One lesson is the importance of universities speaking out and resisting the earliest threats and also uniting whenever possible with other institutions to resist incursions on basic freedoms.[85]

The most effective resistance is when civic leaders and citizens join together in large and politically diverse groups to clearly communicate to a broad public what the ongoing authoritarian incursions are.[86] Diverse leaders and citizens are well positioned to convey clearly why attacks on the freedom of universities are so dangerous, not only (or even mainly) to academics but to the American public. Leaders of American universities—along with leaders of other sectors—need to champion and to communicate a perspective of how teaching and research serve the public by virtue of not being politically subservient. Peaceful public resistance to authoritarian incursions on universities and other institutions serves as an important supplement to reliance on constitutional law.[87]

I have no doubt, given the stakes, that we also should work every promising legal strategy. Yet I worry that too few Supreme Court cases speak directly to academic freedom.[88] Will the Court as it is constituted today and for the foreseeable future rely on past judgments (and in several cases on dicta) in those cases? Lee, am I too pessimistic with regard to the Supreme Court today expanding a university's power to mount a successful legal defense based primarily on academic freedom (rather than on due process and unconstitutional conditions)?

Whatever our courts do, we must take to heart what the history of our country and democracies worldwide teach: laws only stay as strong over time as the democratic culture supporting them.[89] This is yet another reason why as many people as possible need to speak publicly about—and unite in defending—the critical importance of universities serving the public interest, as a public trust. Universities' leaders need to convincingly convey this trust to the American public. The access of American citizens to knowledge uncontrolled by political authorities is essential not only to our basic freedom to hold governments accountable but also to live our lives as we—rather than partisan political authorities—see fit.

We depend on knowledge to make daily decisions much as we rely on oxygen to breathe. We cannot live our lives by constantly inquiring into the sources of knowledge any more than we can constantly inquire into the sources of the air we inhale. When the knowledge we rely upon is polluted by what pleases today's political authorities, our personal and political freedoms are unnoticeably but radically diminished over time.

To be treated as trustworthy, however, it sure helps to be trusted by the public. Gallup polls show that the American public's trust in universities and many other civic associations plunged over the past decade.[90] This presents universities with a profound challenge. To better secure their ability to serve effectively as a public trust, universities need to do what they can to gain the public's trust without succumbing to populist demands that, however popular, violate the university's core mission and make them untrustworthy. Clear and consistent public communication of the university's core mission is essential work that has long been neglected.

In the spirit of never letting a crisis go to waste, university leaders who resist the frontal assault on academic freedom can seize this opportunity to shine a brighter spotlight on the public importance of the university's mission. They can highlight the many creative contributions and lifesaving benefits made possible by university research as they also work to broaden *scholarly* approaches and perspectives in those fields where it would improve research and teaching excellence. By resisting the assaults on academic freedom, universities maintain their integrity while risking the loss of precious research funding, but they also gain a more prominent public platform to tell stories that resonate with diverse audiences who are potential allies. They can show how mightily universities contribute to educational and economic opportunity, and to both the freedom and the prosperity of the American people, starting in their own communities and radiating out across the country.

Recognizing that the democratic foundations of liberty and prosperity are under major assault by the Trump administration today is therefore essential. To the extent that universities recognize and resist the assaults and communicate the stakes of their resistance for their communities and country, they incentivize the support of others. From the very creation of American democracy, its survival and progress have depended on independent institutions and their leaders and members in resisting autocracy.[91] Today we still have a chance to counter and resist the authoritarian attacks on American universities and other institutional (and individual) sources of knowledge. To invoke Benjamin Franklin's wisdom at the time of our nation's creation, "we must hang together, or, most assuredly, we shall all hang separately."[92] Will enough university leaders and others resist these assaults, call out their dangers, and unite in defending endangered individuals and institutions?

Studying the rise of authoritarianism in democracies teaches us that the more civic leaders and citizens who resist threats to freedom and defend those most threatened, the more likely a democracy is to secure freedom and survive in more than name only. Many leaders in America today who recognize the threat are not speaking out or publicly supporting the few who have done so. It's not too late for civic leaders and citizens to use their collective power to bend the arc of American history forward toward freedom. History tells us, however, that time alone is not on our side.

Lee, would you say more about how the judicial system, and in particular the Supreme Court, can better defend the freedom of universities? What would you recommend universities do to make it more likely that they win legal battles and gain more of the public's trust?

Bollinger: Thank you, Amy. Let me just say how much I like your metaphor of how information and knowledge are like the air we breathe, and the oxygen we need to live, and of how we need to be concerned about polluting the processes by which we obtain that air through acts of censorship and distortion for political purposes. The image is especially vivid and apt for what we are facing.

As to your comments and questions about the principle of academic freedom, or freedom of the university, and the potential for the Supreme Court to provide a robust defense of the principle, I have several thoughts. Honestly, I do not know how the current Supreme Court would come out on challenges to the Administration's attacks and intrusions into traditional academic decision-making. The principle itself is noted in several of the Court's decisions spanning over a half century. Yet it is, as we have noted, underdeveloped.[93] That ambiguity about the reach of the First Amendment is compounded by the fact that the administration is threatening to withhold funding rather than to act directly and seize control of universities. In other words, the government today is saying, "We choose not to fund your academic scholarship unless you abide by our conditions for receiving those funds, which include giving over multiple areas of your decisions about hiring faculty, selecting students, and what to teach and how to teach." Under First Amendment jurisprudence as it now stands, that, too, is an area of some uncertainty. The government surely has a "right" under the First Amendment to speak as it wishes, including how it distributes its funds; yet, we also know that, given the massive spending by the federal government, the government could, if left unchecked, easily accomplish through its funding decisions what it is constitutionally forbidden to do through direct censorship. There are a number of cases on this issue of so-called "unconstitutional conditions," but they are few in number and more ambiguous than we might like.[94] Lastly, the authoritarian maneuvers of the Trump administration are largely taken under the guise of noble ends (e.g., preventing invidious discrimination), which will require the Court to look beneath the surface of the legal claims and see these as pretexts for crushing the independent-mindedness and objectivity of universities, which is what really rankles the government.

All that said, I remain optimistic about the Court responding favorably to a strong challenge should it come from threatened universities. The idea of universities having a special standing and deserving special protections under the First Amendment is well-enough established and, certainly, highly consistent with the rationales of freedom of speech and press, and this gives us a head start. That, coupled with the obviousness of the government's overreach into traditional areas of academic decision-making to intimidate universities into submission and reduce disfavored viewpoints, seems to me compelling, even for justices otherwise skeptical of intervening in government funding decisions. I would also note that, in the constitutional area of the First Amendment, there is far more unity of thinking among conservative and liberal justices than in most other areas (abortion, for example). Indeed, many of our strongest First Amendment decisions have been authored by conservative justices and joined by their liberal colleagues.[95] This shared heightened sensitivity to government encroachments into freedom of speech could bode well for the positions universities should be taking.

Still, we have a lot of work to do in building the identity and character of our universities, especially in explaining how they collectively fit within our political and constitutional system. I believe that we have suffered from a prolonged and carefully orchestrated attack on our academic institutions, one filled with misrepresentations and mischaracterizations and designed to weaken public respect and support. Clearly, this movement has sadly had success, as shown by the polls you refer to. But we have also not done well in responding to these attacks and correcting the record. So, we certainly start from a deficit. Yet we also have very far to go once we regain the base of trust and then want to articulate and persuade the public and the courts that the American system of higher education is not only a source of great material benefits but also a profound manifestation, and implementation, of the nation's commitment to carry forward and expand human knowledge. The American press has done a better job, in my view, of developing the identity of an institution devoted to serving the public's right to know, so much so that it merits the title of the Fourth Branch of Government. While that, too, is being contested, and while the emergence of the Internet has undermined the traditional press's economic health and therefore the viability of its special constitutional role, our system of universities has, at the very least, an equally important systemic function in fulfilling the nation's desire for knowledge—all the more critical as the press fades. I would even go so far as to label the American university as the Fifth Branch of Government.

I have no doubt, however, that pursuing a constitutional basis for the principle of freedom of the university, or of academic freedom, is one extremely important route for universities to take. Like you, I am gratified that Harvard has, so far, taken the lead in defending and articulating the principle. But the principle must be strengthened and fortified in our consciousness, both within universities as well as in the society. Because of what we face now, and presumably will continue to face for some time, this is both an immediate task and a long-term mission. If we get through this difficult and dangerous period and then let everything just go back to normal, we will have failed to learn an important lesson about what can befall us if we are not careful.

I am pleased that you raised the Global Colloquium of University Presidents, in 2005, where we gathered US and international universities to speak out about academic freedom. What strikes me now is how tacitly confident we were that nothing like what we are experiencing now would ever happen in the United States. We assembled in order to project the idea of academic freedom out into the world, to express our solidarity with universities abroad that were under threat. At least in my case, I did not have the imagination to foresee how devastating a blow to the independence of universities we would encounter in just two decades here in the United States.

So, we should use this moment to begin placing the building blocks for a much stronger idea of freedom of the university. That will have many different facets. We need to be looking for favorable opportunities for using litigation to articulate and advocate for the principle. (In *University: A Reckoning,* I offer a few examples.) And, we need to put into operation a plan to create support within the public at large for the concept. Much of this has to begin at home, as it were—that is, within universities themselves. We are far too separate and independent institutionally. Collective action among universities is very hard to achieve. Even expressions of support for those inappropriately attacked is not a given; it takes work and convincing. Yet the strongest version of the principle of the freedom of the university is for the system itself, not for discrete universities or individual professors. This need for bringing colleges and universities together in pursuit of the rights of the network will require real and sustained labor and commitment. Eventually, we should hope to see collateral institutions develop that have as their mission defending academic freedom, in the way that we see with a host of organizations that work on freedom of the press. But, in the end, what progress we will make toward strengthening the basic principle will depend on there being a much more unified and common commitment, inevitably at the expense of some institutional independence. As a network, we will be able to do so much more. But we'll need a different mindset among university leaders.

I would conclude by highlighting what you say about the interaction between our political culture and how our laws are interpreted and applied. I think this is profoundly important. These are not independent and unrelated elements of the society. Of course, the whole subject of how the Constitution and laws are understood over generations is one of immense complexity and intense debate. But it seems undeniable that the public's grasp of its deepest commitments and values is, in the end, the most powerful source of what happens over time. Law can help shape that, but the political culture can shape law, too. For the future meaning of freedom of the university, or academic freedom, therefore, universities will need to concentrate and work in all dimensions, whether it's the themes of a "public trust" or a principle of the First Amendment. No theory should go unexplored or unpursued.

Gutmann: Lee, you aptly began our exchange by asking me how to *appraise* the dangers to academic freedom in the Trump era, and then we transitioned to how to *address* them. In concluding, I want only to underscore the need for more work both by universities and also, as you suggest, across many institutions. Universities need to lead with their core values and consistently practice and continually communicate them, including in managing crises when "results will be imperfect."[96] For this crisis not tragically to go to waste, concerned Americans need to engage multiple associations, some as old as (or even older than) our country and others newly created for this effort. We have a lot of work ahead of us.

The "we" begins with all those who lead and care about universities, the press, and other institutions that disseminate knowledge and depend on freedom of inquiry. We must judiciously speak out, calling on our courts and everyone who cares about our Constitution and the rule of law to help by upholding the freedom of universities, and freedom of thought and inquiry more generally. Of greatest and ultimate importance—and a subject worthy of attention in its own right—we must do more to serve, to engage, and to earn the trust of all Americans for the vital role universities have played and must continue to play in furthering freedom, prosperity, and security in our democracy.

NOTES

Opening Dialogue

1. Ellen W. Schrecker, No Ivory Tower: McCarthyism and the Universities (Oxford University Press, 1986).
2. Richard C. Atkinson & William A. Blanpied, *Research Universities: Core of the US Science and Technology System*, 30 *Tech. in Soc'y* 30, 38–39 (2008).
3. Lee C. Bollinger, University: A Reckoning (W.W. Norton, 2026).
4. Nicholas Havey & Xiong Her, *The Politics of the Professoriate: A Social Media Approach*, 48 Rev. of Higher Educ. 583, 597 (2025); Foundation for Individual Rights and Expression, *The Academic Mind in 2022: What Faculty Think About Free Expression and Academic Freedom on Campus* (2022) https://www.thefire.org/research-learn/academic-mind-2022-what-faculty-think-about-free-expression-and-academic-freedom ("Overall, half of the faculty surveyed identified as liberal, 17% identified as moderate, and just over one-quarter (26%) identified as conservative.").
5. Megan Brenan, *U.S. Political Parties Historically Polarized Ideologically*, Gallup (Jan. 16, 2025) (noting that in 2024, 37 percent of Americans described their political views as "very conservative," 34 percent as "moderate," and 25 percent as "very liberal" or "liberal").
6. *See, e.g.*, Gabriel Rossman, How to Get More Conservatives in Academia, City Journal (Feb. 10, 2025), https://www.city-journal.org/article/academia-conservatives-universities-ideological.
7. Foundation for Individual Rights and Expression, *The Academic Mind in 2022: What Faculty Think About Free Expression and Academic Freedom on Campus* (2022), https://www.thefire.org/research-learn/academic-mind-2022-what-faculty-think-about-free-expression-and-academic-freedom (noting that "[o]ne-third of faculty reported that they self-censor on campus 'fairly' or 'very' often, a figure that does not compare favorably to the 21% of students who said they felt this way in FIRE's 2022 CFSR survey," and also that conservative students and faculty report self-censoring more commonly than their moderate or liberal peers).

Chapter 1

1. We might date the official striking of the bargain to the issuance of the authoritative *1940 Statement of Principles on Academic Freedom and Tenure*, which was endorsed by over 180 educational organizations and has become "the general norm of academic practice in the United States." William W. Van Alstyne, *Academic Freedom and the First Amendment in the Supreme Court of the United States: An Unhurried Historical Review*, 53 Law & Contemp. Probs. 79, 79 (1990). *See* Browzin v. Catholic Univ. of Am., 527 F.2d 843, 848 and n.8 (D.C. Cir. 1975) (The *1940 Statement* represents "widely shared norms within the academic community, having achieved acceptance by organizations which represent teachers as well as organizations

which represent college administrators and governing boards"). The *1940 Statement* may be found in American Association of University Professors, Policy Documents and Reports 3–11 (9th ed. 2001) [AAUP Redbook]. The principles of the *1940 Statement* are typically incorporated into contracts between faculty and the university or college that hires them. The *1940 Statement* is quite clear about the underlying bargain that supports academic freedom. It states that "Institutions of higher education are conducted for the common good. . . . The common good depends upon the free search for truth and its free exposition."

2. *German Universities*, 96 North American Rev. 447, 463 (Apr. 1, 1863). At the time, academic freedom frequently designated giving students "the greatest possible freedom in the choice and in the range of . . . studies, instead of forcing upon all alike a single traditional curriculum." *Inaugural Address Delivered to the University of St. Andrews*, 105 North American Review 291, 295 (July 1, 1867). A student's "choice among teachers" was regarded as "a very valuable element in academic freedom for the student." Charles W. Eliot, *Academic Freedom*, 26 Science 1, 7 (1907).
3. D. C. Gilman, The Benefits Which Society Derives from Universities: An Address 16 (1885).
4. On the question of disciplinary knowledge, see Robert C. Post, *Debating Disciplinarity*, 35 Critical Inquiry 749 (2009).
5. When the trustees of the University of Pennsylvania summarily fired radical professor Scott Nearing, refusing to give a reason for their action, trustee George Wharton Pepper explained: "If I was dissatisfied with my secretary or anything he had done, some people might be in favor of calling him in here and sit down and talk it over. Others might think it wiser to dismiss him without assigning cause." Lightner Witmer, The Nearing Case 21 (1915). Pepper, who was a distinguished lawyer, explained that university trustees chose the latter option, as was their legal right.
6. *See* Matthew W. Finkin & Robert C. Post, For the Common Good: Principles of American Academic Freedom 23–52 (2009).
7. The text of the *Declaration* is reproduced in Finkin & Post, *supra* note 6, at 157–81.
8. *Id.* at 166.
9. *Id.* at 163.
10. *Id.* at 160.
11. *Id.* at 162.
12. *Id.* at 164.
13. *Id.* at 164–65.
14. *Id.* at 163.
15. *Id.* at 173.
16. *Id.* at 179–80.
17. *Id.* at 157. The *1940 Statement* describes freedom of research as "full freedom in research and in the publication of results." Freedom of extramural utterance refers to the right of faculty to speak in public as citizens about matters unrelated to their scholarship. Because this component of academic freedom cannot be directly derived from the pursuit of either pedagogy or research, it is theoretically the most controversial aspect of academic freedom. For a discussion, see Finkin & Post, *supra* note 6, at 127–48. In his most recent book, David Rabban argues that extramural speech should not be protected by academic freedom. *See* David M. Rabban, Academic Freedom: From Professional Norm to First Amendment Right 155–61 (2024). For a contrary view, see Judith Butler, *Academic Freedom in a Time of Destruction: Reconsidering Extramural Speech*, 92 Social Research 407 (2025). In this chapter, I discuss only academic freedom of research and of teaching.
18. *1915 Declaration*, *supra* note 7, at 174.
19. *Id.*
20. *Id.* at 167–68. For a discussion of academic freedom of teaching, see Robert Post, "The Classic First Amendment Tradition Under Stress: Freedom of Speech and the University," in The Free Speech Century (Lee C. Bollinger & Geoffrey R. Stone eds. 2019).
21. *1915 Declaration*, *supra* note 7, at 172.
22. *See supra* note 1.

23. The point should not be exaggerated. In contrast to European universities, there had been since the late 19th century a strong native American land-grant tradition of universities aiding in the development of agricultural expertise. During the progressive era, American scholars often saw themselves as publicly-facing experts, so much so that the *1915 Declaration* asserts that a third major purpose of universities is "to develop experts for various branches of the public service." *1915 Declaration, supra* note 7, at 166. It was not until the late 1940s, however, that the nation definitively acknowledged and endorsed the ongoing need for university research to sustain broad economic, medical, and military development.
24. Vannevar Bush, Science: The Endless Frontier: A Report to the President on a Program for Postwar Scientific Research 2 (1990). "[S]ince health, well-being, and security are proper concerns of Government, scientific progress is, and must be, of vital interest to Government. Without scientific progress the national health would deteriorate; without scientific progress we could not hope for improvement in our standard of living or for an increased number of jobs for our citizens; and without scientific progress we could not have maintained our liberties against tyranny." *Id.* at 11.
25. *Id.* at 8. *See id.* at 31.
26. *Id.*
27. *Id.* at 9. *See id.* at 19:

    Publicly and privately supported colleges and universities and the endowed research institutes must furnish both the new scientific knowledge and the trained research workers. These institutions are uniquely qualified by tradition and by their special characteristics to carry on basic research. They are charged with the responsibility of conserving the knowledge accumulated by the past, imparting that knowledge to students, and contributing new knowledge of all kinds. It is chiefly in these institutions that scientists may work in an atmosphere which is relatively free from the adverse pressure of convention, prejudice, or commercial necessity. At their best they provide the scientific worker with a strong sense of solidarity and security, as well as a substantial degree of personal intellectual freedom. All of these factors are of great importance in the development of new knowledge, since much of new knowledge is certain to arouse opposition because of its tendency to challenge current beliefs or practice.

    Industry is generally inhibited by preconceived goals, by its own clearly defined standards, and by the constant pressure of commercial necessity. Satisfactory progress in basic science seldom occurs under conditions prevailing in the normal industrial laboratory. There are some notable exceptions, it is true, but even in such cases it is rarely possible to match the universities in respect to the freedom which is so important to scientific discovery.
28. *Id.* at 12. Bush understood that because "basic research is a long-term process," it was important that the federal grants extend for long periods of time. "Continuity and stability of the program and its support may be expected (a) from the growing realization by the Congress of the benefits to the public from scientific research, and (b) from the conviction which will grow among those who conduct research under the auspices of the agency that good quality work will be followed by continuing support." *Id.* at 33.
29. *Id.*
30. *Id.* at 33.
31. *Id.* at 39. *See* John R. Thelan, A History of American Higher Education 271–72 (3d ed. 2019) ("The watchword was that 'Big Science' was the 'Best Science,' and this meant a system of competitive grants awarded to university scientists who submitted proposals and were then selected by peer review to carry out government projects.").
32. Bush, *supra* note 24, at 21.
33. Erich Bloch, *Foreword*, in *id.* at vi.
34. For a revealing graph of this development, see Jeremy W. Peters & Andrea Fuller, *How Universities Became So Dependent on the Federal Government*, N.Y. Times (Apr. 18, 2025), https://www.nytimes.com/2025/04/18/us/trump-universities.html.
35. National Center for Education Statistics, 120 Years of American Education: A Statistical Portrait Table 24 (Thomas D. Snyde, ed. 1993).
36. *See* Martin Trow, Twentieth-Century Higher Education: Elite to Mass to Universal (2010).

37. Thelan, *supra* note 31, at 322. By 1991, 53.7 percent of the 18- to 24-year-old population attended an institution of higher education. National Center for Education Statistics, *supra* note 35 at Table 24.
38. This transformation is what prompted debates that emerged within academic circles in the 1960s about whether universities should pursue policies of "institutional neutrality," which would require universities to avoid public positions on controverted questions of public policy. See Robert Post, *The Kalven Report, Institutional Neutrality, and Academic Freedom*, (July 25, 2023), at https://papers.ssrn.com/sol3/papers.cfm?abstract_id=4516235.
39. 539 U.S. 306, 332 (2003).
40. The Act is popularly known as the Stop WOKE Act, WOKE in this case being an acronym for "Wrongs to Our Kids and Employees."
41. *See* Pernell v. Florida Board of Governors of the State University System, 641 F.Supp.3d 1218, 1231 (N.D. Fla. 2022). The eight forbidden concepts were:

    1. Members of one race, color, national origin, or sex are morally superior to members of another race, color, national origin, or sex.
    2. A person, by virtue of his or her race, color, national origin, or sex is inherently racist, sexist, or oppressive, whether consciously or unconsciously.
    3. A person's moral character or status as either privileged or oppressed is necessarily determined by his or her race, color, national origin, or sex.
    4. Members of one race, color, national origin, or sex cannot and should not attempt to treat others without respect to race, color, national origin, or sex.
    5. A person, by virtue of his or her race, color, national origin, or sex bears responsibility for, or should be discriminated against or receive adverse treatment because of, actions committed in the past by other members of the same race, color, national origin, or sex.
    6. A person, by virtue of his or her race, color, national origin, or sex should be discriminated against or receive adverse treatment to achieve diversity, equity, or inclusion.
    7. A person, by virtue of his or her race, color, sex, or national origin, bears personal responsibility for and must feel guilt, anguish, or other forms of psychological distress because of actions, in which the person played no part, committed in the past by other members of the same race, color, national origin, or sex.
    8. Such virtues as merit, excellence, hard work, fairness, neutrality, objectivity, and racial colorblindness are racist or sexist, or were created by members of a particular race, color, national origin, or sex to oppress members of another race, color, national origin, or sex.

    Id. at 1231; § 1000.05(4)(a) 1.–8., Fla. Stat. (2022). When Florida's counsel was asked by a judge whether prohibited concept #6 referred to affirmative action, which at that point bore the imprimatur of the Supreme Court of the United States, counsel "answered, unequivocally, 'Your Honor, yes.'" Florida thus sought to defend the position that "the idea of affirmative action is so 'repugnant' that instructors can no longer express approval of affirmative action as an idea worthy of merit during class instruction." 641 F.Supp.3d at 1233.

    The IFA contains "a so-called 'savings clause,' which states that the [statute] 'may not be construed to prohibit discussion of the concepts listed therein as part of a larger course of training or instruction, provided such training or instruction is given in an objective manner without endorsement of the concepts.'" *Id.* at 1231. As the District Court in the case put it, the savings clause means that when it comes to the eight listed concepts, instructors are put to a choice. They "may only discuss them 'in an objective manner'—whatever that means—or they may criticize or condemn the concepts. Defendants admit that the State of Florida is engaging in rank viewpoint discrimination." *Id.* at 1272.
42. Brief of Defendants-Appellants, Pernell v. Lamb, 2023 WL 3021084, at *17 (Apr. 23, 2023) (italics in the original). *See* Ryan Quinn, *Indiana Argues Professors Lack First Amendment Rights in Public Classrooms*, Inside Higher Ed (Aug. 14, 2024), at https://www.insidehighered.com/news/faculty-issues/academic-freedom/2024/08/14/indiana-says-professors-lack-first-amendment-rights (At oral argument, an "appeals court judge asked an attorney representing Florida, 'Could a legislature prohibit professors from

saying anything negative about a current gubernatorial administration?' The lawyer replied, 'I think, your honor, yes, because in the classroom the professor's speech is the government's speech and the government can restrict professors.'").

In making this argument, Florida relied on Garcetti v. Ceballos, 547 U.S. 410 (2006), which held that when speaking "pursuant to their professional duties" government employees would not be able to assert First Amendment rights to protect their speech. *Id.* at 426. In his opinion for the Court in *Garcetti*, however, Justice Kennedy specifically reserved the case of university faculty because of "important ramifications for academic freedom." *Id.* at 425. "There is some argument that expression related to academic scholarship or classroom instruction implicates additional constitutional interests that are not fully accounted for by this Court's customary employee-speech jurisprudence. We need not, and for that reason do not, decide whether the analysis we conduct today would apply in the same manner to a case involving speech related to scholarship or teaching." *Id.*

43. A federal district court found Florida's claim to "unfettered authority to muzzle its professors" to be "positively dystopian." 641 F. Supp. 3d at 1230. By contrast, a district court in Alabama has upheld a statute roughly equivalent to the IFA by explicitly accepting the argument that *Garcetti* should not be interpreted to include an exception for academic scholarship or classroom instruction. *See* Simon v. Ivey, 2025 WL 2,345,845 (N.D. Ala. 2025), at *58; note 50; *infra* note 167.
44. *See supra* text at note 13.
45. *See supra* note 17.
46. Academic freedom does not require that faculty be free to say whatever they wish in the classroom. Academic freedom instead requires that, in the classroom, faculty be governed by professional disciplinary standards of research and pedagogy. For a discussion, see Finkin & Post, *supra* note 6, at 79–111.
47. *See, e.g.*, Josh Moody, *A Clash over Core Curriculum at New College of Florida*, Inside Higher Ed (Oct. 29, 2024), at https://www.insidehighered.com/news/faculty/curriculum/2024/10/29/clash-over-core-curriculum-new-college-florida.
48. The implications of this view of higher education are plain enough. *See, e.g.*, Vimal Patel & David Goodman, *Texas Professor Fired After Accusations of Teaching "Gender Ideology,"* N.Y. Times (Sep. 10, 2025), at https://www.nytimes.com/2025/09/10/us/texas-professor-fired-gender ideology.html ("Republican politicians in the state, including the governor, demanded quick action from the public university, accusing the instructor of 'blatantly indoctrinating students in gender ideology.'"). Statutes like the IFA are now common throughout the nation. "More than 70 bills and policies across 26 states have been introduced to censor higher education," and of these "22 have become law in 16 states. . . . Almost 40% of the U.S. population now live in states affected by state level higher education censorship laws or policies." Laura Benitez, Amy Reid & Jonathan Friedman, *With a Wave of New Bills in 2025, State Legislators Cast a Web of Control over Higher Education*, Pen America (July 24, 2025), at https://pen.org/with-a-wave-of-new-bills-in-2025-state-legislators-cast-a-web-of-control-over-higher-education/ ("With remarkable speed and determination, lawmakers have passed a stunning wave of educational gag orders that directly censor academic teaching.").
49. Jeffrey M. Jones, *U.S. Confidence in Higher Education Now Closely Divided*, Gallup (July 8, 2024), at https://news.gallup.com/poll/646880/confidence-higher-education-closely-divided.aspx.
50. There is "a stark partisan divide in perceptions of colleges. Conservative Americans frequently view higher education institutions as bastions of liberal ideology, contributing to distrust. Meanwhile, Democrats are more likely to associate college with opportunity and upward mobility." *Crisis of Confidence in Higher Education*, The Change Leader, Inc., at https://changinghighered.com/why-public-trust-in-higher-ed-is-declining-and-what-leaders-can-do-about-it/.
51. Jones, *supra* note 49. By contrast, the percentage of Democrats with a great deal or quite a lot of confidence in higher education dropped from 68 percent to 56 percent, and the percentage of independents with a great deal or quite a lot of confidence in higher education dropped from 48 percent to 35 percent. The percentage of Democrats with little or no confidence in 2024 was 12 percent, and of independents 31 percent. On the "education gap" between

Democrats and Republicans, see David A. Hollinger, *The Evangelical Capture of the Republican Party and Its Implications for Academia*, 92 Social Research 525, 526–28 (2025); Craig Volden, Jonathan Wai & Alan E. Wiseman, *On the Decline of Elite-Educated Republicans in Congress*, Perspectives on Politics (Aug. 27, 2025), at https://www.cambridge.org/core/journals/perspectives-on-politics/article/on-the-decline-of-eliteeducated-republicans-in-congress/B50B628CA9CCC799A0D86D9496EA3F6F.

52. Jones, *supra* note 49. Twenty-eight percent of Americans with little or no confidence in higher education report that their lack of confidence is due to the unduly high costs and expenses of colleges and universities. *Id.* One can perhaps detect in these figures a resurgence of class animosity against institutions of higher education.
53. National Conservatism, *J. D. Vance| The Universities Are the Enemy| National Conservatism Conference II*, YouTube (Nov. 10, 2021), https://www.youtube.com/watch?v=0FR65Cifnhw.
54. Thomas B. Edsall, *JD Vance Wanted to 'Aggressively Attack" American Universities*, N.Y. Times (June 3, 2025), at https://www.nytimes.com/2025/06/03/opinion/harvard-trump-vance.html ("a virulent hostility toward America's most elite universities underpins the Trump administration's assaults on higher education").
55. *See, e.g.*, Exec. Order No. 14322, *Improving Oversight of Federal Grantmaking*, 90 Fed. Reg. 38929 (Aug. 7, 2025) ("Discretionary awards must, where applicable, demonstrably advance the President's policy priorities," including the administration's political policies involving race and gender, and including the denial of grants that "promote anti-American values"). Trump's secretary of education, Linda McMahon, made this point explicitly. "Universities should continue to be able to do research," she said, "as long as they're . . . in sync, I think, with the administration and what the administration is trying to accomplish." Quoted in Anthony L. Fisher, *The Trump Administration Just Kicked Its War on Free Speech into Overdrive*, MSNBC (May 30, 2025), at https://www.msnbc.com/opinion/msnbc-opinion/trump-free-speech-harvard-marco-rubio-rfk-jr-censorship-rcna209870.
56. *See, e.g.*, National Conservatism, *supra* note 53. Vance began his speech to conservatives this way: "So much of what we want to accomplish, so much of what we want to be in this movement and in this country, I think are fundamentally dependent on going through a set of very hostile institutions, specifically the universities, which control knowledge in our society, which control what we call truth and what we call falsity, [and which] provide research that gives credibility to some of the most ridiculous ideas that exist in our country." Vance ended his speech by quoting Richard Nixon: "The professors are the enemy."
57. *See, e.g.*, William J. Broad, *Historians See Autocratic Playbook in Trump's Attacks on Science*, N.Y. Times (Aug. 31, 2025), at https://www.nytimes.com/2025/08/31/science/trump-science-autocrats.html.
58. David E. Sanger, *It's a Really Bad Time to Be an Expert in Washington*, N.Y. Times (June 6, 2025), at https://www.nytimes.com/2025/06/06/us/politics/experts-trump-doge-cuts.html; Apoorva Mandavilli, *Will the C.D.C. Survive?*, N.Y. Times (Aug. 29, 2025), at https://www.nytimes.com/2025/08/29/health/cdc-kennedy-public-health.html. *See also, e.g.*, Tom Latchem, *Trump Appoints 22-Year-Old Ex-Gardener and Grocery Store Assistant to Lead U.S. Terror Prevention*, Daily Beast (June 6, 2025), at https://www.thedailybeast.com/donald-trump-appoints-22-y-o-ex-gardener-grocery-store-assistant-as-us-homeland-department-terrorist-chief/.

    The idea that there is no real knowledge, but only opinions invested with the power to brand themselves as knowledge, may have originated in left postmodern thought, but it is now at the root of the conservative attack on expertise. *See, e.g.*, Matt Johnson, *Christopher Rufo's Pyrrhic Victory*, Quillette (May 5, 2025), at https://quillette.com/2025/05/05/christopher-rufos-pyrrhic-victory-gramsci-harvard-trump/; *cf.* Nathan Sperber & George Hoare, *How the Right Hijacked Antonio Gramsci*, Jacobin (Mar. 15, 2025), at https://jacobin.com/2025/03/right-gramsci-de-benoist-trump. Although the practices of argumentation and evidence that define academic disciplines can no doubt be abused and subordinated to political agendas, the ultimate question is whether these practices produce forms of knowing that are in the long run more reliable and useful than the tides of popular opinion that currently sweep the platforms of the Internet. On this question, see Hollinger, *supra* note 51.

59. Adam Geller, *How War, Money and the Quest for Discovery Entwined the US Government and Universities*, Associated Press (Apr. 16, 2025), at https://apnews.com/article/trump-harvard-research-universities-stanford-794eb7f35e55df48be5d03c9e18e383e.
60. Massachusetts v. National Institutes of Health, 2025 WL 702163, at *1 (D. Mass 2025).
61. *Id.* The decision is under appeal. Alongside the general cut to indirect costs, the Trump administration required the National Science Foundation (NSF) to "screen grant proposals for 'topics or activities that may not be in alignment with agency priorities,'" a directive that superimposed a screen of explicitly ideological criteria on the scholarly assessments of merit previously used by the NSF. Kathryn Palmer, *NSF Halts New Funding and Caps Indirect Rate Costs*, Inside Higher Ed (May 5, 2025), at https://www.insidehighered.com/news/government/science-research-policy/2025/05/05/nsf-halts-new-funding-and-caps-indirect-rate. As a result of this screening, grant proposals touching on subjects like diversity, equity, and inclusion, gender ideology, or transsexuality were summarily rejected. Although a federal court condemned this screening process as discriminatory and illegal when applied to NIH grants, APHA v. NIH, 2025 WL 1822487 (D. Mass. July 2, 2025), the court's order voiding the cancellations was stayed by the Supreme Court on the ground that challenges to grant cancellations should be brought before the Federal Court of Claims. NIH v. American Public Health Association, 2025 WL 2415669 (Aug. 21, 2025). This decision throws considerable doubt on the ability of universities to deploy litigation as an effective defense against the Trump administration's policy using grant cancellations to extort university concessions. Eric Kelderman, *Will the Supreme Court's Ruling on Research Grants Sink Harvard's Lawsuit Against Trump?*, Chron. of Higher Educ. (Aug. 27, 2025), at https://www.chronicle.com/article/will-the-supreme-courts-ruling-on-research-grants-sink-harvards-lawsuit-against-trump.
62. Palmer, *supra* note 61. *See* Lauran Neergaard & Kasturi Pananjady, *NIH Research Cuts Threaten the Search for Life-Saving Cures and Jobs in Every State*, Associated Press (Mar. 6, 2025), at https://apnews.com/article/trump-science-medicine-research-cancer-funding-university-0ef3fa47694784e47b0ecd51680410ba ("The administration's unprecedented moves are upending the research engine that has made the U.S. 'the envy of the world in terms of scientific innovation.'"); John Drake, *Former NSF Director Warns of Fragile Future for American Science*, Forbes (June 2, 2025), at https://www.forbes.com/sites/johndrake/2025/06/02/former-nsf-director-warns-of-fragile-future-for-american-science/ ("The scientific enterprise that helped make the U.S. a global leader after World War II—one built on public investment, open collaboration, and an ethos of discovery—is under pressure from political polarization, disinvestment and short-term thinking. And while philanthropy plays an increasingly important role, . . . it is no substitute for government support."); Brandon Roberts, Annie Waldman & Pratheek Rebala, *Gutted: How Deeply Trump Has Cut Federal Health Agencies*, ProPublica (Aug. 21, 2025), at https://projects.propublica.org/federal-health-worker-cuts-rfk-trump-administration/.
63. The day after he took office, Trump issued an executive order entitled *Ending Illegal Discrimination and Restoring Merit-Based Opportunity*, which tasked federal agencies with deterring "DEI programs or principles" by identifying "up to nine potential civil compliance investigations of . . . institutions of higher education with endowments over 1 billion dollars." Exec. Order No. 1473, 90 Fed. Reg. 8633 (Jan. 21, 2025). There is also evidence that the Trump administration is contemplating using accreditation agencies to enforce its ideological agenda. *See* Greg D. Pillar & Laurie Shanderson, *The Weaponization of Accreditation*, Chron. of Higher Educ. (May 22, 2025), at https://www.chronicle.com/article/the-weaponization-of-accreditation. Accreditation is necessary for students at a college or university to be eligible for federal loans to pay for their tuition. Without accreditation, an institution's ability to sustain a steady flow of tuition income is greatly decreased. *See* Susan Svrluga, *Education Department Says Columbia Doesn't Meet Accreditation Standards*, Washington Post (June 4, 2025), at https://www.washingtonpost.com/education/2025/06/04/columbia-university-accreditation-education-department/.
64. Title VI provides that "No person in the United States shall, on the ground of race, color, or national origin, be excluded from participation in, be denied the benefits of, or be subjected to discrimination under any program or activity receiving Federal financial assistance." 42 U.S.C. § 2000d, et seq.; 34 C.F.R. § 100, et seq.

65. 143 S.Ct. 2141 (2023).
66. Craig Trainor, Dear Colleague Letter (Feb. 14, 2025), at https://www.ed.gov/media/document/dear-colleague-letter-sffa-v-harvard-109506.pdf. On July 29, 2025, Attorney General Bondi issued a memorandum providing "Guidance for Recipients of Federal Funding Regarding Unlawful Discrimination" that recapitulated the essential conclusions of the Dear Colleague Letter. *See* Memorandum for All Federal Agencies (July 29, 2025), at https://www.justice.gov/ag/media/1409486/dl?inline.
67. *See* Department of Education, *Press Release: ED Requires K-12 School Districts to Certify Compliance with Title VI and Students v. Harvard as a Condition of Receiving Federal Financial Assistance* (Apr. 3, 2025), at https://www.ed.gov/about/news/press-release/ed-requires-k-12-school-districts-certify-compliance-title-vi-and-students-v-harvard-condition-of-receiving-federal-financial-assistance.
68. National Education Association v. United State Department of Education, 2025 WL 1188160, at *1 (D. N.H. 2025). It is plain that the DOE letter rather vastly overreads the implications of *SFFA*. The letter has been struck down as inconsistent with both the APA and the First Amendment. American Federation of Teachers v. Department of Education, 2025 WL 2374697 (D. Md. Aug. 14, 2025).
69. *Columbia University Caves to Demands to Restore $400m from Trump Administration*, THE GUARDIAN (Mar. 21, 2025), at https://www.theguardian.com/us-news/2025/mar/21/columbia-university-funding-trump-demands. The administration's demands may be found at *Read the Letter to Columbia University*, N.Y. TIMES (Mar. 14, 2025), at https://www.nytimes.com/interactive/2025/03/14/nyregion/columbia-letter.html. The administration charged that Columbia had "failed to protect American students from antisemitic violence and harassment in addition to other alleged violations of Title VI and Title VII of the Civil Rights Act of 1964." *Id.* The legality of the administration's initial freezing of Columbia's funds is highly debatable. The unfolding story is updated in *Tracking Trump's Higher-Ed Agenda*, CHRON. OF HIGHER EDUC., at https://www.chronicle.com/article/tracking-trumps-higher-ed-agenda. Most recently, Columbia entered into an agreement with the Trump administration that included payment of $200 million "to settle claims related to discriminatory practices" and the establishment of "robust oversight, including an independent Resolution Monitor and an Administrator, to ensure Columbia complies with the agreement and federal laws." The White House, *Fact Sheet: President Donald Trump Secures Major Settlement with Columbia University* (July 24, 2025), at https://www.whitehouse.gov/fact-sheets/2025/07/19853/.
70. Trump variously characterized Harvard as "a threat to Democracy," "a liberal mess," and "an Anti-Semitic, Far Left Institution." Amanda Friedman, *"A Threat to Democracy": Trump Continues Bashing Harvard amid Attacks on Major Institutions*, POLITICO (Apr. 24, 2025), at https://www.politico.com/news/2025/04/24/trump-harvard-funding-attack-0030768p. For the larger ideological context of the Trump administration's attack on Harvard, see Christopher F. Rufo, *Harvard and Hegemony*, CITY J. (Dec. 13, 2023), at https://www.nytimes.com/interactive/2025/04/14/us/trump-harvard-demands.html; *Conservative Activist Christopher Rufo on His Push to Scrutinize Higher Education*, PBS NEWS (May 1, 2025), at https://www.pbs.org/newshour/show/conservative-activist-christopher-rufo-on-his-push-to-scrutinize-higher-education.
71. *Read the Trump Administration's Letter to Harvard*, N.Y. TIMES (Apr. 14, 2025), at https://www.nytimes.com/interactive/2025/04/14/us/trump-harvard-demands.html.
72. *See* Letter from William A. Burck & Robert K. Hur to Josh Gruenbaum, *et al.* (Apr. 14, 2025), at https://www.harvard.edu/research-funding/wp-content/uploads/sites/16/2025/04/Harvard-Response-2025-04-14.pdf. On April 21, Harvard brought suit against the administration to prevent the cancellation of grants. *See* Sarah Brown, *Harvard Sues Trump Administration over "Improper Government Intrusion," with Billions at Stake*, CHRON. OF HIGHER EDUC. (Apr. 21, 2025), at https://www.chronicle.com/article/harvard-sues-trump-administration-over-improper-government-intrusion-with-billions-at-stake. Harvard argued that the First Amendment prohibited the federal government from forcing "a private university to adopt a particular ideological agenda" and that the administration had failed to identify "any rational connection between antisemitism concerns and the medical, scientific,

and other research it has frozen." *Id.* Stating that "Now it is the job of the courts to . . . step up, to safeguard academic freedom and freedom of speech as required by the Constitution," a district court recently agreed, ruling that the Trump administration's freezing and cancelling of grants to Harvard violated the First Amendment. President and Fellows of Harvard College v. United States Department of Health and Human Services, 2025 WL 2528380 at * 37 (D. Mass. Sep. 3, 2025). The practical effect of the decision is unclear. *See, e.g.,* Alan Binder, *Harvard Won Its Money Back, but Will It Actually Get It?,* N.Y. Times (Sep. 4, 2025), at https://www.nytimes.com/2025/09/04/us/harvard-federal-funds-court-victory-trump-administration.html, in part because it is unknown whether the Supreme Court will regard the District Court decision as inconsistent with NIH v. American Public Health Association, 2025 WL 2415669 (U.S.S.C. Aug. 21, 2025); *see supra* note 61.

73. *See* Michael C. Bender, *All the Actions the Trump Administration Has Taken Against Harvard,* N.Y. Times (May 27, 2025), at https://www.nytimes.com/2025/05/22/us/politics/harvard-university-trump.html.
74. Bianca Quilantan, *Trump Says He's Yanking Harvard's Tax-Exempt Status,* Politico (May 2, 2025), at https://www.politico.com/news/2025/05/02/trump-harvard-tax-exempt-status-00323192.
75. Collin Binkley & Jocelyn Gecker, *Trump Administration Says Harvard Will Receive No New Grants Until It Meets White House Demands,* Associated Press (May 5, 2025), at https://apnews.com/article/harvard-trump-grant-f677055d7536ab1478ee9b836ca11bf7; Stephanie Saul, *Trump Intends to Cancel All Federal Funds Directed at Harvard,* N.Y. Times (May 27, 2025), at https://www.nytimes.com/2025/05/27/us/harvard-trump-federal-funds.html.
76. Maddie Khaw, *Harvard's Battle with Trump Escalates as Research Money Is Suddenly Canceled,* Chronicle of Higher Education (May 5, 2025), at https://www.chronicle.com/article/harvards-battle-with-trump-escalates-as-research-money-is-suddenly-canceled ("Unlike other cancellations in recent months targeting research focused on topics like LGBTQ health, race, or Covid-19, these sweeping terminations seem unrelated to research content and instead zero in on the institution at large and its response to campus antisemitism."). *See* Emily Badger, Aatish Bhatia & Ethan Singer, *Here Is All the Science at Risk in Trump's Clash with Harvard,* N.Y. Times (June 22, 2025), at https://www.nytimes.com/interactive/2025/06/22/upshot/harvard-funding-cuts.html.
77. Karin Fischer, *Hours After Harvard Sues, Court Blocks Trump's Move to Ban Enrollment of Foreign Students,* Chron. of Higher Educ. (May 22, 2025), at https://www.chronicle.com/article/trump-administration-revokes-harvards-ability-to-enroll-international-students. Harvard promptly sued, alleging violations of the First Amendment, Due Process, and the Administrative Procedure Act, and a court immediately granted a temporary restraining order. *Id.*; President and Fellows of Harvard College v. Department of Homeland Security, 2025 WL 1479 077 (D. Mass. May 23, 2025). The court also blocked a subsequent effort to evade this order and prevent international students heading to Harvard from obtaining visas. Stephanie Saul & Andrés R. Martínez, *Judge Temporarily Blocks Trump's Order Curtailing Foreign Students at Harvard,* N.Y. Times (June 5, 2025), at https://www.nytimes.com/2025/06/05/us/harvard-response-trump-international-students.html. A spokeswoman for the Trump administration defended its action on the ground that "It is a privilege, not a right, for universities to enroll foreign students." Stephanie Saul & Alan Blinder, *Judge Blocks a Trump Effort to Prevent International Students at Harvard,* N.Y. Times (June 20, 2025), at https://www.nytimes.com/2025/06/20/us/international-students-harvard-preliminary-injunction.html. *See* Stephanie Saul, *Judge Blocks Trump Proclamation Barring Harvard's International Students,* N.Y. Times (June 23, 2025), at https://www.nytimes.com/2025/06/23/us/harvard-trump-international-students.html.
78. Karen Fischer, *The Trump Administration Is Scrutinizing Colleges' Foreign Gifts. It's Not the First Time,* Chron. of Higher Educ. (Apr. 18, 2025), at https://www.chronicle.com/article/the-trump-administration-is-scrutinizing-colleges-foreign-gifts-its-not-the-first-time.
79. *Trump Administration Threatens to Strip Harvard University of Lucrative Patents,* The Guardian (Aug. 9, 2025), at https://www.theguardian.com/us-news/2025/aug/09/trump-administration-harvard-patent-review.

80. Dhruv T. Patel & Grace E. Yoon, *Trump Admin Issues Finding That Harvard Permitted Antisemitism in Violation of Civil Rights Law,* HARVARD CRIMSON (June 30, 2025), at https://www.thecrimson.com/article/2025/6/30/harvard-hhs-ocr-antisemitism-finding/. Even though Harvard, unlike many universities, sued to resist Trump's attacks, it has nevertheless been affected by the pressure of the Trump Administration. *See, e.g.,* Stephanie Saul, *Harvard Is Making Changes Trump Officials Want, Even Without a Deal,* N.Y. TIMES (Aug. 23, 2025), at https://www.nytimes.com/2025/08/23/us/harvard-changes-academic-freedom-trump-deal.html.
81. The implications of this turn in conservative policy are fundamentally incompatible with academic freedom of teaching. Exemplary is the recent memorandum of the chancellor of the Texas Tech University system requiring that "course materials, curricula, syllabi, and other instructional documents" follow "applicable law" by recognizing "only two human sexes: male and female." *See* Memorandum from Chancellor Tedd L. Mitchell to Component University Presidents, Texas Tech University System (Sep. 25, 2025), at https://www.texastech.edu/downloads/9-25-25-memo-to-university-presidents-regarding-compliance.pdf. The memorandum illustrates why Hanna Gray was right to fear that the conservative "assault would . . . transform colleges into weapons of ideological advocacy and political manipulation, substituting Trump's own version of correct doctrine for the mandate that is at the heart of a university's foundational mission, that of freely seeking knowledge and understanding." Hanna H. Gray, *Alumni Must Defend Universities from Trump's Assault,* BOSTON GLOBE (May 30, 2025), at https://archive.ph/016Dd. The conservative attack on academic freedom has roots in William F. Buckley, Jr.'s repudiation of the concept of academic freedom as a superstition and a "hoax." *See* WILLIAM F. BUCKLEY, JR., GOD AND MAN AT YALE: THE SUPERSTITIONS OF "ACADEMIC FREEDOM" 123–69 (1951). Buckley explicitly rejected the notion that the aim of a college education was to get a student "to exercise, in behalf of himself, his fullest intellectual powers." William F. Buckley, Jr., *The Aimlessness of American Education,* NEWSDAY (Mar. 5, 1960), at 6M. Because Buckley believed conservatives already knew the truth, he contended that conservatives were entitled to impose that truth on students at colleges and universities:

> Certain great truths have been apprehended. In the field of morality, all the basic truths have been apprehended; and we are going to teach these, and teach, and demonstrate, how it is that those who disregard them fall easily into the alien pitfalls of communism, or fascism, or liberalism.
>
> There is a purpose in life. It is known what that purpose is, in part because it has been revealed, in part because man is endowed with a rational mechanism by which he can apprehend it. Educators should pass on those truths, and endow students with the knowledge of the processes by which they are recognized as such. To do this is the single greatest contribution a teaching institution can make; it is the aim of education, to which all else is subordinate and derivative.

Id. at 7M. Trump's interventions express a similar confidence in the truth of his partisan convictions, a confidence that academic freedom fundamentally repudiates in the name of epistemological humility.
82. The implications of this turn in conservative policy are fundamentally incompatible with academic freedom of research and teaching. *See, e.g.,* Jaweed Kaleem, *Here Are the Details of Trump's $1.2-Billion Call to Remake UCLA in a Conservative Image,* L.A. TIMES (Sep. 15, 2025), at https://www.latimes.com/california/story/2025-09-15/trump-doj-proposed-settlement-demand-letter-ucla-university-of-california ("The 28-page letter . . . lays out in sweeping detail how it wants the university to enforce new policies that adhere to the president's conservative agenda."). The administration made this point unmistakably clear early on in its executive order "Restoring Truth and Sanity to American History," issued on March 27, 2025. Exec. Or. No. 14,253, 90 Fed. Reg. 14,563. The Order asserted:

> Over the past decade, Americans have witnessed a concerted and widespread effort to rewrite our Nation's history, replacing objective facts with a distorted

narrative driven by ideology rather than truth. This revisionist movement seeks to undermine the remarkable achievements of the United States by casting its founding principles and historical milestones in a negative light. Under this historical revision, our Nation's unparalleled legacy of advancing liberty, individual rights, and human happiness is reconstructed as inherently racist, sexist, oppressive, or otherwise irredeemably flawed. Rather than fostering unity and a deeper understanding of our shared past, the widespread effort to rewrite history deepens societal divides and fosters a sense of national shame, disregarding the progress America has made and the ideals that continue to inspire millions around the globe....

Once widely respected as a symbol of American excellence and a global icon of cultural achievement, the Smithsonian Institution has, in recent years, come under the influence of a divisive, race-centered ideology. This shift has promoted narratives that portray American and Western values as inherently harmful and oppressive. For example, the Smithsonian American Art Museum today features "The Shape of Power: Stories of Race and American Sculpture," an exhibit representing that "[s]ocieties including the United States have used race to establish and maintain systems of power, privilege, and disenfranchisement." The exhibit further claims that "sculpture has been a powerful tool in promoting scientific racism" and promotes the view that race is not a biological reality but a social construct, stating "Race is a human invention." ...

It is the policy of my Administration to restore Federal sites dedicated to history, including parks and museums, to solemn and uplifting public monuments that remind Americans of our extraordinary heritage, consistent progress toward becoming a more perfect Union, and unmatched record of advancing liberty, prosperity, and human flourishing. Museums in our Nation's capital should be places where individuals go to learn—not to be subjected to ideological indoctrination or divisive narratives that distort our shared history.

To advance this policy, we will restore the Smithsonian Institution to its rightful place as a symbol of inspiration and American greatness—igniting the imagination of young minds, honoring the richness of American history and innovation, and instilling pride in the hearts of all Americans.

Id. See Jack Dolan, *Trump Bans "Negative" Signage at National Parks*, L.A. Times (June 19, 2025), at https://www.latimes.com/california/story/2025-06-19/trump-bans-negative-signage-at-national-parks-asks-visitors-to-snitch-on-unpatriotic-text.

83. In a recent article, Stanley Kurtz asks *What, to a Conservative, Is Academic Freedom?*, Ethics & Public Policy Center (Apr. 28, 2025), at https://eppc.org/publication/what-to-a-conservative-is-academic-freedom/. Kurtz begins his essay: "'Don't tread on our academic freedom!' shouts Harvard while suing Trump to prove the point. 'Frankly, my dears, I don't give a damn,' replies Trump, while slashing ever more federal dollars to force reform." If standards of academic freedom merely govern the relationship between Harvard and its faculty, Trump can legally ignore them. But if these standards also constitute constitutional limitations on state action, Trump's actions can perhaps be restrained by courts.

84. *See, e.g.*, Walter P. Metzger, *Profession and Constitution: Two Definitions of Academic Freedom in America*, 66 Tex. L. Rev. 1265 (1988).

85. Keyishian v. Board of Regents, 385 U.S. 589, 603 (1967).

86. Rabban, *supra* note 17, at 112. *See* J. Peter Byrne, *Academic Freedom: A "Special Concern of the First Amendment,"* 99 Yale L.J. 251, 253 (1989) ("There has been no adequate analysis of what academic freedom the Constitution protects or of why it protects it. Lacking definition or guiding principle, the doctrine floats in the law, picking up decisions as a hull does barnacles."); Clay Calvert, *Professional Standards and the First Amendment in Higher Education: When Institutional Academic Freedom Collides with Student Speech Rights*, 91 St. John's L. Rev. 611, 621 (2018) ("The unsettled state of academic freedom, particularly as it ties to the First Amendment, is widely recognized."); Robert C. Post, Democracy, Expertise, Academic Freedom: A First Amendment Jurisprudence for the Modern State 61–93 (2012).

87. Zach Greenberg, *The Chilling Effect of Sunlight: Preserving Academic Freedom in the Face of Abusive Open Records Requests*, 29 Geo. Mason U. Civ. Rts. L. J. 145, 148 (2019) ("Commentators have lamented the muddiness of" the "connection" between academic freedom and the First Amendment.); Mark P. Strassser, *The Onslaught on Academic Freedom*, 81 UMKC L. Rev. 657, 658 (2013) ("The degree to which academic freedom is protected by the First Amendment has been a matter of some dispute for over half a century.").
88. Lawrence Rosenthal, *Does the First Amendment Protect Academic Freedom?*, 46 J. Coll. & Univ. L. 223, 238–39 (2021) ("It is, therefore, far from clear that there is a doctrinal basis for recognizing a First Amendment right of academic freedom beyond the more general First Amendment rights of all public employees to be free from official demands for ideological or partisan loyalty.").
89. Complaint, ¶ 2, President and Fellows of Harvard College v. Department of Homeland Security, 2025 WL 1484188 (D. Mass. May 23, 2025). *See supra* note 77.
90. In President and Fellows of Harvard College v. United States Department of Health and Human Services, 2025 WL 2528380 (D. Mass. Sep. 3, 2025), a federal district court held that the Trump administration's freezing of grants to Harvard constituted unconstitutional retaliation under the First Amendment.
91. National Rifle Association of America v. Vullo, 602 U.S. 175, 189 (2024). *See* Lexi Lonas Cochran, *Judge Raises Free Speech Concerns in Trump Administration Effort to Ban Harvard International Students*, The Hill (June 24, 2025), at https://thehill.com/homenews/education/5366177-judge-free-speech-trump-harvard-international-students/.
92. Roberts v. United States Jaycees, 468 U.S. 609, 618, 622 (1984) (an expressive association is formed "for the purpose of engaging in those activities protected by the First Amendment," and the identity of its members affects the First Amendment message it seeks to communicate).
93. 303 Creative LLC v. Elenis, 600 U.S. 570, 586 (2023).
94. *Id.* at 589. *See* Hurley v. Irish-American Gay, Lesbian and Bisexual Group of Boston, 515 U.S. 557 (1995); Boy Scouts of America v. Dale, 530 U.S. 640 (2000).
95. That is why Justice Frankfurter, in a much cited passage, writes that universities can flourish only if they are "left as unfettered as possible," which means left free to enjoy "'the four essential freedoms of a university'—to determine for itself on academic grounds who may teach, what may be taught, how it shall be taught, and who may be admitted to study." Sweezy v. New Hampshire, 354 U.S. 234, 262–63 (1957) (Frankfurter, J., concurring).
96. Boy Scouts of America v. Dale, 530 U.S. 640 (2000).
97. *Id.*; *Hurley*, *supra* note 94, holds that under conditions of expressive association, in which the identity of membership affects the message that an organization sends to the public, to regulate the membership of an organization is to compel the organization's speech. *See 303 Creative*, *supra* note 93; Robert C. Post, *Public Accommodations and the First Amendment:* 303 Creative *and "Pure Speech,"* 2023 Sup. Ct. Rev. 251, 285–86.
98. As reported in the *Wall Street Journal*, the charges of anti-semitism advanced by the Trump administration are part of a larger effort "to combat what they view as the liberal, anti-Western" stance "of American higher education." Eliza Collins, Douglas Belkin, Tarini Parti, & Liz Essley Whyte, *The Punch That Launched Trump's War on American Universities*, Wall St. J. (May 28, 2025), at https://www.wsj.com/us-news/education/trump-college-university-federal-funding-fight-91c2a274.
99. "Leaders in Trump circles have argued that universities were so deeply stewed in progressive ideas that small, incremental changes wouldn't be enough—that the federal government needed to force a major cultural shift." *Id. See* Alan Blinder, *As Trump Attacks Universities, Some Are Agreeing to Negotiate*, N.Y. Times (Sep. 5, 2025), at https://www.nytimes.com/article/trump-university-college.html.
100. Kathleen M. Sullivan, *Unconstitutional Conditions*, 102 Harv. L. Rev. 1413, 1415 (1989). *See* Mahmoud v. Taylor, 145 S.Ct. 2332, 2359 (2025); Perry v. Sindermann, 408 U.S. 593, 597 (1972). *See supra* note 77 for an example of the Trump administration seeking to revive the rights/privilege distinction.
101. Agency for International Development v. Alliance for Open Society International, Inc., 570 U.S. 205, 216–17 (2013).

102. *Id.* at 217.
103. *See supra* note 72. For a discussion of some of the complexities of unconstitutional-conditions doctrine, see Robert C. Post, *Subsidized Speech,* 106 Yale Law J. 151 (1996). The doctrine of unconstitutional conditions, of course, does not apply to the Trump administration's efforts to cut back future research funding. *See supra* text at note 62.
104. Mahanoy Area School District v. B.L., 594 U.S. 180, 189 (2021).
105. Iancu v. Brunetti, 139 S. Ct. 2294, 2302 (2019) (Alito, J., concurring). *See* Rosenberger v. Rector & Visitors of Univ. of Va., 515 U.S. 819, 829 (1995). Justice Brennan has written that "[v]iewpoint discrimination is censorship in its purest form and government regulation that discriminates among viewpoints threatens the continued vitality of 'free speech.'" Perry Educ. Ass'n v. Perry Local Educators' Ass'n, 460 U.S. 37, 62 (1983) (Brennan, J., dissenting).
106. Police Dept. of Chicago v. Mosley, 408 U.S. 92, 96 (1972).
107. Viewpoint discrimination is also indispensable in university education. Grading is a practice that routinely depends upon viewpoint discrimination.
108. It is for this reason that those who attempt to conceptualize academic freedom as analogous to a professor's individual right of freedom of speech fail to theorize the actual contemporary practices of universities. For a discussion of the contrast in this regard between the AAUP and the Foundation for Individual Rights and Expression (FIRE), see Post, *supra* note 20, at 110–22; Sarah Viren, *A Professor Was Fired for Her Politics. Is That the Future of Academia?,* N.Y. Times Magazine (June 6, 2025), at https://www.nytimes.com/2025/06/06/magazine/academic-freedom-politics.html.
109. Allan Gibbard, Thinking How to Live 226 (2003) ("the concept of knowing serves to guide us in relying on some kinds of judgment and not on others").
110. *See* Post, *supra* note 86, at 67–68; William W. Van Alstyne, *The Specific Theory of Academic Freedom and the General Issue of Civil Liberties,* 404 Annals Am. Acad. Pol. & Soc. Sci. 140, 146–47 (1972).
111. *See supra* text at note 16.
112. Jacob T. Levy, *Academic Freedom as Freedom of Complex Association,* in Academic Freedom in a Plural World: Global Critical Perspectives 25–31 (Frédéric Mégret & Nandini Ramanujam, eds. 2024); Robert C. Post, *Academic Freedom and Legal Scholarship,* 64 J. Leg. Educ. 530, 533–34 (2015).
113. Thomas L. Haskell, *Justifying the Rights of Academic Freedom in the Era of "Power/Knowledge,"* in The Future of Academic Freedom 54 (Louis Menand, ed. 1996).
114. Post, *supra* note 86, at 80. It is often debated in legal scholarship whether rights of academic freedom should attach to universities as institutions or instead to individual professors. *See* Neal Hutchens & Vanessa Miller, *Florida's Stop Woke Act: A Wake-Up Call for Faculty Academic Freedom,* 10 J. College & University L. 35, [illegible] (2023) ("Within the contested terrain of constitutional academic freedom, a key issue pertains to whether individual scholars in public higher education possess First Amendment academic freedom rights . . . or, instead, does academic freedom, if a viable constitutional doctrine at all, only exist as a right to be exercised at the institutional level"). In truth, however, academic freedom protects neither the individual rights of professors nor the institutional rights of organizations that happen to call themselves universities. It instead safeguards the professional standards that allow true universities both to teach and to increase knowledge. Either individual faculty or institutions of higher education can be proper parties to assert rights of academic freedom, so long as the substance of the rights being protected are defined in terms of the protection of these standards. *See infra* note 168.
115. Harper & Row Publishers, Inc. v. Nation Enters., 471 U.S. 539, 559 (1985) (quoting Estate of Hemingway v. Random House, Inc., 244 N.E.2d 250, 255 (N.Y. 1968)).
116. *Hurley,* 515 U.S. at 573.
117. *303 Creative,* 600 U.S. at 592.
118. 547 U.S. 410 (2006).
119. *Id.* at 421.
120. *Id.* at 425. *See supra* note 42.
121. Michael K. Park, *A Matter of Public Concern: The Case for Academic Freedom Rights of Public University Faculty,* 26 Communication L. & Pol. 32, 40 (2021) ("Post-*Garcetti,* circuit

courts have not defined the limits of academic freedom, nor have they uniformly recognized special academic free speech rights for university faculty that would limit *Garcetti*'s application."); RABBAN, *supra* note 17, at 128–31. *See* POST, *supra* note 86, at 90–93; Simon v. Ivey, 2025 WL 2,345,845, at *58 (N.D. Ala. Aug. 13, 2025).

122. *Connick v. Myers*, 461 U.S. 138, 147 (1983) ("We hold . . . that when a public employee speaks not as a citizen upon matters of public concern, but instead as an employee upon matters only of personal interest, absent the most unusual circumstances, a federal court is not the appropriate forum in which to review the wisdom of a personnel decision taken by a public agency allegedly in reaction to the employee's behavior.").
123. Timothy Zick, *Faculty Speech, Academic Freedom, and Democratic Backsliding*, *in* THE ELGAR COMPANION TO FREEDOM OF SPEECH AND EXPRESSION (2025) (manuscript at 13), https://papers.ssrn.com/sol3/papers.cfm?abstract_id=5179131.
124. RABBAN, *supra* note 17, at 126. *See* POST, *supra* note 86, at 80–85.
125. There are significant analytic difficulties in doing so, as is clear in the brave (if theoretically hopeless) efforts of the court in Pernell v. Florida Board of Governors of the State University System, 641 F.Supp. 3d 1218 (N.D. Fla. 2022) to wrestle with the distinction between viewpoint and content discrimination.
126. For such an argument, see POST, *supra* note 86, at 61–99.
127. Post, *supra* note 20, at 112–17.
128. UNIVERSITY OF CALIFORNIA PERSONNEL MANUAL, *Section 010* ("Academic Freedom"), at https://www.ucop.edu/academic-personnel-programs/_files/apm/apm-010.pdf.
129. For a full discussion, see Robert C. Post, *Between Governance and Management: The History and Theory of the Public Forum*, 34 UCLA L. REV. 1713 (1987). For a detailed analysis of how courts use doctrine in this way in assessing the constitutionality of speech regulation in public K-12 schools, despite explicit statements to the contrary, see Robert C. Post, *Theorizing Student Expression: A Constitutional Account of Student Free Speech Rights*, 76 STAN. L. REV. 1643 (2024).
130. Post, *Between Governance and Management*, *supra* note 129. Because of its focus on individual rights, the Court has never been able explicitly to acknowledge this point. So, for example, the Court has consistently classified managerial domains as nonpublic fora, and it has consistently asserted that viewpoint discrimination is prohibited in nonpublic fora. *See, e.g.*, Minnesota Voters Alliance v. Mansky, 585 U.S. 1, 12 (2018). But the Court has in fact routinely permitted viewpoint discrimination in nonpublic fora, as can clearly be seen in a decision like Morse v. Frederick, 551 U.S. 393 (2007), which holds that K-12 schools can prohibit speech advocating drug use but nevertheless allow speech opposing drug use. *Morse* graphically illustrates that the relevant constitutional question for the regulation of speech within nonpublic fora is not viewpoint discrimination, but instead whether speech regulation is instrumentally connected to the specific mission of an institution. Consider in this regard the courtroom governance of speech in an ordinary trial.
131. *See, e.g.*, Ronell Andersen Jones & Sonja R. West, *The Disappearing Freedom of the Press*, 79 WASH. & LEE L. REV. 1377 (2022).
132. POST, *supra* note 86, at 61–80.
133. Interpreting the First Amendment in light of the current need for a functioning democracy is no different in theory than the Court's recent efforts to restructure administrative law in light of what it understands to be contemporary democratic requirements. *See, e.g.*, Free Enterprise Fund v. PCAOB, 561 U.S. 477, 497–99 (2010); Noah A. Rosenblum & Roderick M. Hills, *Presidential Administration After* Arthrex, DUKE L. J. (forthcoming 2026), at https://papers.ssrn.com/sol3/papers.cfm?abstract_id=5122594. In its unrelenting efforts to wrest control away from an unelected bureaucracy and place it instead in the hands of a democratically elected president, the Roberts Court is radically changing constitutional law to restructure federal administration in ways that would have been all but unrecognizable to the Framers. *See, e.g.*, Ashraf Ahmed, Lev Menand & Noah A. Rosenblum, *The Making of Presidential Administration*, 137 HARV. L. REV. 2131, 2139 (2024) ("Presidential administration was not an idea working itself pure in real time. It had to be made. It was the result of localized interventions in concrete political and legal fights."); *id.* at 2142 ("the unitary executive theory rests its claims to legitimacy in part on its being a

long-accepted, widely shared theory of constitutional interpretation. But the history reveals otherwise.").

134. Universities possess this authority because they supervise the training and certification of new experts. Of course, the "knowledge" produced by scholars is subject to continuous revision and reformulation, which is why academic freedom of research is itself essential. *See* Joan Wallach Scott, *Academic Freedom & the Politics of the University*, 153 DAEDALUS 1 (Summer 2024). The point, however, is that scholarly debates accompanying the production of disciplinary standards occur within the disciplinary practices of the profession. Because academic judgments must always be exercised within the context of freedom, they are inherently unstable. *See* FINKIN & POST, *supra* note 6, at 56–60. If judgment becomes too intolerant, a discipline can become static and irrelevant. But if judgment is insufficiently rigorous, a discipline can explode into antinomian anarchy.
135. Many organizations in American society, from pharmaceutical companies to Bell Labs, produce knowledge, but their dissemination of this knowledge is protected only by ordinary First Amendment rights. By contrast, institutions of higher education should enjoy a unique constitutional right of academic freedom of research because they alone validate and reproduce the practices that identify expert knowledge and hence that form the foundation for the epistemological independence of citizens.
136. The separation of the sphere of knowledge from the sphere of power is an essential premise of modern democratic thought. CLAUDE LEFORT, DEMOCRACY AND POLITICAL THEORY 15 (David Macey trans., 1988). On the general movement in international law for courts to protect structures that are necessary for the exercise of democratic rights, see Kim L. Scheppele, *Rights into Structures: Judging in a Time of Democratic Backsliding*, 26 GERMAN L. J. 255, (2025).
137. *See supra* text at note 21; AMY GUTMANN, DEMOCRATIC EDUCATION (1987); BENJAMIN R. BARBER, AN ARISTOCRACY OF EVERYONE: THE POLITICS OF EDUCATION AND THE FUTURE OF AMERICA 15 (1992) ("[I]n democracies, education is the indispensable concomitant of citizenship.").
138. *See* Robert C. Post, *The Internet, Democracy, and Misinformation, in* DISINFORMATION, MISINFORMATION, AND DEMOCRACY: LEGAL APPROACHES IN COMPARATIVE CONTEXT 44–45 (Ronald J. Krotoszynski, Jr., András Koltay & Charlotte Garden eds., Cambridge University Press 2025).
139. ROBERT C. POST, CITIZENS DIVIDED: CAMPAIGN FINANCE REFORM AND THE CONSTITUTION 10–19 (2014).
140. 344 U.S. 183, 194 (1952) (Frankfurter, J., concurring).
141. *Id.* at 196–97.
142. *See supra* note 56.
143. Consider, in this light, the administration's attack on the independence of law firms or its dismissal of the head of the Bureau of Labor Statistics. *See* Ben Casselman, *Trump Fired America's Economic Data Collector*, N.Y. TIMES (Aug. 4, 2025), at https://www.nytimes.com/2025/08/03/business/trump-bls-firing-economic-reports.html; Nona Randois, *Trump's Attacks on Lawyers Are Attacks on the Rule of Law*, ALLIANCE FOR JUSTICE (Apr. 30, 2025), at https://afj.org/article/trumps-attacks-on-lawyers-are-attacks-on-the-rule-of-law/.
144. The doctrine of expressive associations, *supra* text at notes 92–99, is so powerful and malleable that it can offer extensive constitutional protections to state efforts to regulate private universities.
145. Indiana Senate Bill 202 (Mar. 13, 2024), at https://legiscan.com/IN/text/SB0202/id/2946990.
146. An opponent of the law characterized the thrust of the legislation as "We don't like the universities, and we wish there were fewer liberals." Representative Ed DeLaney, quoted in Casey Smith, *Despite Changes, Bill to End "Viewpoint Discrimination" Still Draws Ire from College Faculty*, INDIANA CAPITAL CHRON. (Feb. 22, 2024), at https://indianacapitalchronicle.com/2024/02/22/despite-changes-bill-to-end-viewpoint-discrimination-still-draws-ire-from-college-faculty/.
147. Christa Dutton *Changing the Course*, CHRON. OF HIGHER EDUC. (Mar. 5, 2025), at https://www.chronicle.com/article/changing-the-course.

148. *Id.*; *see* Keith E. Whittington, *Intellectual Diversity Mandates and the Freedom to Teach* (Dec. 15, 2024) at https://ssrn.com/abstract=5057350, at 3–4.
149. This difficulty leads to the fallacious reasoning of Meriwether v. Hartop, 992 F.3d 492 (6th Cir. 2021), which appeals to individual free-speech rights to uphold against a motion to dismiss a suit to set aside a college's regulation of pronoun usage in the classroom.
150. The State of Indiana defended its statute in a brief filed in federal court on the ground that faculty speech in the classroom of a public university is "core government speech." *See* Memorandum in Opposition to Plaintiff's Motion for Preliminary Injunction and in Support of the State's Motion to Dismiss for Lack of Subject-Matter Jurisdiction by Intervenor State of Indiana at 12, Carr v. Trustees of Purdue, No. 1:24-cv-00772 (S.D. Ind. July 22, 2024) [*Indiana Brief*]. Citing *Garcetti*, Indiana argued, as Florida had argued in defense of the IFA, *supra* text at note 42, that "[t]he instruction offered by state-employed educators at public universities is . . . government speech," and hence that faculty are without any relevant First Amendment rights. *Indiana Brief* at 12–13. The State argued that the First Amendment protected "teachers' speech" only "when made as 'private citizens.'" "Any speech pursuant to the teacher's 'official duties' and 'professional responsibilities' is subject to state direction." *Id.* at 13. *See* Quinn, *supra* note 42. Shockingly, although both Indiana and Purdue University have internal policies protecting academic freedom of teaching, both institutions at first endorsed this argument. Steve Sanders, *IU, Purdue Are Telling a Court Their Faculty Have No First Amendment Rights in the Classroom*, Medium (Aug. 9, 2024), at https://medium.com/@stevesan/iu-purdue-are-telling-a-court-their-faculty-have-no-first-amendment-rights-in-the-classroom-eeaea6bcc5d1; *see also* Defendant's Motion to Dismiss, Carr v. Trustees of Purdue, No. 1:24-cv-00772 (S.D. Ind. July 22, 2024). Both institutions later recanted this position. *See* Supplemental Notice Reaffirming the Limited Article III Scope of University Defendants' Joinder in State's Brief on Dismissal and Opposition to Preliminary Injunction, *id.* (Aug. 12, 2024). The suit to enjoin Public Law 113 was ultimately dismissed without prejudice on the ground that it was not ripe. Carr v. Trustees of Purdue University, 2024 WL 3,819,424 (S.D. Ind. Aug. 14, 2024).
151. As the Court, speaking in a constitutional register, put it in Rosenberger v. Rector and Visitors of University of Virginia, 515 U.S. 819, 836 (1995), "college and university campuses" are among "the vital centers for the Nation's intellectual life."
152. For the language of "public trust," see *supra* text at note 10. The justification for constitutionally imagining universities as a public trust of this kind is explained *supra* text at notes 131–141.
153. *See* Post, *Theorizing Student Expression*, *supra* note 129, at 1652–58.
154. *See* Legal Services Corp. v. Velazquez, 531 U.S. 533, 545–46 (2001).
155. *See, e.g.*, FCC v. League of Women Voters, 468 U.S. 364 (1984); Post, *Between Governance and Management*, *supra* note 129, at 1765–71; Post, *supra* note 103, at 160–63.
156. About this kind of situation, the *1915 Declaration* states:

> The simplest case is that of a proprietary school or college designed for the propagation of specific doctrines prescribed by those who have furnished its endowment. It is evident that in such cases the trustees are bound by the deed of gift, and, whatever be their own views, are obligated to carry out the terms of the trust. If a church or religious denomination establishes a college to be governed by a board of trustees, with the express understanding that the college will be used as an instrument of propaganda in the interests of the religious faith professed by the church or denomination creating it, the trustees have a right to demand that everything be subordinated to that end. If, again, as has happened in this country, a wealthy manufacturer establishes a special school in a university in order to teach, among other things, the advantages of a protective tariff, or if, as is also the case, an institution has been endowed for the purpose of propagating the doctrines of socialism, the situation is analogous. All of these are essentially proprietary institutions, in the moral sense. They do not, at least as regards one particular subject, accept the principles of freedom of inquiry, of opinion, and of teaching; and their purpose is not to advance knowledge by the unrestricted research and unfettered discussion of impartial investigators, but rather to

> subsidize the promotion of opinions held by the persons, usually not of the scholar's calling, who provide the funds for their maintenance. Concerning the desirability of the existence of such institutions, the committee does not wish to express any opinion. But it is manifestly important that they should not be permitted to sail under false colors. Genuine boldness and thoroughness of inquiry, and freedom of speech, are scarcely reconcilable with the prescribed inculcation of a particular opinion upon a controverted question.

Declaration, supra note 7, at 159–60.

157. *See, e.g.*, Healy v. James, 408 U.S. 169, 171 (1972) ("The college classroom with its surrounding environs is peculiarly the 'marketplace of ideas.'"). In this regard it is disturbing to read in the 2024 Gallup poll, *supra* note 49, that among Americans who have a great deal or quite a lot of confidence in higher education, only 9 percent state as a reason that it "trains students to think for themselves."
158. *See supra* text at note 120 and note 42.
159. Thus, a federal district court has recently upheld the constitutionality of Alabama's equivalent of the IFA on the explicit ground that there is no academic-freedom exception for *Garcetti*. The Court reasoned: "Incanting the phrase 'academic freedom' does not justify giving unique treatment to one subgroup of government employees. Singling out professors for special constitutional treatment would create inequities among public employees, including subsets of the government workforce whose jobs involve expressive work." Simon v. Ivey, 2025 WL 2345845, at *58 (N.D. Ala. Aug. 13, 2025).
160. *See* Whittington, *supra* note 148.
161. *See supra* note 156.
162. On the distinction between the values protected by a right and the identities of those empowered to bring lawsuits to enforce those values, see Robert C. Post, *Democratic Constitutionalism and Cultural Heterogeneity*, 25 Australian Journal of Legal Philosophy 185, 191–95 (2000).
163. *See supra* text at note 113.
164. *Declaration, supra* note 7, at 180.
165. *Id.*
166. *See supra* text at notes 51–52; Billie Wright Dziech, *Higher Ed, We Have a Problem*, Inside Higher Ed (Sep. 20, 2023), at https://www.insidehighered.com/opinion/views/2023/09/20/higher-ed-cant-afford-its-left-wing-bias-problem-opinion. Issues of expense and economic inequality are likely also relevant. *See supra* note 52.
167. *See, e.g.*, Sebastian Kiecker, *The Politics of Populism and Climate Action*, E3G (Dec. 16, 2024), at https://www.e3g.org/news/the-politics-of-populism-and-climate-action/.
168. *See* Robert C. Post, *The Supreme Court's Crisis of Authority: Law, Politics, and the Judiciary Act of 1925*, 100 Notre Dame L. Rev. (forthcoming 2025); Robert C. Post, *Theorizing Disagreement: Reconceiving the Relationship Between Law and Politics*, 98 Calif. L. Rev. 1319 (2010).
169. *Proceedings of the Forty-Ninth Judicial Conference of the District of Columbia*, 124 F.R.D. 241, 338 (1989).
170. *See* Robert C. Post & Reva B. Siegel, *Democratic Constitutionalism*, *in* The Constitution in 2020, at 25 (Jack M. Balkin & Reva B. Siegel eds., 2009); Robert C. Post & Reva B. Siegel, Roe *Rage: Democratic Constitutionalism and Backlash*, 42 Harv. C.R.-C.L. L. Rev. 373 (2007).
171. On the generic necessity for such balancing in the context of regulating professional expertise, see Post, *supra* note 79, at 97–99.

Chapter 2

1. *See* William F. Buckley, Jr., God and Man at Yale: The Superstitions of "Academic Freedom" (1951).
2. *See, e.g.*, *id.* at xv–xvi ("[T]he institution that derives its moral and financial support from Christian individualists . . . then addresses itself to the task of persuading the sons of these supporters to be atheistic socialists.").
3. *See, e.g.*, *id.* at 50–54.

4. *See id.* at 121–23.
5. *See id.* at xv, xix.
6. *See Government Funding for Universities*, IBIS World (July 11, 2024), https://www.ibisworld.com/us/bed/government-funding-for-universities/4073/. In 2023, for example, federal funding for universities amounted to almost $60 billion—55 percent of all university research and development expenditures. *Since the 1950s, Over Half of R&D Expenditures at U.S. Colleges and Universities Have Been Funded by the Federal Government*, Nat'l Ctr. for Sci. & Eng'g Stat. (July 10, 2025), https://ncses.nsf.gov/pubs/nsf25345; *see also* Andrea Fuller et al., *Where Federal Dollars Flow to Universities Around the Country*, N.Y. Times (Apr. 30, 2025), https://www.nytimes.com/interactive/2025/04/30/us/university-funding-research.html. That year, Columbia alone received almost $989 million from the federal government, making it the sixth-biggest university recipient of federal funds. *Table 24. Federally Financed Higher Education R&D Expenditures, Ranked by FY 2023 R&D Expenditures: FY 2010–23*, Nat'l Ctr. for Sci. & Eng'g Stat. (Nov. 2024), https://ncses.nsf.gov/pubs/nsf25314/table/24. Harvard received almost $640 million. *Id.*
7. *See* Christopher Eisgruber, *The Cost of the Government's Attack on Columbia*, The Atlantic (Mar. 19, 2025), https://www.theatlantic.com/ideas/archive/2025/03/columbia-academic-freedom/682088/ ("Robust federal funding helped make American universities the world's best, but it also created a huge risk. Universities had acquired a public patron more powerful than any private donor; their budgets became heavily dependent on that single source. If the United States government ever repudiated the principle of academic freedom, it could bully universities by threatening to withdraw funding unless they changed their curricula, research programs, and personnel decisions.").
8. *DOJ, HHS, ED, and GSA Announce Initial Cancelation of Grants and Contracts to Columbia University Worth $400 Million*, U.S. Dep't of Educ. (Mar. 7, 2025), https://www.ed.gov/about/news/press-release/doj-hhs-ed-and-gsa-announce-initial-cancelation-of-grants-and-contracts-columbia-university-worth-400-million.
9. *See* Letter from Josh Gruenbaum, Comm'r of the Fed. Acquisition Serv., Gen. Servs. Admin., Sean R. Keveney, Acting Gen. Couns., US Dep't Health & Hum. Servs., & Thomas E. Wheeler, Acting Gen. Couns., US Dept. of Educ., to Katrina Armstrong, Interim President, Colum. U., David Greenwald, Co-Chair, Colum. Bd. of Trustees, & Claire Shipman, Co-Chair, Colum. Bd. of Trustees (Mar. 13, 2025), https://static01.nyt.com/newsgraphics/documenttools/6d3c124d8e20212d/85dec154-full.pdf.
10. *Id.*
11. *U.S. Department of Education's Office for Civil Rights Sends Letters to 60 Universities Under Investigation for Antisemitic Discrimination and Harassment*, US Dep't of Educ. (Mar. 10, 2025), https://www.ed.gov/about/news/press-release/us-department-of-educations-office-civil-rights-sends-letters-60-universities-under-investigation-antisemitic-discrimination-and-harassment. The letters warned sixty universities of "potential enforcement actions if they do not fulfill their obligations under Title VI of the Civil Rights Act to protect Jewish students on campus." *Id.*
12. Letter from Josh Gruenbaum, Comm'r of the Fed. Acquisition Serv., Gen. Servs. Admin., Sean R. Keveney, Acting Gen. Couns., US Dep't Health & Hum. Servs., & Thomas E. Wheeler, Acting Gen. Couns., US Dept. of Educ., to Alan M. Garber, President, Harv. U. & Penny Pritzker, Lead Member, Harv. Corp. (Apr. 11, 2025), https://www.harvard.edu/research-funding/wp-content/uploads/sites/16/2025/04/Letter-Sent-to-Harvard-2025-04-11.pdf.
13. I bracket the extraordinary nature of the letter's text, apart from legal questions. Its tone might perhaps be understandable if directed at a university whose principal mission was to promote Communism or Nazism. I also bracket the shameful and horrific history of uses of public power to manipulate institutions of higher education to promote the views and the interests of those in authority. *See generally, e.g.*, Benjamin Tromly, Making the Soviet Intelligentsia (2013); Abraham Wolf, Higher Education in Nazi Germany (1944); *see also* United States Holocaust Memorial Museum, *Higher Education in Nazi Germany*, Experiencing History: Holocaust Sources in Context, https://perspectives.ushmm.org/collection/higher-education-in-nazi-germany (last visited Oct. 12, 2025).

14. In 2025, there were numerous relevant events, and any account will rapidly become dated. It is worth noting that in July, Columbia University settled with the executive branch, with terms that seemed to preserve its autonomy but that also gave a great deal in return, including money. *See* Sharon Otterman, *Columbia Agrees to $200 Million Fine to Settle Fight With Trump*, N.Y. TIMES (July 23, 2025), https://www.nytimes.com/2025/07/23/nyregion/columbia-trump-funding-deal.html; *Fact Sheet: President Donald J. Trump Secures Major Settlement with Columbia University*, THE WHITE HOUSE (July 24, 2025), https://www.whitehouse.gov/fact-sheets/2025/07/19853/.
15. An especially valuable discussion can be found in J. Peter Byrne, *Academic Freedom: A "Special Concern of the First Amendment,"* 99 YALE L.J. 251 (1989).
16. *See* Lawrence Rosenthal, *Does the First Amendment Protect Academic Freedom?*, 46 J. COLL. & U. L. 223, 228 (2021) ("Academic freedom can also be framed as the prerogative of a university to make and enforce academic judgments free from external interference; in the words of Justice Frankfurter, academic freedom consists of 'the four essential freedoms *of a university*—to determine for itself on academic grounds who may teach, what may be taught, how it shall be taught, and who may be admitted to study.'"). A prominent reference to academic freedom appears in *Regents of Univ. of California v. Bakke*: "Academic freedom, though not a specifically enumerated constitutional right, long has been viewed as a special concern of the First Amendment. The freedom of a university to make its own judgments as to education includes the selection of its student body." 438 U.S. 265, 312 (1978) (opinion of Powell, J.); *see also* Keyishian v. Board of Regents of Univ. of State of N.Y., 385 U.S. 589, 603 (1967) ("Our Nation is deeply committed to safeguarding academic freedom, which is of transcendent value to all of us, and not merely to the teachers concerned. That freedom is therefore a special concern of the First Amendment. . . . The Nation's future depends upon leaders trained through wide exposure to that robust exchange of ideas which discovers truth 'out of a multitude of tongues, [rather] than through any kind of authoritative selection.'" (quoting United States v. Associated Press, 52 F. Supp. 362, 372 (S.D.N.Y. 1943))).
17. *See* Geoffrey R. Stone, *Content Regulation and the First Amendment*, 25 WM. & MARY L. REV. 189 (1983).
18. *Id.* at 197.
19. *Id.* at 190.
20. *Id.* at 189.
21. R.A.V. v. City of St. Paul, 505 U.S. 377, 388 (1992); Rosenberger v. Rector & Visitors of the Univ. of Va., 515 U.S. 819, 829 (1995). See, in particular, this illuminating passage from *Rosenberger*:

    > When the government targets not subject matter, but particular views taken by speakers on a subject, the violation of the First Amendment is all the more blatant. Viewpoint discrimination is thus an egregious form of content discrimination. The government must abstain from regulating speech when the specific motivating ideology or the opinion or perspective of the speaker is the rationale for the restriction.

    Id. And note this potentially provocative statement: "If the topic of debate is, for example, racism, then exclusion of several views on that problem is just as offensive to the First Amendment as exclusion of only one." *Id.* at 831.
22. It might be possible to argue that the prohibition on price-fixing is not viewpoint-based, on the theory that the prohibition is designed to prevent not speech but a kind of act. I acknowledge this point without embracing it here. It is tempting, and too easy, to characterize words that one wishes to ban as "acts."
23. On some of the complexities in the academic setting, *see generally* CASS R. SUNSTEIN, CAMPUS FREE SPEECH (2024).
24. *See* Reed v. Town of Gilbert, 576 U.S. 155, 165 (2015) ("[S]trict scrutiny applies either when a law is content based on its face or when the purpose and justification for the law are content based.").

25. For example, a prohibition on perjury is content-based, and so is a prohibition on bribery or child pornography.
26. Consider, for example, an effort to demonstrate that the sun goes around the earth, that the Holocaust never happened, or that dropped objects do not fall. Perhaps it can be said that efforts of this sort are terrible because they cannot meet standards of competence, but viewpoint discrimination, of one kind of another, might be difficult to avoid.
27. *See, e.g.*, Clark v. Cmty. for Creative Non-Violence, 468 U.S. 288, 293 (1984) ("[R]estrictions of this kind are valid provided that they are justified without reference to the content of the regulated speech, that they are narrowly tailored to serve a significant governmental interest, and that they leave open ample alternative channels for communication of the information."); *see generally* Geoffrey R. Stone, *Content-Neutral Restrictions*, 54 U. CHI. L. REV. 46 (1987). There is also a distinction between public forums and nonpublic or limited public forums; the latter may be subject to broader regulation. *See Rosenberger*, 515 U.S. at 829.
28. The basic principles can be gleaned from Schneider v. State, 308 U.S. 147 (1939); Martin v. City of Struthers, 319 U.S. 141 (1943); Bartnicki v. Vopper, 532 U.S. 514 (2001); United States v. O'Brien, 391 U.S. 367 (1968).
29. Pleasant Grove City v. Summum, 555 U.S. 460, 467 (2009); Walker v. Texas Division, Sons of Confederate Veterans, 576 U.S. 200, 207 (2015). For discussion, *see generally* Caroline Mala Corbin, *The Government Speech Doctrine Ate My Class*, 76 STAN. L. REV. 1001 (2024).
30. 500 U.S. 173 (1991).
31. *Id.* at 194 (citation omitted) (citing 22 U.S.C. § 4411(b)).
32. *Board of Regents of Univ. of Wis. System v. Southworth*, 529 U. S. 217, 229, 235 (2000). The reason for the formulation in text—"perhaps no"—is that we can imagine cases that would raise hard questions. Suppose that the government encouraged private employers to hire only Christians. Would that violate the Establishment Clause? The answer is not obviously "No."
33. 524 U.S. 569 (1998).
34. Rosenberger v. Rector and Visitors of the University of Virginia, 515 U.S. 819 (1995); Legal Services Corp. v. Velasquez, 531 U.S. 533 (2001); Agency for International Development v. Alliance for Open Society, 570 U.S. 205 (2013).
35. 20 U.S.C. § 954 (2010).
36. *Finley*, 524 U.S. at 580–81.
37. *Id.* at 583.
38. *Id.* at 587.
39. *See id.* ("[T]he First Amendment certainly has application in the subsidy context. . . .").
40. Rosenberger v. Rector and Visitors of the University of Virginia, 515 U.S. 819 (1995); Legal Services Corp. v. Velasquez, 531 U.S. 533 (2001); Agency for International Development v. Alliance for Open Society, 570 U.S. 205 (2013).
41. *See, e.g., Velasquez*, 531 U.S. at 552–53 (Scalia, J., dissenting) (writing that, absent a threat of "'coercive effect' on those who do not hold the subsidized position," which is "virtually impossible" to prove, government subsidy programs "may allocate . . . funding according to criteria that would be impermissible were direct regulation of speech or a criminal penalty at stake" (quoting *Finley*, 524 U.S. at 587–88)). This dissent was joined by Justices Thomas and O'Connor. *Id.* at 549. *See also Alliance for Open Society*, 570 U.S. at 222 (Scalia, J., dissenting) ("Of course the Constitution does not prohibit government spending that discriminates against, and injures, points of view to which the government is opposed."). This dissent was joined by Justice Thomas. *Id.* at 221.
42. 515 U.S. 819 (1995).
43. *Id.* at 822–23.
44. *Id.* at 833.
45. *Id.* at 833–34.
46. *Id.* at 835.
47. 531 U.S. 533 (2001).
48. *Id.* at 541. For a broader reading, *see Agency for International Development v. Alliance for Open Society International, Inc.*, 570 U.S. 205, 221 (2013) (Scalia, J., dissenting) ("The First Amendment does not mandate a viewpoint-neutral government. Government must choose between rival ideas and adopt some as its own: competition over cartels, solar energy over coal, weapon

development over disarmament, and so forth. Moreover, the government may enlist the assistance of those who believe in its ideas to carry them to fruition; and it need not enlist for that purpose those who oppose or do not support the ideas. That seems to me a matter of the most common common sense."). It should be noted that this view, vigorously supported by Justice Scalia, has been repudiated by the Court on several occasions, but there can be no assurance that it would not be accepted, in some form, in the future.

49. *Velazquez*, 531 U.S. at 541 (quoting Rosenberger v. Rector and Visitors of University of Virginia, 515 U.S. 819, 833 (1995)).
50. In the same vein is Agency for International Development v. Alliance for Open Society, 570 U.S. 205 (2013).
51. We could put some pressure on this conclusion. Suppose that the government ran a grant program about the history of race in the United States and refused to fund applications that celebrated slavery. Or suppose that the government ran a grant program funding historical work on World War II and refused to fund applications that extolled Hitler's virtues and lamented the defeat of Nazi Germany. With such examples in mind, we might be drawn to the conclusion that funding decisions are not subject to restrictions on viewpoint discrimination. *See, e.g.*, *Velasquez*, 531 U.S. at 552–53 (Scalia, J., dissenting) (writing that government subsidy programs "may allocate . . . funding according to criteria that would be impermissible were direct regulation of speech or a criminal penalty at stake"); *Alliance for Open Society*, 570 U.S. at 222 (Scalia, J., dissenting) ("Of course the Constitution does not prohibit government spending that discriminates against, and injures, points of view to which the government is opposed."). But the Court has repeatedly rejected that conclusion.
52. *See Velasquez*, 531 U.S. 533 (2001); *Alliance for Open Society*, 570 U.S. 205 (2013).
53. *See* Daniel Kahneman, Thinking Fast and Slow (2011).
54. *See* Daniel Gilbert, Stumbling on Happiness (2006).
55. *See* Kathleen Sullivan, *Unconstitutional Conditions*, 102 Harv. L. Rev. 1513 (1989).
56. 500 U.S. 173, 197 (1991).
57. 468 U.S. 364 (1984).
58. 47 U.S.C. § 399.
59. *League of Women Voters of California*, 468 U.S. at 400.
60. *Id.*
61. See United States v. American Library Assn., Inc., 539 U.S. 194, 210 (2003).
62. I believe this to be true, though if we do not press hard on the word "relatively," the proposition might be contested, and from high levels. In *Alliance for Open Society*, for example, the Court wrote: "In the present context, the relevant distinction that has emerged from our cases is between conditions that define the limits of the government spending program—those that specify the activities Congress wants to subsidize—and conditions that seek to leverage funding to regulate speech outside the contours of the program itself. The line is hardly clear, in part because the definition of a particular program can always be manipulated to subsume the challenged condition." 570 U.S. 205, 214–15 (2013). Much of the time, I think, it is not possible to manipulate the definition in this way.
63. *See id.* at 218 ("By demanding that funding recipients adopt—as their own—the Government's view on an issue of public concern, the condition by its very nature affects 'protected conduct outside the scope of the federally funded program.'"). Note that this is a different problem from (for example) funding Democratic student groups but not Republican student groups.
64. 505 U.S. 377 (1992).
65. *Id.* at 384.
66. *Id.*
67. *See, e.g.*, Letter from Josh Gruenbaum et al. to Katrina Armstrong & David Greenwald, *supra* note 9 (declaring that "the United States Government would be pausing or terminating federal funding" for Columbia and that it would not engage in "formal negotiations regarding Columbia University's financial relationship with the . . . government" if the university did not, among other things, adopt and promulgate a definition of anti-Semitism that addressed anti-Zionist discrimination against Jews, ban masks, and enforce disciplinary policies against the encampments); Letter from Josh Gruenbaum et al. to Alan Garber & Penny Pritzker, *supra*

note 12 (demanding that Harvard "reform[] programs with egregious records of antisemitism or other bias," "end support and recognition of... student groups or clubs that engaged in anti-Semitic activity," "implement a comprehensive mask ban," and expel and suspend particular students, among other things, in order to "maintain [its] financial relationship with the federal government").

68. The Department of State, for example, lists a wide range of acts it considers anti-Semitic; these range from "[c]alling for, aiding, or justifying the killing or harming of Jews," to "[m]aking . . . stereotypical allegations about Jews," to "[a]ccusing Jews as a people of being responsible for real or imagined wrongdoing committed by a single Jewish person or group, or . . . by non-Jews," to "claiming that the existence of a State of Israel is a racist endeavor." *Defining Antisemitism*, U.S. DEP'T OF STATE, https://www.state.gov/defining-antisemitism/ . The Anti-Defamation League gives its own definition of anti-Semitism, which it says "can range from offensive or biased comments and behaviors based on that person's Jewish identity (or perceived identity), to language, rhetoric or actions that demonize, delegitimize or apply a double standard to the Jewish state, Zionism and Zionists." *Understanding Antisemitism and Anti-Zionism*, ANTI-DEFAMATION LEAGUE (June 16, 2025), https://www.adl.org/resources/tools-and-strategies/understanding-antisemitism-and-anti-zionism. For a compilation of various definitions of anti-Semitism, *see* Rabbi Toby H. Manewith, *Five Definitions of Antisemitism*, UNION FOR REFORM JUDAISM (Apr. 24, 2025), https://urj.org/blog/five-definitions-antisemitism.
69. 524 U.S. 569 (1998).
70. *Id.* at 588.
71. *Id.* at 589.
72. *Id.*
73. *Id.* at 590.
74. *Id.* at 599–600.
75. *National Association of Diversity Officers in Higher Education v. Trump*, 767 F. Supp. 3d 243 (D. Md. 2025); *Santa Cruz Lesbian and Gay Community Center v. Trump*, 508 F. Supp. 3d 521 (N.D. Cal. 2020); *San Francisco A.I.D.S. Foundation v. Trump*, 2025 WL 1621636 (N.D. Cal. Jun. 9, 2025).
76. *San Francisco A.I.D.S. Foundation*, 2025 WL 1621636 at 21.
77. Papachristou v. Jacksonville, 405 U.S. 156 (1972).
78. An open-ended grant could also raise nondelegation concerns, but it is not clear how seriously the Court is taking the nondelegation doctrine. *See* Gundy v. United States, 588 U.S. 128 (2019); Federal Communications Commission v. Consumers' Research, 145 S. Ct. 2482 (2025).
79. *See* David Besanko, *Performance Versus Design Standards in the Regulation of Pollution*, 34 J. PUB. ECON. 19 (1987).
80. 414 U.S. 1142 (1974).
81. *Id.* at 258.
82. As noted, there is a question whether vagueness in funding provisions is subject to the void-for-vagueness doctrine. *See supra.*
83. *See, e.g.*, Rahem D. Hamid & Elias J. Schisgall, *More Than Three-Quarters of Surveyed Harvard Faculty Identify as Liberal*, HARVARD CRIMSON (May 22, 2023), https://www.thecrimson.com/article/2023/5/22/faculty-survey-2023-politics/ (reporting that more than 77 percent of Harvard faculty polled in a 2023 survey identified as either "very liberal" or "liberal"; Meimei Xu, *More than 80% of Surveyed Harvard Faculty Identify as Liberal*, HARVARD CRIMSON (July 13, 2022), https://www.thecrimson.com/ (reporting that 82 percent of Harvard faculty polled in a 2022 survey identified as either "very liberal" or "liberal"); Buckley Institute, *A Report on Faculty Political Diversity* (Sept. 2024), https://buckleyinstitute.com/content/uploads/2024/09/Faculty-Research-Report-2024_compressed.pdf (reporting that, among surveyed Yale faculty, 77 percent registered as Democrats or had "conducted political activity that heavily or exclusively supports Democrats" and under 3 percent are Republican).
84. The classic text is WILLIAM F. BUCKLEY, JR., GOD AND MAN AT YALE (1951). *See generally* Steven M. Teles, *Why Are There So Few Conservative Professors?* CHRONICLE OF HIGHER

EDUCATION (July 1, 2024), https://www.chronicle.com/article/why-are-there-so-few-conservative-professors; Keith E. Whittington, *The Value of Ideological Diversity Among University Faculty*, 37 SOC. PHIL. & POL. 2 (2021), https://www.cambridge.org/core/journals/social-philosophy-and-policy/article/abs/value-of-ideological-diversity-among-university-faculty/6D0D3069588A790AB37A34AEA4101E10.

85. *See supra* notes 1–2 and accompanying text.
86. Letter from Josh Gruenbaum et al. to Katrina Armstrong & David Greenwald, *supra* note 6.
87. *See* CASS R. SUNSTEIN, CAMPUS FREE SPEECH (2024).
88. Grayned v. City of Rockford, 408 U.S. 104 (1972).
89. Dombrowski v. Pfister, 380 U.S. 479 (1965).
90. *See* Keyishian v. Board of Regents of the University of the State of New York, 385 U.S. 589, 603 (1967) ("Our Nation is deeply committed to safeguarding academic freedom, which is of transcendent value to all of us, and not merely to the teachers concerned. That freedom is therefore a special concern of the First Amendment.").
91. Sweezy v. New Hampshire, 354 U.S. 234, 249–50 (1957). For a vivid statement, *see* Robert Post, *Academic Freedom and the Constitution*, in WHO'S AFRAID OF ACADEMIC FREEDOM? 123, 123 (Akeel Bilgrami & Jonathan R. Cole eds., 2016) ("[T]he doctrine of academic freedom stands in a state of shocking disarray and incoherence."). For a brisk, helpful summary of the ambiguous history of academic freedom in the United States, *see* Byrne, *supra* note 15, 267–79. Note, in particular, this suggestion, highly relevant to originalists and to those who focus on history and tradition: "In the old-time college, prior to the Civil War, the concept of academic freedom was literally inconceivable. The goal of higher education was to train young men in religious piety and mental discipline as a preparation for the clergy and other gentlemanly professions, such as law and medicine. The essentially religious objectives of the early colleges demanded and received the assent of faculty to the theological essentials of the Christian sect that founded and supported the college." *Id.* at 270.
92. U.S. CONST. amend. I.
93. *See* Post, *supra* note 91, at 132 ("The value of democratic competence should lie at the core of the constitutional concept of academic freedom. As a constitutional principle, academic freedom must preserve the integrity of disciplinary practices from unrestrained political control. This is consistent with the professional ideal of academic freedom, which essentially claims that the scholarly profession should be self-regulating. Decisions about disciplinary competence cannot be made on the basis of public opinion or on the basis of the personal views of those who happen to provide the funds that support universities.").
94. For a vivid account, broadly supportive of McCarthy, *see generally* WILLIAM F. BUCKLEY, JR., & L. BRENT BOZELL, MCCARTHY AND HIS ENEMIES (1954).
95. *See* Dobbs v. Jackson Women's Health Center, 597 U.S. 215, 231 (2022) (stating that any right held to be guaranteed by a constitutional provision without having been explicitly mentioned "must be 'deeply rooted in this Nation's history and tradition' and 'implicit in the concept of ordered liberty'" (quoting Washington v. Glucksberg, 521 U.S. 702, 721 (1997))).
96. 354 U.S. 234 (1957).
97. *Sweezy*, 354 U.S. at 245 (emphasis added).
98. *Id.* at 250.
99. *Id.*; *see* Post, *supra* note 91, for a sustained elaboration.
100. *Sweezy*, 354 U.S. at 262 (Frankfurter, J., concurring).
101. *Id.*
102. *Id.* at 263; *see also* Keyishian v. Board of Regents, 385 U.S. 589 (1967).
103. *Keyishian*, 385 U.S. at 603.
104. University of Pennsylvania v. Equal Employment Opportunity Commission, 493 U.S. 182 (1990).
105. To know whether there is a right to academic freedom, and to know its scope, we need a theory of constitutional interpretation. We should be able to agree, of course, that academics have freedom of speech, which means that intrusions on the freedom of administrators, professors, lecturers, and students can raise First Amendment issues. But a different conception of academic freedom, entailing some kind of immunity for academic institutions, raises different issues. Post, *supra* note 91, defends academic freedom on something like purposive grounds.

Originalists might struggle to identify anything in the original public meaning that would support academic freedom as such. The majority and concurring opinions in *Sweezy* are also not originalist.

106. *See* Judith Areen, *Government as Educator*, 97 Geo. L.J. 945 (2009); William Van Alstyne, *Academic Freedom and the First Amendment in the Supreme Court of the United States*, 53 L. and Contemp. Probs. 79 (1990); Robert Post, Democracy, Expertise, Academic Freedom (2012); Byrne, *supra* note 15; Finkin, *Toward a Law of Academic Status*, 22 Buffalo L. Rev. 575, 587 (1973); Murphy, *Academic Freedom—An Emerging Constitutional Right*, 28 L. & Contemp. Probs. 447 (1963); *Developments in the Law, Academic Freedom*, 81 Harv. L. Rev. 1045 (1968).
107. *See* Byrne, *supra* note 15, at 251 ("I shall argue that the First Amendment protects the central intellectual efforts of the modern university. These efforts include teaching, scholarship, and experimentation, all of which contribute unique cultural and intellectual values to a free society.").
108. *See Regents of the University of California v. Bakke*, 438 U.S. 265, 312 (1978).
109. *See* Byrne, *supra* note 15, at 312 (suggesting that "judicial protection of institutional autonomy is the appropriate concern of constitutional academic freedom").
110. *Cf. id.* at 267 ("The structural mechanisms within the university that give precedence to peer judgment and the function that this judgment performs in preserving the coherence and promoting the accomplishments of a given discipline determine the content of academic freedom.").
111. *See id.* at 262 ("The term 'academic freedom' should be reserved for those rights necessary for the preservation of the unique functions of the university, particularly the goals of disinterested scholarship and teaching.").
112. *See* Areen, *supra* note 106; Post, *supra* note 106.
113. Byrne, *supra* note 15, at 264.
114. *See* Post, *supra* note 106, for a general discussion.
115. Sweezy v. New Hampshire, 354 U.S. 234, 263 (1957); *see also* notes 279–81 and accompanying text.
116. *See* NAACP v. Button, 371 U.S. 415 (1963).
117. *See* Kent v. Dulles, 357 U.S. 116 (1958).
118. Cass R. Sunstein, *Two Justifications for the Major Questions Doctrine*, 76 Fla. L. Rev. 251 (2024).
119. West Virginia v. EPA, 142 S. Ct. 2587, 2616 (2022) (Gorsuch, J., concurring).
120. *Id.* at 2608 (majority opinion).
121. *See, e.g.*, Dear Colleague Letter: Sexual Violence, from Russlynn Ali, Assistant Sec'y for C.R., US Dep't of Educ. (Apr. 4, 2011), https://www2.ed.gov/about/offices/list/ocr/letters/colleague-201104.pdf (promulgating new guidelines for universities to follow in dealing with sexual-harassment and sexual-assault complaints filed by students and announcing that failure to comply with such guidelines could lead to withdrawal of federal funding).
122. That appears to be the Court's view in *Sweezy*. One version of that view, emphasizing democratic competence, is defended in Post, *supra* note 105.

Chapter 3

1. Quoted in Ellen Schrecker, No Ivory Tower: McCarthyism and the Universities 360 (Oxford Univ. Press, 1986).
2. John Dewey, Academic Freedom (1902), *reprinted in* The Chicago Canon on Free Inquiry and Expression 51–64 (Banout & Ginsburg eds., 2024)
3. John K. Wilson, *100 Years Ago, the Scopes Monkey Trial Discovered Academic Freedom*, Chron. of Higher Educ. (Jul. 10, 2025).
4. Sweezy vs. New Hampshire, 354 US 234 (1957).
5. Lawrence Levine demonstrated that this is a process that has been continuous in American history from the nineteenth century to the present, in The Opening of the American Mind: Canons, Culture, and History (Penguin, 1997).

6. Lee A. Daniels, *Stanford Alters Western Culture Course,* N.Y. Times (Apr. 2, 1988).
7. David Kurlander, *"Out of Ignorance": William Bennett, Stanford, and the Debate over History Education,* Café (Jun. 17, 2021), https://cafe.com/article/out-of-ignorance-william-bennett-stanford-and-the-debate-over-history-education/; *see also* Steven Mintz, *The Culture War. Version 2.0,* Inside Higher Ed (Nov. 8, 2023) (quoting Carl Degler as saying that "[f]ew historians believe that the culture of this country has been seriously influenced by ideas from Africa, China, Japan or indigenous North America." Mintz notes the irony of Degler saying this, given that he was a Pulitzer Prize–winning historian of slavery, race, and gender, but also noting that there was an actual debate on the subject among principled faculty).
8. John Pollack, *Bennett Blasts Fac Sec,* The Stanford Daily (Apr. 19, 1988); Allan Bloom, The Closing of the American Mind: How Higher Education Has Failed Democracy and Impoverished the Souls of Today's Students (Simon & Schuster, 1987).
9. Newsweek Staff, *Curdled Politics on Campus,* Newsweek (May 5, 1991)
10. *See* James Davison Hunter, Culture Wars: The Struggle to Define America (Basic, 1991).
11. See my account of Berkeley between 2012 and 2017 in Nicholas B. Dirks, City of Intellect: The Uses and Abuses of the University (Cambridge Univ. Press, 2024).
12. The critique of liberalism left no consensus in its place, instead opening universities up to the charge that they were hypocritical in their supposedly full embrace of free speech and the open marketplace of ideas.
13. Berkeley was threatened by Trump in a tweet of February 2017, the morning after a riot took place on campus around the visit of Yiannopoulos, with the cancellation of all federal funding. This threat was not activated during Trump's first presidential term, and universities doubtless grew complacent as a result.
14. Stanley Kurtz et al., Goldwater Inst., Campus Free Speech: A Legislative Proposal (2017).
15. John R. Vile, *Campus Free Speech Protection Laws,* Free Speech Ctr. at Middle Tenn. State Univ. (Oct. 31, 2024), https://firstamendment.mtsu.edu/article/campus-free-speech-protection-laws/.
16. *See, e.g.,* Matthew Purdy, *The Techno-Futuristic Philosophy Behind Elon Musk's Mania,* N.Y. Times (May 31, 2025).
17. National Conservatism, *J. D. Vance| The Universities Are the Enemy| National Conservatism Conference II,* YouTube (Nov. 10, 2021), https://www.youtube.com/watch?v=0FR65Cifnhw.
18. H.R. 7, 124th Leg. Reg. Sess. (Fla. 2022).
19. *See* Derrick A. Bell, Race, Racism and American Law (6th ed. 2008); Kimberlé Crenshaw, *Demarginalizing the Intersection of Race and Sex: A Black Feminist Critique of Anti-Discrimination Doctrine, Feminist Theory and Antiracist Politics,* 1989 U. Chi. Legal Forum 139 (1989).
20. Christopher F. Rufo, America's Cultural Revolution: How the Radical Left Conquered Everything (2023).
21. For an excellent review and discussion of the book, see Len Gutkin, *Chris Rufo Can't Decide Between Propaganda and Intellectual History,* Chron. of Higher Educ. (Aug. 4, 2023).
22. Michael Bender et al., *Inside Trump's Pressure Campaign on Universities,* N.Y. Times (Apr. 14, 2025).
23. Rufo, *supra* note 20 at 280–81.
24. *See* Max Eden, *A Comprehensive Guide to Overhauling Higher Education,* Am. Enter. Inst. (Dec. 4, 2024).
25. Rufo, *supra* note 20 at 281–82.
26. Letter from Josh Gruenbaum et al. to Alan M. Garber & Penny Pritzker (Apr. 11, 2025).
27. Joan Scott, *Knowledge, Power, and Academic Freedom,* in Who's Afraid of Academic Freedom? (Akeel Bilgrami & Jonathan R. Cole eds., Colum. U. Press, 2015).
28. *See, e.g.,* Ross Douthat, *Why Liberal Academia Needs Republican Friends,* N.Y. Times (Nov. 4, 2023); Tyler Austin Harper, *America's Colleges Are Reaping What They Sowed,* Atlantic (May 2, 2024).

Chapter 4

1. Thomas Babington Macaulay, The History of England from the Accession of James the Second, vol. II at ch. VIII (1848), https://www.gutenberg.org/files/2439/2439-h/2439-h.htm.
2. *Id.*
3. *Id.*
4. *April 3 Demands to Harvard*, Harvard Crimson (Apr. 4, 2025), https://www.thecrimson.com/widget/2025/4/4/harvard-demands-letter/.
5. *Id.*
6. Letter from Josh Gruenbaum, Comm'r of the Fed. Acquisition Serv., General Services Administration, Sean R. Keveney, Acting General Counsel, US Dep't Health & Human Servs. & Thomas E. Wheeler, Acting General Counsel, US Dept. of Education, to Dr. Alan M. Garber, President, Harvard University & Penny Pritzker, Lead Member, Harvard Corporation (Apr. 11, 2025), https://www.harvard.edu/research-funding/wp-content/uploads/sites/16/2025/04/Letter-Sent-to-Harvard-2025-04-11.pdf.
7. *Id.*
8. Donald J. Trump (@realDonaldTrump), Truth Social (May 2, 2025, 7:25 a.m.), https://truthsocial.com/@realDonaldTrump/posts/114437989795464761.
9. Joint Task Force to Combat Anti-Semitism, *Joint Task Force Letter to Harvard University Concerning Notice of Violation* (June 30, 2025), https://www.gsa.gov/about-us/newsroom/news-releases/joint-task-force-letter-to-harvard-university-concerning-notice-of-violation-06302025.
10. Bob Jones University v. United States, 461 U.S. 574 (1983).
11. James Hankins, A Conservative Harvard Professor on How the University Can Save Itself, Wall Street J. (Apr. 24, 2025), https://www.wsj.com/us-news/education/a-conservative-harvard-professor-on-how-the-university-can-save-itself-e5f9c90a.
12. *Id.*
13. Complaint, President and Fellows of Harvard College v. Department of Health and Human Services, et al., Docket No. 1:25-cv-11048 (D. Mass. 2025) [*Harvard v. DHHS*], available at https://www.harvard.edu/research-funding/wp-content/uploads/sites/16/2025/04/Harvard-Funding-Freeze-Order-Complaint.pdf
14. *Id.* at ¶ 11–12.
15. Douglas Belkin et al., *Harvard President Says Any Move to Revoke Tax-Exempt Status Would Be "Highly Illegal,"* Wall Street J. (May 2, 2025), https://www.wsj.com/us-news/education/trump-harvard-tax-exempt-status-3b114fb7.
16. *Id.*
17. Letter from Linda McMahon, secretary of education, to Dr. Alan M. Garber, president, Harvard University (May 5, 2025), https://www.harvard.edu/research-funding/wp-content/uploads/sites/16/2025/05/5.5.25-Harvard-Letter-from-EdSec-FINAL.pdf.
18. Michael C. Bender & Alan Blinder, *Trump Administration Cuts Additional $450 Million in Grants to Harvard*, N.Y. Times (May 13, 2025), https://www.nytimes.com/2025/05/13/us/politics/trump-harvard-grants-450-million.html.
19. Press Release, Dep't of Homeland Security, *Harvard University Loses Student and Exchange Visitor Program Certification for Pro-Terrorist Conduct* (May 22, 2025), https://www.dhs.gov/news/2025/05/22/harvard-university-loses-student-and-exchange-visitor-program-certification-pro.
20. Joseph Gedeon, White House Targets Harvard Again with Social Media Screening of All Foreign Visitors to School, Guardian (May 30, 2025), https://www.theguardian.com/us-news/2025/may/30/harvard-social-media-screening-visitors-trump-administration.
21. White House, *Enhancing National Security by Addressing Risks at Harvard University* (June 4, 2025), https://www.whitehouse.gov/presidential-actions/2025/06/enhancing-national-security-by-addressing-risks-at-harvard-university/.
22. Order Granting Plaintiff's Motion for a Preliminary Injunction, ECF No. 73, *Harvard v. DHHS* (June 20, 2025), available at https://www.harvard.edu/federal-lawsuits/wp-

content/uploads/sites/17/2025/06/0073.-06-20-2025-Judge-Allison-D.-Burroughs-ORDER-entered.-Preliminary-Injunction-entered-GRANTING-62-Motion.pdf.

23. Memorandum and Order, ECF No. 238, *Harvard v. DHHS* (Sept. 3, 2025), https://www.harvard.edu/federal-lawsuits/wp-content/uploads/sites/17/2025/09/gov.uscourts.mad_.283718.238.0_1.pdf.
24. Letter from Chuck Schumer, Senator, et al., to Heather M. Hill, Acting Inspector General, Treasury Inspector General for Tax Administration (May 2, 2025), https://www.democrats.senate.gov/imo/media/doc/letter_to_tigta_-_schumer_wyden_warren_markey_-_may_2_2025.pdf.
25. Mackenzie Wilkes, *Trump Says Deal Reached to End Feud with Harvard*, POLITICO (Sept. 30, 2025), https://www.politico.com/news/2025/09/30/trump-deal-reached-end-feud-harvard-00588651.
26. Douglas Belkin et al., *Harvard Explores New Center for Conservative Scholarship amid Trump Attacks*, WALL STREET J. (July 10, 2025).
27. Ben Unglesbee et al., *Tracking the Trump Administration's Deals with Colleges*, HIGHER ED DIVE (Oct. 22, 2025), https://www.highereddive.com/news/tracking-the-trump-administrations-deals-with-colleges/803434/.
28. Lexi Lonas Cochran, *Here Are the Colleges Rejecting Trump's Funding Compact*, The Hill (Oct. 21, 2025), https://thehill.com/homenews/education/5558934-colleges-reject-donald-trump-administration-compact/.
29. Macaulay, *supra* note 1.
30. Greg Lukianoff, *Harvard in the Crosshairs*, The Eternally Radical Idea (Substack) (Apr. 24, 2025), https://eternallyradicalidea.com/p/harvard-in-the-crosshairs.
31. *Id.*
32. Atul Gawande, *The Cost of Defunding Harvard*, New Yorker (Apr. 21, 2025), https://www.newyorker.com/news/the-lede/the-cost-of-defunding-harvard.
33. Harvard Presidential Task Force on Combating Antisemitism and Anti-Israeli Bias, *Final Report* at 8–9, 12, (Apr. 29, 2025), https://www.harvard.edu/wp-content/uploads/2025/04/FINAL-Harvard-ASAIB-Report-4.29.25.pdf.
34. *Id.* at 18.
35. *Id.*
36. *Id.* at 19.
37. *Id.* at 149–50.
38. Lukianoff, *Harvard in the Crosshairs*, *supra* note 30.
39. Rahem D. Hamid & Elias J. Schisgall, *More Than Three-Quarters of Surveyed Harvard Faculty Identify as Liberal*, HARVARD CRIMSON (May 22, 2023), https://www.thecrimson.com/article/2023/5/22/faculty-survey-2023-politics/.
40. Lukianoff, *Harvard in the Crosshairs*, *supra* note 30.
41. Rahem D. Hamid & Elias J. Schisgall, *More Than Three-Quarters of Surveyed Harvard Faculty Identify as Liberal*, *supra* note 39.
42. *Id.*
43. *Id.*
44. Students for Fair Admissions v. President and Fellows of Harvard College, 600 U.S. 181 (2023).
45. Matthew Yglesias, *Trump's War on Harvard*, Slow Boring (Substack), https://www.slowboring.com/p/trumps-war-on-harvard.
46. *Id.*
47. Harvard University, *Meet the Class of 2027*, https://features.thecrimson.com/2023/freshman-survey/beliefs/ (last visited Nov. 2, 2025).
48. *Id.*
49. Samuel A. Church & Cam N. Srivastava, *Most Harvard Students Do Not Feel Comfortable Sharing Controversial Opinions in Class, Survey Finds*, HARVARD CRIMSON (Feb. 10, 2025), https://www.thecrimson.com/article/2025/2/10/survey-results-controversial-opinions/.
50. Harvard University, *Meet the Class of 2027*, *supra* note 47.

51. Laura Silver, Younger Americans Stand Out in Their Views of the Israel-Hamas War, Pew Research Ctr. (Apr. 4, 2024), https://www.pewresearch.org/short-reads/2024/04/02/younger-americans-stand-out-in-their-views-of-the-israel-hamas-war/.
52. *Id.*
53. NBC News Stay Tuned Poll Results (Apr. 27, 2025), https://www.documentcloud.org/documents/25919931-nbc-news-stay-tuned-poll-april-27/.
54. More in Common, Is Gen Z Giving Up on Democracy? 4 (2025), https://moreincommonus.com/publication/is-gen-z-giving-up-on-democracy/.
55. *Id.*
56. Emily Hallas, *White House Offers Funding Advantage to Colleges That Sign "Compact for Academic Excellence,"* WASHINGTON EXAMINER (Oct 2, 2025), https://www.washingtonexaminer.com/policy/education/3833857/white-house-funding-advantage-colleges-sign-compact-for-academic-excellence/ (full compact available on same web page).
57. Edward Gibbon, The Autobiography of Edward Gibbon (1788).

Chapter 5

1. Center for American Progress, *Mapping Federal Funding Cuts to U.S. Colleges and Universities* (July 23, 2025), https://www.americanprogress.org/article/mapping-federal-funding-cuts-to-us-colleges-and-universities ("According to the Trump administration, it has terminated awards valuing between $6.9 billion and $8.2 billion.").
2. President and Fellows of Harvard College v. Department of Health and Human Services, 798 F. Supp.3d 77, 2025 WL 2528380 (1st Cir., 2025); Thakur v. Trump, 787 F.Supp.3d 955 (N.D. Cal. 2025), 148 F.4th 1096 (9th Cir. 2025). I am cocounsel in Thakur v. Trump.
3. Jason Cohen, *How Much Federal Funding Do Colleges and Universities Receive?*, URBAN WIRE (May 8, 2025), https://www.urban.org/urban-wire/how-much-federal-funding-do-colleges-and-universities-receive.
4. Collin Binkley & Jonathan Mattise, *With No Takers Yet, White House Sets Meeting with Colleges Still Weighing an Agreement with Trump*, ASSOCIATED PRESS (Oct. 17, 2025), https://www.yahoo.com/news/articles/no-takers-yet-white-house-174246827.html/.
5. Ross Douthat, *The Anti-D.E.I. Crusader Who Wants to Dismantle the Department of Education*, N.Y. TIMES (Apr. 7, 2025), https://www.nytimes.com/2025/04/07/opinion/ross-douthat-christopher-rufo.html.
6. Emma Green, *Inside the Trump Administration's Assault on Higher Education*, NEW YORKER (Oct. 20, 2025), https://www.newyorker.com/magazine/2025/10/20/inside-the-trump-administrations-assault-on-higher-education.
7. American Association of University Professors, *1915 Declaration of Principles on Academic Freedom and Academic Tenure* (1915), https://www.aaup.org/NR/rdonlyres/A6520A9D-0A9A-47B3-B550-C006B5B224E7/0/1915Declaration.pdf.
8. Keyishian v. Bd. of Regents, 385 U.S. 589, 603 (1967).
9. Sweezy v. New Hampshire, 354 U.S. 234, 250 (1954) (plurality).
10. Exec. Order No. 14151, 90 Fed. Reg. 8339 (Jan. 20, 2025).
11. Exec. Order No. 14173, 90 Fed. Reg. 8633 (Jan. 21, 2025).
12. Exec. Order No. 14168, 90 Fed. Reg. 8615 (Jan. 20, 2025).
13. Exec. Order No. 14158, 90 Fed. Reg. 8441 (Jan. 20, 2025).
14. Exec. Order No. 14222, 90 Fed. Reg. 11095 (Feb. 26, 2025).
15. See Department of Government Efficiency, Wall of Receipts, https://doge.gov/savings (last visited Nov. 4, 2025).
16. Complaint at ¶ 112, Thakur v. Trump, 3:25-cv-04737 (N.D. Cal. June 4, 2025).
17. Thakur v. Trump, 184 F.4th at 1108–09.
18. Regan v. Tax'n with Representation of Wash., 461 U.S. 540, 547–48 (1983) (citation omitted).
19. 500 U.S. 173 (1991).
20. *Id.* at 179.
21. *Id.* at 180.
22. *Id.* at 193 (citations omitted) (emphasis added).
23. 524 U.S. 569, 587 (1998).

24. 20 U.S.C. § 954(c)(1)-(10).
25. *Id.* § 954(d)(1); *Finley*, 524 U.S. at 576.
26. *Id.* at 583.
27. *Id.*
28. Thakur v. Trump, 787 F.Supp.3d at 974.
29. Exec. Order No. 14151, 90 Fed. Reg. 8339 (Jan. 20, 2025) (emphasis added); Exec. Order No. 14173, 90 Fed. Reg. 8633 (Jan. 21, 2025) (emphasis added).
30. *See* Alan Blinder & Michael C. Bender, *Trump Wants U.C.L.A. to Pay $1 Billion to Restore Its Research Funding*, N.Y. TIMES, (Aug. 9, 2025), https://www.nytimes.com/2025/08/08/us/trump-ucla-research-funding-deal.html.
31. 600 U.S. 181 (2023).
32. President and Fellows of Harvard College, slip op. at 27.
33. Resolution Agreement Between Brown University and the United States of America (July 30, 2025), https://www.brown.edu/sites/default/files/brown-and-united-states-resolution-agreement_July-30-2025.pdf.
34. *Id.* at 7.
35. Press Release, US Department of Education, Secretary McMahon Statement on Brown University Deal (July 30, 2025), https://www.ed.gov/about/news/press-release/secretary-mcmahon-statement-brown-university-deal.
36. Sharon Otterman, Columbia Agrees to $200 Million Fine to Settle Fight with Trump, N.Y. TIMES (July 23, 2025), https://www.nytimes.com/2025/07/23/nyregion/columbia-trump-funding-deal.html.
37. Letter from Josh Gruenbaum, Comm'r of the Fed. Acquisition Serv., General Services Administration, Sean R. Keveney, Acting General Counsel, US Dep't Health & Human Servs. & Thomas E. Wheeler, Acting General Counsel, US Dept. of Education, to Dr. Alan M. Garber, President, Harvard University, & Penny Pritzker, Lead Member, Harvard Corporation (Apr. 11, 2025) https://www.harvard.edu/research-funding/wp-content/uploads/sites/16/2025/04/Letter-Sent-to-Harvard-2025-04-11.pdf.
38. 42 U.S.C. § 2000(d).
39. President and Fellows of Harvard College, slip op. at 37.
40. Emily Hallas, *White House Offers Funding Advantage to Colleges That Sign "Compact for Academic Excellence,"* WASHINGTON EXAMINER (Oct. 2, 2025), https://www.washingtonexaminer.com/policy/education/3833857/white-house-funding-advantage-colleges-sign-compact-for-academic-excellence/ (full compact available on same web page).
41. *Id.*
42. Snyder v. Phelps, 562 U.S. 443, 458 (2011).
43. Counterman v. Colorado, 600 U.S. 66, 69 (2023) (a speaker can be punished if he "consciously disregarded a substantial risk that his communication would be viewed a threat of violence").
44. ERWIN CHEMERINSKY & HOWARD GILLMAN, FREE SPEECH ON CAMPUS 82 (2017).
45. Bostock v. Clayton County, Georgia, 590 U.S. 644 (2020).
46. 483 U.S. 203 (1987).
47. *Id.* at 211 (citation and internal quotation marks omitted).
48. 567 U.S. 519 (2012).
49. *Id.* at 581.
50. *Id.* at 581–82.
51. *See* text accompanying note 390, *supra*; Jason Cohen, *How Much Federal Funding Do Colleges and Universities Receive*, URBAN WIRE (May 8, 2025), https://www.urban.org/urban-wire/how-much-federal-funding-do-colleges-and-universities-receive.
52. Regan v. Tax'n with Representation of Wash. 461 U.S. 540, 545 (1983) (quoting Perry v. Sindermann, 408 U.S. 593, 597 (1972)).
53. 357 U.S. 513 (1958).
54. *Id.* at 518.
55. *Id.* at 519.
56. 408 U.S. 593, 597 (1972) (citation omitted).
57. 468 U.S. 364 (1984).

Chapter 6

1. John Aubrey Douglass, *The Rise of the Publics: American Democracy, the Public University Ideal, and the University of California*, Rsch. & Occasional Paper Series, Feb. 2018, at 5.
2. This statement somewhat oversimplifies. As Judith Areen has noted, due to the states' involvement in the appointment of lay board members, "[h]istorians still debate whether the earliest American colleges were public, private, or something else entirely." Judith Areen, *Governing Board Accountability: Competition, Regulation, and Accreditation*, 36 J.C. & U.L. 691, 696 (2010).
3. Morrill Act of 1862, Pub. L. 37–130, 12 Stat. 503 (codified as amended at 7 U.S.C. § 301).
4. James A. Maxwell, Federal Grants and the Business Cycle 1 (1952).
5. Agricultural College Act of 1890, Pub. L. 51–841, 26 Stat. 419 (codified as amended at 7 U.S.C. § 321).
6. Hatch Act of 1887, Pub. L. 49–314, 24 Stat. 440 (codified as amended at 7 U.S.C. § 361a). In 1998, Congress amended the 1887 Hatch Act to require states to provide matching funds. Agricultural Research, Extension, and Education Reform Act of 1998, Pub. L. 105–185, 112 Stat. 523 (codified as amended at 7 U.S.C. § 7601).
7. Jonathan R. Cole, The Great American University 19 (2009).
8. *Id.* at 22–23.
9. Elissa Nadworny, *What Losing Billions in Federal Grants Means for Universities, and the Nation*, NPR: Morning Ed. (May 16, 2025), https://www.npr.org/2025/04/25/nx-s1-5375033/trump-federal-grants-cuts-universities-could-mean.
10. Derek Bok, Higher Education in America 16 (2013).
11. Matt Hourihan, *Wartime Innovation: Lessons from the Office of Scientific R&D*, Am. Ass'n for the Advancement of Sci. (Dec. 3, 2020), https://www.aaas.org/news/wartime-innovation-lessons-office-scientific-rd; Jeremy W. Peters & Andrea Fuller, *How Universities Became So Dependent on the Federal Government*, N.Y. Times (Apr. 18, 2025), https://www.nytimes.com/2025/04/18/us/trump-universities.html.
12. Daniel P. Gross & Bhaven N. Sampat, *The World War II Crisis Innovation Model: What Was It, and Where Does It Apply?*, Rsch. Pol'y, Nov. 2023, at 1, 3.
13. Roger Geiger, Research & Relevant Knowledge 3 (2017).
14. *Id.* at 4–5.
15. *Id.* at 3–5.
16. Exec. Order No. 8807, 6 Fed. Reg. 3207 (July 2, 1941).
17. Cole, *supra* note 7, at 86.
18. *Id.*
19. *Id.* at 93.
20. *See generally* Vannevar Bush, Science: The Endless Frontier (1945).
21. Cole, *supra* note 7, at 104.
22. *Id.* at 95–97. *See also* Bush, *supra* note 20, at 9–10 (arguing that postwar research funding should preserve "freedom of inquiry"). Another conflict was between military and national-security demands for secrecy, on the one hand, and scholarly demands for open communication necessary for scientific advances and peer review, on the other. Cole, *supra* note 7, at 92.
23. Cole, *supra* note 7, at 97.
24. *Id.* at 98.
25. *Id.* at 98–99.
26. *Id.* at 99.
27. Jaquelina C. Falkenheim & Jeffrey M. Alexander, *Funding Sources of Academic R&D*, Nat'l Sci Bd. (Oct. 5, 2023), https://ncses.nsf.gov/pubs/nsb202326/funding-sources-of-academic-r-d. Although states provide some research funding to their universities, the majority of research funding comes from the federal government. For example, during fiscal year 2024 at the University of North Carolina at Chapel Hill, the state provided only 8.5 percent of

research funding, whereas the federal government provided almost 66 percent. *Research Funding*, UNIV. OF N.C., https://research.unc.edu/impact/facts-rankings/funding/#sources (last visited Aug. 13, 2025).

28. KAVYA SEKAR, CONG. RSCH. SERV., R41705, THE NATIONAL INSTITUTES OF HEALTH (NIH): BACKGROUND AND CONGRESSIONAL ISSUES 26–29 (2025).
29. *Id.* at 42.
30. *Id.*
31. COLE, *supra* note 7, at 99.
32. *Id.* at 99.
33. Pub. L. No. 104–99, § 128, 110 Stat. 34, 51 (1996).
34. *See, e.g.*, Joceyln Kaiser & Meredith Wadman, *Trump Administration Releases New Details on Fetal Tissue Restrictions*, SCIENCE (July 26, 2019), https://www.science.org/content/article/trump-administration-releases-details-fetal-tissue-restrictions.
35. BOK, *supra* note 10, at 322.
36. 35 U.S.C. § 200.
37. Goshen David Miteu, *Patenting: The Bayh–Dole Act and Its Transformative Impact on Science Innovation and Commercialization*, 86 ANNAL MED. & SURGERY 3192, 3192–95 (2024). In an escalation of his war with Harvard, President Trump has announced that the Department of Commerce is investigating whether Harvard has complied with the requirements for technology transfers. *See* Stephanie Saul & Alan Blinder, *Trump Officials Press New Case Against Harvard, and Add a New Investigation*, N.Y. TIMES (Aug. 10, 2025), https://www.nytimes.com/2025/08/08/us/trump-harvard-patent-investigation-international-students.html.
38. BOK, *supra* note 10, at 322–23.
39. *Id.*
40. *Id.* at 323.
41. *Id.* at 325–26.
42. Brent D. Maher, Regulation and Autonomy: Three Historical Case Studies of Tensions Between Higher Education and the Federal Government 19 (2019) (Ph.D. dissertation, Harvard University), https://dash.harvard.edu/server/api/core/bitstreams/42b3c1c4-4f00-41b4-96c9-39a6ce26037e/content.
43. *Id.*
44. *Id.* at 33–38. Some conservatives were also concerned that universities were training students to be disloyal subversives. *Id.* at 34–35.
45. *Disclaimer Affidavit: Non-Participating and Disapproving Colleges and Universities*, 48, no. 4 AAUP BULL. 331, (1962). https://www.jstor.org/stable/40222919.
46. Maher, *supra* note 42, at 48.
47. 42 U.S.C. § 2000d.
48. 20 U.S.C. §§ 1681–1688.
49. 29 U.S.C. § 794.
50. For a much more in-depth discussion of this topic, *see* Jacob Gersen & Jeannie Suk, *The Sex Bureaucracy*, 104 CAL. L. REV. 881 (2016).
51. Jeremy W. Peters, *Trump Amps Up an Obama Strategy to Crack Down on Universities*, N.Y. TIMES (Aug. 6, 2025), https://www.nytimes.com/2025/08/06/us/politics/trump-universities-title-ix-vi-obama.html.
52. 547 U.S. 47 (2006).
53. 10 U.S.C. § 983.
54. *Rumsfeld v. F. for Acad. & Institutional Rts., Inc.*, 547 U.S. at 70. [*FAIR*]
55. *See* DAVID RABBAN, ACADEMIC FREEDOM: FROM PROFESSIONAL NORM TO FIRST AMENDMENT RIGHT 186–88 (2024) (noting how the Court ignored institutional academic freedom arguments presented in the case); *id.* at 308 (arguing that "institutional commitments to societal rather than educational values [as in *FAIR*] . . . are outside the scope of institutional academic freedom").
56. 603 U.S. 707 (2024).

57. *Id.* at 731 n.4 ("The Court ruled as it did because the law schools' recruiting services were not engaged in expression. The case could not have been resolved on that ground if the regulation had affected what happened in law school classes instead.") (internal citations omitted).
58. Agency for Int'l Dev. v. All. for Open Soc'y Int'l, Inc., 570 U.S. 205, 214–15 (2013).
59. *Id.* at 215.
60. *See* David Pozen, *Regulation by Deal Comes to Higher Ed*, BALKINIZATION (July 23, 2025), https://balkin.blogspot.com/2025/07/regulation-by-deal-comes-to-higher-ed.html (arguing Columbia settlement "gives legal form to an extortion scheme").
61. Lisa Larrimore Ouellette, *The Trump Administration's Multi-Front Attack on Federal Research Funding*, JUST SEC. (July 9, 2025), https://www.justsecurity.org/116486/trump-assault-federal-research-funding/. On September 29, 2025, the Office for Civil Rights at the US Department of Health and Human Services announced it was referring Harvard for "suspension and debarment proceedings." Press Release, US Dep't of Health and Hum. Servs., HHS' Office for Civil Rights Refers Harvard University for Suspension and Debarment Proceedings (Sep. 29, 2025), https://www.hhs.gov/press-room/ocr-refers-harvard-suspension-debarment.html.
62. Alexandra Zimmerman, *FY 2026 R&D Appropriations Dashboard*, AM. ASS'N FOR THE ADVANCEMENT OF SCI. (July 31, 2025), https://www.aaas.org/news/fy-2026-rd-appropriations-dashboard.
63. This is Harvard's indirect cost rate. *See F&A Cost Rates—Federal Sponsors*, HARV. UNIV., https://osp.finance.harvard.edu/fa-rates-federal-sponsors#:~:text=Note%201:%20For%20federal%20awards%20that%20use,for%20fiscal%20year%20ending%20June%2030%2C%202028 (last visited Oct. 5, 2025).
64. *Tracking the Trump Administration's Moves to Cap Indirect Research Funding*, HIGHER ED DIVE (June 24, 2025), https://www.highereddive.com/news/tracking-the-trump-administrations-moves-to-cap-indirect-research-funding/751123/. Federal district courts have enjoined these new policies, but litigation is ongoing. *Id.*
65. 600 U.S. 181 (2023); Michael C. Bender & Anemona Hartocollis, *Trump Administration to Require Universities to Submit Data on Applicants' Race*, N.Y. TIMES (Aug. 7, 2025), https://www.nytimes.com/2025/08/07/us/politics/trump-schools-race-data.html.
66. Emily Badger et al., *These Are the Universities Most Dependent on International Students*, N.Y. TIMES (May 23, 2025), www.nytimes.com/2025/05/23/upshot/harvard-trump-international-students.html.
67. *Id.*
68. *See generally* John Bound et al., *A Passage to America: University Funding and International Students*, 12 A.M. ECON. J.: ECON. POL'Y 97 (2020).
69. Tax Cuts and Jobs Act of 2017, Pub. L. 115–97, § 13701(a), 131 Stat. 2054, 2167 (codified as amended at I.R.C. § 4698).
70. One Big Beautiful Bill Act, Pub. L. 119–21, § 70415 (2025) (codified as amended at I.R.C. § 4968).
71. Gregory Svirnovskiy, *Trump Floats Going After More Schools' Tax-Exempt Status*, POLITICO (May 7, 2025), https://www.politico.com/news/2025/05/07/trump-taxes-harvard-universities-00334582.
72. Rose Horowitch, *The Elite University Presidents Who Despise Each Other*, THE ATLANTIC (Aug. 11, 2025), https://www.theatlantic.com/ideas/archive/2025/08/trump-university-presidents/683803/.
73. Letter from Josh Gruenbaum, Comm'r, Fed. Acquisition Serv., to Dr. Katrina Armstrong, Interim President, Columbia Univ. (Mar. 13, 2025), https://static01.nyt.com/newsgraphics/documenttools/6d3c124d8e20212d/85dec154-full.pdf.
74. Josh Moody, *Columbia Agrees to Trump's Demands*, INSIDE HIGHER ED (Mar. 21, 2025), https://www.insidehighered.com/news/governance/executive-leadership/2025/03/21/columbia-agrees-trumps-demands. The American Association of University Professors and the American Federation of Teachers have brought a legal challenge, but a federal district court dismissed the case for lack of standing, noting repeatedly that Columbia is responsible for most of the actions these groups challenge. Am. Ass'n of Univ. Professors v. U.S. Dep't of Just., No. 25-cv-2429, 2025 WL 1684817 (S.D.N.Y. June 16, 2025).

75. Anemona Hartocollis, Michael C. Bender & Alan Blinder, *Trump Offered Universities an Invitation for a Deal. Some See a Trap*, N.Y. Times (Oct. 2, 2025), https://www.nytimes.com/2025/10/02/us/trump-universities-compact-funding.html.
76. Michael S. Schmidt & Michael C. Bender, *University of Virginia President Resigns Under Pressure from Trump Administration*, N.Y. Times (June 27, 2025), https://www.nytimes.com/2025/06/27/us/politics/uva-president-resigns-jim-ryan-trump.html.
77. *Id.*
78. *Id.* The University of Virginia had received at least $355 million in 2023. *Id.*
79. Cole, *supra* note 7, at 96.
80. Robert Maynard Hutchins, The Higher Learning in America 4 (2d ed. 2009); *see also id.* at 5 (arguing that universities "should have an educational policy and then try to finance it, instead of letting financial accidents determine their educational policy").
81. Russell Kirk, *Massive Subsidies and Academic Freedom*, 28 Law & Contemp. Probs. 607, 607 (1963).
82. *Id.* at 611.
83. *Id.* at 612.
84. Clark Kerr, *The Realities of the Federal Grant University*, *in* The Uses of the University 35, 43 (5th ed. 2001).
85. *Id.* at 43–44; *see also* Am. Ass'n of Univ. Professors, Academic Freedom in the Medical School 125 (1999) [AAUP Medical School Report], https://www.aaup.org/sites/default/files/academic-freedom-medical-school.pdf (noting that the "growing reliance on clinical enterprises at many medical schools" may divert the university's attention from teaching to research and discourage professors from engaging in graduate teaching and university service, which are not financially lucrative).
86. Kerr, *supra* note 84, at 43.
87. AAUP Medical School Report, *supra* note 85.
88. Gordon G. Gallup & Brian B. Svare, *Hijacked by an External Funding Mentality*, Inside Higher Ed (July 24, 2016), https://www.insidehighered.com/views/2016/07/25/undesirable-consequences-growing-pressure-faculty-get-grants-essay.
89. *Id.*
90. *Id.*
91. Derek Bok, Universities in the Marketplace: The Commercialization of Higher Education 350–52 (2003).
92. *Id.* at 351–56.
93. *See, e.g.*, Naija Agarwal, *Penn Faculty Express Concern over Lack of Institutional Support, Funding Cuts for DEI Research*, The Daily Pennsylvanian (Feb. 23, 2025), https://www.thedp.com/article/2025/02/penn-faculty-dei-related-research-concerns (quoting a professor expressing concern that "the University will not fund [DEI research] programs that they have funded in the past because they are afraid of being seen to support this highly politicized area").
94. Ryan Quinn, *Williams Rejects NSF, NIH Grants Over Unclear DEI Ban*, Inside Higher Ed (June 9, 2025), https://www.insidehighered.com/news/quick-takes/2025/06/09/williams-college-rejects-nsf-nih-funds-over-unclear-dei-ban.
95. Am. Ass'n of Univ. Professors, 1940 Statement of Principles on Academic Freedom and Tenure 14 (1940), https://www.aaup.org/sites/default/files/1940%20Statement.pdf.
96. *Id.*
97. Wortis v. Trs. of Tufts Coll., 228 N.E.3d 1163, 1183 (Mass. 2024). The professors' claims were essentially breach-of-contract claims resting on Tufts' policies that incorporated the AAUP's *1940 Statement*. *Id.*
98. *Id.* at 1172.
99. *Id.* at 1167.
100. *Id.* at 1181.
101. *Id.*
102. *Id.* at 1167.
103. *Id.* at 1181.

104. 602 U.S. 175, 180 (2024) ("Government officials cannot attempt to coerce private parties in order to punish or suppress views that the government disfavors.").
105. Am. Ass'n of Univ. Professors, Against Anticipatory Obedience 1 (2025), https://www.aaup.org/sites/default/files/Against_Anticipatory_Obedience.pdf.
106. Letter from Andrew Tripp, Senior Vice President for Legal Affairs & General Counsel, Univ. of N.C. Sys., to the Chancellors of the University of North Carolina System (Feb. 5, 2025) [Tripp Letter], https://www.unc.edu/wp-content/uploads/2025/02/February-5-Memorandum-Regarding-Federal-Contracting-Compliance.pdf.
107. Ryan Quinn, *Citing Trump Order, UNC System Ends DEI Course Requirements*, Inside Higher Ed (Feb. 10, 2025), https://www.insidehighered.com/news/quick-takes/2025/02/10/citing-trump-order-unc-system-ends-dei-course-requirements.
108. Tripp Letter, *supra* note 106, at 2.
109. This curriculum mandate is similar to the decisions by many institutions around the country to dismantle campus DEI offices. *See* Erin Gretzinger et al., *Tracking Higher Ed's Dismantling of DEI*, Chron. of Higher Educ. (Aug. 5, 2025), https://www.chronicle.com/article/tracking-higher-eds-dismantling-of-dei. Such offices do not necessarily violate any antidiscrimination laws; indeed, in some places, the offices have been renamed things like "Student Belonging" to avoid attention as well as claims of illegality. *Id.* Notably, the UNC System made its decision to alter curricular requirements before the issuance of the February 14, 2025, "Dear Colleague" Letter from the US Department of Education, which declared it was "illegal" to have "programming" that "teach[es] students that certain racial groups bear unique moral burdens that others do not." Letter from Craig Trainor, Acting Assistant Sec'y for C.R., US Dep't of Educ., to Institutional Recipients of Federal Financial Assistance (Feb. 14, 2025), https://www.ed.gov/media/document/dear-colleague-letter-sffa-v-harvard-109506.pdf. A subsequent FAQ Memorandum recognized that federal law "prohibit[s] the Department from exercising control over the content of school curricula," but asserted that the Department has the authority to curb "themes in . . . class[es]" when they involve "more extreme practices" such as colleges requiring their students to "take certain positions on racially charged issues" in class, or "mandating courses . . . that are designed to emphasize and focus on racial stereotypes." Memorandum from Craig Trainor, Acting Assistant Sec'y for C.R., US Dep't of Educ., to Institutional Recipients of Federal Financial Assistance (Feb. 28, 2025), https://www.ed.gov/media/document/frequently-asked-questions-about-racial-preferences-and-stereotypes-under-title-vi-of-civil-rights-act-109530.pdf. A federal district court has preliminarily enjoined enforcement of the February 14, 2025, Dear Colleague Letter and the February 28, 2025, FAQs Memorandum against the National Education Association. National Education Ass'n v. US Dep't of Educ., 779 F. Supp.3d 149 (D.N.H. 2025).
110. No. 25-cv-2429, 2025 WL 1684817 (S.D.N.Y. June 16, 2025).
111. *Id.* at *4, *8–10, *14.
112. *Id.* at *14 ("Columbia did not merely implement the steps listed in the March 13 Letter from executive agencies, but rather exercised independent judgment.").
113. Am. Ass'n of Univ. Professors, Statement on Government of Colleges and Universities 120 (2025), https://www.aaup.org/sites/default/files/2025-07/Statement_on_Government_of_Colleges_and_Universities.pdf.
114. *Id.*
115. *Id.*
116. Kenneth P. Mortimer & Thomas Raymond McConnell, Sharing Authority Effectively: Participation, Interaction, and Discretion 6–7 (1978).
117. Weber et al., Am. Ass'n for Higher Educ., Faculty Participation in Academic Governance 1 (1967), https://files.eric.ed.gov/fulltext/ED018850.pdf.
118. Calls for Harvard to establish a faculty senate started during the pro-Palestinian protests in 2024. *See* Tilly R. Robinson & Neil H. Shah, *Awakening the Sleeping Giant: Harvard's Faculty Push for a Role in Governance*, Harv. Crimson (May 23, 2024), https://www.thecrimson.com/article/2024/5/23/harvard-faculty-governance-feature/.
119. For example, Professor Noah Feldman quickly rebutted any suggestion that Harvard consult him as it fights the Trump Administration. *The Face-Off Between Harvard and the Administration*, NPR: Fresh Air (Jun. 4, 2025), https://www.npr.org/2025/06/04/1253616082/

harvard-trump. During an interview on "Fresh Air," Feldman said that these kinds of decisions are best left to the university counsel. *Id.*

120. Douglas Belkin, *Faculty-on-Faculty War Erupts at Columbia as Trump Targets Elite School*, Wall St. J. (Mar. 11, 2025), https://www.wsj.com/us-news/education/columbia-university-trump-faculty-reaction-725a5e87.
121. Against Anticipatory Obedience, *supra* note 105.
122. Universities have had to make difficult funding decisions as a result of the massive loss of state and federal funding. *See, e.g.*, Francesca Pinney, *Stanford to Layoff over 360 Staff Following over $140 Million Budget Cuts*, Stan. Daily (Aug. 7, 2025), https://stanforddaily.com/2025/08/06/stanford-to-layoff-over-360-staff-following-140-million-budget-cuts/; Alan Blinder, *Tuition Increases and Layoffs Are Coming to Broad Set of Universities*, N.Y. Times (Jun. 20, 2025), https://www.nytimes.com/2025/06/20/us/tuition-hikes-layoffs-universities.html; Letter from Laura Rosenbury, President, Barnard College, to Barnard Community (July 31, 2025), https://barnard.edu/news/college-wide-staff-restructuring (announcing elimination of seventy-seven staff positions); Erin Gretzinger & Matt Hartman, *UNC-Chapel Hill Unveils Plan to Cut $70 Million in Response to Funding Pressure*, The Assembly (July 30, 2025), https://www.theassemblync.com/education/higher-education/unc-chapel-hill-unveils-plan-to-cut-70-million/ (noting that in the face of federal and state budget cuts, UNC will consolidate nonacademic teams such as human resources and reduce or cut certain academic programs, among other measures).
123. Kerr, *supra* note 84, at 43.
124. Neal H. Hutchens, *Preserving the Independence of Public Higher Education: An Examination of Constitutional Autonomy Provisions for State Public Colleges and Universities*, 35 J. Coll. & Univ. L. 271, 275 (2009) ("[L]egislative authority over appropriations represents a key check on constitutionally autonomous schools.").
125. Matthew W. Finkin & Robert C. Post, For The Common Good 150 (2009); Bok, *supra* note 91.
126. See Cole, *supra* note 7, at 101–02 (arguing it is "incorrect . . . that science for the public good could be produced without public discourse").
127. Keith Whittington, You Can't Say That 91 (2023).
128. *Id.* at 123.
129. *Id.* at 123–24.
130. *Id.* at 124.
131. *Id.* at 92.
132. *See generally* Am. Ass'n of Univ. Professors, Report of a Special Committee: Political Interference and Academic Freedom in Florida's Public Higher Education System (2023), https://www.aaup.org/sites/default/files/AAUP_Florida_final.pdf.
133. *See generally* Keith Whittington, *The Bounded Independence of American Universities* (Yale Law & Economics Research Paper, Aug. 5, 2025) https://papers.ssrn.com/sol3/papers.cfm?abstract_id=5378989.
134. *See* Eugene Volokh et al., *A Statement from Constitutional Law Scholars on Columbia*, N.Y. Rev. of Books (Mar. 20, 2025), https://www.nybooks.com/online/2025/03/20/a-statement-from-constitutional-law-scholars-on-columbia/.

Chapter 7

1. Edward W. Morley, *Oliver Wolcott Gibbs, 1822–1908*, 49 Proc. Am. Phil. Soc. xix (2010); Jocelyn Wilk, *A Narrative in the Documents: The Gibbs Affair*, Colum. U. Library Blog (Apr. 11, 2014), https://blogs.library.columbia.edu/rbml/2014/11/04/a-narrative-in-the-documents-the-gibbs-affair/.
2. David Pozen, *The Tenth Demand*, Balkinization (March 31, 2025), https://balkin.blogspot.com/2025/03/the-tenth-demand.html; Elisa Nadworny & Jordan Owens, *What We Know About Columbia's $221 Million Settlement with the Trump Administration*, NPR (July 25, 2025), https://www.npr.org/2025/07/25/nx-s1-5479240/columbia-trump-administration-settlement-details.

3. Michael T. Nietzel, *Federal Cuts Force Hiring and Raise Pauses at Johns Hopkins University*, Forbes (June 3, 2025), https://www.forbes.com/sites/michaeltnietzel/2025/06/03/federal-cuts-force-hiring-and-raise-pauses-at-johns-hopkins-university/.
4. Richard Hofstadter, *The Revolution in Higher Education*, *in* Paths of American Thought 269 (Arthur Schlesinger & Morton White, eds., 1963).
5. Morrill Land Grant College Act, ch. 130 §1, 12 Stat. 503 (1862) (codified as 7 U.S.C. § 301)
6. Hofstadter, *supra* note 4.
7. Roger L. Geiger, Research and Relevant Knowledge: American Research Universities Since World War II (2d ed. 2017); Jonathan R. Cole, *The Great American University*, 64 Bull. of the Am. Acad. of Arts and Sciences 27 (2011).
8. Geiger, *supra* note 7, at 30–31; Joel Isaac, *The Human Sciences in Cold War America*, 50 Historical Journal 725 (2007); Rebecca S. Lowen, Creating the Cold War University: The Transformation of Stanford (1997).
9. Philip G. Altbach, *The Past, Present, and Future of the Research University*, 46 Econ. and Pol. Wkly. 65, 65 (2011).
10. Jonathan R. Cole, *Balancing Acts: Dilemmas of Choice Facing Research Universities*, 122:4 Daedalus 1, 2 (1993); Rodney W. Nichols, *Federal Science Policy and Universities: Consequences of Success*, 122:4 Daedalus 197 (1993).
11. On the G.I. Bill, see Geiger, *supra* note 7, at 40–41. Christian K. Arnold, *A Historical Perspective: The Federal Role in Funding Education*, 14 Change 39 (1982).
12. Richard C. Atkinson & William A. Blanpied, *Research Universities: Core of the US Science and Technology System*, 30 Tech. in Soc'y 30, 38–39 (2008).
13. Deborah Welch Larson, *The Cold War and the University*, 24 Diplomatic History 151, 151 (2000); Louis Morton, *National Security and Area Studies: The Intellectual Response to the Cold War*, 34 Journal of Higher Education 142, 147 (1963).
14. Isaac, *supra* note at 8; Nils Gilman, Mandarins of the Future: Modernization Theory in Cold War America (2003).
15. Mark Solovey, *Science and the State During the Cold War: Blurred Boundaries and a Contested Legacy*, 31 Social Studies of Science 165, 168 (2001).
16. Daniel J. Kevles, *The National Science Foundation and the Debate over Postwar Research Policy, 1942–1945: A Political Interpretation of* Science—The Endless Frontier, 68 Isis 5 (1977).
17. Jonathan R. Cole & Cat Warren, *The Biography of the Great American University*, 96 Academe 43, 44 (2010).
18. Atkinson & Blanpied, *supra* note 12, at 41.
19. These results are from, respectively, William M. Bowen & Haifeng Qian, *State Spending for Higher Education: Does It Improve Economic Performance?* 9 Regional Science Policy & Practice 7 (2017); Philippe Aghion et al., *The Causal Impact of Education on Economic Growth: Evidence from US*, 1 Brookings Papers on Economic Activity 1 (2009); Lara Lebedinski & Vincent Vandenberghe, *Assessing Education's Contribution to Productivity Using Firm-Level Evidence*, 35 International Journal of Manpower 1116 (2014). Other studies caution against the risk of upward selection bias in published studies. Nikos Benos & Stefania Zotou, *Education and Economic Growth: A Meta-Regression Analysis*, 64 World Dev. 669 (2014).
20. Paul Pierson, Politics in Time: History, Institutions, and Social Analysis (2004).
21. Edwin Mansfield, *Basic Research and Productivity Increase in Manufacturing*, 70 Amer. Econ. Rev. 863 (1980); Ufuk Akcigit, Douglas Hanley & Nicolas Serrano-Velarde, *Back to Basics: Basic Research Spillovers, Innovation Policy and Growth*, 88 Rev. of Econ. Studies 1 (2021).
22. An informative study of Yale and the University of Cambridge found that the former, but not the latter, has been successful in stimulating local biotech start-ups. Shiri M. Breznitz, The Fountain of Knowledge: The Role of Universities in Economic Development (2014). It concludes that the effects of a university on its local economy vary depending on endogenous factors.
23. Aziz Z. Huq, *The Geopolitics of Digital Regulation*, 92 U. Chi. L. Rev. 833 (2025).
24. Luwei Rose Luqiu & John D. McCarthy, *Confucius Institutes: The Successful Stealth "Soft Power" Penetration of American Universities*, 90 J. of Higher Educ. 620 (2019).

25. Christopher Rufo, *How to Save Higher Ed—and End the Serial Abuse of American Taxpayers*, Free Press (July 14, 2025), https://www.thefp.com/p/the-president-wants-to-fix-higher-education-policy-reform-campus-university.
26. See Benjamin Eidelson & Deborah Hellman, *Antisemitism, Anti-Zionism, and Title VI: A Guide for the Perplexed*, Harv. L. Rev. F. (2025).
27. Meghan O'Rourke, *The End of the University as We Know It*, N.Y. Times (Mar. 16, 2025), https://www.nytimes.com/2025/03/16/opinion/university-defunding-trump-rufo.html.
28. Sarah Mervosh & Michael Schmidt, *What Happens if 'Harvard Is Not Harvard'?*, N.Y. Times (June 11, 2025), https://www.nytimes.com/2025/06/11/us/harvard-funding-trump-administration.html.

Chapter 8

1. This essay discusses a particular speech-suppressive Trump-administration measure that was also deployed by Presidents Obama and Biden. Trump also has taken many other actions that present a unique threat to academic autonomy and free speech on campus, a few of which we summarize here, and many of which are discussed in other chapters in this book.
2. Gloria Pazmino, *First on CNN: Congressional Delegation Visits Mahmoud Khalil and Rumeysa Ozturk in Louisiana Detention Centers*, CNN (Apr. 22, 2025), https://www.cnn.com/2025/04/22/us/mahmoud-khalil-rumeysa-ozturk-louisiana; Zach Montague, Stanford Newspaper Challenges Legal Basis for Student Deportations, N.Y. Times (Aug. 6, 2025), https://www.nytimes.com/2025/08/06/us/politics/stanford-lawsuit-student-activist-deportations.html (describing lawsuit brought by FIRE in August 2025, mounting a First Amendment challenge to a federal statute that Trump has invoked as allegedly justifying these deportations).
3. *International Student Visas Revoked*, Inside Higher Ed, https://www.insidehighered.com/news/global/international-students-us/2025/04/07/where-students-have-had-their-visas-revoked (last visited Oct. 3, 2025).
4. Stephanie Saul & Alan Blinder, *Judge Blocks a Trump Effort to Prevent International Students at Harvard*, N.Y. Times (June 20, 2025), https://www.nytimes.com/2025/06/20/us/international-students-harvard-preliminary-injunction.html.
5. There are many factual disputes about whether particular statements convey hateful or discriminatory messages. One common current example is "From the river to the sea, Palestine shall be free," which some interpret as supporting genocide of Israelis, and others interpret as opposing genocide by Israelis. This essay discusses whether speech may be restricted, even assuming that it may fairly be considered hateful or discriminatory.
6. Sometimes this form of impermissible harassment has been labeled "discriminatory harassment." It is distinguishable from "quid pro quo" sexual harassment, which refers to a form of extortion: when one person, who exercises power over another, demands sexual favors as the price of favorable (or fair) treatment—for example, when a faculty member indicates that a student's grade will turn on the (non)granting of sexual favors. The First Amendment does not protect any expression that is used for purposes of extortion. See text at *supra*, note 6.
7. *U.S. v. Schwimmer*, 279 U.S. 644, 654 (1929) (Holmes, J., dissenting).
8. Government may enforce speech restrictions that are not based solely on disapproval of the speech's viewpoint, but rather on other, contextual factors: if the speech violates a reasonable, viewpoint-neutral time, place, or manner regulation, or if the speech directly causes or imminently threatens certain specific serious harm, such as intentionally threatening or bullying a specifically targeted individual.
9. *See, e.g.*, Nadine Strossen, *Regulating Campus Hate Speech: A Modest Proposal?*, 1990 Duke L. J. 484 (1990); Greg Lukianoff, Unlearning Liberty: Campus Censorship and the End of American Debate (2014).
10. Robert Shibley, *Why the Supreme Court's Davis Standard Is Necessary to Restore Free Speech to America's College Campuses: Part I*, Found. for Individual Rts. and Expression [FIRE] (Oct. 14, 2019), https://www.thefire.org/news/why-supreme-courts-davis-standard-necessary-restore-free-speech-americas-college-campuses-part.

11. 526 U.S. 629 (1999). Title IX applies to federally funded education programs, which includes most K-12 public schools and virtually all colleges, public and private, thanks to federal student grants and loans.
12. *Meritor Savings Bank, FSB v. Vinson*, 477 U.S. 57, 67 (1986).
13. *Davis*, 526 U.S. at 633, 650, 651, 652 and 654.
14. *Id.* at 667 (Kennedy, J., dissenting).
15. *Id.* at 651–52. Speech-protective as the majority's standard was, the four dissenting Justices might well have defined constitutionally unprotected harassing expression even more narrowly. *See id.* at 667 (Kennedy, J., dissenting). Even in an employment setting, where free speech is much less important and much less protected that in an educational setting, the Court has said that "a mere offensive utterance" is unlikely to constitute hostile-environment harassment that violates Title VII's ban on employment discrimination. *Harris v. Forklift Systems*, 510 U.S. 17, 23 (1993). *Accord Faragher v. Boca Raton*, 524 U.S. 775, 787 (1998) (Title VII is not violated by the "mere utterance of an ethnic or racial epithet which engenders offensive feelings in an employee" or by "discourtesy or rudeness" including when caused by a "lack of racial sensitivity").
16. *Davis*, 526 U.S. at 646 ("[T]he nature of [the State's] power [over public schoolchildren] is custodial and tutelary, permitting a degree of supervision and control that could not be exercised over free adults.'"); *Id.* at 649 (Title IX requires educational institutions "to respond to known peer harassment in a manner that is not clearly unreasonable," considering the overall factual context"; since "[a] university might not . . . exercise the same degree of control over its students that a grade school would enjoy," it would be harder to show that a university's response was "clearly unreasonable").
17. Title VI and IX are considered sister statutes, and courts frequently apply the same reasoning to both. *See Cannon v. University of Chicago*, 441 U.S. 677, 696 (1979) ("The drafters of Title IX explicitly assumed that it would be interpreted and applied as Title VI had been. . . .")
18. *See, e.g.*, Henry Louis Gates, Jr., *Let Them Talk: Why Civil Liberties Pose No Threat to Civil Rights*, The New Republic (Sep. 20, 1993), https://newrepublic.com/article/149558/let-talk.
19. *Doe v. University of Michigan*, 721 F. Supp. 852 (E.D. Mich. 1989) (striking down the University of Michigan's code as unconstitutionally vague and overbroad).
20. *See* Erwin Chemerinsky & Howard Gillman, *College Campuses Can't Ban Hateful Speech, but There Are Other Ways to Combat It*, S.F. Chron. (Dec. 12, 2023), https://www.sfchronicle.com/opinion/openforum/article/free-speech-college-campus-18549500.php ("In the early 1990s, over 360 colleges and universities adopted hate speech codes. Every one, without exception, that has come to court was declared unconstitutional as a violation of the First Amendment.").
21. *See, e.g., DeJohn v. Temple Univ.*, 537 F.3d 301, 318–19 (3d Cir. 2008); *McCauley v. Univ. of the V.I.*, 618 F.3d 232, 247–53 (3d Cir. 2010); *Roberts v. Haragan*, 346 F. Supp. 2d 853, 871–73 (N.D. Tex. 2004); *Bair v. Shippensburg Univ.*, 280 F. Supp. 2d 357, 367–70 (M.D. Pa. 2003); *Booher v. Bd. of Regents*, No. 2:96-cv-135, 1998 U.S. Dist. LEXIS 11404, at *21–33 (E.D. Ky. July 21, 1998); *Corry v. Leland Stanford Junior Univ.*, No. 740309, 1995 WL 18262175, at *1–9 (Cal. Super. Ct. Feb. 27, 1995) (slip op.); *UWM Post, Inc. v. Bd. of Regents of the Univ. of Wis. Sys.*, 774 F. Supp. 1163, 1168–77 (E.D. Wis. 1991).
22. *Saxe v. State Coll. Area Sch. Dist.*, 240 F.3d 200, 204 (3d. Cir. 2001).
23. FIRE, Spotlight on Speech Codes 2025, at 4, https://www.thefire.org/sites/default/files/2025/07/Spotlight%20on%20Speech%20Codes%202025.pdf.
24. FIRE, Spotlight on Speech Codes 2024, at 3, https://www.thefire.org/sites/default/files/2024/01/Speech%20Code%20Report_2024_final.pdf.
25. Kristen Lombardi, *Education Department Touts Settlement as "Model" for Campus Sex Assault Policies*, The Center for Pub. Integrity (Dec. 8, 2010), https://publicintegrity.org/education/education-department-touts-settlement-as-model-for-campus-sex-assault-policies/.
26. While "Dear Colleague" letters are intended to provide "guidance" regarding a department's position on current legal requirements, indicating how the government interprets and intends to enforce these requirements (and what might prompt a finding of violation and possible

defunding), they rarely go through "notice and comment" processes that would give them the binding legal force of regulations. *See* Ari Cohn, Did the Office for Civil Rights' April 4 "Dear Colleague" Letter Violate the Law?, FIRE (Sep. 12, 2011), https://www.thefire.org/news/did-office-civil-rights-april-4-dear-colleague-letter-violate-law.

27. Russlynn Ali, Dear Colleague Letter (Apr. 4, 2011), at https://www.ed.gov/media/document/colleague-201104pdf-35042.pdf.
28. Gerald Reynolds, Dear Colleague Letter (July 28, 2003), at https://www.ed.gov/about/offices/list/ocr/firstamend.html.
29. See FIRE, US Department of Education's Office for Civil Rights April 4, 2011, Guidance Letter Reduces Due Process Protections, at https://www.thefire.org/cases/us-department-educations-office-civil-rights-april-4-2011-guidance-letter-reduces-due-process.
30. Letter from DOJ Civil Rights Division and DOE Office for Civil Rights to Royce Engstrom & Lucy France (The University of Montana) at 1 (May 9, 2013), https://www.justice.gov/sites/default/files/opa/legacy/2013/05/09/um-ltr-findings.pdf[Montana Letter].
31. Montana Letter at 8; *see also* US Department of Education, Archived Information About Sexual Harassment (last accessed Oct 3, 2025), https://www.ed.gov/about/offices/list/ocr/docs/ocrshpam.html (citing expression such as "sexual or dirty jokes," "displaying or distributing sexually explicit drawings, pictures, or written materials," and "circulating or showing e-mails or Web sites of a sexual nature" as "[e]xamples of sexual conduct").
32. Montana Letter at 4.
33. Montana Letter at 3.
34. Eugene Volokh, *The Administration Says Universities Must Implement Broad Speech Codes*, VOLOKH CONSPIRACY (May 13, 2013), https://volokh.com/2013/05/13/the-administration-says-universities-must-implement-broad-speech-codes-2/.
35. Candice Jackson, Dear Colleague Letter (Sep. 22, 2017), https://www.thefire.org/research-learn/september-22-2017-dear-colleague-letter.
36. 34 C.F.R. § 106, https://www.ecfr.gov/current/title-34/subtitle-B/chapter-I/part-106.
37. Craig Trainor, Dear Colleague Letter (Feb. 2, 2025), https://www.ed.gov/media/document/title-ix-enforcement-directive-dcl-109477.pdf.
38. Since 2004, under both political parties, the ED's OCR has interpreted anti-Semitism and other forms of mixed ethnic and religious discrimination "to be illegal under Title VI if it is based on a group's 'actual or perceived: (i) shared ancestry or ethnic characteristics; or (ii) citizenship or residency in a country with a dominant religion or distinct religious identity,' rather than the group's religious practices." *See* CONG. RESEARCH SERV., RELIGIOUS DISCRIMINATION AT SCHOOL: APPLICATION OF TITLE VI OF THE CIVIL RIGHTS ACT OF 1964 at 3, https://www.congress.gov/crs_external_products/LSB/PDF/LSB11129/LSB11129.2.pdf.

    The Biden OCR opened Title VI investigations and resolved cases involving allegations of discrimination based on shared Jewish, Israeli, Palestinian, Muslim, and/or Arab ancestry. For example, in December 2024, the OCR secured resolution agreements with the University of Cincinnati and the University of California system to address this range of claims.
39. International Holocaust Remembrance Alliance, *Working Definition of Antisemitism*, https://holocaustremembrance.com/resources/working-definition-antisemitism (last visited Oct. 3, 2025).
40. Kenneth S. Stern, *Will Campus Criticism of Israel Violate Federal Law?*, N.Y. TIMES (Dec. 12, 2016), https://www.nytimes.com/2016/12/12/opinion/will-campus-criticism-of-israel-violate-federal-law.html.
41. International Holocaust Remembrance Alliance, *supra* note 39.
42. Exec. Order No. 13899, §§ 2(a)(ii), 2(b), 84 Fed. Reg. 68779 (Dec. 11, 2019), https://www.govinfo.gov/content/pkg/DCPD-201900859/pdf/DCPD-201900859.pdf./
43. See, e.g., Trovia Smith, *Harvard Agrees to Adopt a Broad Definition of Antisemitism to Settle Two Lawsuits*, NPR, https://www.npr.org/2025/01/22/g-s1-44170/harvard-antisemitism-lawsuits-settlement; *Read the Letter to Columbia University*, N.Y. TIMES (Mar. 14, 2025), https://www.nytimes.com/interactive/2025/03/14/nyregion/columbia-letter.html.
44. Letter from Brian Gnandt, Program Manager, US Dep't of Educ. Office for Civil Rights to Kelly Cruz, Assoc. Gen. Couns. at the University of Michigan at 10 (June

17, 2024), https://www.ed.gov/sites/ed/files/about/offices/list/ocr/docs/investigations/more/15242066-a.pdf.

45. Erwin Chemerinsky & Howard Gillman, *Federal Attempt to Combat Anti-Semitism Puts Universities in an Untenable Position*, SACRAMENTO BEE (Dec. 12, 2023), https://www.sacbee.com/opinion/op-ed/article282921393.html.
46. Catherine E. Lhamon, Dear Colleague Letter at 2–3 (May 7, 2024), https://www.ed.gov/media/document/colleague-202405-shared-ancestrypdf-35100.pdf.
47. *Speech First, Inc. v. Cartwright*, 32 F.4th 1110 (11th Cir. 2022); *Speech First, Inc. v. Fenves*, 979 F.3d 319 (5th Cir. 2020); *Speech First, Inc. v. Schlissel*, 939 F.3d 756 (6th Cir. 2019); *but see Speech First, Inc. v. Whitten*, No. 1:24-CV-00898-JPH-MG, 2024 WL 3964864 (S.D. Ind. Aug. 28, 2024), aff'd, No. 24–2501, 2024 WL 4363740 (7th Cir. Sept. 5, 2024), cert. denied, 145 S. Ct. 701 (2025).
48. *See* Evelyn Douek & Genevieve Lakier, *Title VI as a Jawbone*, KNIGHT FIRST AMENDMENT INSTITUTE AT COLUMBIA UNIVERSITY (Sep. 26, 2024), https://knightcolumbia.org/blog/title-vi-as-a-jawbone (stating that the ED "may be leveraging its power" under Title VI "to get universities to crack down on protected student and faculty speech by threatening them with legal sanctions or investigations").
49. Letter from Beth Gellman-Beer, Director, US Dep't of Educ. Office for Civil Rights to Nicole Hurd, President, Lafeyette College at 8 (June 21, 2024), https://www.ed.gov/sites/ed/files/about/offices/list/ocr/docs/investigations/more/03242029-a.pdf; *see also* Robert Shibley, *Fed Investigation of Lafayette College over Israel-Hamas Protests Highlights New Threat to Free Speech*, FIRE (July 2, 2024), https://www.thefire.org/news/fed-investigation-lafayette-college-over-israel-hamas-protests-highlights-new-threat-free.
50. *See* Gellman-Beer Letter, *supra* note 49 at 13.
51. See *Sweezy v. New Hampshire*, 354 U.S. 234, 245 (1957) (limiting investigative power is "particularly important . . . when the investigative process . . . impinge[s] upon such highly sensitive areas as freedom of speech or press, freedom of political association, and freedom of communication of ideas, particularly in the academic community").
52. Press Release, DOJ, *Justice Department Announces Formation of Task Force to Combat Anti-Semitism* (Feb. 3, 2025), https://www.justice.gov/opa/pr/justice-department-announces-formation-task-force-combat-anti-semitism.
53. Montana Letter, *supra* note 30 at 3.
54. Joint Notice of Violation to Columbia University, US Dep't of Health & Human Servs., Office for Civil Rights & US Dep't of Educ., Office for Civil Rights (Sept. 13, 2023), https://www.hhs.gov/civil-rights/for-providers/compliance-enforcement/examples/national-origin/ocr-joint-notice-of-violation-to-columbia/index.html.
55. *Id.* at III.
56. *Id.* at III.13.
57. *Id.* at III.27.
58. *Id.* at III.61.
59. *Id.* at IV.1.
60. Notice of Violation: Harvard University, US Dep't of Health & Human Servs., Office for Civil Rights at 16 (June 30, 2025), https://www.hhs.gov/sites/default/files/harvard-title-vi-notice-violation.pdf.
61. *Id.*
62. Students for Just. in Palestine, at Univ. of Houston v. Abbott, 756 F. Supp. 3d 410 (W.D. Tex. 2024).
63. Exec. Order No. GA-44 (Mar. 27, 2024), https://gov.texas.gov/uploads/files/press/EO-GA-44_antisemitism_in_institutions_of_higher_ed_IMAGE_03-27-2024.pdf.
64. Students for Just. In Palestine, 756 F. Supp. 3d at 415.
65. *Tinker v. Des Moines Indep. Cmty. Sch. Dist.*, 393 U.S. 503 (1969).
66. *See, e.g., Forsyth County v. Nationalist Movement*, 505 U.S. 123, 134–135 (1992) ("Speech cannot be . . . punished or banned, simply because it might offend a hostile mob.").
67. Students for Just. in Palestine, 756 F. Supp. 3d at 425–26.

68. Jake Offenhartz, *A Columbia Genocide Scholar Says She May Leave over University's New Definition of Antisemitism*, AP NEWS (July 25, 2025), https://apnews.com/article/columbia-university-antisemitism-definition-68d44684f376b12162a28b88104e5d24.
69. *Gartenberg v. Cooper Union for the Advancement of Sci. & Art*, 765 F. Supp. 3d 245 (S.D.N.Y. 2025), *reconsideration denied sub nom. Gartenberg v. Cooper Union for Advancement of Sci. & Art*, No. 24 CIV. 2669 (JPC), 2025 WL 602945 (S.D.N.Y. Feb. 25, 2025).
70. *Landau v. Corp. of Haverford Coll.*, No. CV 24–2044, 2025 WL 1796473, (E.D. Pa. 2025).
71. *Cooper Union*, at 270.
72. *Id.* at 270–271.
73. *Id.* at 271.
74. *Id.* at 260 ("A statute that burdens protected speech must comport with the First Amendment regardless of whether it does so directly, such as by prohibiting certain speech outright, or indirectly, such as by requiring a court adjudicating a 'civil lawsuit between private parties' to apply a rule of law that has the effect of 'impos[ing] invalid restrictions on [the defendant's] constitutional freedom[] of speech.'").
75. *Id.* at 252–53.
76. *Haverford*, 2025 WL 1796473 at *2.
77. *Id.*
78. *Id.* at *3.
79. *Id.*
80. *See, e.g.*, NADINE STROSSEN, HATE: WHY WE SHOULD RESIST IT WITH FREE SPEECH, NOT CENSORSHIP 69–104, 194–201 (2020).
81. Glenn Greenwald, *In Europe, Hate Speech Laws Are Often Used to Suppress and Punish Left-Wing Viewpoints*, THE INTERCEPT (Aug. 29, 2017), https://theintercept.com/2017/08/29/in-europe-hate-speech-laws-are-often-used-to-suppress-and-punish-left-wing-viewpoints/.
82. AMERICAN ASSOCIATION OF UNIVERSITY PROFESSORS, THE HISTORY, USES, AND ABUSES OF TITLE IX (2016), https://www.aaup.org/reports-publications/aaup-policies-reports/topical-reports/history-uses-and-abuses-title-ix.
83. Laura Kipnis, *Sexual Paranoia Strikes Academe*, CHRON. OF HIGHER EDUC. (May 29, 2015), https://www.chronicle.com/article/sexual-paranoia-strikes-academe/.
84. Laura Kipnis, *My Title IX Inquisition*, CHRON. OF HIGHER EDUC. (May 29, 2015), https://www.chronicle.com/article/my-title-ix-inquisition/.
85. FIRE, 2024 College Free Speech Rankings, https://www.thefire.org/research-learn/2024-college-free-speech-rankings.
86. FIRE, 2024 College Free Speech Rankings, https://www.thefire.org/research-learn/2024-college-free-speech-rankings.
87. Sean Stevens, *A Year in Campus Speech Controversies—What Does the Data Reveal?*, FIRE (Oct. 15, 2024), https://www.thefire.org/news/year-campus-speech-controversies-what-does-data-reveal.

Chapter 9

1. Regents of the Univ. of Cal. v. Bakke, 438 U.S. 265, 312(1978) (opinion of Powell, J.).
2. *Id.*
3. Grutter v. Bollinger, 539 U.S. 306 (2003).
4. Students for Fair Admissions, Inc. v. President and Fellows of Harvard Coll., 600 U.S. 181 (2023) [SFFA].
5. *See, e.g.*, Doe v. Univ. of Mich., 721 F. Supp. 852 (E.D. Mich. 1989).
6. SFFA, 600 U.S at 186.
7. US Dep't of Educ., Dear Colleague Letter (Feb. 14, 2025).
8. Char Adams & Nigel Chiwaya, *Map: See Which States Have Introduced or Passed Anti-DEI Bills*, NBC NEWS (Mar. 2, 2024), https://www.nbcnews.com/data-graphics/anti-dei-bills-states-republican-lawmakers-map-rcna140756; Vivian E. Hamilton, *Reform, Retrench, Repeat: The Campaign Against Critical Race Theory, Through the Lens of Critical Race Theory*, 28 WM. & MARY J. RACE GENDER & SOC. JUST. 61, 73–78 (2021) (describing

the rise of legislation opposing critical-race theory after the protests of 2020); Michelle Garcia, *Florida Public Colleges Barred from Using State and Federal Funds for DEI Programs*, NBC News (Jan. 17, 2024), https://www.nbcnews.com/news/nbcblk/florida-dei-rule-board-education-funding-state-federal-rcna134398.

9. Vicki C. Jackson, *Knowledge Institutions in Constitutional Democracies: Preliminary Reflections*, 2021 CJCCL 159.
10. US Dep't of Ed., Dear Colleague Letter (Feb. 14, 2025).
11. *Id.*
12. Letter to Interim President of Columbia University Katrina Armstrong and Columbia Board of Trustees from Comm'r of Fed. Acquisition Serv Josh Gruenbaum (March 13, 2025) [Columbia Letter]. Even prior to this letter, the administration announced the "immediate cancelation of approximately $400 million" in Columbia's federal grants and contracts "due to the school's continued inaction in the face of persistent harassment of Jewish students" and stated that "[t]hese cancelations represent the first round of action and additional cancelations are expected to follow." *DOJ, HHS, ED, and GSA Announce Initial Cancellation of Grants and Contracts to Columbia University Worth $400 Million*, US Dep't of Educ. (Mar. 7, 2025), https://www.ed.gov/about/news/press-release/doj-hhs-ed-and-gsa-announce-initial-cancelation-of-grants-and-contracts-columbia-university-worth-400-million.
13. *See* Resolution Agreement Between the United States of America and Columbia University (July 23, 2025), https://president.columbia.edu/sites/default/files/content/July%202025%20Announcement/Columbia%20University%20Resolution%20Agreement.pdf; Michael C. Bender & Sharon Otterman, *Columbia and White House Enter Final Stage of Talks to End Standoff*, N.Y. Times (July 17, 2025).
14. Complaint, President & Fellows of Harvard Coll. v. Dep't of Health & Hum. Servs., No.1:25-cv-11048, 2025 WL 2528380 (D. Mass. 2025); *see also* Stephanie Saul, *Harvard Sues over Threats to Block Funding*, N.Y. Times, April 22, 2025, at A22.
15. Cecilia Mould, *Letters from DOJ Reveal Threats to U.Va. over Admissions Policies, Ryan's Leadership*, Cavalier Daily (July 1, 2025), https://www.cavalierdaily.com/article/2025/07/letters-from-doj-reveal-threats-to-uva-over-admissions-policies-ryans-leadership (collecting Department of Justice letters addressed to the University of Virginia); Michael S. Schmidt & Michael C. Bender, *University of Virginia President Resigns Under Pressure from Trump Administration*, N.Y. Times, June 28, 2025, at A1.
16. Angela Woolsey, *Trump Administration Demands Apology from George Mason University President for Diversity Practices*, AP News (Aug. 25, 2025), https://apnews.com/article/colleges-and-universities-gregory-washington-donald-trump-donald-trump-es-glenn-youngkin-79920e1359e4820adfc5ecc491a4b2c8.
17. Joseph Fishkin, *Making Policy Based on Falsehoods: The Federal Government vs UCLA*, Balkinization (Aug. 31, 2025), https://balkin.blogspot.com/2025/08/making-policy-based-on-falsehoods.html; Julie Watson, *UCLA Says Trump Administration Has Suspended $584 Million in Grants, Threatening Research*, AP News (Aug 6, 2025), https://apnews.com/article/ucla-trump-funding-cuts-research-antisemitism-0c95177d6fb64695f9f707079fee4e8e.
18. The Trump administration has not been clear or consistent in its explanation for its authority to terminate funds and grants to universities. *See* Defendant's Memorandum in Support of Cross Motion for Summary Judgment, Harvard v. Dep't of Health & Hum. Servs. at 18 (D. Mass. 2025) (No. 1:25-cv-11048-ADB) (arguing the case is not "Title VI or bust" and that the federal government should be able to "us[e] every tool at its disposal to combat discrimination, including negotiating contract terms that require a contractor to take antidiscrimination efforts seriously"); Letter to Harvard University President Alan Garber and Harvard Corporation from Comm'r of Fed. Acquisition Serv. Josh Gruenbaum (April 11, 2025) (stating, among other rationales, that federal "investment[s]" in Harvard are not "entitlement[s]," and that funding will only be restored if the university ends its "ideological capture"); Letter to Agency Senior Procurement Executive from Comm'r of Fed. Acquisition Serv. Josh Gruenbaum (May 27, 2025) (stating, among other rationales, that "being a counterparty with the federal government comes with the deep responsibility . . . to safeguard[] . . . taxpayer money").

19. David Pozen, *Regulation by Deal Comes to Higher Ed.*, BALKINIZATION (July 23, 2025), https://balkin.blogspot.com/2025/07/regulation-by-deal-comes-to-higher-ed.html.
20. Lee Bollinger, Academic Freedom, *in* IN SEARCH OF AN OPEN MIND, at 59 (2025); Healy v. James, 408 U.S. 169, 180 (1972).
21. McKenzie Carrier & Thomas Carothers, *U.S. Democratic Backsliding in Comparative Perspective*, CARNEGIE ENDOWMENT (Aug. 25, 2025), https://carnegieendowment.org/research/2025/08/us-democratic-backsliding-in-comparative-perspective?lang=en.
22. Harvard v. HHS, No.1:25-cv-11048, 2025 WL 2528380, at *23 (citing Regents of Univ. of Mich. v. Ewing, 474 U.S. 214, 226 n.12 (1985)).
23. Blasdel v. Nw. Univ., 687 F.3d 813, 816 (7th Cir. 2012).
24. Carrier, *supra* note 21.
25. Sweeney, 354 U.S. 250.
26. *See* Vicki C. Jackson, *The Trump Administration's Attack on Knowledge Institutions*, VERFASSUNGSBLOG (Mar. 28, 2025), https://verfassungsblog.de/education-democracy-america/; Vicki C. Jackson, *Knowledge Institutions in Constitutional Democracies: Preliminary Reflections*, 2021 CJCCL 159, 159 ("Knowledge institutions are fundamental to the success of constitutional democracy.").
27. *See* Vicki C. Jackson, *The Trump Administration's Attack on Knowledge Institutions*, VERFASSUNGSBLOG (Mar. 28, 2025), https://verfassungsblog.de/education-democracy-america/ ("Knowledge institutions—including universities, the truth-oriented press, government offices with data collection or scientific responsibilities—are crucial for constitutional democracies. They have as a central mission the search for truth or better understandings, through independent application of disciplinary or professional standards of reliability.").
28. Becky Prager, *The Hungarian Gender Studies Ban, and Its Implication for Democratic Freedom*, HARVARD J. OF LAW & GENDER, Jan. 20, 2019, https://journals.law.harvard.edu/jlg/2019/01/the-hungarian-ban-on-gender-studies-and-its-implications-for-democratic-freedom/; Vicki C. Jackson, *Knowledge Institutions and Resisting "Truth Decay," in* DISINFORMATION, MISINFORMATION, AND DEMOCRACY: LEGAL APPROACHES IN COMPARATIVE CONTEXT (Ronald Krotoszynski, András Koltay & Charlotte Garden (ed.), 2025).
29. TAIFHA ALEXANDER ET AL., CRT FORWARD: TRACKING THE ATTACK ON CRITICAL RACE THEORY, https://crtforward.law.ucla.edu/wp-content/uploads/2023/04/UCLA-Law_CRT-Report_Final.pdf (tracking anti-CRT bans and bans on teaching "divisive concepts").
30. ROBERT SCHERTZER & ERIC TAYLOR WOODS, THE NEW NATIONALISM IN AMERICA AND BEYOND: THE DEEP ROOTS OF ETHNIC NATIONALISM IN THE DIGITAL AGE (2022); Richard C. Fording & Sanford F. Schram, *Pride or Prejudice? Clarifying the Role of White Racial Identity in Recent Presidential Elections*, 55 POLITY 106 (2023); ROGERS M. SMITH & DESMOND KING, AMERICA'S NEW RACIAL BATTLE LINES: PROTECT VERSUS REPAIR (2024).
31. Bollinger, *supra* note 20, at 70.
32. Emily R. Chertoff & Jessica Bulman-Pozen, *The Administrative State's Second Face*, 100 N.Y.U. L. REV. 727 (2025).
33. *See* Kim Scheppele, *Autocratic Legalism*, 85 U. CHI. L. REV. 545 (2018); Javier Corrales, *Autocratic Legalism in Venezuela*, 26 J. DEMOCRACY 37, 38–45 (Apr. 2015); *see also* David Landau, *Abusive Constitutionalism*, 47 U.C. DAVIS L. REV. 189 (2013).
34. H.R. Misc. Doc. No. 124, 88th Cong., 1st Sess. 3, 12 (1963).
35. GERALD N. ROSENBERG, THE HOLLOW HOPE: CAN COURTS BRING ABOUT SOCIAL CHANGE? 35–36 (1991).
36. Adams v. Richardson, 480 F.2d 1159, 1164 (D.C. Cir. 1973) (affirming that the Department of Health, Education and Welfare, the precursor to the Department of Education, had failed to properly implement Title VI with respect to developing desegregation plans at colleges and universities); WILLIAM A. KAPLIN & BARBARA A. LEE, THE LAW OF HIGHER EDUCATION 1450–52 (4th ed. 2006) (documenting the *Adams* litigation).
37. Mary Ann Connell, *Race & Higher Education: The Tortuous Journey Toward Desegregation*, 36 J. COLL. & U. L. 945, 955 (2010) (after the *Adams* litigation, HEW began to enforce higher-education desegregation plans in Tennessee, Louisiana, Mississippi, and Alabama).

38. Olatunde C. A. Johnson, Beyond the Private Attorney General, Equality Directives Under American Law, 87 N.Y. U. L. Rev. 1339 (2012).
39. Stephen C. Halpern, On the Limits of the Law: The Ironic Legacy of Title VI of the 1964 Civil Rights Act 37–39 (1995).
40. 42 U.S.C. § 2000d-1 ("Compliance with any requirement adopted pursuant to this section may be effected (1) by the termination of or refusal to grant or to continue assistance under such program or activity to any recipient as to whom there has been an express finding on the record, after opportunity for hearing, of a failure to comply with such requirement, but such termination or refusal shall be limited to the particular political entity, or part thereof, or other recipient as to whom such a finding has been made and, shall be limited in its effect to the particular program, or part thereof, in which such noncompliance has been so found, or (2) by any other means authorized by law. . . .").
41. *See* Halpern, *supra* note 39, at 37.
42. Stephen C. Halpern, On the Limits of the Law: The Ironic Legacy of Title VI of the 1964 Civil Rights Act 37–39 (1995) (describing disagreement over whether to allow any termination power, and the negotiations that resulted in the final statute allowing termination but after following a detailed process).
43. Halpern, *supra* note 39, at 37.
44. 88 Cong. Rec. 5606, 6837–44, 7059, 12714–15 (1964).
45. For the congressional debates, see 88 Cong. Rec. 5606, 6837–44, 7059, 12714–15 (1964); Hearings Before Subcomm. No. 5 of the Comm. on the Judiciary of the H. of Reps. 88th Cong. 1st Sess. on Miscellaneous Proposals Regarding the Civil Rights of Persons Within the Jurisdiction of the U.S., 88th Cong. 1784, 1788, 1890–91, 2404–06 (1963).
46. *See* 42 U.S.C. § 2000d-1 ("Compliance with any requirement adopted pursuant to this section may be effected (1) by the termination of or refusal to grant or to continue assistance under such program or activity to any recipient as to whom there has been an express finding on the record, after opportunity for hearing, of a failure to comply with such requirement, but such termination or refusal shall be limited to the particular political entity, or part thereof, or other recipient as to whom such a finding has been made and, shall be limited in its effect to the particular program, or part thereof, in which such noncompliance has been so found.").
47. *Grove City Coll. v. Bell*, 465 U.S. 555 (1984).
48. *See* Civil Rights Restoration Act of 1987, Pub. L. No. 100–259, 102 Stat. 28 (codified as amended at 20 U.S.C. § 1687(3)(a)).
49. S. Rep. No. 100–64, 100th Cong., 1st Sess. 2 at 20 (1987).
50. Amicus Brief of Former US Agency Officials, Exhibit B, Declaration of Judge David S. Tatel at 1, President & Fellows of Harvard Coll. v. Dep't of Health & Hum. Servs. No.1:25-cv-11048-ADB, 2025 WL 2528380 (D. Mass. 2025) [Tatel Declaration] (former head of HEW from 1977–79 stating that "the voluntary compliance element of Title VI was central to the statutory scheme. No matter how egregious the discrimination, Title VI bars the government from cutting off federal funds unless there is a no genuine chance of voluntary resolution.").
51. *Id.* at 5.
52. *Id.*; Suzanne Goldberg & Olatunde Johnson, *Campus Crises and the Limits of Title VI*, 126 Colum. L. Rev. F. (forthcoming 2026).
53. The Administrative Procedure Act also places limits on government action that is "arbitrary and capricious."
54. U.S. Const. art. I, § 8, cl. 1; Cummings v. Premier Rehab Keller, P.L.L.C, 596 U.S. 212, 219 (2022); Pennhurst State Sch. & Hosp. v. Halderman, 451 U.S. 1, 16–17 (1981).
55. Arlington Cent. Sch. Dist. Bd. of Educ. v. Murphy, 548 U.S. 291, 296 (2006).
56. *See* Cass R. Sunstein, "Our Money or Your Life!": Higher Education and the First Amendment Harv. L. Rev. F. (2025) ("the problem with an unconstitutional condition is that the government is *leveraging its power over federal funds to stop people from saying (or get people to say) what they would otherwise say (or not say), independent of the exercise of that leverage*"), https://harvardlawreview.org/forum/vol-139/our-money-or-your-life-higher-education-and-the-first-amendment/.
57. *See* Evelyn Douek & Genevieve Lakier, *Title VI as a Jawbone*, Knight First Amend. Inst. at Columbia Univ. (Sep. 26, 2024), https://knightcolumbia.org/blog/title-vi-as-a-jawbone.

The 2024 Supreme Court case *National Rifle Association v. Vullo* explains that government's "threat of invoking legal sanctions and other means of coercion" against a third party "to achieve the suppression" of disfavored speech violates the First Amendment. *NRA of Am v. Vullo*, 602 U.S. 175, 176 (2024) (citing *Bantam Books, Inc. v. Sullivan*, 374 U.S. 58, 67 (1963).

58. Julie Johnson, *Reagan Vetos Bill That Would Widen Federal Rights Law*, N.Y. Times, Mar. 17, 1988 at A1; *Forty Years Ago a Supreme Court Case Changed GCC Forever*, Grove City Coll. (Feb. 26, 2024), https://www.gcc.edu/Home/News-Archive/News-Article/forty-years-ago-supreme-court-case-changed-gcc-forever (2024).
59. Jacob Gersen & Jeannie Suk, *The Sex Bureaucracy*, 104 Cal. L. Rev. 881 (2016); Olatunde C. A. Johnson, *Overreach & Innovation in Equality Regulation*, 66 Duke L. J. 1771 (2017).
60. State of Tennessee v. Xavier Becerra, Cause No. 1:24cv 161-LG-BWR (S.D. Miss. filed May 30, 2024).
61. President and Fellows of Harvard Coll. v. US Dep't of Health & Human Services, No.1:25-cv-11048, 2025 WL 2528380 (D. Mass. 2025).
62. *See, e.g., U.S. Department of Education's Office for Civil Rights Sends Letters to 60 Universities Under Investigation for Antisemitic Discrimination and Harassment*, U.S. Dep't of Educ. (May 10, 2025), https://www.ed.gov/about/news/press-release/us-department-of-educations-office-civil-rights-sends-letters-60-universities-under-investigation-antisemitic-discrimination-and-harassment (describing letters sent to fifty-five universities "under investigation or monitoring in response to Title VI complaints filed with OCR" related to anti-Semitism and to five additional universities under OCR-initiated directed investigations).
63. *See, e.g.*, Kiara Alfonseca, *DOE Launches Investigation into Harvard Following Islamophobia, Anti-Arab Complaint*, ABC News (Feb. 6, 2024), https://abcnews.com/US/doe-launches-investigation-harvard-islamophobia-anti-arab-complaint/story?id=106998802; *Muslim Advocates & CUNY Students File Federal Civil Rights Complaint About Anti-Palestinian Racism*, Muslim Advocates (Apr. 16, 2024), https://muslimadvocates.org/2024/04/muslim-advocates-cuny-students-file-federal-civil-rights-complaint-about-anti-palestinian-racism.
64. *See, e.g.*, Letter from Catherine E. Lhamon, Assistant Sec'y for Civil Rights, Office for Civil Rights, US Dep't of Educ., to Colleagues 1 (May 7, 2024), https://www.ed.gov/sites/ed/files/about/offices/list/ocr/letters/colleague-202405-sharedancestry.pdf [https://perma.cc/568B-TJB2] [2024 Guidance] ("Title VI's protections against discrimination based on race, color, and national origin encompass antisemitism . . . when based on shared ancestry or ethnic characteristics.").
65. Timothy C. Shiell, Campus Hate Speech on Trial 4 (2009) (2nd ed.); Wornie L. Reed, *Commentary: The Role of Universities in Racial Violence on Campuses*, 3 Trotter Rev. 3 (Mar. 1989); Walter C. Farrell, Jr., & Cloyzelle K. Jones, Recent Racial Incidents in Higher Education: A Contemporary Perspective, 20 Urban Rev. 211 (1988).
66. 477 U.S. 57 (1986).
67. Davis v. Monroe County Bd. Of Educ. 526 U.S 629, 651 (1999).
68. By some analyses, the use of the disjunctive for peer-on-peer harassment is incorrect. *See* Todd E. Pettys, *Hostile Learning Environments, the First Amendment, and Public Higher Education*, 54 Conn. L. Rev. 1, 20–22 (2022) (using Davis's "and" formulation for peer-to-peer harassment, as opposed to teacher-to-student harassment, because of First Amendment concerns and because "[i]n their dealings with one another, students usually can be expected to protect themselves with the same kinds of self-help strategies they use when managing interpersonal conflicts in the larger community").
69. *See, e.g.*, 2024 Guidance, *supra* note 64, at 4 (May 2023); Office for Civil Rights, US Dep't of Educ., Dear Colleague Letter: Harassment and Bullying, at 2, 4, 6 (Oct. 2010); Racial Incidents and Harassment Against Students at Educational Institutions; Investigative Guidance, 59 Fed. Reg. 11448, 11449 (Mar. 1994); https://www.ed.gov/sites/ed/files/about/offices/list/ocr/docs/dcl-factsheet-201010.pdf.
70. *See* Doe v. University of Michigan, 721 F Supp. 852 (E.D. Mich. 1989); UVM-Post v. Board of Regents of the University of Wisconsin, 774 F. Supp. 1163 (E.D. Wis. 1991).
71. Timothy C. Schiell, Campus Hate Speech on Trial 87 (2009).

72. *See, e.g.*, Kent Greenawalt, Fighting Words 96–98 (1995) (adopting the hostile-environment standard could likely preserve the constitutionality of campus speech codes); Richard H. Fallon, Jr., *Sexual Harassment, Content Neutrality, and the First Amendment Dog That Didn't Bark*, 1994 Sup. Ct. Rev. 1, 46–47 (contending that the *Meritor* standard is consistent with First Amendment principles and could be extended to campus settings without damage to academic freedom in Title IX cases).
73. Kent Greenawalt, Fighting Words 96–98 (1995); Richard H. Fallon, Jr., *Sexual Harassment, Content Neutrality, and the First Amendment Dog That Didn't Bark*, 1994 Sup. Ct. Rev. 1, 46–47.
74. For instance, the Biden Administration's May 7, 2024, guidance stated that nothing in "title VI or regulations implementing it requires or authorizes a school to restrict any rights otherwise protected by the First Amendment to the U.S. Constitution and that OCR enforces the laws within our jurisdiction consistent with the First Amendment."
75. *See* Gartenberg v. Cooper Union for the Advancement of Sci. and Art, 765 F.Supp.3d 245 (S.D.N.Y. 2025).
76. President and Fellows of Harvard Coll. v. US Dep't of Health & Human Services, No.1:25-cv-11048, 2025 WL 2528380 at *24 (D. Mass. 2025) ("Defendants have failed to meet their burden to show they acted with a non-retaliatory purpose for several reasons. First, as discussed, the April 11 Letter specifically conditioned funding on agreeing to its ten terms, only one of which related to antisemitism, . . . while six related to ideological and pedagogical concerns, including who may lead and teach at Harvard, [HHSHarv_00000098–99 ("Governance and leadership reforms"; "Merit-Based Hiring Reform")], who may be admitted [HHSHarv_00000099 ("Merit-Based Admissions Reform"; "International Admissions Reform")], and what may be taught [HHSHarv_00000099–100 ("Viewpoint Diversity in Admissions and Hiring"; "Discontinuation of DEI")].
77. SFFA, 600 U.S. at 187 ("College admissions are zero-sum, and a benefit provided to some applicants but not to others necessarily advantages the former at the expense of the latter.")
78. United States Dep't of Ed., Dear Colleague Letter (Feb. 14, 2025).
79. *Id.*
80. Memorandum on Ensuring Transparency in Higher Education Admissions, 2025 Daily Comp. Pres. Doc. 837 (Aug. 7, 2025), https://www.whitehouse.gov/presidential-actions/2025/08/ensuring-transparency-in-higher-education-admissions/.
81. SFFA, 600 US at 230.
82. Sonja B. Starr, *The Magnet School Wars and the Future of Colorblindness*, 76 Stan. L. Rev. 161, 164–65 (2024); Olatunde Johnson, *Race, Affirmative Action, Antidiscrimination, and the Roberts Court*, 713 Ann. Am. Acad. Pol. Soc. Sci. 124, 129 (2024).
83. Roger L. Geiger, American Higher Education Since World War II: A History (2019); Christopher Eisgruber, *The Cost of the Government's Attack on Columbia*, The Atlantic (Mar. 19, 2025), https://www.theatlantic.com/ideas/archive/2025/03/columbia-academic-freedom/682088/ ("Federal funding helped make American universities the world's best.").
84. Nancy Cantor, Chancellor of Syracuse University, Anchor Institutions—Connecting with Community for Innovation and Opportunity (2011); Susan Sturm, *Activating Systemic Change Toward Full Participation: The Pivotal Role of Boundary Spanning Institutional Intermediaries*, 54 St. Louis U. L. J. 1117 (2010) (discussing the need for an effective bridge); Susan P. Sturm, *Reframing Affirmative Action: From Diversity to Mobility and Full Participation*, 2020 U. Chi. L. Rev. Online 59 (2020).
85. Danielle Allen, *America and Its Universities Need a New Social Contract*, The Atlantic (Apr. 13, 2025), https://www.theatlantic.com/ideas/archive/2025/04/stem-academia-universities-citizenship-civics/682384/.
86. *See, e.g.*, Harvard Univ., *Report of the Antisemitism, Anti-Muslim, and Anti-Arab Advisory Panel* (Apr. 29, 2025), https://www.harvard.edu/wp-content/uploads/2025/04/FINAL-Harvard-AMAAAPB-Report-4.29.25.pdf; Columbia Univ., *Report #2: Task Force on Antisemitism* (Aug. 30, 2024), https://www.columbia.edu/content/report-2-task-force-antisemitism; Columbia Univ., *Student Belonging and Exclusion Survey Report* (June 2025), https://www.columbia.edu/content/sites/www.columbia.edu.

content/files/content/Documents/Columbia-Student-Survey-Report-June-2025.pdf; Univ. of Washington, *Antisemitism and Islamophobia Task Forces: Climate Assessment and Reports* (Oct. 15, 2024), https://www.washington.edu/antisemitism-and-islamophobia-taskforces/; Peter Brest et al., *"It's in the Air": Antisemitism and Anti-Israeli Bias at Stanford, and How to Address It* (May 31, 2024); *Muslim Advocates & CUNY Students File Federal Civil Rights Complaint About Anti-Palestinian Racism*, Muslim Advocates (Apr. 16, 2024), https://muslimadvocates.org/2024/04/muslim-advocates-cuny-students-file-federal-civil-rights-complaint-about-anti-palestinian-racism.

87. Jamal Greene, How Rights Went Wrong: Why Our Obsession with Rights Is Tearing America Apart 240–41 (2021) ("The purpose of a university is not to provide a forum for free speech. It is to prepare students for democratic citizenship.").
88. Lilliana Mason, Uncivil Agreement: How Politics Became Our Identity (2018).

Chapter 10

1. Michael Stephen Steinberg, Sabers and Brown Shirts: The German Students' Path to National Socialism, 1918–1935 103 (1973).
2. *Id.* 175
3. *Id.* 176
4. Geoffrey J. Giles, Students and National Socialism in Germany 99–100 (1985).
5. Jessica Priest, Nicholas Gutteridge & Kate McGee, *How a Secret Recording of a Gender Identity Lecture Upended Texas A&M*, Texas Tribune (Sept. 19, 2025), https://www.texastribune.org/2025/09/19/texas-a-m-welsh-firing-professor-gender-mccoul/.
6. *Id.*
7. @Son_of_Aragorn, X (July 9, 2025, 10:10 p.m.), https://x.com/Son_of_Aragorn/status/1943130625420022176.
8. @Son_of_Aragorn, X (July 9, 2025, 10:51PM), https://x.com/Son_of_Aragorn/status/1943140952987648227; @Son_of_Aragorn, X (July 9, 2025, 10:51PM), https://x.com/Son_of_Aragorn/status/1943140900755882274.
9. @Son_of_Aragorn, X (July 10, 2025, 9:32 a.m.), https://x.com/Son_of_Aragorn/status/1943302411327615143
10. @Son_of_Aragorn, X (July 10, 2025, 11:14 a.m.), https://x.com/Son_of_Aragorn/status/1943328041389711516; @Son_of_Aragorn, X (July 10, 2025, 11:18 a.m.), https://x.com/Son_of_Aragorn/status/1943328041389711516; @Son_of_Aragorn, X (July 10, 2025, 11:20 a.m.), https://x.com/Son_of_Aragorn/status/1943329486423929163.
11. @Son_of_Aragorn, X (July 10, 2025, 11:14 a.m.), https://x.com/Son_of_Aragorn/status/1943328041389711516.
12. @Son_of_Aragorn, X (July 10, 2025, 1:39 p.m.), https://x.com/Son_of_Aragorn/status/1943364582245863493.
13. Brian Harrison (@brianeharrison), X (Sept. 8, 2025, 12:44 p.m.), https://x.com/brianeharrison/status/1965093848520294565 (video of students speaking).
14. *Id.*
15. Emma Whitford, 2 Texas A&M Administrators and Professor Out After Viral Video, Inside Higher Ed (Sept. 10, 2025).
16. Priest et al., *supra* note 5.
17. Brian Harrison (@brianeharrison), X (Sept. 8, 2025, 12:44 p.m.), https://x.com/brianeharrison/status/1965093848520294565.
18. Brian Harrison (@brianeharrison), X (Sept. 8, 2025, 12:44 p.m.), https://x.com/brianeharrison/status/1965093851531444722.
19. Harmeet Dhillon (@AAGDhillon), X (Sept. 8, 2025, 2:58 p.m.) https://x.com/AAGDhillon/status/1965127511228232127.
20. @Son_of_Aragorn, X (Sept. 8, 2025, 1:52 p.m.), https://x.com/Son_of_Aragorn/status/1965111118483128700.
21. Priest et al., *supra* note 5.
22. *Id.*
23. Texas A&M University (@TAMU), X (Sept. 8, 2025, 11:15 p.m.), https://x.com/TAMU/status/1965252609033327010.

24. Greg Abbott (@GregAbbott_TX), X (Sept. 9, 2025), https://x.com/GregAbbott_TX/status/1965467515485860093.
25. Brian Harrison (@brianeharrison), X (Sept. 8, 2025, 12:44 p.m.), https://x.com/brianeharrison/status/1965469671274238448.
26. Brian Harrison (@brianeharrison), X (Sept. 8, 2025, 12:44 p.m.), https://x.com/brianeharrison/status/1965473227209408940.
27. @Son_of_Aragorn, X (Sept. 8, 2025, 1:52 p.m.), https://x.com/Son_of_Aragorn/status/1965396112208252964.
28. JC Flors, (@happyface1973), X (Sept. 9, 2025, 12:46 p.m.), https://x.com/happyface1973/status/1965456724934209859.
29. @Shaughn_A2, X, (Sept. 9, 2025, 1:07 p.m.), https://x.com/Shaughn_A2/status/1965462099481821676.
30. @Aggie_Vet, X (Sept. 9, 2025, 1:44 p.m.), https://x.com/Aggie_Vet/status/1965471505711845732.
31. @Son_of_Aragorn, X (Sept. 8, 2025, 1:52 p.m.), https://x.com/Son_of_Aragorn/status/1965506653496946816.
32. Dylan Chryst Watkiss, *Texas A&M Professor Fired, Leaders Reassigned amid Scrutiny over Course Curriculum*, KBTX (Sept. 9, 2025), https://www.kbtx.com/2025/09/10/texas-am-professor-fired-after-video-showing-clash-over-course-curriculum/.
33. *An Update from President Mark A. Welsh III* (Sept. 9, 2025), https://president.tamu.edu/messages/an-update-from-president-mark-a-welsh-iii.html.
34. *Id.*
35. American Association of University Professors (AAUP), 1940 Statement of Principles on Academic Freedom and Tenure with 1970 Interpretive Comments, https://www.aaup.org/reports-publications/aaup-policies-reports/policy-statements/1940-statement-principles-academic.
36. *Id.*
37. *AAUP-TAMU Response to the Firing of Dr. McCoul* (Sept. 18, 2025), https://aaup-texas.org/blog/f/aaup-tamu-response-to-the-firing-of-dr-mccoul.
38. *Id.*
39. Wieman v. Updegraff, 344 U.S. 183, 196 (1952).
40. Sweezy v. State of New Hampshire, 354 U.S. 234, 250 (1957).
41. Keyishian v. Bd. of Regents of Univ. of State of N. Y., 385 U.S. 589, 603 (1967).
42. Nicholas Gutteridge, *Students and Professors Defend Texas A&M President Mark Welsh amid Calls for His Ousting*, TEXAS TRIBUNE (Sept. 17, 2025), https://www.texastribune.org/2025/09/17/texas-a-m-university-president-mark-welsh-support-letters/.
43. Jessica Priest, *Texas A&M President Mark A. Welsh III to Step Down After a Week of Turmoil over Viral Classroom Video,* TEXAS TRIBUNE (Sept.18, 2025), https://www.texastribune.org/2025/09/18/texas-am-university-president-mark-welsh-resigns/.
44. Priest et al., *supra* note 5.
45. Priest, *supra* note 43.
46. Exec. Order No. 14168, 90 Fed. Reg. 8615 (Jan. 20, 2025).
47. Priest et al., *supra* note 5.
48. Priest et al., *supra* note 5.
49. Christin Bentley (@Bentley4Texas), X (Sept. 8, 2025, 10:13 p.m.), https://x.com/Bentley4Texas/status/1965237014821036231.
50. David J Harris Jr. (@DavidJHarrisJr), X (Sept. 8, 2025, 2:26 p.m.), https://x.com/DavidJHarrisJr/status/1965119626339373243.
51. Josiah Alipate, *Texas A&M Student Chose Bravery over Conformity*, FACEBOOK (Sept. 8, 2025), https://www.facebook.com/watch/?v=1080211620950734.
52. Ed Feulner, *Seeking Safe Spaces on Campus Report*, HERITAGE FOUNDATION (March 9, 2016), https://www.heritage.org/education/commentary/seeking-safe-spaces-campus-report.
53. Texas A&M University, Guidelines for Recording Lectures, https://www.tamiu.edu/disability/guidelines-for-recording-lectures.shtml (last visited Nov. 5, 2025).
54. Texas A&M University Student Handbook 2025–26, Rule 24: Student Conduct Code, https://student-rules.tamu.edu/rule24/ (last visited Nov. 5, 2025).
55. Priest et al., *supra* note 5.

56. Priest et al., *supra* note 5.
57. @Son_of_Aragorn, X (Sept. 9, 2025, 9:19 p.m.), https://x.com/Son_of_Aragorn/status/1965585921191068002.
58. Curtis Bunn & Tyler Kingkade, *How Charlie Kirk's Professor Watchlist Reshaped Free Speech on Campus*, NBC News (Sept. 23, 2025), https://www.nbcnews.com/news/us-news/charlie-kirk-professor-watchlist-free-speech-college-campus-rcna231448.
59. Professor Watch List, Submit a Tip, https://www.professorwatchlist.org/submitatip (last visited Nov. 5, 2025).
60. Professor Watch List, About Us, https://www.professorwatchlist.org/aboutus (last visited Nov. 5, 2025).
61. Professor Watch List, Submit a Tip, https://www.professorwatchlist.org/submitatip (last visited Nov. 5, 2025).
62. Charlie Kirk (@charliekirk11), X, (March 22, 2020, 4:14 p.m.), https://twitter.com/charliekirk11/status/1241820673007161345?ref_src=twsrc%5Etfw.
63. Bunn & Kingkade, *supra* note 58.
64. Anthea Butler, *I'm on the "Professor Watchlist." It's a Ploy to Undermine Free Speech*, Guardian (Dec. 2, 2016), https://www.theguardian.com/commentisfree/2016/dec/02/us-universities-professor-watchlist-free-speech.
65. *Id.*
66. *Id.*
67. *A Profile of Charlie Kirk*, Dartmouth Review (Nov. 1, 2019), https://dartreview.com/a-profile-of-charlie-kirk/.
68. Steinberg, *supra* note 1 at 5.
69. *Id.* at 5.
70. *Id.* at 73
71. *Id.* at 78.
72. Jeremy Noakes, The Nazi Party in Lower Saxony 1921–1933 378 (1971).
73. Steinberg, *supra* note 1 at 100–101.
74. *Id.* at 101
75. *Nazi Minister of Education Orders Probe into Charges Against Professor Cohn*, Jewish Telegraphic Agency, Feb. 16, 1933, https://www.jta.org/archive/nazi-minister-of-education-orders-probe-into-charges-against-professor-cohn.
76. Steinberg, *supra* note 1 at 135
77. *Id.* at 135
78. *Id.* at 136
79. *Id.* at 134
80. Noakes, *supra* note 72 at 397.
81. United States Holocaust Memorial Museum, *Nazi Book Burnings*, https://encyclopedia.ushmm.org/content/en/article/book-burning (last visited Nov. 5, 2025).
82. Richard L. Rubenstein, *The Philosopher and the Jews: The Case of Martin Heidegger*, 9 Modern Judaism 179 (1989).
83. Martin Heidegger, German Students, speech delivered Nov, 3, 1933, at Freiburg University. English translation in R. Wolin, ed., The Heidegger Controversy ch. 2 (MIT Press, 1993).
84. Benyamin Cohen and Hannah Feuer, *Who Was Horst Wessel, and Why Are People Comparing Charlie Kirk to Him?* Forward (Sept. 11, 2025), https://forward.com/news/768607/horst-wessel-charlie-kirk-nazi/
85. Warren J. Blumenfeld, *Horst Wessel and the Propaganda of Ultra-Right Martyrdom*, The Times of Israel (Sept. 26, 2025), https://blogs.timesofisrael.com/horst-wessel-and-the-propaganda-of-ultra-right-martyrdom/.
86. Trump Blames "Radical Left" Rhetoric for Charlie Kirk's Assassination in White House Video Statement, Associated Press (Sept. 10, 2025), https://newsroom.ap.org/editorial-photos-videos/detail?itemid=bc61fde41d814d96ba882132792cc50e&mediatype=video.
87. David E. Sanger, *Trump Downplays Violence on the Right and Says the Left Is the Problem*, N.Y. Times (Sept. 12, 2025), https://www.nytimes.com/2025/09/12/us/politics/trump-charlie-kirk-shooting.html.

88. Tyler Pager & Nick Corasaniti, *Trump Escalates Attacks on Political Opponents After Charlie Kirk's Killing*, N.Y. Times (Sept. 13, 2025), https://www.nytimes.com/2025/09/13/us/politics/trump-kirk-political-opponents.html.
89. Id.
90. Robert McCoy, MAGA Thinks Alleged Kirk Shooter Was Radicalized by . . . College, The New Republic (Sept. 12, 2025), https://newrepublic.com/post/200427/maga-alleged-kirk-shooter-radicalized-college.
91. Kimmy Yam, After Charlie Kirk's death, Teachers and Professors Nationwide Fired or Disciplined over Social Media Posts, NBC News (Sept. 12, 2025), https://www.yahoo.com/news/articles/charlie-kirks-death-teachers-professors-233204452.html.
92. Statement of Robert M. Hutchins, Associate Director of the Ford Foundation, November 25, 1952, in Hearings before the House Select Committee to Investigate Tax-exempt Foundations and Comparable Organizations, pursuant to H.Res. 561, 82d Cong., 2d Sess., quoted in Wieman v. Updegraff, 344 U.S. 183, 196–98 (1952).

Chapter 11

1. *E.g.*, Alvin Powell, *Trump Administration Freezes $2.2 Billion in Grants to Harvard*, Harvard T. H. Chan School of Public Health News (Apr. 15, 2025), https://hsph.harvard.edu/news/trump-administration-freezes-2-2-billion-in-grants-to-harvard/; Ben Unglesbee, *Trump Administration Cuts Off Harvard University from Future Research Grant Funding*, Higher Ed Dive (May 6, 2025), https://www.highereddive.com/news/trump-administration-cuts-harvard-university-grants/747322/; Reuters, *Columbia University Lays Off Nearly 180 Researchers Due to Trump Funding Cuts* (May 6, 2025), https://www.reuters.com/world/us/columbia-university-lays-off-nearly-180-researchers-due-trump-funding-cuts-2025-05-06/; Josh Moody & Ryan Quinn, *NIH Freezes Millions More in Funding for Columbia*, Inside Higher Ed (Apr. 9, 2025), https://www.insidehighered.com/news/government/politics-elections/2025/04/09/nih-freezes-millions-more-funding-columbia; Sara Randazzo & Nidhi Subbaraman, *How Trump Blew Up Northwestern's Business Model*, Wall St. J. (June 15, 2025), https://www.wsj.com/us-news/education/northwestern-funding-freeze-trump-85d49da2?gaa_at=eafs&gaa_n=ASWzDAhxJtrRBQmmwRC65Eg_dlTNmhXrvASVO8eoFGeFkfSn9bwVWSh6T_Ln4agyc7c%3D&gaa_ts=68519773&gaa_sig=UIhmzL29Z050rpSQM0AVa8dXrkIICsuQnHgvK6iKQfBiiBbV56atTBHGFnHcXaSBk98Ic4ylpPKAToqOsWwd7g%3D%3D; Michael C. Bender & Sheryl Gay Stolberg, *Trump Administration Freezes $1 Billion for Cornell and $790 Million for Northwestern, Officials Say*, N.Y. Times (Apr. 9, 2025), https://www.nytimes.com/2025/04/08/us/politics/cornell-northwestern-university-funds-trump.html.
2. *Columbia University Lays Off Nearly 180 Researchers Due to Trump Funding Cuts*, Reuters (May 6, 2025), https://www.reuters.com/world/us/columbia-university-lays-off-nearly-180-researchers-due-trump-funding-cuts-2025-05-06/; Josh Moody & Ryan Quinn, *NIH Freezes Millions More in Funding for Columbia*, Inside Higher Ed (Apr. 9, 2025), https://www.insidehighered.com/news/government/politics-elections/2025/04/09/nih-freezes-millions-more-funding-columbia.
3. Devan Cole, *Federal Judge Indefinitely Blocks Trump Administration from Cutting Off Harvard's Ability to Host Foreign Students*, CNN (June 20, 2025), https://www.cnn.com/2025/06/20/politics/harvard-foreign-students-ruling; April Rubin, *Trump's Tax Fight with Harvard Sends Chill Through Nonprofit Sector*, Axios (May 5, 2025), https://www.axios.com/2025/05/05/harvard-tax-exempt-trump-threats-illegal-irs.
4. Jeffrey Clements, Corporations Are Not People 21–23 (2014); Jeet Heer, *The Powell Memo Helped Create Project 2025*, The Nation (Sept. 6, 2024), https://www.thenation.com/article/society/powell-memo-project-2025-plutocracy/.
5. Memorandum to Mr. Eugene B. Sydnor, Jr., from Lewis F. Powell, Jr., *Attack on American Free Enterprise System* (Aug. 23, 1971), https://www.reuters.com/investigates/special-report/assets/usa-courts-secrecy-lobbyist/powell-memo.pdf.
6. *Id.* at 1.
7. *Id.* at 24.

8. *Id.* at 25.
9. *Id.* at 2–3.
10. *Id.* at 12.
11. *Id.* at 3, 8.
12. *Id.* at 15.
13. *Id.* at 11.
14. *Id.* at 13.
15. *See id.* at 15, 17–20.
16. *Id.*
17. *Id.* at 26.
18. *Id.* at 26–27.
19. *Id.* at 27.
20. Jane Mayer, Dark Money: The Hidden History of the Billionaires Behind the Rise of the Radical Right (2016).
21. Jane Mayer, *How Right-Wing Billionaires Infiltrated Higher Education,* Chronicle of Higher Education (Feb. 12, 2016) [Mayer, Chronicle].
22. *Id.*
23. *Id.*
24. *Id.* The Scaife Foundation spent "some $620 million . . . aimed at influencing American public affairs." Mayer, Dark Money, supra note 20, at 73.
25. Mayer, *Chronicle, supra* note 21.
26. *Id.*
27. *Id.*
28. *Id.*
29. Mayer, Dark Money, supra note 20, at 182–83.
30. Leah M. Litman, Lawless: How the Supreme Court Runs on Conservative Grievance, Fringe Theories, and Bad Vibes 169 (2025).
31. *Id.*
32. Shawn Musgrave, *Leonard Leo Built the Conservative Court. Now He's Funneling Dark Money into Law Schools,* The Intercept (May 29, 2024), https://theintercept.com/2024/05/29/leonard-leo-donor-law-schools/.
33. Mayer, *Chronicle, supra* note 21.
34. Litman, Lawless, *supra* note 30 at 170.
35. *E.g.,* Alvin Powell, *Trump Administration Freezes $2.2 Billion in Grants to Harvard,* Harvard T. H. Chan School of Public Health News (Apr. 15, 2025), https://hsph.harvard.edu/news/trump-administration-freezes-2-2-billion-in-grants-to-harvard/; Ben Unglesbee, *Trump Administration Cuts Off Harvard University from Future Research Grant Funding,* Higher Ed Dive (May 6, 2025), https://www.highereddive.com/news/trump-administration-cuts-harvard-university-grants/747322/; Reuters, *Columbia University Lays Off Nearly 180 Researchers Due to Trump Funding Cuts* (May 6, 2025), https://www.reuters.com/world/us/columbia-university-lays-off-nearly-180-researchers-due-trump-funding-cuts-2025-05-06/; Josh Moody & Ryan Quinn, *NIH Freezes Millions More in Funding for Columbia,* Inside Higher Ed (Apr. 9, 2025), https://www.insidehighered.com/news/government/politics-elections/2025/04/09/nih-freezes-millions-more-funding-columbia; Sara Randazzo & Nidhi Subbaraman, *How Trump Blew Up Northwestern's Business Model,* Wall St. J. (June 15, 2025), https://www.wsj.com/us-news/education/northwestern-funding-freeze-trump-85d49da2?gaa_at=eafs&gaa_n=ASWzDAhxJtrRBQmmwRC65Eg_dlTNmhXrvASVO8eo FGeFkfSn9bwVWSh6T_Ln4agyc7c%3D&gaa_ts=68519773&gaa_sig=UIhmzL29Z050rp SQM0AVa8dXrkIICsuQnHgvK6iKQfBiiBbV56atTBHGFnHcXaSBk98Ic4ylpPKAToqOs Wwd7g%3D%3D; Michael C. Bender & Sheryl Gay Stolberg, *Trump Administration Freezes $1 Billion for Cornell and $790 Million for Northwestern, Officials Say,* N.Y. Times (Apr. 9, 2025), https://www.nytimes.com/2025/04/08/us/politics/cornell-northwestern-univer sity-funds-trump.html.
36. Amanda Holliks Brusky, Ideas with Consequences (2016).
37. Mayer, *Chronicle, supra* note 21.
38. Litman, Lawless, *supra* note 30, at 169.

39. Sheldon Whitehouse, Scheme Speech 9: Amicus Flotillas (Nov. 16, 2021), https://www.whitehouse.senate.gov/news/speeches/scheme-speech-9-amicus-flotillas/.
40. Heidi Przybyla, *"Plain Historical Falsehoods": How Amicus Briefs Bolstered Supreme Court Conservatives*, Politico (Dec. 3, 2023), https://www.politico.com/news/2023/12/03/supreme-court-amicus-briefs-leonard-leo-00127497.
41. Mayer, Dark Money, supra note 20, at 272. It also went to social-welfare groups with similar orientations. *See id.* at 304–05.
42. Litman, Lawless, *supra* note 30 at 168.
43. Litman, Lawless, *supra* note 30 at 170.
44. Nicholas Riccardi & Thomas Beaumont, *Democrats' Win in Wisconsin Court Race Also Is a Big Loss for Elon Musk*, AP (Apr. 2, 2025), https://apnews.com/article/wisconsin-supreme-court-elon-musk-81f71cdda271827ae281a77072a26bad.
45. Maggie Haberman et al., *Musk Donates to G.O.P Members of Congress Who Support Impeaching Judges*, N.Y. Times (Mar. 19, 2025), https://www.nytimes.com/2025/03/19/us/politics/musk-donations-congress-judges.html.
46. Mayer, Chronicle, *supra* note 21.
47. Mayer, Dark Money, supra note 20, at 20.
48. *Id.* at 106.
49. Ronald Reagan, Remarks at a White House Briefing on Proposed Criminal Justice Reform Legislation (Oct. 16, 1987), https://www.reaganlibrary.gov/archives/speech/remarks-white-house-briefing-proposed-criminal-justice-reform-legislation; Bernard Weinraub, *Reagan Says He'll Use Vacancies to Discourage Judicial Activism*, N.Y. Times (Oct. 22, 1985), https://www.nytimes.com/1985/10/22/world/reagan-says-he-ll-use-vacancies-to-discourage-judicial-activism.html.
50. Ronald Reagan, Remarks at a White House Briefing on Proposed Criminal Justice Reform Legislation (Oct. 16, 1987), https://www.reaganlibrary.gov/archives/speech/remarks-white-house-briefing-proposed-criminal-justice-reform-legislation.
51. Bernard Weinraub, *Reagan Says He'll Use Vacancies to Discourage Judicial Activism*, N.Y. Times (Oct. 22, 1985), https://www.nytimes.com/1985/10/22/world/reagan-says-he-ll-use-vacancies-to-discourage-judicial-activism.html.
52. 570 U.S. 529 (2013).
53. Leah M. Litman, Inventing Equal Sovereignty, 114 Mich. L. Rev. 1207, 1229–52, 1268–73 (2016).
54. Litman, Lawless, *supra* note 30 at 116–17.
55. Citizens United v. FEC, 558 U.S. 310 (2010); McCutcheon v. FEC, 572 U.S. 185 (2014); FEC v. Ted Cruz for Senate, 596 U.S. 289 (2022).
56. Citizens United v. FEC, 558 U.S. 310 (2010); see Order List 606 U.S. (Aug. 1, 2025), https://www.democracydocket.com/wp-content/uploads/2024/01/2025-08-01-Order.pdf.
57. New York State Pistol & Rifle Ass'n v. Bruen, 591 U.S. 1 (2022); McDonald v. City of Chicago, 561 U.S. 742 (2010); Masterpiece Cakeshop v. Colorado Civil Rights Comm'n, 584 U.S. 617 (2018); Fulton v. City of Philadelphia, 593 U.S. 622 (2021); 303 Creative v. Elenis, 600 U.S. 570 (2022).
58. Espinoza v. Montana, 591 U.S. 464 (2020); Carson v. Makin, 596 U.S. 767 (2022); Trinity Lutheran v. Comer, 582 U.S. 449 (2017); Catholic Charities Bureau v. Wisconsin Labor & Industry Review Comm'n, 605 U.S. 238 (2025).
59. Rucho v. Common Cause, 588 U.S. 684 (2019); Shelby County v. Holder, 570 U.S. 529 (2013); Brnovich v. Democratic Nat'l Committee, 594 U.S. 647 (2021); LA v. Callais 145 S.Ct. 1164 (Mem) (2025).
60. Michael S. Schmidt & Alan Binder, *Harvard and Trump Restart Talks to Potentially End Bitter Dispute*, N.Y. Times (June 20, 2025), https://www.nytimes.com/2025/06/20/us/politics/harvard-federal-funding-trump.html; Francesca Regaldo, *Columbia Violated Jewish Students' Civil Rights, Trump Administration Finds*, N.Y. Times (May 22, 2025).
61. Katie J. M. Baker, *The Group Behind Project 2025 Has a Plan to Crush the Pro-Palestinian Movement*, N.Y. Times (May 18, 2025).
62. *See supra* text accompanying notes 21–35 and 46–48.
63. Baker, *supra* note 61.

64. *Id.*; Heritage Foundation, Heritage Announces Formation of National Task Force to Combat Antisemitism (Nov. 22, 2023), https://archive.is/njWYq; Vimal Patel, *How to Define "Antisemitism" Is a Subject of Bitter Debate*, N.Y. Times (May 8, 2024), https://archive.is/OW1wQ.
65. Philip Bump, *What Trump Said with His "Very Fine People" Comments vs. What He Meant*, Wash. Post (June 28, 2024), https://www.washingtonpost.com/politics/2024/06/28/what-trump-said-with-his-very-fine-people-comments-vs-what-he-meant/.
66. *Id.*
67. Tom Dreisbach, *Multiple Trump White House Officials Have Ties to Anti-Semitic Extremists*, NPR (May 14, 2025), https://www.npr.org/2025/05/14/nx-s1-5387299/trump-white-house-antisemitism.
68. Tom Dreisbach, *Trump Nominates Official with Ties to Anti-Semitic Extremists to Lead Ethics Agency*, NPR (May 30, 2025).
69. Maggie Haberman & Alan Feuer, *Trump's Latest Dinner Guest: Nick Fuentes, White Supremacist*, N.Y. Times (Nov. 25, 2022).
70. Ben Beaumont-Thomas, *Kanye West Sued and Dropped by Talent Agency over Antisemitism Slurs*, The Guardian (Feb. 12, 2025), https://www.theguardian.com/music/2025/feb/12/kanye-west-sued-dropped-by-talent-agency-and-retail-platform-over-antisemitic-remarks; Faarea Masud, *Adidas Ends "Fight" with Kanye West over Antisemitism*, BBC (Oct. 29, 2024), https://www.bbc.com/news/articles/cgej945wp9xo.
71. Robert Helfand, *Opinion: What Fighting Antisemitism Means to Donald Trump*, CTMirror (May 19, 2025), https://ctmirror.org/2025/05/19/what-fighting-antisemitism-means-to-donald-trump/.
72. Jude Sheerin, *Trump's "Shylock" Comment Draws Outcry from Jewish Groups*, BBC (July 5, 2025), https://www.bbc.com/news/articles/c80p3v0xx53o.
73. Baker, *supra* note 61.
74. *Id.*
75. Aaron Rupar, Bluesky (July 24, 2025), https://bsky.app/profile/atrupar.com/post/3lupiv74kmm2n.
76. Saikrishna Bangalore Prakash, *A Fool for the Original Constitution*, 130 Harv. L. Rev. F 24, 28 (2016); Howard Wasserman, *Scalia, Judicial Ideology, and Flag Burning*, PrawfsBlawg (Aug. 31, 2012), https://prawfsblawg.blogs.com/prawfsblawg/2012/08/stop-talking-about-flag-burning.html.
77. *E.g.*, Robert J. Smith, Antonin Scalia's Other Legacy, Slate (Feb. 15, 2016); Saikrishna Bangalore Prakash, *A Fool for the Original Constitution*, 130 Harv. L. Rev. F 24, 28 (2016); Howard Wasserman, *Scalia, Judicial Ideology, and Flag Burning*, PrawfsBlawg (Aug. 31, 2012), https://prawfsblawg.blogs.com/prawfsblawg/2012/08/stop-talking-about-flag-burning.html.
78. Calvin TerBeek, *Clocks Must Always Be Turned Back*: Brown v. Board of Education *and the Racial Origins of Constitutional Originalism*, 15 a.m. Pol. Sci. Rev. 82–34 (2021); Reva B. Siegel, *The History of History and Tradition: The Roots of* Dobbs's *Method (and Originalism) in the Defense of Segregation*, 133 Yale L.J. Forum 99 (2023).
79. Jamal Greene, *On the Origins of Originalism*, 88 Tex. L. Rev. 1 (2009); Reva Siegel, *Memory Games*: Dobb's *Originalism as Anti-Democratic Living Constitutionalism—and Some Pathways for Resistance*, 101 Tex. L. Rev. 1127 (2023).
80. Litman, Lawless, *supra* note 30 at 19–24.
81. Siegel, *Memory Games*, *supra* note 79 at 1149–51, 1159–60.
82. Litman, Lawless, *supra* note 30 at 23.
83. *See generally* Amanda Hollis-Brusky & Joshua C. Wilson, *Separate but Faithful: The Christian Right's Radical Struggle to Transform Law & Legal Culture* (2020).
84. *Id.*
85. Mayer, *Chronicle*, *supra* note 21.
86. Memorandum to Mr. Eugene B. Sydnor, Jr., from Lewis F. Powell, Jr., *Attack on American Free Enterprise System* (Aug. 23, 1971) 2–3, https://www.reuters.com/investigates/special-report/assets/usa-courts-secrecy-lobbyist/powell-memo.pdf.
87. See Rupar, *supra*.

88. Will Bunch, *Young People Won't, or Can't, Read a Book. Now Democracy Is Dying. Coincidence?*, Philadelphia Inquirer (Apr. 10, 2025), https://archive.is/1IvLW#selection-1465.0–1475.2.
89. Kevin D. Roberts, Foreword: A Promise to America, in Project 2025 15 https://www.documentcloud.org/documents/24088042-project-2025s-mandate-for-leadership-the-conservative-promise/ (emphases added).
90. Mayer, *Chronicle*, *supra* note 21.
91. *Id.*
92. Jason Deparle, *Goals Reached, Donor on Right Closes Up Shop*, N.Y. Times (May 29, 2005), https://archive.is/TvsIS.
93. *Id.*
94. Mayer, *Chronicle*, *supra* note 21.
95. *Id.*
96. Daniel T. Deacon & Leah M. Litman, *Legalistic Noncompliance*, 75 Duke L.J. __ (forthcoming 2026), https://papers.ssrn.com/sol3/papers.cfm?abstract_id=5241936.
97. *See* Katherine Rosman, *Legal Experts Question Trump's Authority to Cancel Columbia's Funding*, N.Y. Times (Mar. 17, 2025), https://www.nytimes.com/2025/03/17/nyregion/columbia-trump-administration-funding-fight.html.
98. Deacon & Litman, *Noncompliance*, *supra* note 96.
99. *See* Adam Liptak, *Supreme Court Keeps Ruling in Trump's Favor, but Doesn't Say Why*, N.Y. Times (July 16, 2025), https://www.nytimes.com/2025/07/16/us/politics/supreme-courts-shadow-docket.html.
100. Deacon & Litman, *Noncompliance*, *supra* note 96.
101. *See* Nate Raymond, *US Judges Cleared of Misconduct over Columbia Clerk Hiring Boycott*, Reuters (Aug. 5, 2024), https://www.reuters.com/legal/legalindustry/us-judges-cleared-misconduct-over-columbia-clerk-hiring-boycott-2024-08-05/; Josh Blackman, *An Interview with Judge James C. Ho*, The Volokh Conspiracy (Nov. 11, 2024), https://reason.com/volokh/2024/11/11/an-interview-with-judge-james-c-ho/.
102. Will Bunch, *Free speech is dead at the American university*, Philadelphia Inquirer (May 18, 2025).

Chapter 12

1. See, e.g., AAUP v. Rubio, 2025 WL 2777659 at *9–37, 45–51 (D. Mass. Sept. 30, 2025) (providing extensive overview of the issues, and summarizing previous litigation in other cases).
2. Institute for International Education, *Million International Students at Higher Education Institutions, Reaching All-Time High* (Nov. 18, 2024), https://www.iie.org/news/us-hosts-more-than-1-1-million-intl-students-at-higher-education-institutions-all-time-high/.
3. See, e.g., American Immigration Council, *Immigrants and the U.S. Educational System* (Aug. 16, 2021) (noting that, as of 2019, there were some 785,000 foreign-born workers in American higher education, making up over 17 percent of total workers), https://www.americanimmigrationcouncil.org/report/immigrants-america-educational-system/.
4. Executive Order No. 14161, 90 Fed. Reg. 8451 (Jan. 20, 2025), available at https://www.presidency.ucsb.edu/documents/executive-order-14161-protecting-the-united-states-from-foreign-terrorists-and-other.
5. For an extensive overview, see AAUP v. Rubio, 2025 WL 2777659 at *9-37.
6. 8 U.S.C. § 1227(a)(4)(C)(i).
7. Massieu v. Reno, 915 F. Supp. 681, 699–703 (D.N.J. 1996), reversed on other grounds, 91 F.3d 416 (3d Cir. 1996).
8. Massieu v. Reno, 91 F.3d 416 (3d Cir. 1996).
9. 8 U.S.C. § 1182(a)(3)(B).
10. See, e.g., Jason Brennan, When All Else Fails: The Ethics of Resistance to State Injustice (2019) (arguing that such resistance is justified in a wide range of circumstances).
11. White House, *Fact Sheet: President Donald J. Trump Takes Forceful and Unprecedented Steps to Combat Anti-Semitism* (Jan. 30, 2025), https://www.whitehouse.gov/fact-sheets/

2025/01/fact-sheet-president-donald-j-trump-takes-forceful-and-unprecedented-steps-to-combat-anti-semitism/.

12. I have argued that the grounds for supporting Israel against Hamas apply with even greater force to supporting Ukraine against Russia, given the much larger scale of the aggression and atrocities by the aggressor in the latter conflict. See Ilya Somin, *Those Who Support Israel Against Hamas Should Also Back Ukraine Against Russia*, Reason (Oct. 12, 2023), https://reason.com/volokh/2023/10/12/those-who-support-israel-against-hamas-should-also-back-ukraine-against-russia/.
13. See, e.g., Edith Lederer, *US Refuses to Blame Russia for Ukraine War, Splitting with European Allies in UN Votes*, Associated Press (Feb. 24, 2025), https://apnews.com/article/un-russia-ukraine-war-resolution-trump-zelenskyy-cde221e5850196776525403e788c272c.
14. Exec. Order no. 14188, 90 Fed. Reg. 8847 (Jan. 29, 2025).
15. White House, *Fact Sheet: President Donald J. Trump Takes Forceful and Unprecedented Steps to Combat Anti-Semitism* (Jan. 30, 2025), https://www.whitehouse.gov/fact-sheets/2025/01/fact-sheet-president-donald-j-trump-takes-forceful-and-unprecedented-steps-to-combat-anti-semitism/.
16. See, e.g., AAUP v. Rubio, 2025 WL 2777659 at *9-37. 45–51 (describing multiple such cases and holding that they violate the First Amendment); Khalil v. Trump, 786 F.Supp.3d 871, 877–79 (D.N.J. 2025) (holding that attempted detention and deportation of former student "chilled" his speech); Ozturk v. Trump, 783 F.Supp.3d 801, 809–11 (D. Vt. 2025) (noting the likelihood of success on First Amendment claims); Mahdawi v. Trump, 781 F. Supp. 3d 214, 229–30 (D. Vt. 2025) (same).
17. Öztürk, 783 F.Supp.3d at 806–11.
18. Rümeysa Öztürk et al., *Try Again, President Kumar: Renewing Calls for Tufts to Adopt March 4 TCU Senate Resolutions*, Tufts Daily (Mar. 26, 2024), https://www.tuftsdaily.com/article/2024/03/4ftk27sm6jkj.
19. See Declaration of Rümeysa Öztürk, Öztürk v. Trump, 783 F.Supp.3d 801(D. Vt. 2025) (No. 2:25-CV-00374) (describing terrible conditions in detention, including denial of needed medical care), https://www.aclum.org/cases/ozturk-v-trump/?document=VT-Pet-Exhibit-1-G-Declaration-of-R%C3%BCmeysa-%C3%96zt%C3%BCrk#documents.
20. Emily Hallas, *White House Offers Funding Advantage to Colleges That Sign "Compact for Academic Excellence,"* Washington Examiner (Oct 2, 2025), https://www.washingtonexaminer.com/policy/education/3833857/white-house-funding-advantage-colleges-sign-compact-for-academic-excellence/ (full compact available on same web page).
21. Lexi Lonas Cochrane, *Here Are the Colleges Rejecting Trump's Funding Compact*, The Hill (Oct. 21, 2025), https://thehill.com/homenews/education/5558934-colleges-reject-donald-trump-administration-compact/; Dan Rosenzweig-Ziff, *University of Virginia Declines Trump Deal for Priority Federal Funding*, Washington Post (Oct. 17, 2025), https://www.washingtonpost.com/education/2025/10/17/uva-trump-compact-agreement-rejection/; Liz Wolfe, *Schools Find Their Spines*, Reason (Oct. 21, 2025), https://reason.com/2025/10/21/schools-find-their-spines/.
22. For explanations of how the compact threatens free speech and academic freedom, see, e.g., Genevieve Lakier, *The Unconstitutional Conditions Doctrine and the Compact for Excellence*, Divided Argument (Substack) (Oct. 3, 2025), https://blog.dividedargument.com/p/the-unconstitutional-conditions-doctrine; Walter Olson, *Universities Must Defend Their Independence by Rejecting Trump's "Compact,"* Cato Institute (Oct. 10, 2025), https://www.cato.org/blog/universities-must-defend-their-independence.
23. Joe Walsh, *Trump Administration Revokes 6 Visas over Comments About Charlie Kirk*, CBS News (Oct. 15, 2025), https://www.cbsnews.com/news/trump-administration-revokes-visas-charlie-kirk/.
24. AAUP, *1940 Statement of Principles on Academic Freedom and Tenure with 1970 Interpretive Comments*, https://www.aaup.org/reports-publications/aaup-policies-reports/policy-statements/1940-statement-principles-academic.
25. *Ibid.*

26. See, e.g., Keith E. Whittington, Speak Freely: Why Universities Must Defend Free Speech 141–51 (2019); Erwin Chemerinsky & Howard Gillman, Free Speech on Campus 65–66 (2017).
27. AAUP, *1940 Statement of Principles.*
28. Chemerinsky & Gillman, *Free Speech on Campus*, 67.
29. AAUP, *1940 Statement of Principles, supra* note 27.
30. AAUP, *Joint Statement on Rights and Freedoms of Students* (1967), https://www.aaup.org/reports-publications/aaup-policies-reports/policy-statements/joint-statement-rights-and-freedoms.
31. See, e.g., Kleindienst v. Mandel, 408 U.S. 53 (1972) (upholding speech-based exclusion of a Marxist academic); AAUP v. Rubio, 2025 WL 2777659 at *45-47 (summarizing relevant precedent and noting the distinction between "exclusion" and deportation).
32. See, e.g., Ilya Somin, *The Case Against Deporting Immigrants for "Pro-Terrorist" Speech*, Reason (Mar. 10, 2025), https://reason.com/volokh/2025/03/10/the-case-against-deporting-immigrants-for-pro-terrorist-speech/.
33. For recent overviews of some of the reasons why remote communication cannot fully replicate the benefits of in-person interaction, see, e.g., Wendy L. Patrick, *Beyond Zoom: How Meeting in Person Creates Connection*, Psychology Today (Oct. 13, 2024), https://www.psychologytoday.com/us/blog/why-bad-looks-good/202410/beyond-zoom-how-meeting-in-person-creates-connection; Elizabeth L. Keating, *Why Do Virtual Meetings Feel So Weird?*, 109 American Scientist 94 (2021), https://www.americanscientist.org/article/why-do-virtual-meetings-feel-so-weird.
34. For my account of this experience, see Ilya Somin, *The Uncertain Limits of Intellectual Freedom in China*, Washington Post (Aug. 7, 2014), https://www.washingtonpost.com/news/volokh-conspiracy/wp/2014/08/07/the-uncertain-limits-of-intellectual-freedom-in-china/.
35. *Ibid.*
36. I eventually decided I should take the risk, and there were no repercussions. *Ibid.* The outcome might well have been less happy in today's more repressive atmosphere in China.
37. See discussion in Part III, *supra.*
38. F. A. Hayek, The Constitution of Liberty 405 (1960).
39. For leading overviews, see, e.g., Bernard Bailyn, The Ideological Origins of the American Revolution (1967); Gordon Wood, The Radicalism of the American Revolution (1991).
40. U.S. Census, Population Clock, https://www.census.gov/popclock/ (last visited Oct. 12, 2025).
41. See discussion in Part I, *supra.*
42. See, e.g., Terri Diane Halperin, The Alien and Sedition Acts of 1798: Testing the Constitution (2016); John Chester Miller, Crisis in Freedom: The Alien and Sedition Acts (1951).
43. See, e.g., Erika Lee, America for Americans: A History of Xenophobia in the United States 139–40 (2019); Adam Hochschild, *When America Tried to Deport Its Radicals*, New Yorker (Nov. 4, 2019), https://www.newyorker.com/magazine/2019/11/11/when-america-tried-to-deport-its-radicals.
44. For an extensive overview, see Alex Nowrasteh & Benjamin Powell, Wretched Refuse? The Political Economy of Immigration and Institutions (2021).
45. These points are developed in more detail in Ilya Somin, Free to Move: Foot Voting, Migration, and Political Freedom 130–34 (2022).
46. See, e.g., Mari Matsuda et al., Words That Wound: Critical Race Theory, Assaultive Speech, and the First Amendment (1993); Jeremy Waldron, The Harm in Hate Speech (2014).
47. For these and other criticisms of hate-speech restrictions, see, e.g., Nadine Strossen, Hate: Why We Should Resist It with Free Speech, Not Censorship (2018); Jacob Mchangama, Heini Skorini & Mathias Meier, *Hate Speech, Holy Prophets, and Human Rights: The Struggle for Free Speech from 1945–2021*, 2 J. of Free Speech 675 (2022).
48. Quoted in AAUP v. Rubio, 2025 WL 2777659 at *17.

49. See, e.g., Flemming v. Nestor, 363 U.S. 603 (1960) (holding that there is no "property right" to Social Security benefits, and Congress can lower them as it chooses).
50. Perry v. Sindermann, 408 U.S. 593, 597 (1972).
51. *Ibid.* at 597–600.
52. For a discussion of why diversity statements are at odds with academic freedom, see Keith E. Whittington, *Diversity Statements, Academic Freedom, and the First Amendment*, 103 Nebraska L. Rev. 643 (2025).
53. *Ibid.*, 646–47.
54. FIRE, 2026 College Free Speech Rankings 23–24 (2025), https://www.thefire.org/college-free-speech-rankings.
55. *Ibid.* at 6–10.
56. On the many benefits of foot voting, see Somin, Free to Move, *supra* note 45 at ch. 1.
57. Heather K. Gerken, *Second-Order Diversity*, 118 Harv. L. Rev. 1099 (2005).
58. See discussion in Part III, *supra*.
59. See Somin, Free to Move, *supra* note 45 at ch. 6; Ilya Somin, *Immigration and the Economic Freedom of Natives*, 37 Public Affairs Quarterly 226 (2023).
60. See Somin, Free to Move, *supra* note 45 at 139–41.

Chapter 13

1. Katrin Kinzelbach et al., *Academic Freedom Index Update 2025*, Friedrich-Alexander-Universität Erlangen-Nürnberg, Varieties of Democracy Project (2025), https://academic-freedom-index.net/.
2. National Conservatism, *J. D. Vance | The Universities Are the Enemy | National Conservatism Conference II*, YouTube (Nov. 10, 2021), https://www.youtube.com/watch?v=0FR65Cifnhw.
3. David Rabban, Academic Freedom: From Professional Norm to First Amendment Right (2024).
4. See Eve Darian-Smith, Policing Higher Education: The Antidemocratic Attack on Scholars and Why It Matters 64–65 (2025).
5. Jacob Levy, *Academic Freedom as Freedom of Complex Association*, *in* Academic Freedom in a Plural World: Global Critical Perspectives 25–39 (Frédéric Mégret & Nandini Ramanujam eds., 2024).
6. Janika Spannagel, *The Constitutional Codification of Academic Freedom over Time and Space*, 14 Global Constitutionalism 46 (2025); *see also* Tom Ginsburg, *Academic Freedom and Democratic Backsliding*, 71 J. of Legal Education 238 (2022).
7. Anna Berry, The German Model of Academic Freedom (unpublished manuscript) (on file with author).
8. E.g., Artículo 3(VII), Constitución Política de los Estados Unidos Mexicanos, CPEUM, Diario Oficial de la Federación [DOF] 05–02–1917, últimas reformas DOF 10–02–2014 (Mexico) (university right to autonomous self-governance); Art. 14, Constitución Nacional [Const. Nac.] (Argentina) (everyone has the freedom to teach and learn).
9. Charter of Fundamental Rights of the European Union, Art 13, https://www.europarl.europa.eu/charter/pdf/text_en.pdf.
10. U.S. Const, art I, § 8.
11. Rabban, *supra* note 3.
12. 547 U.S. 410, 421 (2006) ("We hold that when public employees make statements pursuant to their official duties, the employees are not speaking as citizens for First Amendment purposes.").
13. *Id.* at 425 ("There is some argument that expression related to academic scholarship or classroom instruction implicates additional constitutional interests that are not fully accounted for by this Court's customary employee-speech jurisprudence. We need not, and for that reason do not, decide whether the analysis we conduct today would apply in the same manner to a case involving speech related to scholarship or teaching.").
14. Meriwether v. Hartop, 992 F.3d 492, 505 (6th Cir. 2021); Adams v. Trustees of the Univ. of N.C.-Wilmington, 640 F.3d 550, 562 (4th Cir. 2011); Buchanan v. Alexander, 919 F.3d 847, 852–53 (5th Cir. 2019); Demers v. Austin, 746 F.3d 402, 411–12 (9th Cir. 2014).

15. See, e.g., Heim v. Daniel, 81 F. 4th 212 (2d Cir. 2023).
16. Karlie M. Bischoff, *Advancing Academic Freedom Through State Constitutional Protections,* 52 UC Law SF Const. Q. 3 (2024).
17. Scholars at Risk, Free to Think 2025 (2025), https://www.scholarsatrisk.org/resources/free-to-think-2025/.
18. Mike Ticher, *Long Arm of Law and Justice: The Sydney Professor Under Attack from Poland's Ruling Party,* Guardian (Oct. 3, 2020), https://www.theguardian.com/world/2020/oct/04/long-arm-of-law-and-justice-the-sydney-professor-under-attack-from-polands-ruling-party.
19. *Prosecutors in Thailand Drop Royal Defamation Case Against US Scholar,* CNN (May 1, 2025), https://www.cnn.com/2025/05/01/asia/thailand-lese-majeste-paul-chambers-intl-hnk.
20. Erik Heinze, The Most Human Right: Why Free Speech Is Everything (2022).
21. Jeremiah O Arowosegbe, *African Universities and the Challenge of Postcolonial Development,* 93 Africa 591 (2023); Wathira Kigotho, *How Universities in Africa Lost Their Academic Freedom,* University World News (Feb. 22 2024), https://www.universityworldnews.com/post.php?story=2024022115014069.
22. Kunti Surender, *Evangelist Prof Ch Chengiah Removed as HOD at Sri Venkateswara University, LRPF Seeks Termination,* Voice of the Nation Organizer (Dec. 16, 2024), https://organiser.org/2024/12/16/269633/bharat/andhra-pradesh-evangelist-prof-ch-chengiah-removed-as-hod-at-sri-venkateswara-university-lrpf-seeks-termination/.
23. Scholars at Risk, Free to Think 2025, *supra* note 17.
24. Russell Kirk, *Massive Subsidies and Academic Freedom,* 28 Law and Contemporary Problems 607 (1963).
25. *Id.* at 612.
26. Suzanne Nossel, *Why the Compact Failed,* Chron. of Higher Educ. (Oct. 22, 2025).
27. https://www.indystar.com/story/news/education/2025/08/14/iu-sanctions-professor-indiana-intellectual-diversity-law-202/85643279007/.
28. https://share.google/VJ9lsUTwwXy9YB4um.
29. Foundation for Individual Rights and Expression, Scholars Under Fire Database (last visited Nov. 3, 2025), https://www.thefire.org/research-learn/scholars-under-fire.
30. Anthoula Makkopolou, *Oxford Handbook of Democratic Self-Defense* (unpublished manuscript) (on file with author).
31. Karl Popper, The Open Society and Its Enemies (1945).

Chapter 14

1. Perhaps the most dramatic clash between populists and progressives over academic freedom occurred during the "Scopes Monkey Trial," when populist hero William Jennings Bryan squared off against the progressive icon Clarence Darrow over a state statute banning the teaching of evolution in the public schools. For my analysis of the case and its connection to the trajectory of American constitutional history, see Louis Michael Seidman, *Populist and Progressive Strands in American Constitutionalism,* 53 Conn. L. Rev. 411, 426–31 (2021).
2. *See, e.g.,* Lawrence Goodwyn, The Populist Moment: A Short History of the Agrarian Revolt in America 3–93 (1978).
3. *See, e.g.,* J. M. Balkin, *Populism and Progressivism as Constitutional Categories,* 104 Yale L. J. 1935, 1945 (1995).
4. *See, e.g.,* Richard Hofstadter, The Age of Reform: From Bryan to FDR 61–62 (1955).
5. *See, e.g.,* Michael Kazin, The Populist Persuasion: An American History 52 (2017).
6. For an account, see Mark Tushnet, *The Next Generation of Free Expression Scholarship: A Manifesto (in Memory of Fred Schauer),* 33 Wm. & Mary B. of Rts. J. 999, 1008–1025 (2025).
7. *See Vietnam Commander Westmoreland Dies at 91,* National Public Radio (July 19, 2005), https://www.npr.org/2005/07/19/4760273/vietnam-war-commander-westmoreland-dies-at-91 (attributing quotation to William Westmoreland).
8. Watergate and the White House: The "Third Rate Burglary" That Toppled a Presidency, U.S. News and World Report (Aug. 8, 2014), https://www.usnews.com/news/articles/2014/08/08/watergate-and-the-white-house-the-third-rate-burglary-that-toppled-a-president.

9. *See January 26, 1998: Response to the Lewinsky Allegations*, Miller Center, https://millercenter.org/the-presidency/presidential-speeches/january-26-1998-response-lewinsky-allegations.
10. *See* Seymour M. Hersh, *Who Lied to Whom?*, New Yorker (Mar. 23, 2003), https://www.newyorker.com/magazine/2003/03/31/who-lied-to-whom.
11. *See* Peter Baker, *Don't Call It a Bailout: Washington Is Haunted by the 2008 Financial Crisis*, N.Y. Times (Mar. 4, 2023),https://www.nytimes.com/2023/03/14/us/politics/bailout-biden-financial-crisis.html.
12. *See* Richard Van Noorden, *More Than 10000 Research Papers Were Retracted in 2023—a New Record*, Nature (Dec. 12, 2023), https://www.nature.com/articles/d41586-023-03974-8; R. Grant Steen, Arturo Casadevall & Ferric C. Fang, *Why Has the Number of Scientific Retractions Increased?*, *in* Methodological Issues and Strategies in Clinical Research 55 (4th ed. 2016).
13. For a long list of hoaxes perpetrated by journalists, see *Journalistic Hoaxes*, Wikipedia, https://en.wikipedia.org/wiki/List_of_hoaxes (last visited July 17, 2025).
14. *See, e.g.*, Thomas P. Doyle & Stephen C. Rubino, *Catholic Clergy Sexual Abuse Meets Civil Law*, 31 Ford. Urban L. J. 549 (2004).
15. *See* Mark Tushnet, *Trust the Science but Do Your Own Research: A Comment on the Unfortunate Revival of the Administrative State*, 98 Ind. L. Rev. 335, 347–362 (2023) (discussing shifting government advice on preventing Covid).
16. *See* Daniel Wolfe & Daniel Dale, *"It's Going to Disappear": A Timeline of Trump's Claims That Covid Will Vanish*, CNN (Nov. 31, 2020), https://www.cnn.com/interactive/2020/10/politics/covid-disappearing-trump-comment-tracker/.
17. *See* Tushnet, *supra* note 15, at 351–53; Julia Naftulin, *WHO Says There Is No Need for Healthy People to Wear Face Masks, Days After CDC Told All Americans to Cover Their Faces*, Business Insider (Apr. 7, 2020),https://www.businessinsider.com/who-no-need-for-healthy-people-to-wear-face-masks-2020-4.
18. *See* Cheyanne Mumphrey, *Covid Guidelines Have Changed. Here's When a Sick Kid Can Return to School*, Fortune (Aug. 19, 2024), https://fortune.com/well/2024/08/19/covid-guidelines-sick-kids-return-school/.
19. *See, e.g.*, Brian Leiter, *The Epistemology of the Internet and the Regulation of Free Speech in America*, 20 Geo. J. L. Pub. Pol'y 903 (2022); Bobby Chesney & Danielle Citron, *Deep Fakes: A Looming Challenge to Privacy, Democracy, and National Security*, 107 Calif. L. Rev. 1783 (2019).
20. Keyishian v. Board of Regents, 385 U.S. 589, 603 (1967) (quoting United States v. Associated Press, 52 F. Supp. 362, 372 (S.D.N.Y 1943)).
21. *See* J. Peter Byrne, *Academic Freedom: A "Special Concern of the First Amendment,"* 91 Yale L. J. 251 (1989).
22. *See* Robert C. Post, Democracy, Expertise, Academic Freedom: A First Amendment Jurisprudence for the Modern State (2012).
23. *See id.* at 9 (arguing that "the creation of expert knowledge requires practices that separate true ideas from false ones"); Byrne, *supra* note 21, at 261 (arguing that academic speech should be protected because it is held to high standards).
24. *See* Post, *supra* note 22, at 6–10.
25. For the best-known judicial defense of academic freedom during the Warren period, see Sweezy v. New Hampshire, 354 U.S. 234, 261–64 (1957) (Frankfurter, J. concurring); *see also id.* at 250 (Warren, C.J.); Healy v. James, 408 U.S. 169, 196–97(1972) (Douglas, J., concurring); Keyishian v. Board of Regents, 385 U.S. 589, 603 (1967) (Brennan, J.).
26. United States v. Skrmetti, 602 U.S. 495, 547 (2025) (Thomas, J., concurring) (internal and quotations citations omitted).
27. *Compare* Lee H. Kilmer, Jesse Chou, Christopher A. Campbell, Brent R. DeGeorge & John T. Stranix, *Gender-Affirming Surgery Improves Mental Health Outcomes and Decreases Antidepressant Use in Patients with Gender Dysphoria*, National Institute of Health (2024), https://pubmed.ncbi.nlm.nih.gov/38315125/ (concluding that gender-affirming surgery improves mental health) *with* Hilary Cass, The Cass Review: Independent Review of Gender Identity for Children and Young People (2024) (concluding

that there is no reliable evidence that gender-affirming treatment for young people improves mental health).

28. *See, e.g.*, Thomas C. Leonard, Illiberal Reformers: Race, Eugenics & American Economics in the Progressive Era 109–28 (2016).
29. For an account, *see* J. S. Weiner, The Piltdown Forgery: The Classic Account of the Most Famous and Successful Hoax in Science 1–16 (2009).
30. On the influx of leading academics into the Kennedy administration and how they subsequently supported the Vietnam War, see David Halberstam, The Best and the Brightest (1972).
31. For a summary of "Dunning school" claims about Reconstruction, see Eric Foner, Reconstruction and America's Unfinished Revolution, 1863–1877 at xix–xxi (1988).
32. *See. e.g.*, Jason M. Chin & Katheryn Zeiler, *Replicability in Empirical Legal Research*, 17 Ann. Rev. L. & Soc. Sci. 239, 240 (2021) (observing that "[t]he replication crisis that has struck all scientific fields, from medicine to economics to psychology and beyond, is by now well known"). For a discussion, see Jeffrey Brainard & Jia You, *What a Massive Database of Retracted Papers Reveals About Science Publishing's "Death Penalty,"* Science (Oct. 25, 2018), https://www.science.org/content/article/what-massive-database-retracted-papers-reveals-about-science-publishing-s-death-penalty.
33. *See The Untreated Syphilis Study at Tuskegee Timeline*, Ctr. for Disease Control (Sept. 4, 2024), https://www.cdc.gov/tuskegee/about/timeline.html.
34. *See, e.g.*, *Carnegie Classification of Institutions of Higher Education*, Carnegie Foundation (2025), https://carnegieclassifications.acenet.edu (last visited July 21, 2025).
35. *Cf.* EY Parthenon, Making the Grade: Can Liberal Arts Institutions Reclaim Their Value Proposition (2023), https://www.ey.com/content/dam/ey-unified-site/ey-com/en-us/insights/education/documents/ey-how-liberal-arts-institutions-can-reclaim-their-value-proposition.pdf (showing enrollment at liberal-arts institutions declining as a percentage of overall enrollment in higher education).
36. Duncan Kennedy, *Legal Education and the Reproduction of Hierarchy*, 42 J. of Legal Educ. 591, 615 (1983).
37. *See, e.g.*, Sherry E. Moss & Morteza Mahamoud, STEM the Bullying: An Empirical Investigation of Abusive Supervision in Academic Science (Sept. 8, 2021); Derek Lowe, *Graduate Abuse*, Science (Oct. 18, 2019),https://www.science.org/content/blog-post/graduate-abuse; *Academic Bullying and Graduate Student Abuse: Graduate Schools' Dirty Secret*, Graduate Student Success (July 5, 2022), https://gradstudentsuccess.com/academic-bullying/.
38. *See, e.g.*, Ariel H. Kim & Meinei Xu, *"An Open Secret": Harvard Graduate Students Decry Harassment, Neglect from Faculty*, Harvard Crimson (May 26, 2022), https://www.thecrimson.com/article/2022/5/26/graduate-students-power-dynamics/.
39. *See, e.g.*, Kimberly D. Becker, *Graduate Students' Experience of Plagiarism by Their Professors*, 73 Higher Educ. Q. 251 (Oct. 29, 2018), *available at* https://onlinelibrary.wiley.com/doi/10.1111/hequ.12179.
40. *See*, Lucas Lin, *Duke School of Medicine Plans Salary Cuts for Tenured Faculty Who Do Not Meet Grant Expectations*, Duke Chronicle (July 18, 2025) https://www.dukechronicle.com/article/2025/07/duke-university-school-of-medicine-implements-faculty-productivity-guidelines-external-grant-funding-requirements-salary-reductions.
41. *See, e.g.*, Karen Sloan, *Penn Law Prof Amy Wax Loses Bid to Stop Sanctions over Comments Deemed Discriminatory*, Reuters (June 24, 2025), https://www.reuters.com/legal/government/penn-law-prof-amy-wax-loses-bid-stop-sanctions-over-comments-deemed-2025-06-24/; Reshmi Dutt-Ballenstadt, *An Extraordinary Firing*, Inside Higher Ed (June 3, 2021), https://www.insidehighered.com/views/2021/06/04/universities-fire-tenured-faculty-without-due-process-are-setting-dangerous (recounting instances of tenured faculty fired without due process).
42. Which is not to claim that important people haven't said it. *See, e.g.*, Regents of University of California v. Bakke, 438 U.S. 265, 311–14 (1978) (Powell, J., announcing judgment for the Court) (defending the constitutional status of academic freedom in the context of decisions made by a public university).

43. *See* Students for Fair Admissions v. President and Fellows of Harvard College, 600 U.S. 181 (2023).
44. *See, e.g.*, LAWRENCE A. CREMIN, AMERICAN EDUCATION: THE NATIONAL EXPERIENCE 1783–1876 at 107 (1980).
45. The views I express here roughly correspond to those articulated by John Dewey over a century ago. *See* JOHN DEWEY, DEMOCRACY AND EDUCATION: AN INTRODUCTION TO THE PHILOSOPHY OF EDUCATION 87–88 (1916).

Chapter 15

1. Robert M. Hutchins, *What Is a University?* A Speech Delivered by the President of the University of Chicago, (Apr. 18, 1935), *in* THE CHICAGO CANON ON FREE INQUIRY AND EXPRESSION 35 (Tony Banout & Tom Ginsburg, eds., 2023).
2. West Virginia State Bd. of Educ. v. Barnette, 319 U.S. 624, 642 (1943).
3. R. A. Barnett, *Higher Education: Legitimation Crisis*, 10 STUDIES IN HIGHER EDUC. 241, 248 (1985).
4. JOHN MCWHORTER, WOKE RACISM: HOW A NEW RELIGION HAS BETRAYED BLACK AMERICA (2021).
5. *See* Marina Watts, *In Smithsonian Race Guidelines, Rational Thinking and Hard Work Are White Values*, NEWSWEEK (July 17, 2020), https://www.newsweek.com/smithsonian-race-guidelines-rational-thinking-hard-work-are-white-values-1518333.
6. *See* MCWHORTER, *supra* note 4, at 6; George Packer, *When the Culture War Comes for the Kids*, ATLANTIC (Oct. 2019), https://www.theatlantic.com/magazine/archive/2019/10/when-the-culture-war-comes-for-the-kids/596668/; Tema Okun, *White Supremacy Culture*, https://www.whitesupremacyculture.info/one-right-way.html.
7. *See, e.g.* LAURA W. PERNA, TAKING IT TO THE STREETS: THE ROLE OF SCHOLARSHIP IN ADVOCACY AND ADVOCACY IN SCHOLARSHIP (2018). This problem may be broader, but it is particularly pronounced within the DEI community.
8. Sofia Leung, *Whiteness as Collections*, SOFIA LEUNG (Sep. 30, 2019), sofiayleung.com/thoughts/whiteness-as-collections.
9. For one example in a scientific field, see Chanda Prescod-Weinstein, *Making Black Women Scientists Under White Empiricism: The Racialization of Epistemology in Physics*, 45 SIGNS: JOURNAL OF WOMEN IN CULTURE AND SOCIETY 421 (2020).
10. THOMAS KENEALLY, SCHINDLER'S LIST 167–69 (1982).
11. *See, e.g.*, VALERY N. SOYFER, LYSENKO AND THE TRAGEDY OF SOVIET SCIENCE (Leo Gruliow & Rebecca Guliow, trans., 1994).
12. Many versions of the DEI Glossary exist; the quotations in this essay are from a commonly used one which is discussed here, among other places: Santi Tafarella, *DEI Invades Community Colleges Too*, WALL ST. J. (Feb. 21, 2024), https://www.wsj.com/opinion/dei-invades-community-colleges-too-los-angeles-county-free-inquiry-indoctrination-19058b34.
13. For further elaboration of the inherent anti-Semitism and anti-Asian implications of the rejection of merit, see DANIEL A. FARBER & SUZANNA SHERRY, BEYOND ALL REASON: THE RADICAL ASSAULT ON TRUTH IN AMERICAN LAW 52–71 (1997); Suzanna Sherry, *DEI and Antisemitism: Bred in the Bone*, 19 FIU L. REV. 899 (2025); Daniel A. Farber & Suzanna Sherry, *Is the Radical Critique of Merit Anti-Semitic?*, 83 CALIF. L. REV. 853 (1995).
14. *See, e.g.*, Elizabeth Redden, *DEI Training Gone Wrong*, INSIDE HIGHER ED (June 15, 2021), https://www.insidehighered.com/news/2021/06/16/eeoc-complaint-against-stanford-alleges-dei-program-created-hostile-environment (describing Jewish faculty at Stanford being forced into "white accountability" affinity groups).
15. *See, e.g.*, Martin Kramer, *In the Words of Martin Luther King*, MARTIN KRAMER (Mar. 12, 2012), martinkramer.org/2012/03/12/in-the-words-of-martin-luther-king/ (quoting Seymour Martin Lipset, who quoted what King had said in his presence); *10 Great Moments of Black Jewish Unity*, AM. JEWISH COMM. (Sep. 10, 2020), www.ajc.org/news/10-great-moments-of-blackjewishunity (quoting Vernon Jordan to the same effect).
16. Noah Feldman, *The New Antisemitism*, TIME (Feb. 27, 2024), https://time.com/6763293/antisemitism/.

17. *See generally* STEPHEN HOLMES, THE ANATOMY OF ANTILIBERALISM (1993).
18. *See generally* DAVID A. HOLLINGER, SCIENCE, JEWS, AND SECULAR CULTURE (1996).
19. For some specific examples, see Sherry, *supra* note 13, 19 FIU L. REV. at 901–02 n.14; Geoffrey R. Stone, *Free Speech on Campus: A Challenge of Our Times* (Sep. 22, 2016) *in* BANOUT & GINSBURG, *supra* note 1; *Scholars Under Fire Database*, FOUND. FOR INDIVIDUAL RTS. & EXPRESSION (2025), https://www.thefire.org/research-learn/scholars-under-fire. Although not the focus of this article, it must be noted that some universities—often as a result of pressure from outside sources—have also occasionally punished left-wing speakers. *See, e.g.*, Sarah Viren, *Can Academic Freedom Survive*, N.Y. TIMES MAGAZINE 30 (June 8, 2025). I would argue that the difference is that in most of those cases, it is university administrators, not faculty or student organizations, who instigate and implement the "cancellation." That difference is important because administrators—unlike faculty and students—are usually acting not out of fealty to an ideological commitment but for the same reason they have failed to stop the spread of anti-Semitism: the fear of negative consequences to themselves and their universities—in other words, cowardice.
20. *See, e.g.*, Bret Stephens, *Campus Antisemitism, Free Speech and Double Standards*, N.Y. TIMES (Dec. 9, 2023), https://www.nytimes.com/2023/12/08/opinion/antisemitism-college-free-speech.html.
21. Emma Pettit, *At UC Berkeley, the Faculty Asks Itself, Do Our Critics Have a Point?*, CHRON. OF HIGHER EDUC. (May 21, 2025), https://www.chronicle.com/article/at-uc-berkeley-the-faculty-asks-itself-do-our-critics-have-a-point.
22. Franklin Foer, *Columbia University's Anti-Semitism Problem*, ATLANTIC (Mar. 17, 2025), https://www.theatlantic.com/ideas/archive/2025/03/columbia-antisemitism-israel-palestine-trump/682054/.
23. Frankel v. Regents of the Univ. of Cal., 744 F. Supp.3d 1015, 1020 (C.D. Cal. 2024) (emphasis in original).
24. *See, e.g.*, Bret Stephens, *For America's Jews, Every Day Must Be October 8*, N.Y. TIMES (Nov. 7, 2023), https://www.nytimes.com/2023/11/07/opinion/us-jewish-israel-sept-11.html.
25. University of California Rubric to Assess Candidate Contributions to Diversity, Equity, and Inclusion, reprinted at https://www.thefire.org/research-learn/rubric-assess-candidate-contributions-diversity-equity-and-inclusion. For details on (and a critique of) Harvard's diversity-statement requirements, *see* Randall Kennedy, *Mandatory DEI Statements Are Illogical Pledges of Allegiance*, CHRON. OF HIGHER EDUC. (April 3, 2024), https://www.chronicle.com/article/mandatory-dei-statements-are-ideological-pledges-of-allegiance.
For an early empirical study of diversity statements, see James D. Paul & Robert Maranto, *Other Than Merit: The Prevalence of Diversity, Equity, and Inclusion Statements in University Hiring*, AEI (Nov. 2021), https://www.aei.org/wp-content/uploads/2021/11/Other-than-merit-The-prevalence-of-diversity-equity-and-inclusion-statements-in-university-hi ring.pdf.
26. John Sailer, *Higher Ed's New Woke Loyalty Oaths*, TABLET MAG. (Sep. 6, 2022), https://www.tabletmag.com/sections/news/articles/higher-ed-new-woke-loyalty-oaths-dei.
27. Daniel Ortner, *In the Name of Diversity: Why Mandatory Diversity Statements Violate the First Amendment and Reduce Intellectual Diversity in Academia*, 70 CATH. U. L. REV. 515, 548–49 (2021).
28. *See, e.g.*, Steven M. Teles, *Why Are There So Few Conservative Professors*, CHRON. OF HIGHER EDUC. (July 1, 2024), https://www.chronicle.com/article/why-are-there-so-few-conservative-professors; Rose Horowitch, *The Era of DEI for Conservatives Has Begun*, ATLANTIC (May 27, 2025), https://www.theatlantic.com/ideas/archive/2025/05/conservative-professors-dei-initiatives/682944/.
29. Samuel A. Church & Cam N. Srivastava, *Most Harvard Students Do Not Feel Comfortable Sharing Controversial Opinions in Class, Survey Finds*, HARVARD CRIMSON (Feb. 10, 2025), https://www.thecrimson.com/article/2025/2/10/survey-results-controversial-opinions/; *The Academic Mind in 2022: What Faculty Think About Free Expression and Academic Freedom on Campus*, FIRE, https://www.thefire.org/research-learn/academic-mind-2022-what-faculty-think-about-free-expression-and-academic-freedom (last visited Oct. 10, 2025).

30. Forest Romm & Kevin Waldman, *Performative Virtue-Signaling Has Become a Threat to Higher Ed*, The Hill (Aug. 13, 2025), https://thehill.com/opinion/education/5446702-performative-virtue-signaling-has-become-a-threat-to-higher-ed/amp/.
31. Jon A. Shields, Yuval Avnur & Stephanie Muravchik, Closed Classrooms? An Analysis of College Syllabi on Contentious Issues (July 10, 2025) (unpublished manuscript), https://www.hoover.org/sites/default/files/2025-12/Closed%20Classrooms.pdf; see also Jon A. Shields & Yuval Avnur, *Evidence Backs Trump on Higher Ed's Bias*, Wall St. J. (Aug.t 14, 2025), https://www.wsj.com/opinion/evidence-backs-trump-on-higher-eds-bias-politics-13d4fec0; Emma Pettit, *These Scholarly Topics Are Hotly Debated. So Why Don't Syllabi Reflect That?*, Chron. of Higher Educ. (July 22, 2025), https://www.chronicle.com/article/these-scholarly-topics-are-hotly-debated-so-why-dont-syllabi-reflect-that.
32. Neil Vigdor, *Georgetown Suspends Lecturer Who Criticized Vow to Put Black Woman on the Court*, N.Y. Times (Jan. 31, 2022), https://www.nytimes.com/2022/01/31/us/ilya-shapiro-georgetown-biden-scotus.html.
33. Conor Friedersdorf, *The Fight Against Words That Sound Like, but Are Not, Slurs*, Atlantic (Sep. 21, 2020), https://www.theatlantic.com/ideas/archive/2020/09/fight-against-words-sound-like-are-not-slurs/616404/. This article also contrasts the incident with the lack of reaction to analogous complaints some twenty years earlier, suggesting that the culture has changed significantly.
34. *Id.*
35. 163 U.S. 537, 559 (1896) (Harlan, J., dissenting).
36. *See, e.g.*, Trinity College, Diversity, Equity, and Inclusion Glossary, https://www.trincoll.edu/esc/racial_equity_action_plan/glossary/ (last visited Mar. 17, 2026).
37. Jerome McCristal Culp, Jr., *Telling a Black Legal Story: Privilege, Authenticity, "Blunders," and Transformation in Outsider Narratives*, 82 Va. L. Rev. 69, 90 & n.72 (1996). See also sources cited in Daniel A. Farber & Suzanna Sherry, *Beyond All Criticism?*, 83 Minn. L. Rev. 1735, 1738–39 & nn.6–21 (1999).
38. 438 U.S. 265 (1978).
39. *Id.* at 311.
40. Rahem D. Hamid & Elias J. Schisgall, *More Than Three-Quarters of Surveyed Harvard Faculty Identify as Liberal*, Harvard Crimson (May 22, 2023), https://www.thecrimson.com/article/2023/5/22/faculty-survey-2023-politics/.
41. Leah J. Teichholtz & Meimei Xu, *The Graduating Class of 2024 by the Numbers*, Harvard Crimson, https://features.thecrimson.com/2024/senior-survey/national-politics/.
42. 347 U.S. 483 (1954).
43. Ibram X. Kendi, *Pass an Anti-Racist Constitutional Amendment*, Politico: How to Fix, www.politico.com/interactives/2019/how-to-fix-politics-in-america/inequality/pass-an-anti-racist-constitutional-amendment/ (last visited Oct. 10, 2025).
44. Ibram X. Kendi, How to Be an Anti-Racist 18 (2019).
45. *Id.*
46. Amna Khalid & Jeffrey Aaron Snyder, *Yes, DEI Can Erode Academic Freedom*, Chron. of Higher Educ. (Feb. 6, 2023), https://www.chronicle.com/article/yes-dei-can-erode-academic-freedom-lets-not-pretend-otherwise.
47. As quoted in the University of Chicago Report of the Committee on Free Expression (2015), *reprinted in* Banout & Ginsburg, *supra* note 1 at 160, 161, (also available at https://provost.uchicago.edu/sites/default/files/documents/reports/FOECommitteeReport.pdf).
48. David Reiff, Desire and Fate 113 (2024).
49. *Id.* at 174.
50. *Id.* at 175.
51. *See* Richard Hofstadter, Anti-Intellectualism in American Life (1963).
52. Report of the Committee on Free Expression, *supra* note 47.
53. University of Chicago, Report on the University's Role in Political and Social Action (1967) ("Kalven Report"), *reprinted in* Banout & Ginsburg, *supra* note 1, at 114, (also available at https://provost.uchicago.edu/sites/default/files/documents/reports/KalvenRprt_0.pdf).
54. Report of the Committee on Free Expression, *supra* note 47, at 163–64.

55. Abrams v. United States, 250 U.S. 616, 630 (1919) (Holmes, J., dissenting).
56. Kalven Report, *supra* note 53, at 116.
57. *See* David E. Bernstein & David L. Bernstein, *Supporting Free Speech and Countering Antisemitism on American College Campuses,* Harv. J. L. & Pub. Pol'y Per Curiam (Summer 2025), at 22–24.
58. *Id.* at 13.
59. *See, e.g.,* Daniel Patrick Moynihan, The Negro Family: The Case for National Action (1965); Stuart Buck, Acting White: The Ironic Legacy of Desegregation (2011).

Chapter 16

1. Michael T. Nietzel, *Gallup: Public Perception of a College Education Hits a 15-Year Low.* Forbes (Sep 13, 2025), https://www.forbes.com/sites/michaeltnietzel/2025/09/13/gallup-public-perception-of-a-college-education-hits-a-15-year-low/.
2. *See e.g., Historic Overview: The GI Bulge,* Syracuse Univ., https://veterans.syracuse.edu/why-su/history/gi-bulge/ (last visited Nov. 4, 2025).
3. Harry Edwards, *The Growing Disjunction Between Legal Education and the Legal Profession,* 91 Mich. L. Rev. 34 (1992).
4. *Climate Change Evidence,* NASA, https://science.nasa.gov/climate-change/evidence/ (last visited Nov. 4, 2025).
5. *The Global School of Sustainability at LSE,* London School of Economics and Political Science, https://www.lse.ac.uk/global-school-of-sustainability (last visited Nov. 4, 2025).
6. Melina Walling & Seth Borenstein, *Trump Calls Climate Change a "Con Job" at the United Nations. Here are the Facts and Context,* PBS News (Sep. 25, 2025), https://www.pbs.org/newshour/politics/trump-called-climate-change-a-con-job-at-the-united-nations-here-are-the-facts-and-context.

Chapter 17

1. *See* Smith v. Allwright, 321 U.S. 649 (1944).
2. Henry J. Hyde and George M. Fishman, *The Collegiate Speech Protection Act of 1991: A Response to the New Intolerance in the Academy,* 37 Wayne L. Rev. 1469 (1991).
3. *See* The Leonard Law, Cal. Educ. Code § 94367, (1992) ("No private postsecondary educational institution shall make or enforce any rule subjecting any student to disciplinary sanctions solely on the basis of conduct that is speech or other communication that, when engaged in outside the campus or facility of a private postsecondary institution, is protected from governmental restriction by the First Amendment to the United States Constitution or Section 2 of Article 1 of the California Constitution."); *see also* Taylor J. Barker, *Expressive Association Claim for Private Universities,* 76 Stanford L. Rev. 1787 (2024).
4. See Erwin Chemerinsky, *Trump's "Compact" with Universities Is Just Extortion,* N.Y. Times (Oct. 2, 2025), https://www.nytimes.com/2025/10/02/opinion/trump-compact-universities-constitution.html (artguing that imposition is just as objectionable issuing from the White House and coercive bargaining as it is issuing from Congress and legislation). *Cf.* Danielle Allen, *Why I'm Excited About the White House's Proposal for a Higher Ed Compact,* The Renovator (Oct 5, 2025), https://therenovator.substack.com/p/why-im-excited-about-the-white-houses (either mode of imposition represents an undermining of independence and competition in higher education); Brian J. Gross, letter to the editor, *What Would Jefferson Think of Trump's Pact,* Wall St. J., (Oct 14, 2025), https://www.wsj.com/opinion/what-would-jefferson-think-of-trumps-pact-funding-preference-uva-00490863 ("The White House's new compact is central planning in academic dress.").
5. Derek Bok, *Protecting Freedom of Expression on the Campus,* Boston Globe, Mar. 25, 1991.
6. *See* Cohen v. California, 403 U.S. 15 (1971). This chant by pledges of a Yale fraternity in 2010 led to the group's suspension. Zach Howard, *Yale Punishes Fraternity for Sexist Chanting,* Reuters (May 17, 2011).
7. *See* Cass R. Sunstein, Campus Free Speech: A Pocket Guide 82–83 (2024).

8. *See* David French, *Why Trump Can Do No Wrong*, N.Y. Times (Nov 2, 2025), https://www.nytimes.com/2025/11/02/opinion/trump-corruption-zelensky-johnson-biden.html.
9. Whether discrimination based on anti-Semitism should be viewed as a type of discrimination covered by Title VI is a more complicated question than generally recognized. *See* Benjamin Edelson & Deborah Hellman, Antisemitism, Antizionism, and Title VI: A Guide for the Perplexed, 139 Harvard L. Rev. 1 (2025). The applicability of Title VI to anti-Semitic discrimination is assumed for the purposes of this essay.
10. *See* Eugene Volokh et al., *A Statement from Constitutional Law Scholars on Columbia*, N.Y. Review (Mar. 20, 2025), https://www.nybooks.com/online/2025/03/20/a-statement-from-constitutional-law-scholars-on-columbia/.
11. Kelsey Walsh, Lalee Ibssa & Soo Rin Kim, *Trump Suggests if He Loses Election, Jewish Americans Would "Have a Lot to Do with That,"* ABC News (Sep. 20, 2024), https://abcnews.com/Politics/trump-israel-eradicated-win/story?id=113853150.
12. *See* Naftali Bendavid, *Many Jews Say Trump Is Politicizing the Fight Against Antisemitism*, Wash. Post, (Apr. 25, 2025), https://www.washingtonpost.com/politics/2025/04/25/antisemitism-trump-jews-israel/; *Broad Coalition of Mainstream Jewish Organizations Release Statements Rejecting False Choice Between Jewish Safety & Democracy*, Jewish Council for Public Affairs (Apr. 15, 2025), https://jewishpublicaffairs.org/press-release/jewishcommunalstatement/; Jason DeRose, *Most American Jews Say Trump Is Using Antisemitism as an "Excuse" to Silence Free Speech at Universities*, NPR (Sep. 17, 2025), https://www.npr.org/2025/09/17/nx-s1-5543212/study-most-american-jews-dont-agree-with-trumps-tactics-for-combating-antisemitism; *Donald Trump's Record on Antisemitism*, Jewish Democratic Council of America (Nov. 3, 2025), https://jewishdems.org/donald-trumps-antisemitic-record/.
13. Michael S. Roth, *Trump Is Selling Jews a Dangerous Lie*, N.Y. Times (Apr. 7, 2025), https://www.nytimes.com/2025/04/07/opinion/trump-jewish-antisemitism-wesleyan.html.
14. David French, *Cruelty, Bigotry, and Rage. What's Not to Like?*, N.Y. Times (Nov. 9, 2025), https://www.nytimes.com/2025/11/09/opinion/right-wing-america-politics-culture.html; Rick Klein, *Trump Said "Blame on Both Sides" in Charlottesville, Now the Anniversary Puts Him on the Spot*, ABC News (Aug. 12, 2018), https://abcnews.com/Politics/trumpblame-sides-charlottesville-now-anniversary-puts-spot/story?id=57141612.
15. *See* Benjamin Eidelson & Deborah Hellman, *Antisemitism, Anti-Zionism, and Title VI: A Guide for the Perplexed*, 139 Harvard L. Rev. 1 (2025).
16. *See, e.g.*, Franklin Foer, *Columbia University's Anti-Semitism Problem*, Atlantic (Mar. 17, 2025), https://www.theatlantic.com/ideas/archive/2025/03/columbia-antisemitism-israel-palestine-trump/682054/.
17. *See* Steven Pinker, *Harvard Derangement Syndrome*, N.Y. Times (May 23, 2025), https://www.nytimes.com/2025/05/23/opinion/harvard-university-trump-administration.html.
18. Joint Task Force Letter to Harvard University Concerning Notice of Violation, June 30, 2025.
19. Madeline Halpert, *Growing Backlash over Harvard Students' Pro-Palestine Letter*, BBC News (Oct. 10, 2023), https://www.bbc.com/news/world-us-canada-67067565.
20. Claudine Gay, *Remarks at Harvard Hillel*, Harvard Office of the President (Oct. 27, 2023), https://www.harvard.edu/president/speeches-gay/2023/remarks-at-harvard-hillel/.
21. *See Id.*
22. Alan. M. Garber, *Announcement of Presidential Task Forces*, Harvard Office of the President (Jan. 19, 2024), https://www.harvard.edu/president/news/2024/announcement-of-presidential-task-forces/; Emma H. Haidar and Cam E. Kettles, *Garber Announces Presidential Task Forces on Antisemitism, Islamophobia at Harvard*, Harvard Crimson (Jan. 19, 2024), https://www.thecrimson.com/article/2024/1/19/garber-presidential-task-forces/.
23. *See* President & Fellows of Harvard Coll. v. Dep't of Health & Hum. Servs., No.1:25-cv-11048, 2025 WL 2528380 (D. Mass. 2025).
24. Leo Terrell (@TheLeoTerrell), X (Oct 20, 2024), https://x.com/TheLeoTerrell/status/1848085166297686207.
25. Letter from Josh Greenbaum, Comm'r, Fed. Acquisition Serv., to Alan Garber, President, Harvard Univ., & Penny Pritzker, Lead Member, Harvard Corp. (Mar. 31, 2025).

26. April 3 Letter from Josh Greenbaum, Thomas E. Wheeler & Sean R. Kaveney to Alan Garber & Penny Pritzker (Apr. 3, 2025).
27. April 11 Letter from Josh Greenbaum, Thomas E. Wheeler & Sean R. Kaveney to Alan Garber & Penny Pritzker (Apr. 11, 2025).
28. Letter from William A Burck & Robert K. Hur, Quinn Emanuel Urquhart & Sullivan, to Josh Gruenbaum, Sean R. Keveney & Thomas E Wheeler (Apr. 14, 2025).
29. *See* President & Fellows of Harvard Coll. v. Dep't of Health & Hum. Servs., No.1:25-cv-11048, 2025 WL 2528380 at *25–27 (D. Mass. 2025).
30. *Id.* at 31.
31. *Id.* at 36.
32. *See* Alvin Powell, *"Antisemitism and Other Forms of Hate Have No Place at Harvard,"* Harvard Gazette (Dec. 5, 2023), https://news.harvard.edu/gazette/story/2023/12/president-gay-details-fight-against-threats-harassment-bigotry-at-house-hearing/; Emma H. Haider & Cam E. Kettles, *Garber Says Harvard Can and Should Condemn Hateful Speech Under Institutional Voice Policy,* The Crimson, (Dec. 11, 2024) https://www.thecrimson.com/article/2024/12/11/garber-condemns-hateful-speech/.
33. *See* Aaron Terr & Angel Aduardo, *Why Everything Pam Bondi Said About 'Hate Speech' Is Wrong,* Foundation for Individual Rights and Expression (Sep. 16, 2025), https://www.thefire.org/news/why-everything-pam-bondi-said-about-hate-speech-wrong.
34. Sam Cabral, *Claudine Gay: Harvard President Sorry for Remarks on Antisemitism,* BBC (Dec. 8, 2023), https://www.bbc.com/news/world-us-canada-67662871.
35. For a further discussion, see, Nadine Strossen, HATE: Why We Should Resist It with Free Speech, Not Censorship (2018).

Chapter 18

1. American Association of University Professors, *1940 Statement of Principles on Academic Freedom and Tenure with 1970 Interpretive Comments,* available at https://www.aaup.org/reports-publications/aaup-policies-reports/policy-statements/1940-statement-principles-academic; Henry Reichman, Understanding Academic Freedom (2nd ed. 2025).
2. Keith E. Whittington, *Academic Freedom and the Scope of Protections for Extramural Speech,* 105 Academe 20 (2019); Peter J. Byrne, *Academic Freedom: A "Special Concern of the First Amendment,"* 99 Yale L. J. 251 (1989); Matthew W. Finkin & Robert C. Post, *Freedom of Extramural Expression, in* For the Common Good: Principles of American Academic Freedom 127–48 (2009); David M. Rabban, Academic Freedom: From Professional Norm to First Amendment Right (2024).
3. Peter J. Byrne, *Academic Freedom: A "Special Concern of the First Amendment."* 99 Yale L. J. 251 (1989); Neil W. Hamilton, *Peer Review: The Linchpin of Academic Freedom and Tenure,* 83 Academe 14 (1997); Finkin & Post, *Conclusion: On Professional Responsibility, in* For the Common Good: Principles of American Academic Freedom 149–56 (2009).
4. Robert J. Zimmer, *What Is Academic Freedom For?, in* Whose Afraid of Academic Freedom 239–46 (Akeel Gilbrami & Jonathan Cole eds., 2015).
5. Victor S. Navasky, *On Civil Liberties on Campus,* 136 Daedalus 108 (2007) (reference to "little Eichmann" comment); Robert M. O'Neil, *Academic Freedom as a "Canonical Value,"* 76 Social Research 437 (2009) (Holocaust denial); Doug Criss, *College Professor Wanted "White Genocide" for Christmas,* CNN (Dec. 26, 2016), https://www.cnn.com/2016/12/26/health/drexel-professor-white-genocide-trnd; Ryan Quinn, *Claremont Institute, Home of "Stop the Steal" Lawyer, Returns to Political Science Conference,* Inside Higher Ed (Sep. 20, 2024), https://www.insidehighered.com/news/faculty-issues/academic-freedom/2024/09/10/claremont-home-stop-steal-lawyer-back-apsa.
6. Thomas Sowell, *Arthur Jensen and His Critics: The Great IQ Controversy,* 5 Change 33 (1973); Edward O. Wilson, Sociobiology: The New Synthesis (1975); Peter Duesberg, *HIV Is Not the Cause of AIDS,* 241 Science 514 (1988); Jon Cohen, *The Duesberg Phenomenon,* 266 Science 1642 (1994); Lisa Littman, *Parent Reports of Adolescents and Young Adults Perceived to Show Signs of a Rapid Onset of Gender Dysphoria,* PLOS One (Aug. 16, 2018), https://journals.plos.org/plosone/article?id=10.1371/journal.pone.0202330; Bruce Gilley, *The Case for Colonialism,* 31 Academic Questions 167, (2017); Tom Young, *The Gilley "Debate,"* 57 J. Modern African Studies 325 (2019); J. Mark Ramseyer, *Contracting for*

Sex in the Pacific War: A Response to My Critics (Harv. L. Sch. John M. Olin Center Discussion Paper No. 1075, 2022), https://papers.ssrn.com/sol3/papers.cfm?abstract_id=4000145.

7. P. K. Gupta, *The 2005 Nobel Prize in Physiology or Medicine: Helicobacter Pylori and Its Role in Gastritis and Peptic Ulcer Disease*, 89 Current Sci. 1651 (2005).
8. Marco Romano & Richard L. Cifelli, *100 Years of Continental Drift*, 350 Science 915 (2015).
9. P. Balaram, *Seeing Is Believing: Quasicrystals and the Demise of Perfect Order*, 101 Current Sci. 981 (2011); Dan Shechtman, Nobel Lecture (Dec. 8, 2011), https://www.nobelprize.org/prizes/chemistry/2011/shechtman/lecture/.
10. Deborah Josefson, *The Prion Hypothesis Is Finally Accepted by the Establishment*, 315 British Medical J. 972 (1997); Rosie Mestel, *Putting Prions to the Test*, 273 Science 184, 184 (1996).
11. Arturo Casadevall, *The mRNA Vaccine Revolution Is the Dividend from Decades of Basic Science Research*, J. Clinical Investigation (Sep. 24, 2021).
12. Timothy H. Lim, The Dead Sea Scrolls: A Very Short Introduction (2nd ed., 2017); Jewel Spears Brooker, *Sleuthing Around in "The Waste Land,"* 29 J. Modern Literature 194 (2006); K. A. Cuordileone, *The Torment of Secrecy: Reckoning with American Communism and Anticommunism After Venona*, 35 Diplomatic History 615 (2011); Paul Gifford & Pierpaolo Antonello, *Rethinking the Neolithic Revolution: Symbolism and Sacrifice at Göbekli Tepe*, *in* How We Became Human: Mimetic Theory and the Science of Evolutionary Origins 261–88 (2015).
13. Peter N. Stearns, *Social History and History: A Progress Report*, 19 Journal of Social History 319 (1985); Sherry B. Ortner, *Theory in Anthropology Since the Sixties*, 26 Comparative Studies in Society and History 126 (1984).
14. Robert J. Gordon et al., *Postwar Macroeconomics: The Evolution of Events and Ideas*, *in* The American Economy in Transition 101–182 (Martin Feldstein ed., 1980); Richard H. Thaler, *Behavioral Economics: Past, Present, and Future*, 106 The Am. Econ. Rev. 1577 (2016).
15. Harry Levin, *Successions in Psychology*, 236 Science 1683 (1987) (review of *The Cognitive Revolution in Psychology* by Bernard Baars).
16. Kristen Renwick Monroe, *Pathologies of Rational Choice Theory: A Critique of Applications in Political Science*, 25 Political Theory 289 (1997) (review of book by Donald P. Green & Ian Shapiro); Steve Chan, *In Search of Democratic Peace: Problems and Promise*, 41 Mershon International Studies Rev. 59 (1997); David Kinsella, *No Rest for the Democratic Peace*, 99 American Political Science Review 453 (2005).
17. Ellen Schrecker, No Ivory Tower: McCarthyism and the Universities (1986).
18. Gary Werskey, *Review: Science and Ideology in the Soviet Union*, 8 British Journal for the History of Science 240 (1975); Michael D. Gordin, *Lysenko Unemployed: Soviet Genetics After the Aftermath*, 109 Isis 56 (2018); Scholars at Risk's Submission to the Third Cycle of Universal Periodic Review of Turkey 35th Session of the United States Human Rights Council to be Held in January 2020, https://www.scholarsatrisk.org/wp-content/uploads/2019/07/Scholars-at-Risk-Turkey-UPR-Submission-Full.pdf (accessed September 29, 2025); Franklin Foer, *Viktor Orbán's War on Intellect*, Atlantic (June 2019), https://www.theatlantic.com/magazine/archive/2019/06/george-soros-viktor-orban-ceu/588070/; András L. Pap, *Academic Freedom in a Hybrid Illiberal Regime: Risks, Threats and Resources for Resilience*, 72 Journal of Legal Education 96 (2022).
19. Joseph Schumpeter, Capitalism, Socialism, and Democracy (1942); Israel M. Kirzner, *The Alert and Creative Entrepreneur: A Clarification*, 32 Small Business Economics 145 (2009).
20. Steve Mentz, *Phlogiston*, *in* Elemental Ecocriticism: Thinking with Earth, Air, Water, and Fire 55 (Jeffrey Jerome Cohen & Lowell Duckert eds., 2015).

Chapter 19

1. I use this term to also include all post-secondary educational institutions.
2. Steven Poskanzer, The University's Voice: Principled Silence and Purposeful Speech (Johns Hopkins Univ. Press, 2025).
3. 354 U.S. 234, 263 (1957) (Frankfurter, J., concurring); *see also* Regents of the Univ. of Michigan v. Ewing, 474 U.S. 214, 226 n. 12 (1985) ("Academic freedom thrives . . . [in part] on autonomous decision making by the academy itself.").

4. Keyeshian v. Board of Regents, 385 U.S. 589, 603 (1967).
5. Some commentators argue for elevating academic freedom to its own domain of free expression. *See* David Rabban, Academic Freedom (Harvard Univ. Press, 2024).
6. Another funding stream is *indirect* public appropriations channeled to universities through students or their families, as with many loan programs.
7. Exec. Order No. 14151, 90 Fed. Reg. 8339 (Jan. 29, 2025) ("Ending Radical and Wasteful Government DEI Programs and Preferencing"); Exec. Order No. 14279, 90 Fed. Reg. 17529 (Apr. 28, 2025) ("Reforming Accreditation To Strengthen Higher Education").
8. Letter from Craig Trainor, Acting Assistant Sec'y for Civil Rights, US Dep't of Educ. (Feb. 14, 2025).
9. *U.S. Department of Education Initiates Reduction in Force,* US Dep't of Educ. (Mar. 11, 2025).
10. Ariane de Vogue, Mary Kay Mallonee & Emanuella Grinberg, *Trump Administration Withdraws Federal Protections for Transgender Students,* CNN (Feb. 23, 2017).
11. Michael Bender, *All the Actions the Trump Administration Has Taken Against Harvard,* NY Times (May 22, 2025), https://www.nytimes.com/2025/05/22/us/politics/harvard-university-trump.html.
12. *See,* e.g., *DOJ, HHS, ED, and GSA Announce Initial Cancelation of Grants and Contracts to Columbia University Worth $400 Million,* U.S. Dep't of Educ. (Mar. 7, 2025).
13. *See, e.g.,* Nate Raymond, *Trump Administration Seeks to Make Harvard Ineligible for Federal Funding,* Reuters (Sept. 29, 2025), https://www.reuters.com/legal/government/trump-administration-seeks-make-harvard-ineligible-federal-funding-2025-09-29/.
14. *See, e.g.,* Andy Rose & Taylor Romine, *Trump Says the Government Will Revoke Harvard's Tax-Exempt Status. The University's President Says That Would Be Illegal,* CNN (May 2, 2025), https://www.cnn.com/2025/05/02/us/white-house-harvard-tax-status.
15. *E.g., Harvard University Loses Student and Exchange Visitor Program Certification for Pro-Terror Conduct,* Dep't of Homeland Sec. (May 22, 2025).
16. *See, e.g.,* Luke Barr & Julia Reinstein, *Trump Authorizes ICE to Target Courthouses, Schools and Churches.*
17. Memorandum from Todd Blanche, Deputy Attorney General (May 19, 2025) (announcing Civil Rights Fraud Initiative targeting universities engaged in "illegal DEI" for violations of the False Claims Act and encouraging private suits under the Act).
18. *See, e.g.,* Amanda Friedman, *"A Threat to Democracy": Trump Continues Bashing Harvard Amid Attacks on Major Institutions,* Politico (Apr. 24, 2025), https://www.politico.com/news/2025/04/24/trump-harvard-funding-attack-00307689.
19. One Big Beautiful Bill, Pub. L. No. 119–21, 139 Stat. 72.
20. Fla. Stat. §1000.05(4)(a)1–8 (2022); Fla. Stat. §§1004.06 (2)(b), 1007.55 (1)(b), and 1007.25 (3)(c) (all 2023); Wyo. Stat. Ann. §§9-25-101(a), (b) (2025); Miss. House Bill 1193 §3(f) (2025), https://legiscan.com/MS/text/HB1193/2025.
21. Letter from Anti-Semitism Task Force to Columbia University (March 13, 2025) [Columbia Letter]; Letter from Anti-Semitism Task Force to Harvard University (April 11, 2025) [Harvard Letter].
22. Letter from Craig Trainor, Acting Assistant Sec'y for Civil Rights, US Dep't of Educ (Feb. 14, 2025).
23. Even if such mission-related stances are motivated by self-interest, they are still legitimate and may be compelling.
24. For instance, the Harvard Letter envisions transferring academic hiring for a recalcitrant department to a cognate department or field—as if academic units are interchangeable in their expertise.
25. This is a pointed jab to embarrass Harvard for the controversy surrounding former President Claudine Gay's scholarship.
26. University of Chicago, Kalven Committee Report on the University's Role in Political and Social Action (Nov. 1, 1967), https://provost.uchicago.edu/reports/report-universitys-role-political-and-social-action.
27. *See* Alan M. Garber, *The Promise of American Higher Education,* Harvard Office of the President (Apr. 14, 2025), https://www.harvard.edu/president/news/2025/the-promise-of-american-higher-education/.

28. *Stand Up for Princeton and Higher Education,* PRINCETON, https://standup.princeton.edu/ (last visited Sept. 30, 2025).
29. *A Call for Constructive Engagement,* AMERICAN ASSOCIATION OF COLLEGES & UNIVERSITIES (Apr. 22, 2025), https://www.aacu.org/newsroom/a-call-for-constructive-engagement.
30. Natalie Schwartz, *Senate Panel's Proposal Would Hike Endowment Tax Less Than House Bill,* HIGHER ED DIVE (June 17, 2025), https://www.highereddive.com/news/senate-panels-proposal-would-hike-endowment-tax-less-than-house-bill/750992/.
31. 5 U.S.C. §§ 551–559.
32. RESOLUTION AGREEMENT BETWEEN THE UNITED STATES OF AMERICA AND COLUMBIA UNIVERSITY (July 23, 2025).
33. Jeffrey Jones, *U.S. Confidence in Higher Education Now Closely Divided,* GALLUP (July 8, 2024).

Chapter 20

1. Letter from Thomas Jefferson to Charles Yancey (Jan. 6, 1816) in *Founders Online, National Archives.*
2. Letter from Josh Gruenbaum, Comm'r of the Fed. Acquisition Serv., Gen. Serv. Admin., Sean Keveney, Acting Gen. Couns., US Dep't Health & Human Servs., and Thomas Wheeler, Acting Gen. Couns., US Dep't of Educ., to Dr. Alan Garber, President, Harvard Univ., & Penny Pritzker, Lead Member, Harvard Corp., N.Y. TIMES (Apr. 11, 2025), https://www.nytimes.com/interactive/2025/04/14/us/trump-harvard-demands.html.
3. Joint Task Force to Combat Anti-Semitism, *Joint Task Force Statement Regarding Harvard University* (Apr. 14, 2025), US Dep't of Health & Human Servs.
4. *See* Letter from Josh Gruenbaum, Comm'r of the Fed. Acquisition Serv., Gen. Serv. Admin., Sean Keveney, Acting Gen. Couns., US Dep't Health & Human Servs., and Thomas Wheeler, Acting Gen. Couns., US Dep't of Educ., to Dr. Katrina Armstrong, Interim President, Columbia Univ., David Greenwald & Claire Shipman, Co-chairs, Columbia Bd. of Trs., N.Y. TIMES (Mar. 13, 2025), https://www.nytimes.com/interactive/2025/03/14/nyregion/columbia-letter.html (delineating broad demands on Columbia's administration); US Dep't of Educ., Office for Civil Rights, *U.S. Department of Education's Office for Civil Rights Finds the University of Pennsylvania Has Violated Title IX* (Apr. 28, 2025), https://www.ed.gov/about/news/press-release/us-department-of-educations-office-civil-rights-finds-university-of-pennsylvania-has-violated-title-ix (demanding Penn remove a transgender athlete's records); *accord* Letter from Robert F. Kennedy, Jr., Sec'y, US Dep't of Health & Hum. Servs. & Linda McMahon, Sec'y, US Dep't of Educ., to Vincent Price, President, Duke Univ., Adam Silver, Chair, Duke Bd. of Trs., & Mary Klotman, M.D., Dean, Duke Univ. Sch. of Med. (July 28, 2025), https://www.hhs.gov/sites/default/files/duke-health-joint-letter.pdf (notifying Duke Med of allegations of racial preference in hiring and student admissions).
5. First enumerated by T. B. Davie in 1953. Repeated by Justice Felix Frankfurter in Sweezy v. New Hampshire, 354 U.S. 234, 261 (1957) (concurring in result) (the "academic freedom" of a university is "to determine for itself on academic grounds who may teach, what may be taught, how it shall be taught, and who may be admitted to study").
6. Letter from Gruenbaum et al. to Garber & Pritzker, *supra* note 2.
7. *Id.* at 2.
8. *Id.* at 3.
9. *Id.* at 5.
10. *Id.* at 3.
11. *See id.* at 2; Letter from Gruenbaum et al. to Armstrong et al., *supra* note 4.
12. *See* Nobel Prize laureates and research affiliations, https://www.nobelprize.org/prizes/lists/nobel-laureates-and-research-affiliations/.
13. W. Bently McLeod & Miguel Urquiola, *Why Does the United States Have the Best Research Universities? Incentives, Resources, and Virtuous Circles,* 35 J. ECON. PERSP. 185 (2021).
14. *Id.* at 199.

15. Futao Huang, *Building the World-Class Research Universities: A Case Study of China,* 70 Higher Educ. 203, 208 (2015).
16. Qiang Zha, *Intellectuals, Academic Freedom, and University Autonomy in China,* in University Governance and Reform 209 (H. G. Schuetze, W. Bruneau & G. Grosjean eds., 2012).
17. *Sweezy,* 354 U.S., *supra* note 5.
18. "Unfortunately, the Supreme Court's glorification of academic freedom as a 'special concern of the First Amendment' has produced hyperbolic rhetoric but only scant, and often ambiguous, analytic content. The Court has never systematically explained the theory behind its relatively recent incorporation of academic freedom into the first amendment, a problem occasionally acknowledged by the justices themselves." David Rabban, *A Functional Analysis of "Individual" and "Institutional" Academic Freedom Under the First Amendment,* 50 L. & Contemp. Probs. 227, 230 (1990) (quoting *Keyishian v. Board of Regents,* 358 US 589, 603 (1967)); *See also* Robert Post, *Academic Freedom and the Constitution,* in Who's Afraid of Academic Freedom? 123 (Akeel Bilgrami & Jonathan Cole, eds., Columbia Univ. Press, 2015).
19. Academic freedom of faculty was first institutionalized in the United States in 1915 and restated in 1940 by the American Association of University Professors; *see* Am. Ass'n of Univ. Professors, *1915 Declaration of Principles on Academic Freedom and Academic Tenure* in Policy Documents & Reports 291 (Robert B. Kreiser, 9th ed., 2001) [hereinafter 1915 AAUP Declaration]; Am. Ass'n of Univ. Professors, *1940 Statement of Principles on Academic Freedom Tenure* in Policy Documents & Reports (Robert B. Kreiser, 9th ed., 2001).
20. *See* Robert C. Post, Democracy, Expertise, and Academic Freedom: A First Amendment Jurisprudence for the Modern State (Yale Univ. Press, 2013); Amy Gutmann, *Academic Freedom and Freedom of the Academy,* in Democratic Education 175 (rev. ed., Princeton Univ. Press, 1999); Amy Gutmann, *Is Freedom Academic?* in NOMOS XXV: Liberal Democracy 257 (1983); Lee C. Bollinger, University: A Reckoning (W.W. Norton, 2026).
21. *See* Ellen Schrecker, *Academic Freedom and Political Repression from McCarthyism to Trump,* in The Right to Learn: Resisting the Right-Wing Attack on Academic Freedom 17 (Valerie C. Johnson, Jennifer Ruth & Ellen Schrecker, eds., Beacon Press, 2024); Klint Alexander, *Shadows of McCarthyism: The New Era of Government Intervention in Higher Education and Its Legal Implications for Academic Freedom on Campus,* 50 J. of Educ. Fin. & L. 108 (2025).
22. Letter from Gruenbaum et al. to Garber & Pritzker, *supra* note 2.
23. The Administration's "Compact for Academic Excellence in Higher Education," rolled out in October 2025, included this condition along with others in its offer that would restrict academic freedoms. Michael Bender, *Trump Administration Asks Colleges to Sign "Compact" to Get Funding Preference,* N.Y. Times (October 2, 2025), https://www.nytimes.com/2025/10/02/us/politics/trump-college-funding.html.
24. Christopher L. Eisgruber, Terms of Respect 94–112 (Basic Books, 2025) (on the civic mission of universities and nine recommendations to improve campus discourse); Sigal Ben-Porath, Cancel Wars: How Universities Can Foster Free Speech, Promote Inclusion, and Renew Democracy 111–152 (Univ. of Chicago Press, 2023) (on free speech on college campuses and its democratic function).
25. Am. Ass'n of Univ. Professors, *supra* note 19, at 298.
26. John Tomasi & Jonathan Haidt, *You Can't Pursue Truth Without Viewpoint Diversity,* Inside Higher Ed (Oct. 29, 2025). The level of trust among Republicans, it also bears noting, declined much more and to a significantly lower level than among Democrats and Independents. See Jeffrey M. Jones, *U.S. Confidence in Higher Education Now Closely Divided* (July 8, 2024), https://news.gallup.com/poll/646880/confidence-higher-education-closely-divided.aspx.
27. *Id.*
28. As recognized by the 1915 AAUP Declaration, *supra* note 19 at 294 (describing universities as a "public trust"); Joan Wallach Scott, *Knowledge, Power, and Academic Freedom* in Knowledge, Power and Academic Freedom 39, 45–46 (Columbia Univ. Press, 2019)

(developing the concept of the university as a public trust and establishing the roots of public trust language from the AAUP's original declarations).

29. President Dwight D. Eisenhower, *Farewell Address*, Nat'l Archives & Records Admin. (Jan. 17, 1961).
30. U.S. Dep't of Health & Human Servs, *supra* note 3.
31. Letter from William Burck, Quinn Emmanuel Urquhart & Sullivan, LLP and Robert Hur, King & Spalding, LLP, to Josh Gruenbaum, Comm'r of the Fed. Acquisition Serv., Gen. Serv. Admin., Sean Keveney, Acting Gen. Couns., US Dep't Health & Human Servs., and Thomas Wheeler, Acting Gen. Couns., US Dep't of Educ., Harvard University 1 (Apr. 14, 2025), https://www.harvard.edu/research-funding/wp-content/uploads/sites/16/2025/04/Harvard-Response-2025-04-14.pdf.
32. *See* Alan M. Garber, *Upholding Our Values, Defending Our University* (Apr. 21, 2025), https://www.harvard.edu/president/news/2025/upholding-our-values-defending-our-university/ (Harvard University President Alan Garber addressed the Harvard community in defiance of the Trump Administration's demands.).
33. For the meaning of a "rotten compromise," *see* AVISHAI MARGALIT, ON COMPROMISE AND ROTTEN COMPROMISES 54–67 (Princeton Univ. Press, 2013).
34. Letter from Burck & Hur to Gruenbaum et al., *supra* note 31, at 2.
35. *E.g., Pres. & Fellows of Harvard Coll. v. U.S. Dep't of Health & Hum. Servs.*, No. 1:25-cv-11048 (D. Mass. filed Apr. 21, 2025) (Harvard suing the Trump Administration for pulling federal funding on APA and First Amendment grounds); *Pres. & Fellows of Harvard Coll. v. U.S. Dep't of Homeland Sec.*, No. 1:25-cv-11472-ADB, 2025 WL 1737493 (D. Mass. June 23, 2025) (Harvard suing Trump's attempt to block the University from enrolling international students).
36. *See, e.g.,* Ben Casselman & Colby Smith, *Trump's Attacks on Institutions Threaten a Bulwark of Economic Strength*, N.Y. TIMES (Aug. 22, 2025), https://www.nytimes.com/2025/08/22/business/trump-federal-reserve-bls.html; Pien Huang & Will Stone, *Trump Administration Restricts CDC Research and Messaging with Layers of Oversight,* NPR (Feb. 14, 2025), https://www.npr.org/sections/shots-health-news/2025/02/13/nx-s1-5297177/cdc-scientists-publications-trump-administration; Justin Spike & Nicholas Riccardi, *Trump's Moves Against Media Outlets Mirror Authoritarian Approaches to Silencing Dissent,* PBS NEWS (Sept. 18, 2025), https://www.pbs.org/newshour/politics/trumps-moves-against-media-outlets-mirror-authoritarian-approaches-to-silencing-dissent.
37. Justin Lahart et al., *Trump Orders Firing of Bureau of Labor Statistics Chief,* WALL ST. J. (Aug. 1, 2025) (quoting Donald J. Trump (@realDonaldTrump), Truth Social (Aug. 1, 2025, 3:44 p.m.), https://truthsocial.com/@realDonaldTrump/posts/114955222046259464).
38. Peter Nicholas, *Trump Orders Firing of Bureau of Labor Statistics Chief,* WALL ST. J. (Apr. 9, 2020), https://www.wsj.com/politics/policy/trump-orders-firing-of-bureau-of-labor-statistics-chief-d8eaa272.
39. Eric Revell, *Trump Slams Powell as "Moron" and Calls for Fed's Board to Take Control of Policy Moves,* FOX BUS. (Aug. 1, 2025) (quoting Donald J. Trump (@realDonaldTrump), Truth Social (Aug. 1, 2025, 6:32 a.m.), https://truthsocial.com/@realDonaldTrump/posts/114953049546233760).
40. Alejandra O'Connell-Domenech & Nathaniel Weixel, *Huge Cuts to mRNA Research Sparks Fears About Future Pandemics,* THE HILL (Aug. 6, 2025) (quoting Dr. Jerome M. Adams (@JeromeAdamsMD), X Post No. 1952905490662629640 (Apr. 30, 2025, 3:15 p.m.), https://x.com/JeromeAdamsMD/status/1952905490662629640).
41. For a summary of the proven results and potential of mRNA vaccines for saving lives, improving the quality of life, and helping communities prosper, *see* Rick Bright, *America Is Abandoning One of the Greatest Medical Breakthroughs,* N.Y. TIMES (Aug. 18, 2025); *see also* Jeff Coller, *RFK Jr.'s Dangerous Attacks on mRNA Research,* WALL ST. J. (Aug. 18, 2025).
42. *See* Lahart et al., *supra* note 37.
43. Josh Moody, *How Trump Forced Cuts at Wealthy Universities,* INSIDE HIGHER ED (Aug. 7, 2025), https://www.insidehighered.com/news/business/cost-cutting/2025/08/07/how-trump-forced-cuts-wealthy-universities; Cheyanne Mumphrey, *College Endowment Tax Is Leading to Hiring Freezes and Could Mean Cuts in Financial Aid,* PBS NEWS (Aug.

8, 2025), https://www.pbs.org/newshour/education/college-endowment-tax-is-leading-to-hiring-freezes-and-could-mean-cuts-in-financial-aid.

44. See Pres. & Fellows of Harvard Coll. v. U.S. Dep't of Homeland Sec., *supra* note 35; *cf.* Gretzinger et al., *Tracking Higher Ed's Dismantling of DEI*, CHRON. OF HIGHER EDUC. (Aug. 26, 2025), https://www.chronicle.com/article/tracking-higher-eds-dismantling-of-dei.
45. *See* Stephen Woolf et al., *The Potential Impact of the Trump Administration Policies on Health Research in the USA*, 405 THE LANCET 2114 (June 2025); Institute for Macroeconomic & Policy Analysis, *Preliminary Estimates of the Macroeconomic Costs of Cutting Federal Funding for Scientific Research* (Apr. 30, 2025).
46. Victor J. Dzau, Nat'l Acad. of Med., *Effectiveness of COVID-19 Vaccines Under Operation Warp Speed* (Sept. 5, 2025).
47. *See* Dan Garisto, *Trump Order Gives Political Appointees Vast Powers over Research Grants*, SCI. AM. (Aug. 12, 2025), https://www.scientificamerican.com/article/trump-order-would-give-political-appointees-power-over-science-funding/; Ryan Quinn, *Trump Order on Grants Puts Politics Above Peer Review, Researchers Say,* INSIDE HIGHER ED, (Aug. 13, 2025), https://www.insidehighered.com/news/government/science-research-policy/2025/08/13/trump-order-puts-politics-above-peer-review.
48. For a full explanation of the basis of the distinction in human cognition, *see* DANIEL KAHNEMAN, THINKING, FAST AND SLOW (Farrar, Straus & Giroux, 2011) (as Kahneman explains, when confronted with a hard question, we often answer an easier one instead without even noticing, a form of fast thinking called "intuitive heuristics").
49. *See, e.g.,* Thomas B. Edsall, *Trump Wants to Drown Us in a Sea of Chaos*, N.Y. TIMES (Sept. 2, 2025), https://www.nytimes.com/2025/09/02/opinion/trump-winning-imperial-presidency.html ("Every day Trump sows confusion and uncertainty as his overall strategy of drowning voters in a sea of chaos keeps a majority of Americans in the dark, unable to distinguish truth from fiction amid the cacophony of political and legal charges, countercharges and—because Trump is a master prevaricator—lies.")
50. Haidt & Tomasi, *supra* note 26; *see* Jonathan Haidt, *Why Universities Must Choose One Telos: Truth or Social Justice*, HETERODOX ACAD. (Oct. 22, 2016), https://heterodoxacademy.org/blog/one-telos-truth-or-social-justice-2/; *see also* John Tomasi, *A University the World Has Never Seen*, FREE THE INQUIRY (Oct. 8, 2024), https://heterodoxacademy.substack.com/p/a-university-the-world-has-never. Jonathan Haidt and John Tomasi are founders of the Heterodox Academy, an organization dedicated to open inquiry, diversity of scholarly perspectives, and constructive disagreement in universities.
51. For an exemplary statement in this regard, *see* Robert P. George, Tom Ginsburg, Robert C. Post, David M. Rabban, Jeannie Suk Gersen & Keith E. Whittington, *Our Politics Differ, but We Agree: Trump's "Compact" Violates Academic Freedom*, CHRON. HIGHER EDUC. (October 16, 2025), https://www.chronicle.com/article/our-politics-differ-but-we-agree-trumps-compact-violates-academic-freedom.
52. Whitney v. California, 274 U.S. 357, 377 (1927) (Brandeis, J., concurring).
53. Jefferson Letter, *supra* note 1.
54. A foundational principle in American political theory; *see* The Federalist No. 51 (J. Cooke ed. 1961) (A. Hamilton & J. Madison); C. MONTESQUIEU, THE SPIRIT OF THE LAWS (Hafner, 1949).
55. Similarly foundational, *see* JEREMY BENTHAM, THE HANDBOOK OF POLITICAL FALLACIES (Harold A. Larrabee ed.; Harper & Bros., 1962), at 13 (on the functions of politics as a game and politicians as players, "Insincerity in all its shapes, disingenuousness, lying, hypocrisy, fallacy—are all instruments employed by players on both sides for obtaining advantages in the game."); ALEXIS DE TOCQUEVILLE, DEMOCRACY IN AMERICA, 1213 (Eduardo Nolla ed., James T. Schleifer trans.; Liberty Fund, 2010) (1840).
56. For example, see DAVID BROMWICH, WHAT WENT WRONG: ASSESSING OBAMA'S LEGACY (Harper's Magazine, June 2015); JACK GOLDSMITH, POWER AND CONSTRAINT: THE ACCOUNTABLE PRESIDENCY AFTER 9/11 (W.W. Norton, 2012). For charges of misleading communications in defending school shutdowns by members of the Biden Administration during the Covid-19 pandemic, *see* STEPHEN MACEDO & FRANCES LEE, IN COVID'S WAKE:

How Politics Failed Us (Princeton Univ. Press, 2025), and David Zweig, An Abundance of Caution: American Schools, the Virus, and a Story of Bad Decisions (MIT Press, 2025).

57. *See generally*, Schrecker, *supra* note 21.
58. Christopher L. Eisgruber, *The Cost of the Government's Attack on Columbia*, Atlantic (March 19, 2025), https://www.theatlantic.com/ideas/archive/2025/03/columbia-academic-freedom/682088/.
59. *See also* Eisgruber *supra* note 24, for his extensive analysis of threats to academic freedom and free speech.
60. Mark Warren, *Accountability and Democracy*, in The Oxford Handbook of Public Accountability 39 (Oxford Univ. Press, 2014).
61. *See* Bollinger, *supra* note 20.
62. *See* Steven Levitsky & Lucan Way, *The New Competitive Authoritarianism*, 31 J. Democracy 51 (2020).
63. *See* Emily Falk, What We Value: The Neuroscience of Choice and Change (W.W. Norton, 2025) (explaining the neuroscience of individual choice, including relating to communities); Wendy Pearlman, *Moral Identity and Protest Cascades in Syria*, 48 British J. Pol. Sci. 877 (2016); Larson et al., *Social Networks and Protest Participation: Evidence from 130 Million Twitter Users*, 63 a.m. J. Pol. Sci. 690 (2019); Emily Falk, *Here Is the Science of Why You Doomscroll*, N.Y. Times (Jul. 6, 2025).
64. Christina H. Paxson, Pres. Brown Univ, Letter (October 15, 2025), https://www.brown.edu/sites/default/files/brown-response-federal-compact-10-15-2025.pdf. The universities that rejected the "Compact" are M.I.T., Brown, Univ. of Pennsylvania, Univ. of Southern California, Univ. of Virginia, Dartmouth, and Univ. of Arizona. Without rejecting it, Vanderbilt did not accept. Without accepting it, Univ. of Texas Austin said it was open to it and honored to be selected. Connor Greene, "The Seven Colleges That Rejected Trump's 'Compact,' and Two Still Weighing the Proposal," https://time.com/7327437/trump-universities-compact-federal-funding/.
65. Bollinger, *supra* note 20.
66. *See* Steven Levitsky & Daniel Ziblatt, When Democracies Die (Crown, 2018); Erica Chenoweth & Maria J. Stephan, Why Civil Resistance Works: The Strategic Logic of Nonviolent Conflict (Columbia Univ. Press, 2012).
67. *See, e.g.*, Sweezy v. State of N.H. by Wyman, 354 U.S. 234 (1957); Keyishian v. Bd. of Regents of Univ. of State of N. Y., 385 U.S. 589 (1967); Grutter v. Bollinger, 539 U.S. 306 (2003).
68. *See* 1915 AAUP Declaration *supra* note 19.
69. *See* Scott, *supra* note 28, at 45–46; Gary A. Tobin, Aryeh Kaufmann Weinberg & Jenna Ferer, The UnCivil University: Intolerance on College Campuses, 14 (Lexington, 2005) ("The public trust originates in the long-standing connection between American universities and the government."); Matthew W. Finkin, *On "Institutional" Academic Freedom*, 61 Tex. L. Rev. 817, 832 (1983) ("The court held that an institution so heavily imbued with a public purpose was, in effect, a public trust," referencing a Dartmouth University case in the New Hampshire Supreme Court).
70. *See* Owen Fiss, *The Democratic Mission of the University*, 76 Alb. L. Rev. 735 (2013).
71. *See, e.g.*, John H. Bryant & Anvar Velji, *Global Health and the Role of Universities in the Twenty-First Century*, 25 Infectious Disease Clinics of N. Am. 311 (2011).
72. Elizabeth Popp Berman, Creating the Market University: How Academic Science Became an Economic Engine (Princeton Univ. Press, 2012).
73. *See generally*, 1915 AAUP Declaration, *supra* note 19.
74. *Id.* at 295.
75. Am. Ass'n of Univ. Professors, *Timeline: First 100 Years*, https://www.aaup.org/about/history/timeline-first-100-years.
76. Melissa De Witte, *Academic Freedom's Origin Story*, Stanford Graduate School of Education (May 1, 2023).
77. 1915 AAUP Declaration, *supra* note 19 at 294.
78. Sweezy, *supra* note 5.
79. *See generally*, Schrecker, *supra* note 21.

80. Global Colloquium of University Presidents, Academic Freedom Statement of the First Global Colloquium of University Presidents (May 26, 2005), https://www.columbia.edu/~md2221/academicstatement.doc.
81. Former College and University Presidents, *Higher Education Must Do Better, but Politically Driven Government Intervention Is Not the Solution,* Fortune (Apr. 8, 2025), https://fortune.com/2025/04/08/colleges-universities-education-politics/.
82. *See* Christopher L. Eisgruber, *The Cost of the Government's Attack on Columbia,* Atlantic (Mar. 19, 2025), https://www.theatlantic.com/ideas/archive/2025/03/columbia-academic-freedom/682088/; Garber, *supra* note 32; A. Martínez & Destinee Adams, *Wesleyan University President Says Trump's Antisemitism Fight Doesn't Protect Jews,* NPR (Apr. 17, 2025), https://www.npr.org/2025/04/17/nx-s1-5366667/trump-defunding-university-antisemitism-wesleyan; Laura Spitalniak, *George Mason University Leader Rebukes Trump Administration's Apology Demand,* Higher Ed Dive (Aug. 26, 2025), https://www.highereddive.com/news/george-mason-university-leader-rebukes-trump-apology-demand-Gregory-Washington/758690/.
83. *See* Amy Lai, In Defense of Free Speech in Universities 42 (Univ. of Mich. Press, 2023); Leo L. Rockwell, *Academic Freedom: German Origin and American Development,* 36 Bulletin of the American Association of University Professors 225 (1950).
84. Ferenc Laczó, *The Tragedy of Central European University,* 119 Current Hist. 83 (2020).
85. *See* Henry Reichman, The Future of Academic Freedom (Johns Hopkins Univ. Press, 2019).
86. *See* Levitsky & Ziblatt, *supra* note 66; Hinck, Hawthorne & Hawthorne, *Authoritarians Don't Deliberate: Cultivating Deliberation and Resisting Authoritarian Tools in an Age of Global Nationalism,* 14 J. Pub. Deliberation 16 (2018).
87. *See generally* Andreas Schedler, *Disturbing the Dictator: Peaceful Protest Under Authoritarianism* in Crisis in Autocratic Regimes 43 (Johannes Gerschewski & Christoph H. Stefes eds., Lynne Rienner, 2018) (arguing for the political normative power of protest in authoritarian rule); Pavlo Lysenko, *Nonviolent Resistance and Repression: Examining Civil Resistance and Authoritarian Adaptation in Post-Soviet States,* 10 J. Baltic Sec. 26 (2024) (examining authoritarian repression by leaders like Putin and efficacy of civil resistance); Robert M. Press, *Sierra Leone's Peaceful Resistance to Authoritarian Rule,* 1 Afr. Conflict & Peacebuilding Rev. 31 (2012) (applying Western frameworks of resistance to Sierra Leone).
88. *See* Rabban, *supra* note 18.
89. *See* Seana Valentine Shiffrin, Democratic Law 189 (Hannah Ginsborg ed., Oxford Univ. Press, 2021) ("[a democratic legal system]'s success will depend upon a complementary ethos emerging in the culture. . . . Our understanding of why people follow the law . . . will be informed by such things as how, in the culture, we speak about compliance, our common enterprise, and about each other.").
90. Jeffrey M. Jones, *U.S. Confidence in Higher Education Now Closely Divided,* Gallup (July 8, 2024), https://news.gallup.com/poll/646880/confidence-higher-education-closely-divided.aspx; *accord* Carl Latkin et al., *An Assessment of the Rapid Decline of Trust in US Sources of Public Information About COVID-19,* 25 J. Health Comm. 764 (2021); Ashley Mowreader, *More Americans Trust Public Universities Than Private Ones,* Inside Higher Ed (June 23, 2025), https://www.insidehighered.com/news/quick-takes/2025/06/23/more-americans-trust-public-universities-private-ones.
91. *See* Tocqueville, *supra* note 55.
92. Library of Congress Prints and Photographs Division, *"Either We Hang Together or . . ."* (n.d.) (attributing the quote to Benjamin Franklin).
93. *See* Bollinger, *supra* note 20.
94. *Id.*
95. *See, e.g.,* Matal v. Tam, 582 U.S. 218 (2017) (unanimous decision authored by Justice Alito).
96. Eisgruber, *supra* note 24 for nine recommendations for strengthening campus discourse.

INDEX

For the benefit of digital users, indexed terms that span two pages (e.g., 52–53) may, on occasion, appear on only one of those pages.

www.ingramcontent.com/pod-product-compliance
Ingram Content Group UK Ltd.
Pitfield, Milton Keynes, MK11 3LW, UK
UKHW040919150926
475595UK00002B/19

9 780197 854839